A CAPTIVE LAND

The politics of agrarian reform in the Philippines

James Putzel

First published 1992 by the Catholic Institute for International Relations, Unit 3 Canonbury Road, 190a New North Road, London N1 7BJ, UK

and

Monthly Review Press, 122 West 27th Street, New York, NY 10001, USA

First published in the Philippines by Ateneo de Manila University Press, Bellarmine Hall, Loyola Heights, Quezon City, PO Box 154, 1099 Manila, Philippines.

Exclusively distributed in South East Asia by Ateneo de Manila University Press.

British Library Cataloguing in Publication Data

Putzel, James
  Captive Land: Politics of Agrarian Reform
  in the Philippines
  I. Title
  338.109599

Library of Congress Cataloging-in-Publication Data

Putzel, James.
    A captive land: the politics of agrarian reform in the
  Philippines / by James Putzel.
      p.   cm.
    Includes bibliographical references and index.
    ISBN 0-85345-842-1 (pbk.) : $22.00
HN1333.P6P88   1992
333.3'1599—dc20   92-12667
                                                                      CIP

ISBN 1 85287 084 2   CIIR
ISBN 0 85345 842 1 Monthly Review Press

Cover and text design by Rich Cowley
Cover photo by Jenny Matthews
Printed in the United Kingdom by Bell & Bain Ltd, Glasgow

A CAPTIVE LAND

The politics of agrarian reform in the
Philippines

James Putzel

Acknowledgements

I would like to express my gratitude to the many institutions, organizations and individuals who helped make this study possible and from whom I learned a great deal. The staff of the Philippine Peasant Institute in Manila and the Alternative Forum for Research in Mindanao facilitated my travels throughout the archipelago and offered a wealth of knowledge based on their many years of research. Many peasant families and organizers welcomed me to their *barrios* and into their homes and patiently explained the realities of their lives. Government officials, landowners and corporate executives, kindly agreed to interviews and provided crucial documentation for this study. Former Assistant Secretary of Agrarian Reform, Gerry Bulatao, spent many hours with me, allowing me a unique insight into the policy-making and implementation processes in the country. The staff, faculty and students of the Department of Political Science and the School of Economics at the University of the Philippines provided a base from which to conduct my research. Jesus Calaguas, Petite Peredo and their family provided a home away from home. Craig Nelson and Elizabeth McQuerry, at the National Security Archive in Washington DC, helped in locating important US government documents. The Philippine Resource Centre kept me in almost daily contact with the Philippines while in the UK.

My work on this topic began almost seven years ago in Canada where Professor Sam Noumoff encouraged my first forays into the study of agrarian reform. I owe a great debt to Lorraine Shanley Putzel and Daniel J. Putzel whose support allowed me to pursue my studies over so many years. In Oxford, my doctoral dissertation was supervised by Dr. Keith Griffin and Dr. Peter Carey, whose criticisms and advice have been invaluable. I am also grateful for suggestions made by Lawrence Whitehead and Professor Otto van den Muijzenberg who examined my dissertation. Irene Gedalof, Dr. James Meadowcroft, Phil Spires and Professor Reginald Green read portions of the manuscript and provided helpful advice.

The Catholic Institute for International Relations in London has supported me in all my work and allowed me the opportunity to write this book. I am especially grateful to Caroline Spires without whose continual support and patience this book may never have been published. To all of these and many others whose names are not mentioned I express my deepest gratitude. However, responsibility for the views expressed here, and for any errors, is mine alone.

CONTENTS

LIST OF TABLES

LIST OF FIGURES

ACCP	American Chamber of Commerce in the Philippines
AFP	Armed Forces of the Philippines
AFRIM	Alternative Forum for Research in Mindanao
AMA	Alliance of Makati Associations
AMA	Aniban ng Manggagawa sa Agrikultura (Alliance of Agricultural Workers)
AMG	American Military Government - South Korea
ANGOC	Asian NGO Coalition for Agrarian Reform and Rural Development
ARBA	Agrarian Reform Beneficiaries Association
ARSP	Agrarian Reform Support Program - US
ARI	Agrarian Reform Institute
ARTO	Agrarian Reform Team Offices
BARC	Barangay Agrarian Reform Council
BAYAN	Bagong Alyansang Makabayan (New Patriotic Federation)
BBC	Bishops Businessmen's Conference for Human Development
BCLP	Barrio Committees on Land Production
CA	Commonwealth Act
CAC	Cabinet Action Committee on Agrarian Reform
CAFGU	Civilian Armed Forces Geographical Units
CAMP	Cory Aquino Movement for President
CAPP	Council of Agricultural Producers of the Philippines
CARP/CARL	Comprehensive Agrarian Reform Program (LAW) 1988
CAT	Centrál Azucarera de Tarlac
CIA	Central Intelligence Agency
CIDA	Canadian International Development Agency
CG	Convenors Group
CHDF	Civilian Home Defense Forces
CLOA	Certificate of Land Ownership Award
CLT	Certificate of Land Transfer
COCOFED	Philippine Coconut Producers Federation
CON-COM	Constitutional Commission (1986)
CON-CON	Constitutional Convention (1971)
CPAR	Congress for a People's Agrarian Reform
CPP	Communist Party of the Philippines
CRC	Centre for Research and Communications

CSJ	Committee on Social Justice of Constitutional Commission
DA	Department of Agriculture
DAR	Department of Agrarian Reform
DARBCI	Dole Agrarian Reform Beneficiaries Cooperative
DENR	Department of Energy and Natural Resources
DF	Department of Finance
DJ	Department of Justice
DoD	Department of Defence
ECA	Economic Cooperation Administration - US
EDCOR	Economic Development Corps
EDMS	Economic District Management System
EO	Executive order
EP	Emancipation patent
FAITH	Federation of Agricultural and Industrial Toiling Hands
FAO	United Nations Food and Agricultural Organization
FELDA	Federal Land Development Authority - Malaysia
FFF	Federation of Free Farmers
FOA	Foreign Operations Administration - US
GDP	Gross Domestic Product
GSIS	Government Service Insurance System
HB	House Bill
HLI	Hacienda Luisita Inc.
HMB	Hukbong Mapagpalaya ng Bayan (People's Liberation Army)
HYV	High-yielding varieties (mainly rice)
IATFAR	Inter-Agency Task Force on Agrarian Reform
ICA	International Cooperation Administration - US
IFC	International Finance Corporation (World Bank)
IMF	International Monetary Fund
IRRI	International Rice Research Institute
ISH	Integrated Survey of Households
ISI	Import-substitution industrialization
JCC	Journal of the Constitutional Commission
JCRR	Joint (US - Republican China) Commission of Rural Reconstruction
JICA	Japan International Cooperation Agency
JUSMAG	Joint US-RP Military Group
KBL	Kilusang Bagong Lipunan (New Society Movement)
KMP	Kilusang Magbubukid ng Pilipinas (Peasant Movement of the Philippines)
KMT	Koumintang (Nationalist Party - China)
KOMPIL	Kongreso ng Mamamayan Pilipino (Congress of the Filipino People)
LABAN	Lakas ng Bayan (Power of the People)
LBP	Land Bank of the Philippines
LDP	Lakas ng Demokratikong Pilipinas (Strength of Philippine

	Democracy)
LE	Landed Estates
LMMMP	Lakas ng Magsasaka Manggagawa at Mangingisda ng Pilipinas (Strength of the Awakened Farmworkers in the Philippines)
LOI	Letter of Instruction (from President)
MAF	Ministry of Agriculture and Food
MAI	Multilateral Aid Initiative
MAR	Ministry of Agrarian Reform
MBC	Makati Business Club
MF	Ministry of Finance
MNR	Ministry of Natural Resources
MSA	Mutual Security Agency - US
NACUSIP	National Congress of Unions in the Sugar Industry of the Philippines
NAGRICO	National Agricultural Investment Company
NAMFREL	National Movement for Free Elections
NARRA	National Rehabilitation and Resettlement Administration
NCRDC	National Capitol Region Defense Command
NDC	National Development Corporation
NDCF	National Defense Council Foundation - US
NDF	National Democratic Front
NEDA	National Economic Development Authority
NFA	National Food Authority
NFSP	National Federation of Sugar Planters
NFSW	National Federation of Sugar Workers
NGO	Non-governmental organization
NGPI (NGEI)	NDC-Guthrie Plantations (Estates) Inc.
NPA	New People's Army
NRDF	Negros Rural Development Fund
NRS	Natural Resources Section of SCAP - Japan
NSC	National Security Council - US
NUC	National Unification Committee
ODA	Official Development Assistance
OIC	Officers in Charge
OLH	Operation Leasehold
OLT	Operation Land Transfer
OP	Office of the President
PA	Public Act
PAGRICO	Private Agricultural Investment Company
PAKISAMA	Pambansang Kilusan ng mga Samahang Magsasaka (National Movement of Farmer Unions)
PARC	Presidential Agrarian Reform Council
PARCCOM	Provincial Agrarian Reform Coordinating Committee
PARCODE	People's Agrarian Reform Code
PBSP	Philippine Business for Social Progress

PC	Philippine Constabulary
PCA	Philippine Coconut Authority
PCCI	Philippine Chamber of Commerce and Industry
PCGG	Presidential Commission on Good Government
PCGR	Presidential Commission on Government Reorganization
PD	Presidential Decree
PDCP	Private Development Corporation of the Philippines
PDP	Philippine Democratic Party
PDSP	Partido Demokratiko Soyalista ng Pilipinas (Philippine Social Democratic Party)
PHILDHRRA	Philippine Partnership for the Development of Human Resources in Rural Areas
PHINMA	Philippine Investment and Management Corporation
PKP	Partido Komunista ng Pilipinas (Philippine Communist Party)
PKM	Pambansang Kaisahan ng mga Magbubukid (National Peasants Union)
PMA	Philippine Military Academy
PNB	Philippine National Bank
PnB	Partido ng Bayan (Party of the People)
PPI	Philippine Peasant Institute
PRRM	Philippine Rural Reconstruction Movement
PSA	Philippine Sugar Association
RA	Republic Act
RAM	Reform the Armed Forces Movement and later, Rebolusyunaryong Alyansang Makabayan (People's Revolutionary Alliance)
SB	Senate Bill
SCAP	Supreme Command(er) of the Allied Powers
SEC	Securities and Exchange Commission
SN	Samahang Nayon (Barrio Unions - cooperatives)
SWS	Social Weather Station, Inc.
TADECO	Tarlac Development Corporation
TLA	Timber Licensing Agreement
TNC	Transnational corporation
TUCP	Trade Union Congress of the Philippines
UCPB	United Coconut Planters Bank
UFFAP	United Farmers and Fishermen's Association of the Philippines
UNIDO	United Nationalist Democratic Organization
UPLB	University of the Philippines at Los Baños
US	United States
USAID	United States Agency for International Development
VOS	Voluntary Offers to Sell
WCARRD	World Conference on Agrarian Reform and Rural Development
YOU	Young Officers Union

AWSJ	Asian Wall Street Journal
BD	Business Day
BS	Business Star
BT	Business Times
BW	Business World
DG	Daily Globe
FEER	Far Eastern Economic Review
FT	Financial Times
IHT	International Herald Tribune
MB	Manila Bulletin
MC	Manila Chronicle
NYT	New York Times
PDI	Philippine Daily Inquirer

adelantado	Governor general
Ang Bayan	'Of the People' (CPP central organ)
aparcero	Sharecropper
barangay	Village community
barrio	Village neighbourhood, or precinct
Batasang Pambansa	National legislature (Marcos' parliament)
cabeza de barangay	Local official
cacique	Local political boss
caudillos	Overseers
cedula	Head tax
chungbo	Korean measure, roughly one hectare
colonos	Tenant settlers
datu	Traditional village chieftain
delicadeza	Scrupulousness
estancias	Large ranches
hacenderos	Owners of traditional plantations
haciendas	Traditional plantations
Huks	Hukbo ng Bayan laban sa Hapon (Hukbalahap or People's Anti-Japanese Army); after the war, HMB
huweteng	Gambling racket (numbers game)
ilustrados	Highly educated Chinese and Spanish *mestizos*
inquilinos	Fixed-rent tenants
insulares	Philippine-born Spaniards ('islanders')
kalayaan	Freedom
kapataz	Foreman
kasamá	Share-cropping tenants
Listasaka	Government's land registration programme
Lumad	The term by which indigenous tribal peoples in Mindanao are known
maharlika	Village 'nobility'
Manindigan	'Take a Stand' (businessmen's organization)
mestizo	Mixed-race
palay	Unhusked rice
pasyon	'Story of Christ'
peninsulares	Iberian-born Spaniards

xvi

picul	A measure used mainly for sugar (usually 63.25 kilograms; 139.44 lb)
principalia	Indigenous notables under the Spanish
sacada	Migrant sugar cane harvesters
utang-na-loób	Debt of gratitude
yangban	Traditional landowners in Korea

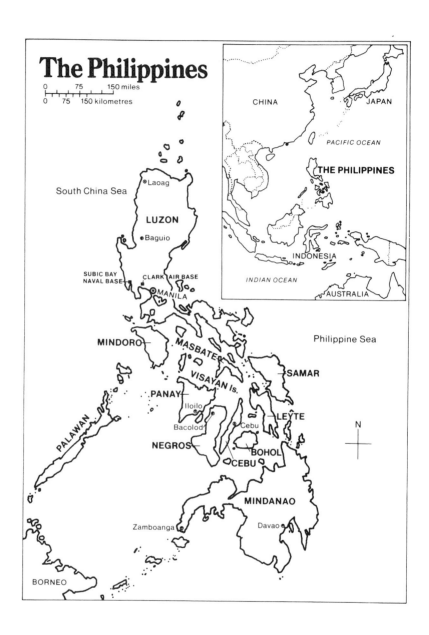

The Philippines

0   75   150 miles

0   75   150 kilometres

South China Sea

Laoag

LUZON

Baguio

SUBIC BAY
NAVAL BASE

CLARK AIR BASE

MANILA

CHINA

JAPAN

PACIFIC OCEAN

THE PHILIPPINES

INDONESIA

INDIAN OCEAN

AUSTRALIA

Philippine Sea

MINDORO

MASBATE

SAMAR

VISAYAN Is.

PANAY

Iloilo

LEYTE

Bacolod

Cebu

NEGROS

BOHOL

CEBU

N

MINDANAO

Zamboanga

Davao

PALAWAN

BORNEO

AGRARIAN REFORM IN A CAPTIVE LAND

The Philippines is a nation of contrasts. The vast majority of the archipelago's people live and work in rural *barrios*, or villages, trying to earn an income by cultivating the land. A tiny minority of the population live in palatial homes surrounded by servants, work in air conditioned high-rise office buildings in Makati - the capital's financial district - and travel to foreign cities to conduct business with partners or vacation with the more fortunate citizens of the North whose lifestyle they share. The institutions of government, the press and the courts, are formally democratic but exist side-by-side with a factionalised military that wants a bigger share of power having tasted authority during thirteen years of martial law. A constitutional regime, which claims to enshrine equal rights for all citizens, presides over a political and economic system so riven by inequality that it has given rise to an armed peasant-based movement fighting what it calls a revolutionary war.

The contrasts are all-pervasive. People who communicate with friends and neighbours in thriving Malay languages have been forced to speak first Spanish and then English in the conduct of their national affairs. Christianity and Catholicism hold sway, yet local politics are conducted through violence and intimidation. For six years a woman held the presidency, yet rural women fled unpaid work in farm homes and fields to sell themselves as mail-order brides, 'entertainers' and domestic helpers in Hong Kong, Tokyo, London and Los Angeles. Politicians speak of national independence and identity, while the national exchequer is depleted through servicing one of the biggest foreign debts in Asia and paying for luxury and capital goods imported from abroad. American films and pop music dominate the cinemas and airwaves.

In Metropolitan Manila, capital of the republic's 7,100 islands, the homes of the wealthy are surrounded by gardens in neighbourhoods encircled by high walls topped with bits of broken glass and barbed wire where the gates are manned by armed guards. The vast majority of the capital's people live in improvised housing, made of scrap wood, metal and cardboard, that lines the roads and highways and the slopes surrounding better-off middleclass suburbs. Manila is a city of eight million people with an infrastructure designed to accommodate two million, and it is bursting at the seams. People have flocked to the urban shanties because of the most striking contrast of all: the Philippines is primarily an agricultural country but those who work on the land are hungry.

This book is about agrarian reform in a captive land. It asks why, despite the central place accorded to agrarian reform on the political agenda in the Philippines throughout most of the 20th century, no significant land redistribution occurred. The definition of agrarian reform is itself a matter of controversy. Here agrarian reform refers to programmes, usually introduced by the state, that have the intention of redistributing agricultural land to its tillers and providing them with secure property rights and the means to earn an adequate living. From this perspective agrarian reform seeks both poverty alleviation and national economic development. But agrarian reform does not mean the same thing to all Filipinos. Nor is its definition agreed upon by the many foreigners who provide perhaps too much advice and too much 'assistance' as they seek to influence policy in the country. Debates about the meaning of reform are themselves a reflection of political struggle and are explored in Chapter 1.

The term 'a captive land', which originated in a speech by peasant leader Jaime Tadeo, has many layers of meaning.[1] On one level it illustrates the relationship between the state and the elite. There is an increasing interest in studying Philippine politics and agrarian reform policy-making within the perspective of state-society relations, an interest which is explored in Chapter 1. In many ways the state in the Philippines can be seen as a 'captive' of elite interests, or more specifically, of the clans which dominate political life. At the same time, it is a fractured state where factional interests like those of the military and bureaucrats beholden to private patrons prevent the consolidation of stable political institutions. Agrarian reform policy has been influenced both by the structural characteristics of the state and economy, and by the part played by individual political actors. Chapter 1 presents a framework in which to understand the role played by both in the policy-making process.

This framework suggests that agrarian reform experience in the Philippines has been characterized by a confrontation between 'conservative' and 'liberal' approaches to reform. Advocates of each have been active among both US and Filipino policy-makers. Few who have looked at reform experience in the Philippines, or elsewhere in Asia, have fully appreciated the nature and consequences of this confrontation. The analysis of the contention between these two approaches forms a thread running throughout this study. It is essential to an understanding of reform experience not only in the Philippines, but also in countries like South Korea. It is also vital if the active role played by the United States is to be properly comprehended.

Agricultural land in the Philippines is also 'captive' to a far smaller percentage of the population than anyone has realized. Chapter 1 examines new data on landownership and provides an analysis of the extent of landlessness, ownership concentration and poverty, as well as the basic characteristics of the agricultural sector. Chapter 2 traces the historical origins of the elite and the manner in which it captured the land through 350 years of Spanish colonial rule, the short-lived First Philippine Republic, and a half century of rule under the United

States. This and subsequent chapters covering debates about reform during the years following independence, through the years of Marcos dictatorship and the Aquino restoration, argue that this economic structure and pattern of landowner-ship were not the 'inevitable' consequence of colonialism and elite domination. Rather, they were the result of specific historical processes and political choices of both Filipino and US policymakers.

Jaime Tadeo also used the term 'captive land' to describe what he believed to be the country's 'foreign dominated economy'. To a large extent, economics, politics and even, to some degree, culture have been the captive of foreign influences, particularly those emanating from the United States. There is much confusion over the role the US has played in agrarian reform efforts in the Philippines and elsewhere in the third world. A major thesis of this study is that the US has been extremely influential both directly and indirectly in framing debates about agrarian reform right through the 1980s. US thinking about counterinsurgency has dominated policy-makers' response to persistent rural protest, while US biases against redistributive reform – partly promoted in terms of fighting 'world-wide communism' – have coincided with those of the elite.

At the same time, these dominant positions have not gone unchallenged, even among US policy-makers themselves. Chapter 3 explores the historical role of the US in reform debates in Asia after World War II. Subsequent chapters follow its influence in the Philippines right through the Aquino period. *A Captive Land* questions why the US supported reform efforts in Japan, Taiwan and South Korea, while it never did so in the Philippines. Such a perspective should provide some insight into whether or not the US is likely to support redistributive reforms in the wake of the decline of the socialist world.

In the Philippines, not only is the land a captive to the elite, bus so also is the peasantry. This was nowhere more poignantly illustrated than with the arrest and imprisonment of Tadeo himself.[2] Notorious figures like Eduardo 'Danding' Cojuangco Jr. and Juan Ponce Enrile, who had greatly expanded their corporate landholdings at the expense of the peasantry during the Marcos years, were not only free but actively engaged in the nation's politics in 1990. General Fidel Ramos became a national hero when he deserted President Marcos to support Corazon Aquino in 1986 and was actively campaigning for the presidency in 1991-92. For many years he had commanded the Philippine Constabulary which carried out some of the worst abuses against the peasantry during the Marcos dictatorship. Meanwhile Tadeo was locked in maximum security prison on charges of 'swindling' first levelled against him during the Marcos years. The peasant movement has been largely responsible for putting agrarian reform on the nation's political agenda and the role of its organizations remains a constant theme throughout this study.

Chapter 4 summarizes the experience of reform under Marcos and emphasizes the general pattern of support he received from most of the elite during the early years of martial rule. Particular attention is accorded to the role of Cojuangco, Enrile and other politicians and their clans, who were preparing their political revivals in the early 1990s. Chapters 5 to 10 explore in detail debates about reform during the Aquino years. Based on an examination of unpublished documents, interviews with many of the key players, and field research throughout the country, these chapters attempt to provide a record of the debates. The study documents the stance taken on reform during the crucial first two years of the government by all of the major elite politicians. New insights are offered into the origin of the controversial corporate stock-sharing plan which allowed President Aquino's family to hold on to its famous sugar estate, Hacienda Luisita, and into the role of the US, the military and the business community in shaping reform policy.

The multi-dimensional character of agrarian reform

Agrarian reform is a multi-dimensional issue encompassing a wide range of economic, political and social problems. Among what are usually considered as 'economic' problems are: poverty and inequality; the low productivity of agriculture; technical change; the balance of agricultural production between export and domestic markets and between food and non-food crops; regional disparities; the balance between urban and rural investment and lending; and sluggishness in the development of non-agricultural productive activities, especially in the manufacturing and industrial sectors. The problem of rapid demographic growth leading to increasing pressure on finite land resources clearly has social, economic, political and cultural causes and consequences.

'Social' and 'political' problems include: the concentration of property rights that have contributed to growing landlessness among agricultural tenants, workers, marginal farmers, fisherfolk and other rural poor, as well as the denial of the traditional but unrecorded rights of the indigenous peoples to their ancestral lands; monopolies in land, labour and capital markets; the unequal distribution of power in the political system between classes, groups and clans; the problems of finance, bureaucratic inefficiency and corruption in the institutions of the state stretching from central to local village government; and competition for authority and resources between state institutions and among factions within them, not the least of which involve the military. A further problem addressed by agrarian reform is the rapid ecological destruction of the countryside.

Touching on all these domains is continued social violence including: the on-going organized warfare between the Armed Forces of the Philippines (AFP) and the New People's Army (NPA), and the smouldering confrontation of the former with the Muslim armies fighting for self-determination in Mindanao, both of which are fuelled by conflicts over land; the perpetual violence of the political system in the Philippines where large landowners and rural monopolists mount their own armed groups, eject peasants from the land, and regularly carry out political assassinations of rivals; as well as the culture of criminal violence like cattle poaching, robbery and summary killings which flourish in a poverty stricken environment.

Many problems related to agrarian reform in the Philippines also have international dimensions. These include: foreign influence over the armed forces in strategic, ideological and material terms; and foreign participation in the agricultural economy through aid, investment and the models of development which accompany them. Most studies of agrarian reform in the Philippines and in Asia have largely ignored the role played by the United States and other foreign actors. Yet this dimension is crucial to understanding the experience of agrarian reform in the Philippines and elsewhere.

Agrarian reform can also play a role in confronting the hardships suffered by rural women. These include discrimination in property rights, long and unpaid household and agricultural production work, and rape inside and outside the household, as well as the direct and indirect coercion of young rural women into occupations as domestic workers, brides and prostitutes at home and abroad.

Of course, all these issues cannot be examined in one study on agrarian reform. But the recognition of the multi-dimensional character of agrarian reform and the problems it touches on has important implications for the study of agrarian reform policy-making. The scope of this study is both broad and narrow. It attempts to present an overall portrait of the multi-dimensional character of debates about reform past and present, while also delving into some of the minute detail so crucial to understanding the realities of policy-making.

There are important reasons why debates and popular campaigns concerned with the agricultural sector have focused on 'agrarian' or 'land' reform rather than simply on 'agricultural development'. Agrarian reform places the issue of agricultural development on political terrain. It is concerned not only with the technical mechanisms of farm production and distribution, but with property rights and control over the resources used in production. Agrarian reform focuses debates about agricultural development on people and their relations with one another rather than on inputs *per se*. While every national debate over 'agrarian' or 'land' reform policy must be understood in its own historical context, there has been a common thread running through most debates. Debates everywhere have seen a confrontation between those who believe that agrarian reform must be centred on the *redistribution* of ownership rights and effective control over productive agricultural land and those opposed to extensive redistribution who wish reform to focus on measures to raise agricultural productivity.

There are advantages and disadvantages in writing about the Aquino reform so soon after its passage and early implementation. While this account, written near the end of Aquino's term in office, will need to be amended, or even revised as other information becomes available, at the same time it can put on the record 'historical facts' that might otherwise escape notice. In this sense this book is offered as a contribution to what must be an on-going process of study about agrarian reform. The struggle for land has long preoccupied not only the people of the Philippines, but also people throughout the third world. Given the intransigence of both landed elites and aid donors in the developed countries, it is a struggle that is likely to continue to occupy the energies and imagination of future generations.

Notes

1. Tadeo, 1986, p. 15.
2. See Chapter 10.

1
LANDLESSNESS, AGRARIAN REFORM AND THE STATE

1.1 Introduction

After President Aquino assumed power in February 1986, it was difficult to find anyone in the political arena in the Philippines who voiced open and clear-cut opposition to agrarian reform. Everyone from the Communist-led National Democratic Front (NDF) to large landowners and state officials, including some military officers, voiced their endorsement for 'agrarian reform'. The Communist Party and the NDF continued to implement their 'revolutionary land reform program' in the areas which they controlled, and the policy statements of both emphasized this programme.[1] The biggest landowner organization in the country, the Council of Agricultural Producers of the Philippines (CAPP) in 1988 expressed its commitment to a 'truly just, workable, and effective Comprehensive Agrarian Reform Program.'[2] Lt.Col. Victor Corpus, in his book recommending that the armed forces adopt a more effective counterinsurgency strategy, stated, 'it is the problem of the peasant farmers - the issue of agrarian reform - which is most urgent and primary.'[3]

Among foreign aid donors, there have long been similar expressions of general support for agrarian reform. Since the early 1950s, the United Nations Food and Agricultural Organization has endorsed land reform. In 1979 it organized a World Conference on Agrarian Reform and Rural Development, setting out a programme of action.[4] As early as 1975, the World Bank published a policy paper endorsing, in general, the contribution of land reform to development.[5] In the early 1970s, even the United States Agency for International Development (USAID), which has been the most hostile to programmes of land redistribution, joined the chorus.[6]

Far from representing a consensus, the near universal endorsement of 'agrarian reform' or 'land reform' in the third world and among the aid officials of the developed countries hides sharp divergencies over the meaning and content of such reform.[7] Agrarian reform has been the subject of wrenching debates over state policy in the Philippines and elsewhere in Asia. This chapter examines the basic facts about the agricultural production structure in the Philippines in order to explain why agrarian reform debates have been so important in the country. It also provides a theoretical framework for understanding those debates.

Alternative definitions of agrarian reform have been at the heart of political confrontations over proposals for land redistribution. They are themselves a reflection of opposing views about development strategy and opposing interests in predominantly agricultural societies. Arriving at a meaningful definition of reform provides the first step in understanding what has been at stake in the debates. It is suggested here that agrarian reform remains so central because of peasant reaction to landlessness and land concentration.

Agrarian reform is a complex policy issue touching on a myriad of problems in the social, economic and political life of a third world nation. Authors writing on the state and agrarian reform have discussed a number of important propositions about the political and economic factors determining state policy. A critical assessment of their work raises important questions about the relationship between state and society in the process of agrarian reform policymaking in the Philippines. An alternative approach is offered here, encompassing the multi-dimensional character of reform. It also provides a more interpretive and historically oriented approach to state-societal relations, and a framework to analyse the intersection of interests between domestic and foreign actors in the policy-making process.

One of the most striking aspects about Philippine agrarian reform debates has been the participants' lack of accurate knowledge about the structure of landownership. Here, an effort is made to present as accurate an assessment as possible of the extent of landlessness and ownership concentration. While the paucity of data necessitates only indicative conclusions, the picture that emerges is one of widespread landlessness and poverty, and a much higher degree of landownership concentration than has been previously believed.

1.2 Why agrarian reform?

In one form or another 'agrarian reform' has been on the political agenda in the Philippines since the United States replaced Spain as colonial rulers of the archipelago in 1898. Its roots could be traced even further back to the numerous peasant uprisings that occurred periodically during nearly 350 years of Spanish rule. Since the Philippines was granted Commonwealth status under US authority in 1935, agrarian reform has figured prominently in policy and legislative debates of successive administrations. Manuel Quezon, first as Senate President (1916-1935) and then as Commonwealth President (1935-1942), introduced tenancy legislation. After the country was granted independence in 1946, major pieces of agrarian reform legislation were passed during the presidency of Ramon Magsaysay (1954-1957) and that of Diosdado Macapagal (1962-1965). Shortly after he declared martial law in 1972, President Marcos proclaimed 'the whole country as [a] land reform area.'[8] Almost immediately upon assuming office in February 1986, President Aquino's government was confronted with demands that it institute a comprehensive programme of agrarian reform.

After World War II, redistributive land reform became an issue of international concern as third world 'peasant populations' played an increasingly important role in national/anti-colonial independence movements and in the post independence policy debates of new state rulers.[9] This tendency was reinforced after the success of the Chinese revolution in 1949 when knowledge of China's radical agrarian reform became known in the third world. Third world state authorities, as well as the United States and other developed countries which began to provide foreign assistance to them, had to confront growing political instability as peasant-based political movements organized around demands for access to land. Since the mid-1950s, rather than directly oppose demands for reform, many third world states, as well as aid donors in the developed world, have tended to minimize the redistributive content of reform programmes and the definition of reform itself.[10]

In a strict sense, 'land reform' can be said to refer particularly to a change in the legal or customary institution of property rights and duties, which define the rights of those who own or use agricultural land. Ownership is best conceived of as a 'bundle of rights' representing varying degrees of control over things: the right to possess, use, manage, earn an income from, lend, transfer, or sell, as well as to pass these rights on to heirs. Land reform seeks to alter the distribution of any or all of these rights. In this sense, it has been employed to refer both to the outright redistribution of the entire bundle of rights over land to those who cultivate the soil, as well as a single adjustment of the conditions under which a tenant, or other cultivator, gains access to the land (for example, the amount of rent in cash or kind, the security of the tenancy arrangement or land use right, or the obligation of tenants and owners to one another).[11]

Since the late 1950s, the term 'agrarian reform' has increasingly replaced 'land reform' in policy discussions both within third world states as well as among foreign aid officials in developed countries. The shift in terminology was brought about by two contradictory influences. On the one hand, policy-makers opposed to redistributive reform have chosen the term 'agrarian reform' over 'land reform' with one specific political objective: to take the focus off land redistribution and concentrate on land settlement and productivity programmes within existing property institutions.[12] On the other hand, the use of the term 'agrarian reform' by the advocates of redistributive reform reflects both their concern with placing reform on the terrain of human relations, and their recognition that any reform programme must encompass more than the redistribution of property rights.

The term 'agrarian' has, in fact, long held a connotation associated with land redistribution. An 'agrarian' in 1818 England was 'one in favour of a redistribution of landed property', and 'agrarianism' in 1861 referred to 'political agitation...arising from dissatisfaction with existing tenure of land'.[13] Thus the term 'agrarian reform' implies not only the physical redistribution of land, but a transformation in rural relations. It has been adopted by the advocates of redistributive reform who realise that land redistribution must be accompanied by other changes in the agricultural production structure, such as the introduction of credit programmes, the provision of extension services, or the reform of farm input and produce markets that allow beneficiaries profitably to engage in farming.[14]

3

In a predominantly agricultural society like the Philippines, the creation and use of agricultural infrastructure is always influenced by local power relations, which in turn reflect the control of land. This is why land redistribution must be at the centre of any meaningful concept of agrarian reform.[15] The opponents of redistributive measures have, however, attempted to define agrarian reform as any change in agriculture, whether it be minor adjustments to rental fees for land or the introduction of programmes to improve agricultural productivity. These would be better labelled tenancy reforms or agricultural development programmes.

1.3 The state and agrarian reform

The debate over agrarian reform in the Philippines and elsewhere has historically occurred as a debate over state policy. Agrarian reform involves policy decisions affecting existing property rights that are central to the consensus whereby the powerful in society continue to support the state.[16] Agrarian reform also involves decisions about economic organization that affect the whole of society. This can only be addressed at the level of the state. What is more, since reform emerges on the agenda as a response not only to poverty and landlessness, but also to potential or actual political instability, it touches on the central issue of order in society which is one of the basic preoccupations of the state. Agrarian reform is also crucially related to 'state capacity', or the – historically evolved – technical, administrative and financial resources within the institutions which compose the state.

The most interesting studies of agrarian reform policy-making have either explicitly or implicitly situated the problem in an analysis of the state and its relationship with society. In the Philippines, the importance of discussing agrarian reform in relation to the state was highlighted by one of the country's leading experts on the issue, Mahar Mangahas, during the debate over reform in 1987:

> Today's great inequities in the distribution of land in the Philippines have been mainly the doing of the state...The root of the land distribution problem has been the abuse of state prerogatives, over the centuries, to grant land and any other natural resources to the merely powerful and hence socially undeserving few.[17]

He argued that, since the state was the source of the problem, then the state had the responsibility to provide the solution. Authors who have looked at agrarian reform from the perspective of state-society relations raise questions crucial to understanding reform experience in the Philippines.

The first question which emerges from these studies is whether state policy on agrarian reform is primarily determined by the socio-economic structural characteristics of a society, or by the ideology and action of individuals in positions of power. In other words, is agrarian reform policy essentially a reflection of the level of economic development and the alignment of classes in a society, or is it determined by the ideas and action of state leaders?

The 'structural determinists' have regarded state policy on agrarian reform as essentially determined by the material development of the system of agricultural production, the struggle between classes within that system and the manner in which the system is integrated into the world economy. From this perspective, reforms are seen to be functional to the transition from 'pre-capitalist' to 'capitalist' forms of farming, and also to the maintenance of forms of capitalist accumulation that perpetuate the dependent position of third world economies.[18]

In direct opposition to the determinist view are those who assume or claim that redistributive reforms are possible where state leaders have both the 'political will' and an adequate development strategy to proceed. From this perspective, state policy on agrarian reform is principally determined by the character and commitment of individual political leaders. This idea has been widely promoted on the Philippine political scene and in the academic community.[19] Others, inspired by Weberian ideas, have opposed the structural determinist approach by arguing that state policies on agrarian reform were not simply derivative of class relationships in society, 'but were influenced by the development ideologies adopted by state elites', the 'political entrepreneurship' of specific individuals and the bargains struck between state elites and social groups.[20]

The structural-determinist argument underlines the necessity of examining the complexities of the Philippine production structure, the way in which it has influenced decisions about reform, and the impact that those decisions have had on the agricultural economy.[21] Structural determinists also highlight the import-ance of foreign capital in a third world country integrated in the world economy. By the late 1980s, foreign corporations still played a significant role in the Philippine economy. Of the country's top 2,000 corporations in 1988 (measured in terms of gross revenue), 220 were foreign-owned companies. The US had by far the largest number with 123, while Britain came a poor second with 23. No less than 42 of these foreign companies had significant interests in agribusiness.[22] Besides plantation agriculture, foreign transnationals were particu-larly important in the agricultural chemicals sector (pesticides and herbicides) through companies like the US Monsanto, France's Rhone Poulenc or the British-Dutch Shell Chemical Company. By the late 1980s, 60 to 70 per cent of all fertilizer was imported, as were substantial amounts of animal feed, chemicals, breeder stock for poultry and livestock, and, of course, wheat.[23]

The structural determinists therefore raise questions that are essential to understanding the context in which policy debates occur, and also the economic and political constraints faced by decision-makers. However, by reducing all policy to mere reflections of the development of modes of production, the structural determinist approach cannot explain the diametrically opposed views on agrarian reform that have characterized policy-debates in the Philippines and among US foreign aid officials in Asia. The Weberian-inspired approach points to the necessity of examining the real impact of the ideas and actions of particular leaders on policy outcomes at different moments in Philippine history. On the other hand, this perspective tends to ignore the socio-economic structure that influences both the development ideology and the actions of state leaders and, in the Philippine case, the intervention of the US and other foreign actors. Thus, to understand agrarian reform policy-making it is necessary to combine the insights from both schools of thought.

The most interesting propositions about the process of state policy-making on agrarian reform emerge out of debates about the role of authoritarian regimes, state capacity and the 'relative autonomy' of the state in determining policy outcomes. In other words, do state institutions and leaders enact agrarian reforms to expand their authority, or are agrarian reforms only possible when state institutions already enjoy concentrated authority and considerable technical and administrative resources?

The state's action on agrarian reform has been explained by some authors as both a measure of, and a means to expand, state 'autonomy' from specific interests in society.[24] Grindle argued that states in Latin America, in line with their own goals as opposed to those of dominant classes, used agrarian reform to coerce large-scale farmers into modernizing. She suggested that state officials also employed agrarian reform to establish a 'dependent clientele of reform benefi-ciaries.' In the Philippine context it is necessary to investigate whether the state's adoption of measures to encourage large-scale farmers to modernize their operations during the Marcos and Aquino years was a reflection of the state's autonomy or a reflection of state control by elite groups with an interest in a particular modernization programme. It must be asked whether agrarian reform programmes were adopted by state officials, autonomous from dominant classes, to develop peasant loyalty and dependence on the state, or whether they were adopted by state officials, representing one elite faction, in their attempt to defeat rivals.

A number of authors have considered authoritarian 'governments', 'regimes', or 'states', as the best agents to implement agrarian reform, assuming implicitly or explicitly that they were also the most autonomous.[25] This assumption has been made about the martial law regime established by President Marcos in the Philippines in 1972.[26] This perspective assumes that the expansion of the state's role in society necessarily weakens the landed oligarchy.[27] In doing so, it ignores the possibility that members of the oligarchy might very well control those state institutions which are expanding. It also ignores the potential for reform under more competitive political systems. In the Indian state of Kerala and in neighbouring Sri Lanka, far more was achieved through the mobilization of rural people for reform than in the noncompetitive regimes of Pakistan.[28] It is difficult to accept a priori that authoritarian regimes are either more autonomous from society or more likely to implement redistributive reforms.

In a related argument, some authors have seen agrarian reform policy as essentially determined by the historically evolved 'capacity' of state institutions. Hayami et al argued that redistributive reform of the type pursued in Japan, Taiwan and South Korea could not be carried out in the Philippines because of the lack of competent governmental bureaucracy, the absence of land records, and weak tenant organization.[29] Agrarian reform requires technical expertise in planning, mapping, administration, taxation, extension services and a range of other functions. The presence or absence of systematic land-titling procedures and records of landownership can make an enormous difference in the efficacy of a reform programme. However, the absence of a bureaucratic machinery capable of carrying out reform and the lack of adequate land records cannot be considered simply as characteristics of the Philippine political system. State capacity is not engraved in stone, but is, at least in part, determined by the political choices of those who control state power.

If there are problems in understanding the role of the state in relation to agrarian reform, there are just as many in the conceptualizing of society. The most important is associated with the analysis of classes. Characteristic of many attempts to analyse societal determinants of agrarian reform policy has been the work of Hayami *et al.* They assume that those who demand agrarian reform include both the rural landless and the urban business and middle class, which has an interest in political stability and the expansion of domestic markets for urban goods and services.[30] While this is a logical assumption, it is not necessarily an accurate one. It is necessary to examine whether or not an independent urban business sector favouring redistributive reform has ever existed. In analysing classes in the Philippines, the 'national bourgeoisie' is often discussed, yet few authors have ever described precisely who belong to this class.[31] Authors often write about the 'agrarian elite' or the 'rural elite' without examining who they are and what their specific characteristics are in any given national and historical context.[32]

The analysis of classes is extremely important to an understanding of agrarian reform policy-making.[33] But, while the concept of 'class' is useful in analysing the determinants of agrarian reform policy, the particular characteristics of classes are historically and society-specific. As E.P. Thompson put it, 'Classes do not exist as abstract, platonic categories'.[34] Looking at classes in society means looking at groups defined primarily by their role in the process of production and distribution of wealth. Whether a 'manufacturing class' is more or less distinct from a 'landowning class' is primarily a question to be resolved by historical enquiry. Whether a 'working class' is a leading force for change and development, a minor player, a passive group, or even a conservative force must be decided through historical investigation.[35]

The labels accorded to groups and classes in society also need to be defined. In this study, the 'peasantry' is broadly defined, in accordance with practice in the Philippines itself.[36] However, this does not mean that there are not important distinctions within the peasantry which have major consequences for agrarian reform.[37] What is more, 'class' is not the only significant form of organization or identity in society. In the Philippines it is necessary to look at gender, clan, status, religious and, in some regions, 'tribal' organizations and identities to understand how societal forces influence state policy-making. 'Political clans' - or alliances of powerful, and often landowning, families built on patronage

7

networks from municipal to provincial and national levels – appear to be the most important form of political organization among the elite.[38]

In order to understand the agrarian reform policy-making process it is crucial to analyse action at the level of the state. Individual state leaders and the ideas they adopt do make a difference to policy outcomes. An anatomy of state institutions can help to understand the central issue of a state's capacity to undertake a specific reform programme. However, it is also important to remember that the state 'emerges' from society.[39] While the state has an institutional identity, it can only be understood through the identification of its societal sources of support, and the manner in which both state personnel and particular institutions relate to both domestic and foreign interests.

An examination of agrarian reform experience in the Philippines must be grounded in an historical analysis that takes into account conflicting interests in Philippine society, as well as opposing ideas and strategies held by domestic societal, state and foreign actors. A framework for such an analysis should be able to situate the Philippine reform experience in a broader comparative and historical perspective.

1.4 Contrasting approaches to reform

Agrarian reform emerged at the centre of the state's political agenda in the Philippines and elsewhere in Asia largely as a reaction to emerging revolutionary movements supported by peasant populations. It has seldom been realised that the debates over reform which came to preoccupy the attention of state leaders in the Philippines and other Asian countries after World War II were characterised by a confrontation between 'liberal' and 'conservative' approaches to the issue. Agrarian reform was endorsed by revolutionary movements as well as conservative and liberal reformers. However, these three agrarian reform currents were based on distinct and contrasting ideas about what reform should actually entail. These focused on: (1) their position toward the redistribution of property rights in agricultural land; (2) their objective *vis á vis* the maintenance or transformation of the principal institutions of the state; and (3) the process by which they proposed to transform or maintain agrarian and property relations.

1.4.1 Revolutionary agrarian reform

Redistributive agrarian reform has played an important part in post-war revolutionary struggles throughout the third world. Revolutionary movements have attempted to draw upon peasant unrest and demands for land in their efforts to capture and consolidate state power. From the revolutionary perspective, agrarian reform means the expropriation of land, with or without compensation, from non-tiller owners and its redistribution to the agricultural producers. Agrarian reform is seen as a comprehensive restructuring of the agricultural sector, undertaken with the participation of the peasantry and their organizations, and providing producers with access not just to land, but to the means to make it productive.

8

The ultimate objective of agrarian reform for most revolutionary movements has been to consolidate rural support for newly established state institutions under the control of the movements' own organizations. To date, most revolutionary movements have seen agrarian reform as the first step toward the creation of forms of cooperative and collective farming. However, this need not be a defining characteristic of the revolutionary model. What is important about revolutionary agrarian reform, in contrast to opposing conservative and liberal approaches, is the *process* by which it attempts to transform agrarian and property relations, not its commitment to establishing socialism.[40] Although revolutionary agrarian reform has generally been associated with those whose ultimate objective has been collectivization and socialism, conceivably it could be directed toward establishing a system of individual property and a market economy.[41]

In Asia, such reforms were an essential part of the revolutionary process in China, North Vietnam and North Korea.[42] Agrarian reform also played a crucial part in the Cuban and Nicaraguan revolutions.[43] William Hinton's classic account of land reform in China underlined the central role it played in transforming the social structure of the countryside. Peasant participation in the process of identifying lands for expropriation and then in redistribution was crucial to undermining relations of dependency between owners on the one hand, and tenants, workers and marginal farmers on the other.[44]

What is labelled here as 'revolutionary agrarian reform' is distinct from the more general experience of socialist agricultural development. The process of rural change led by the Chinese Communist Party was qualitatively different, at least from the late 1920s to the late 1950s, from Stalin's forced collectivization in the USSR. First, the Chinese Party had much experience in the countryside and many of its leaders spent their formative years organizing peasants. Second, agrarian reform was an integral part of the Party's overall strategy after 1928, throughout the fight against Japanese occupation (1937-45) and during the Civil War (1945-49). Finally, the Chinese Party attempted to involve local peasant communities in the process of change rather than simply imposing a new organizational form from above.[45]

The Chinese experience served as an example to revolutionary movements throughout Asia during the post-war period. In the Philippines during World War II, the *Hukbalahap*, or People's Anti-Japanese Army, mobilized peasants against Japanese occupation largely around the issue of land. When the peasant army again became active in the late 1940s, at least part of the movement drew inspiration from the Chinese Communist Party's rural struggle.[46] However, it was only when the reconstituted Communist Party of the Philippines (CPP) was formed in 1968, that the Chinese experience was fully incorporated in the Philippine Party's own 'Revolutionary Guide to Land Reform.'[47]

Those supporting revolutionary agrarian reform have operated mainly outside policy debates in the Philippine and other third world state institutions. They have served as the catalyst in initiating debates within the state, while offering

9

the peasantry a radical alternative reform in the context of a wider revolutionary change. Revolutionary agrarian reform has, therefore, never been a 'policy option', but rather a radical alternative to both the liberal and conservative approaches to reform.

1.4.2 The dominant conservative approach

During the post-war period, the threat to political stability emanating from land-hungry peasants in many third world countries made it a political imperative for state officials to put agrarian reform on the policy agenda. However, more often than not they attempted to minimize the redistributive content of reform and sought only to bolster the legitimacy of their governments. The vast majority of agrarian reform legislation in the third world has been of a decidedly conservative character. This 'conservative approach' has focused on introducing agrarian reform legislation in response to peasant demands, while minimizing any disturbance to existing property rights.

The conservative perspective is based on the proposition that a healthy economy requires the operation of land, labour and capital markets free from state intervention, including state initiated land redistribution.[48] From the conservative perspective, the problem of poverty is not founded in unequal distribution of assets, but rather in low productivity. It is traceable to population growth which has also made redistributive reform all but irrelevant.[49] Large estates, when run with modern agribusiness management, are seen to be more efficient than small farms, while tenant farmers are considered just as efficient or even more efficient than small owner-cultivators. Agrarian reform is perceived as irrelevant to wage workers.[50]

Under certain conditions the state may employ tenancy reforms involving adjustments in the level of land rents or the transformation of sharecroppers into fixed-rent leaseholders.[51] Alternatively, the state may launch resettlement programmes providing incentives for the landless to move to untitled public lands, or to engage in productivity enhancement programmes like those associated with the 'green revolution'.[52] However, large landowners and domestic and transnational agribusiness corporations that run on modern management principles, whether on large estates or through various forms of contract farming, are best placed to inject new investment into agriculture and to lead the way in producing crops for export. Large landowners and existing trading and credit networks are seen to play an irreplaceable functional role in rural economies.[53]

Advocates of the conservative approach oppose redistributive reform on the grounds that it violates the 'natural rights' of the individual to private property. They also object that it is disruptive to the legal system of property and that it would introduce insecurity and frustrate expectations. This would result in a decline in production and so in the general welfare of society.[54] If any land is to be expropriated by the state, owners should be offered incentives to part with their property voluntarily and compensated for their land at its full market value.

During the post-war period, most agrarian reforms in Latin America, the

Indian subcontinent and the Middle East, as well as those in Southeast Asia, have embodied this conservative approach.[55] In his discussion of reforms in India, Kohli pointed out that it is common for regimes in private property-based market economies 'to adopt a rhetoric of reform, while eschewing any serious attempts to take such actions.' He rightly emphasized that 'the state's incapacity to counter dominant social interests constitutes a normal state of affairs.'[56] It is not surprising, then, that the conservative approach to agrarian reform has been the dominant one in the Philippines and in most third world countries.

1.4.3 The liberal challenge

While the conservative approach has been dominant in the Philippines, it has not remained unchallenged. At the end of World War II, largely in response to the success of the Chinese Communist Party in winning peasant support and the potential threat that its example posed to Western interests in Asia, an alternative 'liberal' approach to redistributive reform was articulated by a vocal minority in the United States foreign aid bureaucracy who worked with like-minded officials in Asia. This approach was best expressed in the work and writings of Wolf Ladejinsky, who headed US efforts to implement reform during the occupation of Japan.[57] Like revolutionary agrarian reform, the liberal approach places redistribution of land at the centre of a strategy for rural change. But while the revolutionary model seeks to overthrow existing state structures, the liberal approach regards agrarian reform as the surest means to consolidate existing state authority and to defeat or pre-empt revolutionary movements in the countryside.

Liberal reformers assert that monopoly power prevents the operation of free markets in land, labour and agricultural inputs and produce. They believe that it is an important source of poverty and allocative inefficiency in the rural sector. Large landowners have easy access to credit, since they possess land collateral or have political connections both to bankers and government, so they often engage in capital investments such as labour-saving mechanization.[58] Land redistribution is considered necessary in order to undermine monopoly power, to tap the greater efficiency of small-owner cultivators in a labour-abundant and capital-scarce economy, and to alleviate poverty.[59] Such a reform is also seen as a necessary condition to bring down population growth in countries where large percentages of the population live in rural poverty.[60] In most cases tenancy reform is impossible to enforce, while resettlement programmes are prohibitively expensive and infringe on the rights of those already cultivating 'public' lands.[61]

The advocates of redistributive reform recognize the central role of technological innovation and programmes like the 'green revolution', but argue that these must be accompanied by agrarian reform if they are to have a positive impact on poverty and development.[62] However, advocates of the liberal approach have provided no clear assessment of the role of agribusiness corporations, especially in export production, in the context of redistributive reform. They assert that the state can initiate the provision of credit, extension and other services to the beneficiaries.[63]

A central proposition in the liberal approach to agrarian reform is that land redistribution would actually strengthen the institution of private property.[64] However, land is seen as a special case of property and individual rights over it are subject to certain limitations.[65] Because land is a finite endowment of nature, its unlimited appropriation by some will sooner or later deny the equal rights of others to benefit from its bounties.[66] The liberal reformers also argue that because redistribution will increase productivity and establish political stability, it is justified for the state to expropriate land.[67]

The advocates of the liberal approach believe that landowners have a right to compensation, but at a level less than market value in order to ensure a real resource transfer to the landless and to guarantee the fiscal viability of reform.[68] Compensation to landowners has been seen as necessary to overcome land-owners' political, and very likely violent, opposition to reform.[69] The US reform advocate, Roy Prosterman who played an important role in the Philippines, argued that landowners could be expected to accept less than market value compensation, or even as little as '50 per cent of current market value', as long as they were not treated disparagingly by the state.[70]

Aside from the well-known examples of redistributive reform in Japan, Taiwan and South Korea, the liberal approach to reform emerged in many other settings. In India, advocates of the model have long been active, but perhaps minimally successful in implementing their approach only in the states of Kerala and West Bengal.[71] In South Vietnam, after supporting a conservative approach to reform under Ngo Dinh Diem, the United States threw its weight behind what was essentially a liberal redistributive reform model adopted by the Nguyen Van Thieu government in 1969.[72] In the Philippines, the predominant conservative approach supported by state officials and the elite more generally, was first challenged in the early 1950s during the Communist-led Huk uprising.[73] At every stage in the reform debate in subsequent years, Filipino advocates of the liberal approach have been active - sometimes supported by those on the fringes of the US and other foreign aid organizations working in the Philippines.

1.4.4 Counterinsurgency and agrarian reform

The conservative and liberal approaches to agrarian reform involve sharply different perceptions about the nature of peasant-based revolutionary movements and the best means to safeguard existing structures of the state. Despite the fact that agrarian reform has almost always emerged on the agenda of third world states in response to significant peasant protest and rebellion, usually in conflict with the armed forces, few analysts have examined the influence of dominant military ideas on agrarian reform policy.[74]

The advocates of the conservative approach to agrarian reform find common ground with dominant thinking about 'counterinsurgency' in many third world military establishments and in the Pentagon.[75] For the counterinsurgency strategist, peasant-based revolutionary movements cannot be defeated by military force alone. Concerted action on the political and economic front by central and local government administration is also required.[76] However, redistributive agrarian reform has rarely been accepted as a necessary part of such a strategy and has often been opposed by counterinsurgency theorists as a destabilizing and counter-productive measure.

French Commandant David Galula summed up the lessons of counterinsurgency in Algeria and Indochina, arguing that the first step in fighting a guerrilla army is militarily to destroy or expel the guerrillas from an area and then to work with local elites to consolidate political control.[77] For Karl Jackson, a Berkeley counterinsurgency expert and former US Deputy Assistant Secretary of Defence, while 'it remains a truism that land reform is a good thing', reform is not a necessary condition for successful counterinsurgency. In fact, he argued that military efforts 'to protect and encourage progovernment rural élites' were 'the hallmark of successful counter-insurgency in Malaysia, Indonesia and the Philippines.' While underlining the need for military reform in many third world countries, Jackson nevertheless asserted that leadership is a matter of combining 'political savvy with outright coercion'. Successful counterinsurgency requires 'rather ruthless local commanders'.[78]

In direct contrast to the liberal approach, counterinsurgency theorists and the advocates of the conservative approach believe that redistributive reforms cannot be implemented 'in the midst of an insurgency', and that such reforms are politically impractical given the opposition that they would elicit from landowners.[79] For Jackson, even more important than implementing a general programme of reform, was the 'promise of reform,' and its 'selective' implementation in well-chosen regions. This was because 'image may be vastly more important than reality'.[80]

Earl Kulp, a disciple of Commandant Galula, whose career in third world and Philippine development work has overlapped with many counterinsurgency operations supported by the US government, provided the clearest example of the common ground between counterinsurgency theory and the conservative approach to reform.[81] Kulp devoted one chapter of his influential manual on development planning to the basic counterinsurgency principles elaborated by Galula.[82] In his view, 'rural development includes the paramilitary and civil aspects of counterinsurgency, the environment and the planning techniques of which are basically the same'.[83] In an extremely revealing passage, Galula acknowledged that the most effective way to defeat an insurgency would be to implement the reforms around which the insurgents have rallied support. However, to do so would likely undermine the very social forces which the counterinsurgency operation was designed to keep in power.[84] The central question for the counterinsurgent and for the advocates of the conservative approach to agrarian reform, was asked by Galula, 'how far can he go in the way of reforms without endangering his power, which, after all, is what he – right or wrong – is fighting to retain?'[85]

The proponents of the liberal approach argue that landlessness and poverty provide the breeding grounds for protest and revolution. While they share with the conservatives the same objectives of maintaining the existing structure of the state, they feel that long-term political stability is unattainable without a fairly sweeping redistributive reform.[86] By virtue of their control over land, argue the liberals, big landowners enjoy political influence and power far beyond that which is warranted by their numbers or their economic contribution.[87]

The liberals' claim that landownership is often a major source of political power is not disputed by the advocates of the conservative approach, but the two come to very different conclusions. The US agrarian reform expert Wolf Ladejinsky argued that the one lesson to be drawn from the communist revolutions of the 20th century was that governments will stand or fall on their relationship to the peasantry.[88] Citing the US political scientist Samuel Huntington, the US reform advocate Roy Prosterman argued that landlessness was a major source of revolutionary violence.[89] Contradicting the conservatives, Prosterman asserted that there is a close correlation between landlessness and revolution. He developed an 'index of rural instability' based on the percentage of landless families in the population as a whole. He stated that this could serve as a barometer to predict the likelihood of revolutionary upheaval in a developing country. On this basis he predicted 'a substantial danger of major revolution for any country 25 per cent or more of whose total population consisted of landless peasants.'[90]

For Prosterman the only alternative to redistributive reform would be the 'violence' and 'despotism' of 'revolutionary Marxism'.[91] While not all advocates of the liberal approach have endorsed such apocalyptic images, most have agreed that a redistributive reform is necessary to avoid violent revolution. Although clearly motivated by anti-communism, Prosterman argued directly against military formulae, like that of Jackson, which stressed the need for 'ruthless local commanders'. Strategies that relied too heavily on military force to suppress rebellion would be both ineffectual and costly. He deplored the use of 'death squads', which he said create 'a sense of rage and injustice' and only contribute to further rebellion.[92]

Redistributive reform is seen by the liberals as a vehicle for changing the balance of power in rural society and, by some, as a means to foster democracy.[93] The proponents of the liberal approach reject the conservative argument that redistributive reform is politically unfeasible. In commenting on the various approaches to reform, Herring stated, 'the political realists seem to assume, rather curiously, that it is politically realistic to leave the status quo in place.'[94] While the advocates of the liberal model argue that redistributive reform must alter the distribution of political power in the countryside, they tend to believe this can be achieved by existing state authorities. Much as they believe that landowners can be 'won over' to something less than market-value compensation for their property, they believe that a redistributive reform can be instituted in a developing country if only the state's leaders can be convinced of its utility.[95]

Of course these two approaches represent only broad trends. Not every advocate of an agribusiness-led rural development strategy would support the counterinsurgency formula outlined here. In a similar fashion, not all who support an essentially liberal prescription for reform do so with the same anti-communist vigour of Roy Prosterman. Reality seldom fits into such neat boxes. Nevertheless, a significant and continual debate along the lines of the liberal and conservative approaches has occurred throughout the post-war period.

While these two approaches have dominated the debate about agrarian reform, they both suffer from serious limitations. The debate on property rights and agrarian reform has occurred in terms defined by Western legal and political discourse and traditions. This reflects the reality of the Philippines and many other former colonies in the third world where these traditions now dominate. However, both the liberal and conservative conception of property rights clash with the indigenous peoples' concepts of the relation between human society and land, and also with Islamic ideas about property in the Muslim areas of Mindanao.[96] The two approaches also have little to say about the plight of rural women since they both embody the gender biases inherent in Western legal tradition.[97] Furthermore, Western conceptions of private property have severe limitations in curtailing the rapid destruction of the environment in the third world.

The conservative approach appears retrogressive in its outright rejection of expressed peasant demands for land. The liberal approach, however, fails to account for the role of agribusiness in implementing agrarian reform, and places enormous confidence in the capacity of the state to manage reform. The conservative faith in a military-centred counterinsurgency strategy to bring about rural peace seems unwarranted, yet the liberal belief that landowners can easily be made to accept redistributive reform is also questionable.

In this sense, while the two approaches have dominated the policy debate, they do not represent the final word on agrarian reform. In examining the policy debates in the Philippines and post-war Asia, it is necessary to consider alternatives to both these approaches and to consider both the problems and possibilities presented by the revolutionary model of agrarian reform.

1.5 Agriculture as a starting point for development

While agrarian reform has been at the centre of policy debates about development in the Philippines in the past, it is reasonable to ask whether it remains relevant in the late 20th century. Development, considered to be the improvement of the material well-being of people in a society, should focus on the economic sectors and geographical areas where most people live and work. By the mid-1980s over 60 per cent of all Filipino people still lived and worked in the rural areas. Half of the working population and 40 per cent of all families earned the major part of their income directly through agricultural activities (Table 1.1). Development, from this perspective, also means the reduction of the number of people who live in poverty.

15

Table 1.1: Families Living Below Subsistence (1985)

Main Sectoral Income Source Sector	Number of Families	% Total Families	Number Below Subsistence[1]	% by Sector	% Urban by Sector	% Rural by Sector
Agriculture	**3,917,293**	**39.8**	**1,810,442**	**46.3**	**7.9**	**92.1**
Wage & Salary	901,972	9.2	473,044	52.4	8.8	91.2
Own Account (crops, livestock, forestry)[2]	2,335,758	23.7	1,059,560	45.4	6.1	93.9
Own Account (Fishing)	471,396	4.8	230,894	49.0	13.5	86.5
Share of Others'agricultural production (net share produce)	208,167	2.1	46,944	22.5	12.6	87.4
Non-Agricultural	**4,283,477**	**43.5**	**776,946**	**18.1**	**40.1**	**59.9**
Wage & Salary	3,064,210	31.1	535,694	17.5	42.0	58.0
Own Account	1,219,267	12.4	241,252	19.8	36.0	64.0
Other Sources	**1,646,569**	**16.7**	**388,830**	**23.6**	**19.6**	**80.4**
Cash Receipts (from abroad)	568,524	5.8	19,866	3.5	21.9	78.1
Cash Receipts (domestic sources)	339,617	3.4	116,575	34.3	27.2	72.8
Family Sustenance Activities	243,297	2.5	158,386	65.1	7.2	92.8
Other (pension, urban rental, etc.)	495,131	5.0	94,003	19.0	30.4	69.6
TOTAL	**9,847,339**	**100.0**	**2,976,218**	**30.2**	**17.9**	**82.1**

[1]Subsistence defined by World Bank as bottom 30% of families in readjusted income data.
[2]Forestry, with about 34,100 families below subsistence out of a total of 57,000, has highest percentage below subsistence at 60%, while livestock and poultry, with about 27,700 families below subsistence out of 78,700, has the lowest at 36%.
Source of Basic Data: National Census and Statistics Office, Family Income and Expenditure Survey, 1985 and report on this survey in World Bank, *The Philippines: The Challenge of Poverty*, 1988, p. 118.

Poverty is endemic in the Philippines and is most widespread in the rural areas. By the mid-1980s the country had one of the worst levels of poverty in Southeast Asia.[98] Government statistics on income and poverty levels - and World Bank estimates based on them - at best, only approximate reality. Based on sample surveys they do not capture the great diversity which exists from *barrio* to *barrio*, nor do they incorporate the extensive unreported economic activity which is so much a part of every third world economy.[99] It is difficult to compare poverty between countries since the poor within every society are, to some extent, defined by their relative position to the rich. Yet in one respect useful comparisons can be made, since in every country those who are hungry are poor.[100] In 1986, the Philippine government estimated that 67 per cent of rural families and 57 per cent of urban families were living beneath the poverty threshold. The government set the poverty line at an income level necessary for a family's minimum nutritional requirements and basic expenditures.

Employing a lower estimate of required nutrition, a World Bank study still affirmed that as of 1985, 58 per cent of rural families and 42 per cent of urban dwellers lived below the poverty line.[101] The World Bank identified a 'core poverty' group as those who did not receive the minimum food intake necessary for survival. The overwhelming majority of people in this category lived in the rural areas. The Bank estimated that this group was roughly correlated with the poorest 30 per cent of families. Almost 50 per cent of all agricultural households fell into this category (Table 1.1).[102] Despite the predominant place of agriculture as a source of livelihood for the population, malnutrition was widespread, particularly among the rural poor.[103] Even the urban poor had largely agricultural roots, since the increasing numbers of squatters in Manila, Cebu, Davao and other urban centres fled there in the hope of escaping poverty in the countryside.[104]

Development, considered as the growth of society's overall level of production, must focus and build upon those sectors of the economy where human and material resources are concentrated. From this perspective, by the late 1980s the Philippine economy no longer appeared to depend primarily on agriculture for its production. Agriculture, defined as the production of crops, livestock, poultry, forestry and fishery, accounted for only about 27 per cent of Gross Domestic Product (GDP) in 1988 (see Table 1.2). Yet, if looked at in terms of 'agribusiness' - or agriculture plus all directly related manufacturing activities - the importance of the sector to the overall economy appeared overwhelming.[105] The direct contribution of agribusiness amounted to 41 per cent of GDP in 1988. When it is considered that a good portion of the service sector, whether in wholesale and retail trade, transport and storage, or government and private services, is directly related to agribusiness activity, the total contribution was probably well over 50 per cent.

The majority of agricultural lands and labour are devoted to the production of rice, corn and coconut (Table 1.3).[106] Rice lands occupy about 3.7 million hectares, or 40 per cent of farm-land and produce the staple food crop for about

Table 1.2: Gross Value Added 1981-1988*
(Millions Pesos at Constant 1972 Prices and Percentage)

	1981	1982	1983	1984
Agriculture[1]	24608 (25.6)	25378 (25.6)	24845 (24.9)	25409 (27.1)
Agroindustrial[2] Manufacturing	13143 (13.7)	13424 (13.5)	13612 (13.6)	13297 (14.2)
Agribusiness Sub-Total	37751 (39.2)	38802 (39.2)	38457 (38.5)	38706 (41.2)
Industry[3]	21820 (22.7)	22290 (22.5)	22343 (22.4)	18985 (20.2)
Services[4]	36636 (38.1)	37907 (38.3)	39120 (39.1)	36236 (38.6)
TOTAL VALUE ADDED	**96207**	**98999**	**99920**	**93927**
	1985	1986	1987	1988
Agriculture[1]	26252 (29.2)	27110 (29.7)	26834 (28.1)	27752 (27.23)
Agroindustrial[2] Manufacturing	12299 (13.7)	12129 (13.4)	12995 (13.6)	13983 (13.7)
Agribusiness Sub-Total	38551 (42.9)	39239 (43.4)	39829 (41.7)	41735 (41.0)
Industry[3]	16701 (18.6)	16251 (17.8)	17566 (18.4)	19298 (18.9)
Services[4]	34551 (38.5)	35674 (39.1)	38039 (39.9)	40725 (40.0)
TOTAL VALUE ADDED	**89803**	**91164**	**95434**	**101758**

*GVA is computed by deducting the total value of intermediate inputs from the value of each sector's gross output. Figures may not total due to rounding.
[1]Crops, Livestock, Poultry, Fishery and Forestry.
[2]Sub-section of Industrial Manufacturing: Food, Beverages, Tobacco, Textile, Wood and Cork, Furniture and Fixtures, Paper, Leather and Rubber products.
[3]Industry less Agroindustrial manufactures: Mining and Quarrying, Other Manufactures, Construction and Utilities.
[4]Transport and storage, Wholesale and Retail Trade, Banks, Non-banks and Insurance, Real Estate, Ownership of Dwellings, Government Services, Private Services.
Source: *Agribusiness Fact Book*, 1986. Manila: Centre for Research and Communications, 1987, pp. 5-10.

80 per cent of the population. Rice is generally produced in the low fertile valleys on both irrigated and rain-fed farms throughout the country. Corn is grown on about 1.9 million hectares, or 20 per cent of farm-land. It is the staple food for about 20 per cent of the population, as well as an important feed crop for livestock, and is generally grown on higher and unirrigated lands.[107] The Philippines is the world's largest exporter of coconut products, with trees planted on about 29 per cent of farm-land concentrated on higher ground in Southern Mindanao and Southern Tagalog, and to a lesser extent in the rest of Mindanao, the Eastern Visayas and Bicol.

The balance of farm land - about 1.2 million hectares or 12 per cent of the total - is devoted to other commercial crops, mainly oriented towards export production. The largest area among these - about 300,000 hectares - has been

Table 1.3: Farm Area and Number By Crop Type (1980)

Crop	FARM AREA Hectares	% Area	NUMBER Number	% Total
Principal Crops	**9,192,000**	**97.79**	**3,341,035**	**97.68**
Rice (Palay)	3,755,700	38.60	1,610,529	47.09
Coconut	2,842,900	29.20	709,626	20.75
Corn	1,955,000	20.10	753,632	22.03
Sugar	312,800	3.20	34,634	1.01
Fiber (Abaca)	60,100	0.62	16,054	0.47
Banana	79,700	0.82	20,570	0.60
Pineapple	28,100	.29	2,331	0.07
Mango	9,000	0.09	2,100	0.06
Coffee	123,800	1.27	37,301	1.09
Tobacco	8,100	0.08	5,302	0.16
Citrus	16,800	0.17	3,548	0.10
Other Permanent and Temporary[1]	**318,600**		**145,408**	
Tuber/Root/Bulb	131,600	.35	76,765	2.24
Vegetables	47,700	0.49	28,580	0.84
Other Permanent	86,700	0.89	17,467	0.51
Other Temporary	52,600	0.54	22,596	0.66
Livestock/poultry	**181,600**	**1.87**	**52,211**	**1.53**
Cattle	128,700	1.32	6,579	0.19
Hog	22,700	0.23	23,127	0.68
Other livestock	16,900	0.17	7,846	0.23
Chicken	12,600	0.13	13,467	0.39
Other poultry	700	0.01	1,192	0.03
Other	33,000	0.34	27,077	0.79
TOTAL	**9,725,200**		**3,420,323**	

	AQUACULTURE		
	Brackish Water		**Fresh Water**
Private	123,701		14,239
Public	81,300		141
TOTAL	**205,001**		**14,380**

[1]Includes: tuber/root/bulb, vegetables, other permanent and other temporary.
Source: Census of Agriculture 1980 as compiled in Agribusiness Fact Book, CRC, 1986, p. 22-23.

planted with sugarcane. From the late 1960s through the 1980s, other commercial crops produced mainly for export became increasingly important on the remaining 650,000 hectares of farm land devoted to crop production.[108] Among the most important were pineapples, bananas, mangoes and, more recently, other fruits and vegetables like citrus and black peppers. Some new crop types, like oil palms, were still in their infancy in the late 1980s and not yet produced for the export market.

Livestock and poultry were produced on about 200,000 hectares of farm land. Deep-sea and inland fishing have been an extremely important source of food for the archipelago and an increasingly valuable export product. Survey data conservatively reported about 200,000 hectares of fishponds in 1986, the vast majority of which were brackish water.[109] Finally, logging, somewhat dubiously grouped together with agriculture, has long been a major export earner. As in much of Southeast Asia, rampant logging has led to the rapid depletion of forest area.[110] By the end of the 1980s, of the country's nearly 15 million hectares of classified forest lands, only 6 million hectares were left with tree cover and only 1 million hectares of 'virgin forest' remained.[111]

Traditionally, agricultural products made up as much as 85 per cent of all exports (Table 1.4). By the late 1980s coconut and forest products still made up the bulk of agricultural exports, but the contribution of sugar declined sharply while that of pineapple, bananas and other fruits and vegetables increased significantly. The overall contribution of agriculture to export earnings declined to only 45 per cent by 1979, while during the 1980s they made up only 25 per cent of total export earnings. Both the internal shift in the composition of agricultural exports and their decline relative to manufactured (particularly clothing and electronic) products was caused by a sharp reduction in world commodity prices. However, the real shift may be somewhat less drastic since the new high export earners relied heavily on imported inputs.

While agriculture's position in the national account had declined by the late 1980s, it remained absolutely central to economic life in the country. This had crucial consequences both for the producers (the poor in Philippine society), and for the wealthy (the large landowners, managers, business and financial executives) and the political alliances they financed and organized. The destiny of rich and poor alike, as well as the fate of the nation as a whole, was largely bound up with what would happen in the agricultural sector.

By the late 1980s, there was a general consensus, at least in rhetorical terms, that agriculture had to be the starting point of any overall plan for national development.[112] Only a relatively small group of 'elite nationalists' still regarded focusing development policy on agriculture as keeping the nation in backwardness.[113] More often than not, they were supported by those with considerable investments in inefficient protected manufacturing establishments. Some of these were large landowning families who feared that emphasis on agricultural production would inevitably lead to government intervention and agrarian reform undermining their control over land.[114] However, although there was a general consensus on the importance of the agricultural sector, there was no consensus over the controversial issue of agrarian reform.

1.6 Landlessness and insecurity

The overwhelming reason why agrarian reform has remained on the political agenda in the Philippines must be located in peasant reaction to increasing insecurity on the land, and the concentration of landed property and other rural assets in the hands of a small number of powerful families. In a predominantly agricultural society, the 'landless' - or tenants, marginal farmers, farmworkers

Table 1.4: Philippine Exports by Major Commodity Group (Selected Years) (US $ Millions)

	1965			1979			1987		
	US $ Mill	% of Exports (Agr)	(Total)	US $ Mill	% of Exports (Agr)	(Total)	US $ Mill	% of Exports (Agr)	(Total)
Coconut Products	271	40.33	34.05	1024	49.11	22.26	560	40.11	9.79
Sugar Products	147	21.88	18.47	240	11.51	5.22	78	5.59	1.36
Abaca Products	26	3.87	3.27	38	1.82	0.83	47	3.37	0.82
Tobacco Products	16	2.38	2.01	33	1.58	0.72	23	1.65	0.40
Forest Products	195	29.02	24.50	536	25.71	11.65	306	21.92	5.35
Pineapple Products	12	1.79	1.51	96	4.60	2.09	136	9.74	2.38
Banana (Fresh)	2	0.30	0.25	100	4.80	2.17	121	8.67	2.12
Other Fruits & Veg	3	0.45	0.38	18	0.86	0.39	125	8.95	2.19
Subtotal Agricultural	**672**	**100.00**	**84.42**	**2085**	**100.00**	**45.32**	**1396**	**100.00**	**24.41**
Mineral Products	70		8.79	831		18.06	224		3.92
Mineral fuel & Lub	6		0.75	42		0.91	79		1.38
Chemicals	2		0.25	112		2.43	246		4.30
Textiles	5		0.63	39		0.85	68		1.19
Miscellaneous Manufactures & Other	39		4.90	1463		31.80	3558		62.20
Re-exports	2		0.25	29		0.63	149		2.60
TOTAL	**796**		**100.00**	**4601**		**100.00**	**5720**		**100.00**

Source: National Census and Statistics Office, 1988.

21

and other rural poor groups who enjoy no secure access to land - can never be certain of meeting their basic needs for survival.

Rapid demographic expansion has resulted in an increasing population density, putting severe pressure on land resources.[115] By the late 1980s the Philippines had one of the fastest growing populations in Southeast Asia. The government estimated a 1989 population of 60.1 million growing at an annual rate of 2.34 per cent. Independent demographers believed that the population was actually growing at a rate of 2.8 per cent annually and they estimated a mid-1989 population of approximately 64.9 million. At that rate the population would reach 130 million by the year 2,020.[116]

Despite years of discussions about agrarian reform, the degree of landlessness and the extent of ownership concentration remain unknown. The government's apparent underestimate of population growth makes any assessment of landlessness difficult. The problem is compounded by the paucity of accurate statistics on employment and landownership. However, if government statistics are used carefully, and it is remembered that the basic underestimate of population leads to conservative estimations of landlessness, they can still shed considerable light on the dimensions of landlessness and inequality. Nevertheless, it must be stressed that this discussion of the dimensions of landlessness and land concentration can only lead to indicative conclusions.

By all estimates, the vast majority of those who earned their living in agriculture owned little or no land. By the mid-1980s, government figures suggested that half of the 10 million individuals earning agricultural income were farmworkers. In 1986, about 2.1 million people were listed as wage and salary employees, most of whom were farmworkers working either on small farms or in large plantations (Table 1.5).[117] Almost one-third of those employed in agriculture, or 3.2 million people in 1986, were unpaid family workers - a fact almost always omitted when the government aggregates figures on agricultural employment.[118] While the majority of these unpaid workers were probably members of what government household surveys categorize as farming families engaged in 'own account' or 'entrepreneurial' activities, a significant number belonged to households which had agricultural wage work as their major source of income. This is because wherever male farmworkers work on a piece-rate basis - whether on the sugar *haciendas* in Negros Occidental, on the oil palm plantations in Agusan del Sur, or on smaller farms devoted to rice production - their wives and children usually work beside them to increase earnings.[119]

The other half of those employed in agriculture, or 5.1 million individuals in 1986, were labelled by the government as 'own account' farmers (Table 1.5). The majority of agricultural households, or almost 3 million families, fell into one of four groups included in this category in 1985 (Table 1.6). The first were owner-cultivators, who can be defined as families who have legal title to their land on either an individual or 'tribal' basis, and who cultivate it primarily with their own labour. The second group were share and leasehold tenants, who turn over either a share of their crop production or pay a fixed cash rent to the

Table 1.5: Employment by Sector 1984-1986 (Thousands)*

Sector	1984		1985		1986	
	Number	% 0.0[1]	Number	% 0.0	Number	% 0.0
Agriculture	**9,740**	**50.30**	**10,085**	**49.62**	**10,416**	**49.77**
Wage & Salary	2,149	(22.06)	2,255	(22.36)	2,102	(20.18)
Own Account	4,957	(50.89)	5,029	(49.87)	5,154	(49.48)
Unpaid Family Workers	2,634	(27.04)	2,801	(31.77)	3,160	(30.34)
Industry	**2,845**	**14.69**	**2,798**	**13.77**	**2,790**	**13.33**
Manufacturing	1,931	9.97	1,926	9.48	1,906	9.11
Wage & Salary	1,240	(64.22)	1,303	(67.65)	1,267	(66.47)
Own Account	487	(25.22)	0,493	(25.60)	530	(27.81)
Unpaid Family Workers	204	(10.56)	0,130	(6.75)	109	(5.72)
Other[2]	914	4.72	0,872	4.29	884	4.22
Services	**6,541**	**33.78**	**7,022**	**34.55**	**7,259**	**34.69**
Trade	2,125	10.97	2,308	11.36	2,467	11.79
Wage & Salary	506	(23.81)	591	(25.61)	641	(25.98)
Own Account	1,619	(76.19)	1,717	(74.39)	1,826	(74.02)
Social & Personal Services	3,170	16.37	3,461	17.03	3,586	17.13
Wage & Salary	2,891	(91.20)	3,128	(90.38)	3,210	(89.51)
Own Account	279	(8.80)	333	(9.62)	376	(10.49)
Other[3]	1,246	6.43	1,253	6.16	1,206	5.76
Other Family Workers	**237**	**1.22**	**420**	**2.07**	**463**	**2.21**
TOTAL	**19,363**		**20,325**		**20,928**	

*Fourth quarter. Distribution of unpaid family workers estimated from sectoral aggregates.
[1]Parenthesis denotes percentage of sectoral category.
[2]Mining (100,000), construction (600,000) and utilities (60,000), the majority are wage and salary.
[3]Transportation, storage and communication (700,000) and financing, insurance, etc. (350,000).
Source: National Census and Statistics Office, report on Integrated Survey of Households as reported in World Bank, *The Philippines: The Challenge of Poverty*, 1988, p. 130.

landowner in exchange for the right to use the land. The third group were marginal farmers, or those individuals or 'tribal communities' who cultivate marginal, usually rain-fed sloping lands, on which they have no effective legal standing. Finally, noncultivating landowners who earned most of their income through farm rents or business and corporate profits from farming would also be included here.[120]

There is no data that can be employed to arrive at an accurate estimate of how many families fell into each of these categories. The Department of Agrarian Reform (DAR) has taken the overall agricultural employment figure of 10 million people and estimated the composition of the agricultural labour force in terms of land tenure, concluding that 85 per cent had no secure title to the land. Veteran farmer leader, Jeremias Montemayor, applied the same method to arrive at a somewhat more detailed assessment and the conclusion that 70 per

Table 1.6: Families by Main Source of Income 1985

Main Sectoral Income Source	Number of Families	% of Total Families	Number Urban	% Urban by Sector	Number Rural	% Rural by Sector
Agriculture	**3,917,293**	**39.8**	**430,474**	**11.0**	**3,486,820**	**89.0**
Wage & Salary	901,972	9.2	110,965	12.3	791,007	87.7
Own Account (Crops, livestock, forestry)[1]	2,335,758	23.7	188,999	8.1	2,146,759	91.9
Own Account (Fishing)	471,396	4.8	73,491	15.8	397,905	84.2
Share of Others' agricultural production (net share produce)	208,167	2.1	57,019	27.4	151,149	72.6
Non-Agricultural	**4,283,477**	**43.5**	**2,513,064**	**58.6**	**1,770,412**	**41.4**
Wage & Salary	3,064,210	31.1	1,852,689	60.5	1,211,520	39.5
Own Account	1,219,267	12.4	660,375	54.2	558,892	45.8
Other Sources	**1,646,569**	**16.7**	**782,511**	**47.5**	**864,058**	**52.5**
Cash Receipts (From Abroad)	568,524	5.8	343,909	60.5	224,615	39.5
Cash Receipts (Domestic Sources)	339,617	3.4	138,382	40.7	201,236	59.3
Family Sustenance Activities	243,297	2.5	18,832	7.7	224,466	92.3
Other (Pension, Urban rental, etc.)	495,131	5.0	281,388	56.8	213,741	43.2
TOTAL	**9,847,339**	**100.0**	**3,726,049**	**37.8**	**6,121,290**	**62.2**

[1]Includes livestock, poultry, forestry, hunting, and crop farming, but majority are in crop farming.

Source: National Census and Statistics Office, Family Income and Expenditure Survey, 1985.

cent of cultivators were landless.[121] While the DAR, and most analysts, have portrayed these figures as fact, they represent no more than guess-work.[122]

There are two important problems with these figures. First, these estimates relate to the number of people in farming, rather than the number of households. Many families have two or three members employed in farming on a paid or unpaid basis. If the object in discussing landlessness is to propose a redistribution of land to increase the number of owner-cultivators, it is important to know how many *families* own land. Of course not all landless or near landless families would necessarily be included in a programme of land redistribution. Many families who earn their main income from fishing, wages or non-agricultural activities would not necessarily be deemed eligible, nor would they necessarily desire, to become owner-cultivating farmers. Second, households and even individuals cannot easily be labelled as uniquely tenants, workers, or owner-cultivators. It is common, particularly among the poor majority, to hold a tenancy contract on a small piece of land, while working as a wage labourer on neighbouring farms.[123]

In the absence of more accurate nationwide surveys of landownership and land tenure, it is possible to arrive at only an indicative estimate of the extent of landlessness, as reported in Table 1.7.[124] On the basis of income and poverty surveys in 1985, it is clear that out of the 3.9 million households recorded as dependent on agricultural income, at the very least 2.2 million, or 56 per cent, had little or no land. They were workers, marginal farmers, fishermen and tenants. Those families earning their main source of income from fishing, who fell below the level of subsistence, are counted among the landless because many poverty-stricken rural families without access to land have had to turn to fishing.[125] At the most, about 1.2 million or 29 per cent of agricultural families could be deemed viable owner-cultivators and 332,000, or 8 per cent, noncultivating landowners. This is an extremely conservative estimate of the numbers of the landless. The 332,000 noncultivating landowning families would represent only those whose main income was derived from agriculture. The actual number of non-cultivating landowners was probably higher, but non-cultivating owners with more than 3 hectares of land were unlikely to have numbered more than about 500,000 families, and most of these did not derive their main income from agriculture.[126]

The number of owner-cultivating families was probably even lower than the estimate in Table 1.7. The government's *Listasaka*, or land registration programme, indicated in 1988 that there were approximately 1.3 million owners with holdings of less than three hectares.[127] This is the average upper limit likely to be farmed primarily with family labour.[128] However, many of these were non-cultivating small landowners who belonged to the large group of middle-class urban dwellers, who invest in small pieces of land for speculative purposes or for security on retirement.[129] What is more, many of these holdings were very likely tenanted, or run with hired labour or both. Because labour is so abundant, even the smallest owners and the more well-off tenants often hire

Table 1.7: Approximation of Minimum Magnitude of Landlessness/Near-Landlessness (1985)

Family Principal Income Source	Number of Families	% Agricultural Families
Landless/Near-Landless Families		
Fishing (below subsistence)[1]	230,900	5.9
Agricultural wages	902,000	23.0
'Own Account' farming (below subsistence)	1,059,600	27.1
Subtotal Landless/Near-Landless	**2,192,500**	**56.0**
Viable Owner Cultivators[2]		
'Own Account' farming (above subsistence)	1,151,800	29.4
Fishing (above subsistence)	240,500	6.1
Non-Cultivating Owners[3]	332.500	8.5
Total Dependent on Agriculture	**3,917,300**	**100.0**

[1]Many rural poor families have turned to fishing since they lack access to land for farming.
[2]'Own account' agricultural families above subsistence less those living in urban areas.
[3]'Own account' agricultural families residing in urban areas less those living below subsistence plus families whose income derives from their share of the agricultural produce of other families.
Sources of basic data: National Census and Statistics Office, Family Income and Expenditure Survey, 1985 and report on this survey in World Bank, *The Philippines: The Challenge of Poverty*, 1988, p. 118.

farmworkers or informally engage tenants or sub-tenants to farm the land.[130] Initial tabulation of a nationwide survey by the Philippine Peasant Institute (PPI) in 1990-91 showed that owner-cultivators made up only 25 per cent of total agricultural households, while landless tenants, marginal farmers and workers comprised some 70 per cent. Their study indicated that the largest group of landless were in fact share and leasehold tenants.[131]

There are several reasons why the number of those living and working in the agricultural sector, and the number of the landless among them, was probably far higher than is immediately apparent from government statistics. First, independent studies have indicated that there could be as many as eight to ten million people farming upland areas, many of whom would not be reflected in government employment statistics.[132] Many of these people were part of indigenous 'tribal' communities, whose claim to the land is 'original' but who often have no legal title. Others are marginal farmers who have been forced off profitable lowlands and have sought a living in the uplands. Second, the number of unpaid family workers was probably far higher than household surveys reflected. Women and children under 15 years of age, who do extensive unpaid farming work, are generally not counted or under-represented in employment surveys.[133] Third, about a quarter of a million rural families depend on what the government describes as 'sustenance activities', or non-market subsistence activities, and these certainly must be considered among the landless poor.[134]

It would probably be more accurate to assess the extent of landlessness as a percentage of *all rural families*. In this case, it was likely that by the late 1980s 72 per cent of all rural households could be counted among the landless or near-landless population.[135] A large number of rural families who derived their principal income from non-agricultural activities should probably be counted among the landless farmers. Many farming families were so poor that the work that members of their families did in non-agricultural employment brought in more income than their farming. This was particularly evident among the half-million rural families who relied on non-agricultural income but fell below the level of subsistence (Table 1.1). The magnitude of the problem of landlessness would be even greater if those among the urban poor who have fled the countryside were to be considered. In Manila and the other urban centres, as well as in provincial towns, every middle-to-upper class family has either live-in or day labour (the number increasing with family income), often coming directly from the rural areas, to wash, clean, cook, drive and do repairs.

Inequality was reflected not only in landownership but also in the overall distribution of income. The World Bank reported that while income distribution improved slightly over the 1970s, by 1985, the top 10 per cent of the population still had more than 15 times the income of the poorest 10 per cent, while average rural incomes were less than half the size of average urban incomes.[136] The top 20 per cent of families earned 50.8 per cent of total income, while the bottom 20 per cent earned only 5 per cent. Before implementing a programme of land redistribution, Taiwan had exactly the same level of inequality, but after redistribution, the richest 10 per cent earned only four times the income of the poorest 10 per cent, while the gap between rural and urban incomes was sharply reduced.[137]

The combined effect of landlessness and poverty meant that by the late 1980s, the average Filipino lived in the countryside, owned no land and was very poorly nourished. Those who fled the countryside for Manila, Davao, Cebu or other large regional urban centres were most likely to find only tertiary employment or to work in the informal economy, thus remaining poor and under-nourished. While this group of people formed the base of the social pyramid and the major source of support for those demanding redistributive agrarian reform, at the pinnacle were a small group of wealthy families, most of whom owned considerable amounts of land and had done so over generations.

1.7 Concentration of landownership

While successive governments recognized that landownership was unequal, they appear to have greatly underestimated the extent of inequality. In justifying a call for land redistribution, the government and particularly the Department of Agrarian Reform have often proclaimed that, 'Only 20 per cent of the population owns 80 per cent of the land'.[138] In fact, the government's land registration programme in 1988 demonstrated that not more than 5 per cent of all families owned 83 per cent of farm land.[139] This data must be treated with

Table 1.8: Size Distribution of Farms 1980

Farm Size (ha.s)	No. of Farms (%)		Area (%)	Area (ha.s)
Under 0.5	289,962	8.5	0.7	68900
0.50 - 0.99	485,829	14.2	3.1	300200
1.00 - 1.99	964,220	28.2	12.2	1189900
2.00 - 2.99	613,824	18.0	13.7	1332300
3.00 - 4.99	588,151	17.2	21.2	2066700
5.00 - 7.00	283,585	8.3	16.6	1612100
7.01 - 9.99	76,421	2.2	6.5	630900
10.00 - 24.99	103,723	3.0	14.5	1406300
25.00 and above	14,608	0.4	11.5	1117800
TOTAL	**3,420,323**			**9725100**

Source: 1980 Census Table 1.1 and Institute of Agricultural Statistics, 1987, p. 11.

caution for reasons that will be discussed below. Nevertheless, it offers a glimpse at the possible extent of ownership concentration in the late 1980s and provides added weight to the argument that census data cannot be used to estimate ownership concentration.

For many years, landowners and government officials have employed census data to claim that most privately owned lands were held by small landowners, and that the scope for land redistribution was extremely limited (see Table 1.8).[140] The census data has often been misinterpreted by both government and non-government actors in the Philippines, who concluded that because 67 per cent of the land was in farms of under 7 hectares, most land was held by small owners.[141]

Philippine census data, like agricultural census data in much of the third world, have been designed to disguise landownership.[142] The census counts only the size and number of farms, failing to identify who owns the land or landowners who own more than one farm. Typically owners have holdings in many different *barrios* (village neighbourhoods), municipalities and even provinces, but the census provides no means of identifying these multiple holdings. Lands devoted to the production of coconut, rice and corn are generally divided into small farms, however, absentee ownership is still widespread in these crop sectors.[143]

In 1988, as part of its preparations for agrarian reform, the government launched '*Listasaka*', a land registration programme. Even the initial reports from this programme, covering about 80 per cent of officially listed farm area, demonstrated that landownership was far more concentrated than previously believed.[144] While the data is far from conclusive it provides considerable insight into the skewedness of landownership and demonstrates conclusively why census data cannot be employed as any measure of ownership distribution.

Only 90,000 people, or 5.8 per cent of all landowners, reported holdings of more than 12 hectares. These owned 3.8 million hectares of land, or 50 per cent

Table 1.9: Concentration of Agricultural Landownership (1988)

Farm Size (Hectares)	Number Owners	% of Owners	Area Hectares	% of Area	% Rural Families	% Agric'l Families
<3.0	1021446	65.71	1257074	16.40	16.66	26.06
3.1 - 7.0	319595	20.56	1471149	19.19	5.21	8.15
7.1 - 12.0	123507	7.94	1126197	14.69	2.01	3.15
12.1 - 15.0	27243	1.75	363173	4.74	0.44	0.70
15.1 - 24.0	37797	2.43	710844	9.27	0.62	0.96
24.1 - 50.0	16781	1.08	545475	7.11	0.27	0.43
50.1 - 100.0	4990	0.32	337843	4.41	0.08	0.13
>100.0	3235	0.21	1854888	24.19	0.05	0.08
TOTAL	**1554594**	**100.00**	**7666643**	**100.00**	**25.35**	**39.67**

Agricultural Families = 3919241; Rural Families = 6132339.
Source: DAR (1988) Confidential 'Listasaka I: Final Report on Landholders Registration by Regions as of July 18 1988', mimeo. Manila, DAR.

of the total land reported. Even if each owner reported the total holdings of their families, which they surely did not, these owners represented only 1.5 per cent of all rural families or less than 1 per cent of all families in the Philippines.[145] On the other hand, over 1 million people, or 65 per cent of all landowners, owned only 16.4 per cent of total farm area in holdings of less than 3 hectares (Table 1.9).

Figure 1.1 and Table 1.10 provide two illustrations of the inequality in land distribution. The Gini coefficient of overall inequality in landownership based on 1988 data was 0.647, denoting a high degree of inequality. A graphic representation is presented by the Lorenz curve. Table 1.10 provides more detail about the inequality in landownership by illustrating the ratio of the percentage of owners to the percentage of land in each size category. It shows that those with 100 hectares and more owned 116 times their 'equal share' of the land, when considered against all reporting landowners, while those with less than 3 hectares had only 25 per cent of their fair share. It is likely that the Listasaka itself underestimates the extent of inequality in landownership, since owners probably did not report the full extent of their holdings, and there was no way of identifying owners who registered lands in more than one province or who were part of a larger landowning family.

1.8 Land tenure patterns and productivity

There is no conclusive evidence about the correlation between land inequality and poverty in the Philippines.[146] However, the skewed pattern of landownership and control has led to the development of a complex pattern of land tenure that appears to contribute not only to poverty but also to a low rate of agricultural productivity. Land tenure patterns differ widely across different crop sectors and different regions of the country.

Other than on large corporate estates, rice and corn are generally cultivated by share and leasehold, tenants, owner-cultivators or farmworkers on small plots of

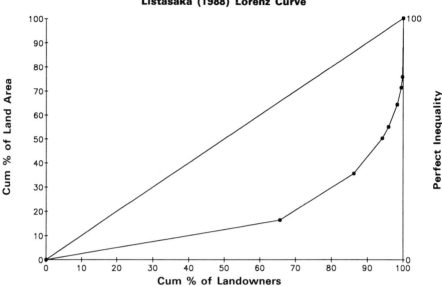

**Figure 1.1: Landownership Inequality
Listasaka (1988) Lorenz Curve**

Depicts a Gini coefficient of 0.647. A perfectly equal distribution would render a coefficient of 0.0 and a curve which followed the diagonal from 0. A perfectly unequal distribution would arrive at a coefficient of 1.0 and its curve would follow the x and y axis. Thus the Lorenz curve shows a high degree of inequality.
(Methodology for calculating the Gini coefficient from William I. Greenwald, Statistics for Economics. Columbus: Charles E. Merrill Books, Inc., 1963, p.26).

Table 1.10: Land Concentration and Inequality (1988)

Farm Size	% of Owners	% of Area	Coefficient of Equality	% of Rural Families	Coefficient of Equality
< 3.0	65.71	16.40	0.25	16.66	0.98
3.1 - 7.0	20.56	19.19	0.93	5.21	3.68
7.1 - 12.0	7.94	14.69	1.85	2.01	7.29
12.1 - 15.0	1.75	4.74	2.70	0.44	10.66
15.1 - 24.0	2.43	9.27	3.81	0.62	15.04
24.1 - 50.0	1.08	7.11	6.59	0.27	26.00
50.1 - 100.0	0.32	4.41	13.73	0.08	54.16
> 100.0	0.21	24.19	116.27	0.05	458.64
TOTAL	**100.00**	**100.00**		**25.35**	

*The Coefficient of Equality represents the ratio between the percentage of owners and the percentage of area they own (Brockett, 1988, p.73). Source: Department of Agrarian Reform, Confidential: 'Listasaka I: Final Report on Landholders by Regions as of July 18, 1988', mimeo. Manila: DAR.

Table 1.11: Coconut and Sugar Farm Size (1985/1982)

| | <5 Hectares | | 5-20 Hectares | | >20 Hectares | | |
	No./Area	%	No./Area	%	No./Area	%	TOTAL
Coconut							
Farm Number	653380	91.0	50300	7.0	14300	2.0	718000
Farm Area	915600	33.0	628300	22.0	1256100	45.0	2800000
Sugar							
Farm Number	20795	60.1	9930	28.7	3495	10.1	34600
Farm Area	38474	12.3	83830	26.8	190495	60.9	312799

Sources: For Coconut: Philippine Statistical Yearbook as reported by World Bank, *Philippines Agricultural Strategy Review.* Report No. 6819-PH, vol. II, 21 October 1987. Washington, D.C.: World Bank. For Sugar: PHILSUCOM, Research and Development Office, Statistical Series on Sugar, Vol. 1, 1982, cited in World Bank, *Agrarian Reform Issues in the Philippines: An Assessment of the Proposal for an Accelerated Land Reform.* Draft, Strictly Confidential. Report No. 6776-PH. Projects Department: East Asia and Pacific Regional Office. Washington, D.C., 12 May 1987, p. 6.

land. Sharecroppers on rice and corn lands pay anything from about 25 per cent of their harvest (if they shoulder all expenses for farming) to 50 per cent of their harvest (if the landowner shoulders all expenses) as rent. Among the better-off tenants on irrigated rice lands close to urban centres, systems of sub-tenancy have emerged. Among the poorest in the rural areas are those landless workers who are hired, even by poor small owner-cultivators and tenants, to weed and harvest the crops.

Almost 40 per cent of all families who derive their income from agriculture work in the coconut farms.[147] There are many large holdings in this crop sector. Data on the operational holdings on coconut lands indicate that 91 per cent of farms occupy only 33 per cent of farm area, while just 2 per cent of coconut farms occupy 1.25 million hectares, or 40 per cent of the total area. Based on the earlier discussion of the nature of operational holdings, it can reasonably be assumed that ownership is even more concentrated (Table 1.11). Coconut lands are operated under a variety of complex systems of tenure and labour employment. During the 1970s and 1980s the area under coconut was greatly expanded, mainly in Mindanao, through the establishment of large commercial plantations run with hired labour. More widespread are sharecropping tenants who pay from 50 to 90 per cent of their production as rent to the landowners.[148] However, many landowners divide lands into 5 hectare farms, which are then administered by caretakers who hire workers or engage tenants to pick the nuts, make copra or tap the trees for tuba.[149]

Ownership is also concentrated in lands devoted to sugarcane. As with coconut, data on operational holdings reveals extreme inequality in landholdings, likely to be much worse in terms of ownership (Table 1.11). Just under 5 per cent of all sugar cane farms were reported as over 50 hectares in size, occupying 43 per cent of the total sugarcane area. Traditionally sugar was second only to coconut as an export earner. Production was carried out mainly in large *haciendas* in Negros Occidental, Iloilo and Central Luzon. It was cultivated by permanent workers and the seasonally hired *sacada*, or cane-cutters, who, by the mid-1980s, numbered between 300,000 and 500,000 people. A smaller amount of production was undertaken by tenant farmers, particularly in Luzon. Sugar lands occupied a comparatively small percentage of total land. However, due to the concentration of landholdings among a small number of families in geographically specific regions who commanded sizeable revenues from exports, the *hacenderos* in the sugar sector, along with the owners of the nation's sugar mills, traditionally played a central role in the nation's politics.[150]

In the commercial crop sector devoted to the cultivation of high-value export crops, production has been carried out almost exclusively by agricultural corporations. This has taken place either on large plantations like the Mindanao pineapple estates of Dole and Del Monte on land rented from government and large landowners, or through contract arrangements with large and medium size landowners as in the production of Cavendish bananas. All cultivation is carried out by hired workers under the management of agricultural corporations, that are either foreign-owned or Filipino corporations linked to transnationals. In the livestock and poultry sector, while a great deal of production has been carried out by small farmers on a 'back-yard' basis, intensive production for the urban centres was increasingly undertaken by large corporations and ranchers employing hired labour or contracting with smaller owners.

The fishing industry includes both small coastal and inland fisherfolk and farming families, as well as wage and contract workers for larger operators and corporations. From the mid-1980s large landowners in coastal areas and the biggest agricultural corporations greatly expanded the area of brackish-water ponds devoted to production of prawns for export to Taiwan and Japan.

Since World War II, most logging has been undertaken by domestic companies operating under 25-year 'timber licensing agreements' (TLAs) granted by the government. While these forest lands have been legally classified as 'publicly owned', most form part of land claims made by communities of the indigenous peoples. Concessionaires were typically allotted 40,000 to 60,000 hectares each, though by law they were allowed up to 100,000 hectares.[151] It has been widely believed that many went far beyond their licensed area. By the late 1980s there were 130 of these TLAs still in effect. By 1987, in contrast to the vast areas covered by TLAs, the government had issued stewardship contracts under its Integrated Social Forestry Programme to 64,000 individuals and seven communities of indigenous peoples covering only 460,000 hectares of forest land. The rapid deforestation of the archipelago has brought about a decline of the logging industry, and, much more importantly, has threatened not only the livelihood of the indigenous peoples traditionally inhabiting these areas, but also the overall ecological systems of the country.

While agriculture remained central to the welfare and development prospects for the nation as a whole, overall productivity in the sector was still extremely low. In practice, the state and the wealthy starved the sector as a whole of credit and new investment. In 1988, only 7.4 per cent of total credit went to the agricultural sector.[152] Despite the much-heralded effect of 'green revolution' programmes in the Philippines, agricultural productivity measured as production per hectare performed poorly in comparison with other countries in the region. In 1985, value-added generated directly from crops, livestock, poultry and fishery came to only $655 per hectare harvested. The comparable figure in China was $2,500, $5,000 in Taiwan, $7,000 in South Korea and $10,000 in Japan. Land was thus greatly under-utilized.[153]

Inequality in landownership would be much less significant if alternative sources of employment existed for the workforce. Most peasants, however, cannot escape this cycle of poverty. With incomes so low for the majority of the population, there has been little stimulus to the development of a manufacturing sector. The percentage of the labour force employed in the industrial sector actually declined between the mid-1960s and the mid-1980s. In 1965, industry provided employment for 16 per cent of the labour force, but by 1986, only 14.5 per cent were employed in industry.[154]

1.9 Conclusion: an approach to the study of agrarian reform

Persistent problems of landlessness and land concentration as well as the continuing importance of the agricultural sector to the Philippine economy have kept agrarian reform on the political agenda. Inequality in landownership is much more pronounced than even those advocating liberal reform have realized. The estimates presented here are cautious ones, thus the situation is probably much worse. The problems in identifying the extent of landlessness are themselves political rather than technical in nature. Aside from the still limited *Listasaka* land registration programme, there has never been a concerted effort to collect ownership data - and this in a country that has been talking about agrarian reform since independence in 1946. While agrarian reform has remained on the political agenda, it has continued to be the subject of intense debate over state policy.

The strength of the liberal approach is its recognition that land redistribution must be at the heart of an agrarian reform programme. The extent to which an agrarian reform programme is actually redistributive can be determined by examining its provisions concerning four central aspects of reform: (1) the overall scope of land to be covered including the amount and type of land that owners are allowed to retain or to have exempted or deferred from coverage; (2) the period of time allocated for programme accomplishment; (3) the type of transfer involved including the payment of compensation to landowners for land expropriated, the posture taken toward 'voluntary land transfers', and the formula for beneficiary payments for land; and (4) the degree to which peasant beneficiaries are involved in the implementation of the programme.

Only a programme that makes land redistribution central to the logic of reform can help to break both the economic and political ties of dependence and subordination between the rural poor and their patrons. This is arguably the most important contribution that redistributive agrarian reform makes to development. The conservatives have never recognized the need for such a catharsis as a precondition for rural progress. Redistributive reform alone, however, cannot guarantee development. As the conservatives have correctly stated, it cannot solve the plight of all of the rural poor. There will be trade-offs between the rights of tenants to own land and the rights of their farmworkers. Many rural producers earn most of their income from non-agricultural activities and will not be able to secure access to enough land to make an adequate living. What is more, a viable programme of agrarian reform must consider what role agribusiness firms, independent merchants, and other rural based enterprises can play in a post-reform scenario. Agrarian reform must be part of an overall development programme that involves both the diversification of agricultural production and the creation of economically and environmentally sustainable non-agricultural productive activities in the rural areas.

The opposing positions on economic development, property rights and military strategy advanced by the conservative and liberal approaches to agrarian reform must be analysed in the context of the relationship between the state and its domestic and international sources of support. An analysis of agrarian reform policy necessarily entails an anatomy of the state that identifies its capacity in terms of human, financial and technical resources, its internal structure, and its relationship with groups and institutions in society. The state is built on an historically evolved consensus among the powerful in society, be they domestic groups and classes or foreign actors. Property rights are an important part of that consensus, as are the other written and unwritten rules governing economic activity and the maintenance of order. The conservative approach to agrarian reform seeks to maintain that consensus essentially unaltered, while the liberal approach proposes a significant modification, particularly in the rights to landed property.

The historical debates between advocates of the conservative and liberal models of reform cannot be understood solely in terms of the conflict between classes in society, or as a reflection of the structure of the Philippine economy and its relation to the world economy. The action of individuals as state leaders, or members of groups within society and state institutions, as well as the development strategies adopted by them, have had an important impact on the final shape of policy. For this reason the political action and ideas of individuals and groups will be accorded particular importance throughout this book. An attempt will be made, however, to describe the constraints under which political action normally operates, as well as the episodes - which might be labelled as 'historical moments of choice' - when the margin for political action was far wider than under normal conditions.

The conservative and liberal approaches to reform can best be described as alternative strategies advanced with the common objective of avoiding revolution and conserving the existing structure of the state. Despite the fact that agrarian reform has often emerged on the political agenda of third world countries as a response to peasant unrest and pressures for revolutionary change, few writers have examined reform policies in the context of military strategy. The debate between the conservative and liberal approaches can only be understood by examining the intersection between differing ideas about economic development, property rights and military strategy.

At the same time, the strategies or 'ideas' about agrarian reform which can be shown to have had an impact on both policy debates and outcomes are in no way proof of the 'relative autonomy of the state'. As the impact of ideas are examined, it is crucial to look at how they relate to interests in society. The role of the military is an interesting example since it has been both a 'carrier' of a particular strategy as well as a group with interests of its own.

An understanding of the agrarian reform policy adopted by the state requires analysis both of state institutions and the social and economic reality over which they preside and out of which they emerge. Those writing from the structural-determinist perspective correctly underlined the importance of looking at the complexities of the agricultural production system and the manner in which it is inserted in both the national and international economy. In this regard, it is crucial to grasp the divergent and common interests among those who own and control land and other rural assets, as well as the common and divergent interests among those broadly labelled as the 'peasantry'. However, it is necessary to examine the characteristics of classes, groups and social institutions - both domestic and foreign - not as ideal theoretical constructs, but rather as they have historically emerged in the Philippines, in order to understand the role that they have played in relation to agrarian reform.

Notes

1. Communist Party of the Philippines, 1987. The draft 'Program of the National Democratic Front,' in circulation in 1987 and 1988 elaborated the NDF's commitment to 'implementing genuine agrarian reform,' pp.16-18.
2. Council [CAPP], 1988.
3. Corpus, 1989, p.183.
4. United Nations FAO, 1951, and subsequent reports and FAO, 1979.
5. World Bank, 1975.
6. USAID, 1970.
7. In this study the term 'third world' refers loosely to the countries of Asia, Africa and Latin America with the exception of Japan and parts of the former Soviet Asia. The original meaning of this categorization (Worsely, 1984, pp.296-332) has been eclipsed by the decline of the 'socialist second world'. However, this grouping still has political and economic significance in that it includes those nations which, by the 20th century, were either late modernizers or former colonies. While encompassing a broad range of diversity, since it groups together nations as disparate as the rich oil exporting countries of the Middle East and the least developed countries of Africa, the term third world is less value-laden than alternatives such as the 'developing countries', while the geographical designation, the 'South'', is simply inaccurate.
8. These reforms will be discussed in Chapters 2 to 4 below.
9. I use the term 'peasantry' loosely, as a political category, to refer to all those who work on the land, whether they do so as tenants, small owner-cultivators, or farm workers, and their dependents, as well as other poor rural dwellers not working on farms. This includes the "rich

peasant" who may not directly engage in labour on the family farm, but whose children do so. Excluded are the small absentee landowner and the large landowner and agribusiness manager whose primary role in production is not on the land. For a similar definition see Grindle, 1986, pp.xi-xii.

10. Warriner, 1969, p.xiv. Broad definitions were employed by Tuma (1966, p.6) and by de los Reyes (1972, p.80) in the Philippines.

11. Herring, 1983, p.13.

12. Olson, 1974, p.6; El-Ghonemy, 1990, p.89.

13. *The Oxford English Dictionary*, Second Edition, 1989, vol.1, p.264. See also the debate on the floor of the Philippine House, Chapter 9 below.

14. Ladejinsky, 1955, p.226 and 1964, p.356.

15. Herring, 1983, p.282.

16. Following Held (1989, p.1) 'power' here is defined broadly as the 'capacity of social agents, agencies and institutions to maintain or to transform their environment, social or physical'. The 'powerful in society', who can also be loosely referred to as 'the elite', are those with a great capacity to maintain and transform their social and physical environment. By the state, we mean the set of institutions or organizations established over time by people within a society, inhabiting a defined territory, that govern the relations among people within the society and their relations with others outside the society's boundaries, according to rules, claimed to be universal, that are coercively enforced. In addition to upholding and presiding over the evolution of property rights, state institutions are responsible for both internal policing and external protection, and whatever other administrative functions that have evolved over time. They also take charge of the collection and allocation of societal resources to accomplish these tasks.

17. Mangahas, 1987, pp.139, 145.

18. de Janvry, 1981, Chapters 1, 3 and 6 and for the Philippines, Quisumbing and Adriano, 1987. For a review of the neo-Marxist literature which has inspired this approach, see Jessop, 1982.

19. Amando Doronila 'Political Will Needed for CARP', *MC* (23 July 1987); Melinda Quinto-de Jesus *PDI*, (23 November 1987); Cardinal Sin, *MC*, (27 February 1988). The causal power of 'political will' was endorsed by Ladejinsky (1964, p.357), Tai (1974, pp.6,266), Herring (1983, p.285n), and Prosterman and Riedinger (1987, p.13 and Chapter 7).

20. Grindle, 1986, p.19; Kohli, 1987. On the Weberian-inspired state-centred approach to the study of politics see Weber, 1968, Chapters 9-13; Stepan, 1978; and Skocpol, 1979, 1985.

21. Quisumbing and Adriano, 1987.

22. Mahal Kong Pilipinas Foundation, 1989. By looking not only at direct ownership, but also at firms operating under licensing agreements, joint ventures, etc. IBON Databank (1988a) estimated 354 'foreign affiliated' corporations among the top 1,000. Of course, there were many more foreign companies active outside the nation's leading corporations, with an intricate web of lesser connections between domestic and foreign firms.

23. *Ibon Facts and Figures*, vol.13, no.20 (31 October 1991).

24. Grindle, 1986, p.133. Also, Herring, 1983, p.218.

25. Tai, 1974, p.434; see also pp.15-16, 139-142, 471; Huntington, 1968, pp.384-87, 392; El-Ghonemy, 1990, pp.64-65, 284.

26. Hawes, 1987, pp.14, 20. See Chapter 4 below.

27. For a similar argument see Stepan, 1985.

28. Herring, 1983, p.234.

29. Hayami et al, 1990, pp.80-82.

30. Hayami et al, 1990.

31. This is true in both orthodox Marxist interpretations as well as those put forward by modernization theorists. For the former see Guerrero, 1970. However, more recent Marxist studies have begun to seek empirical evidence for the existence of the national bourgeoisie (Ferrer, 1989). Wurfel (1988, pp.59-60) also made sweeping statements about a 'national bourgeoisie' without demonstrating who they were. Hawes (1987, pp.20, 37) did the same, from a 'dependency' perspective.

32. Grindle, 1986, pp.4-5; Herring, 1983, p.17.

33. Bell, 1974, p.90.

34. Thompson, 1965, p.261; see also, pp.279-280, 295.

35. In the Soviet Union in the 1980s, wage-workers who enjoyed a certain security appeared to act to put a brake on changes necessary for further economic and social development (Nove, 1983, p.178). The institutionalised interests of trade unions in developed capitalist countries may well act as a conservative force in regard to important developmental issues (Gorz, 1988, p.233).

36. See note 9. The *Kilusang Magbubukid ng Pilipinas* (KMP) includes among its members a broad cross-section of the rural poor.

37. Adriano and Quisumbing, 1987.

38. Institute [IPD], 1987.

39. The state (as defined in note 16), in its relationship with society, can best be described as an 'emergent' phenomenon, in the scientific sense. That is, the state, and the action which it undertakes, results from a combination of causes in society, but cannot simply be understood as the sum of the individual effects of those causes. For a discussion of the use of this concept in social science see Lloyd, 1986, pp.137-47, 171-74.

40. Here we differ with Michael Lipton who drew a distinction between a 'distributionist' and 'collectivist' approach to agrarian reform based on the ultimate organization of agriculture into family farms or collective units (Lipton, 1974, pp.270, 287).

41. Nicaragua under the Sandanista leadership provided some evidence of the possibility. See Wheelock, 1991.

42. On China, Hinton, 1966; on North Korea, King, 1977, Chapter 10; on North Vietnam, Kolko, 1986, Chapters 3-5.

43. Ghai and Peek, 1988; Thorpe, 1990; and Wheelock, 1991.

44. Hinton, 1966; see also Shillinglaw, 1974.

45. The contrast between the Soviet and Chinese models is evident in comparing Hinton, 1966, with Lewin, 1968. Mao Tse-tung's differences with Stalin over the question of collectivization can be seen in Mao, 1977. For a comparison of the two models see Amin, 1981.

46. Kerkvliet, 1977, pp.225-226.

47. Communist Party of the Philippines, 1972.

48. Heady, 1952, p.623.

49. Lal, 1983, pp.89-97 and Graham and Floering, 1984, p.10.

50. Graham and Floering, 1984, p.69.

51. Criticism of sharecropping on the grounds that it provides no incentive for agricultural improvement has been accepted in economic theory since Adam Smith (1776, Book III, Chapter II) and found new expression in the works of Alfred Marshall (1890, Book VI, Chapter X).

52. Brown, 1970 and Lal, 1983, p.97.

53. Tiffin and Mortimore, 1990, p.33; Graham and Floering, 1984, pp.13, 80-82; Lal, 1983, p.97.

54. The appeal to natural rights gives a moral flavour to the conservative approach and mirrors Robert Nozick's (1974) 'theory of entitlement', while the latter argument adds a functionalist flavour and reflects the traditional utilitarian defence of private property found in the work of thinkers such as Bentham (1789).

55. For Latin America, see Grindle, 1986; de Janvry, 1981; Lindqvist, 1979; Barraclough, 1973. For South Asian reforms, see Kohli, 1987; Herring, 1983; and Lehmann, 1974. For the Middle East see, El-Ghonemy, 1990 and Warriner, 1948. On Indonesia see Huizer, 1972 and Tjondronegoro, 1972; and on Thailand see, Feder-Gershon et al, 1988 and Islam, 1983.

56. Kohli, 1987, pp.46-48.

57. Ladejinsky, 1977. His role is more thoroughly discussed in Chapter 3 below and in Putzel, 1986.

58. El-Ghonemy, 1990, p.144-47, 167-74; Dorner, 1972, p.86; Ladejinsky, 1939b, pp.30-39 and

1964, p.355. Griffin (1974, pp.30-36), while not necessarily an advocate of the liberal approach provides evidence for many of its claims.

59.   El-Ghonemy, 1990, p.88, 95 and Herring, 1983, p.262. For the classical defense of the efficiency of small farming see Smith, 1776, Book III, Chapter II and Mill, 1848, Book II, Chapters VI and VII. For the most comprehensive statement of the liberal position see Prosterman and Riedinger, 1987, pp.36-67.

60.   Prosterman and Riedinger, 1987, pp.1, 74, 86, 287-88n.4 and Herring, 1983, pp.283-84. Mill (1848, Book II, Chap VII) made essentially the same liberal argument.

61.   Ladejinsky (1964, pp.356-58) saw the control of land rents and resettlement as a potentially positive first step in reform, while Prosterman and Riedinger (1987, pp.179-82, 190) tended to regard these programmes as potentially negative. See also Lipton, 1974, p.279; El-Ghonemy, 1990, p.89.

62.   Griffin, 1974, pp.48-58.

63.   Prosterman and Riedinger (1987, pp.179, 207, 218, 225) see a role for the private sector.

64.   Ladejinsky, 1964, p.365. See also Dorner, 1972, p.134. For an early version, see Mill, 1848, Book II, Chapter I, p.217.

65.   The liberal approach also appeals to natural rights. It starts from the Lockean notion that individuals have a right to anything that they have found in a 'state of nature' with which they have 'mixed their labour', but only if 'there is enough, and as good left in common for others'. Locke, 1690, 'Second Treatise on Government,' 27, p.288.

66.   Mill (1848, Book II, Chapter I, section 1) argued that land was a special case of property since it was not the produce of labour but the 'raw material of the earth'. This idea was developed to its full extreme by Henry George (1881, p.25), who argued that since the only justification for a natural right to private property is that one has the right to the produce of one's own labour and since land is the product of no one's labour, private property in land can never be justified.

67.   Mill (1848, Book II, Chapter II, pp.231-233) provided a utilitarian justification on these grounds.

68.   Ladejinsky, 1964, p.359; Prosterman and Riedinger, 1987, p.196. Here they part company with Mill (1848, Book II, Chapter II, p.234) who stated that landowners were entitled not only to market value compensation, but to even more if they had a particular emotional affinity to their land.

69.   Prosterman and Riedinger, 1987, pp.13, 179-194.

70.   Prosterman and Riedinger, 1987, pp.194-196. See also Lipton, 1974, pp.308-309.

71.   On reforms in India and Kerala see Herring, 1983, Chapters 6 and 7 and Franke and Chasin, 1990, pp.43-51; and on West Bengal, Kohli, 1987.

72.   Prosterman and Riedinger, 1987, Chapter 5.

73.   See Chapter 3.

74.   Quisumbing and Adriano (1987), who carried out an extensive examination of alternative agrarian reform policy proposals and the groups behind them, failed to make any mention of the military. Herring's (1983) framework for analysing the agrarian reform policy-making process in South Asia, which looks in detail at the role of various branches of the state, does not accord any attention to the military or its strategy in handling peasant rebellions. While Grindle (1986, p.135) mentioned that the military in Latin American countries often ended reform, she did not discuss the impact of the strategies and ideologies promoted by the *juntas* on agrarian reform policy. Wurfel (1983, p.12) underlined the negative role of the Philippine military in relation to reform, but did not analyse the impact of their strategy.

75.   Shafer (1988, p.4) defined 'counterinsurgency' as 'a politico-military strategy to prevent latent insurgencies from breaking out by reinforcing the weak spots in threatened societies'. The terms 'insurgent' and 'counterinsurgent' have an interesting political connotation. Commandant David Galula wrote that it was 'unwise to concede to Mao Tse-tung that the revolutionary's opponent is a "counterrevolutionary", because this would be tantamount to

admitting that the opponents of revolution were "reactionary": Therefore, one side will be called the "insurgent" and his action the "insurgency"; on the opposite side, we will find the "counterinsurgent" and the "counterinsurgency" (Galula, 1964, p.xiii).

76. Galula, 1964, pp.85-90.

77. Galula, 1964, p.77; Jackson, 1986, p.21, 26.

78. Jackson, 1986, pp.5, 35, 27.

79. Jackson, 1986, p.31. A point also stressed by Galula (1964, p.78), Kulp (1970, p.496) and Lal (1983, p.97).

80. Jackson, 1986, p.5, 31.

81. Kulp (1970) was a self-proclaimed disciple of Galula, to whom he dedicated his book. On Kulp in the Philippines, see Chapter 10 below.

82. Kulp, 1970, pp.487-514.

83. Kulp, 1970, p.15.

84. Galula, 1964, p.67.

85. Galula, 1964, p.103.

86. Ladejinsky, 1954, p.208.

87. Ladejinsky, 1964, p.361. See also El-Ghonemy, 1990, pp.146-147.

88. Ladejinsky, 1957, p.280.

89. Prosterman and Riedinger, 1987, p.7. See Huntington, 1968, p.375. He also drew on the work of Ted Gurr (1970).

90. Prosterman and Riedinger, 1987, p.24. For earlier statements of the model see Prosterman, 1972 and 1976. For the conservative view see Jackson, 1986, pp.6-9.

91. Prosterman and Riedinger, 1987, p.2.

92. Prosterman and Riedinger, 1987, p.9 and specifically on El Salvador, p.145.

93. Ladejinsky, 1954, p.209; Dorner, 1972, p.78; El-Ghonemy, 1990, p.97; Prosterman and Riedinger, 1987, p.232.

94. Herring, 1983, p.284.

95. See discussion of 'political will' in section 1.3.

96. Pagusara, 1984.

97. For a criticism of the gender bias see MacKinnon, 1989, pp.161-62.

98. The World Bank (1988a) estimated that while 52 per cent of the Philippine population lived below the poverty line by the mid-1980s, comparable figures in the rest of the region were lower: Indonesia, 39 per cent; Thailand, 31 per cent; and Malaysia, 28 per cent. By comparison, South Korea had only 8 per cent.

99. In this and the next two sections, information from the government's Integrated Survey of Households and Family Income and Expenditure Surveys (FIES) are used, drawing on both government and World Bank reports on this data. The World Bank reports are useful since they present disaggregated data not otherwise available to the author.

100. Sen, 1981, Chapter 2.

101. NEDA, 1986b, pp.51, 83 and World Bank, 1988b, pp.1-3. NEDA estimated an increase over 1985 poverty estimates of 64 per cent for rural areas and 52 per cent for urban areas. Both government and the Bank base the non-food element of the poverty line on the extremely low level of non-food expenditures by the poorest 10 per cent of families in 1971, adjusted for inflation. Poverty thresholds were set at a lower level in rural areas than urban ones. The average per capita nutritional requirement was estimated by the Food and Nutrition Research Institute (NEDA, 1986c, p.65) at 2,032 kilocalories of energy, 50.8 grams of protein and 12.0 grams of iron, against the Bank's estimate of 2,016 kilocalories and 50 grams of protein.

102. World Bank, 1988b, pp.iii, 8-12, 118. As shown in Table 1.1, 82 per cent of the core poor lived in rural areas.

103. NEDA, 1986b, p.223.

104. Van Naerssen, 1991, p.1.

105. Agribusiness was first defined by Davis and Goldberg, 1957, p.2.

106. There is great confusion over the area planted to each crop, because census data reports actual physical farm area while production data reports 'area harvested', counting the same area every time it is harvested. Thus, in 1980, while the census reported 1.9 million hectares in corn farms, production data recorded 3.2 million hectares harvested because corn is often planted two or even three times a year on the same land. It is less clear why rice area harvested (11 million hectares in 1980) was *less* than farm area, given the prevalence of double cropping at least on irrigated lands.

107. On these two crop sectors see Castillo, 1975.

108. Also included here were vegetable and fruit crops grown either for local consumption or to feed the urban centres, with the latter increasingly concentrated in commercial and mainly corporate farms.

109. Center [CRC], 1986.

110. The FAO reported that the Philippines was the 6th biggest loser in absolute forest area, with a depletion of 100,000 hectares per year. This contrasts with Indonesia with 550,000, Thailand with 330,000, Malaysia with 230,000, India with 147,000 and Laos with 125,000 (cited in *PDI* 14 March 1990). However, other estimates put the annual loss in the Philippines at 200,000 hectares per year (World Bank, 1989b, p.11), and it must be remembered that the absolute forest area of a country like Indonesia is much larger.

111. World Bank, 1989b, p.i. From the 1960s through the 1980s, 90 per cent of the old-growth dipterocarp forests were lost to legal and illegal logging activities.

112. Former Communist Party chairman José Ma. Sison (1989, pp. 153-54) said that land reform was essential to national industrialization, while the government's development plan saw agriculture as the leading sector (NEDA, 1986b).

113. The theoretical argument for this view is best presented by Lichauco, 1988.

114. See Chapter 3 below and subsequent discussion of this trend.

115. If independent population data is correct then there were 216 people per sq km by 1989. The official 1986 population data reported a density of 186 people per sq km against 47.4 in Malaysia; 85.8 in Indonesia; 104 in Thailand and 111 in China. Interestingly, it is still a much lower density than in South Korea (419) or Taiwan (540) (Europa Publications, 1987).

116. The National Census and Statistics Bureau put the 1989 population level at 60.1 million with a growth rate of 2.38 per cent per year. The Population Reference Bureau, Washington D.C., placed population at 64.9 million in mid-1989 growing at an annual rate of 2.8 per cent. Cited in *PDI* (27 August 1989).

117. Farm managers and other professionals would also be included in this category, however they probably did not number more than 28,000 people (Institute [IAS], 1987, p.4).

118. The government's most common report on the Integrated Survey of Households (ISH) lists only aggregate totals of employment by sector (NEDA, 1986b, p.7 or NCSO, ISH, 1988). However, the World Bank (1986, vol. III, p.7) presented the disaggregated data mentioning the total of 'unpaid family workers'. Since both reports use fourth quarter data from the ISH, it is possible to estimate the number of unpaid family workers in the agricultural and manufacturing sectors.

119. Field investigations in Luzon, Negros Occidental and Agusan del Sur, 1988-89.

120. In Table 1.6, those landowners who earned most of their income from sharecropping tenants appear to be separated from other 'own account' families and listed as receiving income from the 'share of other household's agricultural production'.

121. DAR, 1987 based on Presidential [PCGR], 1986b, p.7; Montemayor, 1986, pp.56-57.

122. The DAR's estimate does not appear to be based on any empirical source. The government always states that these figures are based on 'various studies,' a euphemism for guess-work which originated in Tadem's work (Presidential [PCGR], 1986b, p.7). Tadem seems to have drawn on Montemayor (1986, p.56). Many authors have uncritically based their assumptions on this guess work (Putzel and Cunnington, 1989, Chapter 2; Riedinger, 1990, p.19 and Congress [CPAR], 1990, p.60).

123. Field research, Bulusan, Sorsogon, March 1989.
124. In what follows, 'own account farmers' below subsistence are assumed not to own the land they till while those above subsistence are assumed to be owners. While neither assumption is necessarily true in all cases, the World Bank (1988b, p.11) reported that 67 per cent of farm families below subsistence had little or no land.
125. The World Bank (1989b, p.42) reported that about 75 per cent of those who earn their income from fishing were involved in small-scale municipal coastal and inland fishing, 21 per cent in aquaculture and only 4 per cent in larger commercial fishing.
126. 533,148 owners reported holdings over 3 hectares in the *Listasaka* programme which covered 7.666 million hectares of farm land (DAR, 1988b). If there were the same ratio for the entire 9.725 million hectares, this would mean a total of some 676,000 families. However, since owners registered individually and not by household or family, it is likely that the number of families is far lower. See the discussion of landownership below.
127. DAR, 1988b. 1.021 million owners registered holdings of less than 3 hectares out of the total 7.666 million hectares of land registered (Table 1.9). The same ratio for total farm land would indicate 1.295 million small owners, approximating the number of own-account farmers above subsistence (Table 1.7).
128. About two hectares of paddy land is considered the upper farm-size limit to be cultivated primarily with family labour (Mauri, 1986, p.90), but other crops would have a higher limit.
129. A survey by the Social Weather Stations, Inc. (1988, p.1), reported that 20 per cent of respondents in Manila stated that their families owned some agricultural land.
130. Hayami and Kikuchi, 1985.
131. In Luzon 47 per cent of farmers were share and leasehold tenants, while the total for Cebu was 53 per cent. Philippine [PPI], 1991a, pp.115.
132. World Bank, 1989b, pp.ii, 22. The Bank report demonstrated that in the past the government has consistently under-estimated upland population.
133. World Bank, 1988b, p.54.
134. Of the 1.8 million rural families who relied on non-agricultural activities for most of their income (Table 1.6), about 335,000 were dependent on trade and another 100,000 on 'manufacturing' (mainly handicrafts, contract sewing, etc.), while the balance were dependent on wages from similar activities (not shown in Table 1.6).
135. There were 6.1 million rural households in 1985 and only 1.7 million could conceivably enjoy secure ownership of an adequate amount of land or an adequate income from fishing (Table 1.7).
136. World Bank, 1988b, p.5.
137. Lee-Flores, 1988, p. 29.
138. DAR, 1987 and Juico, 1989, p.89.
139. DAR, 1988b. While this data covered only 80 per cent of the nation's 9.7 million hectares of farm land, this is probably still an underestimate of land concentration. See discussion below.
140. Interview with Atty. Eduardo Hernandez, President of the Council of Agricultural Producers of the Philippines (CAPP), 2 December 1988. See also Council [CAPP], 1987b, pp.37-43.
141. Institute on Church and Social Issues, in the *MC* (20 February 1987) and IBON, 1988b, p.14.
142. See Panse (1965, pp.10-11,40,218) for early debates about the World Census of Agriculture.
143. The census reported that in 1980, 25 per cent of all farms covering 19 per cent of farm area were tenanted or leased, while 69 per cent were owned or partly owned by their operators covering 77 per cent of farm area. However, there is no way of knowing how much of the 'owned land' was run with hired labour, or tenants declared as labourers, rather than cultivated by the owning family.
144. DAR, 1988b. The discussion here relates to the findings of the first stage of the programme in which 1.5 million people registered ownership of 7.7 million hectares. In 1991, DAR's final report on *Listasaka* (DAR, 1991a, p.9) included 2,062,720 owners on 8.9 million hectares, but detailed information from *Listasaka II* was not made available to the author.

41

C

145 Even as a percentage of total farm land (e.g., including the 2 million hectares not covered by *Listasaka I*) these large owners alone, not counting those still to report, held more than 40 per cent of total farm land.

146 Attempting to correlate *Listasaka* data with poverty data renders no definite trend, but since *Listasaka* data is available only by region and defines regions differently than does the poverty data, the sample size is too small to undertake meaningful regression analysis.

147 This estimate is based on the assumption that each coconut farm can support about two families (718,000 farms and 1.4 million families) (World Bank, 1987a, Vol.II, p.22). While coconut is thus the main source of income for a huge number of people (considering additional jobs in processing, transportation and trading), some make extraordinary claims to the effect that half the Philippine population depends on coconut (*IBON Facts & Figures*, vol.13, no.7, 1990).

148 World Bank, 1987a, Vol.II, pp.23-24; Tiglao, 1981, pp.41-61.

149 Mauri, 1986, pp.82-85.

150 Gonzaga, 1989. The comparison with the coconut sector is interesting here. While coconut was also a major export earner, much larger areas were required to produce a given amount of foreign exchange and owners were spread throughout the country. Significant concentration of landholdings and wealth in the coconut sector was achieved only during the Marcos years, when the largest actors then became much more important politically.

151 World Bank, 1989b, p.18 and Draft Executive Order, 20 May 1987, section 23.

152 *Final Report of the Committee on the Assessment of the Agricultural Sector's Performance Under the Aquino Government*, 1989, p.80.

153 Roxas, 1989. Even if one takes into account subsidies to the farmer in South Korea and Japan which would reduce value-added figures roughly to the level of China, the contrast with the Philippines is still sharp.

154 NEDA, 1986b; World Bank, 1985.

HISTORICAL ORIGINS: THE COLONIAL STATE AND THE LANDED ELITE

2.1 Introduction

In 1565 Miguel López de Legazpi led an expedition to the Philippines accompanied by the Augustinian friar-navigator Andrés de Urdaneta. Thus began a long collaboration between the Spanish Crown and the Catholic Church, particularly its monastic orders, in the colonization of the Philippine islands. It was not Spain's first contact with the islands. Ferdinand Magellan had met his end there in 1521 at the hands of Chief Lapu-Lapu of Mactan, delaying Spanish colonization for almost 50 years. Three hundred and fifty years of Spanish rule followed by half a century of US colonial administration largely set the parameters within which families like the Aquinos, Cojuangcos and Laurels compete for power in today's Republic, while peasants struggle to survive on the land.

A review of the colonial era provides some insight into the origins of the Philippine state, particularly in terms of the system of property rights established and the emergence of institutions like the military. The Catholic Church had a profound influence over the development of the nation. The colonial period saw the rise of a landed oligarchy composed of families which are still prominent in political and economic life. This chapter combines a sketch of the broad historical trends with specific insights into the evolution of corporations such as Tabacalera and Del Monte and families like the Cojuangcos. The means by which they gained rights over lands such as Hacienda Luisita, or the pineapple plantations of Bukidnon, remain important in the debates about agrarian reform in the late 20th century.

Much has been written about the colonial period, but old and new myths about the nature of US colonialism abound, the most potent of which views the overall influence of the US as a 'benign' colonial power. Yet it would seem that the US had a clear understanding of the problems of landlessness and land concentration in their colony. However, successive US Governors-General, supported by powerful politicians and lobbies back home, were more concerned with consolidating a close relationship with the emerging landed oligarchy than with improving the plight of the peasantry. During the colonial period the US also established economic, political and cultural bonds which still tie it closely to the archipelago.

2.2 Origin of the elite under Spanish colonialism

There is still a great deal of debate about the social structure existing on the islands in the pre-Hispanic period. Most agree that the village communities, or *barangays*, that the Spanish found were already experiencing a certain degree of social stratification. This trend was most developed in the Southern island of Mindanao, where Islam, spreading from what is today Indonesia, had made significant inroads. Only the US would bring Mindanao under rule from Manila. In the *barangays* (which were to come under Spanish authority) a *datu*, or chief, ruled assisted by the *maharlika*, or 'nobles', who together formed a group with some claim on the community's surplus produce. Communities on the islands are thought to have participated in an ancient trade in the region, with reports of sugar-cane from the Philippines being used in China as early as the 12th century.[1] Forms of sharecropping and what has been labelled as 'debt peonage' and slavery did exist. However, the barriers between these categories do not appear to have been rigid ones. Most importantly, there was no concept of individual freehold private property in land. This was to be an innovation introduced during colonial rule.[2]

When Spain established its authority in Manila in 1571, it had little interest in developing agricultural production in the archipelago. The Spanish Crown's principal interest in the islands was in establishing Manila as a naval base in the Pacific. In this way it hoped to gain a foothold in the spice trade dominated by the Portuguese in the Far East, to establish a stop-over point in the galleon trade between Mexico and China, and to set up a base for the proselytisation of China.[3] In fact, there was only limited development of the agricultural potential of the colony from the conquest until the late 18th century.

Much of the archipelago consisted of scattered communities who lacked professional military forces to match the firepower of the Spanish. Areas outside the Islamic sultanates of the south and the upland communities of the north were relatively easily subdued, and Spanish authority could be maintained with small garrisons. In fact, the Governor-General of the colony remained under the authority of the Viceroy of Mexico until Mexican independence in 1821. During the early colonial period, royal land grants were bestowed on about 120 individuals. These grants included small parcels of about 42 hectares intended for crop production, as well as larger ones of approximately 1,700 hectares intended for ranching. Most royal land grants included one of the large parcels and several of the smaller areas. They were supposed to cover only unsettled lands, but most of the original 120, as well as later grants, encompassed settled areas.[4]

The colonial state that emerged was virtually a partnership between the Spanish Crown and the Catholic friars, who were able to preserve their autonomy. While Spanish officials limited their activity mainly to the Manila galleon trade, from very early on the Catholic friars established themselves on agricultural land. The Augustinians arrived with López in 1565, the Franciscans in 1577, the Jesuits in 1581 and the Recollects in 1606.[5] For most of the indigenous people their first contact with the colonial regime was with the friars. The religious orders used local languages as they proselytised local communities, thus setting a pattern by which only the elite of each region knew Spanish and could communicate with one another.[6]

At the pinnacle of society were the *peninsulares*, Iberian-born Spaniards who occupied key positions in the state. They shared authority with the Catholic Church and friar orders. Below them were the *insulares*, or Philippine-born Spaniards. The *datus*, who commanded authority in the *barangays* were incorporated as local officials, or *cabezas de barangay*, in the colonial state. It was their responsibility to collect tribute and organize corvée labour, in exchange for a portion of the collection and exemption from labour requirements. They collectively became known as the *principalia*, or the 'prominent ones', and during the first two centuries of colonial rule these local offices were hereditary.

The *estancias*, or large ranches, which developed from land grants made by the Crown to *conquistadores* and early settlers, soon passed to the friar orders. They were the first to establish *haciendas*, or large landed estates, producing grain for both local consumption and for Manila. By 1612, the land grants had been reduced to only 34 *estancias*. Upland areas in Cavite and Batangas were abandoned. The Jesuits and Augustinians were the first to accumulate *haciendas*. Jesuits had no rule against property accumulation and possessed considerable experience in Latin America. The Augustinians ran lands in Cebu from the end of the 16th century. The Dominicans and Recollects followed, while Franciscans were barred from accumulating lands by their statutes. By the end of the Spanish colonial period these lands totalled some 171,000 hectares. In addition, in Laguna, Bulacan and Batangas alone, four archdiocesan estates totalled some 44,000 hectares. In Cavite, there was a solid belt of friar estates covering most of the lowlands by the end of the 19th century. Thus the Church owned much of the best land by the end of the colonial period.[7]

In the early colonial period these estates were devoted mainly to rice cultivation originally with sharecropping tenants, *casamajan*, or *kasama*. The *haciendas* were able to attract such tenants since they could exempt them from the corvée labour required of all households by the state. Through these means the *haciendas* were able to expand cultivation, encroaching increasingly on lands held by independent *barangay* communities. This led to a major agrarian revolt in 1745, when peasants in areas surrounding the estates rose up in anger against encroachments upon their land.[8] By the 18th century *haciendas* were farmed increasingly by *inquilinos*, or tenants who paid a fixed rent in grain.

During the first two hundred years of colonial rule Spain kept the colony closed to most of the outside world. The *peninsulares* and *insulares* were not allowed to visit Asian ports. Chinese from Fukien and Kwantung were attracted to Manila by the presence of Mexican silver. They came to outnumber the Spanish and established themselves in all areas of trade.[9] The Spanish looked down upon the Chinese, and the label 'Sangley', or 'merchant', took on a pejorative connotation. However, by the early 18th century Chinese merchants were already moving into provinces like Pampanga where they rented lands from the *principalia* and established sugar mills for domestic consumption. This was the beginning of the investment of merchant capital in the land.[10] Slowly, a new group of Chinese mestizos began to emerge as merchants intermarried with the *principales*. In what seemed to be an effort to prevent a separate merchant class of Chinese mestizos from assuming the inherited leadership positions of *cabeza de barangay* through marriage, the Spanish abolished hereditary succession to the position and introduced an electoral process among the *principalia* for the post.[11]

The pattern of colonial life changed when, as a result of Spain's alliance with France during the Seven Years War, the British invaded and occupied Manila between 1762 and 1764. The Chinese still living in the archipelago looked favourably upon the occupation, since just seven years earlier the colonial government had ordered the expulsion of non-Catholic Chinese from the islands. They joined the Protestant British in what proved to be a futile effort to defeat the Spanish in territories beyond Manila.[12] After the British departed, the colonial state gradually began to open the colony to international trade. In 1765, because of Chinese support for the British and the competition that they represented to the Spanish, many more of their number were expelled or restricted from travelling through the colony, and further Chinese immigration was halted until the 1840s.[13] With the exclusion of the Chinese lasting nearly a century, the Chinese mestizos filled the gap and made significant investments in business and land.

Other changes were afoot in this period in response to the financial crisis left by the British occupation and the winding down of the galleon trade. Carlos III's governor, José Basco y Vargas (1777-87), was set upon establishing secular rule and fostering commercial agriculture on the lands of the friar estates. As in the rest of the Spanish domain, the Jesuits were expelled from the colony and their estates expropriated.[14] In 1785, the Crown granted the monopoly of all Philippine-European trade to the newly established Royal Philippine Company. While the company remained frequently on the verge of collapse until it was disbanded in 1834, it nevertheless provided large amounts of crop loans to generate the production of exports. Opening the colony to export production stimulated a major change in land tenure. The *hacenderos* began to rent their lands in greater tracts to *inquilinos*, who in turn, engaged *kasama* as sub-tenants to cultivate the land.

In 1781, Ciriaco González Carvajal, the colony's first intendant or financial administrator, became the founding director of the Economic Society of the Friends of the Country, created to promote agricultural and manufacturing production. He implemented a tobacco monopoly that had been introduced nearly twenty years earlier. A system for collecting the crop was introduced whereby *caudillos*, or overseers, from among the *principalia*, were assigned the responsibility of ensuring that only those permitted to grow tobacco did so and that their product was delivered to the state. This led to further encroachment on the lands of the indigenous peoples, and expansion of the colonial authority in the north. In 1785, the Crown extended the monopoly to the sprawling Cagayan province. The effect of the monopoly in Cagayan and elsewhere was to strengthen the position of the *principales vis à vis* previously independent farmers.[15]

González had evidently hoped that the expropriated Jesuit lands would be sold to their cultivators, or leased in hereditary tenures, in an early version of a liberal approach to reform.[16] But in the end, in what might be described as the first in a long series of failures at agrarian reform, they were auctioned in 1790 to Spaniards and *inquilinos* interested in export production.[17] While the colonial state was able to profit from the tobacco monopoly, the failing fortunes of the Royal Philippine Company prompted it to allow the entry of other European merchants in 1789. The first export crops were indigo, cotton, sugar, rice and black pepper.[18] With the opening of the port of Manila in 1834, British and US trading houses became increasingly important in financing agricultural production for export. Subsequently, much of the export trade fell into their hands.

The Spanish families were not entirely left out. With the disbandment of the colonial state's Royal Philippine Company in 1834, its *adelantado* (governor general), Spanish born Antonio de Ayala, joined with the *hacendero* Don Domingo Roxas to form the Ayala Corporation, still one of the country's leading firms.[19] The Ayalas were cousins to another wealthy Spanish family of that era and the present, the Sorianos, who established the San Miguel Corporation in 1890. In 1851, the Zobel-Ayala family corporation acquired one of the formerly Jesuit-owned *haciendas* outside Manila which today forms the nation's exclusive financial district, Makati. In 1851, Antonio de Ayala established the Banco Español-Filipino de Isabel II which would later be known as the Bank of the Philippine Islands.

When the exclusion of the Chinese was lifted in 1850, they flocked back into the country and the Chinese *mestizos* could not compete with them in commerce. As a result another major change occurred in the countryside. The *mestizos* began to turn their attention almost exclusively to leasing and buying land. Consequently the conditions under which *kasama* held the land became increasingly unfavourable.[20] The *kasama* system was expanding rapidly at the close of the 19th century due to increases in tenant indebtedness and land-grabbing. One means used by the elite to accumulate land was the *pacto de retroventa*. Through this system, lenders protected their loans to the peasants by taking control of the latter's land. During the period of the loan the peasant remained the 'owner' of the land but was, at the same time, his lender's *kasama*.[21] If the peasant could not repay the loan on time the land automatically became the property of the lender.

During this period, the Spanish stepped up direct taxation and established the first organized military force based on native recruitment. Due to a need for additional revenues, the colonial state instituted a *cedula*, or head tax, consisting of a three pesos annual fee, or labour service, to be paid to the state. In 1868, the Spanish created the Guardia Civil to protect the expanding property of *hacenderos* in the lowlands.[22] From its beginnings, the Guardia, to which the modern day Philippine Constabulary can trace its origins, was looked upon by the peasantry as an abusive and occupying force. Like its successor in the early years of US rule, the Guardia was a native force commanded by foreigners, designed to relieve the burden on Spanish troops.

The large sugar *haciendas* of Negros Occidental were established after the port of Iloilo was opened to the British in 1855. The first sugar mill in Negros was put up by the British in 1857, and by the turn of the century 274 mills were in operation and the population had expanded ten-fold.[23] While the first producers were British and French, families like the Benedictos, Montelibanos, Ledesmas, Yulos and Lopezes were to follow. The latter part of the 19th century also saw the rapid development of abaca (the palm that furnished Manila hemp), tobacco and coconut for export to the international market. As export production developed, an increasing amount of rice was imported. By the end of the 19th century, most of the friar estates leased only large tracts of land. The family of José Rizal, who would become a leader among the rising group of educated *mestizos*, or *ilustrados*, held 389 hectares in Hacienda Calamba along Laguna de Bay.[24]

During this period another group of elite families emerged, many of which went on to form family empires and political clans that still dominated the country in the late 20th century. In 1870 the first José Cojuangco, who had arrived in the Philippines from China 10 years before and was a carpenter by trade, settled in Paniqui, Tarlac, buying rice and sugar lands.[25] He was the great-grandfather of the two branches of the Cojuangco family now locked in rivalry for control of the country - those allied to brothers José and Pedro Cojuangco and their sister President Corazon Aquino, and those allied to their cousin, Eduardo 'Danding' Cojuangco Jr. By the time of the Philippine Revolution in 1896, the Cojuangcos were already one of the largest landowners in Tarlac.[26]

In 1881, in anticipation of the abolition of the tobacco monopoly the following year, the Compañia General de Tabacos de Filipinas, or Tabacalera, was incorporated in Madrid with Spanish and French capital. It was able to take over many of the operations previously consigned to the state monopoly and became an important producer and exporter of tobacco, sugar, abaca and other agricultural products. By disguising its intentions, one of the company's future directors, Antonio P. Casal, was able to assemble huge tracts of land in the Cagayan Valley, Tarlac, Negros Oriental and elsewhere. In 1882 it established four sprawling estates in the northern province of Isabela, Haciendas San Antonio, Santa Isabel, San Rafel, La Concepción and San Luis, which by 1898 totalled 14,630 hectares. To have a 'captive' labour force, the company recruited tenants from Ilocos to cultivate the land. Their descendants in the late 1980s claimed that the company had promised that after 99 years their families would own the land.[27] However, Tabacalera's official corporate history, not surprisingly, makes no mention of such promises.[28]

In the 1890s in Tarlac, the company established the 10,000 hectare Hacienda Luisita, which would later be acquired by Corazon Cojuangco Aquino's family. In the early 1880s, the company began efforts to acquire the land, a jungle area known as Mapalacsiao, when they realized it was to be traversed by the British-financed Manila-Dagupan railroad. Tabacalera acquired the land from the Spanish Crown and used early settlers - mostly railroad workers - to cut the forests for timber, and to clear and plant the land first with tobacco and abaca and later with rice and sugar.[29]

By the 1860s the Aquino family were already large landowners in Concepcion, Tarlac. At the time of the Revolution they owned the *Casa Grande* (the big house) in neighbouring Murcia. Their rice and sugar fields stretched to the edge of Tabacalera's Hacienda Luisita. The border between the two estates was for many years a matter of dispute between the company and the family.[30]

Three hundred years of Spanish colonial rule had given rise to a landed oligarchy whose fortunes were largely tied to export agriculture. They were composed mainly of two groups, the highly educated Chinese and Spanish *mestizos*, known as the *ilustrados*, who were landowners or well-off tenants, and the *cacique*, the descendants of the *principalia*, usually but not always landed, who were tax-collectors and administrators of local government.[31] From among their ranks would come the generals of the first Philippine army and the leaders of the First Republic. There were also a small number of Spanish families and corporations like the Ayalas and Tabacalera among the landed oligarchy. The friar orders still controlled most of the great *haciendas*, but the emergent Filipino elite began to challenge their pre-eminent position and the colony's relationship with the Spanish Crown.

The legacy of colonial rule was an oppressive land tenure system where political and economic authority were largely based on control over the land. While on the friar estates the peasant *kasama* had some common cause with the *ilustrado* tenants, evidence of the divergence of interest between the emergent Filipino elite and the peasantry was already present during the struggle for independence.

2.3 The first Philippine Republic

The *ilustrados'* agitation began with the Propaganda Movement, which had its origins in the 1870s. They were demanding not independence from Spain, but the curtailment of the power held by the friar orders and the reform of the colony. They were inspired by the 'enlightened liberal ideas' that spread throughout Spain after 1868.[32] Eventually, in 1892, Andres Bonifacio formed a secret brotherhood, the Katipunan, which was committed to full independence.[33] When revolution broke out in 1896, many peasants joined with the Katipunan under the command of their landowning patrons, or encouraged by their Filipino parish priests.[34]

However, peasant support for and participation in the Katipunan was also part of a long tradition of peasant rebellion in the islands. Peasant animosity was directed against the demands of the colonial state for forced labour and the head tax, as well as the abuses of the friar orders.[35] Peasant revolts were launched in a language of folk-Christianity, as demonstrated by Ileto in his study of the role of the *pasyon*, or the 'story of Christ', in peasant rebellion.[36] A revolt in Bohol lasted from 1744 until 1829, when peasants established mountain communities based on principles of self-sufficiency and egalitarianism, and which were opposed to Spanish rule, tribute payments and forced labour. Its leader, Francisco Dagohoy, began the revolt after his rebellious brother was refused a burial by the local Jesuit priest.[37] Movements like the Cofradía de San José in the 1840s, and its successor, the Colorum in the late 1800s, which came to oppose Spanish rule, were sparked by the refusal to allow Filipinos entry to the clergy. The Guardia de Honor, an organization originally founded by the Dominicans themselves, evolved into a peasant movement throughout the provinces in the late 19th century. It came to embody ideas of peasant justice including the 'division of lands among the righteous'.[38]

The Revolution of 1896 represented a juncture between the animosity of the emerging Filipino *ilustrado* elite against the friar orders and Spanish dominance, and the aspirations of the peasantry for *kalayaan*, or freedom. Andres Bonifacio founded the Katipunan in the tradition of secret brotherhoods so common among the peasantry. While Bonifacio was inspired by the writings of José Rizal and other *ilustrados*, he planted the original Katipunan firmly within the tradition of revolts by the poor. The schism between the elite *ilustrado* and the urban and rural poor in the Katipunan found expression in the split that occurred in the movement in 1897.[39] Bonifacio was arrested and executed by General Emilio Aguinaldo's forces who came to lead the Katipunan on behalf of the *ilustrados*.[40] This division was also in evidence as peasants used the occasion of the revolutionary war to seize the lands of the wealthy, especially the friars.[41]

The first wave of the Revolution wound down when Aguinaldo was forced into exile in December 1897, after the pact of Biak-na-Bato negotiated with the Spanish authorities. However, as the United States went to war with Spain and promised to support the Revolution, Aguinaldo was able to return to the country in May 1898, where a reconstituted Katipunan had made significant headway against the colonial forces. They declared independence from Spain and established the Philippine Republic on 12 June 1898.[42] In Rey Ileto's words, Aguinaldo was charged by the *ilustrados* with the task of 'preserving the Filipino elite's conservative definition of the state'.[43] The Republic embodied the aspirations of the *ilustrados* to be masters in their own house, a house that would be run by the landed oligarchy.

The new government imposed its own head-tax, while its local officials attempted to usurp land at the expense of the peasants.[44] It was not surprising, then, that during the short-lived Republic opposition sprung up in the form of rival grass-roots movements. Many had hoped for a regime that would bring about a more egalitarian society. It was also not surprising that it was these groups, whose members were mainly peasants, that carried on the fight against the US colonial government long after Aguinaldo and the other *ilustrados* were captured and resigned to defeat.[45] The 1896 Revolution led to the overthrow of Spanish rule and the curtailment of friar authority, but the land tenure system was left very much intact. The local landed oligarchy that dominated the shortlived Philippine Republic soon came to an understanding with the new colonial authorities.

2.4 The consolidation of the elite under US rule

In its brutal colonization of the Philippines, the US was propelled by its desire to penetrate the markets and natural resources of Asia. While the US government was fully aware of the problems of land concentration in the islands, it chose to strike an alliance with the landed elite. From the consolidation of colonial rule at the turn of the century, until it withdrew from the islands when the Japanese invaded in 1942, US policy served to reinforce the position of that elite. The US built upon the economic and political legacy of Spanish rule, shaping both the economic and state structures that would characterize the Philippines for the rest of the 20th century.

In much the same manner as the Spanish before them, the Americans were first interested in the Philippines for its strategic location as the gateway to China. In a speech from the floor of the US Senate on the eve of colonization, Senator Alfred Beveridge outlined the dual objectives of the US in taking the islands. First, they provided a gateway to 'China's illimitable markets'. Secondly, the fertile 'plains and valleys of Luzon' could produce 'rice and coffee, sugar and coconuts, hemp and tobacco', and the island's forests could 'supply the furniture of the world for a century to come'.[46] US government and public opinion was sharply divided over both the conduct of the war and the decision to establish colonial authority over the islands.[47] However, the claims of some scholars that the US colonization of the Philippines was more 'benign' than other colonial experiences are difficult to reconcile with the historical record.[48]

After promises to Philippine nationalist leaders that the US would support their efforts to establish a Republic, and after Aguinaldo's army had defeated the Spanish and held Manila under siege, Washington dispatched 70,000 troops to 'pacify' the Philippines in what was one of the bloodiest wars of colonization in history.[49] General Arthur MacArthur's proud report home, which claimed that for every 15 Filipinos killed only one was wounded, demonstrated that the US military were murdering the wounded. MacArthur explained that the reason why the ratio of killed to wounded was so much worse among Filipinos than among Americans, was because Anglo-Saxons did not succumb to wounds as easily as men of 'inferior races'.[50] At the start of the campaign to take the island of Samar in 1901, General Jacob Smith epitomized the US approach to the war when he told his men to turn the island into a 'howling wilderness' saying, 'Kill and burn, kill and burn, the more you kill and the more you burn the more you please me'.[51] The US campaign sought to wipe out guerrilla resistance by annihilating the peasantry which sustained it. Over a quarter of a million Filipinos died during the Philippine-American War.

One Filipino historian has argued that the US 'considered *caciquism* under the American flag unthinkable'. However much they may have wanted to abolish it, he argued, 'they possessed neither the spirit nor the know-how to do it effectively, since agrarian reform had not been one of their recent socio-economic problems at home.' In his conclusion he argued that it was US 'naivité' that led them to believe that *caciquism*, or the rule of local political bosses, could be undermined through education.[52] In fact, the US was very much aware of the problems engendered by the dominant position of the landed oligarchy and the means through which it could be challenged, but US officials decided from the outset that the dual interests mentioned by Beveridge - establishing a solid forward base in the Philippines and assuring production of export crops - would best be met by maintaining existing property relations.

This intention was first revealed in the Treaty of Paris in 1898, in which Spain ceded the Philippines to the US, which said that the new colonial power would respect existing property rights of private establishments, ecclesiastical bodies and individuals.[53] This meant that even the land grants bestowed upon the friar orders and companies like Tabacalera would be honoured. The implications of the Treaty were not lost on opponents of US expansionist activities. In 1900, upon his return from Asia, Mark Twain told journalists that he had believed his government's intention in the Philippines was to free the islands of the oppressive system of friar and landlord rule. But, he argued, 'I have read carefully the Treaty of Paris, and I have seen that we do not intend to free, but to subjugate the people of the Philippines...We have also pledged the power of this country to maintain and protect the system established in the Philippines by the Friars.'[54]

President McKinley's letter of instructions to the Taft Commission, which was to serve as the first colonial administration, demonstrated Washington's aware-ness of the land problem, but set the limits of reform as well. The letter, drafted by Secretary of War Elihu Root, said it was the Commission's duty to investigate complaints against individuals and religious orders that hold titles to large tracts of land and seek 'redress of the wrongs which have caused strife and bloodshed in the past'. But he told the Commission that the US was pledged 'to the protection of all rights of property in the Islands,' and reminded them that 'the principle of our own Government which prohibits the taking of private property without due process of law, shall not be violated'. The policy directive set the limits for agrarian reform, saying that 'private property shall not be taken for public use without just compensation'.[55]

During the first decade of the new colonial regime, the basic framework governing property rights in the colony was embodied in legislation passed by the US Congress and the Philippine Commission. The Philippine Organic Act, introduced in July 1902, served as the 'constitution' of the colony until 1916.[56] It limited the size of public lands that could be acquired by individuals to 16 hectares (later amended to 100 hectares) and by corporations to 1,024 hectares.[57] Originally, Governor General William Taft (1901-1903) and the US business lobby in Manila had asked for a limit of 20,000 acres (8,097 hectares) for corporations. But the US farm lobby opposed the proposition and through Congressional representatives was able to limit the size of landholdings.[58] In

November the Philippine Commission passed a law calling for the issuance of Torrens titles covering private and public lands. These were to provide an absolute proof of ownership, but the law made the titling system 'voluntary'.[59] Small peasants were too ill-informed to benefit from the programme. Virtually all of the titles granted by the Court of Land Registration up to 1910 were for large holdings, and even these were limited in number since landowners feared the tax implications of such a measure.[60]

The Public Lands Act passed in October 1903 was supposedly designed to allow the landless and land-poor peasantry to acquire their own farms. Modelled on the legislation used to settle the American west, it allowed anyone to acquire 16 hectares of public land by establishing a homestead and cultivating it for five consecutive years with payment of a nominal fee.[61] Filipinos had no tradition of living on isolated homestead farms, but rather lived in *barrios*, or village neighbourhoods, and few had the resources to avail themselves of such a programme.[62]

In an effort to limit peasant resistance to US rule, in 1902 the colonial state announced its intention to acquire and redistribute the friar lands. As early as 1900, the Taft Commission carried out an investigation into the friar lands and recommended that to avoid 'troublesome agrarian disturbances' it would be wise if the 'government could buy these large *haciendas* of the friars and sell them out in small holdings to the present tenants.'[63] In 1902 the US began negotiations with the Vatican on the purchase of the estates. At the end of 1903 the friar orders agreed to sell 165,000 hectares, or almost 90 per cent of their holdings, for approximately $7 million. The Friar Lands Act of April 1904 specified that preference for sale and lease of the land would be given to the 60,000 share tenants already farming the land.[64]

However, after acquiring the friar estates, the US authorities decided that they would sell the land for the cost of purchase, thus putting it out of the reach of the *kasamas*. Instead, it was the better off *inquilinos* and members of the landed oligarchy, as well as at least one US sugar corporation, who received the lion's share of the friar lands.[65] General Aguinaldo, who had by then decided to cooperate with the US and had returned from exile in Guam, received a 100 hectare farm.[66] Several thousand Filipinos were involved in purchasing the cultivated portions of the estates, but by the 1930s only a small percentage of these lands were farmed by peasant cultivators.[67] Apparently it proved difficult for the government to sell the uncultivated portions of the friar estates, probably for the same reasons that its resettlement and homestead programmes failed.

It is clear that the Philippine Commission's belief that 'redistribution' could and should be accomplished without spending government funds preempted any possible social benefit from its tentative initiatives.[68] In order to sell the San José Estate, a 22,000 hectare holding in Mindoro formerly belonging to the friars, to agents of the American Sugar Refining Corporation, or the Sugar Trust, the Philippine Commission passed a special law that exempted the friar lands from the size limitations imposed on the sale of public lands.[69] An investigation in the

US House of Representatives, led to instructions that further sales of the friar lands had to conform to the limits, but the San José sale was allowed to stand.

Large corporate landowners like Tabacalera faired well under US rule. Its huge *haciendas* in the Cagayan Valley continued to expand, totalling 15,452 hectares by 1913. In 1909 the colonial government began work on the Tarlac Canal, which would eventually provide irrigation to Hacienda Luisita through a diversion of the waters of the O'Donnell River. The canal and irrigation systems connected to it were delayed by incompetent planning, and by 1913 a large part of Luisita's 10,278 hectares was still uncultivated.[70] When the canal was finally completed in 1914, Tabacalera was ensured priority in the use of the water on the grounds that they had given up part of their lands for the construction of the canal. The following year, Tabacalera was brought to court by neighbouring landowners. They traditionally depended on the waters of the O'Donnell, which were being depleted through the diversion to Hacienda Luisita. The Supreme Court ruled in Tabacalera's favour and the company was able rapidly to increase the cultivated area of the *hacienda*.

Over the next decade the company began to plant the land increasingly with sugar-cane to take advantage of the US market.[71] In 1922 it completed construction of an internal rail line to link up with the Manila-Dagupan line, and in 1927 it put up one of the colony's biggest sugar mills on Luisita, the Centrál Azucarera de Tarlac (CAT).[72] It became one of the nation's most productive mills, and the neighbouring Aquino family soon became the biggest suppliers outside Luisita itself. The CAT was said to have milled over 400,000 *piculs* (25,300 metric tons) in its first year and one-half million *piculs* (31,600 metric tons) a year by the mid-1930s.[73] In 1928, just 25 kilometres to the north of Tabacalera's central, José Cojuangco's four grandsons (José II [Don Pepe], Juan, Eduardo and Antonio) established the Paniqui Sugar Central. They owned all the lands servicing the central.[74] The two centrals were subsequently locked in competition.

Far from curbing the power of the landed oligarchy, the US contributed to consolidating its dominance in the colony. The *hacenderos* in the sugar sector found common cause with the Sugar Trust in the United States.[75] Since 1902 the US sugar refiners and the Philippine *hacenderos* had lobbied, against the interests of US growers, for a trade agreement that would allocate to the Philippines a quota in US imports of primary commodities.[76] The Payne-Aldrich Act of 1909 granted a sugar quota of 300,000 tons to the Philippines but blocked tobacco and rice imports. However, all American goods would enter the Philippines free of duties and quotas. In 1913, the Underwood-Simmons Act removed all quota limitations and free-trade continued until 1934, after which it was perpetuated under the Tydings-McDuffie Act.[77] This ensured the preeminence of the 'sugar barons' - the big *hacenderos* - and the landed elite in general on the colonial political scene.

The colonial state took special steps to bend the rules on public land acquisition to encourage the expansion of US business interests in agriculture. It was common for US cattle ranchers to exceed the land limitations in Bukidnon, on the southern island of Mindanao, as long as they remained in the good graces of the governor.[78] In 1926, the Philippine Packing Corporation (PPC), today's Del Monte Philippines, laid the foundations for its huge pineapple plantation in Bukidnon. It was established by the US agribusiness giant, then known as the California Packing Company. According to its official corporate history PPC 'found' lands totalling some 4,324 hectares, under lease to individuals since 1917 and due to expire only in 1942. The company 'succeeded in getting the lessees to turn over their leases to individuals connected with PPC'.[79] There is some evidence that the land was originally held by the PPC pioneer in the region and president of the company from 1938 to 1958, James McNeil Crawford, along with prominent American cattle ranchers.[80] Evidently five individuals associated with the company assumed control over these leases.

The colonial state also facilitated PPC's expansion by establishing an 'agricultural colony' in Bukidnon. The Governor General, Dwight F. Davis, said that this was done by using 'wide areas of vacant agricultural land under arrangements which will provide capital without necessarily amending the present land laws'.[81] One report says that Davis' 'arrangements' actually involved turning the land into a Naval Reservation and that PPC subleased it from the US Navy.[82] Over 14,000 hectares were set aside in Libona and Santa Fe for the colony, called the Bukidnon Pineapple Reservation.[83] PPC was authorized to take up an area within the colony and to finance 'homesteaders' who would settle and raise pineapples. In an arrangement recalling Tabacalera's methods, the 'settlers' had to mortgage their land to the corporation to pay for advances provided by the latter, and were required to sell all their produce to PPC. Farmworkers were recruited in Bohol and placed in camps at the plantation site. The corporation also set up a cannery in neighbouring Bugo, Misamis Oriental.

The US colonial period saw an increase in the percentage of tenants among the agricultural population and a consequent consolidation of landlord political and economic power. Tenancy is said to have increased from 16 per cent in 1903 to 35 per cent of the farming population just before World War II.[84] Central Luzon, the centre of rice production, saw an even higher tenancy rate, particularly in Pampanga, Nueva Ecija and Bulacan. In Nueva Ecija tenancy went from 38 per cent in 1903 to 54 per cent just prior to World War II, and to 60 per cent by 1948.[85] Leasehold tenancy with fixed cash rents declined rapidly, as cash tenants facing exorbitant rents were reduced to sharecropping. By 1939, only 17,000 farms were run by cash tenants, or 1 per cent of the total, while 548,000 were operated by sharecroppers.[86] Usury, with interest rates of up to 100 per cent, kept sharecroppers in a state of debt peonage throughout the period. In general, the land-grabbing practices and tenancy patterns established under the Spanish continued unabated under US authority.

The political system that emerged gave an institutional form to the power-sharing arrangement established between the US colonial authority and the Filipino oligarchy. The Organic Act of 1902 created a bicameral assembly, with the Philippine Commission (appointed by the US Governor) acting as the Upper House and an elected Philippine Assembly as the Lower House. The US banned any Filipino party whose platform included a call for independence and endorsed the Federalistas as the party of their choice. By 1906, with US control firmly established, the ban on promoting independence was lifted and a new party, the Nacionalistas, was formed with independence as the main plank in its platform. Because popular sentiment favoured independence, even the Federalistas changed their name to the Partido Nacional Progresista and included a call for 'eventual' independence in their programme. The Nacionalistas won an overwhelming majority in the 1907 election and were to dominate the colonial political arena until World War II.

The landed elite's control, however, was assured by limiting the franchise to men, 23 years of age or older, who had held office under the Spanish, who owned real property worth at least P500, or who could read, write, and speak Spanish or English.[87] Aside from the gender restriction, the literacy criterion, maintained even after the Commonwealth Constitution of 1935, was the most important limitation of the franchise, and could be surmounted only by those with substantial property. In the first national election in 1907, only 1.4 per cent of the population voted. Of the 80 assemblymen elected, 73 had held office under the Spanish.[88] National politics were characterised by the competition between political clans, based on patronage, rather than political parties. Local politics were similarly controlled by the *cacique*, or local political bosses, just as they had been during the Spanish period. Provincial political power was enhanced by the fact that only the elite spoke a 'national language' which, besides its limitations on the franchise, ensured competition stayed among local rivals.

In 1916, the Jones Law, which superseded the Organic Act as the constitution of the colony, was passed by the US Congress. It replaced the Philippine Commission with a Senate, composed of 22 members elected by districts and two appointed by US authorities. The Philippine Assembly became the House of Representatives with 80 elected members and nine appointed. Under Governor General Francis Burton Harrison (1913-1921), the cabinet and the civil service were rapidly 'Filipinized'. By the end of his term, 90 per cent of 14,000 civil service posts were occupied by Filipinos.[89] In 1919, the National Development Corporation (NDC) was established as a semi-governmental body charged with promoting investment in the colony. Other government corporations included the New Industries Board, Coconut Products Board, the National Cement Company and the National Coal Company.[90] The Steering Committee of the House of Representatives was given control over all government corporations. This enabled politicians representing the oligarchy to use the state to further their fortunes by employing such institutions as the NDC to their advantage.[91] The Philippine National Bank became the biggest milch-cow. Its generous loans to sugar planters in Negros and other enterprises of the oligarchy, often on the basis of non-existent security and for purposes other than those stated openly, nearly bankrupted the colony during its first decade.[92] While independence rhetoric dominated political discourse, most Filipino politicians were willing to accommodate themselves to US objectives.

By the early 1920s, Manuel Quezon emerged as the central figure among the Nacionalistas. Quezon had the support of the local landlord political authorities and most of the legislators were either part of the landed oligarchy or depended upon it for support. A list of the first assembly members' professions revealed a large number of lawyers and a good number of professionals, but most were either from landed families or the 'surrogates' for powerful *cacique*.[93] Quezon came from the southeastern Luzon province of Tayabas which today bears his name. He was born into a poor family but, as with so many Filipino politicians, entered the elite through the legal profession. By the time he reached national prominence he owned several large estates, including a 200 hectare *hacienda* in Pampanga.[94]

The Catholic Church retained a great deal of power and was itself a large landholder, while many of its priests came from landed families.[95] While opposition parties came and went, they were generally split-offs from the Nacionalistas, with the same social composition, and often criticized the government only on specific issues of corruption and graft.

The US colonial administrators created a military establishment in the islands that served both to protect US interests and to reinforce the position of the landed elite. Recruiting veterans of the hated Guardia Civil, the US Army organized an Insular Police Force as early as 1901 to assist in putting down what US officers and the *cacique* referred to as *ladrones* (bandits) and *pulahanism* (fanaticism).[96] In fact, the 'bandits' and 'fanatics' were peasants fighting US occupation. US commanders argued that, unlike the Guardia, the Insular Police (soon renamed the Philippine Constabulary [PC]) was designed to win the confidence of the local population.[97] However, the 6,000 strong PC quickly became perceived as a tool of the landed elite. Kerkvliet described its actions in Central Luzon in the 1930s, 'When landlords needed help, either to guard their fields against tenants who wanted to harvest early or to barge in on peasants' meetings, they only had to ask the local PC commander'.[98]

The Philippine Scouts were established in 1899, as a unit of the US Army to assist the effort to 'pacify' the islands.[99] The US was clearly not interested in building a regular army that might challenge its own preeminence in the archipelago, and by World War II Eisenhower commented that at the time of the Japanese invasion, 'there was no Philippine Army to speak of'.[100] The Scouts, recruited mainly from the Macabebe tribe in Pampanga and later to be reincarnated as the Scout Rangers, eventually numbered 7,000.[101] They were better trained, equipped and paid than any other Filipino force, but they remained a unit of the US Army until independence. Kessler commented on their role in the Philippine-American War, arguing that they were '75 per cent cheaper to maintain' than US troops and could be employed as a 'means by which American troops could be withdrawn from fighting the increasingly unpopular war'.[102]

2.5 Peasant unrest and 'reform' under the Commonwealth

By the 1930s, the system of landlord rule and economic depression had given rise to widespread agrarian unrest.[103] Peasant uprisings occurred in many areas, but were particularly strong in the areas of widespread tenancy on the large landed estates in the interior of Central Luzon. The Partido Komunista ng Pilipinas (PKP), or Communist Party of the Philippines, and the Socialist Party each claimed to have 100,000 peasant followers.[104] Partly in response to these protests and popular pressure for independence, the US granted the Philippines the status of a Commonwealth in 1935 and Quezon became its first President.[105] The Armed Forces of the Philippines (AFP) were formally organized in 1936 after the institution of the Commonwealth. General Douglas MacArthur, who had served in the Philippines under his father in 1903, again from 1922 to 1925, and as head of the Philippine Department of the US Army from 1928 to 1930, became Quezon's military adviser and 'Field Marshal' of the tiny AFP which he was charged with organizing. The PC remained the biggest contingent of the AFP right up until the Marcos years.[106] Quezon employed the PC extensively against the peasant movement during the 1930s. Military officers and landowners alike made no distinction between the peasant movement and the Communist and Socialist political movements for revolutionary change.[107]

During the Commonwealth period the colonial state made some halting attempts at rural reform, to supplement its heavy-handed response to the growing peasant movement. The 1935 Constitution, the basic law of the Commonwealth and of the Republic from 1946 to 1972, empowered the National Assembly to expropriate private lands for redistribution, but enshrined the requirement that owners receive 'just compensation'.[108] The Constitution embodied the same limitations on public land acquisition as were contained in the early Organic Acts, however it allowed leases for grazing lands of up to 2,000 hectares. It also required that the use of public lands be limited to Filipinos or corporations at least 60 per cent owned by Philippine citizens.[109]

In language borrowed from Roosevelt's 'New Deal', Quezon advocated a 'Social Justice' programme.[110] In 1936 he requested the Department of Labour to conduct a fact-finding survey of the rural areas. The survey reported the 'complete penury' among tenants throughout the countryside who were denied 'constitutional and inalienable civil and political rights'.[111] The colonial state had begun an effort to quell peasant unrest with the passage of the Sugar Cane Tenancy Contract Act in 1933.[112] Two years later, the Rice Share Tenancy Act called for a standardization of a 50-50 sharing agreement for tenants and a 10 per cent ceiling on interest rates.[113] But the law could not be implemented in a municipality unless it was enacted by the municipal council. That only one council enacted the law demonstrated the widespread dominance of landlord interests in local governments. The Act was amended in 1936 to allow the

President to implement the law. Quezon ordered its implementation throughout Central Luzon. But because landlords were only required to give a one-year contract to tenants, by 1939 tenants were faced with widespread evictions as landowners sought to undermine peasant claims to the land.[114]

In 1936, the Quezon government also passed a law to facilitate the redistribution of public lands and created the National Rice and Corn Corporation.[115] Two years later, Commonwealth Act 461 authorized the expropriation of private lands, and on this basis the Rural Progress Administration was established in 1939 to purchase large estates.[116] But the law was ineffectual since no limits were set on the amount of land that could be retained by owners.[117] The National Land Settlement Administration was put up in 1939 mainly to organize settlement and cultivation on public lands.[118] Subsequently it opened the Koronadal Valley, the Allah Valley in Cotabato and the Mallig Plains in Isabela. However, by 1950 it had resettled only 8,300 families at the astronomical cost of P11 million.[119]

Despite the noises in favour of reform, little land was acquired or redistributed by the Quezon government (1935-42). In fact, the Commonwealth period saw an acceleration of land concentration. Most notable were the special efforts of President Quezon to facilitate the security and expansion of foreign companies like the Philippine Packing Corporation. The leases on five parcels of public land covering 4,000 hectares of the PPC estate were due to expire in 1942. In 1938, in a presentation before the House of Representatives, Quezon praised PPC's contribution to the development of the economy of the colony. Quezon introduced a plan, later passed into law, to convert the National Development Corporation into a fully-owned government enterprise authorized to lease from the government 'all the lands that may be necessary for the development of the pineapple industry and for the NDC to enter into a suitable agreement with the Philippine Packing Corporation in regard to this industry'. Thus, through Commonwealth Acts Nos 182 and 311, the 1935 Constitution's requirements for national ownership were by-passed and NDC allowed 'to hold public agricultural lands in excess of the areas permitted to private corporations, associations, and persons by the Constitution and by the laws of the Philippines, for a period not exceeding twenty-five years'.[120] An agreement was signed between NDC and PPC on 18 August 1938, which required PPC to pay the minimal sum of one peso per hectare for the use of 10,000 hectares of public lands in Tankulan, Bukidnon.[121]

While corporate landholdings became more secure, by the outbreak of World War II tenancy had become more widespread and landlord power more firmly entrenched in the Philippines than ever before. Shortly after the Japanese bombed Pearl Harbour in December, 1941, they launched their assault on the Philippines. On 2 January 1942, they occupied Manila. Much as the Americans before them, the Japanese enlisted the cooperation of Filipino political leaders and left the landlord order basically intact.[122] As in much of Southeast Asia, armed resistance to the Japanese was largely carried out by the peasantry whose fight was directed both at the invaders and at local landlords. Just as most of the landed elite defected to the Japanese during the war, so too did most of the armed forces. Seven of the nine generals in the Army and 80 per cent of its officers defected to the Japanese, and the Constabulary was used by them to suppress anti-Japanese peasant guerrillas.

The *Hukbalahap* (Hukbo ng Bayan Laban sa Hapon – People's Anti-Japanese Army) was formed in the tenant dominated region of Central Luzon in March 1942. They worked together with the PKP, but never came entirely under the direction of the party. The first armed groups were formed in Pampanga, Bulacan and Nueva Ecija, where peasant organization had been strong since the 1930s.[123] By the end of the war, the Huks, as they became known, succeeded in seizing significant areas in Central Luzon and freeing them from landlord rule. The peasants' experience in the 1930s, and even more so, in the fight against the Japanese, led them to a new sense of their own power. Their aspirations for rural reform become more focused in demands for agrarian reform after the war.

2.6 Conclusion

The colonial period gave rise to an economic and political system where a relatively small group of initially landed families enjoyed considerable monopoly power. US corporate interests held a privileged place within the economy and many in the elite were tied to the United States, either through education, market opportunities or investment ventures. The state that was bequeathed to the Philippines at independence was largely a captive of these interests. Government corporations and institutions like the military were linked closely to particular interests in civil society. During the US colonial era, the image of the military as an institution on the side of the wealthy was reinforced by its structural ties to the US armed forces.

The process of land acquisition by the elite, through royal land grants, land-grabbing and privileged access to legal formalities, created a system of property rights which tended to appear arbitrary to peasants in the *barrios*. It made the claims for the 'sanctity of private property' more questionable in later debates about redistributive agrarian reform. Conversely, peasant and the indigenous peoples' claims to land tended to be reinforced as a result of this tradition. Because the institutions of the state appeared so intimately tied to sectional interests in civil society they had little claim to the loyalty of peasants.

From the outset of US colonial rule, the US bias against redistributive reform was apparent in the treatment of the friar lands sale. For them, land redistribution was no more than a state-managed market transaction. Specific US corporations benefited enormously from the special treatment accorded them during the colonial period, a fact that must be kept in mind as one assesses their overall contribution to the Philippine economy. The assessment of US colonial rule must be based not only on the formal actions of its administration, such as establishing schools and literacy programmes, but also must take into account the deals made with foreign corporations by successive Governors General. Legal limits on the amount of land that corporations and individuals could acquire were regularly by-passed.

Colonial rule promoted the interests of elite families, or political clans, and domestic and foreign corporations against those of the rural majority. This brief review, which has explored the origin of families such as the Cojuangcos and corporations like Tabacalera and Del Monte, points to the necessity for more research on the historical process of land acquisition in the country. This is particularly true for the acquisition of public lands. A detailed history of the National Development Corporation would probably prove particularly reward-ing, since this was the state institution most involved in appropriating public lands for use by powerful private interests. The continuities between the colonial and post-colonial period were particularly evident in the history of institutions such as the Philippine National Bank. In the 1910s the bank was providing huge loans to sugar planters that were secured by unproductive upland areas over which the planters had no proper legal title. This was similar to practices in the latter part of the 20th century.

Peasant pressures for reforms were present from the early Spanish period, through the First Philippine Republic, and during both the initial and later Commonwealth periods of US colonial rule. The refusal of the parish priest to bury Dagohoy's brother, which sparked the peasant revolt in Bohol in the late 18th century, sounds extremely similar to the refusal of a parish priest to allow a church burial for a KMP peasant activist that so angered the local peasant movement in San José, Mindoro, in October 1987.[124] While the content of peasant demands evolved as the peasantry became more aware of modern ideologies, there was a continuity through all their struggles. By the end of World War II, their demands came to be focused clearly on securing access to land.

Notes

1. Quirino, 1978, pp.1476-79. For a discussion of the problems in interpreting this social structure see Scott, 1978 and Rafael, 1988, chapter 5.
2. Douglas, 1970, p.65.
3. Rizal, 1890, p.360.
4. Roth, 1977, chapters 2 and 3.
5. Roth, 1977, pp.25-26; Roth, 1982, p.132.
6. Anderson, 1988, p.6. For the double-edged consequences of the impact of Spanish as the language of the colonizer see the fascinating study by Rafael, 1988.
7. Roth, 1977, pp.1-6, 21, 134.
8. Roth, 1982, pp.137-42.
9. Sturtevant, 1976, p.29; see also Wickberg, 1965.
10. Roth, 1977, p.35.
11. de Jesus, 1980, p.22.
12. de Jesus, 1980, pp.19-20.
13. Anderson, 1988, p.7.
14. Roth, 1977, pp.50-51.
15. The most thorough account of the monopoly is de Jesus, 1980.
16. For an interesting insight to his reformism, see his memorial published as an appendix to Roth, 1977.
17. Roth, 1977, pp.50-51.

18. Roth, 1977, p.33.
19. Lee-Flores, 1987, p.15.
20. Roth, 1977, p.119.
21. McLennan, 1982, pp.69-73.
22. For Sturtevant (1976, pp.34-35), the tax certificates and police function were the first representations of the 'legal paraphernalia of the modern state'.
23. Nagano, 1982, p.1; Steinberg, 1986, p.44.
24. Roth, 1977, p.143.
25. Yoshihara, 1988, p.155.
26. Evidently it was the elder José's daughter, Ysidra, who built up the family fortune (Yoshihara, 1988, p.155).
27. Interviews with tenants on the estates, April 1989.
28. Instead, Tabacalera says it recruited labour by offering to pay off the debts of Ilocano peasants and transfer them to the estates in Isabela. They were installed as *colonos* (tenant settlers) on small plots of land and all their tobacco had to be turned over to the company which set a value on the produce according to quality. The value was then divided into three parts, with one third collected as land rent. One quarter of the remainder was deducted to repay the company for the *colonos'* debts (those paid off in Ilocos, transport costs, food, etc.) and the rest turned over to the *colono* in ready cash. If and when all debts had been repaid, the *colono* had the choice of leaving the *hacienda* or staying on as an *aparcero* (sharecropper) under the same conditions, save that they could retain the full two-thirds value of their harvest. Raventos, 1981, pp.42-45.
29. Raventos, 1981, pp.76-82.
30. Joaquin, 1986, p.73.
31. Salamanca, 1984, p.10.
32. See the writings of José Rizal (1886; 1891).
33. Its full name was the Kataastaasan Kagalanggalang Katipunan ng mga Anak ng Bayan - The Highest and Most Honourable Society of the Sons of the Country.
34. May, 1987, Chapter 3.
35. In 1622 a revolt against Jesuit authorities began in Bohol. It was led by Tamblot, a native priest, who promised a life of abundance without paying tribute to government or dues to the churches. In 1649, there was a revolt in Samar, led by a ship pilot against forced labour (Sturtevant, 1976, p.80ff.).
36. Ileto, 1979, pp.15-28.
37. Constantino, 1975, pp.98-99.
38. Sturtevant, 1976, p.112.
39. Aguinaldo claimed that the split between Bonifacio's Magdiwang faction and the *ilustrado's* Magdalo faction was due to the former's monarchist tendencies and the latter's republican orientation. He claimed that Bonifacio planned a monarchist coup. Ileto (1979, p.136) was convinced that Bonifacio drew the ire of the leading citizens of Cavite, not the people, as the former considered him nothing more than a 'bandit'.
40. Ileto, 1979, Chapters 3 and 4.
41. Guerrero, 1977, cited in May, 1987, p.181.
42. Agoncillo, 1960, p.225.
43. Ileto, 1979, p.142.
44. The personal *cedula* was replaced in February 1898 with a property tax (Agoncillo, 1960, p.259).
45. Ileto, 1979, pp.131, 146-54, 257.
46. Congressional Record. U.S. Senate 9 January 1900, pp.704-711 cited in Schirmer and Shalom, 1987, p.23.
47. See Schirmer, 1972.
48. This is the impression given by Salamanca, 1984, especially pp.25-36, 46, 80. In response to

what had long been a benevolent view of US colonization promoted by both US and Philippine historians (e.g., Taylor, 1964), a revisionist nationalist scholarship emerged in the 1960s and 1970s (see Agoncillo, 1960 and Constantino, 1975, 1978). In recent years US historians have undertaken yet another revision criticizing nationalist scholarship (See May, 1987, Stanley, 1984). While May (1987, p.23) rightly took to task scholars like Constantino for ideological bias and 'criticizing the Americans for things they did not do', his own ideological bias becomes clear when (1987, Chapter 9) he accepts the legitimacy of colonialism as given and asks how can scholars best evaluate colonial performance.

49. Zinn, pp.306-309. For a graphic description of what took place, see Francisco, 1973; Schirmer, 1972, Chapter 16.
50. Miller, 1984, p.29.
51. Francisco, 1973, p.312. Smith was later brought to court martial but was only 'admonished' and forced to retire (Schirmer, 1972, p.239).
52. Salamanca, 1984, pp.80, 163.
53. See Article VIII of the Treaty of Paris, reprinted in Agoncillo, 1960.
54. *New York Herald*, 16 October 1900, reprinted in Twain, 1972, p.10. For a fuller statement of Twain's position see 'To the Person Sitting in Darkness,' February 1901 *North American Review*, reprinted in the same volume, pp.74-96.
55. President William McKinley's Letter of Instructions to the Taft Commission, 7 April 1900, reprinted in Salamanca, 1984, pp.237-245.
56. Act No.235, 1 July 1902, cited in Salamanca, 1984, p.130.
57. Amendment on individual limit in Public Act No.2874, 1919.
58. Francisco and Fast, 1985, pp.260-262.
59. Act No. 496, 6 November 1902, cited in Salamanca, 1984, p.129.
60. Forbes, 1928, Vol.1, p.316, cited in Constantino, 1975, p.299.
61. Act No. 926, 7 October 1903, cited in Salamanca, p.130.
62. Salamanca, 1984, pp.130-31.
63. Cited in Salamanca, 1984, p.41.
64. Act No. 1120, 26 April 1904, cited in Salamanca, 1984, p.132.
65. Constantino, 1975, pp.297-299.
66. Rocamora and O Connor, 1977, p.68.
67. Roth, 1977, p.1.
68. May, 1980, p.172; Salamanca, 1984, pp.130-33. Stanley (1974, p.157) reported the Commission's worry about the cost (three quarters of which were 'administrative' and only a quarter for surveying and irrigation) of maintaining the lands, illustrating the Commission's belief that redistribution effectively meant sale at cost.
69. Act No.1847, 3 June 1908, cited in Salamanca, 1984, p.222 n.144; Constantino, 1975, p.300. It is unclear whether the Commission knew before Act No.1847 was passed that the Sugar Trust was interested in buying the lands (Stanley, 1974, pp.157-60, 210-11, 221, 240).
70. Stanley, 1974, p.193. Out of 10,278 hectares, 1,200 were devoted to diverse crops, mainly rice and tobacco; 200 were still forested; 8,378 were denuded forest lands; and 500 were unproductive grasslands (Raventos, 1981, p.126). Luisita's land area remained constant to 1940, when Tabacalera reported it at 10,298 hectares. (US War Damage Commission, 1949).
71. By 1935, 5,666 hectares were planted with sugar and 2,575 with palay; an additional 42 were taken up by roads, rail, the canal and residential areas (Raventos, 1981, p.146)
72. Raventos, 1981, p.146.
73. Joaquin, 1986, pp.126, 273. The measure originating in China was used in sugar cane production: one picul = 63.25 kilograms; one metric ton = 15.81 piculs, or 2,200 lbs.
74. Say, 1976, p.7.
75. The American Sugar Refining Company, or Sugar Trust, controlled 98 per cent of all US sugar refining and thus had an interest in cheap imported raw sugar. McKinley had been an important part of the Sugar Trust lobby in the Senate and is said to have received its support

in his 1896 presidential campaign. The best account of the Sugar Trust and its worldwide activities is Francisco and Fast, 1985.

76. May, 1987, p.23.
77. McCoy, 1983, p.140; Constantino, 1975, p.297.
78. Edgerton, 1984, pp.182. The Filipino oligarchy followed suit in the 1920s and 1930s.
79. Colayco, 1987, pp.14,28. Colayco's book is the 'official history' of the corporation.
80. Ravanera (1990, p.4) reported three of the individuals originally associated with this land as Americans, 'Crawford, Kenneth Dy and Gayhart'. Actually, these were probably James McNeil Crawford, Kenneth Day and Frank Gearhart. Since Crawford, was reported as working for PPC from 1923, three years before the corporation was officially established, it is likely that he was sent by California Packing earlier than 1926 in order to acquire land (Colayco, 1987). Day was a big cattle rancher in Bukidnon and was son-in-law of Frederick Lewis, manager of the Agusan Coconut Company ranch, a subsidiary of the American-Philippine Company (APC). Gearhart, also a Bukidnon rancher, was Chief of the Bureau of Animal Industry. Both were close associates of pioneer rancher, former Secretary of the Interior, and APC General Manager, Dean Worcester (Edgerton, 1984, p.185).
81. Cited from Davis's 1929 year-end report in Colayco, 1987, p.14.
82. According to Edgerton (1984, p.182), based on interviews with the powerful Bukidnon Fortich family.
83. Acting Governor General Gilmore, Proclamation No.230, 22 April 1929, cited in Colayco, 1987, p.15.
84. Luzon [LUSSA], 1983, p.6.
85. Olson, 1974, p.74. The overall tenancy rate was probably at least as high as 46 per cent by 1948 according to research conducted by the MSA (Hardie, 1951).
86. Ofreneo, 1980, p.49.
87. Philippine Commission Act No.s 60 and 82, organic law for municipal government, 1901. These criteria were maintained in subsequent electoral legislation (Act No. 1532 in 1907, the first General Election Law), until the 1935 Constitution, which granted literate Filipinos over 21 years old the vote (De Guzman and Reforma, 1988, p.81).
88. Nevertheless, the Americans' preferred party, the Federalista, lost the election (Constantino, 1970, p.90).
89. Anderson, 1988, pp.11-12.
90. Stanley, 1974, p.238.
91. Joaquin, 1986, p.109. The history of the NDC is still largely unknown.
92. Stanley's (1974, pp.237-244) conclusion, however, that this practice was 'an institutional reflection of the dyadic and familial character of Philippine personal ethics' seems unwarranted since, by his own evidence, many American corporations were whole-hearted participants in the practice.
93. Constantino, 1975, p.315.
94. Agoncillo, 1974, p.397; Kerkvliet, 1977, p.55.
95. Koone and Gleeck, 1970, pp.72-73; Agoncillo, 1974, p.397.
96. Salamanca, 1984, p.154.
97. Sturtevant, 1976, p.119.
98. Kerkvliet, 1979, p.54.
99. Kessler, 1989, p.112.
100. Cited in Constantino, 1978, p.22.
101. Friend, 1965, p.6.
102. Kessler, 1989, p.112.
103. Constantino, 1975, p.374.
104. Ofreneo, 1980, p.25.
105. The Tydings-McDuffie Act, March, 1934. The US was also responding to various domestic and often self-interested forces opposed to long-term colonial rule (Friend, 1965, Part III).

106. Constantino, 1978, pp.16-26; Kessler, 1989, p.113.
107. Kerkvliet, 1979, pp.54-57.
108. Constitution of 1935, Article 12, Section 4 and Article 16, Section 4.
109. Constitution of 1935, Article 13, Section 1. The US forced the independent government in 1946 to amend this provision allowing US individuals and corporations to be treated as Filipino citizens.
110. Constantino, 1975, pp.350-354.
111. Ofreneo, 1980, p.25.
112. Public Act No.4133.
113. Public Act No.4054.
114. Constantino, 1975, p.60.
115. Commonwealth Act (CA) 141.
116. CA461, 1938. Under this authority the government purchased the Buenavista Estate in Bulacan on 4 March 1939 and the Bahay Pare Estate in Pampanga on 14 June 1940. The Act also included a provision against the expulsion of tenants on lands covered by the Rice Share Tenancy Act.
117. Tolk, 1989, p.5, 23-24.
118. CA441, 3 June 1939.
119. MAR [circa 1980] Primer, p.50.
120. CA 182, 1936. Colayco, 1987, pp.28-30.
121. Colayco, 1987, p.30; Ofreneo (1980, p.21) reported an area of 8,195 hectares, but this probably represented a subsequent reduction in public land rented. This rental rate stood until 1958 (see Chapter 4).
122. Constantino, 1978, chapters 3, 4 and 5.
123. Constantino, 1978, pp.138-140. The best account is Kerkvliet, 1979, Chapter 3.
124. Field visit to San José Mindoro, October 1987.

3

THE US AND AGRARIAN REFORM IN POST-WAR ASIA AND THE PHILIPPINES

3.1 Introduction

The dynamics of agrarian reform in the Philippines in the immediate post-war and post-independence period can only be understood by looking at its experience in the broader context of Asia. The United States emerged after World War II as a principal actor in Asia and was deeply involved in developments not only in the Philippines, but also in Japan, Taiwan and South Korea. There are many misconceptions concerning the role played by the United States and its relationship with third world elites in the agrarian reforms launched in Asia during the decade and a half following the war. There are also many illusions about the agrarian reform programmes and the nature of the states that implemented them in these countries.

Two problems have vitiated the work of most of those who have analyzed US involvement in agrarian reform efforts in the Philippines and elsewhere in Asia. The first problem relates to the claim that the United States has, by and large, been supportive of agrarian reform in the third world. This was the position of John Montgomery when he stated that, 'From Truman to Johnson there was a general hope that [land reform] might advance prospects of an international order based on democracy and economic progress.'[1] Montgomery argued that the US commitment to agrarian reform stemmed from the American 'popular will' to inject the idealism of the small farmer into US foreign policy. While he recognized that US policy on agrarian reform was not consistent, he nonetheless argued that, at least through the 1970s, the United States supported agrarian reform in the third world.[2]

A similar position was recently advanced by Riad El-Ghonemy, who stated that after World War II the United States was an enthusiastic advocate of agrarian reform until the Reagan administration in the 1980s. This pro-reform consensus, El-Ghonemy claimed was dominant among the entire developed country foreign aid community and among development theorists until the 1980s revolution of 'supply side' and monetarist economics.[3] In fact, an examination of the history of US involvement with agrarian reform suggests that the conservative approach has dominated US foreign policy since the early 1950s. Advocates of the liberal approach at the end of World War II had to fight an uphill battle in US policy-making circles to win support for their position in Japan, Taiwan and South Korea. While their influence soared in the late 1940s, they were attacked for supposed communist sympathies in the 1950s. Since that time, the liberal approach to reform has been a minority trend in the US foreign aid establishment as well as the multilateral agencies.

The second problem in the analysis of the US role is the failure of some authors to identify the minority trend that has advocated US support for a liberal model of reform. There is a tendency to see only a monolithic policy of opposition to 'genuine' agrarian reform.[4] These observers have felt that because US officials or multilateral agencies have endorsed agrarian reform with ulterior motives, their version of reform is somehow not 'genuine'. These two misinterpretations stem from a failure to analyze the schism in post-war US foreign policy in Asia between the conservative and liberal approaches to agrarian reform. A similar division existed to varying degrees within the third world countries themselves, as can be seen in debates over reform policy in both the Philippines and South Korea. The agrarian reform experience in the Philippines can only be understood by analysing the confrontation between these two approaches and situating it in a comparative perspective.

Discussions about reform debates in South Korea and the Philippines have also failed to place them in the context of the relationship between state institutions and social actors on the one hand, and the relationship of both these with external and particularly US interests on the other. What is more, the importance of agrarian reform in South Korea has been neglected by authors of all political persuasions. The division of Korea and the dominance of US-allied dictatorial regimes in the South have led many to ignore the dynamics and consequences of one of the most sweeping redistributive reforms in recent history. Others have held Korea up as a model of successful third world industrialization without according any attention to its experience with redistributive reform, which was arguably the basis on which all other development was built. The reform experience in South Korea provides a contrast with that of the Philippines, which can aid in interpreting the latter's experience during the 1950s as well as in subsequent years under Marcos and Aquino.

3.2 US agrarian reformers in Japan and Taiwan

The traditional conservative bias of the United States against redistributive reform was evident in its administration of the colonial state in the Philippines before the war. Its land policy had never extended beyond using the colonial state to force an essentially market sale of the friar estates and to stimulate resettlement projects modelled on the US conquest of the Western territories of North America. However, in the post-war occupation of Japan, the US broke from that tradition and endorsed a liberal approach to redistributive reform.

US involvement in implementing the liberal approach to agrarian reform was largely the result of the tireless efforts of Wolf Ladejinsky.[5] Ladejinsky, the son of a Ukrainian landowner, emigrated to the US after the Bolshevik Revolution. In 1935 he joined the Office of Foreign Agricultural Relations of the Department of Agriculture under Raymond T. Moyer. His studies of Asian agriculture won him a reputation as the Department's expert on Japanese agrarian problems. By the end of the war he was lecturing on Japanese rural society to US personnel preparing for the post-war occupation of Japan. In 1945 he was seconded to the staff of General Douglas MacArthur, Supreme Commander for the Allied Powers (SCAP), to assist in articulating and implementing the occupation's agricultural policy.

From the outset, US policy-makers did not share a common appreciation of the political consequences of tenancy in Japan or more generally in Asia. However, during the occupation of Japan and the Kuomintang's (KMT) flight from mainland China to Taiwan, those who advocated the liberal approach to agrarian reform as a means to achieve stability and provide relief to an impoverished peasantry temporarily gained the upper hand.

3.2.1 The reform debate in Japan

In his first articles on Japan, Ladejinsky identified tenancy as the major source of political instability in the country. He showed how Japanese militarists had mobilized support among tenants in their rise to power.[6] The Japanese army had won the support of peasants through the promotion of conservative traditional ideas that idealized rural life and stressed the unity of the village community, thus masking class differences.[7] In Washington, Ladejinsky was involved in an effort to convince the government of the need to implement a land reform in Japan once the war was over. In this he was joined by Robert A. Feary who worked in the State Department's Office of Far Eastern Affairs. Feary was responsible for a series of studies on rural Japan that advocated reform as a means to undermine militarism. Feary's boss, Joseph Clark Grew, Undersecretary of State and US Ambassador to Japan before the war, endorsed the proposal as part of his broader campaign for a quick post-war rehabilitation of Japan. Perhaps more than any US official at the time, Grew argued that Japan, purged of its militarists, was potentially a solid US ally in the Pacific.[8]

Even during this period the liberals were in a minority at the State Department. Opposition to redistributive reform was fuelled by the belief that its challenge to the 'private property' of the landlords would open, rather than close, the door to communists in Japan's rural areas.[9] This argument would resurface in later attacks on the liberal approach and attempts to apply it in the Philippines. But advocates of the liberal approach went on an offensive toward the end of the war. In training programmes established to prepare US officers for the post-war occupation, luminaries of the US social science establishment, like Talcott Parsons, joined Ladejinsky in pushing for land reform.[10] Ladejinsky's writings served as a 'primer' for those training sessions.

It was Parsons who first injected an anti-communist thrust into advocacy for land reform in Japan. He warned that after the war Japan would be particularly susceptible to a communist take-over by 'a small well-organized group' holding 'affiliations with the communists in Soviet Russia and North China'. As in Russia, he argued, 'there exists much agrarian discontent' which 'can be exploited without too much difficulty in a radical rather than a conservative direction'.[11] Parsons argued that the Japanese peasantry presented the greatest potential threat and basis for the emergence of a radical communist movement in the immediate post-war period. Peasant economic and political life had to be transformed, Parsons emphasized, if the danger of a revolutionary communist regime was to be avoided.

Division over the agrarian reform issue persisted in the State Department even as MacArthur landed in Japan on 30 August 1945. This was reflected in the fact that the first statement of US policy on the occupation of Japan made no mention of agrarian reform.[12] There was also division over agrarian reform among members of the Japanese government. The Minister of Agriculture, Matsumura Kenso, and the Director of the Agricultural Administration Division of the Ministry, Wada Hiroo, had both worked in the Ministry before the war and were supportive of agrarian reform. Hiroo, who had been arrested during the war for 'thought offenses', clearly advocated a liberal approach to reform. They began working on reform legislation in October 1945, but early drafts that proposed sweeping measures were opposed by other Cabinet members.[13]

In October 1945, Feary was transferred to the staff of George Atcheson Jr, the State Department representative at MacArthur's headquarters. There he convinced Atcheson to endorse a memorandum calling for agrarian reform, which he and Ladejinsky had drafted in Washington.[14] The 'Atcheson-Feary Memorandum' became the basis for the occupation's agrarian reform policy, but there were those in MacArthur's headquarters who opposed its prescription for the implementation of a sweeping redistributive reform.[15] The Japanese Cabinet presented its own bill on agrarian reform to the Diet, or legislature, on 6 December 1945. Ladejinsky arrived in Tokyo at the beginning of December to begin work in the Natural Resources Section of SCAP. He and other supporters of the liberal approach convinced MacArthur to issue an endorsement for reform, despite objections from some in Washington and on the General's own staff. On 9 December, MacArthur issued a directive instructing the Japanese government to submit 'a program of rural land reform' to his headquarters no later than 15 March 1946.

While MacArthur's directive ensured that the Cabinet's bill was not thrown out by the Diet, the Japanese legislators nevertheless watered down the proposal and passed an essentially conservative reform at the end of December 1945. In February 1946, Ladejinsky and fellow liberal reform advocate Lt. William Gilmartin, both with the Natural Resources Section (NRS) at MacArthur's headquarters, met with Wada Hiroo to inform him that the new law was not acceptable. Its provision allowing landowners to retain a minimum of five hectares of land was far too high, the period for implementation was too long and provisions for tenant security on unredistributed lands were too weak. Nevertheless, the Japanese government submitted the law unaltered to MacArthur on 15 March. Over the next month and a half, Ladejinsky and the NRS, in consultation with liberal reform advocates like Wada Hiroo who had become Agriculture Minister, prepared a critical assessment of the law and an alternative programme. However, MacArthur made no public criticism of the Japanese government proposal. Opponents of liberal reform on his staff and in Washington continued to be vocal and pressure was increasingly put on SCAP for a speedy rehabilitation of the Japanese government.

MacArthur's efforts to remain silent on reform were thwarted when the Soviet member of the Allied Council for Japan asked that land reform be put on the Council agenda on 30 April 1946. While the Council enjoyed only consultative status and all executive power within the occupation remained in MacArthur's hands, the battery of questions posed by the Soviet representative meant that the issue had to be dealt with. On 9 May, Ladejinsky's team at the NRS delivered to MacArthur a draft directive outlining what was clearly a liberal programme of agrarian reform. Concerned about the developing opposition to US action on the matter, MacArthur did not issue the directive to the Japanese government. Rather, on 25 May he placed the issue of reform on the agenda of a meeting of the Allied Council scheduled just four days later. He forwarded to the Council only the Japanese government's law and implementing guidelines and their memorandum claiming that these complied with the SCAP instructions on land reform of the previous December. The criticism and alternative programme proposed by Ladejinsky and his staff were not included, and it was left to the Council to decide if the legislation was adequate.[16]

With only four days to prepare for the meeting, Eric Ward, the assistant to the British Commonwealth representative to the Council, W. Macmahon Ball, arranged an unofficial meeting with Ladejinsky and Gilmartin. Ladejinsky gave him a copy of the criticism and draft programme that he had submitted to MacArthur, together with all the relevant statistical information already collected. Ball was thus in a position to deliver 'initial thoughts' on the Japanese programme criticising the high land retention limits allowed to landowners and the many loopholes in implementation procedures. At the meeting the Soviet representative put forward a radical proposal calling for the complete abolition of tenancy and a three hectare limit of landownership for owner-cultivators. He also proposed a sliding scale for land compensation, which would pay landowners a fixed government price for the first three hectares acquired, half price for the next three, and nothing for land area exceeding six hectares or for idle lands.

The Soviet proposal posed a challenge to the US and the Allied Council. This led the Commonwealth delegation to present a counter-proposal to the next Council meeting. After examining the statistics on landownership and detailed discussions with Ladejinsky and his staff, Ward took up the NRS draft, but stipulated a lower land retention limit of one hectare on tenanted lands. He reiterated the three hectare limit for owner-cultivators and most of the other provisions outlined by Ladejinsky. Thus Ladejinsky's programme was eventually transmitted to the Japanese government in the form of the Allied Council proposal. In order to bolster the image of the Japanese government's independence, the proposal was not given the form of a directive but was accompanied by the strong message that SCAP would look very unfavourably on the adoption of anything less. By October 1946, the Japanese government adopted all the essentials of the plan as its new agrarian reform law.

Some authors have argued that the key role in the decision by the US and the Allies to support reform was played by General MacArthur.[17] Ladejinsky himself lent credence to such a conclusion when, in 1951, he said that MacArthur became the driving force behind reform in Japan as a result of the lessons he and his father had learned in the Philippines.[18] MacArthur's own account suggests that he carried out agrarian reform single-handedly.[19] However, the General's hesitance to support the Ladejinsky plan was clear. Ladejinsky's comments about MacArthur's role were made after he had come under attack from the conservatives and were probably more an attempt to seek legitimacy for his option than a sound evaluation of the General's contribution. That MacArthur had no proclivity towards agrarian reform can be seen in the role that he played in both pre-war and post-war Philippines, where he was tied to some of the biggest landowning families in the country.[20] Clearly, if the advocates of the liberal approach had not won the debate among key State Department officials, and the Soviets had not placed a challenge to the occupation, MacArthur would not have endorsed reform.

The Australians heading the British Commonwealth delegation to the Allied Council played a crucial role in the tactical manoeuvres around the reform issues convincing the US reform advocates to lower the retention limit on tenanted land. However, the central work in drafting the programme was done by Ladejinsky and his staff.[21] The Soviet proposals to the Council gave a new urgency to the question and allowed Ladejinsky, Ward and other supporters of the liberal approach to consolidate support for their programme. Agrarian reform was launched in Japan with a two-fold objective. On the one hand, promoting the owner-cultivator and agrarian capitalism would remove a primary source for the revival of Japanese militarism. On the other hand, it would undermine communist mobilization of the peasantry.[22]

Ladejinsky and the liberal reformers had their next chance to implement their programme in Taiwan. In 1947 Ladejinsky replaced Raymond T. Moyer as chief of the Far East Division of the Office of Foreign Agricultural Relations. In 1949 Moyer, who was by then one of two US officials on the Joint (US - Republican China) Commission of Rural Reconstruction (JCRR) requested Ladejinsky's help in implementing agrarian reform in Sichuan and later on in Taiwan.[23] The JCRR was set up by the United States and Chaing Kai-shek's Kuomintang (KMT), in October 1948 in Nanking in a belated effort to introduce rural reform in China.

Ladejinsky was on the Chinese mainland for only about one week, in October 1949. Moyer described land reform efforts there as a 'rear guard action'.[24] Ladejinsky stated that there were two motives for US actions there: firstly, the United States wanted to prove that the communists did not have a monopoly over agrarian reform; secondly, agrarian reform represented an 'investment' in future action in China: 'The rent reduction program therefore in its immediate and direct impact upon the farmers of Szechwan or Kwangsi, leaves a mark that may not be expunged. The seeds thus planted may not all be lost when the Nationalist government has disappeared from the mainland of China and the Communists have taken over.'[25] Ladejinsky went on to work closely with KMT officials in Taiwan to implement a programme of liberal agrarian reform.

3.2.2 The model of reform as it emerged in Japan and Taiwan

Liberal reformers believed that agrarian reform encompassed both land redistribution and tenancy reforms such as rent reduction and the provision of secure leases. However, they saw redistribution as being most effective.[26] Writing of Japan, Ladejinsky argued that endowing the tenant with land ownership would remove the central source of conflict in rural society – 'the dependency of two sets of people on one piece of land and the unequal returns they share'.[27] Ownership was preferable to regulated tenancies because the scarcity of land in Asia made maintenance of the latter extremely difficult. Tenancy regulation was promoted as a 'second best' 'minimum programme'.

The Japan and Taiwan reforms abolished absentee ownership and set a low ceiling on land that could be retained by landlords. In Japan, the ceiling was put at one hectare for tenanted land and three hectares for land farmed by owner-cultivators. Ladejinsky argued that the 'acreage retained by the landlord must be fixed retroactively' and on the basis of 'land owned by a household', in order to avoid the landlord taking measures to evade the reform.

The advocates of the liberal approach were against confiscatory reforms, but promoted the payment of compensation at below market levels. In Japan, land value was decided by capitalizing annual rent payments and paying landlords 40 times the rental value of a rice field. In Taiwan compensation was based on the production value of the land, and landlords received 2.5 times the annual value of all crops.[28] In designing the programme in Japan, the liberal reformers opposed landlord-tenant negotiations over price or direct transactions between them. They argued that government must purchase land and that sale to the government had to be compulsory. Governments could rarely compensate the landlord in cash and therefore should offer interest-bearing bonds. The liberals stressed that tenants acquiring land should enjoy flexible terms of payment, since if they were too rigid, new owners would soon be forced to sell-out and revert to tenant status.[29]

The liberals emphasized that the success of agrarian reform lay largely in enforcement and that tenants' participation was central to the process. In Japan, tenants participated through Land Commissions that were established on the local, prefectural and national level. The two lower levels were elected, with the local committees including five tenants, three landowners and two owner-cultivators, thus guaranteeing the producers a majority vote.[30] Ladejinsky saw tenant participation as crucial not only to the land valuation and redistribution process, but also to developing democracy in the rural areas. It was his efforts to push tenant participation that made reform in Taiwan a success.[31]

The reforms in Japan and Taiwan also instituted secure tenure for those who did not become owner-cultivators. In Taiwan this meant that tenants received six-year lease contracts that the landlord could not terminate unless the tenant died, migrated or failed to pay rent for two years. Landlords were not allowed to repossess the land even after the lease expired if they could not till it themselves, if they already had sufficient income, or if by taking the land they would deprive the tenant family of their subsistence. Security of tenure, in the liberal model, meant a written lease with a fixed rent. Finally, the liberals believed that if a government was successfully to carry out an agrarian reform, it would have to commit itself to providing agricultural inputs, marketing, irrigation facilities and credit at terms that a new owner-cultivator or leasehold tenant could afford.[32]

The liberal approach to reform in Japan and Taiwan involved a real transfer of power and wealth in the countryside. In Ladejinsky's words, 'These reforms involved a drastic redistribution of property, income, political power and social status at the expense of the landlords'.[33] He emphasized that the reforms were carried out peacefully. In fact, they succeeded in co-opting 'grateful' tenants into the existing political order, making reform appear as a 'gift from the top'.[34] Landlords were not entirely dispossessed, but their monopoly of wealth was significantly diminished and they rechannelled their capital into other avenues of enterprise.

Although the social structure was reformed and the absolute privileges of the landowning class were curbed, the landlords still enjoyed advantages over the tenants and often became the 'bosses' of modern rural Japanese politics.[35] Historian Alfred McCoy stressed that while many Japanese peasants were freed from tenancy, the agrarian reform also effectively undermined the basis for peasant solidarity, 'leaving much of the substance of dependency relations untouched', and allowed landlords to integrate into the expanding class of capitalists.[36] Political scientist Garry Olson argued that in Taiwan tenants were also co-opted and their interests channelled to 'consumerism' and 'low level KMT activity'.[37]

Olson and McCoy tended to underplay the extent to which the tenant plight was alleviated in these countries. Griffin pointed out that in Taiwan, despite its autocratic government, the degree of economic equality was striking in relation to other third world regions.[38] The reforms in Japan and Taiwan did accomplish precisely what the advocates of the liberal approach set out to do - they achieved political stability in the rural areas and the basis for a solid alliance between these governments and the United States. It was this model of successful reform in Japan and Taiwan that Ladejinsky, and those he trained in Japan, would use in attempting to 'sell' the idea of agrarian reform to governments throughout Asia, including the Philippines.

3.2.3 Agrarian reform to counter communism

Despite the decision of the United States to support an agrarian reform programme in Japan, Ladejinsky and his team of liberal reformers had not won over all US policy-makers to their approach. As US policy-makers became increasingly concerned about the 'communist threat' in Asia, Ladejinsky encountered more and more opposition to his reform strategy. By 1949, while all US officials were united on the central objective of countering the 'communist threat' after the Chinese revolution, a sharp division had begun to emerge over how this could best be accomplished.

In Ladejinsky's writings after the late 1940s, he made two main criticisms of US policy-makers' perception of the communist threat in Asia. Firstly, he criticized those who failed to perceive the indigenous source of support for communist movements - the impoverished peasantry. Secondly, he argued against those who failed to understand the nature and extent of Asian nationalism. The policy-makers were advocating direct US intervention to counter communism and relied on dollars, guns and technology, while proposing no change to the status quo in the rural class structure of these countries. Ladejinsky called for a more 'enlightened' struggle against communism. His articulation of agrarian reform as a central component of an anti-communist strategy in Asia emerged only toward the end of his work on the reform programme in Japan.

At the outset, the reform programme in Japan had the dual objective of preventing a military resurgence and undermining the basis for a radical and revolutionary peasant movement. As a communist victory in China became imminent, the thrust of the US occupation in Japan became increasingly anti-communist.[39] In the United States, prominent figures like the sociologist Talcott Parsons saw this as a primary objective before the occupation even began. MacArthur wrote in 1964 that anti-communism was the main thrust of the reform from its inception.[40] The conservative Prime Minister of Japan, Yoshida Shigeru, was finally won over to support redistributive reform, saying that without it the farmers might have made common cause with urban protesters and 'the results would have been incalculable'.[41]

Ladejinsky spoke of the anti-communist objectives of the Japanese agrarian reform only after 1948. He went to Japan with the zeal of a New Deal reformer, conscious that reform was the means to co-opt the peasantry and secure a politically stable ally for the United States. It was in 1949 that he began to argue that land reform was a crucial element in the fight against Asian communists. In a memorandum addressed to the JCRR after his brief visit to the Chinese mainland, Ladejinsky bemoaned the fact that the Nationalist government had not done more about land reform sooner.[42] Not long after, he warned in the popular *Saturday Review of Literature* that Stalin was using the peasants' plight in Asia to further his crusade against the 'capitalist West'.[43]

McCoy believed that Ladejinsky underwent a transformation during this period, when his land reform model became a political weapon in the fight against peasant insurgency.[44] Olson claimed that in Taiwan Ladejinsky and Moyer were probably genuinely motivated by concerns for 'social and economic justice' in their advocacy of agrarian reform. However, their superiors in Washington supported the measures only as an instrument through which to assure a rural base of support for Chiang.[45] Yet these assessments are only partially correct. Ladejinsky did seem to undergo a public transformation with the onset of the Cold War. He believed that only by being concerned with issues of 'social and economic justice' could the United States protect its interests in the face of Asian communism. However, Ladejinsky's liberal approach to agrarian reform had always implicitly contained a thrust to counter peasant radicalism. After 1949 this became explicitly anti-communist.

It was during this period (1950-1951) that the prestige of the liberal model and its supporters reached its zenith, ironically just before both were to be attacked by McCarthy's followers in Washington.[46] Ladejinsky attended top level State Department meetings.[47] With the victory of Mao Tse-tung's agrarian revolution, the US began to parade the Japanese agrarian reform as an alternative to communism. In an address to the Fifth General Assembly of the United Nations in 1950, then Secretary of State Dean Acheson strongly endorsed land reform. In 1951, Channing Tobias, the US Delegate to the General Assembly, claimed that Acheson was the first to introduce the issue of land reform to the General Assembly.[48] In fact, it was Poland's introduction of a resolution supporting land reform at the UN in 1950 that had provided the US with an occasion to launch its challenge to communist leadership on the issue.[49]

The theme of Western-oriented reform as an alternative to communism dominated the International Conference on Land Tenure and Related Problems in World Agriculture, held at the University of Wisconsin in 1951. The conference was paid for by the US Technical Cooperation Administration and the Economic Cooperation Administration, and brought participants from all over Asia including the Philippines. Kenneth Parsons, in his introduction to the published proceedings, summed-up the thrust of the meeting:

> The central question of world tenure policy therefore is this: Will the revolution on the land which is building up over so much of the world go the way of the West toward freedom - roughly the road of the French Revolution - or the way of the Marxist Russian revolution?[50]

In 1950 President Truman issued a strong endorsement of land reform in the third world, which was followed by a campaign by then Secretary of Agriculture Charles Brannon.[51] This, however, was before Truman's 1949 'Point IV' concerning technical aid to the third world had fully taken shape, and before the full impact of the 'loss of China' had been generally felt in US policy-making circles.[52] The division in Washington over how to best fight communism, simmering since the end of the war, was about to boil over. Liberal reformers' brand of anti-communism would prove to be in the minority.

Before Ladejinsky joined the government, and during his early years there, he was tasked with examining Soviet agriculture. In his early articles on the topic, he was wary about the potential of the socialist agricultural model and convinced that only by allowing peasants a margin of autonomy could their political support for the state be maintained. However, his articles were even-handed assessments rather than ideological treatises.[53] Ladejinsky's vision of combating communism in Asia was thus based less on the ideologically inspired view that was the common fare of the Cold War, than on a measured appraisal of why the communists gained support and how the West could 'beat them at their own game'. He argued that communists understood the political importance of land and used land reform to win the support of Asian peasants. Even while they were 'exploiting agrarian discontent for their own political ends', the support that they won among the peasants was genuine and they succeeded in mobilizing indigenous movements.[54]

Ladejinsky tried to convince US state officials and Asian leaders that as long as they continued to support the status quo and left the landlord order in the countryside intact, communism would thrive. He argued against those in Washington who saw land reform as 'communistic', and reiterated that supporting agrarian reform and opposing the landlord order was in the national interest of the United States:

> If for no other reason than enlightened self-interest, in the contest with the Communists in Asia, the United States cannot be friendly to agrarian feudalism simply because we are against Communist totalitarianism. Our attitude should be one of positive support to Asian democracy. We should lend our influence and prestige in whatever form possible to the agrarian reforms already in being and those yet to come. We shall thereby help cut the political ground from under the feet of the Communists and aid the forces that make for a middle-of-the-road, stable rural society.[55]

He argued that, in their defense of the status quo, the landlords and the ruling groups based on landlord power 'are unwitting and unwilling allies of Communism'.[56] While Ladejinsky admitted that land reform could not solve all the peasants' problems, it would address their 'basic needs' and 'it is the struggle for the satisfaction of those basic needs that has led Communism to grow at such an extent as to threaten world peace today.'[57] In 1951, he stated that in Japan, 'General MacArthur stole the Communists' thunder and made the landless peasant's dream of a piece of land he could call his own come true. In Japan we have forged an economic and political weapon more potent in Asia than the strongest battalions and blandishments the communists could put forth.'[58]

Ladejinsky opposed not only those who supported the status quo landlord-based governments of Asia, but also those who failed to recognize and respect Asian nationalism.[59] In his comments to a Ford Foundation conference on land tenure in India in 1952, he emphasized that the US itself could not implement land reform. The best way to push for agrarian reform, he said, was for private agencies to fund and encourage those Indians who favoured the idea.[60]

Lastly, in promoting the liberal model of agrarian reform as a weapon in the fight against communism, Ladejinsky opposed those in the US who felt that financial and technical aid could bring about stability and create allies without challenging the status quo in the rural power structure. His view of US aid contrasted sharply with the final form assumed by Truman's Point IV Programme. For Ladejinsky, the model of how the US could provide assistance through agrarian reform was embodied in the work of the JCRR, first in China and later in Taiwan. The JCRR ruled out costly projects that required modern equipment and never introduced new enterprises that might compete with those already in existence. There was no preconceived notion of what was good for the farmer, and there was a focus on short-term projects that would bear fruit quickly. The choice of a project was determined by what the farmers wanted most.[61]

Ladejinsky was critical of the average aid official who made little effort to relate to the people on their own terms.[62] He advocated a cooperative administration of aid with Asian nationals taking the lead. If such an arrangement was employed, the US might avoid 'the accusation that we harbour ulterior motives in offering assistance'. Finally, he emphasized, 'This novel concept of combining technical aid with that of remedying social inequities strikes at the fundamental causes of peasant discontent' and lays the 'foundation for a middle-of-the-road, stable rural society'.[63]

This was the 'enlightened' anti-communism of the liberal approach to agrarian reform. US support for agrarian reform was not limited to Japan and Taiwan. After much debate, the American Military Government in South Korea also endorsed it as a weapon in the fight against communism.

3.3 Conservative and liberal confrontation in South Korea

When US forces arrived at Inchon on 8 September 1945, they had two broad objectives: first, to implement a policy of 'trusteeship' over Korea, south of the 38th parallel, ensuring that the Soviet Union would not extend its authority in the south; and second, to prevent the leftist oriented anti-Japanese movement from gaining authority in the south. To this end, General MacArthur had already instructed the Commander of the Japanese forces in Korea to maintain order and authority until the US arrived. General John Hodge was ordered to set up an American Military Government (AMG), and President Truman declared that Korean efforts to found their own government be disregarded.

Thirty-six years of Japanese colonial authority had created a particularly oppressive land tenure system in Korea.[64] Japanese corporations and settlers had been able to gain control of 15 per cent of all cultivated land in the South including the best agricultural land.[65] By 1945 only 2.7 per cent of rural households owned two-thirds of all cultivated lands, while 58 per cent of rural households owned no land at all. The *yangban*, or big Korean landowners, still controlled 80 per cent of the land.[66] However, they lost much of the power that they had enjoyed under the Yi Dynasty, as they were pushed out of government office by the Japanese.[67] The landowning class nevertheless collaborated with the colonizers and earned the hatred of much of the peasantry.

Before US forces arrived in Korea, 'People's Committees' had been established throughout the country. They were formed by those who had been involved in the anti-Japanese resistance. They operated first under the aegis of the Preparatory Committee for Korean Independence and later under the Korean People's Republic. The leadership was in the hands of communists and left-of-centre nationalists who enjoyed considerable support throughout the South. People's Committees were established in most local government offices and, by August 1945, had virtually taken over the administration of the country. At this time the Committees, which enjoyed widespread support among tenant farmers, began imprisoning landlords. Their objective was to implement a sweeping programme of agrarian reform.[68]

3.3.1 The reform debate in the American Military Government

The People's Republic and all its local components were outlawed by the AMG in December 1945. Instead of relying on the People's Committees to administer authority, the AMG set up a police force almost entirely composed of members of the Japanese-led colonial police.[69] They also relied on the central and local government bureaucracy inherited from the Japanese to administer day-to-day affairs. Syngman Rhee, who had spent decades in the US promoting the Korean nationalist cause, returned to Seoul in October 1945. The US backed him and his right-wing coalition in a 'less than democratic' election for a Korean Interim Legislative Assembly.[70] The Assembly was set up in October 1946 with 90 members, half of whom were 'elected' and half appointed. The AMG did not allow universal suffrage for fear that the left would sweep the polls. Instead, the right were given a free hand to determine the results.[71]

Occupation authorities were divided over what attitude to take toward agrarian reform. Recognizing that the popularity of the People's Committees in rural Korea stemmed largely from their position on agrarian reform, the AMG passed ordinances that reduced farm rents to one-third of production and required written lease agreements between landowners and tenants. These measures were limited to former Japanese lands under AMG control. The Military Governor, General Archer L. Lerch, defended a conservative approach to agrarian reform. He was against redistributive reform on the grounds that it smacked of communism.[72] Old hands at the State Department tended to support his position. The State Department's initial position in Korea was that land reform was 'a long-range problem that the Koreans will have to work out for themselves'.[73]

Although the People's Committees were undermined by US military authorities in the South, they became the principal organs of government in the early period in North Korea. In March 1946, the Committees in the North implemented an extensive land reform on all private lands. Landowners were allowed to retain five hectares for their own cultivation.[74] The new owners paid a yearly tax of 27 per cent of their crop to the government.[75] These measures led to the creation of a system of small farming that persisted until 1954. The North Korean reform was accomplished relatively peacefully and it was a major factor in winning support and legitimacy for the newly emerging communist government.[76] As unrest mounted in the South, land reform became an object of political competition between the North and the South. By the late 1940s, North Korea was clearly winning the race.

After Ladejinsky, Feary and other supporters of the liberal approach won the debate over reform in occupied Japan, the State Department reversed its position on Korea. The escalation of rural opposition to the AMG and Rhee's right-wing policies, and 'the delay in uniting the country', were cited as reasons for the reversal. In September 1946, it announced that one of the AMG's major objectives was to implement land reforms that would 'replace wide-spread tenancy with full ownership of the land by the individual farmer'.[77] Taking the classic conservative view toward reform, Lerch persisted in his opposition. It was only after he died in September 1947 that the AMG began to take action.

When the issue of reform was introduced in the Interim Assembly, Rhee and his supporters were vehemently opposed. When Rhee had first returned to Korea he received the support of the Korean Democratic Party (KDP), which had been formed in 1945 mainly by wealthy landowners.[78] At the same time, Rhee's paid lobbyists in the US were known to be putting pressure on Washington not to go ahead with reform.[79] Although Rhee broke with the KDP after the election, he still hesitated to antagonize the landowners before full independence was achieved, especially as he wanted their support for his bid to be placed at the head of the new government. Thus the majority of Assembly members were determined to block land reform measures. In order to proceed, the AMG had to abolish the Interim Assembly. It set up the National Land Administration (NLA) to redistribute former Japanese lands under AMG control.[80] In March 1948, the NLA began land redistribution and succeeded in transferring 240,000 hectares, or 10 per cent of cultivated land, to former tenants.[81]

Thus it was only after a protracted struggle that the advocates of the liberal approach among US reformers defeated the conservative position. The US reform covered only 10 per cent of the land, but it set the tone for further debate and contributed to a spate of landowner divestment of lands that would characterise the whole Korean reform. The AMG's implementation of redistribution just before the 1948 elections and independence raised tenant expectations and forced South Korean politicians to confront the problem of agrarian reform. The US land redistribution is widely credited with having foiled a communist-led election boycott among the rural majority.

3.3.2 Reform under Syngman Rhee

All parties included land reform in their election platforms and the new Assembly included a commitment to land reform in the Constitution of 1948.[82]

However, as the Philippine experience under both Marcos and Aquino would later demonstrate, this was by no means a guarantee that the government would actually implement a redistributive programme. President Rhee's overwhelming concern was to establish his authority within the state. To this end he began constructing the foundations of his particular version of an authoritarian regime. He excluded from Cabinet posts all members of the Korean Democratic Party, his main rival within the Assembly. Most of those appointed to his first Cabinet, or State Council, were conservatives, entirely dependent on Rhee, who enjoyed no power base of their own.[83]

The appointment of Cho Pong-am as Minister of Agriculture was one exception. He was a former Communist who had a good deal of support among the farmers, which was clearly the reason why Rhee included him.[84] Cho advocated a liberal redistributive reform and played a similar role to Wada Hiroo in Japan. He made public a land reform draft law in November 1948. The draft proposed to redistribute rapidly all the cultivated lands in the South and to provide only a low level of compensation to landowners, allowing them to retain only two hectares.[85]

Rhee and his State Council took a conservative stance toward reform and opposed the draft. Before submitting it to the Assembly they raised both the retention limit and compensation payments to landowners, as well as the price that beneficiaries would have to pay for the land. Cho later left the Cabinet and was elected to the Assembly in 1950, but after several attempts to build what was essentially a social democratic alternative to Rhee, he was arrested and executed in 1958 as a North Korean spy.[86]

The debate over the reform programme in the legislature that started in 1949 demonstrates why no simple conclusions can be drawn about an authoritarian regime's proclivity to agrarian reform. The respective roles of Rhee's Cabinet and the Legislature were the opposite of what would be expected by those who advocate the modernizing potential of authoritarian regimes. The Legislature, which was largely composed of representatives tied to the landowners, opposed the watered-down draft submitted by the Cabinet essentially because it was not a radical enough programme. In taking this action they were interested both in improving their image among the peasant majority and in curbing Rhee's executive power. The Assembly passed a more radical programme and Rhee vetoed it. But the Assembly voted to override his veto and Rhee was forced to sign the Land Reform Act on 21 June 1949. However, Rhee delayed implementation of the programme and pushed the Assembly to revise the law. A revised law was passed, and signed by Rhee in March 1950. Rhee, however, did not begin implementation until one week before the Korean War broke out on 25 June 1950.[87]

Within two months, troops from North Korea occupied the entire area of the South except for the small perimeter around Pusan. As many as 18,000 farmers' committees were established in most of the districts in the South. Some 573,000 *chungbo* (one *chungbo* is roughly equivalent to one hectare) were distributed for *free* to 1,267,809 farm families or 66 per cent of the total number of farm households in areas under the territorial command of Northern forces.[88] North Korea's policy of land reform probably played a decisive role in winning the support of rural inhabitants and keeping local resistance to the Northern armies to a minimum. When US–UN forces recaptured the territory of the South, these reforms were declared null and void.

Implementation of the Rhee administration's reform did not occur until after the US–UN forces had reoccupied the South.[89] With full backing from the US Economic Cooperation Administration (ECA) in October 1950, Rhee's government announced the resumption of the land reform programme and, in January 1951, began redistribution with a vengeance.[90] By December 1952, the government had essentially completed the programme.[91] The redistribution programmes after 1945, combined with private sales, changed the structure of land tenure in the country. By the end of the reform no more than 7 per cent of farm families were tenants.[92] The area of cultivated land under tenancy had fallen from almost 65 per cent in 1945 to only 18 per cent in 1965.

It is fair to say that the landlord class as such was wiped out by the reform. As in the period between 1945 and 1950, landowners continued to sell their land during the implementation of the Rhee administration's reform programme. Many landowners were ruined by the reform. Most bonds were used for investment in industry, but for the majority of landowners the low value of their bonds did not allow them to make worthwhile investments. Only the biggest landowners and big businessmen, who had substantial capital reserves, profited by buying up the bonds at their low market value.[93]

Rhee was in a position to promote the interests of those businessmen who agreed to support him. By controlling access to licensing, foreign exchange, and loan and aid resources, he made the new business sector very dependent on the presidency. He made sure that supporters of the opposition did not get access to privileges in business.[94] Rather than relying on the KDP, Rhee had turned to the bureaucracy and police to enforce his authority. He used the coercive power of the state to control the National Assembly, often arresting rivals to intimidate the Assembly into doing his bidding. In 1951, he launched his own organization, the Liberal Party, whose inner council was almost entirely drawn from officials of the Japanese colonial government.[95]

It seems that Rhee presided over the emergence of a new 'ruling class' during this period. In a survey of the business sector conducted during the late 1970s, it was found that the majority of businessmen (47 per cent) came from big landowning families. The remainder emanated from the families of bureaucrats, managers and merchants who had enjoyed a privileged place under Japanese rule. The *chaebol*, or business conglomerates, got their start under Rhee. In subsequent years the state was able to curb and shape the development of the business sector principally through control over lending and through severe policing measures.[96]

After considerable debate the US ended up supporting redistributive reform in South Korea. The South Korean regime, despite the prominent place of landowners within it, also supported an essentially liberal approach to reform. The outcome in post-war Philippines was to be far different.

3.4 Liberal reformists routed in the Philippines

When MacArthur returned to the Philippines at the end of 1944, he was intent on preserving the continuity of the pre-war colonial administration, which essentially meant the maintenance of landlord power. He also ensured the exclusion of the guerrilla forces, most active in fighting the Japanese, from participation in post-war politics. During the war, the Hukbalahap had established local governments in many towns and had even carried out some land redistribution.[97] In addition, peasants had taken over large tracts of land abandoned by landlords during the war. MacArthur saw the Huks as the biggest threat to future stability and US interests. He ordered the arrest of their leaders and the disbanding of their armed units. In a move that paralleled US action in Korea, the general also ordered the return of all lands to the landlords.[98] Unlike in Japan, MacArthur made no proposals for agrarian reform to ease rural instability.

Before leaving the Philippines to take up his post as SCAP commander in the occupation of Japan, MacArthur took measures to ensure that his choice, Manuel Roxas, would replace Sergio Osmeña and become the first President of an independent Philippines.[99] Roxas had been close to MacArthur and Quezon before the war, and was one of the few members of the pre-war colonial government to have avoided a prominent government post until the last days of Japanese occupation. In December 1945, Roxas left the Nacionalistas and formed the Liberal Party. He took with him much of the traditional landlord support as well as backing from large US interests. The Philippine Constabulary also lent its support, believing that Roxas would be more sympathetic to those who had collaborated with the Japanese. In May 1946, Manuel Roxas became President.[100] On 4 July 1946, the Philippines was granted independence and had at its helm a Liberal Party government committed to defending the power of the landed oligarchy and the interests of the United States.

The US not only revived the pre-war political status–quo, but also took steps to ensure its economic and military interests in the islands. They revived the export agricultural sector that had been decimated during the war, thus assuring the continued supremacy of the 'sugar barons' on the political scene. The Bell Trade Act was signed in October 1945, and provided for the resumption of free-trade with the United States. It also gave 'equal rights' to American citizens and corporations to exploit Philippine natural resources.[101] In 1946, the Military Bases Agreement gave the US free use of 23 base sites for 99 years (later amended to expire in 1991).[102]

The landlords saw these post-war developments and the election of Roxas as 'their chance to destroy the mass movement' that had emerged during the war.[103] Huk *barrios* were raided and peasants killed. Big landowners established their own private armies to enforce their authority.[104] This prompted the reactivation of the Huk army and its expansion from Central Luzon to other provinces.[105] After the war, the Huks had organized the *Pambansang Kaisahan ng mga Magbubukid* (PKM) or National Peasants Union, with the active participation of the PKP. In 1948 the party changed the name of its peasant army, the Hukbalahap, to Hukbong Mapagpalaya ng Bayan (HMB) or the Army of National Liberation. They demanded land reform and the restoration of a 'democratic peace'. In August 1948, President Elpidio Quirino, who had assumed the presidency after the death of Roxas in April, responded with the mobilization of thousands of troops in a military campaign to rid the rural areas of HMB and communist influence.[106]

At the same time, the free-trade regime had brought about an enormous foreign exchange drain as duty-free imports flooded the Filipino market. A mission sent to the Philippines by the International Monetary Fund (IMF) in 1950 concluded that the single biggest problem blocking development of the economy was free trade.[107] Only the big landowners involved in export-oriented agriculture had benefited from the free-trade arrangements. Peasant insurgency in the countryside was threatening Quirino's government, while an emerging nationalist sentiment among those who aspired to national industrialization threatened to disrupt the unity of the ruling class and its alliance with the US.

The US viewed these developments with apprehension, particularly after the communist victory in China. A 1949 secret report from the US National Security Council (NSC) designated Japan, the Ryukyus and the Philippines as 'our first line of defense and in addition our first line of offense from which we may seek to reduce the area of Communist control'. In 1950, another NSC report stated, 'the security interests of the United States require that the Philippines become and remain stable, anti-communist, and pro-American.'[108]

How the US was to achieve this objective would become the subject of intense controversy. After throwing its weight behind the traditional landlord order in re-establishing the status quo, the US now faced a major peasant uprising that threatened both landlord and US interests in the country.

3.4.1 The first attempt to apply the liberal model

One year later the NSC set the guide-lines for the US response to the growing crisis in the Philippines. In a 1950 report they said that the US must 'use all appropriate measures to assure that the Philippine government effects political, financial, economic and agricultural reforms in order to improve the stability of the country'.[109] On the economic level, the US allowed the imposition of import and foreign exchange controls partly as an effort to court national business interests. This was sufficient to prevent a major rupture in the elite, or elite mobilization around an anti-US platform. The US was then able to focus on what it perceived as the greatest danger - the rise of an armed and communist-led peasant movement.

In the summer of 1950, despite the protests of President Quirino, the US sent

Table 3.1: Scope of Hardie's Land Reform Programme*

Category of Owner	Retention Allowance (Hectares)	Number of Owners Affected	Purchasable Area (Hectares)
Absentee Landlord	None	909	255,484
Resident non-cultivating owner	4	n.a.	n.a.
Owner-cultivator	8	83,293	1,272,732
Part Owner	8	n.a.	n.a.
Other Owners	n.a.	n.a.	n.a.
Total Purchasable Area			1,528,216

*Based on 1938 Census data.

Source: R.S. Hardie, Philippine Land Tenure Reform: Analysis and Recommendations (Manila: USA Special Technical and Economic Mission to the Philippines, 1951), p. 16.

Daniel Bell, Undersecretary of the Treasury, to lead a survey of the Philippine economy. The Bell Mission's report was the first to propose widespread land redistribution as the only solution to agrarian unrest.[110] It recommended a $250 million grant and further loans if reforms were implemented. In 1951, the US Mutual Security Agency (MSA) commissioned Robert S. Hardie to study the tenancy problem in the Philippines. Hardie had worked on the land reform programme in Japan between 1946 and 1949.[111] Accompanying Hardie was another Ladejinsky associate in Japan, Mark Williamson, who was appointed as Hardie's assistant.[112] Ladejinsky himself visited the Philippines in 1948 and on many subsequent occasions.[113]

Hardie's report was released in December, 1952. It proposed a land reform programme that included all the essential components of the model outlined by the liberal reformers in Japan. His definition of land reform corresponded to Ladejinsky's and emphasised land redistribution while also instituting measures to increase agricultural productivity.[114] His recommendations called for: abolishing absentee ownership; low ceilings on land retained by landlords; government purchase of land and a ban on negotiations between landlord and tenant; a land price fixed by the government and compensation in non-negotiable government bonds; a flexible system of amortization payments by tenants; and tenant participation in the reform through land commissions like those that had been established in Japan. His report also called for tenancy reform for those who would not receive land, involving written contracts, cash rents at no more than 25 per cent of the harvest, and a ban on 'extra' services and payments.

Hardie said that the reform would distribute land to 395,908 tenants, or almost 70 per cent of the total number of tenants in the country. As can be seen from Table 3.1, some 1.5 million hectares would be distributed, or what Hardie estimated was 91 per cent of all land operated by tenants (or 23 per cent of total farm area).[115]

Hardie argued that the cost of acquiring the land could be borne by the tenants themselves. The bonds issued to landowners as compensation for their lands would bear 4 per cent interest per annum and would mature in 25 years. Tenants would pay for the land at its purchase price and their payments would also be spread over 25 years at 4 per cent interest per annum.[116] He stressed that the government would be flexible when tenants experienced bad crops. Hardie rejected fixing the land price to a percentage of the annual production, as he wanted to avoid drawn-out conflicts over setting the production value of land. Such a formula would also avoid any sharp increase in the rate of inflation.

Hardie said that it was past the time for 'further study of the problem', arguing that land reform proposals had been on the table since the turn of the century. He proposed speedy action to complete purchase and sale of the land to new owners within two years. The administration of the programme would require P23 million (or US$11 million) for each of the first two years and P4 million for each year thereafter.[117] Hardie stressed that this was only an approximation. Since land acquisition would be financed with bonds to be covered by tenant payments, only administrative costs would need to be met. The Economic Cooperation Administration would provide $15,000 a year in technical assistance, but the P23 million would be raised in 'counterpart funds' within the Philippines.[118] Hardie emphasized that the cost was low, 'compared to the increasing costs for enforcement of law and order.'

That Hardie fully shared Ladejinsky's outlook is demonstrated by his insistence that the cause of rebellion in the Philippines was the oppressive land tenure system: tenancy, insecurity of tenure, rack-renting, unfair feudalistic tenancy practices, inadequate credit and distribution facilities, regressive taxation and the lack of primogeniture in inheritance customs.[119] He also countered the arguments of those in Washington and in the Philippine Congress who claimed that agrarian reform was 'soft' on communism. The mere fact that tenants wanted individual ownership of land, he said, was proof that they were not inclined toward communism. Echoing Ladejinsky, he argued that it was in the national interests of the United States to push for agrarian reform:

> Until remedied, the land tenure system stands as an obstacle thwarting all efforts of the United States to foster the development of a stable democratic economy...Continuation of the system fosters the growth of communism and harms the United States position. Unless corrected, it is easy to conceive of the situation worsening to a point where the United States would be forced to take direct, expensive and arbitrary steps to insure against the loss of the Philippines to the Communist bloc in Asia.[120]

To support his call for reform, Hardie appended to his report public statements in favour of reform by prominent individuals and members of the Church in the US and the Philippines.[121] Hardie and Williamson also won support for their proposal from US Ambassador Raymond Spruance (1952-1956), MSA chief Roland Renne and most of the local US aid officials.

There are two views that are characteristic of most examinations of Hardie's role in the Philippines. Starner argued that Hardie's report was an unrealistic application of the land reform model implemented in Japan, because it ignored the degree of landlord resistance and the Constitutional guarantees recognizing private property in the Philippines. She claimed that only piecemeal reforms were possible.[122] Koone and Gleeck, expressing USAID official views in 1970, claimed that Hardie's proposals were 'unnecessarily militant' and represented a 'largely emotional dedication to land reform', ignoring economic realities.[123] On the other hand, Olson claimed that Hardie's proposals, while perhaps controversial, represented no significant departure from US policy since they were 'designed primarily for the protection of US economic interests'.[124]

Contrary to Koone and Gleeck's claim, Hardie did recognize the need to increase agricultural productivity by means of new technology. However, he argued that tenants would have little incentive to increase productivity or apply new technology if landlords were able to claim half the gains, while high lending rates disallowed use of fertilizers, insecticides and pesticides. As long as rentier wealth was tied up in land, he said, the necessary capital for industrialization would not be available. Hardie emphasized that lands were idle and rentier wealth was leaving the country due to agrarian unrest caused by the tenancy system. Resettlement was not a solution because eventually the same tenancy practices would beset new areas of settlement.

Hardie pointed to the basic weakness of alternative resettlement programmes, arguing that even if the highest tenancy rates were only found in Central Luzon and agrarian unrest was largely centred there, a nationwide reform covering all crop areas was necessary. Central Luzon was but a foretaste of what lay ahead in every region. Common Law in the Philippines was based on 'feudal culture', he said, while the Constitution protected the property rights of landlords. Hardie proposed changes in the Constitution and basic structural changes in rural society to undermine future peasant revolts.[125] A reading of the Hardie Report suggests that he took into account the Constitutional provisions, the political climate and the economic realities in the Philippines. Contrary to Olson's argument, the Hardie report was a significant departure from the standard conservative approach to agrarian reform. Yet, like the conservatives, Hardie was wholly committed to promoting US interests. He recommended a break with past policies based on short-term US interests and maintenance of landlord power in order to defend the long-term interests of the United States.

However, Hardie, like Ladejinsky, underestimated the degree to which the state was controlled by the landed oligarchy in the Philippines, and the extent of animosity toward reform among policy-makers and US corporate lobbyists in Washington. Nonetheless, rather than being an unrealistic morally inspired pipe-dream, as his later critics claimed, Hardie's report identified the roots of peasant unrest in the Philippines that would continue to threaten stability and US interests and lead to future efforts to undertake rural reform.

3.4.2 Counterinsurgency and reform

In September 1950, at the same time as the US was urging rural reform through the Bell Mission, they sent Colonel Edward Lansdale to launch a counterinsurgency campaign against the HMB guerrilla movement. Lansdale was officially attached to the Joint US-RP Military Group (JUSMAG), but was in fact the chief of the Central Intelligence Agency's Office of Policy Co-ordination (CIA-OPC) in the Philippines.[126] Another CIA agent in the OPC explained that the mission of the Office was, 'to conduct covert psychological warfare, political action, and paramilitary action including sabotage, counter-sabotage and support for anti-communist guerrilla groups.'[127] There were two main thrusts in Lansdale's work during this period. The first was to launch a reform of the military and a programme of rural reform and psychological warfare. The objective was to undermine the Huk guerrilla movement and to create a reformist alternative in the countryside. The second thrust, linked to the first, was to groom then Defense Minister and long-time friend of the US, Ramon Magsaysay, to run on a populist reform programme as an alternative to what was now seen as a corrupt Liberal Party government under Quirino.

Lansdale was ostensibly designated the JUSMAG adviser to the Secretary of Defense. Immediately upon his arrival, he struck up a close relationship with Magsaysay, to the point where the latter moved into the JUSMAG complex, sharing quarters with Lansdale.[128] Magsaysay was not from a landowning family, but had risen in the ranks through his connection with a US guerrilla unit during the Japanese occupation. After the war, he joined the Liberal Party and was elected to Congress where he headed the Committee on National Defense. He first met Lansdale in Washington in 1949. In August 1950, upon urging from the US Embassy and JUSMAG, Quirino appointed him Secretary of National Defense.[129]

Quirino's army had conducted a ruthless campaign against the Huks. Lansdale urged Magsaysay to clean up the Armed Forces and promote the army as defenders of the peasants. This involved the consolidation of the armed forces and the formation of a crack anti-guerrilla force based on the original Macabebe Scouts, which was renamed the Scout Rangers. It also involved launching a programme of rural reform. Lansdale initiated the formation of a psychological warfare unit, which was to be known as the Civil Affairs Office of the Armed Forces.[130] The tactics of psychological warfare ranged from methods of armed combat and black propaganda in the media, to organized programmes of rural reform among the peasantry. One former CIA agent explained that black propaganda was more effective than preaching the dangers of communism, 'If we produced a copy of an order to massacre and mailed it to the *Manila Times*, ostensibly from a disillusioned Huk, we would gain a lot more credibility'.[131] Retired US Air Force Colonel, L. Fletcher Prouty, in charge of liaison between the Pentagon and the CIA, said the agency also encouraged Magsaysay to have his own troops masquerade as Huks, committing atrocities in the countryside.[132]

McCoy stated that Hardie's proposal for land reform was 'given additional support by Colonel Edward Lansdale'.[133] However, while Lansdale encouraged general reforms like the liberalization of rural credit, his direct involvement in agrarian reform was limited to the formation of the Economic Development Corps (EDCOR). It was assigned the task of resettling Huk fighters on land granted to them in exchange for laying down their arms. In fact, only eight of the 547 families settled by EDCOR were Huks and the programme served mainly as part of the propaganda campaign to defuse the radical peasant movement. Writing of the programme in 1955, James Emerson, an official in the US International Cooperation Administration, said that, although few Huks were resettled, 'this offer of amnesty and a better life was a powerful propaganda weapon to diminish the Huk movement and its Communistic influences'.[134] Raymond E. Davies, who had been with Ladejinsky in Japan and was Land Settlement Adviser in the Philippines from 1952 to 1957, attested to the fact that EDCOR was mainly a tool in psychological warfare.[135] In the end, EDCOR and resettlement programmes were employed as an alternative to Hardie's proposals for redistributive agrarian reform.

According to Lansdale, there was resistance in Washington even to the limited reforms that he found essential to his counterinsurgency programme.[136] Former CIA operative, Joseph Smith, cited a comment by George Aurell, Chief of the CIA-OPC Far East Division, on the resettlement programme and Lansdale's support for rural reform: 'I'm glad to help fight the Huks, but is it our job to rebuild a nation?'[137] However, Ambassador Spruance lent his support to Lansdale's efforts, just as he had endorsed Hardie's proposals.

The drive to promote Magsaysay as an alternative to the corrupt Quirino government in the 1953 elections began with the Senatorial elections in 1951. The CIA-OPC recruited New York lawyer and politician George Kaplan to assist Magsaysay in his presidential campaign. Kaplan was appointed Deputy Chief of the Manila OPC branch and entered the country under the cover of a CIA-supported Asia Foundation.[138] His first job was to establish the National Movement for Free Elections (NAMFREL), which would work with Magsaysay and the Armed Forces to prevent election fraud by the ruling Liberal Party. The result was an all-round victory for the Nacionalistas and the canonization of Defense Secretary Magsaysay as the guardian of democracy.[139]

In an ostensibly 'unauthorized move', Ambassador Spruance released the Hardie Report to the press in December 1952. Two months later Magsaysay resigned from Quirino's Liberal Party government and announced his intention to run as the presidential candidate on the Nacionalista ticket. Magsaysay ran on a platform of general rural reform and 'clean government', and he clearly had the support of the US. Kaplan and Lansdale played a crucial role in bringing together a coalition behind Magsaysay, and in the formation of the Magsaysay for President Movement (MPM).[140] Key figures were drawn into the coalition, including Senator Lorenzo Tañada and his Citizen's Party, within which were Claro M. Recto and Raul Manglapus. Manglapus became the MPM's campaign manager. Major José Crisol, chief of the military's Civil Affairs Office, became the MPM's head of Public Relations. The MPM made a direct appeal to the population, and particularly the peasants, in order to reach beyond the traditional network and image of the Nacionalistas.[141] But although all parties - the Liberals, Nacionalistas and the Progressive Democratic Party (PDP) - included rural reform in their platforms, none outlined a specific programme for land redistribution.[142]

Magsaysay worked to capture the support of the rural population through the creation of peasant organizations that could replace the radical PKM and other Communist-led organizations. In 1952, the Philippine Rural Reconstruction Movement (PRRM) was established on the model of the JCRR in China. It had the active participation of Y.C. James Yen, whose philosophy of rural development had propelled the movement in pre-revolutionary China. However, PRRM did not adopt a redistributive model of agrarian reform as the JCRR had done in Taiwan with Ladejinsky's help. Instead, PRRM was used by leading Filipinos close to Magsaysay to promote rural programmes based on increasing agricultural productivity as an *alternative* to redistributive agrarian reform. Its work was funded by the CIA, CARE Inc, and numerous Philippine and US corporations.[143] Leading members of the elite, like José Cojuangco II, sat on its founding board.

The Federation of Free Farmers (FFF) was organized in 1953 by a group of Catholic laymen. They were headed by Jeremias Montemayor, who emanated from one of the big landowning families in Pangasinan. That the FFF's main purpose was to undermine communist influence in the rural areas was later revealed by Montemayor himself. He said that after the defeat of the HMB in 1952, 'we organized the FFF to fill the leadership vacuum. No one else was doing it except the communists, and if we failed to fill the vacuum, the communists would again. So we beat them to it.'[144] One of the major sources of FFF finances over the years was the then CIA-funded Asia Foundation.[145] The Catholic Church and the American Federation of Labour – Congress of Industrial Organizations were also notable contributors.[146]

Almost the first act of the FFF was to endorse Magsaysay's candidacy. The elections took place under the scrutiny of NAMFREL, which Lansdale's group had helped to establish. Smith stated that the Manila OPC station 'orchestrated' the mobilization of foreign journalists to quell Liberal Party dirty tricks at the polls.[147] Magsaysay won an overwhelming victory in the elections. The pre-election counterinsurgency effort combined with promises of reform had almost completely defused the peasant insurgency in the countryside. Nationalist historian Renato Constantino noted that the Hardie Report contributed to the victory of Magsaysay in the 1953 election, 'by forcing Quirino and other Liberal Party leaders to reveal their anti-peasant position'.[148] One lesson that the CIA and Washington apparently drew from the experience was that it was possible to counter a radical peasant movement without directly challenging landlord power through a far-reaching programme of agrarian reform. In the words of Berkeley counterinsurgency expert Karl Jackson, the 'promise of reform' was more important than the reform itself.[149]

3.4.3 Landlord opposition and US focus on productivity

When the Hardie Report was released it drew the immediate condemnation of the landlords and their representatives in Congress. Liberal Congressman Diosdado Macapagal, who was backed by landed interests in Pampanga, took a delegation of tenants to Malacañang to tell the President that Hardie's recommendations were unfounded.[150] President Quirino called the Hardie Report a 'national insult'. The House Special Committee on Un-Filipino Activities, inspired by its American cousin, accused the Report of being 'communist inspired'.[151] Congress had shown little overt opposition to the Bell Mission's call for agrarian reform in 1950, but in 1953 it was emboldened by the success of the counterinsurgency drive against the HMB.[152] The strength of landlord opposition to reform and the success of Lansdale's counterinsurgency campaign coincided with a changing political tide back in Washington.

In 1953, liberal reform advocates Hardie and Williamson were recalled. The immediate thrust of US policy remained unclear since Ambassador Spruance and Ronald Renne continued to support Hardie's proposals. However, it was soon clarified by two MSA replacements sent by Washington, John Cooper and Arthur Raper, who had both worked with Ladejinsky in Japan. Cooper released his report in 1954 and demonstrated that he was less faithful to the Ladejinsky model than his predecessor. Cooper's report rejected Hardie's proposals and suggested that with the Huk defeat only minor reforms were necessary.[153] The revival of peasant revolt could be prevented with just enough reform to keep the tenancy rate below 60 per cent of the agricultural population, which he judged to be the danger threshold.

Most authors agree that Magsaysay, who was not a landowner and who had been a good student of Colonel Lansdale, was open to a programme of rural reform.[154] But even given his popular support, if Magsaysay had pursued Hardie's programme without a strong commitment on the part of the US it would have been political suicide. Landowning interests had a stranglehold over the political and economic system. Cooper worked with Magsaysay to institute three pieces of legislation, all of which were to accommodate landlord interests. The Agricultural Tenancy Act was passed in 1954.[155] It spelled out the regulations for share and leasehold rentals and was similar in both intent and effectiveness to Quezon's legislation 20 years before. In June 1955 the Act Creating a Court of Agrarian Relations was passed to enforce the new regulations governing tenancy.[156]

The third piece of legislation was the Land Reform Act of 1955, which created the Land Tenure Administration to acquire large tenanted rice and corn estates and resell them to the tenants.[157] Even though the Bill introduced to the Congress was based on Cooper's much more limited perception of reform, it once again drew the fire of landed representatives. The debate over the Bill revealed the determination of landowner interests among the Nacionalistas themselves to assert their authority over Magsaysay and to remind him to whom he was beholden. Charges that the reform was communistic abounded once again, and the House majority leader (Nacionalistas), Arturo Tolentino, said that reform should be limited to resettlement on virgin lands. The National Rice Producers Association, which included most of the big *palay* producers in Central Luzon, was an active lobby in Congress. Its spokesman, Manuel Gallego, echoed sentiments in the US Department of Agriculture at the time:

{The} history of land reform in the Philippines has all the earmarks of the Chinese Communist land reform system under the guise of democracy, and apparently, under the sponsorship of the United States Technical Advisers as promoters and Philippine tutors of the democratic way of life.[158]

Congress amended the legislation so that only 'lands in excess of three hundred hectares of contiguous areas' if owned by individuals and 600 hectares if owned by corporations could be expropriated. Since few landowners held 300 hectares of 'contiguous' land the law turned out to be quite ineffective. What is more, the law provided that land could be expropriated only 'when a majority of tenants therein petition for such purchase'.[159] As political economist Ronald Herring argued, a tenant would have to be 'irrational' to make such demands given the economic and political power of the landlord.[160] The most indicative aspect of the 1955 Act was the budget allocated for land acquisition, which amounted to a grand total of P300,000.[161] With the provisions stipulated by Congress, Magsaysay's reforms did not even bring about minimal changes.

Ambassador Spruance was recalled in 1955 and in the only interview he granted to the media, he stressed the urgency of land reform.[162] A report issued in 1956 by James Emerson, Deputy Chief of the Agricultural Division of ICA in Manila, made the new US policy quite clear. Emerson set out to reassure the landed oligarchy that the US was now focusing only on issues of productivity, with no challenge to the existing property structure:

The outstanding characteristic of land reform in the Philippines has been the creation of a nationwide environment favourable for natural economic forces to uplift tenants and other small farmers...Drastic and sudden changes in ownership at huge cost to the public treasury, with attendant economic and social chaos, have been avoided to date.[163]

To justify the new thrust, Emerson stressed that the Philippines was very different from both Japan and Taiwan. But much of his argument was based on the sanctity of private property as guaranteed by the Constitution and the 'unpreparedness' of Filipino tenants to assume ownership of land. He redefined land reform, saying that its principal concern should be the establishment of cooperative credit and marketing.[164] The lion's share of US aid in Emerson's budget report went to commodity aid, particularly to the Bureau of Agricultural Extension, with no funds granted to 'Ownership Transfer'. Finally, disregarding

Hardie's warnings, Emerson praised the role of resettlement programmes and community development projects as an antidote for the tenant's plight and for peasant insurgency.

The National Rehabilitation and Resettlement Administration (NARRA), headed by Eligio J. Tavanlar, was set up by Magsaysay in 1954 with US support to 'hasten the free distribution of public lands to landless tenants'.[165] It was responsible for distributing a grand total of 2 per cent of all patents on public lands by 1975.[166] Emerson's 'community development projects' became the key focus of CIA activities after Magsaysay's election. Kaplan worked to push his man in NAMFREL, Jaime Ferrer, into community development work.[167]

3.4.4 Magsaysay and the landowners: the acquisition of Hacienda Luisita

While little land was redistributed to the peasants through Magsaysay's reform programmes, elite families faired much better. The decline of the sugar industry caused by World War II and peasant mobilization in Central Luzon during the late 1940s and early 1950s led several of the foreign owners of large sugar estates to sell their properties. In 1956 the US sugar giant, Spreckles, sold the Pampanga Sugar Mill to the powerful Lopez family, who had owned vast sugar lands in Negros since the 19th century. The Lopez family and the sugar bloc had played a strategic role in electing Magsaysay to the presidency.[168] At the same time Magsaysay saw them as potential rivals.

In 1957 the Spanish corporation Tabacalera informed the President that they wanted to sell their 6,400 hectare sugar estate, Hacienda Luisita, and the Central Azucarera de Tarlac (CAT) after continued labour unrest.[169] Rather than consider the estate for purchase by the government and redistribution to tenants and farmworkers, Magsaysay wanted to block the Lopez family from acquiring still more land in Luzon. With this in mind Magsaysay turned to his young supporter Benigno Aquino, who had married into the powerful clan in Tarlac headed by José Cojuangco II, and asked Aquino if his father-in-law would be interested in acquiring the estate.[170] Aquino wanted to ensure that the Central and the *hacienda* stayed in the immediate family and would not be shared in by the other Cojuangcos. This decision led to the first major rift in the Cojuangco family – one that would prove to have significant consequences for the nation's politics.[171]

Magsaysay's facilitation was only partly responsible for the family's ability to acquire such a large private estate at a time when the government was supposedly promoting land redistribution. They also needed considerable financing. They turned to the Government Service Insurance System (GSIS) to borrow P7,000,000 to purchase the central and the estate. In their loan application they stated that 4,000 hectares of the estate would be divided into four equal parcels and made available to bonafide sugar planters, while the balance of 2,453 hectares would be subdivided for distribution to barrio residents to be paid for on an instalment basis.[172] On 27 November 1957, the GSIS Board approved a loan of

P5,910,000 to José Cojuangco and Associates Inc., arguing that the purchase would mean placing one of the nation's premier sugar centrals in the hands of Filipino businessmen, and that it would allow redistribution of the agricultural estate to the rural poor. It included as a condition for the loan, 'that the lots comprising the Hacienda Luisita shall by [sic] subdivided by the applicant-corporation among the tenants who shall pay the cost thereof under reasonable terms and conditions.'[173] This was inserted to comply with the government's social justice programmes.

The Cojuangcos also needed to secure foreign finance since Tabacalera required partial payment in dollars. They were able to obtain a loan of $2,100,000 from the Manufactures Trust Company of New York.[174] José Fernandez, then working in the Cojuangco family's Philippine Bank of Commerce, is said to have helped package the loan request.[175] Since foreign exchange controls were in effect at the time, the family needed Central Bank approval for their foreign loan. The Monetary Board also stipulated that a clause be inserted in the contract stating that the Cojuangcos were buying Hacienda Luisita 'with a view to distributing this hacienda to small farmers in line with the Administration's social justice program'.[176] It was understood that the land would be distributed within ten years. Benigno Aquino himself said years later that, 'The idea was to buy the hacienda, turn it into a viable operation, then subdivide it and sell it either to the workers or to agricultural cooperatives'.[177]

According to a Cojuangco company official, the family never had any intention of redistributing the land. He said that at the time of purchase, Juan Ponce Enrile was the lawyer for Tabacalera. The Cojuangcos asked Enrile if there were any tenants on the land and he told them that there were none.[178] Then on 5 February 1957 José Cojuangco wrote to the GSIS Board, requesting that the conditions for the loan be altered. Meeting that same day, the Board passed a new resolution that restated the condition for land redistribution. It said 'the lots comprising Hacienda Luisita...shall be sold at cost to the tenants, *should there be any*, and whenever conditions should exist warranting such action under the provisions of the Land Tenure Act'.[179] This amendment opened the doors for the Cojuangcos' later arguments against distribution, saying that there were no tenants on the land. The reference to the Land Tenure Act implied that redistribution would only be warranted if violence erupted on the estate. However, the Monetary Board's resolution requiring distribution within ten years remained on the books; it mentioned distribution not to tenants, but to small farmers.[180]

Benigno Aquino became the first manager of the *hacienda* for the Cojuangcos and was there from 1958 through 1960. He introduced many 'livelihood' projects employing staff from the University of the Philippines at Los Baños, Jesuits from Ateneo de Manila University, the Philippine Rural Reconstruction Movement (PRRM) and an organization called 'World Neighbours'.[181] In later years USAID also established projects there. By employing these organizations, Aquino and the Cojuangcos aimed to improve labour relations on the *hacienda* and to keep independent worker organizations from developing. Luisita's ties with the Americans were not limited to USAID projects. During Aquino's tenure, the hacienda was also used for 'non-agricultural' purposes. In 1958, President Garcia asked Aquino to provide a part of Hacienda Luisita for the training of the Indonesian Colonels working to overthrow Sukarno and a training camp was subsequently established.[182]

3.4.5 Nationalists opposed to agrarian reform

Much like those in the elite who had taken up the nationalist cause against Spain, the elite nationalist movement in the 1950s never endorsed calls for agrarian reform. The US decision to allow the imposition of import and foreign exchange controls in the late 1940s had a significant impact on the economy and politics of the country. In the first four years, between 1949 and 1953, 5,000 industries sprouted. The industrial sector's contribution to GNP rose from 8 per cent in 1949 to 17 per cent in 1960. Industry grew by 12 per cent per annum between 1950 and 1957. Such a development might have been expected to give rise to a manufacturing class distinct from the landed elite, with significant interests in developing the domestic market and supportive of redistributive agrarian reform. The nationalist economic historian Alejandro Lichauco argued that a national manufacturing class did emerge and that it had substantial representation in Congress by the late 1950s.[183]

With a staunchly pro-American government in place in Manila, the US began to backtrack on import and exchange controls. The Laurel-Langley Trade Agreement, signed in 1954, extended US parity privileges to all business activities in the country. Once again, nationalist sentiments rose to the surface, finding their most eloquent spokesman in the person of Claro M. Recto. During the late 1950s, he emerged as the most outspoken critic of US economic domination in the Philippines.[184]

There are several reasons why Recto and other elite nationalists failed to rally to the cause of liberal agrarian reform. Many of these 'nationalists' were members of Spanish families, who spoke Spanish themselves and were extremely suspicious of US motives. Often their families were landed and their views of the countryside 'idyllic'. It is probably a misnomer to regard those who profited from the imposition of controls as a 'national manufacturing class', or to see the controls themselves as purely, or even primarily, a 'concession' to Filipino nationalists. In reality, in the immediate post-war period the US actively supported controls in the Philippines and elsewhere as long as US enterprises were allowed to operate behind the tariff walls and profit from their protection.[185] They achieved this in the Philippines with the institution of parity rights for US citizens and corporations who were able to profit from import-substitution industrialization (ISI).

It is probably more accurate to regard those who profited from ISI as a faction of the oligarchy that became dependent on protectionism for its expansion into manufacturing activities. In fact, many of them did so in alliance with US corporations, either investing behind tariff barriers or exporting intermediate and capital goods into the Philippines.[186] Manufacturing growth during the 1950s was mainly in light industries like shoes, textiles, processed foods and finished consumer products, and remained highly dependent on imported inputs and capital goods.[187] Rather than representing a new class, those families whose economic fortunes rose with ISI often invested in agricultural activities and land, while the majority who profited from ISI were already part of the oligarchy and had simply diversified their activities during this period.

Claro M. Recto, himself born into a prominent family of the *principalia*, was ambivalent about agrarian reform.[188] Perhaps Recto, like Lichauco after him, represented a Bismarckian approach to national development. Like many nationalists in the post-war third world he tended to equate agriculture with backwardness. He opposed the agrarian reforms endorsed by the United States, arguing that they were designed to keep Filipinos as 'suppliers and providers of raw materials and consumers of foreign manufactured goods'. On other occasions, he said that he would support agrarian reforms that increased the purchasing power of farmers, yet he never whole-heartedly endorsed redistributive reform.[189] In fact, except for a brief period during the late 1960s, only the political left would bring about a junction between the movements for nationalist industrialization and peasant movements for agrarian reform.

By the mid-1950s, the landed oligarchy had overcome the challenge to its continued dominance presented by Hardie's proposals. Advocates of the liberal approach had no support among elite nationalists. On the strength of its counterinsurgency success, the US had rejected the liberal approach to reform. It opted instead to put exclusive attention on productivity programmes within the existing framework of property relations. The retreat from the liberal model was not limited to the Philippines.

3.5 The conservative reaction in the United States

Just two years after Hardie was withdrawn from the Philippines, a major attack was launched against his tutor, Wolf Ladejinsky. Aside from the newspaper reports of the day, very little has been written about the 1954 attack that pinpointed Ladejinsky as a 'national security risk' and ultimately drove him out of US government service.[190] This failure to look at the significance of the controversy is part of the general failure to appraise fully the sharp divisions between advocates of the conservative and liberal approaches within US policy-making circles. On the other hand, the fact that Ladejinsky was accused of being a 'national security risk' and was driven out of official government service has probably contributed to the 'progressive' allure that adorns his reputation in Asia. In fact, Ladejinsky continued to work closely with an active minority inside the US government whose views on defending US interests abroad coincided with his own.

By 1950, after the 'loss' of China and with the outbreak of the Korean War, those advocating a primarily military response to communism in Asia began to gain ground against the land reformers. During that year Senator Joseph McCarthy launched his anti-communist witch-hunt and the State Department - especially its Far Eastern Division - was particularly targeted. Many who had been in the foreign service in China and had successfully argued against increased US military intervention on the side of Chiang Kai-shek were purged from the government. They were condemned for having seen the Chinese Communists only as 'agrarian reformers'.

By 1951, Ladejinsky was already writing that he had been 'called a Communist or radical in Japan'.[191] In 1953, he told the Director of the Division of Overseas Activities of the Ford Foundation that American officials visiting Japan had 'closely questioned' MacArthur on 'whether the Japanese land reform was in consonance with American notions about private property and free enterprise'.[192] Like those in the China service, Ladejinsky recognized the nature of Asian nationalism and the political nature of the conflicts in Asia. He saw that military force could not defeat the communists and progress could be made in the fight only by solving the plight of the impoverished peasantry. But he also demarcated himself from those in the China service, criticizing those who mistakenly assumed that the Chinese communists were 'mere agrarian reformers'.[193]

Ladejinsky therefore escaped the purge of US officials working in the Far East, as did his friend and immediate superior Raymond Moyer. They had proven their conservative credentials in Taiwan through their efforts to consolidate Chiang Kai-shek's rule. While Robert Hardie and Marc Williamson, who had worked with him in Japan, came under attack in the Philippines for their land reform proposals in 1952, Ladejinsky continued to promote his model from Tokyo.

However, by the end of 1954, after Eisenhower's Republican Administration had finished its second year in office, Ladejinsky and other advocates of the liberal model were on the defensive. In November 1954, the office of the Secretary of Agriculture, Ezra Taft Benson, informed Ladejinsky that he would not be accepted back to the department in what most had seen as a routine transfer of foreign agricultural attachés from the State Department to Agriculture. In December, the story broke that Ladejinsky was being dropped by the Department of Agriculture because he was a 'national security risk'.[194] For the next month it would occupy the front pages of many newspapers across the United States and throughout the world.

Benson based his public case against Ladejinsky on a series of accusations tying the Russian emigré to the Soviet Union. He cited as evidence the facts that Ladejinsky had three sisters in the Soviet Union, that he had visited that country in 1939 and that he had been a member of two 'Communist front organizations'.[195] One of the 'front organizations' was the Washington Committee for Democratic Action. Ladejinsky responded that he had not been a member of any front organization and that he had not heard from his sisters for the past seven years. He added that his superiors had approved his trip to the USSR.

Most incriminating, argued Benson, was that Ladejinsky had worked for Amtorg Trading Corporation. Ladejinsky had arrived in the US in 1922 and enrolled in Columbia University in 1926. During 1931 he was briefly employed as an interpreter along with many other White Russians at Amtorg, a Soviet firm attempting to encourage trade with the US.[196] Ladejinsky insisted that his job there had been only a menial one and refused to resign, forcing Benson to fire him and putting the controversy in the public eye.

The attack on Ladejinsky represented more than the ill-conceived plan of over-zealous 'anti-communists' in the Department of Agriculture. A conservative journalist, James Rorty reported at the time that, 'in off-the-record interviews some of Secretary Benson's aides have branded the Japanese land distribution as "socialistic". He quoted Benson himself saying, 'I don't know much about land reform policy in Asia, nor about what Ladejinsky did in Japan. But I would not want to see such a programme in this country'.[197] Hubert Humphrey, then a member of the Senate Agriculture Committee, suggested that the charge against Ladejinsky signalled a change in US policy toward land reform.[198] He urged Congress to investigate the link between the charges and the US stand toward 'world land reform' to determine whether the attack on Ladejinsky was 'actually a tip-off of a major change in United States policy'. He further noted that the government was no longer actively pursuing land reform.[199]

Although Eisenhower stood by Benson, his Administration was forced to backtrack on its accusations against Ladejinsky, as prominent Republicans and the State Department came to his defense. Most notable among them was ex-China mission Representative Walter Judd, a Republican member of the House of Representatives who was a prominent participant in the China Lobby and a long-time supporter of Chiang Kai-shek. Judd described Ladejinsky as 'staunchly anti-Communist in both deed and word', adding that his land reform work was 'about the only successful anti-Communist step we have taken in Asia'.[200] Other voices from the right, among them James A. Mitchner, wrote to the press in defense of Ladejinsky.[201]

On 5 January 1955, Harold Stassen, Director of the Foreign Operations Administration and himself once an outspoken supporter of McCarthy, offered to hire Ladejinsky to 'fight Communism in the Far East'.[202] Ladejinsky was to leave immediately for Vietnam to direct a land reform programme. However, just one year later, Ladejinsky was forced to resign from his post with the US aid organization after John B. Hollister, the newly appointed chief of the International Cooperation Administration (ICA) (the successor organization to the FOA), visited Asia. He was forced out ostensibly because he had purchased stocks in a Taiwanese glass factory that was receiving US assistance.[203] Hollister subsequently travelled to the Philippines where he announced that the US would apply no further pressure for agrarian reform.[204]

The attack against Ladejinsky can only be understood in relation to his advocacy of agrarian reform. With his departure from government service, the United States ceased championing the cause of agrarian reform and placed its efforts primarily on developing a military response to 'communist insurgency' and economic and technical aid, without challenging the status quo in rural power structures. In 1951, reflecting US efforts to champion reform, Truman had established an Inter-agency Committee on Land Reform Problems. However, after the Eisenhower Administration took over in 1953, the Committee was never reconvened.[205] Hollister's appointment at the head of the aid establishment reflected a more general shift in US aid policy during the late 1950s. Whereas Stassen had advocated a long-term approach to US development assistance in Asia, many in the Eisenhower period seemed poised to phase out the aid programme in favour of US private sector intervention in the region.

Secretary of State John Foster Dulles reflected that view in 1956, telling the Senate that while the US had to continue investing in military assistance, 'I hope that part of the task which relates to the development of the newly developing countries may more and more be taken over by private capital'.[206] In the mid-1950s, Hollister was at the centre of those proposing to reduce foreign aid. In 1956 he promised US farm interests that there would be no aid to develop recipient countries' potential for production of any crop that the US produced in surplus.[207]

The US never stated that it was opposed to land or agrarian reform, but rather sought to water down the definitions of these terms. Thus in 1959, one US aid official commented, 'we consider agrarian reform in the broad technical framework of rural institutions and services in relationship to agricultural productivity'.[208] Reform emerged as one plank in Kennedy's Alliance for Progress in Latin America in the early 1960s.[209] But by 1963, it was already clear that the US was not serious about pursuing anything more than a conservative approach.

3.6 Liberal reformers and counterinsurgency

In the anti-Huk campaign in the Philippines, the US had employed a two-prong approach in its effort to bolster the weakened position of the elite: sending Robert Hardie and his team, who proposed a liberal model of agrarian reform; and employing Col. Lansdale to conduct military and psychological warfare against the peasant movement. Both approaches were a departure from traditional US policy, and both appreciated the need for some degree of reform. They shared common objectives as could be seen in subsequent activities by Lansdale and Ladejinsky in Vietnam.

Having achieved success in the Philippines, Lansdale went on to Vietnam in 1954, where he attempted 'to do for Ngo Dinh Diem what he had done for Magsaysay'.[210] Lansdale was evidently behind Hollister's request for Ladejinsky's services in Vietnam. When Ladejinsky arrived in Vietnam, it was Lansdale who recommended him to Diem.[211] After Ladejinsky was forced to resign from his ICA post in Saigon, Diem immediately hired him as his personal adviser.[212] Lansdale recounted that Ladejinsky was given a house next to the Presidential Palace and that he joined Diem for breakfast every morning.[213]

Lansdale's approach to counterinsurgency was based on the same understanding of Asian societies that underlay Ladejinsky's approach to agrarian reform. Lansdale was a critic of those who tried to fight Asian communism with conventional military might and financial-technical aid programmes. Echoing Ladejinsky, he argued that the US 'couldn't afford just to be against the Communists. We had to be for something ourselves'.[214] He argued that the US must come to an understanding of 'political struggle' and 'people's war' in Asia. Whereas this understanding led Ladejinsky to propose redistributive reform, it led Lansdale to work to convince the Pentagon that conventional warfare of the type that they had faced in Korea would not be the norm in Asia.[215] Rather the US had to develop skills in 'psychological warfare' and 'black propaganda' campaigns to discredit communist leaders, while instituting reforms to win over the peasantry. Lansdale's reforms, however, did not go beyond what Ladejinsky considered as his 'minimum programme'.

Ladejinsky and Lansdale must have worked very closely together during Ladejinsky's first two years in Vietnam. Ladejinsky's principal work in Vietnam involved the settlement of some 800,000 refugees from the North.[216] Lansdale, by his own account, was instrumental in getting Diem to adopt the programme. He also brought a team of Filipinos who had worked with him during the Magsaysay campaign to launch 'Operation Brotherhood' as part of the effort.[217] The CIA was interested in dramatizing the flight of thousands of peasants, mainly Catholics, from North Vietnam in order to bolster the US stance against holding general elections in the country.[218] Ladejinsky pushed Diem to support more sweeping reforms in Vietnam, but when the Vietnamese leader showed no interest Ladejinsky was content to work on resettlement programmes. As personal adviser to Diem on issues of agrarian reform, he was very much a participant in Diem's agrarian programmes. These were seen by many as an effort to actually consolidate landowner support in the South. He stayed in Vietnam until the end of 1961, but according to some accounts became increasingly disillusioned with Diem and his lack of commitment to land reform.[219]

Ladejinsky's collaboration with Diem and Lansdale offers two important insights into the liberal approach to redistributive reform. First, Ladejinsky was willing to settle for the implementation of a 'minimum programme'. Secondly, he demonstrated on many occasions his willingness to work with dictatorial regimes to implement his model, an attitude not unlike that of supporters of the liberal approach in Taiwan and South Korea. The conclusion that can be drawn is that the strategic objective behind his work was first and foremost the consolidation of states friendly to the US and only secondly the resolution of the plight of the rural poor. Liberal reformers who had worked with Ladejinksy were also involved in the team that replaced Robert Hardie in the Philippines, and they went on to work within the framework of a conservative approach, as did Filipinos who had been close to Magsaysay and his early proposals for more sweeping reforms. In later years in the Philippines this conciliatory attitude would emerge as a consistent trait among Filipino advocates of the liberal approach.

Lansdale's version of counterinsurgency shared some insights with the liberal approach to reform, but did not incorporate the basic proposition on the necessity of redistribution for future economic development and political stability. In this sense his formula, insofar as it deals with rural reform, must be considered as one version of the conservative approach. Supporters of Lansdale would remain somewhat marginal to the mainstream in the Pentagon in later years.

After Vietnam, Ladejinsky went on to work for the Ford Foundation and the World Bank in India in the 1960s and 1970s. However, he was generally involved only in advancing his 'minimum programme', which seldom went beyond the regulation of tenancy and improvement in provision of agricultural services. He had great hopes, however, for the Marcos reform in the Philippines. While the liberal approach to reform saw a revival in the late 1960s in Vietnam, it never regained the prominence that it enjoyed during the immediate post-war period.

3.7 Conclusion: a comparative assessment

The review of US post-war intervention in Asia demonstrates beyond a shadow of a doubt that there was more than one position on agrarian reform among policy-makers of the period. The traditional conservative bias against reform evident during the US colonial period in the Philippines was challenged by a group of liberal reformers who succeeded in securing State Department support for their approach. While Ladejinsky and his 'disciples' won US backing for reform in Japan, Taiwan and South Korea, they never succeeded in seriously uprooting the conservative approach to confronting peasant unrest in the third world. As was seen in the US colonial experience in the Philippines, the conservative approach was founded in ideological beliefs about property rights and the nature of peasant movements, as well as in US political and economic interests.

The ideological proclivity of US politicians against any meddling with private property was revealed in the assault on the policies of Ladejinsky. Even the US backing of reform in Japan, which took place within a policy of speedy rehabilitation of Japanese capital, was subject to the suspicions of US politicians who queried the correctness of redistributing land. The vehemence against the liberal approach was manifested in the McArthyite persecution inflicted on Ladejinsky. The US military establishment's bias against redistributive reform was evident in the resistance of General Lerch in South Korea and the readiness to abandon reform after the success of Col. Lansdale's operations in the Philippines. Hardie's proposals were abandoned in the Philippines when they appeared to threaten the alliance between the Filipino elite and the United States.

From this perspective, agrarian reform proposals of Ladejinsky, Hardie and the other liberal reformers appear as aberrations in the US foreign aid experience.

They were a departure from the norm, rather than part of a Jeffersonian tradition or American will to inject the idealism of the small farmer into US foreign policy.[220] While the liberal reformers presented a distinct alternative to the traditional conservative response to peasant unrest, they were themselves committed to developing a formula that could undermine movements for revolutionary change. This was understood by the conservative supporters of Ladejinsky in 1955. The liberal approach to redistributive reform was, in this sense, not an alternative to counterinsurgency but a different, and in the eyes of its supporters, a more effective approach to counterinsurgency. While it might be assumed that Ladejinsky was a New Deal reformer who only spoke in anti-communist terms after 1949 to win acceptance for his reform model, his relationship with Col. Lansdale in Vietnam during the 1950s would tend to prove otherwise.

The experience of reform in the decade following the war also permits some tentative conclusions about the causal factors underlying the adoption of the liberal approach in Japan, Taiwan and South Korea and its rejection in the Philippines. The most often repeated explanation has been that US occupation in Japan, the American Military Government in South Korea and the KMT's occupation of Taiwan permitted the reform to go ahead, both because occupation forces possessed centralized authoritarian power and because they had no direct interests in landed property themselves. Another explanation places more emphasis on the authoritarian nature of the regimes in Taiwan and South Korea and the implied autonomy of the state from landed interests. Still another has it that redistributive reform was the result of the political will and commitment to carry out reform of leaders either of the occupation forces or the state.

Foreign occupation certainly played a major role in the adoption of reform in both Japan and Taiwan. Japan, however, is a special case and offers only marginal insights for the process of reform in the third world. While the agricultural production system in Japan was still characterized by landlord authority, it had undergone significant development since the Meiji Restoration in the 19th century, and the nation's economy was already an industrial one by the time agrarian reform was introduced. During the 1920s and 1930s, in an effort to spur agricultural production, Japan's rulers had taken measures to deal directly with tenants both in procuring farm produce and in levying taxes, thus reducing significantly the role of landlords.[221] Japan's agriculture was the most advanced in Asia and had already demonstrated its capacity to serve as a basis for industrialization. The capacity of the Japanese industrial sector to provide opportunities for the investment of landed wealth was greatly increased by the post-war reparations policy. Most reparations were to be paid in kind, and thus represented a boon for the manufacturing sector.[222] The US occupation and the Ladejinsky reform plan were decisive in terms of bringing about a rapid redistribution, but the environment in which they were introduced was distinctly different to that prevailing in the third world.[223]

Moyer, Ladejinsky and other US officials with the JCRR played a crucial, though not necessarily determinate, role in advancing agrarian reform in Taiwan. Moyer was in a position to pressure the KMT regime, since he was simultaneously commissioner of the JCRR and chief of the Economic Cooperation Administration branch in Taiwan, and the new regime depended on US assistance for its existence.[224] Taiwan's agrarian production structure had also been developed under Japanese colonial authority, which eased the process of reform. Of more importance was the fact that the Nationalists who established government in Taiwan with US military backing were quite distinct from the local landed elite. What was most significant in Taiwan was that the indigenous landowning elite, who had cooperated with Japanese colonizers, had virtually no access to state power after the KMT established its authority on the island. This was not because the KMT state was somehow autonomous from class forces, since most of its leaders had significant economic interests even if these had been substantially reduced by their flight from the mainland. Nor was it due to the 'authoritarian' character of the KMT regime, but rather to the fact that its authority was in no way dependent on those who stood to lose from reform. This, too, made Taiwan somewhat unique from the situation prevailing in most third world countries.

In both Japan and Taiwan, those who stood to lose from reform had little access to state power. If there was 'political will' to carry out reform, it emanated in the first instance from this fact. In South Korea the situation was more complex and in some ways more similar to the Philippines, since the regime of Syngman Rhee, like that of Magsaysay, relied substantially on landed interests. In South Korea, while the US was responsible for the first episode of reform covering formerly Japanese-owned lands, these represented only 15 per cent of the cultivated area. Syngman Rhee was not a natural advocate of the liberal approach to reform, since he came into power at least partly because of landowners' support.

Some observers have argued that the reform was consistent with an 'ideology of equal opportunity' in South Korea.[225] This is reminiscent of Grindle's proposition that the development ideology of state elites inspires relatively autonomous action. Others argued that the rapid completion of reform was a reflection of Rhee's 'deep commitment and devotion to the principles of land reform'.[226] Neither seem plausible since Rhee was known neither for his commitment to equality nor to reform. His hesitancy on land reform was evident both in his early activity lobbying against the AMG's reform and in his conduct in the National Assembly debate. Magsaysay probably had greater 'political will' to pursue the liberal approach than did Rhee.[227]

The first difference between Korea and the Philippines was in the different effects of colonial rule. In Korea, the Japanese authorities had done much to weaken the power of the old *yangban* land-owning class that had wielded authority during the Yi Dynasty. In the Philippines, the United States quickly came to an accord with the land-owning *hacenderos*, whose economic and political power actually increased during the US colonial period. Landowners who had made peace with the Japanese colonizers were tainted by collaboration and became a target of the rural population once the Japanese were defeated. While landowners had collaborated with the Japanese in the Philippines as well, the period of occupation was so short that the effect was not nearly as severe as in Korea. However, the issue of landowners' collaboration with the Japanese cannot adequately explain why the regime was able to move to implement redistributive reform against the landowners' interests. After all, the police and bureaucracy in South Korea, which were both creatures of the Japanese, were successfully integrated within Rhee's South Korea and wielded enormous power in the post-war period.

It is also not possible to see the adoption of the liberal approach in South Korea as the result of an authoritarian regime bent on modernizing the nation. The complex political environment during the debate over reform in the National Assembly in 1949 prevented polarization between 'pro' and 'anti' landlord camps, or between a modernizing authoritarian executive and a landowner dominated legislature. A number of big landowners remained in the Rhee camp. What is more, in an effort to win popular support, the opposition Korean Democratic Party and its successor, the Democratic Nationalist Party, attempted to distance themselves from the sectional interests of the landlords during the debates over the Land Reform Act between 1949 and 1951.[228]

Rhee's action in the debate with the Assembly demonstrated that he was not a classic example of an authoritarian modernizer confronting landowner intransigence. It was not in his interest to have an autonomous landowner political organization capable of mounting opposition to his government, but he did need the cooperation and backing of wealthy interests in the country. He had to ensure, however, that they were beholden to him and his government for their position. In the end he backed an agrarian reform programme, while ensuring that some of the biggest former landowners, with whom he had a relationship of mutual dependence, were able to secure a position within a new emerging ruling class.

This was not the natural proclivity of an authoritarian regime to implement redistributive reform, nor the action of a state characterized by what Tai called an elite 'separated' from landed interests. Rather, it was the hijacking of the state by a faction of the ruling class. Rhee reluctantly went along with redistributive reform once he could ensure its coincidence with his consolidation of power. However, the contradictions within the ruling circles cannot explain the absence of significant opposition from Korean landowners, who controlled 80 per cent of tenanted land before the reform and lost 50 to 75 per cent of their assets as a result of the measure.[229] This, together with Rhee's endorsement of reform, can only be explained in terms of the threat posed by North Korea and its successful reform. It was clear that the US decision to have the AMG carry out the earlier reform was due in no small measure to the example that had been set by the North. This combined with US prodding provided the climate for the National Assembly to pass its own law in 1949 and 1950. But the passing of the law in the

South was no guarantee that it would be implemented. Here the experience of the Korean War was decisive. It is likely that it was the bitter experience of Northern occupation that persuaded many landowners to submit to reform during the two years that followed.

South Korea was devastated by the war, and clearly it was to the landowners' advantage to receive compensation for even 25 per cent of their assets rather than no compensation at all. Equally attractive was a government that was prepared to ignore their compromised activities during the Japanese colonial period. When the war broke out, Rhee had lost a great deal of popular support. He needed to win the confidence of the rural majority in order to maintain rule over the territory re-captured by US-UN forces. Land reform was essential for his government's legitimacy. What is more, Rhee desperately needed grain. The tenants' payment of 30 per cent of their harvest to the government in return for land was essential to Rhee's efforts to feed his troops. The Korean War was truly an 'historical moment of political choice'. Landowner resistance was so diminished that political authorities could act on reform.

In the Philippines, Magsaysay was a captive to landlord interests. Despite his reformist platform, his nomination as presidential candidate 'was manoeuvred by traditional politicians through traditional political channels, and it was primarily these men who attained political power as a result of his election'.[230] Landowners had not mounted significant opposition to the reform proposals of the US under Quirino until after the Huk threat had subsided. It is possible that if the US had sent only Hardie and not Lansdale and had stuck to Hardie's proposals, Magsaysay might have had more room for choice and action. However, if the US had not sent Lansdale, it is more than likely that Magsaysay would not have been elected to the presidency. In South Korea, the conflict with the North was the crucial factor that led the ruling circles in the South to pass a sweeping agrarian reform and to implement it so quickly and thoroughly. In the Philippines, no threat of this magnitude ever confronted the state.

Even in Taiwan the KMT's willingness to go along with the liberal approach after resisting it on the mainland can only be understood if it is perceived as a reaction to the threat posed by the successful reform undertaken by the communists in China. KMT leaders were keenly aware of the consequences of not dealing with the plight of an impoverished peasantry and consequently displayed little resistance to reform. The victory of the US proponents of the liberal approach should probably be seen in the same light. Outside Japan, the US only endorsed the liberal approach in situations where the alternative was likely to be a victory of radical, peasant-based revolutionary movements. This situation arose toward the end of US involvement in Vietnam, but never in subsequent debates about reform in the Philippines.

Notes

1. Montgomery, 1984, p.132.
2. Montgomery, 1984, pp.119-120.
3. El-Ghonemy, 1990, pp.1, 56-59.
4. Pomeroy, 1974; Kerkvliet, 1979; Constantino, 1987, p.12.

E

5. Ladejinsky's ideas were referred to in Chapter 1.

6. Ladejinsky, 1939, p.48.

7. Dore, 1959, pp.95-109.

8. Olson, 1974, pp.25-26; Halliday, 1975, pp.154-55, 164-67; Bergamini, 1972, pp.60, 135-36; Schaller, 1985, pp.31ff.

9. Feary cited by Olson (1974, p.26); Dore, 1959, p.131.

10. US participants in the agrarian reform programme in Japan saw the Stateside training of officers at Presido Monteray in the spring and summer of 1945 as key to consolidating the US position in favour of land reform (Williamson, 1951, pp.169-170).

11. Parsons, 1946, pp.110-112.

12. The 'United States Initial Post Surrender Policy for Japan', (29 August 1945) and the 'Basic Initial Post-Surrender Directive to Supreme Commander for the Allied Powers,' did not include any mention of agrarian reform among the many reforms listed (Ward, 1990, chapter 2).

13. Ward, 1990, pp.40-41.

14. Dore, 1959, p.131. Walinsky (Ladejinsky, 1977, p.5) cites Feary as saying that the memorandum of the 26 October 1945 was largely the work of Ladejinsky.

15. Foremost among these was the head of the Agriculture Division, Major Warren H. Leonard (Ward, 1990, p.47).

16. This account is based on Ward, 1990, chapters 5 and 6.

17. Olson, 1974, p.28.

18. Ladejinsky, 1951, pp.148-150.

19. MacArthur, 1964, p.313.

20. Shalom, 1986, pp.5-6.

21. Lawrence Hewes (1955, p.68), who served on the US land reform team, testified to the centrality of Ladejinsky's role in the agrarian reform programme, when he said, 'he knew more...about the general topic of land reform in its historical, political, and economic aspects than anyone else'.

22. It was largely the vision of peasant society promoted by social scientists like Talcott Parsons (1946, pp.111-112) that led the US to assume that peasants were either militarists or communists.

23. Ladejinsky, 1949a, pp.127-128.

24. Cited in Walinsky's editorial notes, Ladejinsky, 1977, p.114.

25. Ladejinsky, 1949a, pp.127-128.

26. Ladejinsky, 1964 p.356.

27. Ladejinsky, 1947, p.86.

28. Ladejinsky, 1964 p.358-59.

29. Ladejinsky, 1947, pp.87-88.

30. Ladejinsky, 1949, pp.109-113.

31. Klein, 1958, pp.59,62.

32. Ladejinsky, 1964, pp.357, 364 and 1951, pp.146-147.

33. Ladejinsky, 1964, p.356.

34. Dore, 1959, p.172.

35. Dore, 1959, pp.317-329.

36. McCoy, 1971, p.19.

37. Olson, 1974, p.65.

38. Griffin, 1976, pp.253-276.

39. Dore, 1959, p.315.

40. MacArthur, 1964, p.314.

41. Cited in Ward, 1990, p.112.

42. Ladejinsky, 1949a, p.129.

43. Ladejinsky, 1950, pp.131-132.

44. McCoy, 1971, p.23.
45. Olson, 1974, p.62.
46. The intellectual argument for reform was put well at this time by John Kenneth Galbraith (1951).
47. Ladejinsky attended at least one of these meetings - Interdepartmental Meeting on the Far East at the Department of State, 11 May 1950 - which discussed emergency aid to Southeast Asian countries to ward off the communist threat (*Foreign Relations of the United States*, 1950 vol. 6).
48. Tobias (State Department), 1951, pp.661-64.
49. Warriner, 1969, p.57.
50. Kenneth Parsons, 1956, p.14. The participants from the Philippines included José E. Velmonte, Dean of the College of Business Administration at the University of the Philippines, and Luis Lichauco, then Chairman of the Board of Directors of the Land Settlement and Development Corporation. The University of Wisconsin would later go on to establish the Land Tenure Center, which worked in tandem with USAID and the Ford and Rockefeller Foundations and has been quite active in the Philippines.
51. Cited in McCoy, 1971, pp.22-23.
52. Packenham, 1973, p.43. Point IV of Truman's 1949 inaugural address stressed limited light industrialization from which US exporters of capital equipment and foreign investors could benefit, as well as agricultural programmes focused on exporting US farm inputs and capital investment in agribusiness to the third world (Maxfield and Nolt, 1987, pp.11-13).
53. Ladejinsky, 1934 and 1938. In a letter to the *New York Times* (August 11, 1934), he even argued for the long-term superiority of collectivization.
54. Ladejinsky, 1950, p.131.
55. Ladejinsky, 1949a, p.129.
56. Ladejinsky, 1954, p.205. He put it even more bluntly in 1950, p.134.
57. Ladejinsky, 1951, p.150.
58. Ladejinsky, 1951b, p.151.
59. Ladejinsky, 1950, p.134.
60. Ladejinsky, 1952, p.196. He would drive home this same point with World Bank officials nearly 20 years later. Ladejinsky, 1970, p.475.
61. Ladejinsky, 1950a, p.138.
62. Ladejinsky, 1950a, p.141. Six years later, after Ladejinsky had left the US government he would write to a friend in the State Department criticizing the International Cooperation Administration and the attitude of Americans in Vietnam. He said that the Americans were seen to live apart and even the 'French cut a better figure' (Ladejinsky, 1956, p.277).
63. Ladejinsky, 1950a, p.141-142.
64. Koreans themselves often refer to the era as one of military occupation rather than colonial government. It is probably most accurate to see the administration in Korea as lying somewhere between a purely military colony, like the one they established in Manchuria, and a civilian colony like Taiwan. The result was an extremely repressive regime bent on the 'Japanization' of the Korean nation. See Henderson, 1968, pp.72-74, 401n.
65. The Japanese owned 204,330 hectares of rice land (18.3 per cent of the total) and 153,500 hectares of dry crop land (8.7 per cent of the total) (Mitchell 1949, p.345).
66. Ban et al, 1980, p.284.
67. Rhee, 1980, pp.343-344.
68. Olson, 1974, pp.38-41.
69. Han, 1974, p.8.
70. Halliday, 1978, p.49.
71. Olson, 1974, p.44 and Han, p.8.
72. Olson, 1974, pp.42-43.
73. *Department of State Bulletin* 14 (27 January 1946), p.109 cited in Olson, 1974, p.43.
74. Ravenholt, 1981, p.53.

75. Mitchell, 1949, p.348.
76. Cummings, 1981, vol.1, pp.416-17.
77. *Department of State Bulletin* 15 (8 September 1946), p.482 cited in Olson, 1974, p.44.
78. Han, 1974, p.33 and Kim, 1975, p.124.
79. Olson, 1974, p.47. Robert T. Oliver of Syracuse University was registered as a lobbyist for Rhee, as were John W. Staggers and Jay Jerome Williams, president and vice-president of the American World Trade Export-Import Co. Inc.
80. Mitchell, 1949, p.346.
81. Ban, 1980, p.285.
82. Article 86 of the Constitution stated,'farmland shall be distributed to self tilling farmers. The method of distribution, the extent of possession, and the nature of restrictions of ownership shall be determined by law' (cited in Ravenholt, 1981, p.48).
83. Rhee, 1980, p.327.
84. Han, 1974, p.79.
85. Rhee, 1980, pp.330-331.
86. Rhee, 1980, p.332 and Han, pp.83-84.
87. Whang, p.6 and Rhee, pp.334-335.
88. Rhee, 1980, pp.335-336.
89. Henderson (p.197) claimed that most land was redistributed in May and June 1950. He has since been proven wrong (Cummings, 1990, p.472).
90. Cummings, 1990, p.918n.
91. Rhee, 1980, p.337.
92. Whang (1982, p.31) puts the figure at 2 per cent.
93. Rhee, 1980, p.339.
94. Kim, 1975, p.154.
95. All but one of its leading members were trained as lawyers and served as prosecutors or judges under the Japanese, and all had close links to the police (Han, 1974, p.15ff).
96. Mason, 1980, pp.244-294.
97. Constantino, 1978, p.165.
98. Sison, 1965, p.151; Constantino, 1978, pp.147-149.
99. Constantino 1978, pp.161, 170-171, 186.
100. Constantino, 1978, pp.181-188.
101. Constantino, 1978, pp.198-199; Olson, 1974, p.77.
102. Simbulan, 1983, pp.76-79. Under heavy popular pressure in the Philippines, talks between Philippine Secretary of Foreign Affairs Felixberto Serrano and US Ambassador Charles Bohlen between 1955 and 1961 led to a formal agreement in 1966 to reduce the lease on US bases to 25 years (pp.93-95).
103. Constantino 1978, p.206.
104. Ofreneo, 1980, p.31.
105. Kerkvliet, 1979, is the authority.
106. Constantino, 1978, pp.213-221.
107. Cited in Lichauco, 1982, p.29. For an alternative explanation see below and Maxfield and Nolt, 1987.
108. Both NSC reports are cited in Constantino, 1978 pp.227, 239.
109. Cited in Rocamora and O'Connor, 1977, p.69.
110. Ofreneo, 1980, p.34.
111. McCoy, 1971, p.24; Olson, 1974, p.82. See the excellent study of the Hardie report and its impact in the Philippines by Monk (1990).
112. McCoy, 1971, p.28. Williamson had co-authored a report with Ladejinsky on the Japanese land reform (Ladejinsky et al, 1948).
113. Ladejinsky, 1963, p.325.
114. Hardie, 1951, p.13.

115. Hardie (1951, p.13) noted that these were conservative estimates. His calculation is based on 1938 census data stating a total farm area of 6,691,000 hectares, of which 5 million hectares were tillable. Tenants operated approximately 1,673,000 hectares.

116. Hardie, 1951, pp.20-31.

117. Hardie, 1951, pp.5, 19-20. At the time the exchange rate was P2 = US$1, as set by the Bell Trade Act.

118. Hardie, 1951, Appendix I, pp.I1-2.

119. Hardie, 1951, pp.6,10-12. Rack-renting is an extortionate form of rent roughly equal to the total annual value of the land.

120. Hardie, 1951, pp.6-8.

121. These included Harry S. Truman, William O. Douglas, Barbara Ward, Pope Pius XII, Senator Justiniano Montano, Salvador Araneta, Amando M. Dalisay (PHILSUCA) and Ramon Magsaysay. Of course, many of these individuals, including Truman, Magsaysay and Araneta would later turn their backs on such statements.

122. Starner, 1961, p.120.

123. Koone and Gleeck, 1970, pp.7-8.

124. Olson, 1974, p.93.

125. Hardie, 1951, pp.7-8.

126. Constantino 1978, p.235.

127. Smith, 1976, p.66.

128. Lansdale, 1972, pp.67-68.

129. Constantino, 1978, pp.232-235.

130. Lansdale, 1972, pp.47-48.

131. Smith, 1976, p.66.

132. Prouty, 1973, p.34.

133. McCoy, 1971, p.28.

134. Emerson, 1956, p.43.

135. Cited in Olson, 1974, p.80.

136. Lansdale, 1972, pp.99-106. Smith, 1976, p.106.

137. Smith, 1976, p.106.

138. Smith, 1976, pp.148, 164, 258. This was formerly the Committee for a Free Asia. Later his cover was switched to the Catherwood Foundation of Bryn Mawr, Pennsylvania. After an exposé on the CIA appeared in Ramparts (no. 5, March) in 1967, CIA funding to the Asia Foundation was said to have come to an end (Marchetti and Marks, 1974, pp.46, 178-79).

139. Constantino, 1978, pp.245-247.

140. Constantino, 1978, pp.250-260; Smith, 1976, p.108. Lansdale attempted to underplay his role in the negotiations (Lansdale, 1972, p.104), but Constantino proves otherwise. Carlos P. Romulo also left the Liberal Party and formed the Progressive Democratic Party (PDP) to run for President. The PDP was largely composed of representatives of the 'sugar barons', while the Nacionalistas shared the backing of the rest of the landed oligarchy with the Liberal Party. Smith (1976, p.110) said that, under CIA pressure, Quirino's Vice-president Fernando Lopez joined the PDP slate as V.P. candidate. Later Romulo decided to endorse Magsaysay's candidacy. Thus, the coalition was endorsed by the traditional politicians of the landed oligarchy as well as various nationalists representing business and middle class interests.

141. Starner, 1961, p.6.

142. Starner, 1961, pp.41-44.

143. Shalom, 1986, pp.124 and passim.

144. Cited in Po, 1980, p.43. Information on the FFF is based on Po's account, pp.39-54.

145. Po, 1980, p.47.

146. Hollnsteiner et al, 1978, pp.70-76.

147. Smith, 1976, p.112.

148. Constantino, 1978, p.263.

149. See Chapter 1, section 1.4.4.
150. Constantino, 1978, p.318.
151. Ofreneo, 1980, p.36; McCoy, 1971, p.28; Starner, 1961, p.268n.
152. Ofreneo, 1980, p.37.
153. McCoy, 1971, p.29.
154. McCoy, 1971, p.29; Starner, 1961, pp.137-38; Olson, 1974, 1980, p.83.
155. RA 1199.
156. RA 1267.
157. RA 1400.
158. Cited in Smith, 1976, p.112.
159. Constantino, 1978, p.264.
160. Herring, 1983, p.8.
161. Emerson, 1956, appendix.
162. Starner, 1961, p.137.
163. Emerson, 1956, p.6.
164. Emerson, 1956, p.26.
165. RA 1166.
166. See Appendix I and Inoferio, 1979, pp.13-14.
167. Kaplan also developed the 'Digest of the Provincial Press', to help raise support for Magsaysay's programmes. His budget was running at a quarter of a million dollars a year (Smith, 1976, pp.252-53, 268-70).
168. Shalom, 1986, pp.90-91; Gonzaga, 1989, pp.82-83.
169. On the history of Tabacalera see Chapter 2, section 2.4 above. On 22 October 1947, under Commonwealth Act 539, the government had already acquired 3,300 hectares of the Tabacalera estate (Ministry of Agrarian Reform, 1985).
170. Joaquin, 1986, p.274. Manuel Manahan was on the board of Tabacalera at the time and very close to President Magsaysay, the Americans and Benigno Aquino. This facilitated the deal.
171. On the history of the family see Chapter 2, sections 2.2 and 2.4. In 1938 the family established the Philippine Bank of Commerce, with José Cojuangco II as its first president. He and his three brothers seem to have had a 'gentlemen's agreement' that any investment entered into by one would be entered into by all of them. On the later rift in the family, see Chapter 4, section 4.5.3.
172. Memorandum for Board of Trustees, Government Service Insurance System, from Domingo Garcia of the Real Estate Department, GSIS, 3 May 1957.
173. GSIS Board of Trustees, Regular Meeting No. 129, 27 November 1957, Resolution number 3202.
174. This is now Manufacturers' Hanover Trust, one of the country's biggest creditors. Cited in Manila Regional Trial Court 'Decision' Civil Case no. 131654.
175. Interview, V. Francisco Varua, Vice-President for Marketing, José Cojuangco & Sons, 31 July 1989, Makati.
176. Central Bank Monetary Board, Resolution No. 1240 on 27 August 1957. Cited in the Manila Regional Trial Court's 'Decision' Civil Case no. 131654. In this later Court decision, there is an implication that Tabacalera itself suggested such a condition be tied to the sale of the Hacienda. Judge Bernardo P. Pardo wrote: 'Jose Cojuangco and associates represented that as a condition imposed by the owners of the Compañia General de Tabacos de Filipinas, they agreed to acquire Hacienda Luisita, with a view to distributing this hacienda to "small farmers in line with the Administration's social justice policy". This would not be unprecedented, since it seems that Tabacalera made a similar commitment to the families who worked their Haciendas San Antonio and Santa Isabel in Isabela province. There, tenants were told that after 99 years the Tabacalera land would be distributed to their heirs. Interview with the heirs of the original Tabacalera tenants, Hda Santa Isabel, June 1989.
177. Cited in Joaquin, 1986, p.274.

178. Interview, V. Francisco Varua, Vice-President for Marketing, José Cojuangco & Sons, 31 July 1989, Makati. Varua said that after the sale the Cojuangcos hired Enrile as their own lawyer.

179. GSIS, Board meeting no. 15, resolution no.356, 5 February 1958.

180. The case for distribution would later be pursued by the Marcos government. See Chapter 4, section 4.5.3.

181. The PRRM was set up in 1952 as part of the campaign to stop the expansion of the Hukbalahap in the countryside. José Cojuangco II was on its founding board.

182. Joaquin, 1986, p.271. Aquino even returned to Indonesia with the colonels on a covert operation to set up a listening post to help coordinate the coup against Sukarno. This was but one of many Aquino adventures connected with US policing operations in Asia - including his stint at 'American spy schools' (p.252), in Korea as a war correspondent (pp 201-202), his travels throughout Southeast Asia in preparation for the establishment of SEATO (pp.229-230) and a visit to Vietnam (p.229).

183. Lichauco, 1982, p.30; see also Bello et al, 1982, p.128; Rivera, 1982, pp.7-8.

184. Constantino, 1978, pp.269-273, 291-293.

185. Maxfield and Nolt, 1987.

186. Villegas, 1982, p.53.

187. Bello et al, 1982, p.129.

188. Constantino, 1969, pp.2-3.

189. Starner, 1961, p.168. See also Constantino, 1978, pp.293-294.

190. McCoy (1971, pp.32-33), hinted that the attack was linked to Ladejinsky's promotion of agrarian reform, but described what he thought was the principal motivation by saying, 'another agriculturalist, covetous of Ladejinsky's position in Tokyo, covertly accused him of being a security risk'.

191. Ladejinsky, 1951, p.148.

192. Ladejinsky, 1953, p.199.

193. Ladejinsky, 1950, p.131.

194. NYT, December 19, 1954, 30:1, 2. Eisenhower was apparently informed by Benson before action was taken. In fact, Eisenhower stuck by Benson through the ordeal and retained him throughout his presidency.

195. NYT, December 23, 1:4.

196. Amtorg was established in New York in 1924 as part of Soviet efforts to encourage trade with the West (Carr, 1979, p.94).

197. Rorty, 1955, p.328, 334.

198. NYT, December 22, 1954, 14:3.

199. NYT, December 27, 1954, 5:3.

200. NYT, December 19, 1954, 30:1,2 and December 23, 1.

201. James A. Mitchner, author of Tales of the South Pacific, wrote an interesting letter to the New York Times, 24 December 1954. Mitchner asserted first that he had 'done a good deal of anti-Communist work' himself in Asia, and went on: 'Mr. Ladejinsky is known throughout Asia as Communism's most implacable foe and about the only American who has accomplished much in actually stopping the drift of all Asian farmers to communism'. Another letter, from Frank Traeger who was assigned to Japan in 1953 under the Point IV Program, said that Ladejinsky was the key official assigned to him in his 'classified mission' (NYT, December 29, 22).

202. NYT, January 5, 1955, 16 and January 19, 1955, 6.

203. NYT, 5 February 1956, 1:6, IV, 2:3. The article captured the irony of the means used to push Ladejinsky out: 'A capitalistic venture has forced the resignation of Wolf Ladejinsky, Government official who was once ousted from service for alleged Communist leanings.' See also NYT, 6 February 1956. Ladejinsky was replaced at the ICA post in Vietnam by John Price Gittinger, a Harvard land reform specialist (McCoy, 1971, p.33; Olson, 1974, p.62). A reading of Gittinger's (1961, p.205) evaluation of US agrarian reform efforts suggests that he

too became critical of the US failure to vigorously promote reform in Asia.

204. Olson, 1974, p.84.
205. Gittinger, 1961, p.197.
206. Cited in Montgomery, 1962, p.299.
207. Montgomery, 1962, pp.210, 132.
208. H.E. Henderson, 1959, p.887.
209. Olson, 1974, p.108.
210. Constantino, 1978, p.260.
211. Ladejinsky, 1977, p.215.
212. *NYT*, February 8, 1956.
213. Lansdale, 1972, pp.355-356.
214. Lansdale, 1972, p.369.
215. Lansdale, 1972, p.99.
216. *NYT*, 13 January and 6 and 11 February 1956.
217. Lansdale, 1972, p.165-170; Smith, 1976, p.179.
218. Kolko, 1986, pp.95-96; Constantino, 1978, p.260.
219. Paul L. Montgomery, Ladejinsky's obituary in the *New York Times* (July 4, 1975, p.26).
220. This was where analysts like El-Ghonemy, and the otherwise excellent account of Hardie's experience in the Philippines by Paul Monk (1990), went wrong. Monk has done more than anyone else to date to demonstrate that there actually was a debate in US policy over reform. While he exposed the fallacy behind claims by Montgomery and others that the US always supported reform, he failed to demonstrate that Hardie's position was in fact a *deviation from the norm* in US policy-making. This weakness in Monk's analysis was demonstrated by his constant reference to the subsequent anti-reform position as part of an agenda *first* elaborated by John Foster Dulles in the mid-1950s.
221. Raper, 1951, p.182. Waswo (1988) demonstrated that the reform was a culmination of a 50-year process of rural change.
222. Yanaga Chitoshi, 1968, especially pp.202-221.
223. On the impact of the occupation see Dore, 1959, pp.148,171,192; Raper, 1951, p.182
224. Olson, 1974, p.65.
225. Whang, 1982, p.5. Whang drew his inspiration for this point of view from Lee (1968, p.79), who mentioned Rhee as a 'youthful reformist', but also underlined that, 'The passage of time had eroded his youthful zeal for reform'.
226. Whang, 1982, p.25. This echoed Tai and Ladejinsky's arguments about 'political will' (see Chapter 1).
227. Starner, 1961, p.125.
228. The KDP was renamed the Democratic Nationalist Party in 1949 when Assembly Speaker Shin Ik-hui led his Korean Nationalist Party to the KDP. It was transformed into the Democratic Party in 1955, when the DNP united with a number of independent Assembly members and the Chosen Democratic Party (made up largely of North Korean refugees).
229. Ban et al, 1980, pp.284, 290.
230. Starner, 1961, p.192.

MARCOS AND AUTHORITARIAN REFORM

4.1 Introduction

When Ferdinand Marcos declared martial law in September 1972, both Filipino and US advocates of the liberal approach to agrarian reform saw a new opportunity to introduce a land redistribution programme that would once and for all eliminate the source of rural underdevelopment and protest. They believed that what had been done under US occupation in Japan, under KMT rule in Taiwan and under Syngman Rhee in South Korea could be done under Marcos. A basic proposition of the liberal approach was that concerted political will was the prime ingredient for successful implementation of redistributive reform. From their perspective, the best means to achieve political will was to concentrate political power and state authority at the top and to eliminate the negative influence of landowner dominated legislatures.

After their rout in the 1950s, advocates of the liberal approach to reform continued to challenge the conservative status quo both in the Philippines and within the US foreign policy and foreign aid establishments. Ladejinsky became personally involved in the Philippines in the 1960s and 1970s, and another American, Roy Prosterman, played an important and still much misunderstood role in the reform debate during the early years of martial law. In fact, the US, through both its action and its inaction, had considerable influence over the ultimate shape of Marcos' agricultural development strategy.

While martial law brought a new alliance to power within the Philippine state and a new opportunity for action on reform, there was a great deal more continuity with the past than many analysts have realized. Marcos placed agrarian reform at the centre of what he said was an effort by the state to build a 'New Society'. An examination of the fate of agrarian reform in the years preceding and during martial law provides considerable insight into the nature of the Philippine state and its relation to society

4.2 Prelude to martial law: agrarian reform in the 1960s

When Magsaysay was killed in a plane crash in March 1957, Vice-president Garcia, who was a traditional politician in the Nacionalista Party, replaced him as President. No new agrarian reform legislation was passed during Garcia's administration (March 1957 to 1961). However, 19 large estates and six smaller ones, totalling about 14,000 hectares, were acquired by the government under the Land Reform Act, more than under any other administration until Marcos's second term in office (Table 4.1). Only two new land settlement projects were launched during the period (Table 4.2). Garcia's government implemented the programmes introduced during Magsaysay's term, but remained within the limits of the conservative approach to reform.

While the liberal reformers had little influence over Garcia, Recto's elite nationalists were able to make their voices heard in Malacañang during his presidency.[1] By the time he came to office, the US was intent on removing barriers on the free flow of capital to and from the Philippines. In 1957, Garcia's application to the IMF for a $25 million loan was turned down. The IMF made future loans contingent on the lifting of controls and a devaluation of the peso.[2] The US had not counted on Garcia's presidency and he was not one of the 'Magsaysay boys'. They disliked the prominent position that he gave to the Recto group. Although they opposed Garcia in the 1957 presidential election, he won at the polls. With a growing nationalist movement in the country, Garcia introduced a 'Filipino First Policy', promoting the domestic industrial sector just as the IMF was calling for an open economy.[3] This action quickly drew fire from the American Chamber of Commerce in the Philippines. Interestingly, one of the more vocal opponents of the 'Filipino First Policy' was the Liberal Party's Ferdinand Marcos, who, after having served in the House since 1949, won the most votes for Senator in the 1959 elections.

When Liberal Party candidate Diosdado Macapagal (1962-1965) ran for president in 1961, he opposed the 'Filipino First Policy' and targeted the corruption of the Garcia Administration. The Nacionalistas had been in power for eight years, so graft and corruption, made more acute by the application of import and foreign exchange controls, were particularly evident. It was an effective campaign issue. Macapagal swept the polls and then quickly acceded to pressures exerted by the IMF and World Bank to devalue the peso and remove foreign exchange controls.[4] In return, the agencies granted some $450 million in loans.

Macapagal was silent about agrarian reform during his first year in office, and land acquisitions by the government under the old legislation almost ground to a halt. Only two landed estates were purchased in 1962, totalling about 1,500 hectares. However, in January 1963, Macapagal, who had opposed Hardie's recommendations a decade earlier, appointed a Presidential Land Reform Committee to draft new legislation. Among the eight people appointed were several who had been involved in Magsaysay's rural programmes. These included Jeremias Montemayor, leader of the Federation of Free Farmers, and Teodoro Locsin, one of the journalists who had been in Magsaysay's inner circle. Sixto K. Roxas, Macapagal's top economic adviser and head of the influential Program Implementation Agency (PIA), was appointed secretary. The committee also included liberal reform advocates Dioscoro L. Umali, Dean of the Agricultural College at Los Baños and later Under-secretary for Agriculture, and economist Orlando Sacay.[5] Of those in the Committee, Montemayor, Umali and Sacay could be considered advocates of a liberal approach to reform.[6] The Committee produced a draft Agricultural Land Reform Code, which was sponsored in

Table 4.1: Landed Estates Programmes (1940-1985)

Year	Major Estates* Number	Area (Ha.s)	Minor Estates* Number	Area (Ha.s)	Total Estates Number	Area	Benefic.s Number (Ha.s)	Deeds Number
Quezon (1935-1942)	2	5825			2	5825	2955	
Roxas (1945-April 1948)	4	9251	2	144	6	9395	6139	
Quirino (April 1948/1950-1953)	6	33700	1	23	7	33723	15435	
Magsaysay (1954-March 1957)	2	1182	1	12	3	1194	1149	
Gardia (March 1957/1958-1961)	19	14092	6	306	25	14397	9708	
Macapagal (1962-1965)	5	3309	1	32	6	3341	2293	720
Marcos (1966-1969)	7	2448	5	279	12	2727	2254	4937
Marcos (1970-Sept 1972)	33	10629	42	1825	75	12453	7277	3064
Marcos (Oct 1972 - Jan 1986)	10	16412	13	461	23	16874	5773	6369
TOTAL	**88**	**96848**	**71**	**3082**	**159**	**99929**	**52983**	**15090**
Accomplishments (1986)	Area 19600		% Total Area 20.2		Families w/deeds 12270		% Beneficiaries 23.2	

*Major Estates are those >99.99 ha.s and Minor Estates those <99.99 ha.s.
Source: Ministry of Agrarian Reform, Land Reform Statistics, 1985; On 1986 accomplishment: Presidential Commission on Government Reorganization (1986) Eduardo C. Tadem, *Handbook on the Reorganization Proposals of the Ministry of Agrarian Reform*. Manila: PCGR (December). p. 25.

Table 4.2: Resettlement Programmes (1950-1985)

	Year Proclaimed	Number	Area	Families
Quirino	(April 1948/1950-1953)	12	254678	
Magsaysay	(1954-March 1957)	6	166968	
Garcia	(March 1957/1958-1961)	2	18953	
Macapagal	(1962-1965)	2	60000	36944
Marcos	(1966-1969)	4	42360	3338
Marcos	(1970-Sept 1972)	4	22436	6517
Marcos	(Oct 1972 - Jan 1986)	16	181441	11863
TOTAL		**46**	**746836**	**58662**

Accomplishment (1986)

Area Under Patents	% Total Area	Families w/Patents	% Beneficiaries
95117	12.74	16998	28.98

Source: Ministry of Agrarian Reform, Land Reform Statistics, 1985. On accomplishments: Presidential Commission on Government Reorganization (1986) Eduardo C. Tadem, *Handbook on the Reorganization Proposals of the Ministry of Agrarian Reform*. Manila: PCGR (December), p. 25.

Congress by Senators Raul Manglapus and Genaro Magsaysay, close supporter and brother of the late President, and Representative Juanita Nepomuceno, from Macapagal's own Pampanga district.

The Presidential Committee proceeded cautiously, producing a draft which, while bolder than any legislation enacted in the past, was timid in comparison with the programmes introduced in Taiwan and South Korea. It remained within the limits of the conservative approach, restricting redistribution to rice and corn lands of 25 hectares and over and specifically exempted export crops. Landowners whose land would be covered by reform would be given the option to purchase up to 1,000 hectares of undeveloped public lands from the government. The draft proposed a reorganization of state institutions charged with implementing reform, creating a National Land Reform Council, a Land Authority merging the Land Tenure Administration and the NARRA, and a Land Bank - the brain-child of Sixto K. Roxas - to facilitate the financing of land acquisition. It called for the abolition of sharecropping and the institution of leasehold tenancy in farm-lands other than those devoted to fishponds, saltbeds, and lands principally planted to citrus, coconuts, cacao, coffee, durian and other tree-crops. A bill of rights for agricultural workers granting them the right to organize and to a minimum wage was also included.[7]

Macapagal's reform was no more successful than previous programmes. The Congress subjected the Code to over 200 amendments.[8] The Code was watered down under a concerted effort by such landowner spokesmen as Senators Alejandro Almendras and Lorenzo Sumulong, as well as the elite nationalist bloc led by Senator Lorenzo Tañada.[9] It was at this time that José Cojuangco Jr., then a young congressman from Tarlac, had his first experience in dealing with agrarian reform legislation as vice-chairman of the House Committee on

Agrarian Reform, which helped to whittle down the proposed legislation in that Chamber. Not only were lands with permanent crops exempted, but Congress increased the allowed land retention limit to 75 hectares. In the draft Code, compensation to landowners was to be based on the land's rental income, calculated at 25 per cent of the crop's annual value. Congress succeeded in returning to the traditional definition of 'just compensation' as compensation at the land's market value. The original draft included a plan for a progressive land tax that would have provided both a disincentive to maintain large landholdings and a significant source of funds to carry out the programme. However, this chapter was entirely deleted. The worst blow dealt by Congress was its allotment of less than P1 million for the program, against an estimated cost of P200 million for the first year and P300 million for the next three years.[10]

By the end of Macapagal's administration it became clear that the President's introduction of the Code was primarily a ploy to win tenant support for his re-election in 1965.[11] Roxas, later said of Macapagal that, 'land reform was only a symbol for him'.[12] Even the new agencies called for in the Code were not established until a year after its passage. In 1964, Roxas was appointed as first head of the Land Authority, and the young José Medina, who would become a permanent presence in the agrarian reform bureaucracy, became Chief of Planning.[13] Only three estates were purchased in 1963, covering some 540 hectares, and just one estate of 1,058 hectares was acquired during 1964 and 1965 (Table 4.1). Most attention remained focussed on the supposed conversion of sharecropping tenants to leasehold and the development of programmes to raise agricultural productivity, aspects of the Code that were clearly within the limits of a conservative approach to reform.[14] In fact, it was these aspects on which Macapagal focused when he launched his call for new legislation in March 1963.[15] This approach remained dominant, not only in the Macapagal administration, but also among US advisers.

The 1960s saw a renewed US thrust to open up the Philippines for US investment and trade while at the same time promoting a number of 'modernizing reforms'. The nationalist orientation of the Garcia administration led Washington to lend its support to Macapagal in the 1961 election. A former CIA agent claimed that during the Magsaysay years a 'deep cover agent' established contact with Macapagal and that the CIA supported his candidacy under the banner of the United Opposition.[16] During Macapagal's term, the US pushed a policy of 'liberalization' and 'free enterprise', where foreign investment and export-oriented production were to generate growth.

On the agrarian front attention was focused on increasing productivity. In 1960 the Rockefeller and Ford Foundations and the United States Agency for International Development (USAID) provided the lion's share of funding to establish the International Rice Research Institute (IRRI). It was set up in Los Baños, Laguna, in Southern Tagalog - a major rice and coconut region - to develop new high-yielding varieties of rice (HYVs) that would solve the food problem in Asia.[17] The foundations' lead in financing IRRI would be supplemented in later years by small donations from the corporations who stood to profit from increased purchases of fertilizers and pesticides required by the new seed varieties.[18] The rapid adoption of HYVs throughout the country, and the accompanying increase in rice production, would provide ammunition over the next two decades to those who argued that the agrarian problem in the Philippines and Asia could be solved by technology without a direct challenge to existing landownership patterns.

In December 1962, the US liberal reformer Wolf Ladejinsky travelled to the Philippines on behalf of the Ford Foundation. He visited IRRI and the Agricultural College at Los Baños and toured Pampanga, one of the centres of rice production in Central Luzon. His report was an indictment not only of the continuing conditions of penury among rural tenants, but also of USAID-sponsored 'community development projects' promoted since the rejection of the Hardie Report. He noted that in Pampanga, which had been the centre of HMB guerrilla action in the 1950s, 90 to 95 per cent of farmers were still tenants. Most tenants had no knowledge of the tenancy legislation and worked under a 50-50 sharing arrangement still coupled with a heavy debt burden.[19]

Ladejinsky was sceptical about what could be accomplished by IRRI without carrying out institutional changes involving land ownership. He argued that it would be 'irrational' for a tenant 'to apply to the land practices that make for higher production, knowing full-well that a lion's share of this would go to the landlord, moneylender or merchant'. Ladejinsky met with highly placed Filipino officials, including Sixto Roxas and Dioscoro Umali who would sit on the Presidential Land Reform Committee, as well as Vice-President Emmanuel Pelaez and Dr. Cesar Virata, Vice-President of the University of the Philippines and later a prominent figure in the Marcos regime. Among these, only Umali seemed to understand the importance of redistributive reform. In his report Ladejinsky minced no words about the complacency of these officials in the face of what he regarded as an urgent need for redistributive reform:

'In the stately homes of Manila, one hears comments to the effect that the peasants are lazy; that they are docile anyway and no danger to the status quo.'[20]

Ladejinsky pointed out to his hosts that it had not been long since the 'Philippine-bred Huks' had risen in the countryside, adding that, 'The notion that the people prefer to live in poverty is spurious anthropology'. Ladejinsky's major recommendation was for quick and speedy action by the President to initiate an agrarian reform. He warned that without such action agrarian revolt was likely to emerge with renewed force. Ladejinsky's strongest conviction was that significant land reform was possible in the Philippines if only the 'political will' was there to carry it out 'from the top'.[21] He was to maintain this conviction and welcomed the martial law regime ten years later, believing that its concentration of authority could ensure reform implementation.

While Ladejinsky's December 1962 visit may have had some effect on the decision by Macapagal and his close advisers to put reform back on the political agenda the following January, mainstream US policy remained firmly within the conservative mould. This was reflected in a major policy paper on the Philippines prepared by the State Department at the end of the Macapagal administration.[22] The paper demonstrated an awareness of the centrality of rural poverty as an obstacle to development and the part played by the landed oligarchy. It even advanced an endorsement for 'land reform' in general saying, 'Land reform, thus far successfully opposed by the politically dominant agricultural aristocracy, is urgently needed if agricultural output (and thus agrarian income) is to be increased'.[23]

However, the key to understanding what the State Department meant by 'land reform' can be seen in their almost exclusive focus on raising agricultural output. They offered no criticism of the Agricultural Land Reform Code, and argued that the US should support its implementation, which they saw as adequate to bring about 'far-reaching land reform'. The Department believed that the passage of the Code indicated that reforms in landownership had 'become fundamentally accepted objectives of government'.[24] The paper argued that the US wanted a climate favourable to a 'sustained flow of US investment capital' and the 'continuation of a high level of bilateral trade', which would encourage joint ventures with US companies 'to permit a continued orientation toward the US economy'. It called for a cultural offensive on TV and radio to 'intensify and exploit Philippine interest in US culture'.[25]

According to the State Department, subversion could be tackled 'largely by socio-economic means'. This would involve support for implementation of the Land Reform Code through 'Food for Peace' loans. A proposal was advanced to establish one or two 'pilot projects in an AID-assisted systematic "packaged" approach to increased agricultural productivity'. After one year the FAO and World Bank were to be enlisted to help create a 'Joint Philippine US Authority for Agricultural-Rural Development'. It would be necessary, however, to 'stimulate prior demands on the part of Philippine farmers groups in Central Luzon for such direct US partnership help in meeting the specific needs of a specific area.'[26]

While the language of a 'joint authority' sounded similar to that employed by US liberal reform advocates in Taiwan, the content was centred on an 'integrated package' of productivity measures rather than on redistributive reform. Roxas, who was of the belief that Ladejinsky's insights were irrelevant to the Philippines, said that US officials at the time felt that even he and his colleagues were 'too radical and extreme'. 'They thought us naive in relating agricultural productivity to land redistribution...Philosophically, they believed the only way to go was plantation agriculture and modern agribusiness, like Dole and Philippine Packing.'[27] In fact, the State Department's policy paper argued that, given the success in putting down the Huks in the past, the US should endorse the expansion of 'civic action' programmes employing 'Food for Peace' and US as well as Philippine military personnel. It stated that the US would 'seek to encourage the Philippine armed forces in broader, more penetrating, civic action and internal defense programs'.[28]

Assessing the Agrarian Reform Code in 1969, a UN mission to the Philippines labelled it as no more than a 'land productivity policy'.[29] Rather than combining land productivity programs with structural change as proposed by the advocates of the liberal approach, USAID encouraged an 'agrarian reform' programme that focused on disseminating IRRI's 'green revolution' technology to increase productivity. USAID revealed in 1966, that just as in the mid-1950s, its main prescription for responding to peasant unrest in the third world was the promotion of the private sector, without challenging the structure of power.[30]

In 1965, Ferdinand Marcos left the Liberal Party and, running on the Nacionalista ticket, defeated Macapagal in the presidential election. Macapagal's defeat was due in no small measure to the fact that he had antagonized many in the elite and yet had not delivered his promised reforms to the poor.[31] Marcos appointed Conrado Estrella, former Governor (1954-1963) and Nacionalista political clan leader of Pangasinan, as head of the Land Authority. Estrella would be the only Cabinet member to last the full duration of Marcos' twenty-year presidency. While Marcos revived the rhetoric of reform, during his first term in office (1966-1969) only 12 estates totalling 2,726 hectares were purchased for redistribution to tenant farmers (Table 4.1). In 1965, Marcos had said that 350,000 share-tenants would be converted to leasehold by 1969. However, by the end of crop year 1968-1969, only 31,463 tenants had registered written leasehold contracts.[32]

Instead, emphasis was placed on an agenda that appeared to parallel that outlined by the US Policy Paper in 1966. Deregulation, introduced by Macapagal, had been a boon for the large landed interests producing agricultural products for export. Transnational agribusiness corporations also accelerated their drive to develop new export crops, particularly on plantations in Mindanao.[33] In 1963, Dole Philippines succeeded in establishing a plantation to rival Del Monte, leasing 8,903 hectares from the government's National Development Corporation. The plantation came into full operation during Marcos' first term.[34] Rice production was increased through the use of new IRRI technology and a rapid increase in irrigated land.[35] But tenants, often still paying at least 50 per cent of their crop to landlords, were charged interest rates of up to 100 per cent on credit advanced to purchase inputs. What is more, most irrigation facilities were controlled by landlords who charged exorbitant fees for water.[36]

Marcos' rural programme centred on infrastructure development and 'civic action' programmes, financed through increased foreign borrowing.[37] Through these programmes the military assumed a far greater role in the civilian sector than ever before. By concentrating such resources in the President's office, Marcos was able to increase his own control over patronage networks through-out the country. In 1966, Marcos expanded the Filipino army engineering corps in Vietnam in exchange for increased US aid, including funds for additional army engineering construction battalions to be used within the Philippines.[38]

In the cities the decade of deregulation gave rise to a growing popular movement among students and the unemployed that could not be ignored by the traditional politicians in Congress. In 1968, Speaker of the House José B. Laurel set up a Congressional Economic Planning Office. In May 1969, the Office introduced 'House Joint Resolution No.2,' later to be called the 'Magna Carta of Social Justice and Economic Freedom'. Encouraged by, and perhaps fearing, the growing popular movement, the Laurel group challenged the free trade economy ruled by foreign investment. It called for an end to parity rights (which allowed US individuals and corporations equal rights with Filipinos in the economic sphere), restrictions on foreign corporations, the Filipinization of the economy and provision of credit, protective tariffs, and import and exchange controls. President Marcos was forced to sign the resolution into law, in August 1969, only to retreat from it after his re-election later that year.[39]

In fact, the 1969 presidential elections broke the tradition of 'elite democracy', when Marcos became the first incumbent President to be elected to a second term. The elections were marked by extreme corruption and violence as Marcos broke all records in campaign spending.[40] There was a rapid expansion of private armies under the authority of provincial politicians allied to Marcos. This gave rise to wide-spread protests, strikes and demonstrations. Largely as a result of student demonstrations, Congress passed a law calling for a Constitutional Convention to rewrite the basic charter of government. Special elections were held in November 1970 and the Convention convened in June 1971. Until martial law was declared, the Convention became a major arena of debate on fundamental reforms of the structure of the state as well as the economic organization of society and its relations with the world economy.[41]

International investors responded to growing popular unrest by pulling out their capital, with a net disinvestment between 1970 and 1973 of some $55 million. A Standby Agreement was signed by the IMF, but only after another 60 per cent devaluation of the peso. Inflation spiralled from 1.3 per cent in 1969 to 14.8 per cent in 1970.[42] In 1972, as the mainstream opposition took up the nationalist cause, the Supreme Court issued the now famous 'Quasha Decision'. It ruled that lands acquired by Americans since 1946 had been acquired illegally and would be subject to sale or confiscation by 1974. Another decision banned foreigners from holding executive jobs in industries reserved for Filipinos.[43] As the nationalist movement gained headway in the Congress and institutions of the state, its popular wing in the cities began calling for land reform, thus establishing a link between the nationalist and peasant movements.

The failure of the Agricultural Land Reform Code to achieve any change in the countryside led to increased peasant unrest, as liberal reform advocates had predicted. Organizations sprang up throughout the agricultural sector demanding land reform and improved conditions for agricultural labourers. The National Federation of Sugar Workers (NFSW) emerged in Negros and began organizing the sugar cane plantations. Even the Federation of Free Farmers, which had been set up as a reformist alternative under Magsaysay, became radicalized during this period. It was active in Luzon, Mindanao and the Visayas where its younger and more militant members began to initiate 'peasant mass actions'. As a result, its membership sky-rocketed to some 500,000 on the eve of martial law.[44] A popular movement within the Church, inspired by Latin American 'liberation theology' as well as the indigenous tradition of Catholic dissent, also began organizing in the countryside.

In 1968, the Communist Party of the Philippines (CPP) was established and the following year it launched the New People's Army (NPA) in the rural areas. The party was formed through the merger of a small group of dissident members of the old PKP led by José Maria Sison alias Amado Guerrero, and a guerrilla group of the old HMB led by Bernabe Buscayno, alias Commander Dante. Since its conciliation with Magsaysay in the mid-1950s, the PKP was no longer a threat to the government. It had lost control over much of its armed wing, the HMB, and many of the armed groups had totally abandoned the peasant cause.[45]

One of the reasons for the rapid expansion of NPA numbers and influence was that the young intellectuals leading the new Communist Party launched the NPA as a political force, rather than an exclusively military force like the old HMB. When the army became active in a *barrio*, its members would teach agricultural skills, provide medical training, set up makeshift irrigation, conduct adult education and provide rudimentary local administration, often more effectively than was done by either local or central government agencies. They launched their own agrarian reform programme, which involved land rent reduction, limits on usury, and even outright redistribution in more stable guerrilla fronts.[46] While their influence was spreading rapidly in the early 1970s, the young CPP and NPA - concentrated mainly in Central Luzon - were in no position to bring down the government in 1972, as Marcos would claim when justifying his assumption of absolute powers.

In late 1970, as a response to the growing popular clamour for agrarian reform, both chambers of Congress set up committees to conduct hearings that launched the first agrarian reform initiative ever to emerge in Congress rather than the Executive branch of the state. With peasants and their supporters camping out in front of Congress, by the end of a fifth special session in early September 1971, RA6389 had been passed amending Macapagal's Code and changing its name to the Code of Agrarian Reforms.[47] The amended Code included a lowered land retention limit, a measure opposed by the President, and a new Department of Agrarian Reform. The President and those Congressmen opposed to reform did succeed in reducing the original Senate proposal to substantially increase funding for the programme.

In the committees of the Constitutional Convention, reformist delegates gained approval for constitutional provisions that would provide the basis for much more far-reaching agrarian reform. The Committee on Social Justice approved a proposal that would allow private property to be appropriated by government upon payment of 'compensation equivalent to the tax assessed value'.[48] One of the major constitutional obstacles to redistributive reform had long been the requirement that government could only expropriate land in return for 'just compensation' defined as compensation at market value.

The combined effect of peasant pressure for reform, congressional action and debates in the Constitutional Convention, led the administration to step up its reform activity. Between January 1970 and September 1972, 75 landed estates covering a total of 12,453 hectares were purchased by the government (Table 4.1). At the same time, Marcos used the growing desire for change among both the elite and the popular movement to win allies in his bid to perpetuate his rule. It would soon become clear that Marcos had decided to manipulate popular wishes for reform in his plan to extend his tenure in office beyond its constitutional limits.

4.3 Martial law and authoritarian agrarian reform

With his term in office about to expire and in the face of a growing nationalist and peasant movement, Marcos declared martial law in September 1972. He suspended the Congress and closed the mass media, arresting Senator Benigno Aquino and other opposition leaders who had been poised to support the Senator in his bid for the presidency in 1973. Marcos secured control over the Constitutional Convention in order to produce a charter that would provide a 'legal' justification for the perpetuation of martial law rule, and to eliminate the more radical proposals of the Convention's committees. Marcos and his 'ghost writers' later borrowed the terms of American political scientist Samuel Huntington to justify the martial law regime as an experiment in 'authoritarian modernization' to create a 'New Society'.[49] Marcos began an immediate military build-up and acted quickly to set up a state machinery and a network of urban and rural organizations to provide support for his new regime.

Recalling its origin as a tool to fight the communists in the 1950s, the Federation of Free Farmers returned to its roots and, immediately following the declaration of martial law, Jeremias Montemayor presided over a purge of 30 per cent of its members. Years later, he defended his action and his consistent support for Marcos, saying:

> There was a rift in the top leadership at our convention in Leyte. The military came to arrest four of my men for plotting to kill the President. I was afraid to defend them as it might jeopardize the FFF. I made a list of whom to remove from the organization while in Leyte...They were infiltrators...I opposed the lifting of martial law.[50]

By 1974, FFF membership was back down to about 200,000.[51] In 1972 its constitution was revised stating that, 'clearance from the government's military intelligence service is a requirement for becoming an FFF leader'.[52] The FFF and other rural organizations were to serve as a conduit for Marcos agrarian programmes.

After assuming absolute powers, one of the first actions taken by Marcos was to launch a programme of agrarian reform. In number two of what would amount to some 2,000 Presidential Decrees (PD), he proclaimed 'the whole country as a land reform area' in order to accelerate the implementation of reform both to stimulate agricultural development and to remove the source of rural unrest.[53] When it was launched, the stated objectives of the land reform programme were to abolish sharecropping, transform tenants to owner-cultivators, increase agricultural productivity, create a market for industry and undermine the cause of rural rebellion.

Marcos called a meeting to discuss his plans, bringing together Montemayor, Eligio Tavanlar, who had presided over the land settlement programme under Magsaysay, and Luis Taruc, leader of the Huk Army in the 1950s who was arrested upon the declaration of martial law and later released by Marcos when he promised to support a new reform programme.[54] Then he established a committee to draft a more detailed decree. This included top presidential adviser Alexander Melchor, who was Executive Secretary and close to the United States, his assistant Jacobo Clave and Arturo Tanco, an agribusiness executive who was appointed Secretary of Agriculture by Marcos. Marcos also recruited Tavanlar and Sacay, both of whom had sat on Macapagal's reform committee and worked as consultants for the Ford Foundation and the UN. J.D. Drilon and Estrella's number two at DAR, José Medina, also joined the committee.[55] Estrella stressed that it was Marcos who wrote the final version of the reform decree, but these men clearly had a major influence over the shape of the programme.[56]

The programme took shape in the three months following the declaration of martial law. On 21 October, Presidential Decree 27 laid out the essential contours of the reform. First, the objective of eliminating tenancy was reduced to include only rice and corn lands. The decree stipulated that tenants would be given a family-size farm of 5 hectares on non-irrigated land or 3 hectares on irrigated land. Landowners would be allowed to retain seven hectares, but only if these were to be self-cultivated. The decree also included a formula for land valuation and compensation. The landlord would be compensated at two and a half times the average value of the three normal crop years preceding the decree. This was the same formula as had been employed in the Taiwan reform. Landowners were to be guaranteed compensation, but not at market values.[57]

The tenants were to bear the cost of land acquisition in 15 annual amortization payments at 6 per cent interest per annum, while the government would guarantee payment to the owner through stocks in government-owned corporations.[58] Tenants were further required to join cooperatives as a precondition for receiving land. The cooperative would assume responsibility for any default on amortization payments. Land granted to the tenant could only be transferred by hereditary succession or to the government. Finally, the Rules and Regulations for implementation were to be formulated by the Department of Agrarian Reform (DAR) before transfers could occur. The programme became known as Operation Land Transfer (OLT).

Under the programme, central government had first to identify tenants,

Table 4.3: Changing Scope of Marcos Programme (1972-1986)

Year	Operation Land Transfer (OLT)			Operation Leasehold (OLH)		
	Tenants Number	Area Hectares	Owners Number	Tenants Number	Area Hectares	Owners Number
1972	393778	759015	39550	521136	663973	371129
1977	400082	750469	50438	619647	760575	438553
1979	396082	730734	49221	609042	731836	435209
1982	427623	716520	56574	527667	562030	424838
1986*	587775	822069	65419	same	same	same

*1986 figures pencilled in by MAR officials, confirmed in 'Summary: Land Transfer and Leasehold Operation as of September 30, 1988' Department of Agrarian Reform, 1988.
Source: *Land Reform Statistics*, Ministry of Agrarian Reform, 1985.

landowners and the land to be covered. After this a land survey would be undertaken and Certificates of Land Transfer (CLT) printed at the National Computer Centre. The CLTs then had to be registered with the proper government offices and if found faulty they had to be returned to the Centre to be reissued. Only after registration could the CLTs be distributed to beneficiaries. An assessment of the land value had to be carried out and once approved by the Land Bank, after the landowner submitted extensive documentation, the compensation procedure could begin. Beneficiaries would receive an Emancipation Patent (EP), or title to the land, only after they completed the 15-year amortization period.[59]

Tenancy reform was not mentioned in PD 27, since PD 2 had reaffirmed the Agrarian Reform Code of 1963 that prohibited sharecropping on all lands but those devoted to permanent tree crops, in favour of leasehold contracts with a fixed rent. The DAR, in a November memorandum, stated that all tenancy relations were to be leasehold.[60] Efforts to convert share-tenants to leasehold status would soon become known as Operation Leasehold (OLH). In this way the Marcos programme combined a programme of redistribution with one of tenure security, as had been carried out in liberal land reforms elsewhere in Asia.

By December, Marcos further reduced the scope of reform, stating that it would be carried out in stages beginning with owners of holdings greater than 24 hectares.[61] In fact, the DAR began with holdings over 100 hectares.[62] It was not until November 1974 that Marcos authorized implementation on holdings down to the 7 hectare limit, but then the requirement that the landowner must cultivate the land was dropped.[63] Table 4.3 illustrates the changing scope of OLT over the years. When it was launched, the programme was to transfer about 759,000 hectares of land to 394,000 tenants, with the tenants receiving on average just two hectares per family. By the end of Marcos' rule, the number of beneficiaries to be covered increased slightly to 427,000, while the area they were to receive was reduced to 717,000 hectares.

Land transfer and conversion to leasehold were to be accompanied by an agricultural productivity programme, including cooperative, credit and irrigation projects. In April 1973, Marcos called for the establishment of 'pre-cooperatives' to be known as Samahang Nayon (SN), or Barrio Associations.[64] The SN was to be a means of educating tenants and small owner-cultivators in the new IRRI technology, amassing capital at the *barrio* level and assuring 'the enforcement of discipline' among the farmers. In order to receive land under the programme, a tenant had to become an SN member. Members were required to use IRRI's high-yielding varieties and the chemical fertilizers and pesticides needed for their cultivation. In addition, the tenant had to pay a membership fee, annual dues, contribute 5 per cent of any institutional loan (to be deducted at source) to the Barrio Savings Fund and turn over 1 cavan (50kg) of *palay* (unhusked rice) per hectare per harvest to the Barrio Guarantee Fund. The objective of the SN was to lay the basis for a fully-fledged cooperative movement. It was to act as a substitute for 'services once rendered through landlordism'.[65]

Coupled with the cooperative campaign was the *Masagana* 99 programme, launched in May 1973, to provide credit to tenants and smallholders to purchase the new agricultural inputs.[66] To obtain a loan a farmer was supposed to fill out a farm plan to determine farm inputs needed. Chits would then be given to purchase fertilizers, chemicals and cash to pay for planting, weeding and harvesting. The government instigated a massive drive to disperse farm credit as quickly as possible.

Marcos planned to exercise direct authority over the land reform programme assisted by the Secretary of Agrarian Reform, Conrado F. Estrella, who would be responsible only to the President. Initially Marcos stipulated that landlords would be required to submit a statement on their holdings (size, harvests, number of tenants, etc.) to the Provincial Commander of the Philippine Constabulary (PC).[67] This indicated that he would use the authority of the armed forces under his command to enforce reform. In December 1972, Marcos instructed Estrella to establish pilot projects in the Central Luzon areas of Nueva Ecija, Pampanga, Tarlac and Bulacan, precisely to counter peasant insurgency.[68] In fact, following the State Department policy paper of 1966, USAID had already initiated pilot 'integrated area development' projects in land reform districts in Nueva Ecija. By January 1973, DAR had set up 17 pilot projects - all in areas where the NPA and other rural organizations were active.[69]

Thus the Marcos programme combined objectives of land transfer with tenancy reform and a drive to increase productivity. At the same time, the programme was introduced as a means to respond to peasant unrest. When Marcos first announced that the whole country would be a land reform area, he seemed poised to use his authoritarian power to introduce a radical liberal model of agrarian reform. Even after he reduced the scope of reform to rice and corn lands, he consistently reiterated that his whole project for the New Society hinged on the success of land reform. On the first anniversary of the programme he said, 'The land reform program is the only gauge for the success or failure of the New Society. If land reform fails, there is no New Society'.[70]

The most pronounced difference between the Marcos programme and the liberal model concerned the administration of the programme and tenant participation in implementation. The liberal model called for decision-making powers to be delegated regionally to facilitate swift action, while the Marcos programme retained considerable authority in Manila. It established Barrio Committees on Land Production (BCLP) with roughly the same composition - a balance between tenant and owner representatives - as the village Land Commissions in Japan. But the role of the BCLPs was limited to setting the value of land, and landlords could easily boycott them.[71] On the other hand, Marcos's Agrarian Reform Team Offices (ARTO), charged with carrying out the same functions as the Land Commissions in Japan, differed significantly from the latter. Members of the ARTO in the Philippines were all government employees and their jurisdiction often covered a whole municipality or more, usually including about 20 *barrios*. In Japan, the Land Commission covered only one village (a village is roughly equivalent to a *barrio*) and was composed of elected representatives of the tenants and owners.[72]

Both of these discrepancies are linked to the tension in the liberal approach itself, where there is a proclivity toward an authoritarian state to ensure implementation, but also a desire to promote democratic participation on the part of the tenants. This tension was clearly in evidence when Secretary Estrella, operating under martial law which dictated the suspension of all civil liberties, commented that, 'The primary objective of land reform is the creation of a strong citizenry that will have a real stake in our democracy'.[73] While the Marcos programme was not a strict application of the liberals' 'maximum' model, it was a great deal more than the 'minimum' model of tenure reform that had dominated previous programmes.

During the first two years of martial law, it was not clear just how far Marcos was prepared to go in the implementation of reform. Among those who participated in drafting his programme, there were advocates of both the liberal and conservative approaches.[74] The language and objectives that Marcos employed in his initial decrees on reform were clearly borrowed from the radical liberal models of reform introduced in Japan, South Korea and Taiwan. While the reduction in the scope of reform and the centralist character of the ARTOs were early indications of Marcos' resistance to important precepts of the liberal model, supporters of the liberal approach believed that his programme could form the beginning of a major transformation of the countryside. The US and international agencies like the World Bank, which continued to be major actors in Philippine affairs throughout the Marcos years, would play an important part in influencing the extent and direction of reform implementation.

4.4 The US and the Marcos agrarian reform

There is a great deal of confusion over the role that the United States played in the Marcos agrarian reform programme. This confusion stems in part from the fact that there was more than one US attitude toward reform and the US position appeared to change over time. The confusion has also resulted from the less than accurate portrayal of US involvement that emanates from both Washington officials and the Marcos regime itself. In February 1980, when questioned about Marcos's low level of achievement on agrarian reform, USAID told the US House of Representatives that, 'At no time...was there any AID involvement in the policy aspects of land reform'.[75] In fact, US consultants, embassy staff and USAID personnel had been intimately involved with those planning the Marcos programme in October and November 1972.

4.4.1 Roy Prosterman's involvement in the Marcos reform

Just two weeks before martial law was declared, the US land law expert Roy Prosterman, visited the Philippines at the end of a stint of fieldwork in South Vietnam and elsewhere in Asia. He met with DAR Secretary Conrado Estrella to explain the sweeping reform implemented in South Vietnam and to argue for a similar programme in the Philippines. A few weeks later Marcos declared martial law, and in October 1972, after returning to the US from a field visit to Brazil, Roy Prosterman found a telegram waiting for him from Estrella asking him to come immediately to the Philippines to advise on Marcos's newly announced agrarian reform programme. Prosterman was in the Philippines repeatedly over the next two years, when he met many times with DAR officials and Marcos himself to discuss the progress of reform.[76] But after he became critical of the programme, Marcos had veteran newspaper columnist Teodoro Valencia write a series of articles in the Manila press vilifying Prosterman and claiming that he was an interfering American who had never been invited to the country.[77] Estrella defended this story until he was confronted with the facts years later, when he claimed that he had sent the telegram inviting Prosterman because the US embassy had asked him to do so.[78]

By 1969, Prosterman had become the leading US advocate of the liberal approach to reform when his draft 'Land-to-the-Tiller' programme, embodying a maximum application of the liberal approach, was adopted as policy by the government of Nguyen Van Thieu.[79] According to Prosterman, his first involvement with the issue of land reform came after reading an article in a law review which claimed that reform was impossible without revolution. He countered with his own article, elaborating the essentials of the liberal approach apparently without any knowledge of Ladejinsky's previous work or any experience in foreign affairs.[80] He says that it was on the basis of this article that he was recruited in 1967 by the USAID-funded Stanford Research Institute project set up to investigate the prospects for employing rural development programmes in the war against the peasant-based communist movement in South Vietnam.[81] However, Prosterman's contacts with those in US foreign policy circles probably began earlier when he worked for the New York-based Sullivan and Cromwell law firm, which produced the Dulles brothers and many other high level government officials in post-war decades.[82]

In response to Estrella's invitation, Prosterman arrived in Manila in early November 1972. He was enthusiastic about the potential of reform to undermine the communist-led peasant movement, saying, 'Land ownership [through land reform] is the one thing that stops insurgents cold'.[83] He participated in the Philippine government committee charged with drafting the guidelines for the implementation of Marcos's reform programme. Prosterman advocated reducing the retention limit on tenanted rice and corn lands to zero and allowing only those landowners already cultivating their land to retain it for personal cultivation. He also urged that in the redistribution process the link between beneficiary and former landowner be entirely broken, so that tenants would pay the government and the government would compensate the landowner.[84] These measures would have ensured that the scope of the Marcos reform would cover a much greater number of rice and corn tenants. Prosterman met with Marcos himself to explain his ideas.

While Prosterman was supported in his argument on a zero retention limit by Secretary Abad Santos and Jeremias Montemayor, other members of the Agrarian Reform Coordinating Council, charged with approving the Draft Guidelines, opposed the measure. These included Executive Secretary Jacobo Clave, Agricultural Secretary Arturo Tanco and Finance Secretary Cesar Virata.[85] Estrella himself said that such a measure would 'adversely affect the small landowners who actually belong to the middle class composed of teachers, soldiers, and other government employees...we do not intend to see an emergence of a new discontent [sic] group'.[86] Prosterman said of the zero retention limit, 'I suspect that Marcos, pressed by the Ilocano landlords, was unwilling to accept this'. He said that it was the rejection of the limit 'combined with the administrative lethargy, that was probably, in retrospect, the death-knell' of the reform.[87]

The Coordinating Council did approve a detailed elaboration of the 'Rules and Regulations to Implement Presidential Decree No. 27', as the decree itself had called for. But in a memorandum to Estrella and Virata on 25 November 1972, Marcos ruled, 'We shall postpone promulgation of the Rules and Regulations', and they were never to be approved.[88] Thus Marcos and his Cabinet demonstrated even before the end of 1972 that they were far from committed to implementing a liberal approach to reform. However, in characteristic fashion, both US and Filipino advocates of the liberal approach continued to believe that at least part of their objectives could be achieved in the context of the Marcos programme, and that Marcos himself could be convinced to move toward a more vigorous implementation of land redistribution.

At Estrella's invitation, Prosterman returned to the country a month later and met with Marcos on 15 December. The President told him, 'I cannot overstate the fact that everything in terms of our overall national reforms, hinges on land reform, and bringing satisfaction to the landless'. The main message that the President wanted to transmit through Prosterman to Washington was, however, clear when he said that his government would be 'grateful if our friends chose to help in this hour of need'.[89] Marcos was appealing to the US for funding for land reform. Prosterman felt that the only way that the programme could advance was to substantially *increase* compensation to landowners, and the only way to do this was 'to find external resources that could complement the internal Philippine resources available for landlord payment', as the US had done in Vietnam. He wanted the US to 'express its willingness to provide, over a 2-3 year period, approximately $100 million in support to the Philippine land-reform program, to be released as performance goals are met'. He stressed that, 'This approximately equals the cost of one day of the Vietnam war at 1969 levels', indicating that if land reform was not implemented, '[a]nticipated results would range from a toppling of Marcos and a scramble for power to all-out civil war, in which one participant would be a greatly strengthened NPA'. The US should also seek to gain support of the World Bank Consultative Group, with special help from Japan.[90] Prosterman revisited the country in February, April and June of 1973 to work on proposals for financing reform, and met with Marcos again.[91]

Prosterman's proposals were implicitly supported in a major report by the International Labour Office (ILO) submitted to the government in early 1974.[92] The ILO mission visited the country at the end of 1973 and was chaired by development economist Gustav Ranis. Mission members generally endorsed the potential for reform but expressed worries over the implementation of the Marcos programme. They were more cautious than Prosterman in assessing the contribution which reform could make to increasing agricultural productivity, but nevertheless felt that the government should move quickly to implement its programme. Echoing Prosterman's advice during the previous year, they called for immediate action by the President on guidelines for reform implementation and recommended a zero retention limit. They also called for lower levels of compensation to large landowners. Members of the mission had included both Filipino and foreign advocates of the liberal approach, who had seen at least some of Prosterman's work.[93]

4.4.2 The conservative approach wins out again

By the end of 1972 Marcos had shown his hesitancy to push ahead with a liberal approach to reform. However, a major US effort to encourage Marcos to implement the programme and to provide funding along the lines suggested by Prosterman might have changed his mind. In South Korea, Syngman Rhee had also demonstrated resistance to implementing reform until he was convinced it was in his interests to do so. However, while the US Embassy initially favoured greater backing for the programme, Washington demonstrated its bias against a liberal approach right from the start. Before Marcos announced PD27, the State Department told Ambassador Byroade that if he should receive a request from Marcos to fund land reform, 'our response should be to offer to study the GOP proposal, indicating that, depending upon the nature of the proposal and upon available funds, we might develop a plan for expanding assistance'.[94]

Immediately after Marcos announced his programme, Ambassador Henry Byroade (1969-1973), who was said to be close to the Marcoses and the CIA, indicated to Washington that he believed Marcos was serious about reform and that the US should provide significant funding.[95] He said that the programme was written by an 'able group [of] technocrats', including Melchor, Tanco, Sacay and Tavanlar, who were proceeding 'very responsibly and in close contact with [the] US mission'. In Byroade's opinion, it was a 'serious effort directed to full eradication [of] tenancy'. He said that he expected Marcos to request funds from the US and other members of the World Bank Consultative Group. 'Given the greatly improved environment now existing for land reform in the Philippines, the mission looks forward to a positive review of prospects for US support during AID Assistant Administrator's visit.' [96]

As if to reassure the opponents of redistributive reform in Washington, Byroade added that Marcos would not touch sugar and other commercial crops like coconut, pineapples and bananas, and that 'indications are that he [is] keeping careful watch that rights [to] private property [are] protected and that [the] program does not alienate too many people'. Contrary to later assertions by Washington, Byroade confirmed US involvement in the early stages of planning, saying that the USAID director and staff had been invited to participate in planning sessions in the two weeks leading up to the proclamation of PD27.[97] Byroade also said that, 'In response to special GOP request we arranged with Saigon for [a] technician knowledgeable in rapid land titling to visit Manila.' This confirmed that the US Embassy, and perhaps the CIA, did enlist US personnel like Prosterman, who had experience in the Vietnam programme, to participate in the early stages of the Marcos reform.[98]

Many years later, Eligio Tavanlar, who participated in the committee drafting PD27, made the fantastic claim that the US, through Senators Magnusson and Inouye, had offered Marcos $7 billion to pay for a sweeping reform programme and Marcos turned it down.[99] The director of USAID-Manila (1969-1975), Thomas Niblock, put the blame for this story on Prosterman. He had no recollection of Inouye being present, but said that Magnusson 'happened to be on a year-end cruise and wound up in Manila'. Prosterman arranged a meeting with Marcos and the 'headline the next day was, "US is Going to Provide a Billion Dollars for Philippine Land Reform"...I think Prosterman was trying to force the US government's hand and I think Magnusson...did not dissuade him from his work.'[100]

Niblock believed that if Washington had decided to fund the programme, Marcos might have taken it much further. In early 1973 USAID-Manila 'recommended...in a key message to AID Washington that the United States participate in the compensation process.'[101] Top policy makers in the US were aware that without US funding, Marcos' reform would not amount to anything.[102] Nevertheless, in mid-1973, Washington turned down the funding request. Niblock stated that in the end, 'The US administration never recommended cash financing of land reform.'[103] Once Washington had made itself clear, Byroade and Niblock backed off and, according to Prosterman, the former 'provided no encouragement' while the latter was 'lukewarm' toward efforts to encourage Marcos or Washington to reconsider.[104]

The dominant thinking in USAID Washington and in the State Department remained locked within the conservative approach. A major report on 'Philippine Insurgency and US Policy', submitted to the State Department at the end of 1972, reinforced the traditional bias against redistributive reform. It concluded that, while rural poverty and landlessness were widespread, 'land reform does not appear to be a short-run solution to the lack of productivity increase and the food problem in the Philippines'.[105] Instead, it expressed the hope that, 'the action arms of the central, provincial, and local governments, perhaps aided by a certain stiffening of will supplied by the military, will take upon themselves the task of righting the economic imbalance of the past 20 years'.[106] It said the US should encourage 'progressives in the military', help to expand the AFP engineer construction battalions and, in areas of NPA activity, fund such organizations as Montemayor's FFF and the Philippine Rural Reconstruction Movement (PRRM), which had played such a successful role in the 1950s.[107] When the State Department's Director of Philippine Affairs, Richard E. Usher, was questioned about the lack of progress in Marcos' agrarian reform by Prosterman-supporter and head of AFL-CIO International Affairs, Harry Goldberg, in April 1973, Usher responded, 'we shouldn't judge Marcos on the basis of whether he goes ahead now with his land reform plan, in view of the obvious problems he faces with it'.[108]

Between 1974 and 1978, US assistance to the Marcos programme amounted to no more than $2,382,000, or two per cent of the cost of the programme and about 1.3 per cent of the total USAID budget for the Philippines.[109] As in the past, USAID's role in the programme was restricted almost exclusively to training and administrative procedures.[110] One analyst commented that, not only did USAID 'not use its leverage to push the regime faster, but encouraged a sophisticated and costly data gathering format that slowed land tenure conversion at the very point when Marcos began to have second thoughts about his "cornerstone".[111] Its minimal role was maintained, in part, through the Land Tenure Center at the University of Wisconsin. In 1978 the Center testified to its close relationship with USAID as well as the Ford and Rockefeller Foundations.[112] It provided personnel on a regular basis to USAID and the DAR in Manila and brought a constant stream of DAR officials to the Center in Wisconsin for training.[113]

In August 1974, just three months after the ILO mission's report had endorsed many of his reform recommendations, Prosterman returned to the country to assess the progress of the compromised land transfer programme. He wrote a scathing report which he presented to Executive Secretary Alexander Melchor, documenting widespread landowner evasion, administrative obstacles to reform and over-reporting of progress by the government. The process for correcting Certificates of Land Transfer (CLTs) had broken down and the Land Bank had increased the documentation required from owners resulting in a 'drastic slow-down in progress'. Prosterman revised his assessment of the retention limit, saying that if the 7-hectare limit were enforced the programme could still be effective. He reiterated his call for increased foreign funding and compensation to speed up implementation. However, he argued that unless drastic measures were taken by the end of the year there would be a 'complete disintegration and failure of the land reform program' and 'security problems in the countryside will multiply'.[114]

Ambassador William Sullivan (1973-1977), who had replaced Byroade, sent a copy of Prosterman's report to Washington, saying that it was a 'real irritant' to Marcos. He reported that in a 16 August policy review before the Philippine Chamber of Commerce and Industry, Marcos made no mention of reform in his prepared speech, but added afterward that, 'some foreign experts made [the] mistake of measuring progress on land reform solely on [the] basis of [the] speed of land transfers', and went on to talk about achievements in providing credit, rural electrification, irrigation, feeder roads, fertilizer subsidies and rice and corn marketing. While Sullivan reported that Prosterman's observations were confirmed in another study by US political scientist David Wurfel, he nonetheless added that the Embassy believed, 'Prosterman's predictions of dire social and political consequences are overdrawn'. Sullivan's telegram went on to refute each point made by Prosterman, stressing that Marcos, Finance Secretary Virata and National Economic Development Authority (NEDA) head, Gerardo Sicat, favoured putting funds into infrastructure and productivity programmes rather than land transfer. Sullivan argued that this side of the programme had shown good performance.[115]

In what appeared to be an act of damage control, Sullivan then invited his old friend Wolf Ladejinsky, who was working for the World Bank in India, to visit the country and present a more palatable assessment to Marcos.[116] Ladejinsky had always been even more open to compromise than Prosterman. Ladejinsky had met Secretary Estrella in 1969 and discussed the main outlines of his approach to reform. He arrived in Manila in late September 1974 and met with Marcos on 10 October. In his subsequent report to Secretary Estrella and Robert McNamara, then President of the World Bank, he said that he was impressed with the conceptual basis of the programme and felt that any errors could be corrected by 'political and administrative will'. He suggested that landlord resistance and the government's bureaucratic 'foot-dragging'', common everywhere during land reforms, were surmountable if the regime used its command of force to push the reform.[117] Although he recognized that the reform had slowed down he retained some confidence that a liberal model of reform would be carried out because there was a strong leader in power. He urged Marcos to ensure that lands down to the seven hectare ceiling would actually be covered.

Sullivan told Washington that Ladejinsky covered many of the same points as Prosterman but in a 'less apocalyptic tone and his overall assessment is favorable.' Ladejinsky was widely seen as more 'wise' and 'balanced' than Prosterman by both US and Philippine officials.[118] This seemed to suit the purposes of the Embassy. The ambassador reported that Marcos was pleased with the visit, especially, the President said, since Ladejinsky was 'the personal representative of "our friend" and "benefactor" McNamara.' Marcos asked Ladejinsky whether the World Bank could fund compensation and the next day the Marcos press gave wide publicity to the meeting.[119] By the end of 1974, the Embassy began to excuse the lack of progress on reform and to accept at face value all Philippine government reports about the programme, steering clear of either pressuring Marcos to take firmer action or encouraging him to do so with more funds.

Prosterman returned to the Philippines in January 1975 when he was again granted an audience with President Marcos. His report submitted to the Philippine and US government was short, outlining six points of immediate action required to save the programme, all of which involved direct intervention by the President.[120] On 3 March he did a long interview and, for the first time, publicly criticized the programme, warning that without immediate action to speed up implementation, 'the Philippines may endure a cyclone of revolution'. The article was turned down by the Marcos controlled media, but later appeared in the US armed forces' *Pacific Stars and Stripes*.[121] Marcos was evidently incensed and instructed Teodoro Valencia to write a series of articles condemning the meddling American. Prosterman said that when he made a final trip to the country the following year, 'no one from the government would meet with me'.[122] On 18 March 1975 Prosterman met with Philip Habib and Benjamin Fleck at the State Department to deliver his verdict on the Marcos programme.[123]

Later that year political scientist David Wurfel (University of Windsor) presented a detailed criticism of the programme in a public talk and private discussion with the US Embassy. Sullivan was no more impressed by Wurfel's assessment than he had been by Prosterman. The ambassador reported that Wurfel had documented not only the problems in implementing Marcos' programme, but many cases of Marcos and his associates having acquired large tracts of land. On Wurfel's criticism of land give-aways to agribusiness corporations, Sullivan reported that USAID staff felt that his statistics were in error and that he had an over-emphasis on Mindanao, 'where he was thoroughly exposed to the emotionally anti-government views of Bishop Claver and other activist Church leaders'. Besides, Sullivan added, 'one can hardly deny that the foreign exchange bonanza earned by banana growers must be weighed against the alleged injustice'.[124]

In 1976, Sullivan's Embassy introduced a new element in reports on the Marcos reform programme that would characterize all subsequent reports back to Washington. In an analysis of the third year of martial law, the Embassy acknowledged that the Marcos programme could not effect far reaching changes, 'A truly revolutionary agrarian reform program would have to address such problems as the plight of the sugar plantation workers and the marginal incomes of tenants and smallholders whose income is derived from other crops'. But rather than arguing to step up the pace of reform, the report said that, 'The rhetoric with which Marcos proclaimed the inauguration of land reform was unfortunate'. In other words, the main problem was not the limited nature of the reform, but the high expectations raised by Marcos through the manner in which it had been introduced. The programme was judged a success in bringing 'substantial...benefits to one key sector of the rural population'.[125]

Advocates of a liberal approach made one final intervention in an effort to change US policy on agrarian reform during the Marcos years. In late 1977, a meeting to discuss the Marcos programme was held at the offices of the Rand Corporation, a "think-tank" that had long worked on contract for the US government.[126] The corporation had a mixed record in regard to agrarian reform. In 1967 it had commissioned a report on South Vietnam which argued against US support for redistributive reform, but two years later the same author had written a report supporting redistributive reform in the Philippines.[127] However, the report on the meeting discussing the Marcos programme not only came out decidedly in favour of a liberal approach to reform, but also condemned the Marcos programme in no uncertain terms. Roy Prosterman, who was invited to attend, had a major influence over the final report drafted by anthropologist Gerald Hickey and USAID official John Wilkinson.[128] The report endorsed and went beyond Prosterman's earlier recommendations and his criticisms of the Marcos government's programme. US officials responsible for Philippine policy evidently had no intention of endorsing the report. However, in 1978 one Washington official showed it to a Philippine diplomat and the report reached Marcos. The President was outraged by the criticisms of his land reform and asked the US government to withdraw from its limited involvement in the programme.[129]

Despite assurances by US officials that Washington did not endorse the Rand Corporation study, Marcos did not back down and USAID had nothing more to do with his land reform programme after 1978. Nevertheless, in what appeared to be an effort to demonstrate their endorsement of Marcos' conservative approach, US officials continued to praise his land reform programme. In December 1979, USAID prepared a report on the Marcos programme in response to Congressional inquiries on the lack of progress. The report presented a positive assessment of the programme but said that its goals had been 'overly optimistic' and only 35 per cent of targeted tenants had yet received titles to their land.[130] This was a misrepresentation of the facts, as can be seen in the discussion of accomplishments in the following section. A month later Ambassador Richard Murphy (1978-1982) presented an assessment of the land reform programme to USAID in Washington that was virtually the same text, purged of the few critical comments and stating that 70 per cent of beneficiaries had received titles.[131]

While the US did not encourage agrarian reform, both the US government and the private sector did provide considerable support to Marcos in other spheres. Shortly after Marcos had declared martial law, the American Chamber of Commerce in the Philippines (ACCP) sent a telegram to Marcos offering its support and cooperation.[132] Official policy was to avoid 'any comment about the imposition of martial law which could be taken as a sign of approval or disapproval by Marcos or by the Philippine public'.[133] However, Niblock minced no words, saying that he welcomed martial law and, 'I think that our Ambassador and AID Director and all concerned in the Philippines welcomed this move and hoped that it would succeed and that it would be a substantial measure'.[134]

The World Bank, which, during the 1960s, had increasingly assumed US economic projects in the third world, gave its clear endorsement to martial law and the Philippines was labelled a 'country of concentration'.[135] In 1974 the Philippines received a World Bank loan of $165 million, when Bank assistance in the previous five years had averaged only $30 million per year. From 1950 to 1972 the Bank granted a total of $326 million in loans. After martial law was declared, from 1973 until 1981, the Bank put $2.6 billion into 61 projects.[136] However, the Bank would not participate in funding the reform programme. Prosterman met with Bank president McNamara twice urging that they put resources into the programme, 'but the Bank said land reform doesn't create new assets'.[137] Niblock commented, 'I don't think the Bank staff ever considered any substantial funding of land reform apart from a willingness to consider loans for irrigation and roads in the rural areas'.[138]

A slight shift in the Bank position occurred in the mid-1970s when they came out with a policy paper supporting land reform.[139] A World Bank mission to the Philippines in 1975 concluded that the 'rationale for land reform is that it would help raise productivity by providing the incentive of ownership to former tenants'.[140] The mission praised the M-99 credit programme and the work of IRRI and gave general endorsement to the programme. Subsequently three loans were directed to the land reform programme: a $16 million loan for beneficiary support directed through the Land Bank; a $35 million loan to the Ministry of Agriculture to finance extension services; and a $15 million loan to the Ministry of Agrarian Reform (MAR) to support resettlement programmes. At the same time as Prosterman was writing off the Marcos programme, another Bank Mission working in Mindoro concluded that the 'government is committed to agrarian reform and is moving ahead rapidly with its program to transfer land ownership'.[141] However, in 1978 the Bank acknowledged that the programme had stalled due to poor land records, a lack of leadership, inefficient management and landowner opposition.[142] The Bank decided to direct its efforts more exclusively to the productivity programmes and, much like the State Department, concluded that many 'tenants were not ready for a shift in tenure status..and prefer the protection of the landlord'.[143]

In the US, supporters of both the liberal and conservative approaches to agrarian reform also welcomed the declaration of martial law, believing that Marcos could guarantee stability in the country and protect US interests. Contrary to later claims, Embassy and USAID officials were very much involved in the early planning of the reform. The US refusal to push Marcos to go further with his programme or to provide funds ensured that he would not implement even the minimal programme introduced. At the outset of martial law, there was some support among US officials in Manila for Prosterman's liberal approach and its counterinsurgency potential, no doubt due to the high profile that it had enjoyed in Vietnam after 1969. However, the traditional bias against redistributive reform in Washington quickly marginalized Prosterman. After 1975, US officials took an almost cynical attitude toward the Marcos reform, praising accomplishments that had no foundation in reality and directing most of their economic support to programmes to build infrastructure and increase productivity, while providing military support to deal with unrest. US priorities came to reflect those of the Marcos state and the social forces that sustained it.

4.5 Marcos, agrarian reform and the Philippine state

During the Marcos years, while little land was redistributed to rural producers, a significant amount of land was concentrated in the hands of a small group of families and agribusiness corporations. Two years after the reform was launched, Secretary Estrella declared that, 'The backbone of feudalism for centuries has at last been broken.'[144] Some analysts have said that Marcos used the agrarian reform programme to undermine the traditional landed oligarchy and that the state, under his control, achieved a new autonomy from society.[145] In a related argument, the Marcos state was said to have undermined the traditional landed oligarchy by constituting an unholy alliance between technocrats and 'cronies', with the former group supported by international agencies like the World Bank and the latter dependent on the personal favour of the president.[146]

While there is some validity in such a portrayal of the Marcos state and its use of agrarian reform, it is a picture that tends to overestimate both the impact of Marcos' limited land redistribution programme and the extent to which the oligarchy was displaced. It also tends to underestimate the influence of societal forces within the state and to exaggerate the role of technocrats during the period.

4.5.1 The record of reform and the DAR bureaucracy

By the end of the programme's first year, the Department of Agrarian Reform had issued, though not necessarily distributed, certificates of land transfer (CLTs) covering the land of 144,540 tenants, or 36 per cent of all those who were to benefit under the programme (Table 4.4). However, in the following years the pace of printing the certificates slowed down considerably. Moreover, the number of CLTs issued is a deceiving figure since many were not received by the tenants. The government inflated its success rate in agrarian reform by reporting accomplishments according to the number of CLTs printed.[147] Yet Table 4.4 shows that although certificates were issued for 230,580 tenants by 1976, only about 100,000 tenants had actually received them by the end of that year.[148]

Even tenants who received CLTs were a long way from possessing title to their land. By 1981, only 1,799 tenants had received emancipation patents (EPs), or official titles, to 1,645 hectares of rice and corn land (Table 4.4). In 1982, as the government began facing serious economic difficulties and the New People's Army began to gain support in the countryside, the decision was taken to issue emancipation patents to tenants who had made at least two successive payments on their land.[149] As can be seen in Table 4.4, this boosted the apparent accomplishment rate of the programme considerably during the final years of the Marcos regime.

However, this too was deceptive, both because these numbers represented only EPs printed and not necessarily distributed to the beneficiaries and because the emancipation patents became worthless and tenants risked losing their land if they failed to meet the remaining 13 amortization payments.[150] In 1986, after the Marcos government was defeated, the National Economic and Development Authority reported that only 13,590 beneficiaries, about three per cent of those targeted, had actually received emancipation patents covering 11,000 hectares, or 1.5 per cent of the area under Operation Land Transfer.[151] It was not even clear whether this number had completed all payments for their land.

During the Marcos years, land transfer also continued under the old Resettlement and Landed Estates programmes. Sixteen new settlement sites were proclaimed covering 180,000 hectares and involving 12,000 families (Table 4.2). The actual issuing of deeds of sale, however, proceeded no faster than under previous governments. Under the Landed Estates Programme, 23 estates were acquired covering some 17,000 hectares for distribution to 6,000 beneficiaries. However, two-thirds of this land, or 11,400 hectares, was accounted for by the Tabacalera estates in Isabela, which were acquired only in 1981 and still not paid for by the end of the Marcos regime.[152] In many cases this land was counted twice by the government in its accomplishment reports, since it was also reported under Operation Land Transfer.

The record of Operation Leasehold is even more dubious. By the end of 1985, the Ministry of Agrarian Reform reported that 645,808 tenants had leasehold contracts over 690,207 hectares, representing 122 per cent accomplishment in terms of tenants.[153] However, surveys taken in the late 1970s and early 1980s revealed that share tenancy was still extensive. A 1978 study reported that 44 per cent of rice and corn farmers were share tenants and that it was the dominant form of tenancy in seven out of 11 regions surveyed.[154] Another study found that share tenancy was still widespread in the Bicol region in 1977. At a National Peasant Conference held in August 1984, peasants from Bicol reported the share-tenancy rate at 54 per cent.[155] Leasehold operations have always been difficult to enforce, since they require an enormous investment in supervision.

There were many reasons for the low level of reform accomplishments. During the Marcos years, a conservative vision of reform dominated the agrarian reform bureaucracy within the state. Some Department of Agrarian Reform (DAR) officials believed that such low estimates of accomplishments were misleading. Long-time second-in-command at DAR, José Medina, argued that

Table 4.4: Accomplishment of Marcos Reform (1972-1986)

Year	CLTs Printed		EPs Printed		Owner Compensation (Claims Received & Verified)		
	Benif.s	Area	Benif.s	Area	Owners	Benif.s	Area
1972	295	682	-	-	-		
1973	144245	258666	-	-	-		
1974	44645	77790	-	-	223	14025	18032
1975	19513	29875	97	52	759	25658	35162
1976	21882	33642	534	604	1364	22772	34186
1977	27500	44241	600	485	1800	22377	40947
1978	28146	46812	287	263	1318	16556	30929
1979	46561	53520	82	51	524	6051	19140
1980	34187	26556	84	83	961	11782	14391
1981	50361	74907	115	107	1320	12246	17600
1982*	42524	54544	34913	45592	1695	15277	23508
1983	34768	55717	62782	71131	1194	10637	17599
1984	12277	19765	21208	44770	1825	15095	26328
1985	4038	11458	17229	20453	597	6809	9100
Adjustment	-66665	-21545					
TOTAL	**444277**	**766630**	**137931**	**183591**	**13580**	**179285**	**286922**
% Scope**	103.89	106.99	32.26	25.62	24.00	41.93	40.04

NEDA Report of Actual Accomplishments by 1986

	CLTs Issued		EPs Distributed		Compensation Approved	Paid	
	Benif.s	Area	Benif.s	Area	Owners	Owners	Area
1986	440239	755172	13590	11087	12391	4339	262357
% Scope**	102.95	105.39	3.18	1.55	21.90	7.67	36.62

*After 1982 Emancipation Patents were issued after the beneficiary paid two amortization payments and signed a Deed of Undertaking with Real Estate Mortgage in favour of the Land Bank of the Philippines. MAR, 1983, p. 26.
**Percentage of scope as it stood at the end of 1985 (Table 2.3).
Source: Land Reform Statistics, Ministry of Agrarian Reform, 1985.

the accomplishment rate was very nearly 100 per cent, because all tenants on land covered by PD27 were deemed owners after the declaration of the programme in 1972. DAR's job became essentially paperwork, 'merely a documenting process'. Medina said that agrarian reform should be seen as an 'evolutionary process' where each government offers 'innovations'.[156] It was precisely this vision of agrarian reform, as essentially a documentation process carried out over a long series of bureaucratic steps, that was the ruling philosophy of the DAR during Secretary Estrella's long tenure at the helm of the Department.

The reform bureaucracy, like most state institutions under Marcos, was characterized by patronage and corruption. Estrella was a survivor and a good friend of Marcos. USAID's Thomas Niblock referred to him as 'a local politico'. 'He was a Marcos man. His job was to provide the fanfare.'[157] In October 1972

139

Ambassador Byroade called him a 'weak administrator with [a] reputation as [a] rather traditional politician', believing that Marcos was to keep him on merely as a figure-head at the Department, leaving young technocrats to run the programme.[158] In fact, Marcos entrusted the running of the entire programme to him, shunting aside more competent officials like Orlando Sacay who appeared more committed to redistributive reform.[159] Accomplishment reports were made to look positive and Estrella produced a stream of publications, many with his name as author, extolling the virtues of the programme.[160]

The overwhelming preoccupation of the Land Tenure Operations office in DAR was the process of landowner compensation. Each landowner had a file at DAR Central Office, many of which stood two and a half feet high. Inside was a huge set of documentation, almost all of which was concerned with the valuation of the land. The fact that the office was organized around landowners rather than beneficiaries was indicative of the programme's character.[161] The process of land valuation and of issuing, registering and distributing CLTs and EPs was so long and tedious, involving such reams of paper work, that there was plenty of room for corruption to set in.[162] The process had to pass through a multiplicity of central government agencies and the Land Bank was the most notorious for slowing it down.

True to the conservative approach, the Marcos programme also did not break the dependent relationship between landowners and tenants. From the start it allowed beneficiaries to make direct payments to their landowners, a measure that Prosterman had vigorously opposed. At the end of 1973, Marcos and Estrella decided to allow land valuation through a 'Landowner-Tenant Production Agreement', thus by-passing the Barrio committees.[163] Since tenants were either afraid or unwilling to challenge landowners alone, those valuations that were agreed often favoured the landowner. In many cases, beneficiaries who received CLTs ended up turning over to their landowners 'amortization payments' after each crop was harvested - payments that were equal in value to the land rent collected from their neighbours who were still tenants. This was the case in one *barrio* in Bicol, where a CLT holder said that his landowner never gave receipts for these payments. He was unaware of a date when the payments would end. Probing the issue more deeply, the CLT holders in the *barrio* said that they felt the owner still had a right to receive a payment from them.[164] Without strong and independent peasant committees, a challenge to traditional relationships in the countryside was unthinkable.

In some cases peasants covered by the Marcos programme believed themselves worse off. Many of those tenants covered by Operation Leasehold actually began opting to return to a sharecropping arrangement. Because of the landlord monopoly over land, the rent that leaseholders were charged was extremely high. As a result, the whole return on the leaseholder's capital outlay for agricultural inputs accrued to the landlord in rent, leaving the leaseholder with barely a subsistence wage. This seems to be the main reason for many leaseholders opting to return to sharecropping.[165] Peasants who received CLTs were working under a burden that was often much heavier than when they were tenants. They had to pay for the land, a home plot and also had to pay land tax, irrigation fees and all the fees required by the Samahang Nayon cooperative. On top of this, CLT recipients and leaseholders alike were confronted with the rising costs of fertilizers and pesticides needed to cultivate the IRRI high-yielding varieties.

As in past programmes, many of the beneficiaries under the Marcos programme quickly lost control over what little land they were awarded. A large proportion of peasant beneficiaries of the Landed Estates programme and recipients of CLTs or EPs under the Marcos programme sold or mortgaged their land rights either to their original owner or a better-off neighbour. In Bulan, Sorsogon, Adminvado Luzuriaga owned 100 hectares, part of which was covered by PD27 in 1975. In 1989 he said that since the land had been covered by land reform, 90 per cent of his former tenants had sold their newly acquired rights. He recovered the rents from one-third of the tenants, while the rest were acquired by a retired teacher, a local director of the National Irrigation Authority, a retired city councillor and a few merchants. In 1989, Luzuriaga was still determined and confident that he would be able to recover the rest of his land rents.[166]

Beneficiaries of agrarian reform gave up their rights to land for many reasons. Most commonly, they were victims of debt or precarious circumstances. If a crop failed or a family member was ill they would need cash. Often the former owner of the land, or the trader who bought their rice and sold them fertilizers, was willing to advance the money in exchange for a claim to the produce of their land. There were also speculators or merchants who approached CLT holders offering them P5000 for a hectare of unirrigated land - more money than the average poor farmer ever sees at one time - in exchange for their CLTs, knowing that the land could be sold on at a big profit. In some cases, the CLT holders behaved like traditional absentee owners and, rather than working to make the land productive, mortgaged their CLT first to one person for P10,000, and later to another for P15,000, being content to live off the margin gained.[167] DAR never carried out a study on the extent of this problem.[168] Since it was formally illegal for beneficiaries to sell their rights, such a study was beyond the mandate of a government agency. Privately, officials at both local and central DAR offices acknowledged that the problem was widespread. They argued that the solution would be the provision of appropriate support services and productivity programmes to agrarian reform beneficiaries.

However, government administered credit programmes like 'Masagana 99', and extension services that operated through government established cooperatives like the Samahang Nayon, failed significantly to improve the position of rural producers, despite the praise that they received from US and World Bank officials. By the end of the Marcos administration, many of these organizations had fallen into disrepute, having been used by landowners and rich farmers to syphon government funds into their own pockets while providing little service

141

to the peasants.[169] They became networks of political patronage, often in the hands of Marcos' Kilusang Bagong Lipunan (KBL) *barangay* officials.[170] Loans under the Masagana 99 programme never reached the majority of tenants and smallholders. At its peak, in 1974, only 36 per cent of small rice producers were involved.[171] By July 1983, only 27,538 farmers were borrowing from the programme.[172] Among those who did receive loans, the tendency to fall into arrears or default on payment was high. The loans were tied to the purchase of imported inputs. The price of petroleum-based fertilizer quadrupled from $4.00 per bag in 1973 to $17.00 per bag in 1974.[173] The costs of pesticides also steadily increased over the years of the programme.

Significant gains were made in rice production during the 1970s, but by the mid-1980s there were signs that they could not be sustained. The high-yielding varieties developed by IRRI not only required imported inputs, but performed best on irrigated land, which was beyond the reach of most peasants. By 1980 the ecological impact of the technology, as well as its dependence on expensive imported inputs, led to a decline in rice production. Due to the high cost of imported fertilizers and pesticides, the real income of rice farmers between 1976 and 1979 was estimated by the government to have fallen by 53 per cent.[174] At the end of 1984, farmers' harvests were 50 per cent under target due to their inability to pay for high-priced imported inputs.[175] In December 1984, the Philippine press reported a serious rice shortage of approximately 600,000 metric tons. By the mid-1980s, food 'self-sufficiency' in the Philippines proved to be an elusive goal. The very notion that the country ever achieved food self-sufficiency is doubtful. In those years in which the country exported more rice than it imported, all that was achieved was the production of enough rice to satisfy market demand. However, market demand for rice is not the same as the population's need for rice. Hundreds of thousands of sugar workers in Negros were on the brink of starvation in 1985 and 1986, but they had no income with which to influence market demand.

Many of the gains of the 'green revolution' were confined to specific geographical regions and specific groups of rural producers. As early as 1970, Ishikawa documented changes in the production structure in the rice producing regions of Central Luzon. He pointed to the emergence of a 'new type of commercial farmer' and the development of farm management firms. Yet where this was occurring, the new farmer was rarely the previous tenant but was almost always the landlord himself. Ishikawa acknowledged that the new technology was making the poor still poorer, but argued that they would benefit in the long run.[176] Numerous studies in the 1970s documented the affect of the new technology on production relations in the rice sector.[177] But most of these studies were carried out in areas of Central Luzon that were relatively close to urban centres and accessible to IRRI. There, irrigation was widespread, tenant contracts were under scrutiny and farmers had access to National Food Authority stations to sell their produce at the government support price. In these areas, Marcos' land reform combined with the productivity programmes and an influx of resources from migrant labourers did bring about a process of social and economic differentiation. In some cases a significant minority of village residents were able to dramatically improve their living conditions.[178]

However, by the early 1980s, although the area irrigated had expanded, irrigated lands still comprised only 1,370,000 hectares.[179] One study noted that 58 per cent of rice farmers surveyed had no access to irrigation and therefore most of these only produced one crop a year.[180] In many areas local marketing of the imported fertilizers and pesticides needed to grow high-yielding varieties, as well as the marketing of peasants' produce, was concentrated in only a few hands. Although the National Food Authority (NFA) set a uniform producers' price for rice, most peasants could not get their produce to a NFA station and were obliged to sell at very low prices to local landlords and traders.[181] Kerkvliet described how far from breaking down traditional social relations, the productivity programmes that surrounded Marcos' agrarian reform and received the backing of international agencies often reinforced traditional debt dependency.[182]

The low level of accomplishment after thirteen years of programme implementation reflected not only the weakness of the laws passed through presidential decree, but also the DAR approach, which perceived reform as no more than a process of paper work. From Estrella down to the provincial and municipal DAR offices, the bureaucracy was riddled with patronage. By allowing the tenant-landowner relationship to continue, and by relying on central government agencies and government established organizations, the Marcos state prevented the kind of peasant involvement that was needed to implement and maintain redistributive reform, even on the small scale dictated by the scope of PD27. While little progress was made in redistribution, the productivity programmes, which from the conservative perspective offer an alternative path to rural development, failed to improve the lot of the rural poor. Instead, the agrarian reform programme became just one more instrument through which the Marcos state and its civilian supporters augmented their own economic and political position in the country.

4.5.2 Technocrats and modernizers or a conservative alliance?

The US government, the World Bank and Marcos himself attempted to portray the martial law regime as one in which technocrats and the military had a new role to play within a state committed to modernization. In fact, many of those portrayed as 'technocrats' were no more than representatives of the vested interests of the business community, and are better understood as a group within the oligarchy than a class apart. While the military continued to expand its role in the state and society as it had during Marcos' legal term in office, it was no more committed to reform and rural development than other state institutions or the oligarchy as a whole.

It is true that Marcos expanded central state institutions and tapped the services of technocrats to staff agencies like the National Economic and Development

Authority (NEDA). Gerardo Sicat, educated at MIT, was appointed to head NEDA and later worked for the World Bank. He outlined the 'export-oriented industrialization' strategy adopted by Marcos and could best be described as a technocrat. The same could probably be said of Onofre D. Corpus, Marcos' Secretary of Education. However, many of those often described as technocrats, including Finance chief, Cesar Virata, Trade and Industry head, Roberto Ongpin and Agriculture Secretary, Arturo Tanco can be better understood as representatives of the business community.[183] The term 'technocrat' should be restricted to describe those individuals, based either in academic or bureaucratic institutions, rather than in political networks or the business community, who have arrived in government and remain there primarily by virtue of their technical expertise. It has too often been used to refer to businessmen in government who may at times assume a 'technocratic posture' (i.e., the view that society and economy should be organized on principles established by technical experts).[184] The failure to make the distinction has led to an exaggeration of the influence of 'independent' technocrats during the Marcos years.

The representatives of the business community, such as Virata, were, nevertheless, distinct from traditional politicians in the Cabinet (such as rural banker and provincial politician Conrado Estrella, who had his own provincial political machine), but they had their own constituency in the board rooms of domestic and foreign corporations. Technocrats like Orlando Sacay, who could see the potential of redistributive reform, were marginalized early on.[185] Virata and his associates were much more interested in promoting the interests of domestic and foreign agribusiness.

Cesar Virata, educated at Wharton in the US, began his career with SyCip, Gorres and Velayo, who were hired as consultants by the Dole Corporation. Virata helped Dole establish operations in the country in the early 1960s and hired much of the original Filipino staff for the corporation.[186] Arturo Tanco, educated at Cornell, originally worked for the del Rosario family's PHINMA, leading agribusiness consultants, and had his own agribusiness firm, Management Investment and Development Associates, before joining Marcos. He was not concerned with agrarian reform and never mentioned it in his reports to the President.[187]

Marcos also facilitated the acquisition of land by agribusiness corporations. In May 1974 he issued 'General Order No. 47', which allowed corporations with 500 employees or more to acquire and cultivate their own rice lands, ostensibly to feed their employees.[188] By 1981, 95 corporate farms had been established, encompassing 86,000 hectares of prime rice lands – far more land than beneficiaries were granted title to under Operation Land Transfer by the end of the Marcos years. While the farms were not enormously successful, they did allow firms to acquire additional lands. Marsman Estates Plantation Inc., a contract banana grower for Del Monte, set up Nova Vista Management and Development Corporation with a corporate rice farm of 600 hectares.[189] One community worker stated that 200 to 400 hectares were originally public land

and people were evicted to establish the farm.[190] By 1978 the project was abandoned, but at least part of the farm was incorporated into the Marsman plantation and planted to Cavendish bananas.[191] Most of the corporate rice farms were set up in the Southern Tagalog and Southern Mindanao Regions, where major agricultural estates were operating. The programme was yet another means by which corporations could amass land.

Marcos expanded the role of the National Development Corporation (NDC), which had been used in the past to by-pass constitutional limits on the land area that foreign corporations could control. In 1980 he passed a series of decrees that allowed NDC to assume actual ownership of over 40,000 hectares of land in Agusan del Sur. Under the direction of Roberto Ongpin, NDC entered into a series of joint ventures with transnational corporations to establish oil palm production, promising to provide sufficient unoccupied agricultural lands.[192] All but two of these ventures were abandoned when it became clear that much of the land was already being cultivated by settlers and indigenous peoples' communities. However, the joint venture between NDC and the then British-owned oil palm giant, Guthrie Overseas Holding Ltd., pushed ahead with the establishment of NDC-Guthrie Plantations Inc. on 8,000 hectares of land. A vicious campaign ensued to win effective control over the land from Manobo tribesmen and settlers who already occupied parts of it. This involved everything from duplicity in offering compensation, to the employment of the notorious Col. Carlos Lademora and his 'Lost Command' to disrupt farmer organizations and coerce submission to the plantation project.[193]

During the years of Marcos' agrarian reform, the military was ostensibly to play a support role in the programme. Advocates of the liberal approach to reform, like Prosterman and Ladejinsky, welcomed this arrangement, believing that the deployment of authoritarian force would ensure reform implementation. What they failed to realize was that the military, in much the same manner as the state bureaucracy, was part of the prevailing class alignment in the country. In the beginning Marcos saw a counterinsurgency potential in the agrarian reform programme, but he viewed it as a tactical weapon while the advocates of the liberal approach saw it in strategic terms.

In June 1973 Philippine Constabulary Chief, General Fidel Ramos, called a co-ordinating conference of all government agencies involved with settling agrarian disputes.[194] DAR and the Department of National Defense were to cooperate in implementing reform. During 1973 there was a direct correspondence between the regions with the highest number of CLTs issued and the areas where the NPA was most active.[195] These were the areas where the government had launched its pilot projects. However, the AFP never looked upon agrarian reform as a precondition for eliminating peasant support for the NPA. In fact, in instances where military officers owned lands they intervened directly to oppose the programme.[196] DAR's Annual Report for 1973-1974 referred to the 'uncooperative attitudes of some military personnel.'[197]

The military's counterinsurgency strategy was, if anything, hostile to the notion of redistributive agrarian reform. During martial law, military expenditure increased four-fold, from $169 million in 1971 to $447 million in 1979, while the number of troops under arms increased from 59,000 in 1971 to 156,000 in 1978.[198] In addition Marcos ordered the organization of the paramilitary Civilian Home Defense Forces (CHDF) and the Integrated National Police, which together totalled 116,000 by 1985.[199] The military assumed roles in local government, the judiciary and state-controlled enterprises on an unprecedented scale.[200] Their counterinsurgency strategy was modelled on the early US 'search and destroy' missions in Vietnam, which inflicted heavy losses on rural civilian populations.[201] This involved bombing entire villages, strategic hamletting (herding local populations into 'protected' villages) and the arbitrary 'salvaging' of village residents - a euphemism for military murder.[202] There was little room for redistributive reform within such a strategy.

It was a new alliance that assumed control of the state in the Philippines in 1972, but rather than representing the 'autonomy' of the state from society, it represented its capture by a coalition between Marcos, the military, and selected members of the oligarchy drawn from both the business community and from powerful provincial political clans. Far from undermining the power of the oligarchy, Marcos' agrarian reform programme was used to raise certain families and their corporate interests to new heights of power and wealth.

4.5.3 Agrarian reform, the oligarchy and the state

It became clear fairly early on that although Marcos claimed he would break the oligarchy through martial law, he needed the support of landowners and provincial political clans to enforce his rule throughout the country. Marcos' refusal to challenge the landowners head-on was clear when he restricted reform to rice and corn lands. Even here he allowed phased implementation, which gave landowners time to take evasive measures. One indication of Marcos' buckling under landowner pressure was his decision, in January 1973, to allow landowners to submit statements on their holdings to municipal mayors instead of PC Provincial Commanders.[203] Municipal authorities remained centres of local landowner power and had little interest in implementing the reform. Most mayors were landowners, and Marcos' instructions did not require them to impose any penalty on landowners for false statements on the extent of their holdings and tenant numbers on their land. In addition, in the local courts where landlord-tenant conflicts were handled, the judges were usually landowners or closely connected to them.[204]

What is more, Marcos was himself a large landowner and used martial law to increase his own landholdings as well as those of his extended family. By the early 1980s he and his immediate family were said to have acquired thousands of hectares. These reportedly included 16 *haciendas* and the La Carlota sugar central in Negros Occidental, 30,000 hectares in the northern provinces of Cagayan and Isabela, and several hundred hectares in Davao, other parts of Mindanao and Panay.[205] In a private discussion with the US Embassy in December 1975, political scientist David Wurfel reported one case in Davao where 'Marcos front-men took over land which was already being processed for distribution for tenants, who were ejected".[206] Of course, Marcos' most important land acquisitions were not in the Philippines at all, but rather included prime real estate in New York City and other US locations.[207]

Marcos' early hesitance on reform and his own reputation as a landowner were a signal to owners that the regime was not intent on reform and effectively encouraged landowner resistance. Owners formed associations to apply unified pressure for higher land prices, and these hired batteries of lawyers to contest every facet of the reform.[208] One such group called itself the 'Association of Landowners for Agrarian Reform' (ALARM). This group was based in Nueva Ecija and included most owners affected by OLT in Central Luzon. ALARM organized a uniform opposition to every stage of the land reform pro-gramme.[209] In January 1973, DAR memorandums began to cite widespread examples of landlord evasion. The landlords were said to be forcing tenants to sign statements claiming that they were paid labourers. Landlords also subdivided their lands among relatives, giving each less than seven hectares to avoid redistribution. Some laid criminal charges against their tenants as grounds for eviction.[210] A USAID adviser provided evidence of landlords using eviction and coercion of their tenants to avoid land redistribution.[211] Landowners also shifted to crops other than rice and corn, or accused their tenants of being illegal squatters.[212]

The central state's bureaucracy remained open to pressure and patronage from provincial political networks. As one Agrarian Reform Technician from Region 2 related, 'The local DAR official must give the Mayor due respect. The Mayor will do you a favour - give you a bottle of whiskey or any gift. After that you cannot refuse his request. You can lose your job, or get transferred or there are the goons...' and he moved his finger across his neck.[213] Local DAR personnel were often related to landowners and were sympathetic to their reluctance to part with their lands.[214] Thus, Marcos did not attempt to use the state to undermine the oligarchy as a whole, but to strike out at specific powerful opponents. Marcos's rejection of the 'Rules and Regulations' for the implemen-tation of the reform, which were drawn up by the DAR in 1972, left the programme vague and therefore more easily employed as a means to reward supporters and punish opponents.[215]

An analysis of the list of landowners covered by the programme between 1972 and 1981 revealed that only 264 owners had blocks of land of 99 hectares or over purchased by the government, totalling 62,209 hectares.[216] By the late 1980s, there were still at least 3,200 owners of farms of over 100 hectares, covering a minimum of 1.8 million hectares.[217] Only three landowners appear to have had 1,000 hectares or more covered by PD27: Senen J. Gabaldon had 1,700 hectares covered by the programme; Ramon Cojuangco's family had 1,008 hectares covered (which possibly formed part of the land swap arranged by Marcos and discussed below); José Cojuangco and associates had 1,148 hectares covered.

Even José Cojuangco's family, however, which included Marcos' arch rival Benigno Aquino, was able to hold on to most of its lands, including Hacienda Luisita. Marcos threatened several times to seize their estate in accordance with conditions that the government had originally imposed on its purchase.[218] In March 1967, ten years after the acquisition of Hacienda Luisita, the Cojuangcos had received a letter from Conrado Estrella, Governor of the Land Tenure Administration, asking them what they planned to do to implement the Monetary Board's resolution requiring them to distribute their land. They answered by saying that there were no tenants and as far as they were concerned there was nothing to implement.[219] Nothing else happened until 1978, when Benigno Aquino, then in prison, announced his candidacy for the elections to the Interim Batasan (the legislative assembly mandated by Marcos' 1973 Constitution), which Marcos had called to create a semblance of democracy in the country. The Cojuangcos then received a letter from the Central Bank and the Monetary Board asking them when they planned to implement the land transfer. The Cojuangcos sent back the same reply as they had eleven years before.[220]

They did not hear from the government again until Aquino was about to leave detention for a by-pass operation in the United States in May 1980. The day before he left, the government filed a case.[221] The plaintiffs evidently included the Central Bank (or Monetary Board), the Government Service Insurance System and the Ministry of Agrarian Reform. The case remained in its preliminary stages until August 1983 when Aquino was assassinated. It was only then that the government began to conduct hearings, but there was still no urgency to the case. However, the government's attitude changed at the time of the snap elections in February 1986, when the Aquino-Cojuangco clan once more emerged as a major threat to Marcos. On 3 December 1985, one day after Cory Aquino filed her candidacy, Judge Pardo of the Regional Trial Court denied the appeal and ruled that the family had to transfer their lands. The judge made his ruling even before summary arguments were presented, suggesting that Marcos had intervened to ask for a quick decision.[222] The Cojuangcos immediately submitted an appeal that was to carry their case into Cory Aquino's presidency and guarantee their hold over the family's prime lands.[223]

The nature of the Marcos state and its relationship to the oligarchy and agribusiness is best illustrated through the role of the other branch of the Cojuangco family, allied to Eduardo 'Danding' Cojuangco Jr. He was the sole civilian present at the meeting where the President decided to declare martial law, and became known as the number-one 'crony' of the President.[224] In scrutinizing Cojuangco's role, it is necessary to reevaluate whether he is most accurately seen as a 'crony' dependent on Marcos, or whether the ties of dependence, may, in fact, have run in the opposite direction.

The split between the families of the Cojuangco brothers, José II and Eduardo Sr., assumed national significance in the 1960s.[225] Eduardo Cojuangco Jr. was one of Marcos' most important supporters in his bid for the presidency, while Benigno Aquino, who had married into the José Cojuangco family, became one of the President's most powerful opponents. After Marcos was elected in 1965, Aquino, who was Governor of Tarlac, did not run for re-election and the post was filled by Eduardo Cojuangco. As Governor, Cojuangco was known as an ardent opponent of agrarian reform. In 1968, he had told Estrella, 'I am against land reform...[the lessees] won't be able to hold onto the land...[With] one bad crop...they'll be out of business. In ten years there will be just a few big holdings again.'[226] After Marcos declared martial law, Eduardo Cojuangco seemed poised to help make this forecast a reality.

Right from the start of martial law, Eduardo Cojuangco used the agrarian reform programme, and the state's agricultural programme more generally, to build up his own growing fortune. Cojuangco decided to move into the coconut sector shortly before martial law was declared.[227] In 1971, the Philippine Coconut Producers Federation (COCOFED), an organization dominated by large landowners, succeeded in passing a law instituting a coconut levy in order to raise money for establishing domestic coconut processing. With the help of the Institut des Recherches Pour Les Huiles et Oléagineux, Cojuangco identified Bugsuk Island off the coast of Palawan as an ideal area for the cultivation of a new high-yielding hybrid coconut variety developed by the Institute.[228]

When Marcos took his decision to delay the adoption of the Rules and Regulations governing the implementation of PD 27 in November 1972, he announced that 'landowners will be encouraged to sell or swap their lands...with government lands'.[229] Soon after, Marcos issued a special Letter of Instruction (LOI) ordering the Bureau of Lands, then under Arturo Tanco's Department of Agriculture and Natural Resources, to allow landowners to swap one hectare of developed rice and corn lands for ten hectares of public lands. The LOI was used only once before it was repealed, and this was to allow the heirs of Eduardo Cojuangco Sr. and Ernesto Oppen to swap 1,600 hectares of land located in Tarlac, Nueva Ecija, Pangasinan and Antique in exchange for 16,000 hectares of public land.[230]

The agreement, which was initiated by Cojuangco, had to be completed before 17 January 1973, when Marcos proclaimed his new Constitution, which prohibited the transfer of public lands to private corporations and limited transfer to individuals to 24 hectares under a homestead programme.[231] The land was acquired under the authority of a law passed in Quirino's time which permitted such land swaps.[232] Cojuangco acquired Bugsuk Island, totalling some 11,000 hectares, and later received the balance of 5,000 hectares located in Agusan del Norte on Mindanao. According to Narciso V. Villapando, director of the Bureau of Lands at the time, 'some of the title holders [on Bugsuk Island] refused to leave'. In order to have a contiguous holding Cojuangco had to purchase land rights from 600 families who were then relocated to the southern tip of Palawan by the government. The land was registered as the property of Agricultural Investors Inc., owned by Cojuangco.[233] While beneficiaries under OLT secured absolute title to only 11,000 hectares during the 13 years of implementation of the programme, in one stroke Cojuangco was able to secure title to 16,000 hectares of land.

In March 1974, Cojuangco entered into an agreement with the government to establish a 100 hectare seed farm devoted to raising the hybrid coconut on part of the Bugsuk property. Later that year, Marcos passed a decree authorizing the Philippine Coconut Authority to launch a Nationwide Coconut Replanting Program that would distribute for free the hybrid coconut seedlings to farmers all over the country.[234] The same law established the Coconut Industry Development Fund to pay for the project. In 1975, with legislation provided by Marcos and funds provided in part by the Philippine Coconut Authority, Cojuangco was able to buy out the First United Bank from his estranged cousins and to set up the United Coconut Planters Bank (UCPB).[235]

Over the following decade, Cojuangco, along with Defence Secretary Juan Ponce Enrile, Maria Clara Lobregat and a handful of other large landowning families, established control over the coconut sector through a state-sponsored monopoly over the processing and marketing of coconut oil.[236] They were able to acquire vast tracts of land and secured appointment to the boards of all the state institutions established within the sector. In a similar fashion, Roberto Benedicto was able to secure control over the sugar industry.[237]

Another attempt by Cojuangco to use the agrarian reform programme to secure vast tracts of land, this time in the northern province of Isabela, was thwarted by a concerted and costly peasant mobilization. By the late 1960s, the declining Tabacalera empire had decided to follow up the sale of Hacienda Luisita and divest itself of its three great *haciendas* in Isabela. Productivity had fallen sharply and the estates had become a liability. The first to go was the remaining portion of Hacienda San Luis, which was sold in 1969 to Monterey Farms, owned by the agribusiness giant San Miguel Corporation.[238] When tenants on Haciendas San Antonio and Santa Isabel were registered with the government following the passage of RA 6389 in 1971, the company decided that it was time to unload these estates as well. It made an enticing proposal to the government, offering to sell the 11,448 hectare properties for an immediate cash payment of between one-fifth and one-tenth of their value with the balance to be paid in 20-year Land Bonds. The Executive put the proposal to Congress, which accepted it in principle and set up a committee to work with the Land Bank to assess the land's value. However, when Marcos declared martial law the whole plan came to a halt. The company had still heard nothing from the government by 1980, when it was approached by 'some Filipino capitalists' who offered to buy the land at a favourable price.[239] Activists guessed that they paid about P7,000 per hectare for the land.[240]

The land was transferred on 30 May ostensibly to ANCA Corporation, a company registered with the Securities and Exchange Commission on 1 April 1980. Antonio Carag, a businessman close to Defense Minister Juan Ponce Enrile, was listed as the principal shareholder of the corporation.[241] Retired General Tomas Diaz was the Project Director for ANCA.[242] It soon became clear that Cojuangco was behind the project when he participated in meetings and Carag spoke openly about his mentor's role in the project. The company planned to transform the two estates into a plantation devoted primarily to coconut and cotton, inter-cropped with coffee, yellow corn and mongo beans. Since there were about 2,000 hectares of tenanted rice lands, Cojuangco had to take account of the agrarian reform programme. The company attempted to turn this to their advantage by offering to implement agrarian reform on the estates and provide double the amount of land that the government could distribute to the tenants. About 8,000 hectares were officially listed as cultivated area, with the balance in mountainous pasture land. ANCA wanted a contiguous area of 4,000 hectares, with 4,000 hectares to be turned over to the tenants, who would, however, have to leave the lands that they were currently tilling.[243]

A group of 25 tenants was taken to Manila to meet with Cojuangco, Carag and Secretary Estrella. Carag warned them that if they did not agree they would get no land at all. But when the tenants realized that many among them were to be transferred 'to the mountains' (the pasture land), they decided to fight back. They argued that the land being turned over to them was of poorer quality and was already occupied by other cultivators. In early August, while a meeting was being held between the tenants and Deputy Minister of Agrarian Reform Labayen, the company and soldiers brought in bulldozers and 367 families were ejected. One tenant leader said that the company told them that if the tenants did not move, 'they will block our houses with hollow blocks and we will rot in them. And we cannot pass through the land...because that is Cojuangco's land'.[244] In the demolitions that followed, tenants were killed, wounded and constantly harassed by the military.[245]

Assisted by their local priest, the writer and activist Fr. Pedro Salgado, the tenants filed a petition with the Ministry of Agrarian Reform, sent a letter to the President and sought out the help of national opposition leader and human rights lawyer, former Senator José Diokno. When Diokno met the tenants on 29 August 1980, he told them that he would not take the case unless they were determined to see it through to the end. He pleaded for non-violence and strength and unity among the tenants. He said of the military's removal tactics, 'Do not fight back...they will see you are one. Do not give them a reason to shoot you. You have no arms. You can tell them: We are the same Filipinos. You soldiers, why do you exploit us? We have a petition at the MAR, why don't we wait for that before you eject us....What we will use is moral force not physical'. He went on tell them about Ghandi's strategy in India and then had a long discussion with them about tactics.[246]

By November the tenants had formed an organization and conducted seminars with thousands of residents. On 15 December 1980, Cojuangco was so worried that he travelled to the site with Carag and Diaz to hold a dialogue with the priests and Bishop Purugganan of the Ilagan Diocese. Cojuangco argued in favour of the plan, while Carag claimed that opposition to the project was being instigated by the New People's Army. Nonetheless, ANCA admitted that at least 5,000 people would be relocated. The priests pointed out that those who had already been relocated were given only half the amount of land that they had cultivated before. When the priests suggested that the company had been responsible for the assassination of a tenant organizer, Cojuangco protested that the man was killed because of some local political feud, adding, 'I only play my politics in Tarlac, Father...in Tarlac I don't earn my livelihood...I don't play politics in Negros and Mindanao'. Then the priests asked why even the meeting they were having was surrounded by the military. Carag answered:

> All right, the military, Father...we asked the company of the military, Father, for our self-protection. They did not come here to intimidate you, Father. You should not be intimidated. ...Danding has threats, I have, the General has. If we don't bring the military, Father, we will bring a private army to protect ourselves. We believe that it is better to get hold of protection from the government, legitimate, lawful protection than bring our own body-guards, Father...It was the New People's Army who killed these people because they were for Anca.[247]

The struggle over the land continued throughout 1981. Cojuangco began a high profile campaign to portray himself as implementing the government's agrarian reform programme. On 1 March 1981, the President awarded 144 EPs to tenants on the *haciendas*.[248] Two weeks later, Cojuangco brought Governor Faustino Dy to the site and, with much publicity, distributed titles to 114 tenants.[249] Even PC Provincial Commander Lt. Col. Oscar Florendo came to the *hacienda* to support Cojuangco's project, and the Deputy Commander was regularly present with troops. Marcos' favourite journalist, Teodoro Valencia, wrote a scathing article condemning the Bishop's opposition to a laudable agribusiness project.[250] The tenants responded to the combined onslaught of the regime by organizing an Easter Sunday march of 10,000 with placards that read, 'We want the land free! Stop military operations and harassment of the people! Raise the prices of the farmers' products!'[251]

During 1981 the protests were widely covered and began to have a national impact. This led Cojuangco to back down and announce his withdrawal in December. On 4 March 1982 Marcos announced with great fanfare that the Land Bank would purchase the *haciendas* immediately and, minus 2,000 hectares that would be set aside for an experimental farm, they would be distributed to the tenants under the Landed Estates Programme.[252] Marcos assumed blanket authority for determining the value and price of the land. It would appear that he set a total value of P103 million, which was presumably the amount that the Land Bank paid to Cojuangco.[253] Bishop Purugganan said that Cojuangco had originally paid only P8 million for the land, but other estimates put the figure closer to P80 million.[254]

Cojuangco nevertheless managed to emerge from the failed project with a profit, and, while he was not able to extend his empire to Isabela, he made inroads elsewhere.[255] Carag went on to be elected to the Batasan as the Enrile-supported candidate in 1984. Cojuangco, more than anyone else, illustrated

Marcos' dependence on old money and old political clans to maintain his rule. His alliance with the military to expand his control over property demonstrated the links that even that state institution had with the oligarchy.

While the tenants on Haciendas Santa Isabel and San Antonio defeated Cojuangco, they did not succeed in gaining ownership of the land. Some tenants had been killed, and many of their homes had been destroyed. By 1989, local organizers said that most residents had only received CLTs for homelots, and among those who had CLTs for farm lands, many had sold or mortgaged their rights.[256] However, coming at a moment when Marcos had officially lifted martial law, their struggle inspired the development of a new and militant period of peasant organizing that would eventually contribute to the final downfall of Marcos.

4.6 Conclusion

While the advocates of the liberal approach believed that Marcos' introduction of authoritarian rule would speed up agrarian reform, Marcos proved that such a regime has no special proclivity towards reform. Marcos did not attempt to undermine the oligarchy and landowner power, but only those families who presented obstacles to him or his closest supporters, including Eduardo Cojuangco, Roberto Benedicto and Juan Ponce Enrile. Marcos did not use the powers of martial law to speed up the acquisition of large estates for redistribution. In fact, calculated on an annual basis, the Marcos government 'purchased' slightly more land from large landowners in the year and a half preceding martial law than during the nine and a half years that followed.[257]

The acceleration of land acquisitions during the period immediately preceding martial law was a direct result of the pressure put on government by the peasant movement and its supporters. In an unprecedented success they had persuaded Congress to amend the Land Reform Code independently from, and in opposition to, the Executive branch of government. In fact, the reversal of the traditional positions on agrarian reform between the Executive and Legislature in 1970 to 1971 bore a striking resemblance to the debate that occurred between Syngman Rhee and his legislature in the early 1950s. The forces at play were also similar, with a broad popular movement in favour of redistributive reform, and a contest for power fought out between a President bent on increasing executive authority and a legislature determined to reduce such authority.

However, with the declaration of martial law, the parallel ends. Authoritarian power provided Marcos with room to manoeuvre and the opportunity to choose between a liberal or conservative approach to reform. There were advocates of both positions in the committee that Marcos established to draft his reform legislation in September and October 1972. Roy Prosterman was also on the scene and articulated the liberal position in great detail, demonstrating that Marcos was aware of the options. With the power to remake the Constitution and full legislative and executive authority, Marcos could have decided to implement a sweeping liberal reform with the potential to effect profound changes in the countryside. There are several reasons why he did not take such a course of action.

Firstly, while martial law provided an opportunity for Marcos to choose to implement a liberal reform, it also enabled him to choose to do little about reform. Martial law meant that Marcos, or whoever would succeed him in 1974, would no longer have to compete with Congress for popular support or heed the appeals of an increasingly radical peasant and popular movement for effective land redistribution. In other words, it ensured that a South Korean scenario could not happen in the Philippines.

Secondly, Marcos was dependent on the oligarchy and the military to maintain martial law rule throughout the country. His strongest supporters in the ranks of the political clans and the business community had little interest in redistributive reform. In fact, they saw martial law as an occasion to increase their control over land and other sources of wealth in the country, as did the President himself. The state bureaucracy and the military were tied through relations of patronage to these elite supporters of Marcos and had no concept of agrarian reform as a means to accomplish either their institutional or individual goals.

Thirdly, support for redistributive reform was not forthcoming from the US. A concerted US effort to pressure Marcos to take up reform, and to provide the funds necessary to implement a liberal programme, might have allowed Marcos to bring his major supporters behind the reform option just as Rhee had mobilized his elite and military allies behind reform. Both Filipino and US advocates of the conservative approach often argued that Marcos could not advance with reform for fear of upsetting the base of his support among smaller landowners. In fact, the smaller landowners could not have sustained any prolonged opposition to reform if Marcos had brought to bear the full power of the state. The most powerful elite actors could have been accommodated outside agriculture as they had been in South Korea. Since the military underwent a more than three-fold expansion, largely funded by the US, they could have been trained with the liberal reform prescription as part of their orientation. However, the bias against the liberal approach in Washington precluded such a scenario.

Finally, and perhaps most fundamentally, neither Marcos and his supporters nor the US believed that the threat mounted by the peasant movement warranted the kind of challenge to property rights and the rural power structure that the liberal approach called for. The peasant movement, both in its legal expressions and in its support for the newly formed New People's Army, had not developed to a point where it threatened to overturn the basic structures of the state. Both Marcos and his allies, as well as policy-makers in Washington, apparently believed that a strengthened military and an expanded traditional rural development programme would be sufficient to check the growth of the radical movement.

The Marcos years also highlighted some of the weaknesses within the liberal approach to reform, raising questions about its advocates' identities and objectives. These weaknesses appear to stem from the fact that the advocates of the liberal approach were motivated more by their objective to use reform to safeguard existing state structures than to solve the plight of the landless rural poor. Thus one of the most striking characteristics of both US and Filipino liberal reformers was their illusions about the potential of authoritarian rule to implement reforms from the top down. While they realized that successful reform required peasant involvement, they believed that such involvement could be parented or initiated by the President, central government agencies and the armed forces.

Furthermore, figures like Ladejinsky, Prosterman, Montemayor, Umali, Sacay and others, were always prepared to compromise and to work within the context of programmes confined to the conservative approach. Ladejinsky's whole career had been pursued within such compromises. Montemayor's collaboration with Marcos, long after it became clear that his programme was not going to redistribute land to most of those who needed it, contributed to discrediting his organization and the liberal approach in general. Prosterman eventually condemned the Marcos programme, but for three years he had helped to legitimate the Marcos regime in both the domestic and foreign arenas.

Filipino and US advocates of the liberal model of redistributive reform had distinct objectives. Prosterman was motivated in great measure by a desire to defend what he perceived as long-term US interests in the fight against communism in Asia. Montemayor and other Filipino liberal reformers were clearly more interested in promoting what they perceived as their own national interests. What the two groups shared was an abhorrence of radical change and a tendency to equate militant peasant movements with communism. Montemayor was introduced to rural organizing when he tried to pre-empt the re-emergence of radical organizations in Central Luzon in the mid-1950s.

Ladejinsky and Prosterman had clearly enjoyed some support for their activities inside the US government. Ladejinsky was working for Diem in Vietnam at a time when Col. Lansdale was co-ordinating all US personnel in the country in a covert counterinsurgency campaign.[258] It is unimaginable that Ladejinsky did not maintain close contact with those involved in the campaign. Prosterman worked with General Thieu a decade later and clearly had high-level contacts in the US government that opened doors for him in Vietnam, the Philippines, El Salvador and other countries where he worked. Prosterman's early involvement with the firm of Sullivan and Cromwell no doubt brought him into contact with those who would be highly placed in policy-making circles later on. The publication of his article in *Pacific Stars and Stripes* for distribution in the Philippines also suggests friendly contacts in the Armed Forces. Yet, except for a brief period in Vietnam and in El Salvador, Prosterman, like Ladejinsky before him, remained on the margins of US official policy toward agrarian reform.[259]

Finally, the Marcos years pointed yet again to the fundamental problems of the conservative approach to reform. In some communities, particularly in

Central Luzon, the Marcos programme led to greater differentiation among the peasantry and contributed to the creation of new groups of 'rich' peasants. However, without more widespread redistribution, the productivity programmes spun from IRRI's new seed varieties, together with schemes for community and integrated rural development, did not improve - and in some cases worsened the conditions of many landless peasants and tenant farmers. While military search and destroy missions could momentarily weaken the armed underground peasant movement their long-term effect would be to bolster the CPP-NPA and other radical organizations. Marcos' failure to implement agrarian reform, combined with the overall mismanagement of the economy during his 20 years in office, eventually led to a broadened popular movement for change and the erosion of the elite support that had been almost universal when he first declared martial law. These basic failings set into motion a process that would culminate in Marcos' flight from the country in 1986 and the coming to power of Corazon Aquino as President.

Notes

1. Constantino, 1978, p.203. On Recto see Chapter 3, section 3.4.6.
2. Lichauco, 1982, p.31.
3. Constantino, 1978, pp.299-304.
4. Constantino, 1978, pp.310-11.
5. Acting Secretary of Labour Bernardino Abes was appointed to head the committee. Also appointed were Secretary of Agriculture Benjamin Gozon and Attorney Santiago, the Agrarian Legal Council at the Land Tenure Authority. Interview Sixto K. Roxas, 1 September 1989. Wurfel (1983, p.5) reported Locsin as a member.
6. Even they were hesitant advocates of the approach. Montemayor had shown during the Magsaysay years that he was more interested in the FFF as a vehicle to replace the communists than as an organization committed to achieving redistributive reform (see Chapter 3, section 3.4.3). In 1966, as Chairman of the government's Rice and Corn Study Committee, Umali would argue that 'The implementation of a land reform program should be done cautiously...as fast as we can effect human changes. Otherwise it will boomerang on the Administration'. Committee Report, 8 January 1966, cited in Castillo, 1975, p.313.
7. RA 3844. Reference to the draft is based on Manglapus, 1967.
8. Constantino, 1978, p.319; Manglapus, 1967.
9. Manglapus, 1967.
10. RA3844; Manglapus, 1967, chapter 5; Sison, 1965, p.163; Constantino, 1978, p.319.
11. Wurfel, 1983, p.5.
12. Interview Sixto K. Roxas, 1 September 1989.
13. Interview José Medina, 17 March 1989.
14. RA3844, Chapters I and VI.
15. 'Legislative Message on Tenancy Abolition and Other Land Reforms' reproduced in Lynch, 1972, pp.247-261.
16. Smith, 1976, pp.253, 290-320. Smith claims that Macapagal approached the CIA for support in the 1959 Senatorial elections, but the Agency gave him only $50,000 while $200,000 was given to the 'Grand Alliance', a coalition of politicians centred on Magsaysay supporters drawn from the Party for Philippine Progress, the Nacionalistas, and the Liberal Party. With the victory of Macapagal's Liberals, the CIA gave him its full support in 1961.
17. Philippine Peasant Institute [PPI], 1984, pp.6-7. The Rockefeller Foundation began this work as early as 1944 in Mexico researching high yielding varieties of wheat. With the help of other agencies it set up the International Center for Maize and Wheat Improvement (Farmers Assistance Board, 1978, pp.10-11). Los Baños was the original home of the University of the

Philippines, which was established there by the Americans as an Agricultural School in 1909, later becoming the Agricultural College of the university based in Manila (Gleeck, 1981, p.44).

18. IRRI Annual Reports, 1966, 1972 and 1984.

19. Ladejinsky, 1963, p.326. This report was to Walter Rudlin of the Ford Foundation who was based in Kuala Lumpur.

20. Ladejinsky, 1963, p.328.

21. Ladejinsky, 1963, pp.328-30.

22. 'National Policy Paper on the Republic of the Philippines', 1966, submitted on 1 December 1965 and approved and signed by Secretary of State Dean Rusk on 3 March 1966. Hereafter, NPP, 1966.

23. NPP, 1966, Part I, p.7; Part II, p.66.

24. NPP, 1966, Part II, pp.36, 66.

25. NPP, 1966, Part I, pp.7, 23, 71.

26. NPP, 1966, Part I, pp.24, 75.

27. Interview Sixto K. Roxas, 1 September 1989.

28. NPP, 1966, Part I, pp.77, 82.

29. Cited in Jacoby, 1971, p.210.

30. That year USAID stated: 'AID believes that a vigorous private sector is essential to sound and adequate economic growth of developing nations. It further believes the [sic] American private enterprise not only can greatly assist this process through investment overseas, but that it must do so in recognition of its own stake in further peace.' Cited in Farmers Assistance Board, 1978.

31. Doronila, 1985, p.110.

32. MAR, 1985.

33. Ofreneo, 1980, chapter 4; Constantino, 1978, pp.329-330.

34. A further 3,000 hectares was leased from private owners. Interview, Mani Lopez, Industrial Relations Director, Dole Philippines, 8 May 1989.

35. Koone and Gleeck, 1970, p.47. They state that between 1956 and 1967 irrigated lands increased from 600,000 hectares to 1.35 million hectares (p.66).

36. Bello et al, 1982, p.69.

37. At the end of 1965, the foreign debt stood at $599.5 million. After four years of the Marcos administration, in 1969 it hit $1.9 billion (Bello et al, 1982, p.132; Doronila, 1985, p.111).

38. Doronila, 1985, p.112-113.

39. Lichauco, 1982, p.43. This was not the first nor the last time that Marcos feigned a nationalist position to further his aims. In the crisis of 1981, he did so to resist IMF pressures. In the 1986 presidential campaign he again adopted the language of nationalism in the attempt to resist US pressure to oust him.

40. Doronila, 1985, pp.113-115.

41. Wurfel, 1988, pp.106-113.

42. Bello et al, 1982, pp.20-23.

43. Bello et al, 1982, pp.138-139.

44. Po, 1980, pp.51-53. Po cited a 1975 USAID commentary on the FFF which claimed that the radicalization of the organization was a result of 'communist infiltration', but Po attributed it to 'the intransigence of the rural elite'. In an interview in August 1984, an underground member of the National Democratic Front in Negros explained that the process of radicalization was in fact the reverse of the USAID claim. He and many others had been in the FFF, but were pushed toward a more radical stand both through landlord intransigence and the declaration of martial law.

45. This account is primarily based on Nemenzo, 1984, pp.71-103.

46. Nemenzo, 1984, p.81. Interviews with underground cadre on the history of the CPP in Bicol, September 1989.

47. Wurfel, 1983, pp.6-7.
48. Wurfel, 1988, p.100.
49. Marcos, 1980, pp.23-25; Huntington, 1968.
50. Interview, Jeremias Montemayor, 14 September 1987.
51. Po, 1980, p.53; Hollnsteiner et al, 1978, p.76.
52. Hollnsteiner et al, 1978, p.72. 21.
53. Marcos, 'Presidential Decree (PD) No.2,' 26 September 1972.
54. Interview, Conrado Estrella, 26 February 1989.
55. Interview, José Medina, 17 March 1989. Tanco's participation was reported in Byroade to State, 24 October 1972.
56. Interview, Conrado Estrella, 26 February 1989.
57. Marcos, PD No.27.
58. Marcos, PD No.27. A month later Marcos stipulated that payment might also be in the form of government land, cash or annuities ('Memorandum', 25 November 1972), later reiterated in PD No.85. In PD 251 (21 July 1973), it was stipulated that cash payments would include only 10 per cent of compensation, with the balance in 25-year Land Bank bonds bearing 6 per cent interest.
59. Interview, Gerardo Bulatao, 15 March 1989; see also Luzon [LUSSA], 1983, pp.29-30 and Takigawa, 1974, p.13.
60 Estrella, 'Memorandum,' 9 January 1973.
61. Marcos, 'Letter of Instruction (LOI) No.46'.
62. Estrella, 'Memorandum,' 9 January 1973.
63. Marcos, LOI No.227, 16 November 1974.
64. PD 175. Earlier Marcos had issued LOI No.7 (November 1972), establishing a Bureau of Agricultural Cooperatives under the Department of Local Government, moving to the Ministry of Agriculture only in 1980. This account is based on Po, 1980, pp.76-82.
65. Van Steenwyk (USAID), February 1975, p.12.
66. See Wurfel, 1977, pp.18-21.
67. Marcos, LOI No.41, 27 November 1972.
68. Marcos, LOI No.46, 7 December 1972.
69. Takigawa, 1974, p. 16. In 1970, the USAID provided P20 million to support the Nueva Ecija project. In 1971, it was renamed the Nueva Ecija Land Reform Integrated Development Project (NELRIDP). For assessment of the project by those most intimately involved see: DAR, 1 January 1989; Lynch et al, 1972; and Mangahas et al, 1976.
70. Cited in Kerkvliet, 1979, p.114.
71. Takigawa, 1974, p.55.
72. Takigawa, 1974, pp.88-89.
73. Estrella, 1974, p.25, cited in Takigawa, 1974, p.55.
74. According to Prosterman (Interview, 30 November 1989), Montemayor and Sacay supported a liberal approach.
75. 'Answer on Land Reform' December 1979, p.3, appended to USAID, 4 February 1980, where the statement was reiterated.
76. Prosterman letter to the author, 18 April 1989 and interview, 30 November 1989.
77. Jeff Riedinger, a later assistant to Prosterman, in conversation with the author, 25 February 1989.
78. Interview, Conrado Estrella, 26 February 1989. USAID-Manila director, Thomas Niblock (Interview, 11 December 1989) maintained the fiction, saying of Prosterman, 'He invited himself. As soon as he smelled land reform, he was in heat'.
79. See Prosterman, 1970; Bredo, 1970 and Prosterman and Riedinger, 1987, Chapter 5.
80. Prosterman, 1966. He met Ladejinsky only once at the USAID Spring Review on Land Reform in June 1970 and says he 'probably read a couple of his published articles by the late '60s'. Prosterman letter to the author, 18 April 1989.
81. Interview, Prosterman, 30 November 1989. Jeff Riedinger, in conversation with the author, 25 February 1989.

82. After law school Prosterman worked for the firm from January 1959 to August 1965 (Prosterman, letter to the author, 1 October 1991). On Sullivan and Cromwell in US foreign policy, see Kolko, 1969, pp.17-22.

83. In an interview with his friend Jack Doughty, 13 November 1972, *Seattle Post Intelligencer*, cited in Kerkvliet, 1979, p.118.

84. Prosterman letter to the author, 18 April 1989.

85. Estrella, Memorandum to the President, 22 November 1972 and Agrarian Reform Coordinating Council, 21 October 1972.

86. Estrella, Memorandum to the President, 22 November 1972, p.2.

87. Prosterman letter to the author, 18 April 1989.

88. Marcos Memorandum, 25 November 1972.

89. Prosterman was accompanied by his assistant Charles A. Taylor, Congressman Joel Pritchard from Washington state and journalist Jack Doughty. Prosterman letter to the author, 18 April 1989; Prosterman and Taylor, 18 December 1972.

90. Prosterman and Taylor, 18 December 1972, p.3.

91. Prosterman letter to the author, 18 April 1989.

92. International [ILO], 1974, pp.473-500.

93. Mahar Mangahas, Yujiro Hayami, Akira Takahashi, Albert Berry and Ranis himself were among those very supportive of the liberal approach. The mission report makes reference to Prosterman, 1973.

94. State and USAID to Embassy, 17 October 1972.

95. On Byroade and his intelligence connections, see Bonner, 1988, pp.3-4 and passim.

96. Byroade to State, 24 October 1972.

97. Byroade to State, 24 October 1972. USAID-Manila director, Thomas Niblock (Interview, 11 December 1989 Washington), confirmed this, 'Once the political announcement was made in 1972, there were many joint discussions between AID staff and the Philippine government. In fact, during those years, USAID staff was regularly invited into discussions such as the planning for land reform as friendly colleagues and co-workers.'

98. Byroade to State, 24 October 1972. However, Byroade's request may have referred to the transfer of USAID *staff* directly from South Vietnam. In October 1973, Michael Korin joined USAID Manila to work on land reform, and in mid-1974 Keith Sherper arrived (Monk, 1990, pp. 111-14).

99. Transcript of a discussion on agrarian reform, José, ed., 1986, pp.8-9. Tavanlar said that Thomas Niblock and US Senators Magnusson and Inoye were present, but he referred to Niblock as the US ambassador when in fact he was the head of USAID Manila, indicating that his memory was far from exact. Tavanlar probably meant to say pesos (though he repeated the figure several times), equivalent to US $1 billion at the time.

100. Niblock said, 'I was not at the meeting so I don't know how that came about.' Interview, Thomas Niblock, 11 December 1989. It is likely that Prosterman had simply advanced his proposition of $100 million aid and the Philippine press reported it as $1 billion.

101. Interview, Thomas Niblock, 11 December 1989.

102. The Bureau of Intelligence and Research at the State Department (15 January 1973), the US government institution least supportive of Marcos, pointed out that Marcos 'cannot actually implement land reform without money for credit and marketing aid to farmers, and without expert administrative staff...Only the US can provide the financial aid and the appearance of political backing he badly needs.' For a general assessment of the Bureau see Bonner, 1988, 129-133 and passim.

103. Interview, Thomas Niblock, 11 December 1989.

104. He argued that only two lesser USAID officials, Keith Sherper and Doug Tinsler, who ran the Bicol Integrated Rural Development Project, remained supportive. Interview, Roy Prosterman, 30 November 1989.

105. Development Alternatives Inc. to State Department, 1 December 1972, IX, p.22, VIII, p.8.

106. Development Alternatives Inc. to State Department, 1 December 1972, VIII, p48.

107. Development Alternatives Inc. to State Department, 1 December 1972, XV, p.18.

108. Usher, Memorandum, 13 April 1973.

109. USAID, 4 February 1980 and Rocamora and O'Connor, 1977, p.76.

110. USAID, 4 February 1980. A 1971 study for USAID on the potential for reform spoke of the 1963 Agrarian Reform Code as 'too ambitious' in that it called for a 'change in the very social structure'. The study's major recommendations were for administrative reorganization and personnel training (Panganiban, 1971).

111. Richter, 1982, p.178.

112. Land Tenure Center, 1978, p.2, E6.

113. USAID's Dunkin Harkin and David J. King both emanated from the Center. Among the DAR officials trained there, were Naomi Capinpin, Isidro DeLeon, Floriano C. Fortum, Severino T. Machonio, Josefina Nuñez, Eduardo Santiago and Lilia C. Panganiban (Land Tenure Center, 1978).

114. Prosterman and Taylor, 11 August 1974.

115. Sullivan to State 28 August 1974.

116. USAID's Louis Gleeck had written to Ladejinsky as early as May 1974 asking him to come to Manila, but Ladejinsky said he could not make the trip before August (Monk, 1990, p. 113).

117. Ladejinsky, 1974, p.553.

118. Sullivan to State, 11 October 1974, The comparison was made by: Conrado Estrella, 26 February 1989; Interview, Thomas Niblock, 11 December 1989.

119. Sullivan to State, 11 October 1974.

120. Prosterman and Taylor, 12 March 1975.

121. Jack Doughty, *Seattle Post-Intelligencer* (3 March 1975).

122. Prosterman letter to the author, 18 April 1989.

123. State to Embassy, Memo of Conversation, 18 March 1975.

124. Sullivan to State, 29 December 1975.

125. US Embassy to State, 29 January 1976. Ambassador David Newsom (1977-1978) reported that while the programme had fallen short of its 'ambitious original targets', it had 'registered considerable progress during the past five years' (Newsom to State, 8 June 1977). In 1979, Ambassador Richard Murphy said that the programme had been 'effective in breaking up huge holdings of rice and corn lands and distributed them among impoverished tenants' and had only 'begun to bog down administratively' (Murphy to State, 30 January 1979).

126. The Rand Corporation was one of the first private "think tanks" to play a major role in US strategic planning and had been working for the Pentagon at least since 1948.

127. See Mitchell, 1967 and 1969 and Prosterman and Riedinger's discussion of these reports (1987, pp.130-132).

128. Hickey and Wilkinson, 1978. Hickey had undertaken research work for many years in South Vietnam in close contact with US officials (Chomsky, 1979, p.64).

129. See Monk's (1990, pp.127-133) discussion of reactions to the Rand Corporation report.

130. 'Effectiveness of the Philippine Land Reform Program' (18 December 1979) appended to USAID, 4 February 1980.

131. Murphy to Sullivan (USAID Washington), 31 January 1980, Appendix E, p.3.

132. ACCP, 26 September 1972, appended to Byroade to State, 27 September 1972.

133. *Current Foreign Relations*, No. 43 (25 October 1972).

134. Interview, Thomas Niblock, 11 December 1989.

135. Payer, 1982, p.209.

136. Bello et al, 1982, p.24.

137. Interview, Roy Prosterman, 30 November 1989.

138. Interview, Thomas Niblock, 11 December 1989.

139. World Bank, 1975.

140. World Bank, 1976, p.110.

141. World Bank, 1975a, p.4 and Annex 2.
142. Cited in Bello et al, 1982, p.75.
143. Cited in Bello et al, 1982, p.77.
144. Cited in Takigawa, 1974, p.25.
145. On attack against the oligarchy see Wurfel, 1977, p.1, 32ff; Fegan, 1982, p.2. On state autonomy see Chapter 1 above.
146. This was the position of the Bank itself revealed in the Ascher Memorandum leaked in 1980 (Bello et al, 1982, p.31).
147. Estrella, 1982, p.58. The process of CLT distribution was more complicated than Table 4.4 indicates. Many beneficiaries received more than one CLT. These often covered plots of land in various parts of the *barrio*, each planted to a different crop (eg. rice, corn or vegetables).
148. Wurfel, 1977, p.8.
149. Hayami et al, 1990, p.67. However, official MAR documents through 1986 continued to state that full payment was required before an EP would be issued (MAR, 1986).
150. In fact, beneficiaries had to sign a Deed of Undertaking with the real estate mortgage in favour of the Land Bank. Hayami et al, 1990, p.67.
151. The Presidential [PCGR] (1986a, p.22) reported an even lower rate of accomplishment.
152. MAR, 1985. The struggle over this land is described below.
153. MAR, 1985. The figure is particularly dubious given that in 1980 78,000 tenants were added to the list, but 25,700 hectares were subtracted. Between 1978, when Marcos established his rubber stamp parliament, and early 1987, when the new Aquino Constitution was passed, executive Departments were called Ministries.
154. International [IDRC], 1978, p.79. These figures may only relate to surveys taken earlier in the 1970s.
155. Richter, 1982, p.86; 'Ang Kalagayan ng mga Magsasaka sa Bicol,' presented at the first National Consultative Assembly of Peasant Organizations, Sacred Heart Novitiate, Quezon City, August 7-12, 1984, p.1.
156. Interview, José Medina, 17 March 1989.
157. Interview, Thomas Niblock, 11 December 1989.
158. Byroade to State, 24 October 1972.
159. Sacay was put in charge of developing the government's cooperative programme.
160. Estrella, 1969, 1971, 1978, 1982.
161. Research at the Land Transfer Operations Centre, DAR, Quezon City, 1988-89.
162. Interviews with DAR officials in Region 2 and Region 5, January to June 1989.
163. DAR, 1973.
164. Field Research Sorsogon, March 1989.
165. Ferrer, 1984, pp.211-212; see also Luzon [LUSSA], 1982, p.16.
166. Interview Adminvado Luzuriaga, 28 March 1989.
167. Interview with DAR official in Region 2, March 1989.
168. In 1983, the Ministry of Agrarian Reform published the results of an evaluation of the ten years of implementation of PD27. The methodology used to assess the situation of 'farmer beneficiaries' precluded the identification of those who may have mortgaged their rights to the land (MAR, 1983).
169. Interview, Professor Luciano Lactao, Isabela 20 June 1989. Luzon [LUSSA], 1982, pp.33-34; Wurfel, 1977, pp.21-25; Po, 1980, pp.83-89.
170. See Po, 1980, pp.90-92; Field investigations Sorsogon and Isabela March-July 1989. The KBL, or New Society Movement, was set up as Marcos' political party when he called elections for an interim Batasan Pambansa, or National Assembly, in 1978.
171. Bello et al, 1982, p.78.
172. Philippine [PPI], 1984, p.13.
173. Bello et al, 1982, p.81.
174. Bello et al, 1982, p.97.

175. *Malaya*, December 24, 1984.
176. Ishikawa, 1970, pp.26, 29, 39, 51.
177. Kikuchi and Hayami (1982, pp. 173-190) claimed that the position of the large tenant leaseholder was strengthened *vis a vis* the landlord; see also Kikuchi, et al, 1977. Cordova (1982, pp.191-206) argued that the agricultural labourers benefited at the expense of landlords.
178. For an interesting case study, see Muijzenberg, 1991.
179. UN FAO, 1984, p.57.
180. Luzon [LUSSA], 1982, pp.213-214.
181. Feder, 1983, p.94.
182. Cited in Feder, 1983, pp.93-94.
183. Alejandro Melchor, also often described as a "technocrat", was educated at the US Naval Academy at Annapolis. He enjoyed a high-profile in Washington and could probably be best understood as a representative of the US inside the Marcos Cabinet (Bonner, 1988, pp.109-110' 439-444).
184. Bello et al (1982) and Wurfel (1988, pp.192, 238-41, 254-55) followed the World Bank in using the term "technocrat" in this erroneous fashion.
185. Those technocrats who maintained powerful positions under Marcos, like Sicat, were generally supported by institutions like the World Bank and demonstrated no interest in redistributive reforms.
186. Interview, Manuel Lopez, Industrial Relations Division Director, Dole Philippines, 8 May 1989. Juan Ponce Enrile, working with the Reina law firm, acted as Dole's lawyer.
187. Interview Philip Juico (16 August 1989), who worked for Tanco first in the private sector and then in government.
188. GO47, 27 May 1974.
189. Luzon [LUSSA], 1982, p.301.
190. Interview with ANAWIM, Sto Tomas, 10 May 1989.
191. Marsman management stated that 108 hectares of the land her been planted to Cavendish since 1978, and Nova Vista was officially purchased by MEPI in 1988. Interview, Ferdinand Gonzaga, Manager Financial Services, MEPI. By 1989, Nova Vista was reported as having 194 hectares (DAR, 20 March 1989).
192. Ongpin, who had started his career with Procter and Gamble and moved on to the prestigious accounting and auditing firm SyCip Gorres and Velayo (SGV), was Marcos' Minister for Commerce and Industry.
193. The most complete documentation is Alternative Forum for Research in Mindanao [AFRIM], 1986. Guthrie was acquired by the Malaysian state-owned firm Permodalan Nasional Berhad in September 1981. The plantation project was financed in part by loans from the British state-owned Commonwealth Development Corporation and the World Bank's International Finance Corporation.
194. Estrella, Department Memorandum No. 15 Series 1973.
195. In descending order from highest number of recipients of CLTs, Nueva Ecija with some 40,000, followed by 12,000 or less in Camarines Sur, Leyte, Tarlac, Pangasinan, Pampanga, Iloilo, Isabela and Cagayan. Takigawa, 1974, p.25.
196. Kerkvliet, 1979, p.127.
197. Cited in Takigawa, 1974, p.72.
198. Figures are in constant 1978 prices. US Arms Control and Disarmament Agency, 1982, p.73.
199. Bello, 1987, p.30.
200. Bello, 1987, pp.33-34; Kessler, 1989, pp.124-126.
201. Bello, 1987, pp.36-39.
202. Kessler, 1989, pp.144-145.
203. Marcos, LOI No.52, 17 January 1973.
204. Takigawa, 1974, p.11, 72. He also said that day-time judges in the local courts worked in the evenings as lawyers for landlord families.

205. The 16 *haciendas* were sequestered by the Presidential Commission on Good Government by April 1987 (B. Aquino, 1987, pp.205–06). The other holdings were reported in Kerkvliet, 1979, p.121.
206. Sullivan to State, 29 December 1975. While the Embassy expected him to publish this story, omitted from his public presentation in Manila at the time, Wurfel's (1977) published account of this research made no mention of the case.
207. See B. Aquino, 1987 and Bonner, 1988.
208. Fegan, 1982, p.4. While civil liberties were suspended under martial law, leading to arbitrary arrests and assassinations of peasant and worker activists, landlords had ample freedom to use the trappings of the legal system to modify or change land reform policy.
209. Ofreneo, 1980, p.66. By framing their name as being 'for' agrarian reform they could claim a non-oppositional stance, while their acronym revealed their real purpose.
210. DAR Memorandum, January 9, 1973. José Medina (1975, p.8) also documented landlord resistance.
211. Harkin, 1975, pp.5–6. Also see Takigawa, 1974, pp.64–70, who documented the mushrooming numbers of tenant evictions after the reform was launched.
212. Fegan, 1982, p.4.
213. Interview, Agrarian Reform Technician, Region 2, March 1989.
214. Richter, 1982, p.64.
215. Harkin, 1975, pp.5–10.
216. MAR, 1981, list of all claims approved by the Land Bank through 1981. Even this figure may hide the fact that fewer families were involved, since it is impossible to distinguish claims by family. By 1981, of all lands approved by the Land Bank for purchase, those of 20 hectares and above totalled a mere 132,212 hectares. This represented 28 per cent of all claims and 62 per cent of the whole area approved for compensation by that year.
217. See Chapter 1, Table 1.9.
218. See Chapter 3, section 3.4.5.
219. Estrella's letter was dated 2 March 1967. José Cojuangco II replied on 14 April 1967 stating, 'it was doubtful whether the Central Bank had the power to impose that condition which was so alien to its function of stabilizing the country's monetary System.' Cited in the Manila Regional Trial Court's 'Decision' Civil Case no. 131654.
220. The Court record, however, states that on 5 May 1977 Central Bank Governor Gregorio S. Licaros wrote to the heirs of the late José Cojuangco II requesting information on action taken to distribute the *hacienda*. On 23 May 1978, Under-Secretary Ernesto V. Valdez of the Ministry of Agrarian Reform wrote another letter asking the heirs what had been done to implement the resolution. The record makes no mention of another letter from the Central Bank before the elections for the Interim Batasan held on 7 April 1978, though there may well have been one. The Cojuangco family's reply came in the form of a letter from TADECO vice-president and widow of the late Don Pépé, Demetria S. Cojuangco, dated 22 June 1978 and addressed to Deputy Minister Valdez. She stated that it was 'extremely unwarranted to make us account for the fulfilment of a condition that cannot be enforced.' Cited in the Manila Regional Trial Court's 'Decision' Civil Case no. 131654.
221. The case was filed on 7 May 1980.
222. Interview, V. Francisco Varua, Vice-President for Marketing, José Cojuangco & Sons, 31 July 1989. Judge Pardo's decision was actually dated 2 December 1985, the same day that General Fabian Ver, Marcos' chief of staff, was cleared of all charges in connection with the assassination of Benigno Aquino. The Court fixed 'just compensation' at P3,988,000.00 (or P620.11 per ha.), the price paid for the land as recorded with the Register of Deeds almost 30 years earlier, when the peso was worth ten times its 1985 equivalent.
223. See Chapter 10.
224. On Cojuangco's presence, see Bonner, 1988, p.468.
225. The split began when José Cojuangco II acquired Hacienda Luisita with the help of his son-

in-law, Benigno Aquino (see Chapter 3, section 3.4.5). It apparently came to a head with the family's acquisition of the First United Bank in the early 1960s.

226. Tai, 1974, p.297, citing *NYT* (12 April 1968, p.14).

227. Interview, José Romero, former chairman Philippine Coconut Authority (1987-89), 21 September 1989. Romero stated that former PCA chairman Fritz Gemperle got Cojuangco interested.

228. According to Romero (Interview, 21 September 1989), it was Senator and coconut landowner Emmanuel Pelaez who established contact with Ian Freemont. Freemont had worked on the development of the 'Mawa' hybrid (crossing the Malayan Dwarf with the West Africa Tall) in West Africa. Pelaez, as chairman of the Senate Science and Technology Committee, secured French funding for Freemont to visit the Philippines, where he was introduced to Gemperle who then introduced him to Cojuangco.

229. Marcos, Memorandum, 25 November 1972.

230. Interview with Narciso V. Villapando, former Director of the Bureau of Lands, 18 July 1989. No record of the LOI was available. When questioned on records dealing with the transfer, Villapando said that shortly after he left the Bureau in 1986 there was a fire in his office which consumed all the records. Cojuangco's wife was Gretchen Oppen.

231. Constitution, 1973, Article XIV, Section 11, allowed only the lease of public lands to corporations.

232. RA 926 (20 June 1953) authorized the President to convey lands and other property in payment of landed estates acquired by the government.

233. Villareal, 1987.

234. PD 582, 14 November 1974.

235. Earlier the Central Bank had declared that commercial banks must have a paid-up capital of P100 million, an amount that the José Cojuangco family could not muster under the conditions of martial law. José Romero (Interview, 21 September 1989) claimed, however, that they were paid handsomely for their bank.

236. Tiglao, 1981; Luzon [LUSSA], 1982; Hawes, 1987; Tadem, 1986.

237. On both monopolies see James Boyce, forthcoming.

238. Interview, Alfredo A. Alog, Isabela Provincial Agrarian Reform Officer, 22 June 1989. Tabacalera's official corporate history says that at the time of the sale the estate totalled 4,500 hectares (Raventos, 1981, p.299). However, 3,300 hectares had already been purchased under the Landed Estates programme in 1958. When questioned, Alog said, 'There has been a hitch in the titling process. The mother title was lost. It is in the process of reconstitution through a judicial process.' Asked why this process had still not been completed 30 years after government purchase, Alog replied, 'The process began in 1986'.

239. This account is based on Raventos, 1981, pp.299-300 and confirmed by Labayen (11 March 1982). Tabacalara retained 150 hectares in perpetuity to maintain its tobacco-buying activities.

240. Dialogue of the Hacienda Farmers with Senator José W. Diokno (29 August 1980). Records of this struggle are in the archives of Bishop Purugganan, Diocese of Ilagan, Isabela province.

241. ANCA Corporation, Articles of Incorporation, 1 April 1980. Other nominal shareholders were Jesus M. Manalastas, Leo J. Palma, Felino M. Ganal and Cezar Tadeo P. Hilado. Romero (Interview, 21 September 1989) said that Carag was formerly with Litton Mills and involved in both textiles and sugar. Their certificate of deposit for the P9 million paid up capital was issued by Cojuangco's United Coconut Planters Bank.

242. Bonner (1988, p.468) reported Diaz as one of the 12 men present when Marcos decided to declare martial law. In his exposé on Marcos, Mijares (1976, p.209) mentioned Diaz as being in league with Major-General Fabian C. Ver, chief of the Presidential Security Command, in smuggling luxury goods into the country.

243. ANCA-Priests' Assembly Dialogue with Cojuangco, Carag, Diaz, 15 December 1980.

244. This account from Diokno (29 August 1980), 'Dialogue'.

245. *Courier*, Social Action Center Diocese of Ilagan, selected issues 1981.

246. Diokno (29 August 1980) 'Dialogue'.

247. ANCA-Priests' Assembly Dialogue with Cojuangco, Carag, Diaz (15 December 1980).

248. Labayen Minutes, MAR, 11 March 1982.

249. *Courier* (24 March 1981).

250. *Daily Express* (19 March 1981).

251. Pete Salgado, 'Trouble Stalks the Haciendas' *Courier* (22 March 1981).

252. Marcos, EO 778 and Letter of Instruction 1180-A.

253. This is calculated on the basis of what beneficiaries would have to pay for the land (Interview, Alfredo Alog, 22 June 1989) and it is assumed that Marcos ordered Cojuangco to be paid at least this much. However, DAR records in 1985 listed the price only as 'under negotiation'. Jovelina L. Serdan, Chair, DAR Committee on LBP Acquired Estates, stated that Cojuangco bought the land for P8 million and sold it to the government for P88 million (*PDI* 3 June 1989).

254. Interview, Bishop Purugganan, 20 June 1989. The latter figure is based on rumours that Cojuangco paid P7,000 per hectare for the land.

255. Cojuangco was able to gain control over 7,000 hectares of sugarland in Negros Occidental between 1975 and 1985 (McCoy, 1991, p.116,121).

256. Interviews with CLT holders, *barangay* officials and residents on the estates, 21 June 1989.

257. In 1971 to 1972 the government expropriated 10,600 hectares of farms of over 100 hectares under the Landed Estates Programme - an annual rate of 7,067 hectares. From September 1972 through 1981 the government approved the purchase of (though did not necessarily acquire) a total of 66,380 hectares of farms of over 100 hectares under the Landed Estates and OLT programmes - an annual rate of 6,987. However, they were not necessarily distributed. Data from MAR, 1981, list of owners and MAR, 1985.

258. 'Lansdale Team Report,' 1955, Pentagon Papers. See Chapter 3 above.

259. Apparently Prosterman had to rely on small amounts of funding from liberal foundations associated with the Democratic Party in the US. These included the Westport Fund, the Norcliff Fund, the Hearst Foundation, the WMM Foundation, the Edna McConnel Clark Foundation, the Curry Foundation and the Joyce Mertz-Gilmore Foundation (Prosterman and Riedinger, 1987, p.ix; Jeff Riedinger, in conversation with the author, 25 February 1989). For instance, in 1987 the Joyce Mertz-Gilmore Foundation distributed $37 million in grants, with almost a third donated to Carnegie Council on Ethics & International Affairs, and $65,000 to the University of Washington, presumably for Prosterman. They also funded such institutions as Freedom House ($55,000) which produced an annual 'index of democracy' (Prosterman and Riedinger, 1987, Chapter 1) used by Prosterman in his argument about the counterinsurgency potential of reform (Council on Foundations, Washington D.C.).

THE ANTI-MARCOS MOVEMENT AND AGRARIAN REFORM

5.1 Introduction

The roots of the Aquino government's agrarian reform policy can be traced to the competing interests and political orientations within the coalition that brought it to power in 1986. The coalition emerged during the two years of escalating protest that followed the assassination of Cory Aquino's husband, Marcos's chief political rival, Benigno 'Ninoy' Aquino, on 21 August 1983.[1] Agrarian reform was not a major point of contention in the debates among the anti-Marcos opposition between 1983 and 1986.

The plight of the poor and especially the rural poor had become so dire by the early 1980s that the entire anti-Marcos movement had to proclaim a commitment to establishing a more equitable economic and social structure. Thus no one in the opposition actually opposed agrarian reform and, when asked, even the most conservative agreed to endorse calls for 'effective land reform'. However, an examination of the competing interests and political orientations of those involved in the effort to overthrow Marcos reveals interesting differences among them, and sheds considerable light on subsequent policy decisions about agrarian reform.

5.2 National-Democrats outside the Aquino coalition

After the declaration of martial law in 1972, and until 1983, the national democratic movement had been the most consistent opponent to Marcos. This encompassed the underground Communist Party of the Philippines (CPP), its armed wing, the New People's Army and the National Democratic Front (NDF), an umbrella organization designed to organize non-communist forces into a united front under CPP direction. It also encompassed a wide array of legal 'sectoral' and 'cause-oriented' groups and individuals sympathetic to the national democratic programme outlined by the CPP.[2] Since the movement derived most of its support from the peasantry, it was also the most determined advocate of redistributive agrarian reform, pursuing a decidedly revolutionary approach. Marcos's failure to implement a significant agrarian reform programme ensured a fertile terrain for the growth of the national democratic movement. One of the reasons that Benigno Aquino chose to return to the country in 1983 was his fear of the mounting strength of the left and the armed peasant movement, and the decline of his own influence after three years of exile.[3]

By 1986, the NPA had about 20,000 combatants of which about half were fully armed.[4] The Communist Party and its army were active in at least 60 of the country's 73 provinces. However, the influence of the Party was much broader than indicated by the size of its army. At least 20 per cent of all *barrios*, or villages, were already organized by the end of the Marcos period.[5] The strength of the communist movement lay in its ability to provide security and services to peasants, while local political leaders and government troops often offered only insecurity and hardship. This is not to deny that, in some instances, NPA authority was brutally applied and peasant taxes exacted through coercion.[6] But these were the exception to the rule. The NPA was established as a political army and included in its work the implementation of land redistribution and rent reduction, as well as the provision of medical services and basic education to peasants.[7]

By the end of the Marcos years, the National Democratic Front was more of an idea, or a political programme, than an independent organizational reality.[8] Nevertheless, the Party's political programme for the NDF established guidelines for party activists to recruit sympathizers unwilling to adhere to the more stringent Party programme. The positions outlined on social reforms, such as land reform and Filipino nationalism, proved to be attractive to a wide cross-section of workers, peasants and urban middle class groups that opposed the Marcos regime. It was therefore possible to identify a significant 'national democratic trend' or 'movement' in the country, even if the NDF as an organization was little more than another name for a branch of the CPP, or for those of its sympathizers not fully integrated into the Party.

A possible exception was the unity established between the communists and Catholic and Protestant activists inspired by liberation theology. The Christians for National Liberation, which became a member organization of the NDF, represented a unique characteristic of the Philippine revolutionary movement. The CPP demonstrated a flexibility and accommodation with non-Communist traditions of protest, such as those found among the indigenous peoples, peasant, radical Christian, and Islamic movements, that was almost unheard of in other communist movements. It demonstrated a significant degree of pragmatism in the development of its strategy and tactics.

The national democrats' persistent efforts played a crucial role in weakening the Marcos regime. They also stimulated the emergence of legal rural and urban 'people's organizations' that openly called for a democratic form of government with a nationalist and equitable economic development strategy and an independent foreign policy. It is probably fair to say that they created the conditions for other legal movements to develop that would later present themselves as alternatives to the more radical communist-led movement. It is also probably fair to say that the national democrats' sectarianism and desire to dominate the coalitions in which they participated opened the space still further for non-communist and anti-communist organizations to develop. However, the national democrats demonstrated that the peasantry had a central role to play in any plan for national transformation and that agrarian reform had to be at the centre of such a plan.

The national democrats contributed directly and indirectly to shaping the initial programme of the coalition that put Aquino into power, especially in relation to agrarian reform and nationalist issues such as the future of the US bases. However, the decision of the CPP and the NDF, as well as the major national democratic legal alliance, BAYAN, to boycott the presidential elections in January 1986 ensured their exclusion from the coalition. It also rendered them impotent in influencing the coalition's ultimate political programme and subsequent events.[9]

5.3 Diokno and Tañada committed to nationalism and social reforms

The Aquino coalition was, in the end, an alliance between a wide spectrum of civilian opposition groups and a section of the AFP that became frustrated with Marcos' personal control of the military and his ineffectual prosecution of the war against the communists. The civilian groups that were to back Cory Aquino's challenge to Marcos in the presidential elections can essentially be divided into three trends: 'liberal–democrats', the 'social–democratic and non-communist Christian left', and 'conservative-reformists'.[10] Acting as a bridge between all three trends, and the national democratic movement as well, were two towering figures who had opposed Marcos from the moment he declared martial law.

Former Senators José W. Diokno and Lorenzo Tañada were committed nationalists and determined human rights advocates who, through years of opposition to Marcos, became increasingly convinced of the need for far-reaching social reforms. They served as father figures to the entire anti-Marcos movement. Their nationalism transcended the rhetorical version traditionally expounded by most Filipino politicians, since they were genuinely devoted to severing the ties of dependency on the US. Their nationalist positions were combined with a basic commitment to social reform. This distinguished them from elite nationalists like Claro M. Recto, and economic nationalists like Alejandro Lichauco who either ignored or overtly opposed redistributive agrarian reform.[11]

It is not surprising that in the months following the Aquino assassination, Diokno and Tañada emerged as leaders of the first alliance that aimed to unite the 'cause-oriented' peoples' organizations of various political trends into a broad anti-Marcos coalition. This was the 'Justice for Aquino, Justice for All' (JAJA) movement. They would go on to play an important role in 1984 in launching a successor organization, the Coalition for the Restoration of Democracy (CORD), and, in 1985, in attempting (abortively) to establish BAYAN as the undisputed centre of the entire anti-Marcos opposition.[12]

Their commitment to liberal democratic ideals of human rights and representative government appealed to those in the elite who had opposed Marcos on these grounds. Their determination to rely on the burgeoning grass-roots

169

G

organizations rather than traditional political parties, and to link opposition to Marcos to demands for basic reforms, appealed to the national democrats, the social democrats and the Christian left alike.

During much of his career, Tañada had been opposed to redistributive reform, very much in the tradition of nationalists like Recto.[13] However, in the 1980s he decided to back organizations like BAYAN that were firmly committed to redistributive reform. Diokno, a lawyer, who had been imprisoned during the first two years of martial law, was a vocal advocate of an essentially liberal approach to agrarian reform. His views on reform were most evident in his legal activities in defence of peasants attempting to gain land during the Marcos years.[14] However, while both Diokno and Tañada exercised a profound influence on events between August 1983 and February 1986, their influence within the Aquino coalition after it came to power would be marginalized, particularly by the conservative reformists.

5.4 Liberal-Democrats and passive support for agrarian reform

The liberal-democrats also began organizing against Marcos immediately after the declaration of martial law in 1972. They were mainly lawyers, leading figures from the traditional political parties and the Protestant church which, unlike the Catholic hierarchy, had taken a stand against Marcos almost from the inception of martial law. They called for the restoration of basic civil liberties and democratic government institutions and opposed human rights violations by the military and paramilitary groups under Marcos. They also advocated, to varying degrees, an independent foreign policy, particularly in relation to the United States. Their stance on basic social and economic reforms was even more varied.

Most of the liberal-democrats did not share Diokno's views on social reform and were only passively supportive of agrarian reform. These included politicians like Jovito Salonga, former Senator, Liberal Party leader and lay Protestant minister; Aquilino Pimentel, founder of the Philippine Democratic Party (PDP) in Mindanao; Rogaciano Mercado, a journalist and member of the National Union for Civil Liberties; and Herherson T. Alvarez, anti-Marcos activist and a founder of the Ninoy Aquino Movement while in exile in the United States. Human rights lawyers like Rene Saguisag also fell within this category. Agapito 'Butz' Aquino, a businessman, was a late-comer to this group, becoming active only after his brother's assassination. Other liberal-democrats proved to be opposed to redistributive agrarian reform, most notably the human rights lawyer Joker Arroyo.

The liberal-democrats would play an important role in the Aquino campaign. Some, together with Diokno and Tañada, became the 'democratic conscience' of the Aquino coalition as it headed into the elections and the first year of government. Many would probably have supported a liberal approach to agrarian reform, but there were none, not even Aquino's first Minister of Agrarian Reform Heherson Alvarez, who were prepared to champion such an approach. This was reminiscent of the 1950s, when nationalists like Claro Recto never took up redistributive reform as part of their cause.

5.5 Social-Democrats and agrarian reform

The most vocal advocates of the liberal approach to reform within the Aquino coalition were those individuals and people's organizations that are best described as the 'social-democratic and non-communist Christian left'. Social democracy as a political current remains rather ill-defined and embryonic in the Philippines.[15] A wide array of individuals and organizations fall into this category.

The most conservative element among the 'social-democrats' had its roots in the Jesuit Order. The origins of this trend lay more in Christian Democracy than European-style social democracy. In the pre-Marcos years this trend was represented by former Senator Raul Manglapus's Christian Social Movement, which before martial law was active notably through such groups as Student Catholic Action. In the late 1960s and throughout the early martial law years, the fiercely anti-communist Jesuit, Fr. José Blanco, was its main reference point.[16] This group never went beyond the endorsement of the kind of conservative agrarian reform advocated by Manglapus during the Macapagal administration.[17] Figures such as Emmanuel Soriano, who would play a major role in Aquino's campaign, were associated with this trend.

In 1987, a reformed Partido Demokratiko Soyalista ng Pilipinas (PDSP - Philippine Social Democratic Party), led by Norberto Gonzales, proclaimed its support for an essentially liberal approach to agrarian reform. The PDSP claimed lineage with a clandestine 'cadre' social-democratic organization during the Marcos years, which had focused on a strategy of urban insurrection.[18] It actively supported the Aquino campaign, and at its National Congress of Reorganization in December 1987 included the 'full and accelerated implementation of a comprehensive agrarian reform program' in its 'Programme of Action for 1987-1991'.[19]

The more radical social-democrats, who prefer to be considered as 'democratic socialists', were represented by a group of intellectuals known as the 'Independent Caucus'. This went on to form BISIG.[20] Associated with this group was a broader nationalist organization known as KAAKBAY, in which Diokno also participated. In its statement of support for Aquino, KAAKBAY demanded from the new government, 'the proclamation of a genuine land reform program'.[21] Together, the social-democrats and Christian left influenced a large number of people's organizations, but while their presence in the peasant sector was not insignificant, their urban origins and orientation made them far less influential than the national democrats. The social-democrats played an important role in mobilizing urban people's organizations to support the Aquino campaign, but had very little influence over its political orientation. Many joined the lower echelons of the new government, hoping to influence its policy on such issues as agrarian reform.

5.6 Conservative reformists take the lead

At the heart of what was to become the Aquino coalition were the 'conservative reformists', who were either enthusiastic advocates or passive supporters of a conservative approach to agrarian reform. They included business leaders, traditional politicians, and most of the hierarchy of the Catholic Church and its associated lay organizations. Some among them, like the Aquino-José Cojuangco clan, were persecuted (though not financially ruined) by Marcos and were active in the opposition movement at home and abroad from the beginning of martial law. Most, however, acquiesced in martial law until the late 1970s or early 1980s, when the economy fell into crisis. A notable example was Salvador Laurel, who had cooperated with Marcos after the declaration of martial law and ran for elections under the Marcos KBL banner as late as 1978. He left the 'strong-man's party' only in 1979 when he formed the United Nationalist Democratic Organization (UNIDO), an electorally-oriented conservative alliance of traditional political parties. Another was Vicente Paterno, who served as Marcos' Trade and Industry Minister until 1982, leaving the KBL only in 1983.

The conservative reformists were most concerned with ensuring a peaceful succession to Marcos and an end to the monopolization of economic opportunities by Ferdinand and Imelda's cronies. They wanted to restore government legitimacy so that they could prosecute the war against the communist movement more effectively and restore business confidence to attract foreign investment. While some became more critical of the United States as it continued to provide support to the Marcos regime, all of them sought to win US support for a successor government.[22]

Many of these individuals or their families owned or controlled, through agribusiness corporations, significant tracts of land. This was the case for Cory Aquino herself, her brother José 'Peping' Cojuangco and her brother-in-law, Ricardo 'Baby' Lopa, the three members of their clan most active in the opposition movement. While Aquino was personally close to some of the leading liberal-democrats, her ties to her paternal family, where she served on the boards of several family companies, seemed stronger as she adopted political positions in line with the conservative reformists. Also in this category were Chito Ayala, who operated vast export-oriented agricultural enterprises in Mindanao, and Ramon del Rosario Jr., former president of the Asian Savings Bank and Anscor Inc. His family owned the Philippine Investment and Management Corporation (PHINMA), managing traditional and modern plantations around the country. The conservative reformists also encompassed those politicians with more traditional agricultural holdings and operations, such as the Laurels, an old political clan whose provincial base was Batangas, and Ramon Mitra, who operated cattle ranches and logging concessions and had significant interests in the coconut sector.

Extremely influential among the conservative reformists were a group of businessmen relatively new to politics, whose opposition to Marcos began as economic crisis set in after 1981. Chief among them was Jaime V. Ongpin, whose brother Roberto was Marcos' sitting Trade and Industry Minister. Ongpin was president of Benguet Consolidated Mines, one of the country's premier mining enterprises, established by the Americans in 1903. Ongpin followed an educational and employment pattern similar to many Filipino business executives. Before joining Benguet in 1963, he studied Business Administration at the Jesuit-run Ateneo de Manila University, worked for the local branch of the US transnational corporation Procter and Gamble, and completed an MBA at Harvard Business School financed by a Fulbright scholarship and a scholarship from the Asia Foundation, which remained active in the Philippines after its initial role in the 1950s.[23]

Ongpin had been one of the first in the business community to criticize the Marcos government after martial law was lifted in 1981. In two articles, he attacked the government for rescuing insolvent firms belonging to Marcos' closest associates and is credited with having given the word 'crony' a new meaning in the Philippines. Ongpin seemed to be appealing not only to fellow Philippine businessmen to take a stand against Marcos and his cronies, but also to the international financial community. He wanted to demonstrate that there were businessmen who agreed with IMF and World Bank strategies. His criticisms came just a year after the World Bank had begun a structural adjustment programme in the country that was focused on curbing the power of Marcos cronies.[24] Ongpin probably decided to publish his articles in the *Asian Wall Street Journal* and *Fortune Magazine* partly for fear they would not be published at home, and partly to ensure that they would have the maximum impact abroad.[25]

In 1982 Ongpin took up a seat on the Board of the newly formed Makati Business Club (MBC), along with Vicente Paterno, political aspirant José Romero, and one of the nation's wealthiest businessmen, Enrique Zobel. The MBC was one of the first organizations in Makati, Manila's modern financial district, to take a critical stand toward Marcos.[26] Paterno, who had been a vocal defender of martial law and was Marcos' Minister of Trade and Industry before Bobby Ongpin, was still a member of the KBL at the time. Zobel had also been a long-time supporter of Marcos.

MBC members' interest in the agricultural sector was centred on the promotion of agribusiness enterprises for export-oriented production. Zobel's transnational business empire included a significant agribusiness component. Ongpin's experience with agriculture began with a study of modern cattle ranching in the Philippines which he pursued at Harvard, where he became a strong advocate of an agribusiness-led strategy of rural development. While not yet talking in terms of agrarian reform, this agribusiness orientation would form the basis of his advocacy of the conservative approach later on.

An important part of the conservative reformist opposition that emerged in the early 1980s came from within the Catholic Church. While many priests and nuns had become involved in people's organizations associated with the national, liberal, and social democrats during the 1970s, the most powerful sectors of the

Church were closest to the business community. Throughout much of the martial law period, Cardinal Sin had expounded a policy of 'critical collaboration' with the Marcos regime.[27]

It might also be said that Marcos had his own policy of 'critical collaboration' with the Catholic Church, realising that it was an alternative power base in society. He promoted the Iglesia ni Kristo and his years of martial law saw the expansion of the influence of Evangelical churches, many of which had connections in the United States.[28] When the Church hierarchy became involved with the conservative reformist opposition in the early 1980s, it probably had several objectives. It was in its interest to encourage the opposition both to thwart the rising influence of evangelical movements in society and in the military and to pre-empt the increasing defection of its flock to the national democratic movement. The Vatican, which had shifted decidedly to the right in the early 1980s after the election of John Paul II, was pressuring Filipino bishops to move their Church away from the national democratic movement.[29]

The Bishops Businessmen's Conference for Human Development (BBC), which was established at about the same time as the MBC, also played an important role leading up to the formation of the Aquino coalition. This organization included advocates of both conservative and liberal approaches to agrarian reform. Co-Chairman Vicente Jayme, a noted banker and president of the Private Development Corporation of the Philippines (PDCP), was typical of the conservative majority in the BBC.[30] José Concepcion, also part of the conservative majority, was head of Republic Flour Mills and chaired the newly resuscitated National Movement for Free Elections (NAMFREL), which had been so active in the Magsaysay election in the 1950s.[31] Mahar Mangahas, a professional economist, had long been an advocate of the liberal approach to reform and secured occasional endorsements from the BBC. Christian Monsod, who had worked for the World Bank, probably fell somewhere between the two.[32]

With the mushrooming of popular protests in the weeks following the assassination of Ninoy Aquino, these business and Church-based groups launched a concerted effort to seize the initiative from the more radical organizations leading the demonstrations in the streets. The first Makati rally was organized on 16 September 1983 by the Alliance of Makati Associations (AMA), in which the MBC figured prominently.[33] At about the same time Cardinal Sin and the BBC called for 'national reconciliation' 'based on truth, justice, freedom and faith', a call that was taken up by the Businessmen's Committee on National Reconciliation.[34] During these weeks the Church and the BBC backed the establishment of an anti-Marcos magazine, *Veritas*, linked to the Church-sponsored radio station of the same name. This was to play a central role in the final effort to push out Marcos. Its management board included Jayme, Ongpin, Paterno, Concepcion and Santi Dumlao, an executive at del Rosario's PHINMA, who had attended the Harvard Business School with Ongpin.[35]

In January 1984, the conservative reformists launched their first major effort to take the lead in the anti-Marcos popular movement. In doing so they made one of their first declarations in support of agrarian reform. Representatives of the underground left had contacted Agapito 'Butz' Aquino, Cory's brother-in-law, suggesting that he initiate a congress of the entire left-right spectrum of the anti-Marcos opposition, and promising the support of their organizations.[36] The meeting, ambitiously called the Congress of the Filipino People (Kongreso ng Mamamayang Pilipino - KOMPIL), which was formally initiated by the Alliance of Makati Associations and Butz Aquino's August Twenty-One Movement, brought together some 2,300 delegates from every tendency within the opposition to attempt to arrive at a united opposition programme.

The left hoped to secure a decision to boycott participation in elections to Marcos' rubber-stamp parliament, the Batasang Pambansa, to take place the following May. A week before the congress, Dr. Alfredo Bengzon, director of Medical City, and Emmanuel Soriano, former President of the University of the Philippines, held a meeting among key personalities in the conservative opposition. They decided to participate in the elections if Marcos met certain conditions, and they succeeded in winning KOMPIL support for their position.[37] The KOMPIL 'Primer' included as part of its 'United Front Platform' a general endorsement of agrarian reform:

> An effective land reform program will be pursued, with attention to the required supportive technologies so that maximum benefit will accrue to the farmers.[38]

The conservative reformists endorsed land reform during this period in an attempt to win over the people's organizations. However, since the document mentioned only an 'effective' land reform, such a statement could appeal both to those advocating a liberal redistributive reform, who felt that redistribution of land had to be accompanied by ancillary support services, as well as those promoting a conservative approach, who wanted to minimize the focus on 'redistributive' measures by specifying only means to increase productivity. The decision reached on possible participation in the elections and the choice of leaders selected by the Congress reflected the dominance of the conservative reformists.[39]

Marcos did not respond to any of their conditions, but Corazon Aquino, Salvador Laurel, business leader Jaime Ongpin and other leaders of the conservative opposition decided nonetheless to support participation in the elections. In this they were urged on by Catholic leader Cardinal Jaime Sin and US officials.[40] The opposition won one-third of the seats, a proportion that Marcos had declared as acceptable before the count was even finished.[41] Salvador Laurel's UNIDO emerged as the major opposition group within the *Batasan*.

5.7 The 'facilitators' behind the Aquino campaign

Shortly after the elections, Soriano and Fr. Joaquin Bernas, Jesuit provincial superior and president of Ateneo de Manila University, organized a small informal group of politicians and businessmen. This would come to be known as the 'Wednesday Group' and, later, as the 'Facilitators'. While it was not apparent at the time, nor has it been widely acknowledged since, this group emerged as a direct challenge to Salvador Laurel's leadership of the conservative opposition.

Bernas's role would prove to be pivotal in the emergence of the Aquino coalition. There was an intimate connection between the conservative reformists in the business community and the Jesuit Order. Like Ongpin, many in the business community started their careers as students at the Jesuit-run Ateneo. Ongpin was appointed to the Board of Trustees of Ateneo in 1984. Ateneo's Institute of Philippine Culture, under the American Fr. Frank Lynch, had played a central role in studies on land reform in the 1960s through the early years of martial law, but had generally limited its studies to government and USAID funded projects.[42] Bernas saw the value of keeping agrarian reform on the opposition agenda, and, while he demonstrated an openness to the liberal approach, he frequently appeared willing to defer to the advocates of conservative reform.

According to Bernas, one of the early meetings of the 'Facilitators', which included among others the agribusiness magnate 'Chito' Ayala, decided to form a new businessmen's organization to be called Manindigan ('Take a Stand').[43] Manindigan included Ongpin, del Rosario, Soriano, Bengzon, Bernas and Narcisa Escaler, who had worked with Ongpin at Benguet. They acted later as a kind of 'cadre' group for Aquino's campaign within the business community. However, it appears that no candidate had yet been selected to field against Marcos if he were to call a snap presidential election. It was to this problem that the Facilitators turned their attention.

In late May 1984 the Facilitators began discussing a 'fast track' method to select a single opposition candidate to challenge Marcos. They decided to establish a 'Convenors Group' (CG), to be made up of prominent individuals capable of calling together the most important potential presidential candidates, or 'Presidential Standard Bearers', with the objective of getting them to agree to a common programme and method of choosing a single candidate to challenge Marcos. Three 'convenors' were chosen: Corazon Aquino, who had emerged as the most popular among the conservative reformists; Jaime Ongpin, considered to hold the respect of the domestic and foreign business community; and Lorenzo Tañada, chosen to legitimize the effort to the more radical peoples' organizations. In attendance, as well as the regulars like Bernas, del Rosario, Soriano and Bengzon, were businessman, Aquino brother-in-law Ricardo Lopa - clearly to look after the José Cojuangco family interests - and Bobby Tañada, evidently invited to help secure the participation of his father. These five would act as the 'staff' of the Convenors Group and would later play a pivotal role in the campaign to elect Cory Aquino.[44]

Aquino, Ongpin and Tañada together with their 'staff' met at the Cojuangco family's corporate headquarters in Makati on 13 November 1986. During the next two weeks they drew up a list of 11 potential presidential candidates and a draft 'Declaration of Unity', which was presented to the eleven on 16 December.[45] The Declaration was clearly designed to win the support of the mass movement and included a programme more radical than that advanced in the KOMPIL primer.

The Declaration stated that, 'An effective land reform program truly beneficial to the underprivileged will be vigorously and honestly pursued'.[46] However, there was a tension in its language which reflected two distinct attitudes toward property, later to emerge as a conflict between the conservative and liberal approaches to agrarian reform. On the one hand it asserted that, 'Social structures that perpetuate the oppression of the poor and the dispossessed will be eliminated' and professed:

[A] belief that ownership of the principal means of production must be diffused and income equitably distributed to promote development, alleviate poverty and ensure the rational utilization of resources.[47]

These statements could form the basis of a liberal redistributive reform, if the 'diffusion' of ownership is understood as redistribution. However, in explaining what was meant by this 'belief', the Declaration left the door open to an essentially conservative approach to agrarian reform:

This means that ownership is stewardship; that material wealth is not just for the welfare of the owner but also for the welfare of all; that the accumulation of profit must not ignore the requirements of social justice; that ostentatious display of wealth is to be deplored; and that the use of resources must be for the benefit of all, especially the underprivileged.

What the Declaration offered with one hand it removed with the other, much as would be done later in drawing up a new Constitution and an agrarian reform programme. The statement that ownership of the means of production must be diffused, was immediately qualified by saying that 'ownership is stewardship'. It did not say that material wealth must be *redistributed*, but rather that its ownership must serve the 'welfare' of all. The Declaration stated that a development course would be pursued to enhance, 'equity in the use of resources and in the distribution of the *fruits* of development'. Taken together, these statements essentially advocated the idea that property has a 'social function', an idea that would later be incorporated in the Aquino government's agrarian reform law.[48] In many Latin American agrarian reform programmes, such a notion was used as an 'anti-reformist tool' to justify the expropriation of only a few estates and full compensation to owners in cash. Ernest Feder argued that the concept focused attention only on the use of land and diverted it from the injustices of the sharply unequal distribution of land. It was often employed, he said, to argue that it is unjust to expropriate land from those of the elite who use it productively.[49]

By 26 December, all the presidential hopefuls, except Salvador Laurel and Eva Kalaw of UNIDO, signed the Declaration of Unity.[50] Laurel and Kalaw both refused to sign, partly because the Declaration included a provision arguing for the removal of US bases, but perhaps even more importantly because they felt that UNIDO, an essentially traditional political party, had the right to lead the opposition into an election.[51] Interestingly, the Facilitators' initial position on the US bases had been much more conservative and later Aquino would revert to the conservative position.[52]

Through this process by early 1985 the Convenor Group emerged as an alternative centre to Salvador Laurel and his UNIDO party in the conservative opposition. Laurel had hoped to take the mantle of the opposition through the UNIDO-initiated National Unification Committee (NUC), which was an alliance of traditional political parties. By January 1985, the Convenors, with the Facilitators behind them, were negotiating with the NUC almost as equals, and in the process minimizing the role of the grass-roots people's organizations. In response, the Diokno-Tañada-led CORD launched a new enterprise to reconstitute the alliance of grass-roots organizations into a more disciplined body capable of capturing the initiative from the elite politicians. This was the Bagong Alyansang Makabayan (BAYAN - New Patriotic Federation), which between March and May 1985 attempted once again to unite the opposition behind a more radical and nationalist orientation. Ongpin and others, supported by the Facilitators, participated. Whether such an agglomeration of diverse interests could ever have been consolidated within one organization under a unified leadership cannot be known, but the attempt to form BAYAN as a coalition was undermined when the national democrats moved to seize the leadership by force of numbers. [53] This provided an excuse for figures like Ongpin to turn away from the grass-roots movement and concentrate on their own agenda. Basic social reforms like agrarian reform were not high on that agenda.

5.8 The armed forces and the Aquino coalition

The Convenors and Facilitators did not limit their attention to civilian politicians and the grass-roots movement. As early as May 1985, Ongpin contacted the Reform the Armed Forces Movement (RAM), a group of young officers in the AFP whose later rebellion would spark the final downfall of the Marcos regime. Their rebellion ensured the military, another advocate of the conservative approach to reform, an important place in the coalition behind the new government. Ongpin was able to set up a meeting with Captain Rex Robles, one of the most outspoken in RAM, through retired Captain Antonio O. Tansingco, who was an executive at an affiliate of Ongpin's Benguet Corporation.[54] At about the same time, Pentagon representatives conducted their first official meeting with RAM officers.[55]

The RAM was formally organized in 1984 by a group of about 15 officers, most of whom were graduates in the Class of 1971 at the Philippine Military Academy (PMA), the Philippine version of West Point. It emerged under the wing of Defence Minister Juan Ponce Enrile, who had been increasingly eclipsed after Marcos appointed General Fabian Ver as Chief of Staff in 1981. Enrile and

Ramos represented what Marcos perceived to be a growing threat from the military, whose political ambitions to succeed him were already evident as early as 1981.[56] The RAM officers, led by Col. Gregorio Honasan, served as Enrile's personal faction to counter his growing isolation in the Marcos administration. They received further encouragement from General Fidel Ramos, who had also been increasingly marginalized by Marcos and Ver. The 'RAM Boys', as they would later be known, exploited growing factionalism and discontent within the armed forces.

By the 1980s, PMA graduates serving in the AFP became disillusioned with Marcos. They disliked the networks of patronage that Marcos had set up within the armed forces in order to ensure their loyalty to Malacañang, and which led to the promotion of politically appointed officers rather than those trained at the PMA. They were also dissatisfied with Marcos' direction of the counterinsurgency campaign against the CPP/NPA, where they felt that officers and enlisted men on the front lines were not accorded the salaries, equipment and support needed to carry out the war effectively. On both counts they had considerable sympathy from the Pentagon.[57] While the 'RAM Boys' organized within the military around a platform of reform, they were themselves very much the product of Marcos' martial law regime.

The RAM has often been portrayed as a group of 'reform-minded', 'professional' soldiers, who were devoted to clean government and a modern and efficient military establishment.[58] In reality, the core of RAM were a group of officers who had spent their formative years in military intelligence as the jailers and torturers of political prisoners.[59] The AFP was allocated enormous leeway to suppress any form of opposition to the government.[60] Under Marcos, the AFP became increasingly politicized, with the military assuming extensive roles in the administration of civil society.[61] Leaders of RAM, like Col. Honasan and his deputy Col. Red Kapunan, had positions in government controlled corporations and were paid out of Enrile's share of coconut monopoly funds.[62] The US provided both political and financial support to the movement as a means to pressure Marcos to institute reforms.[63] By 1985, RAM and Enrile were planning to overthrow Marcos through a coup d'état. Their primary objective was to seize power, but there is no evidence that they intended to use such power to institute social reforms.

There is no indication that the RAM, or any other group within the armed forces, supported redistributive agrarian reform as part of an effort to defeat the revolutionary movement. They generally subscribed to the counterinsurgency strategy outlined during the Marcos years. They simply felt that it was never properly implemented. They wanted what Marcos had always promised and what the US had been prescribing: an 'integrated' approach that combined military and psychological warfare, the expansion of local government institutions cooperative with the military, and the extension of economic development programmes in AFP-controlled regions. The young officers wanted the military to have unbridled authority over this process, and believed that they should have a say in who would lead them. Redistributive reform was not set out as an option.[64]

Ongpin arranged at least three meetings between RAM officers and the businessmen and politicians most closely involved with the Aquino campaign. The first meeting on 10 July 1985 took place at the officers' club in Camp Aguinaldo and included members of the MBC and the BBC.[65] The second meeting, on 1 August 1985, included businessmen, conservative Church representatives and liberal democrats.[66] A third meeting was also organized for the members of Manindigan.[67] In October Ongpin told a group of American executives that, 'The military reform movement is one of the most important developments in the Philippines today'. Cory Aquino provided a similar endorsement of the RAM on 1 October when speaking to an international business group in Singapore.[68]

Ongpin became an important fund-raiser for RAM and a bridge between them and the public before the events of February 1986. Aquino's brother, José Cojuangco, apparently organized his own links with RAM, meeting with Col. José Almonte shortly after Marcos called the snap elections. According to RAM officers, Cojuangco was informed of their coup plans and agreed to help by mobilizing support in Tarlac.[69] It seemed that the conservative reformists wanted to ensure their place in the post-Marcos era by whatever course was necessary. The US almost certainly encouraged the process through its overt support for both anti-Marcos initiatives.[70]

The Facilitators and Convenors also remained in contact with American officials in an effort to secure their endorsement and precipitate a break with Marcos.[71] Several of their group met regularly with US officials, especially after 1983. Both Ongpin and José Cojuangco were on good terms with the Embassy.[72] Concepcion's NAMFREL had received financial support from the US.[73] On 6 November 1985, former Assistant Secretary of State Richard Holbrooke met with Aquino, her brother José Cojuangco, Butz Aquino and supporters of Laurel, to urge them to integrate a firm stand against communism into their campaign and to soft-pedal their criticism of the US bases.[74]

By the time of the elections, the Aquino campaign had a team of US public relations experts working in Washington.[75] Robert Trent Jones Jr. had met Cory Aquino's family when he constructed the world class golf course on their Hacienda Luisita in the 1960s. He had lobbied unsuccessfully in Washington to get Ninoy Aquino released from prison in 1974. During the campaign he approached Secretary of State George Schultz and Democratic Senator Sam Nunn on Aquino's behalf.[76] William Overholt, vice-president of Bankers' Trust in Hong Kong, was an adviser to Mrs. Aquino's campaign policy committee, which was chaired by Ongpin.[77] Overholt would have been clearly aware of the political importance of agrarian reform to her campaign, as he had worked as a consultant for the Marcos reform in its early years and had written on the subject.[78] It is unlikely that any other American at this time was encouraging Aquino to endorse reform.

Marcos called for the snap presidential elections in an interview on American television on 3 November 1985. It is not clear how early the Facilitators had decided that Cory Aquino would be the best candidate to field against Marcos. However, by August 1985 it was no doubt clear to them that she was the only rival to Salvador Laurel capable of generating popular support, uniting the liberal and social democrats and the conservative reformists, and securing the support of Marcos critics in the US. Laurel only conceded to serve as Aquino's running-mate at the eleventh hour, but the campaign to elect her as president was already in full-swing by October 1985, even before Marcos announced the snap elections. On 22 October Aquino agreed that in the event of a snap presidential election she would run if a million signatures were collected on a petition asking her to do so. It was around this time that the anti-Marcos newspaper publisher Chino Roces launched the Cory Aquino Movement for President (CAMP).[79] Thus, in a move reminiscent of the launching of the Magsaysay Movement for President, Aquino was able to be parachuted into the race as a candidate of the 'centre' who was not closely linked to any of the traditional political parties.

5.9 The Aquino campaign and its feint toward agrarian reform

Jaime Ongpin acted as the unofficial campaign manager for Aquino - a job that he apparently began well before the campaign was officially under way. In the process he turned to the economist Bernardo Villegas, who would have an important influence on the shape of the Aquino coalition's economic programme and a crucial impact on the new government's stance on agrarian reform. Villegas and Ongpin were life-long friends, together first at Procter and Gamble, and then as fellow Fulbright-funded students at Harvard. They were both on the Makati Business Club Board after 1982, and in 1984 both were lecturing on behalf of the MBC's Speakers Bureau. Villegas represented important interests within the business community as well as the right-wing of the Catholic Church.

During the Aquino campaign and the early years of the new government, Villegas was an influential advocate of the conservative approach to agrarian reform, sometimes drawing on Catholic doctrine to justify his position. He headed the influential Manila think-tank and school, the Centre for Research and Communications (CRC), which hosted the meeting between RAM and the businessmen of Manindigan. The CRC was established in 1967 as a project of the Southeast Asian Science Foundation. It was funded both by individuals and corporations in the domestic private sector, and foreign groups such as the German Christian Social Union's Hans Seidel Foundation.[80]

According to its own publicity brochure, the CRC drew its moral inspiration and its 'spiritual and doctrinal guidance' from Opus Dei,[81] a shadowy conservative movement within the Catholic Church which was made a personal prelature of Pope John Paul II shortly after his election in 1978.[82] Ever since its establishment in Spain in 1929, Opus Dei was known for its commitment to anti-communism and the promotion of the 'free-market'.[83] While the CRC proclaimed that the 'involvement of Opus Dei in CRC...is strictly in the sphere of ethics', Villegas was himself a member of Opus Dei, at least since his days at Harvard in the early 1960s.[84]

From about July through November 1985, Ongpin and Villegas launched a curious campaign to promote the potential of agribusiness investment in the Philippines. In July, in the midst of intensifying street protests and while he was making contacts with RAM, Ongpin found time to introduce Steve Lohr of the *New York Times* to a new Benguet Corporation joint venture, the Philippine Cocoa Estates Corporation. Managing the new corporation was Carlos Villa-Abrille, who had attended the first Ongpin session with RAM. The $2 million venture, co-financed by Sime Darby, had assembled 2,000 hectares in Davao on the southern island of Mindanao, and the plantation was to come into production in 1988. Ongpin commented, 'In my 25 years of business, I have never seen an investment that looks this attractive'. Lohr's subsequent article put across the intended message, 'Starting Over in Mindanao: Agribusiness is the New Hope for a Stagnant Economy'.[85]

On 1 October, Ongpin and Villegas organized a CRC seminar in Singapore for foreign investors, to which Aquino was invited. Ongpin told the audience how bullish he was on the prospects for expansion of agribusiness ventures in citrus and tropical fruits:

> Regardless of the unprecedented crisis conditions prevailing in the Philippines, selective opportunities remain which are exceptionally attractive, especially in non-traditional agribusiness...[86]

The seminar was evidently designed to introduce Aquino to the international financial community and to demonstrate that she had the backing of competent businessmen who would promote opportunities for foreign investment. Her talk on that occasion already sounded like an election speech. Interestingly, she told the representatives of international business that she based her confidence on four factors: 'first, the capacity of the opposition parties to unite; second, the electoral militancy of the awakened Filipino; third, the moral leadership of the Church; fourth, the reform movement in the military'.[87] This was not only an accurate prediction of events to come, but also a vivid portrait of her coalition.

Six days later, Villegas published an article in the *Wall Street Journal*, explaining his own vision of agrarian reform.[88] Referring to the well-known advocate of the 'open economy model', Hla Myint, Villegas called for the implementation of policies 'to encourage labour-intensive, export-oriented industries'.[89] His line of argument essentially followed the structural adjustment prescription advocated by World Bank missions to the country throughout the early 1980s. He called for strengthening existing small farmers, providing them with access to adequate credit, inputs and markets, a formula quite similar to that expounded by the Bank and the Marcos regime throughout the 1970s. Yet he added a new element.

Villegas provided the first glimpse of the emerging Aquino coalition's vision of agrarian reform. In a distinct departure from past government policy, he called for land reform in the sugar and coconut regions 'where the threat of social upheaval is directly correlated with poverty'. His model of reform was based on the 'Foodland' project that had been initiated in Negros Occidental in response to famine conditions that had set in after a rapid decline in international sugar prices. Here land reform was essentially a 'land-sharing scheme', where the starting point was not the landless worker but rather the 'well-to-do planter'. The programme involved 'providing planters with funding assistance for the cultivation of alternative crops' on the condition that the planter 'agree[s] to transfer a *portion* of his farm to his sugar workers'. Villegas summed up the approach:

> [A] partnership among well-to-do planters, private foundations, the government and the small farmers can be an effective antidote to insurgency and a long-term solution to rural development.

The crucial elements of the Villegas proposal encapsulated elements of the conservative approach that would characterize future government policy: land reform should be an essentially voluntary programme, it should involve only a limited portion of cultivated lands, and it should rely on existing landowners to take the lead in diversifying and modernizing crop production.

During her election campaign, Aquino made four major policy speeches, which appear to have been drafted mainly by Ongpin, Bernas and the other Facilitators. In two of the four speeches she claimed that her government would implement an invigorated land reform. Her first speech, outlining her economic programme, was delivered to an audience of 700 people organized by the Makati Business Club and the Management Association of the Philippines (MAP) at the Intercontinental Hotel in Makati on 6 January 1986. The main theme of this speech, initially drafted by Ongpin, was her commitment to rely primarily on the private sector to get the nation's economy back on track. However, within that context she said that she was not prepared to sacrifice 'social equity and justice'. She pronounced her commitment to land reform for the first time, and yet her statement remained general enough to allow the audience to apply their own definition of reform:

> We will review the allocation of our precious and limited arable land for domestic food crops and export crops. While we need export crops to generate foreign exchange, especially to pay the enormous debt that is Mr. Marcos's legacy to us, our first obligation is to provide for the basic food needs of our people. We are determined to implement a genuine land-reform program which will provide the beneficiaries of land reform with adequate credit and the marketing and technological support to enable them to become self-reliant and prosperous farmers.[90]

The emphasis here was on the productivity-enhancing components of agrarian reform, rather than redistribution.

A further hint of what Aquino, Ongpin and their supporters meant was provided when she said that, 'Labor has the inherent right to an equitable share in the fruits of the joint efforts of labor and capital'. This reflected the basic tension on agrarian reform among her supporters. Those who wanted liberal redistributive reform felt that tenants and farmworkers had a right to an equitable share of landed property, while those promoting a conservative approach believed it was sufficient to talk about an equitable share 'in the fruits' of production. Aquino promised consultation with all sectors including the farmers. She said that her government's response to 'the problem of unemployment and mass poverty' was to be 'an essential part of our response to the problem of insurgency'. In response to a question from the floor she attempted to lay to rest a previous statement about the communists that had worried her American supporters, saying, 'I would like to assure everybody here that I will not appoint a Communist to my cabinet'.[91] She held out hope to sugar and coconut planters excluded by the Marcos regime by calling, as the World Bank had been for some time, for 'the immediate dismantling of monopolies in the coconut and sugar sector'.

If the Makati speech tilted toward a conservative interpretation of agrarian reform, her second major speech delivered in Davao on 16 January, which was initially drafted by Fr. Bernas but later incorporated the advice of Ongpin and others, included elements of the liberal approach.[92] In the speech, devoted to an exposition of her social policy, she placed land reform as her first priority and defined it in terms of redistribution of ownership:

> The two essential goals of land reform are greater productivity and equitable sharing of the benefits and *ownership* of the land. These two goals can conflict with each other. But together we will seek viable systems of land reform suited to the particular exigencies dictated not only by the quality of the soil, the nature of the produce, and the agricultural inputs demanded, but *above all* by the needs of small farmers, landless workers, and communities of tribal Filipinos...

One can see here the hand of the conservatives in introducing the idea that reform might be differentially applied depending on crop type and productivity considerations, but the emphasis remained on redistribution of ownership:

> For long-time settlers and share tenants, *land-to-the-tiller* must become a reality, instead of an empty slogan. For the growing number of landless workers, resettlement schemes and *cooperative forms of farming* can be introduced.

Here there is a clear endorsement of redistributive reform on settled and tenanted lands, reinforced by a statement toward the end of her speech when she said, 'I stand for efficient use and equitable *distribution of ownership* of land'. But she excluded land worked by farmworkers and therefore both traditional and agribusiness plantations, showing the influence of the conservative reform advocates. Aquino followed up these comments with an explicit commitment that her family's Hacienda Luisita would be covered by reform - a commitment that would return to haunt her later:

> You will probably ask me: Will I also apply it to my family's Hacienda Luisita? My answer is yes; although sugar land is not covered by the land reform law, I shall sit down with my family to explore how the twin goals of maximum productivity and *dispersal of ownership* and benefits can be exemplified for the rest of the nation in Hacienda Luisita.

But even in this statement there was room for both a conservative and liberal interpretation of her promise. By stating that sugar lands were not covered by the land reform law, she betrayed a lack of clarity as to whether her government would actually aim to introduce a new law. While she said that Hacienda Luisita would be subject to measures to 'disperse' ownership, there was no commitment to outright redistribution.

Aquino's emphasis on the 'twin goals' of productivity and 'dispersal of ownership' foreshadowed the corporate stock-sharing plan that would later be introduced to help families like the Cojuangcos maintain control of their agribusiness operations. In fact, Francisco Varua, who was vice-president of her family's corporation, José Cojuangco and Sons, admitted that the company started planning the corporate stock-sharing option as an alternative version of agrarian reform when the snap election was called.[93] Thus, while her speech raised expectations for agrarian reform and went far enough to encourage the advocates of the liberal redistributive approach, a careful reading of what she said reveals the influence of conservative reformist thinking.

Aquino's two other major policy speeches made no reference to agrarian reform. Her talk before the Rotary Club at the Manila Hotel on 23 January outlined her political programme. Her final policy speech to the joint Philippine and foreign chambers of commerce on 3 February outlined her views on foreign relations.[94] While agrarian reform was not the central issue in Aquino's campaign, she promised to put it at the top of her agenda for social reform. During her first year in office, President Aquino would be reminded of this promise by the peasant movement, as well as the grass-roots people's organizations that had supported her campaign and those that had called for a boycott.

5.10 Conclusion

The Aquino campaign succeeded in uniting much of the broad anti-Marcos opposition, except for the militant national democratic movement. The group calling itself the 'Facilitators' played a central role in building the coalition and catapulting Aquino to the leadership. In retrospect, this group appears to have emerged in the wake of the May 1984 Batasan elections as a tacit alliance between the powerful right wing of the Catholic Church (including movements such as Opus Dei), the business community and the Cojuangco clan, with three broad objectives.[95] First, they were intent on preempting the candidacy of Salvador Laurel, who, through his UNIDO organization, seemed poised to capture the nomination of the traditional political parties in the opposition. Secondly, the Facilitators aimed to bring as much of the militant grass-roots movement as possible actively into the electoral campaign, both to legitimize their candidate and to marginalize the extra-parliamentary opposition. In an interview with Nick Joaquin, Ramon del Rosario Jr. stated that the main objective behind the Convenors Group was, 'to relate to the so-called cause-oriented groups: that was Tañada's principal role'.[96] The final objective was to come up with a single opposition candidate capable of gathering popular support as well as the endorsement of the elite and the US.

The Aquino campaign rallied supporters of both the conservative and liberal approaches to agrarian reform. The conservative reformists' inclusion of agrarian reform in some of their earliest unity statements was prompted by several factors. The most important was that the grass-roots movement, starting with the underground CPP/NDF/NPA, succeeded in demonstrating that rural poverty was one of the nation's most pressing problems, and in organizing peasants into a potent political force. Diokno and the social democratic and Christian left, as well as some of the liberal democrats, believed that a post-Marcos regime must implement a liberal redistributive reform for two reasons: first, they believed that reform could alleviate poverty and allow the rural poor to escape political manipulation by the left and the right; second, they felt that reform was essential if a violent revolution was to be avoided. They therefore lobbied for the inclusion of reform in the platform of the opposition. The Facilitators also realised that in order to challenge Marcos successfully, they had to enlist the support of as much of the grass-roots movement as possible. This was the reason for their early endorsement of a stance against the US bases and in favour of agrarian reform.

Consequently, in their election campaign, Aquino and her advisers put agrarian reform at the top of her list of social priorities. But there was a tension in her speeches between two very different approaches to reform. This reflected the basic tensions in the alliance of interests that decided to back her campaign. Most of the businessmen involved in the Facilitator Group and such organizations as Manindigan and the MBC had significant interests in agribusiness and were prone to a conservative approach to reform. This was most clearly articulated by Ongpin and Villegas. The only support for a liberal approach from within the conservative Catholic organizations came half-heartedly from Fr. Bernas, and with more commitment from a minority within the BBC represented by figures like Mahar Mangahas. Most of the traditional politicians, like Laurel and Aquino's brother José Cojuangco, had large landholdings and important agribusiness interests. The Cojuangcos were already considering how they could address the agrarian reform issue without endangering their control over Hacienda Luisita. Thus, while Aquino promised land reform in her campaign speeches, she and those drafting the speeches were careful not to define precisely what such a reform would encompass. Their vision of reform would emerge only in the first two years of the Aquino presidency.

Notes

1. The best account of the assassination is Burton (1989). De Dios et al (1988) provide a good overview of the development of the elite opposition as well as dissent in the military.

2. 'Sectoral' organizations were peasant, women, worker, teacher, church, student organizations and the like, while 'cause-oriented' organizations emerged to promote issues such as the exposure of human rights violations and the plight of political prisoners, or to campaign against the US economic and military presence. Later all these organizations were referred to as 'people's organizations'.

3. Burton (1989), p.112 citing Ernesto Maceda. See also Aquino, 1983.

4. The military estimated that as of May 1987, the NPA had 23,260 regulars. Office of Security and National Defence, 'Department of National Defence Statistical Data: ST/FA', 1987, p.4, cited in Miranda and Ruben, 1987, p.24. The NPA itself claimed to have 7,000 armed regulars and 'tens of thousands of part-time fighters', *Ang Bayan* cited in *PDI* (21 November 1987).

5. A US Senate investigation in 1984 estimated that the CPP influenced 40 per cent of all areas outside the major urban centres (US Senate, 1984).

6. Kessler, 1989, pp.149-53.

7. Nemenzo, 1984. See Chapter 4, section 4.2.

8. This conclusion is based on my own interviews with Party cadre and sympathizers between 1987 and 1989.

9. Bagong Alyansang Makabayan (BAYAN - New patriotic Federation), 'Persevere in Correct Struggles, Boycott the Sham Snap Election,' reproduced in Schirmer and Shalom (1987, pp.344-45). It must be stressed that this decision guaranteed their exclusion from the coalition. It is almost certain that Aquino's closest supporters would have excluded the national democrats even if they had decided to support her election campaign, due to their anti-communist stance and their desire to accommodate the military as well as the United States. The political cost of doing so, however, would have been far greater.

10. The conceptual designation of 'liberal democrats' and 'conservative reformists' (sometimes called 'bourgeois reformists') originates in the 'class analysis' articulated by the Communist Party of the Philippines outlined in the Central Committee's publication *Ang Bayan*, vol.16, no.2 (January 1985), pp.4-12. Because of its wide adoption within the popular movement, it has found its way into mainstream scholarship. See Landé (1986), pp.124-126 and passim.

11. See the selected writings of Diokno (1987).

12. The best account of their role is provided by Diokno, 1988. See section 5.7 below.

13. See his debate with Senator Manglapus around the 1963 Code of Agrarian Reform in Manglapus, 1967, pp.3-104.

14. See Chapter 4, section 4.5.3.

15. It nonetheless has important historical antecedents intimately linked with the peasant movement and its struggle for land. A Socialist Party of the Philippines was formed as early as 1929, and in 1938 it merged with the old Philippine Communist Party (PKP). See the memoirs of peasant leader Luis Taruc (1953). The SPP of the 1960s had its base in the trade unions and many of its members subsequently joined the CPP.

16. In 1977 the United Democratic Socialist Party of the Philippines, or the Nagkakaisa ng Partido Demokratiko ng Sosyalista ng Pilipinas (NPDSP), was established by another Jesuit, Fr. Romeo Intengan. See Wurfel (1988), pp.218-223.

17. See Chapter 4, section 4.2.

18. The PDSP grew out of the early work of Fr. Blanco and Fr. Intengan. Taking a less conservative position than the two Jesuits, it attempted to establish its anti-Marcos and progressive credentials through a position of critical support to two 'social-democratic' trends

in the 1970s: firstly Ninoy Aquino's Lakas ng Bayan or LABAN (formed from his jail cell to contest the first Batasang Pambansa elections in 1978); and secondly the urban bombing campaigns launched by moderate businessmen opposed to Marcos, like the 'Light a Fire Movement' in late 1979 involving such personalities as businessman Eduardo Olaguer, and the 'April Sixth Liberation Movement' associated with Steve Psinakis whose first actions occurred in 1980 (E. deDios, 1988, pp.71-75).

19.   Partido [PDSP], 1987. It should be noted, however, that much like the CPP, and in a more categorical fashion than the NDF, the PDSP's 'Maximum Programme' calls for 'the collectivization of agriculture'.

20.   Independent Caucus, 'A Philippine Vision of Socialism' September 1985; excerpts reproduced in Schirmer and Shalom (1987, pp.386-391).

21.   'KAAKBAY Supports Cory Aquino's Quest for Freedom and Democracy,' 9 December 1985, reproduced in Schirmer and Shalom (1987, pp.347-348).

22.   On 26 December 1984, Mitra and Cory Aquino both signed the 'Declaration of Unity: Joint Manifesto of Opposition Leaders and Convenor Group', which called for the removal of US military bases from the country. On 21 November 1985, several other conservative reformists signed a minimum programme of the Convenors' Group - National Unification Committee which also called for the removal of the bases. These included Mitra, Jaime Ongpin, John Osmeña and Emmanuel Soriano (Diokno, 1988, pp.152-58). In an interview with the *New York Times* (16 December 1985), Aquino expressed this view. But after the intervention of Americans who helped her campaign effort, Aquino reversed her position, saying that the existing treaty would be respected and a future government 'would keep its options open' as to a new one (Bonner, 1988, pp. 397-404).

23.   For an interesting, if somewhat overly reverential, biography of Jaime Ongpin see Joaquin (1990), on which this background information is based. Ongpin had ascended to the presidency of Benguet in 1974 when majority control of the corporation passed into the hands of a Philippine investments firm, which was later revealed as a front for Marcos and Imelda's brother Kokoy Ramualdez. On the Asia Foundation in the 1950s, see Chapter 3, section 3.4.3.

24.   See Bello et al, 1982, Chapter 6 and Broad, 1988, Chapters 4 and 5.

25.   Joaquin, 1990, pp.2, 201. *AWSJ* (6 June 1981) and *Fortune Magazine* (24 August 1981). In January 1981, just before lifting martial law, Marcos signed a secret decree authorising use of the death penalty against any publisher who allows a 'subversive article to be printed in his newspaper' (Aquino, 1983, p.77).

26.   While Zobel was a long-time friend of Ninoy Aquino (who had originally introduced Zobel to Marcos), he was very close to Marcos through the 1970s. But by September 1983, Marcos loyalists were demonstrating outside Zobel's Bank of the Philippine Islands. However, Zobel was to abandon the Aquino group just weeks before the election and support Marcos (Burton, 1989, pp.48, 60, 106, 155, 324).

27.   On the role of the Church see Wurfel, 1988, Chapters 8 and 10 and Youngblood, 1987.

28.   Wurfel, 1988, p.50, 213-215. On the Evangelical movement, Sabug, 1989; Brock, 1988; and Clad, 1987.

29.   Wurfel, 1988, p.279. On the politics of the Vatican see Naylor, 1987, Chapter 7.

30.   Between 1979 and 1982 Jayme was Chairman of the National Social Action Council created by Marcos in 1973 to ensure cooperation between the churches, the private sector and the government. The NASAC was created by Executive Order 182-A (18 September 1973). Jayme's PDCP, World Vision Philippines and Philippine Business for Social Progress (PBSP) were among the representatives of the private sector. National [NSAC], (1986).

31.   Concepcion and his brother Raul, who headed Concepcion Industries, represented a more 'protectionist' group within the business community than were Ongpin and others, since their enterprises depended on barriers to foreign imports. However, they seemed to be united in their endorsement of agribusiness in the agricultural sector. On NAMFREL, see Chapter 3, section 3.4.3.

32. On Monsod's World Bank orientation see Lichauco, 1988, p.238.

33. The AMA later changed its name to the Alliance of Metropolitan Organizations, and by 1984 the Alliance of Multi-Sectoral Organizations, when future senator José Lina Jr. was its secretary general.

34. The best account of these activities is Diokno, 1988. Endorsing this call were the Financial Executives Institute of the Philippines (FINEX), the Philippine Chamber of Commerce and Industry (PCCI), the MBC and the BBC.

35. Joaquin, 1990, p.224. The first issue was published on 21 November 1983. Ongpin arranged a P1.8 million loan from Jayme's Private Development Corporation of the Philippines. The board held its meetings either at the Benguet Corporation or the PHINMA offices in Makati. Also included were Br. Rolando Dizon and Felix Bautista as editor-in-chief.

36. CPP leader José Ma Sisson (1989, pp.114-16) said that the congress had been his idea. This was confirmed by another ex-cadre (Interview, 1990).

37. Bengzon, in an interview with Joaquin (1990, p.236). Those present were: Aquino's brother José Cojuangco, Butz Aquino, UNIDO leader Salvador Laurel, Catholic business leader José Concepcion, Apeng Yap, Francis Garchitorena, Jesuit Provincial Superior Fr. Joaquin Bernas, and Fr. Beinvenido Nebres.

38. 'Primer of the Kongreso Ng Mamamayang Pilipino (KOMPIL),' Quezon City, 7-8 January 1984. Excerpt reproduced in DeDios et al, 1988, p.602.

39. For a list of chosen leaders see Diokno, 1988, p.150. Of the fifteen leaders, seven were clearly in the conservative group: former Senator Domocao Alonto Jr., UNIDO vice-president Eva Estrada Kalaw, UNIDO president and MP Salvador Laurel, former Justice and MP Cecilia Muñoz-Palma, former Senator Francisco Rodrigo - a close friend of the Aquinos and influential in the Catholic Church as former President of Catholic Action, former Justice Claudio Teehankee and business magnate Enrique Zobel.

40. Ongpin, 1988, p.44; Wurfel, 1988, p.286; Burton, 1989, pp.199-220; Diokno, 1988, pp.151-52, 163-66.

41. Wurfel, 1988, p.286; Burton, 1989, pp.199-220; Diokno, 1988, pp.151-52, 163-66. Lewis Burridge, head of the American Chamber of Commerce in the Philippines, stated, *before* the election, that a 30 per cent vote for the opposition would be acceptable both to himself and to Marcos.

42. Lynch, who was trained in Chicago, had been involved with numerous US-funded studies, including a major one funded by the US Department of Defence through the Office of Naval Research (Lynch, 1968, pp.1-6; Yengoyan and Makil, 1984, pp.1-14; Guthrie, 1971, pp.xi-xii; Mijares, 1986, pp.395-99). By focusing only on the existing political perceptions of both landowners and tenants, as reported in surveys carried out under the parentage of government agencies, these studies generally arrived at the conclusion that redistributive reform on a large scale was not feasible. For reports of their findings see Lynch 1972 and Magahas et al, 1976.

43. Bernas interview cited by Joaquin (1990, p.233). Also present were Soriano, Bengzon, Narcisa Escaler, Bertie Lim an executive at del Rosario's Anscor Inc. and Dr. Antonio Perlas. Later meetings of Manindigan also included Manuel Lopa, Manny Colayco, Narz Lim and Francisco Licuanan.

44. Joaquin, 1990, pp.

45. The 'presidential standard bearers' were: Butz Aquino, José W. Diokno, Teofisto Guingona Jr., Eva Kalaw, Salvador Laurel, Raul Manglapus, Ramon Mitra, Ambrosio Padilla, Aquilino Pimentel, Rafael Salas and Jovito Salonga (Diokno, 1988, p.154).

46. 'Declaration of Unity: Joint Manifesto of Opposition Leaders and Convenor Group', Quezon City, 26 December 1984. This and following citations are taken from a reprint of the document in Schirmer and Shalom, 1987, pp.305-308.

47. This formulation appeared as early as 12 June 1983, in a joint statement from the 'coalesced opposition parties', 'Declaration of Common Principles of the Allied Opposition' (Aquino, 1983, appendix 2, p.88) but it was not attached to any endorsement of land reform.

48. This demonstrated the influence of a trend in the Church's teachings on 'private property', anchored in the discussion of the 'social function of property' in the work of St. Thomas Aquinas. During the debate on reform in 1987 Bernardo Villegas, a disciple from another wing of the Church, would actively promote such an interpretation of agrarian reform based on Catholic doctrine. See below and Chapter 7.

49. Feder, 1971, pp.194-98.

50. Diokno, 1988, p.154.

51. This interpretation is supported by the fact that both Laurel and Kalaw signed the 'Declaration of Common Principles of the Allied Opposition' (Aquino, 1983, appendix 2, p.87), which explicitly called for the removal of the US bases, as early as 12 June 1983.

52. The original draft of the Declaration had said only that 'the status of all military bases will be reviewed with the end in view of resolving the issue in the national interest with the direct participation of our people in the ultimate decision'. Nationalist leaders Diokno and Tañada argued for stronger language calling for the removal of the bases. As at the KOMPIL congress, the most likely reason for the Convenors and the other presidential hopefuls going along with this position, was their desire to bring as much of the grass-roots movement behind their leadership as possible (Diokno, 1988). See note 22.

53. Diokno resigned his position, though Tañada remained with BAYAN. Liberal democrats like Butz Aquino and the social democrats hurried to form BANDILA, an alternative and rival 'mass oriented' alliance. Diokno, 1988, pp.158-62. For an alternative assessment of what transpired see the account by Sison (1989, pp.115-17).

54. Joaquin, 1990, p.252.

55. Burton (1989, p.345) reported that this visit took place in May 1985.

56. See Benigno Aquino (1983, p.78) for an early insight on the military role.

57. The US called for reform in the AFP in the 'National Security Study Directive', a study by the US National Security Council dated November 1984 that was purposely leaked to the press in early 1985. Reprinted in Schirmer and Shalom, 1987, p.3.

58. This was the portrait painted by USAF Lt.Col. William M. Wise, assistant for regional policy and congressional affairs, East Asia and Pacific, Department of Defense (Wise, 1987, 435-448). Kessler (1989, pp.128-35) painted a different, but equally flawed portrait of an idealistic group parallel to the NPA and devoted to social transformation.

59. For a thoroughly researched and revealing portrait of the RAM see McCoy (1988).

60. See Amnesty International, 1981 and International Commission of Jurists, 1984, pp.11-39.

61. Benigno Aquino (1983, p.84) pointed to military tribunals and the appointment of military men as ambassadors, officials in Transportation, Motor Vehicles, Housing and Electricity Departments, and in the regional development authorities, and to serve as governors and mayors, bankers, and corporate executives. In fact, this process began even before Marcos declared martial law, but was greatly accelerated after September 1972 (Doronila, 1985).

62. McCoy, 1988; Bonner, 1988, p.450.

63. Bonner, 1988, p.415.

64. US Defense attaché Lieutenant Colonel Victor Raphael was RAM's contact with the Embassy at the time of the election. It seems that he introduced RAM to Jeffery Race, an 'independent risk analyst' close to the Pentagon who had served in the Vietnam War, and who happened to be in Manila at the time on business. Supposedly some RAM officers read Race's book (Race, 1972) criticizing US counterinsurgency strategy in that war (Burton, 1989, pp.337-338). However, there is no evidence that RAM subscribed to the lessons about land tenure invoked by Race, and Burton's account of the meeting makes no mention of Race discussing the issue. Only later would RAM make any pronouncements about agrarian reform (see Conclusion below).

65. Present were José Concepcion and Vicente Jayme of the BBC, Vicente Paterno and José Romero of the MBC, Emmanuel Soriano and Ramon del Rosario from the Facilitators, and businessmen Rizalino Navarro, Carlos Villa-Abrille, Ricardo Romulo and José Cuisia, as well as Jun Sanchez representing Bernardo Villegas (Joaquin 1990, pp.252-256).

66. Bernas and Bengzon from the Facilitators attended, as well as businessmen Cesar Buenaventure and Dante Santos. Rene Saguisag, who was the liberal democrat most intimately involved with the inner circle during the Aquino campaign, was also present, as was Br. Rolando Dizon from the *Veritas* board (Joaquin 1990, pp.252-256).

67. Included were Narcisa Escaler from the Facilitators, Manuel Lopa, Manny Colayco, Narz Lim and Francisco Licuanan.

68. Pauker, 1987, p.295. On this meeting see below.

69. Burton, 1989, pp.339-341.

70. Whether the US actively encouraged the groups to meet together is not known. Burton (1989, p.338) indicates that there was at least some American advice in this direction.

71. The Reagan White House remained behind Marcos until the very end. The most authoritative account of the changing US position is Bonner (1988), but see also Bello (1985).

72. On Ongpin: Bonner, 1988, p.370; On Cojuangco: Burton, 1989, pp.299

73. NAMFREL requested funding from the National Endowment For Democracy, then headed by Carl Gershman, a former aide to Jeane Kirkpatrick (Bonner, 1988, p.414, 523).

74. Bonner, 1988, pp.394-96.

75. The 'Friends of Aquino' in the US were described by Bonner, 1988, Chapter 16, especially pp.401-04.

76. Bonner, 1988, pp.148-50, 401-03, 427; Burton, 1989, pp.319.

77. Bonner, 1988, p.402. Also involved were Mark Malloch Brown, formerly with *The Economist* and the firm he was to join, D.H. Sawyer and Associates, which waived its normal fee of $250,000.

78. Overholt, educated at Harvard and Yale, was a land reform consultant from the Hudson Institute during the early years of the Marcos programme, who had initially been quite positive about Marcos' programme (Overholt, 1976). He was married to the daughter of a retired Filipino general and an old friend of the Aquinos. Karnow claimed that he brought a former Australian intelligence officer and a British secret service agent disguised as a journalist to protect Aquino during the campaign (Overholt, 1987, p.98, 104; Karnow, 1989, p.412).

79. Other figures like Concepcion and Luis Santos were also involved in the CAMP (Burton, 1989, pp.314-15).

80. Interview with Rolando Dy, head of CRC's Agribusiness Unit, 30 September 1987.

81. Center [CRC], n.d., p.27.

82. Opus Dei was founded in Spain in 1929 by Msgr. José Maria Escrivá de Balaguer. Escrivá supported Generalissimo Franco in his fight against republicanism and Freemasonry during the Spanish Civil War. In Franco's Spain, Opus Dei struggled against the statist orientation of the fascist Phalange, advocating a 'neo-liberal' economic policy. Escrivá is said to have been a close supporter of Polish Cardinal Karol Wojtyla before he ascended to the Papacy, whose anti-communist views coincided with those of Escrivá. Under Pope John Paul II, Opus Dei was granted autonomy from local Bishops, and its position was strengthened in the Vatican supposedly to counter the influence of radical Jesuits. The movement has been said to have played a role in the seamier side of Vatican financing, and to have been involved in the Iran-Contra Scandal and other nefarious undertakings. See Naylor, 1987, pp.110ff, 127, 157.

83. Naylor (1987, p.128) commented, 'in 1958 some of [Opus Dei's] members produced El Plan del Estabilizacion Economica, a watershed in Spanish economic policy...[which] could have been drafted by the IMF: it called for austerity, trade liberalization, an export drive, and convertibility of currency. It also set off a massive flight of now-convertible currency...to Switzerland, as Spanish capitalists discovered how to use accredited diplomats as cash couriers to evade...exchange-control laws.' On Opus Dei's importance in the new Aquino government see Wurfel, 1988, p.308 and Clad, 1987.

84. Joaquin, 1990, p.119.

85. *NYT* (28 July 1985).

86. Ongpin, 'Philippine Investment Projects: A Micro View,' Country Risk Seminar on the

Philippines, 1 October 1985, Pavilion Intercontinental Hotel, Singapore (Ongpin, 1988, p.57). See also Joaquin, 1990, p.246.

87.   Cited in Pauker, 1987, p.295.

88.   Villegas, 1985.

89.   Villegas thus identified himself with what Griffin (1989, p.97n) labelled as the 'extremist version' of the open economy model, also advocated by Anne Kruger, where not only are biases against exports removed, but government actually intervenes to establish biases in favour of exports.

90.   'Building From the Ruins', 6 January 1986 cited in Pauker, 1987, p.303. Most of the speech was reprinted in DeDios et al, 1988, pp.690-92, but this section was not included. On Ongpin's role in drafting it, see Joaquin, 1990, p.240.

91.   Burton,1989, p.321.

92.   'Broken Promises in a Land of Promise' delivered in Davao on 16 January 1986. Excerpts reprinted in Schirmer and Shalom, 1987, pp.339-43. Emphases in the following citations are my own. On Bernas' role in drafting this and the third speech, see Joaquin, 1990, p.240.

93.   Interview with V. Francisco Varua, vice-president of José Cojuangco & Sons Inc., Makati, 31 July 1989.

94.   'Tearing Down the Dictatorship, Rebuilding Democracy,' 23 January 1986 cited in Pauker, 1987, p.297ff. 'Rescue from Disgrace in a Pharoah's Prison,' 3 February 1985 cited in Pauker, 1987, p.302ff.

95.   It is important to stress the fact that this was a tacit alliance and not a 'conspiracy'. The participants apparently came together only slowly as their common interests became apparent.

96.   Joaquin, 1990, p.241.

AQUINO'S RESTORATION: LAYING THE FOUNDATIONS FOR CONSERVATIVE REFORM

6.1 Introduction

During the presidential campaign and on election day, 7 February 1986, Marcos again attempted to employ a combination of bravado, vote-buying, ballot box stuffing and intimidation to claim victory over the Aquino-Laurel ticket. Thousands of official ballot papers were signed 'Marcos - Tolentino', thumb-printed and, still bound in their original pads, distributed throughout the country.[1] In the weeks leading up to the election Marcos tried to capture the support of both landowners and the peasantry. On 14 January he tried in vain to cover up his government's dismal record on agrarian reform by issuing a presidential memorandum that authorized the immediate distribution of Emancipation Patents to designated beneficiaries of his reform programme, regardless of whether they had completed payments for the land.[2] On 27 January, speaking in Bacolod, Negros Occidental, Marcos signed a presidential decree ordering interest rates on loans to sugar planters to be lowered from 42 per cent to 16 per cent.[3] But Marcos' old tactics proved to be of no avail as his traditional sources of support abandoned him.

The Aquino coalition claimed victory and international observers lent credence to their claim, but Marcos refused to concede. The tide was turned on 22 February when, in an effort to avoid arrest for their plans to stage a coup d'état, Defence Minister Juan Ponce Enrile and his RAM Boys enlisted General Fidel Ramos and staged a rebellion. The small group of rebel soldiers, hoping to spark a wider defection in the armed forces, were pitted against General Ver and the bulk of the AFP in a military showdown. Leaders of the Aquino coalition, Cardinal Sin and the Catholic hierarchy called on the population to support the rebel soldiers and defy the troops and tanks sent against them by Marcos. What followed was the now famous 'People Power' 'peaceful revolution' which, after three days, culminated in Marcos' hasty flight by US Air Force transport to Hawaii on 25 February. That same day, at the elite Club Filipino, Corazon Aquino took her oath of office in the presence of Enrile, Ramos, the leading members of RAM and the leading members of the civilian coalition.

6.2 The first cabinet's inaction on agrarian reform

Aquino's first Cabinet was broadly representative of the coalition that brought her to power, and as such was made up primarily of the advocates of the conservative approach to agrarian reform. The one Cabinet portfolio left unfilled during Aquino's first two months in office was that of agrarian reform - an ominous indication of the low priority that it would receive under the new government. High-level appointments were shared out between her key supporters in the business community from the Facilitators and Manindigan, leaders of the traditional opposition parties, close friends of the President and her late husband, and those involved in the military rebellion.

In the first group, Jaime Ongpin was given the powerful position of Minister of Finance and José Concepcion was rewarded with the Ministry of Trade and Industry. Alfredo Bengzon was made Minister of Health and Emmanuel Soriano was given the sensitive National Security portfolio. Narcisa Escaler became Aquino's Appointments Secretary, while Vicente Jayme was appointed to the Philippine National Bank and Vicente Paterno to the Philippine National Oil Company. Thirteen sitting opposition MPs and one other former Senator received Cabinet appointments. Ramon Mitra, former Senator, and MP, a leader of the 'Laban wing' of PDP-Laban and long-time supporter of Ninoy Aquino, was appointed Minister of Agriculture. Aquilino Pimentel, leader of the 'PDP wing' of PDP-Laban, elected but ousted from the Batasan, was named Minister of Local Government. Former Senator and Liberal Party leader Jovito Salonga was named to head the Presidential Commission on Good Government (PCGG), in charge of tracking down and sequestering the illicit funds and property accumulated by the Marcoses and their cronies.[4]

Only six members of Vice-president Laurel's UNIDO party, all sitting MPs, received appointments and three of these had defected early to the Aquino camp. Former Senator, MP and UNIDO leader Laurel was given the prestigious post of Foreign Affairs, where his friendship with the US could be maximized and his influence on the shape of the new government minimized.[5]

Eight of those appointed were close friends of the President or her late husband. Aside from Mitra, these included the controversial human rights lawyer Joker Arroyo, who was made Executive Secretary, Teodoro L. Locsin Jr., who was put in charge of Public Information, and Teodoro Benigno, who became Presidential Press Secretary.[6] Aside from Arroyo, two other figures disliked by the military received high-level appointments: Augusto S. Sanchez was made Labour Minister; and Rene Saguisag, who had played an important role in Aquino's campaign, became Special Legal Counsel to the President. Others close to the grass-roots movement were Mita Pardo de Tavera, former chairwoman of the women's organization Gabriela, who was made Minister of Social Services, and Teofisto Guingona, a pre-martial law head of the Philippine Chamber of Commerce and Industry and prominent member of Butz Aquino's BANDILA, who was made Audit Chairman. In a move which angered the military, José Diokno was named to head the Presidential Commission on Human Rights.

However, the power in the Cabinet remained in the hands of conservative reformists and the military. Reflecting the crucial role that the military played in the establishment of the regime, Juan Ponce Enrile, the original architect of martial law, was retained as Defence Minister. General Fidel Ramos was promoted to his long-coveted post as Chief of Staff of the AFP. Central Bank governor, José Fernandez was also kept on, partly due to Ongpin's strong support and the international financial community's desire for continuity in debt management, and partly due to Fernandez's long relationship with the Cojuangco clan.[7] The most powerful economic positions were in the hands of conservative reformists Ongpin, Concepcion, Fernandez and Mitra. These were not 'technocrats', if that label is to have any meaning, but rather representatives of powerful business and political interests in society. The only truly technocratic figure in the new Cabinet was the UP economist Solita Monsod, appointed as head of Economic Planning and the National Economic Development Authority (NEDA).[8]

There was a great deal of division and tension in the Cabinet, reflecting the uneasy alliances that had brought President Aquino to power. The liberal democrats were intent on restoring basic civil liberties and curbing the authority of the military. They put pressure on the President to fulfil her campaign promise of releasing political prisoners and seeking negotiations with the CPP/NDF/NPA. The traditional politicians, both liberal democrats and conservative reformists, were anxious to rebuild their party machines and undermine the organized structure of Marcos' KBL political networks. Here they were divided between the alliance that had formed around the Facilitators and Convenors' Group during the election campaign, represented by figures like Mitra and Pimentel, and Vice-president Laurel who was already marginalized in the new Cabinet.

Defence Minister Enrile and the RAM colonels, whose rebellion had sparked the popular uprising that placed the new government in power, had hoped to gain a more prominent position in the government. Their plan had been to take power themselves through a coup against Marcos; instead they found themselves underlings again to a civilian government dominated by traditional politicians. They were particularly antagonistic to the liberal democrats in the Cabinet and to the President's decision to release CPP leaders from prison and negotiate with the revolutionary movement.[9] But while divided on these issues, the Cabinet appeared to be united in relegating agrarian reform to the back burner.

While most Cabinet positions were filled within two days of assuming power, Aquino did not name anyone to the Ministry of Agrarian Reform (MAR) until late April 1986. It seems that the President's team first considered appointing Tarlac landowner, provincial politician and presidential friend José V. Yap, who served as deputy governor of the Land Authority under Macapagal, and who headed Aquino's first Task Force to the MAR.[10] Meanwhile, a faction of the traditional politicians in the Islamic community in Mindanao, many of whom were landowners who had supported Aquino's campaign, were lobbying for former KBL member, Omar M. Dianalan MP, to be appointed to the top post in MAR.[11]

Vice-president Laurel had his own candidate for the position. In early March UNIDO MP for Negros Occidental, Wilson Gamboa, turned up at MAR and told the former Minister Conrado Estrella that he had been named as the new

Minister by President Aquino in the presence of Vice-president Laurel.[12] Estrella held a ceremony to hand over the reins to Gamboa, only to discover to his embarrassment that Gamboa had not been given the post by the President.[13] If Estrella is to be believed, President Aquino even asked him to stay on as Minister. If true, this demonstrates that, as with Defense and the Central Bank, Aquino's people had little intention of changing the old regime's approach to reform.[14] But there were other indications that the new government's initial vision of agrarian reform did not go beyond Marcos' limited programme.

It was not until 12 April that Aquino chose Heherson Alvarez, a close friend of Ninoy Aquino during their exile in the US, to be her Minister of Agrarian Reform. He took up his post only on 29 April. Alvarez was a liberal democrat from the northern province of Isabela who, as a delegate to the Constitutional Convention (Con-Con) of 1971, had supported a resolution prohibiting Marcos from seeking another term in office. His brother was brutally killed by Marcos military men in 1974. After martial law was declared, Alvarez fled the country for the US, where he established the Ninoy Aquino Movement. He had virtually no experience with agricultural issues nor had he concerned himself previously with agrarian reform. Clearly, like many politicians previously in the opposition, he was appointed to the new Cabinet as a close friend of Ninoy Aquino and in repayment of a 'debt of gratitude' (*utang-na-loób*) by the presidential family.[15] Like so many in the Cabinet, Alvarez would use his position as a stepping stone to future political office. Alvarez, together with eleven of his Cabinet colleagues, would run for election to the Senate in 1987, and all but the left-leaning Sanchez would be elected.[16]

6.3 Agribusiness and corporate stock-sharing as the 'centre-piece'

While the government delayed appointing a steward for the MAR, other ministers, as well as the President, began to reveal the government's stand on agrarian reform. Finance Minister Ongpin took the lead in laying out the new government's economic programme. He joined the Aquino team out of disgust at the economic mismanagement of the Marcos years. He was convinced that the economic fortunes of the country could be turned around by eliminating the corrupt practices and favouritism of the dictatorship, and by giving a free hand to private enterprise. During his first week in the new job, he began to elaborate on the ideas that he and Villegas had promoted during the election campaign.

At a press conference on 4 March he said, 'I think the government should get out of business completely. Privatize everything'. The government would have to deal with structural problems, he said, which meant dismantling the farm monopolies like those established by Marcos and his cronies in the coconut and sugar sectors, and establishing a fairer system of taxation. In addition, the government was committed to implementing a land reform based on the non-confiscatory Malaysian model.[17] Here he was referring to Malaysia's nucleus estate programme. The Malaysian model would be referred to often over the next two years, as those promoting the conservative approach attempted to recycle the nucleus farming model as the centre of the new government's agrarian reform programme.[18]

After 4 March 1986, Ongpin seldom spoke about his agricultural development programme in terms of 'agrarian' or 'land' reform.[19] In an important speech delivered at the Carnegie Endowment in Washington on 7 April, he outlined plans for an 'agricultural restructuring fund', which he labelled the 'centre-piece of our recovery and development strategy'. The government, he explained, hoped to concentrate future development efforts and income flows to the agricultural sector by establishing a capital fund that could finance the diversification from traditional crops, such as coconuts, sugar, timber and rice, to non-traditional products, such as cacao, oil palms, fruit trees, coffee and aquaculture. Emphasizing the classic agribusiness argument, he said that the programme's 'major emphasis will be on ensuring good management', since the agricultural sector had been 'not only under-financed, it has also been undermanaged'.[20]

In late April Ongpin elaborated on the 'centre-piece of the new government's agricultural program' in preparation for a sub-committee meeting of the World Bank's Consultative Group for the Philippines.[21] The plan was developed in more detail by Rolando Dy, head of the Agribusiness Unit at Villegas' CRC.[22] It called for the establishment of a National Agricultural Investment Company (NAGRICO), which would be jointly financed by the World Bank's International Finance Corporation (IFC). Organized as an investment holding company, NAGRICO would invest in agricultural corporations, or channel funds to financial intermediaries who would lend to corporations. This would finance diversification into non-traditional crops and the establishment of nucleus farming operations.

At this early date Ongpin's plan included a stock-distribution scheme to improve the position of farmworkers, almost identical to the corporate stock distribution option that would later become the most controversial component of the Aquino agrarian reform program. In the Ongpin-CRC plan, nucleus farms would provide small farmlots to worker families on which they could raise food for home consumption, an idea mooted by Villegas during the election campaign. In addition, ten per cent of the profits made on the nucleus farms would be distributed in the form of equity shares in the corporation to its employees until they could acquire a 50 per cent share in the ownership of the company.

Ongpin's 'centre-piece program' was widely perceived as an *alternative* to redistributive agrarian reform. On 29 April, in an early Hearing before the US House of Representatives on future US aid to the country, Rep. Steven Solarz questioned expert witness Gustav Ranis about Ongpin's plan. He asked Ranis 'whether land reform is really a viable policy option in the Philippines', given the argument of Ongpin and others that small farmers do not have access to sufficient credit. Interestingly, while providing a detailed description of the NAGRICO stock-sharing programme, Solarz described it as 'One *alternative* for land reform, in the traditional sense, [which] has been made by Minister

Ongpin'. Winding up his question, he asked Ranis, 'What is your response to this argument *against land reform*, on the grounds that it will not work - that the farmer will not be able to get credit?' Ranis responded:

> I do worry a bit about this proposal of Mr. Ongpin, whom I, otherwise, admire very much. I have a feeling that he is fixed on the large scale project. It comes from his background...'[23]

That Ongpin's plan was indeed an alternative to redistributive reform was quickly perceived by observers in the Philippines. The plan was soon criticized by long-time advocate of the liberal approach to agrarian reform, the BBC's Mahar Mangahas, who argued that the plan was unclear on where these nucleus farms would acquire their land from. He said that the plan would require a huge allocation of government funds that would be better spent by channelling them directly to farmers. After Cabinet criticisms of the plan on the grounds that it called for establishing another huge government corporation, Ongpin reformulated the idea as an entirely private sector venture, the Private Agricultural Investment Company (PAGRICO).[24] However, the stock-sharing proposal would later surface in debates about the government's agrarian reform programme.

During her first months in office, President Aquino herself seemed anxious to steer the government's agricultural policy away from redistributive reform. Less than a week after assuming office, she explained her own approach to agrarian reform:

> [I]t is not so much a matter of distributing land but of enabling people to *share profits*. By sharing out the land, you only create more problems because sugar cultivation, for instance, is definitely uneconomic if carried out in small plots.[25]

The President's vision of agrarian reform as 'profit sharing' fitted in well with Ongpin's alternative to agrarian reform. On 6 April 1986, President Aquino addressed the Asian Development Bank's Board of Directors, outlining her administration's early efforts to trim down the state's bureaucracy and privatize government assets. She then went on to explain what she called 'the core of our recovery and development strategy', which was to improve the conditions of 70 per cent of the population living and working in the countryside:

> This can be achieved through agrarian reform and a package of credit, marketing and technological support. This *means providing a support system* that will enable farmer cultivators to move from subsistence agriculture into the market economy, as both producers and consumers. Most immediately, we must provide post-harvest facilities to hasten delivery and consumption of farm products. The objective is to develop the purchasing power of the rural population, achieve self-sufficiency in food production and establish a sound foundation for industrial growth.[26]

Here, President Aquino seemed to resolve the tension in her election speeches by defining reform primarily as a package of productivity-enhancing measures rather than in redistributive terms.

The President's initial action on agrarian reform was limited to her order, in May, that 9,000 hectares of foreclosed sugar land be transferred through the Philippine National Bank to 3,000 farmworkers in famine-ridden Negros Occidental.[27] Talking to the press in June 1986 about her first 100 days in office, the President said that only idle public lands would be included in the government's land reform programme. She indicated that there were no tenants on her family's Hacienda Luisita, where workers earned more than they could if they were each given a hectare of land.[28] Thus by June President Aquino had ruled out redistributive reform on her family's estate, and had limited the definition of agrarian reform largely to a programme that would provide support services to small farmers, stimulate profit-sharing by agribusiness corporations and redistribute only idle public lands.

Ramon Mitra, who was appointed Minister of Agriculture, seemed to be thinking along similar lines in the first week after the government came to power, when he outlined the ministry's program for agricultural reforms:

> Our major goal is to make farming profitable. This can be done through the extension of modern farming technology, more agricultural credit, appropriate marketing assistance and other farm incentives to the country's farmers.[29]

Mitra asserted that, besides dismantling sugar and coconut monopolies, the new government's agricultural policies would be 'just, consistent and fair' in order to promote stability and encourage big agricultural ventures. He clearly was not considering redistributive agrarian reform. Mitra quickly began a shake-up in the Ministry of Agriculture and Food (MAF) and recommended the appointment of Carlos Dominguez, vice-president for agribusiness at Zobel's Bank of the Philippine Islands, as Deputy Minister. He expressed a desire to centralize in the MAF all the various agencies that deal with agriculture.

On 14 May, the MAF made public its short-term recovery programme. The document stated that one of the government's long-term goals was 'to provide the farmer, especially the poor farmer, with access to land'. Interestingly, in explaining the Ministry's approach to reform, it cited Aquino's election campaign economic policy speech that spoke of 'genuine land reform' primarily as a 'package of credit, marketing and technological support' services. The plan proposed resettlement on public and sequestered lands, the transfer of idle private lands to the landless, encouragement of voluntary land reform in sugar areas and accelerated implementation of the Marcos programme.[30] It did not offer a clear perspective for expanding the reform or instituting new legislation on the issue. A close adviser to Mitra at the time said that they had decided it was not the right time to move into agrarian reform or 'to alienate the big farmers'. Mitra and his staff decided to limit their public pronouncements on 'agricultural reforms' to a general commitment to build infrastructure in preparation for an eventual distribution of land.[31] In fact, their statements were explicitly directed at stimulating new opportunities for agribusiness expansion, which won Mitra considerable support among the business community and landowners. Shortly after Ongpin announced his plans for a World Bank funded NAGRICO and PAGRICO, Mitra came out with a similar agribusiness programme labelled 'Private Investment for Development', to be funded by USAID.[32]

After Heherson Alvarez finally assumed his post as Minister of Agrarian Reform at the end of April 1986, he initially tried to inject a more redistributive content into the government's plans for agrarian reform. Upon taking up office he announced that the government would extend its land reform programme beyond rice and corn lands to cover sugar and coconut areas. Mitra attacked the idea, rushing a memorandum to the President arguing that reform on rice and corn lands should be completed before proceeding further. Alvarez was quick to clarify that he only meant that his Ministry was merely considering such recommendations.[33] Thereafter, he mounted no further challenges to the dominant view in Cabinet.

Alvarez left much of the day-to-day operation of the Ministry to José Medina, number two man at the MAR throughout the Marcos years. According to his successor, in contrast to Mitra, Alvarez left the Marcos MAR organization essentially intact, using the Ministry as little more than 'a parking space'.[34] There is some evidence that Alvarez spent a fair amount of his time in the Ministry cultivating political relationships and renewing contact with his provincial base in Isabela. Inocencio Uy, a large landowner and Mayor of Roxas, Isabela during the Marcos years, said that Alvarez was a close friend whom he helped in his senatorial campaign and who later helped Uy negotiate the sale of his land to the government.[35] Little was accomplished during Alvarez's tenure at MAR, but the responsibility for that must be shared by the whole Aquino Cabinet.

Solita Monsod, who was Minister for Economic Planning and NEDA head, was the only advocate of the liberal approach to reform in the Cabinet. She was out-numbered by Ongpin, Mitra and Concepcion, the other members of Cabinet responsible for the government's economic strategy. She lacked faith in the ability of domestic and foreign agribusiness corporations to take the lead in developing the agricultural sector, and recognized the need to focus on relieving the plight of the rural poor as the starting point for development. She believed that military and strong-arm tactics would only increase rural unrest, and that rural peace had to be based on justice for the rural poor and an end to arbitrary military and paramilitary action.

In April, Monsod outlined a rural development strategy focussed on improving the condition of the rural poor. She said that, 'the only long-term solution to the poverty problem is to endow the poor target groups with income-generating assets'. However, reflecting the Cabinet's lack of concern for the issue, she argued that the 'implementation of a truly effective agrarian reform program' remained an issue 'to be resolved' in the future.[36] On 1 May 1986, a group of economists from the University of the Philippines submitted a study to Monsod that would serve as the basis for the government's 'Policy Agenda for People-

Powered Development' released later that month.[37] In their report, the UP economists urged that a comprehensive agrarian reform programme covering public and private lands be rapidly adopted by the new government. They argued that agrarian reform would not lower productivity on private lands and rejected arguments limiting reform to rice and corn lands and the public domain.

Monsod wholeheartedly supported the study and adopted it as NEDA's draft 'Policy Agenda', which was submitted to Cabinet.[38] There was no debate on reform in the Cabinet. Nevertheless, the final 'Policy Agenda' did not incorporate the UP economists' recommendations on reform. Each Department modified the section that concerned them, indicating that the section on reform was diluted by the DAR.[39] The NEDA plan approved by the Cabinet argued for immediate action to raise rural incomes and for a rural-based development strategy. Emphasis was placed on assisting small farmers, and the agribusiness orientation promoted by Ongpin and Mitra was rejected: 'There will be no government equity participation in agribusiness operations of private corporations'. Yet the plan emphasized that, for the foreseeable future, the government would work within the confines of the Marcos programme, putting off the expansion of reform to an unspecified moment in the future when the first priority would be public rather than privately owned lands:

> The previous land reform program shall be reviewed and redirected to accomplish its original objectives. Genuine agrarian reform shall therefore be pursued to serve justice to those who till the land...Agrarian reform shall *eventually* be expanded to include natural resources and other crops. The reform effort shall be intensified to benefit the greatest number of small farmers. Alienable and disposable lands under the *public domain shall be the priority* target for land justice.[40]

Aside from implementing the Marcos programme, the 'Policy Agenda' asserted that the 'stewardship of idle lands shall be encouraged', and stated that the government would 'provide safeguards to protect the interest of farmers in tenurial arrangements', a point already included in the Marcos Operation Leasehold. The plan endorsed an argument commonly advanced in the conservative framework when it stated that 'In order to pave the way for a more successful program, peace and order conditions in the countryside must be *first* improved'. However, it argued that the means to guarantee peace and order was to disband all private armies and to ensure a democratic process for the selection of local officials. It called for improved measures in land surveys, titling and registration of ownership as well as an expanded credit programme to assist small farmers.

In the following months Monsod directed the preparation of the government's six year Medium Term Development plan. The terms of the plan were ambiguous enough to accommodate the views of both Ongpin and Monsod on agricultural development. Ongpin, discussing its contents at a Business Conference organized by the Philippine Chamber of Commerce and Industry in late

H

November, made no mention of agrarian reform.[41] When published in December 1986, the plan's ambiguous treatment of government intentions to expand reform disappointed the advocates of redistributive reform. The plan stated that the inclusion of lands devoted to sugar and other crops in an 'expanded agrarian reform program is now under *serious consideration*'.[42]

However, the plan's physical targets for land redistribution over the six year period covered only the completion of programmes under existent legislation. In fact, by error or design, the plan presented a deceptive portrait of the quantity of land actually covered by reform.[43] The plan stated that, 'Some 998,000 hectares of sugar, coconut, tobacco and abaca lands are expected to be covered under the program'. However, careful reading of the plan's presentation of the data revealed that these lands were not slated for redistribution, but rather for coverage under tenancy regulation.[44] The only expansion of land area slotted for redistribution to the landless related to 1.3 million hectares of public lands targetted for resettlement programmes. In terms of finance, no funds were allocated for the redistribution of private lands other than rice and corn lands covered by the Marcos programme.[45] Indeed, in the government's budget approved for 1987, no funds were allocated for the expansion of agrarian reform.[46] In summary the plan concluded:

> Over the next six years, the major programs and projects of the subsector will largely concentrate on the acceleration and completion of activities, particularly under operation land transfer, leasehold operation and resettlement.[47]

According to Monsod, during the Aquino government's first year in office the Cabinet never discussed agrarian reform. Monsod, essentially a technocrat, with few direct links to either the Makati groups supporting agribusiness or the networks of landowning traditional politicians, was more open to discussing an expanded agrarian reform programme than any other Cabinet minister, including Alvarez. But, while Monsod supported a liberal approach, during the government's first year in office she did not sense the urgency of moving beyond accepted notions of agrarian reform inherited from the Marcos regime. In June 1986, Monsod said that farmers would have to wait at least three years before the government would implement a new agrarian reform programme.[48] The publication of NEDA's plan in December gave some idea of the limited character of the new programme that she had in mind.

6.4 Lesser officials advocate the liberal approach

Those promoting a liberal approach to agrarian reform were in evidence in the lower echelons of the new government, where they soon began pushing for immediate action to implement a comprehensive programme. On 13 March 1986, President Aquino issued executive order No. 5 establishing the Presidential Commission on Government Reorganization (PCGR), which dispatched Survey Teams to all government departments. The PCGR Survey Team to the MAR was headed by Ernesto Ordoñez, and included advocates of redistributive reform like UP political science professor and BISIG member Eduardo Tadem, and former Federation of Free Farmers (FFF) peasant organizer and political detainee Victor Gerardo J. Bulatao. They worked closely with newly appointed officials in the MAR who were pushing for a rapid expansion of the agrarian reform programme.

On 15 April 1986, two weeks before Alvarez took up his post, MAR officials presented reorganization proposals to the Survey Team. These would prove to be the most radical agrarian reform proposals ever advanced by a government body in the Philippines.[49] They included an extraordinary recommendation advocating early implementation of a sweeping redistributive agrarian reform programme that would cover virtually all public and private lands in the country. One of their most significant recommendations was compensation to landowners based on land values 'assessed by government' rather than market-values. They also proposed the adoption of an 'Agricultural Land Tax scheme that will prevent land hoarding and/or speculation'.

The recommendations called for granting to the Ministry 'quasi-judicial powers' to enable it to implement a redistributive reform programme without getting bogged down in the usual drawn-out court proceedings allowed by all previous reform laws. The MAR report also suggested that the Minister of Agrarian Reform replace the Minister of Finance as ex-officio chairman of the Board at the Land Bank of the Philippines (LBP). This was clearly to ensure that the LBP would no longer be able to act on behalf of landowners to slow down the implementation of redistribution, as it had done consistently during the Marcos years. While the Survey Team insisted that it 'did not in any way attempt to influence or guide the Ministry in the formulation...of the plan',[50] it is clear that these radical proposals coming from MAR represented only a minority view within the Ministry. They were largely the views of newly appointed officials and not those of outgoing Minister Conrado Estrella or his deputy José Medina.[51]

On 15 May the Survey Team's own recommendations endorsed almost all of the MAR proposals.[52] Its chairperson, Ernesto Ordoñez, was convinced that the government should not spend its money on compensating landowners, but rather direct its resources to farmer beneficiaries.[53] The Team's additional recommendations reflected Tadem's own orientation, placing more emphasis than the MAR proposals on cooperative forms of farm organization and the independence of farmer organizations from the Ministry. In their consensus proposal, the Survey Team and the MAR asserted that, 'Farmers and farmworkers have the right to organize themselves in order to protect and advance their sectoral interests'. They emphasized that rural associations must be involved 'in all stages of the agrarian reform program from policy formulation to program implementation and monitoring and evaluation'. However, since the mandate of the PCGR was to work with MAR on proposals for the reorganization of the Ministry, and not to propose new legislation on agrarian reform *per se*, most of the recommendations were simply ignored at the highest level of government.

Survey Team members and MAR officials involved in making these proposals were clearly in contact with those peasant organizations and the grass-roots movement that were advocating the institutionalization of 'people power' during the government's first year in office. Supporters of the liberal approach in the lower echelons of government also received support from the United Nations Food and Agricultural Organization (FAO), who had long been involved in promoting agrarian reform in the country. The FAO sent a mission to the Philippines from 24 August to 6 September 1986 to explore 'Rural Development and Agrarian Reform'. This lent support to those at the lower echelons of government advocating the rapid expansion of agrarian reform.[54] However, the impact of their proposals would only be felt during the following year.

Many of the proposals outlined by the MAR and the PCGR Survey Team would be taken up by the advocates of the liberal approach in later policy debates. However, neither Minister Alvarez nor anyone else in Cabinet decided to champion them during this early period. In its 15 May report, the Survey Team urged President Aquino to make a major policy announcement on 12 June, Philippine Independence Day, stating that 'Agrarian Reform is the core of the government's rural development strategy' and that the 'government is committed to place Hacienda Luisita under agrarian reform'. Instead, Minister Ongpin was promoting his NAGRICO stock-sharing plan as the 'centre-piece' of the government's rural development strategy. And in June President Aquino told the press that she believed the workers on her family's Hacienda Luisita would be ill-served by agrarian reform.

Not only was the new Cabinet not prepared to endorse a liberal redistributive approach to reform, but they appeared to believe that agrarian reform was not an urgent issue for the new government. This was reflected by the delay in appointing an Agrarian Reform Minister, as well as the absence of any new reform initiatives in the government's early economic programme. Ministers Ongpin and Mitra placed a priority on developing incentives for agribusiness expansion, while Minister Alvarez confined his proposals on reform to the existing Marcos programme. During the government's first year in office, the debate between advocates of the conservative and liberal approaches to reform did not take place in President Aquino's Cabinet, but rather in the commission that she appointed to draft a new Constitution.

6.5 Constitutional provisions on agrarian reform

Saddled with a Constitution introduced by Marcos in 1973 under martial law constraints, and a legislative Assembly where Marcos' KBL had always been assured a majority, Aquino's closest advisers counselled radical action. Almost immediately upon his appointment, Local Government Minister Aquilino Pimentel began replacing local officials with his own appointees to serve as 'Officers In Charge' (OICs) until elections could be held. In a more significant move, on 25 March 1986 the President issued Proclamation No.3 which suspended the 1973 Constitution, introduced a provisional 'Freedom Charter' and abolished the Batasang Pambansa. Aquino assumed law making powers until a new Constitution could be drafted and submitted to a plebiscite so that national and local elections could be held.

Peasant organizations and other supporters of redistributive agrarian reform urged the President to use her extraordinary powers to act quickly and implement a sweeping reform programme. They wanted Presidential action before a new Constitution was ratified and a legislative assembly elected, since both would almost certainly curb presidential authority and open the way for the opponents of reform to take evasive action. Meanwhile the first objective of the advocates of a conservative approach to agrarian reform was to ensure that President Aquino would not use her decree-making powers to launch a reform programme before a new Congress could meet and begin deliberations on the issue. The conservatives won the first battle, and arguably the most important, with the drafting of the Constitution in October 1986.

6.5.1 The Constitutional Commission

In fact, it could be argued that the first battle was won by the conservatives with the appointment of the Constitutional Commission on 25 May 1986. Jaime Tadeo, head of the Kilusang Magbubukid ng Pilipinas (the KMP or Peasant Movement of the Philippines), was the sole peasant representative on the Commission. Tadeo has said that at no time did more than nine of the 48 commissioners support constitutional proposals that would have opened the way to agrarian reform.[55]

While the President vowed not to interfere in Commission proceedings, her advisers virtually guaranteed the outcome by hand-picking the 48 commissioners.[56] From the Aquino campaign team, Fr. Joaquin Bernas and Bernardo Villegas played a prominent role. At least four of the commissioners were close friends of the President's family, including the Commission president Cecilia Muñoz-Palma.[57] Law professor Flerida Ruth Romero became Secretary General of the Commission.[58] Ten commissioners had been delegates to the 1971 Constitutional Convention.[59] By appointing a preponderance of former senators, congressmen and Supreme Court justices, as well as representatives of the conservative Catholic hierarchy and the business community, the Commission's work was virtually guaranteed to be more of a restoration of the pre-martial law constitutional order than a fresh start.[60] Commissioner José B. Laurel Jr., brother of Vice-president Laurel and head of the clan, kept up the family tradition of having participated in every constitutional convention in the nation's history.[61]

The Commission set up a number of committees to draft sections of the new charter. The advocates of redistributive reform concentrated their efforts in the Committee on Social Justice (CSJ), which was responsible for drafting the provisions on reform. In the past, agrarian reform programmes in the Philippines and elsewhere were often undermined by appeals to constitutions that prohibited any intrusion on private property rights. Supporters of redistributive reform wanted to ensure a constitutional mandate for an effective agrarian reform programme. An initial draft of provisions on agrarian reform that was based on the demands of farmers' organizations and NGOs was submitted to the CSJ.

The process of debate in the committee might be described as the transformation of a basically revolutionary approach to reform into a liberal approach.[62] The nine advocates of redistributive reform mentioned by Tadeo held a majority in the 17 member CSJ.[63] The committee drafted constitutional provisions that would enable the government to implement a comprehensive redistributive reform. Interestingly, Tadeo later commented that Fr. Bernas had been extremely supportive of the minority effort to give substance to agrarian reform provisions in the Constitution.[64] Thus it appears he threw his support behind a liberal approach to reform. However, the Commission in plenary session struck out most of the CSJ's provisions.

6.5.2 Limits placed on 'just distribution'

The Constitution went further than either the Commonwealth charter of 1935 or Marcos' 1973 Constitution in declaring that agrarian reform would cover all agricultural lands and in enshrining specific rights of farmers and farmworkers. Yet, with provisions concerning the definition of the scope, timing, compensation and voluntary land-sharing associated with reform, the Constitution gave ample room to the opponents of redistributive reform to limit the scope of such a programme:

> The State shall, by law undertake an agrarian reform program founded on the right of farmers and regular farmworkers, who are landless, to own directly or collectively the lands they till or, in the case of other farmworkers, to receive a just share of the fruits thereof. To this end, the State shall encourage and undertake the just distribution of all agricultural lands, subject to such priorities and reasonable retention limits as the Congress may prescribe, taking into account ecological, developmental or equity considerations, and subject to the payment of just compensation. In determining retention limits, the State shall respect the right of small landowners. The State shall further provide incentives for voluntary land sharing.[65]

The tone of the Commission's plenary debates on agrarian reform was best exemplified by Commission Vice-president, former Senator Ambrosio B. Padilla. He argued that delegates should not enshrine in the new charter the abolition of what was actually the desirable institution of tenancy, nor should they allow universal coverage of all lands under agrarian reform.[66] Commissioner Bernardo Villegas, of the CRC and Opus Dei and active participant in Aquino's campaign, constantly reminded the Commission that it did not possess the expertise to mandate a clear-cut programme, implying that it should leave such a task to the experts.[67] In the end they would leave much of the task to Congress.

While the Constitution endorsed the 'just distribution' of 'all' agricultural lands, at the same time it limited the meaning of 'just distribution'. One of the most important limitations was the provision that delegated to Congress the authority to determine three of the most important defining characteristics of any reform programme: scope of coverage, timing and phasing, as well as the amount of land that owners would be allowed to retain. The Committee on Social Justice (CSJ) itself agreed to enshrine the right of landowners to retain land and to allow Congress to determine the amount that could be retained. Allowing a right to land retention was consistent with a liberal approach to reform if the retention limit remained small. However, this was clearly an important concession by those who supported redistributive reform since they knew that it would be difficult to secure low retention limits in Congress.[68]

The Constitution also enshrined the rights of small absentee landowners by stating that, 'In determining retention limits, the State shall respect the right of small landowners'. While no definition was provided for 'small landowner', the Commission understood the term to refer to 'teachers, clerks, nurses and other hardworking and frugal people'.[69] Thus small owners cultivating their own land were put on the same footing as absentee landlords whose land was farmed by tenants or agricultural workers. The provision implicitly set an absolute floor to retention limits equivalent to some arguable average-size small holding.[70] Not only could this clause limit the amount of land available for an agrarian reform programme, it also provided a constitutional mechanism that could be exploited by those wishing to evade redistribution.

The way was left open to landowners to expel tenants from their land and hire farmworkers in order to evade reform. A classic tactic of large landowners has been to divide their land into small holdings, transferring ownership to relatives and clients. Many absentee owners have small holdings, so an unquali-fied 'right of small landowners' could result in an enormous reduction in the amount of land available for redistribution. The original proposal presented by the CSJ, which spoke of not 'unduly' depriving small owners of their lands, provided scope for assessing the type of small holding. It did not establish a 'right of small owners' over and above the stated right of tenants to own the land they till. In defending the provision, Commissioners Christian S. Monsod of the BBC and NAMFREL and Bishop Teodoro C. Bacani argued that tenants on land retained by these small owners could be resettled on public lands.[71] The Constitution emphasized resettlement on public lands as a major component of reform. This would provide the basis for later arguments to undertake resettle-ment and the distribution of public lands before touching privately owned lands.[72]

The Commission's decision to grant Congress the power to determine 'priorities' in a future agrarian reform programme introduced an important ambiguity in the coverage of commercial crop lands controlled by large owners and agribusiness corporations. For several commissioners, the term 'priorities' referred to Congress' power both to decide when farms of certain sizes should be distributed, and when farm land planted to specific crops should be covered. Commissioner Villegas from the CRC stated that this clause empowered

Congress to 'prioritize the coverage of different kinds of crop lands'.[73] This view was shared by Commissioner Ricardo J. Romulo, lay Catholic and NAMFREL member and one of the businessmen whom Ongpin had introduced to RAM. It was also supported by Commissioner Francisco A. Rodrigo, former senator long active in conservative Catholic organizations, and thought by many to have been one of the 'US contacts' on the Commission.[74] Rodrigo had been in the minority in the CSJ and let full vent to views that were well-received by the Commission in plenary session. Commission vice-president Padilla also supported this interpretation of Congressional authority. José N. Nolledo, a professor who had been Palawan's delegate to the 1971 Con-Con, argued that by determining priorities, Congress was empowered to exempt agro-industrial corporations from the programme or to limit reform to rice and corn lands covered by Marcos before proceeding to other crops.[75] The views of these commissioners were important since they could be used as the basis of future constitutional challenges to reform legislation.

Peasant leader Jaime Tadeo opposed the inclusion of this clause and was supported by Commissioner Rene V. Sarmiento, a human rights lawyer who worked with Diokno during the Marcos years, as well as Commissioner Minda Luz M. Quesada, a grass-roots health worker, and Commissioner José E. Suarez, who had been a Pampanga delegate to the 1971 Con-Con and a leader of BAYAN. They argued that the insertion of this clause opened the door for exempting or delaying the implementation of reform on non-food commercial crop lands. It also provided a constitutional basis for Congress to decide the timing of future reform programmes. Timing is a crucial determinant of the effectiveness of an agrarian reform programme, since the longer the time allotted, the greater the leeway for evasive action by landowners.

Another limit imposed on 'just distribution' made it subject to 'ecological, developmental or equity considerations'. Commissioner Ponciano L. Bennagen, a nationalist professor of social anthropology, evidently proposed this phrase with the intention of ensuring that reform would be both equitable and ecologically sound. However, the use of the word 'developmental' provided constitutional grounds to the conservative approach, which argues that redistribution should be limited since it will hinder the potential contribution of large farms to development. This was precisely the meaning attached to this clause by Commissioner Villegas.[76]

Another extremely important qualification of 'just distribution' was the Constitution's affirmation that, 'The State shall further provide incentives for voluntary land-sharing'.[77] As has been demonstrated repeatedly, 'voluntary' arrangements are anathema to redistributive reform because they risk leaving the nexus of landowner power over tenants and farmworkers intact. The provision was suggested by Commissioner Florangel Rosario Braid, Dean of the Asian Institute of Journalism. He wanted to encourage the type of land-sharing then being undertaken in Negros in cooperation with the business community and its protegé, a well-known NGO called Philippine Business for Social Progress (PBSP). This was the same model promoted by Villegas during the election campaign.[78] Landowners who engaged voluntarily in sharing a portion of their lands with tenants or farmworkers would thereby have a means to avoid outright redistribution of their lands. While Commissioner Hilario G. Davide Jr., who had been a Cebu delegate to the 1971 Con-Con, warned that this provision could negate reform altogether, Commissioner Nolledo pushed hard for its adoption and succeeded with a 16 to 14 vote.

With an eye to the land rights of indigenous peoples and cultivators who had lost control of their lands to agribusiness corporations, the CSJ's original proposal stated that agrarian reform would be applied in public lands including those 'under lease or concession' (a specific reference to lands leased to domestic and foreign agribusiness) subject to 'prior rights of original inhabitants'. The phrase, 'original inhabitants', however, was struck from the final version, which, although guaranteeing the 'rights of indigenous communities to their ancestral lands', also opened the way for agribusiness corporations to escape land reform under the rubric of 'prior rights'.[79]

While the original CSJ text recognized the 'primacy' of the rights of 'farmers and farmworkers' in the reform process, the final version only mentioned 'the right of farmers and regular farmworkers who are landless'. This excluded a large section of agricultural producers who can be considered 'seasonal workers', like the *sacadas*, or cane cutters of Negros, and the landless labourers who now find employment only at harvest and planting time in other crop sectors. In the final version of the Constitution, regular farmworkers were guaranteed only a 'just share' of the fruits of production, and not the right to receive land. This was the phrase that Aquino had used in her Makati campaign speech on 6 January 1986. In legal parlance a 'just share' can easily be said to mean no more than a guarantee that regular farmworkers have the right to wages dictated by the 'free market'. In an economy where landowners enjoy monopsony power in labour markets (where a small number of landowners can determine wage levels), 'market justice' cannot appear very attractive to farmworkers. At its best, this provision could mean that regular farmworkers have a right to the government legislated minimum wage for agricultural work.

The Constitution not only failed to provide a framework for farmworkers to receive land, it was also silent on the situation of marginal farmers. The farmer who owns a tiny plot and must work for others to earn a subsistence income was given no constitutional grounds to benefit from agrarian reform. By striking out the 'primacy of rights' accorded to farmers and farmworkers, the Commissioners removed the one clause that would have recognized the small producers' rights as paramount in an agrarian reform programme. The original CSJ formulation would have meant that a tenant actually farming the land could not be legally ejected by a small absentee landowner.[80] The final version accorded no such protection.

6.5.3 The right of landowners to 'just compensation'

As well as enshrining the right of Congress to determine retention limits, the Constitution's guarantee that land redistribution would be subject to 'the payment of just compensation' was a major concession to the landowners. Originally, the CSJ proposed 'a fair and progressive system of compensation'. This was an effort to break from the concept of 'just compensation' first introduced under US colonial reforms and enshrined in the 1935 and 1973 Constitutions.[81] 'Fair and progressive' compensation meant that small landowners would be compensated at a higher rate than large landowners, while 'just compensation' had a precise traditional and legal interpretation in the Philippines as meaning payment at the 'market value'. The CSJ based its proposal for 'fair and progressive' compensation on a plan outlined by liberal reform advocate Mahar Mangahas.

The issue of compensation is one of the central problems raised by agrarian reform. As we have seen, liberal advocates of redistributive reform have always had difficulty in reconciling the need to redistribute assets with the traditional right of compensation implied by the principles of private property.[82] The advocates of redistributive reform argued that if landowners had any claim for compensation it had to be justified both on the basis of improvements they made to the land and proof that their title to the land was legitimately acquired. They argued that, in many cases, peasant producers had already paid for the land several times over by paying exorbitant rents to the landowners or working for wages well below the minimum.

The conservative majority in the Commission was determined to preserve the traditional right of landowners to market-value compensation for any land covered by agrarian reform. Several commissioners argued that since 'just compensation' meant 'fair market value' under the eminent domain clause of the Constitution's Bill of Rights, it should mean the same in relation to agrarian reform.[83] Four commissioners were particularly outspoken on this issue. Once again, Commissioner Rodrigo, who was an ardent advocate of Congressional authority over reform, fully endorsed market-value compensation to landowners. He was joined in this by Commissioners Efrain B. Treñas, Florenz D. Regalado - both Deans of law - and Roberto R. Concepcion, former Chief Justice. Commissioner Bernas stressed that while landowners would receive 'full market value' for their land, the government was mandated to subsidize the purchase of this by farmer beneficiaries.[84]

Commissioner José F.S. Bengzon, a corporate lawyer who was a Pangasinan delegate to the 1971 Con-Con and a close relative to Health Minister and Aquino confidant Alfredo Bengzon, argued that 'just compensation' meant not only market-value but immediate payment to landowners. This interpretation was supported by Commissioner Regalado, who styled himself as a defender of landowners' rights. He stated that landowners should be paid the entire market value of their land *before* any action was taken by government.[85] However, no government could afford to make direct immediate payment to landowners at market value without causing spiralling inflation and huge budget deficits. In other words, arguments for immediate payment for land acquired by government amounted to arguments against redistributive reform.

Commissioner Tadeo and his supporters regarded this provision as a clear indication that they had lost the battle to establish a constitutional mandate for redistributive reform. For agrarian reform to be affordable to the nation, the level of compensation must be limited either by a discretionary policy or by offering compensation over time, which would allow inflation to whittle down landowners' earnings. Tadeo and others argued that only a policy of progressive compensation constitutes any actual redistribution of assets. Only this, therefore, would allow the launch of an affordable programme of reform beneficial to the landless. Many of the provisions inserted by the advocates of the conservative approach to reform merely deferred a resolution of the reform debate to future debates over legislation. However, the provision on 'just compensation' enshrined a traditional landowner right in the new Constitution. This tilted the balance of power in future debates decidedly in favour of the advocates of the conservative approach. This provision afforded a constitutional basis for reducing agrarian reform to little more than a government sponsored 'market transaction', negating the concept of *redistributive* reform.

On 12 October 1986, the Commission voted 45 to 2 in favour of the draft Constitution, with only Tadeo and Suarez dissenting, and submitted the draft to President Aquino.[86] It was overwhelmingly approved by a plebiscite on 2 February 1987. However, there was little ground to perceive the vote as an endorsement of any of the specific constitutional provisions. As is so often the case in conducting a plebiscite, the government conducted its campaign for a 'yes vote' as a referendum for or against the leadership of President Aquino. This fact was driven home by University of the Philippines president José Abueva, former Secretary of the 1971 Con-Con, a close supporter of Aquino and a strong advocate of a 'yes' vote:

> Whatever else may be on the minds of the leaders and the voters in the campaign and plebiscite on the 1986 Constitution, the whole political exercise is a referendum on President Aquino's leadership and her popularity with the people.[87]

In fact, it could be argued that the inclusion of the provisions proposed by the CSJ, which would have laid a constitutional basis for redistributive reform, would not have substantially altered the vote.

The fact that these provisions were excluded from the Constitution was therefore not motivated by the government's desire to win support for its charter. Rather, the debate over the Constitution was the first indication of the influence wielded by the advocates of the conservative approach within the Aquino government. Abueva, in a forceful argument in favour of the charter, recognized its limits, 'As the creation of a selected group of human beings it necessarily reflects their shared values, consensual ideas, and compromises.'[88] The shared values and ideas of the Constitutional Commission's majority were consistent with the vision of agrarian reform articulated by President Aquino and her Cabinet during their first year in office.

6.6 Conclusion

Cory Aquino and her civilian supporters captured the presidency in the wake of a military revolt against President Marcos. While Aquino and her closest advisers took some initial steps against the wishes of the AFP, they made repeated concessions to the military authorities to avoid an outright rupture with the majority of the officer corps. Thus the politicized armed forces remained a major actor within the government, reinforcing the conservative bias of the most powerful civilians in the Aquino coalition.

Aquino's first Cabinet was dominated by the conservative reformists who had played such an important role in her election campaign. There was little interest in redistributive reform among the ministers in charge of the government's economic policy. Minister of Trade José Concepcion was most concerned with maintaining a degree of economic protection and government subsidy for industries, like his own, which depended on such measures for their survival. He was also anxious to attract foreign capital for both direct investments and joint ventures. Agricultural Minister Ramon Mitra was, above all, a traditional politician intent on securing an important position in the new political order. He consequently promoted an agricultural policy compatible with both landowning and agribusiness interests.

Finance Minister Jaime Ongpin was committed to a vision of rural development where domestic and foreign agribusiness would play a leading role. It has not been generally recognized that, as early as 1986, the controversial corporate stock-sharing programme, which would exempt agribusiness firms from land redistribution under the 1988 agrarian reform law, was essentially elaborated by Ongpin as the 'centre-piece' of the government's rural development strategy. Agrarian Reform Minister Heherson Alvarez expressed an openness to the ideas of the liberal reform advocates during this period, but was unwilling to champion such an approach. Alvarez's plans for reform remained within the confines of the Marcos agrarian reform programme. Economic Planning Minister Solita Monsod had endorsed the proposals for a liberal reform in the draft 'Policy Agenda', but backed away from proposals in the face of Cabinet indifference. The most radical members of the Cabinet, like Labour Minister Augusto Sanchez, were urban-based and lacked experience of agricultural affairs. They contributed little to debates about agrarian reform before they were forced out of the government. Executive Secretary Joker Arroyo, disliked by both the military and the conservatives in Cabinet, would play a decidedly negative role in the future debates over presidential action on agrarian reform.

While President Aquino's first year in office offered a unique opportunity for action on agrarian reform, the new government failed to act decisively. In fact, the President herself resolved the ambiguity that had characterized her campaign pronouncements on agrarian reform. She spoke about reform mainly in terms of productivity enhancing programmes rather than land redistribution, and indicated that land redistribution would be inappropriate on her family's *hacienda*. The early confusion and long delay over the appointment of an Agrarian

Reform Minister initiated a pattern of revolving Secretaries and a lack of leadership in this Department that persisted over the next five years. Yet the President retained overwhelming popular support despite her equivocation on agrarian reform.

Those who were most committed to a liberal approach to redistributive reform were confined to the lower echelons of government. From that position, they laid out a clear plan for the expansion of the government's reform programme and called for immediate presidential action to implement a reform covering all agricultural lands. However, their plans were largely ignored by those occupying leadership positions within the state. They also formed a small, but active minority within the Constitutional Commission, but failed to win over enough support to ensure a constitutional basis for redistributive reform.

Villegas, supported by many other commissioners who had been active in the Aquino election campaign, ensured that the Commission's work would be faithful to the demands of the conservative reformists who had been instrumental in Aquino's rise to power. The minority in the Commission, which had sought to make the Constitution a new beginning, rather than an instrument of restoration, believed that they had a popular mandate to lay the foundation for redistributive reform. Indeed, there was ample evidence during the government's first year in office that a broad spectrum of opinion favoured rapid and decisive action to implement a redistributive programme. The advocates of the liberal approach persisted in their efforts to gain presidential endorsement for a redistributive programme during the government's second year in office.

Notes

1. After the election I was able to examine stacks of official ballot papers, still bound on their original pads, pre-signed 'Marcos-Tolentino' and thumb-printed, in the possession of former Sorsogon Governor Raul Lee. There are numerous accounts of the election (see Diokno, 1988; Burton, 1989).

2. 'Memorandum of the President' 14 January 1986 cited in Alvarez, 1986.

3. Burton, 1989, p.324.

4. Antonio V. Cuenco, MP, from the prominent Cebu clan and leader of the regional opposition party *Pinaghi-Usa* formed in 1983 in the central Visayas, was made Political Affairs minister. Victor S. Ziga, MP, was put in charge of General Services. Later, Omar M. Dianalan, MP and KBL member until he defected to Aquino in 1985, was put in charge of Muslim Affairs (Noble, 1987, p.426).

5. Hernando B. Perez, MP, was made Transportation Minister and Luis Villafuerte, Bicol landowner and MP, was put in charge of Government Reorganization. Of the three whose loyalty to Laurel and UNIDO was questionable, Neptali Gonzales, MP, received the Justice Ministry, while Ernesto Maceda, former Senator, MP and close friend of Ninoy Aquino, was made Minister of Energy and Natural Resources, and Alberto G. Romulo, MP, was put in charge of Budget Management.

6. José Antonio U. Gonzales had long been close to Ninoy Aquino and was made Minister of Tourism (Burton, 1989, pp.105-07). Other presidential family and friends included Bengzon, Maceda and Herminio S. Aquino, the President's uncle, who was put in charge of Imelda Marcos's Ministry of Human Settlements. This was soon to be dismantled allowing him to go on to represent the family in the Tarlac constituency of the new Congress. Heherson Alvarez, close friend to Ninoy Aquino in the US, would later be named Secretary of Agrarian Reform.

7. On Fernandez's relationship with President Aquino's family see Chapter 3, section 3.4.5.

8. Applying the title 'technocrat' to businessmen like Ongpin and Fernandez tends to mask their principal role as representatives of specific class interests. These were manifested both in their personal command of capital and in their participation in professional and social organizations associated with the business community. See Chapter 4, section 4.5.2. Solita Monsod may have been appointed in part because she was the wife of prominent Catholic businessman and leading member of the BBC and NAMFREL, Christian Monsod. But her position once in the Cabinet was determined almost entirely by her technical expertise. Minister of Science Antonio V. Arizabal might also be placed in this category.

9. See McCoy, 1988.

10. Kiunisala, 1987, p.13. The Yap family were a Chinese Mestizo family long allied to the José Cojuangco clan in Tarlac. José Yap served as the President's aide-de-camp, and would later head the ruling party's provincial organization and be elected to Congress.

11. On 12 March 1986, the Islamic Conference of the Philippines passed a resolution asking for his appointment to the top post at MAR (Noble, 1987, p.426).

12. While Gamboa was born to a *sacada* family, like other Filipino politicians of humble origins he entered the elite by becoming a lawyer and accountant.

13. Kiunisala, 1987, p.13.

14. Interview, Conrado Estrella, former Minister of Agrarian Reform, Makati, 26 February 1989.

15. The President may also have picked Alavarez since he came from the north, a stronghold of support for the deposed dictator and presidential rivals like Defense Minister Juan Ponce Enrile.

16. Neptali Gonzales, Guingona, Maceda, Mercado, Pimentel, Romulo, Saguisag, Salonga and Ziga were all later elected to the Senate on the government's slate, while Enrile was one of two opposition Senators elected. In addition, Mitra, Cuenco and Herminio Aquino were elected to the House, while Villafuerte became Governor of Camarines Sur.

17. Paul A. Gigot, 'Manila's Economic Revolutionary', Wall Street Journal (5 March 1986), p.32, reprinted in Schirmer and Shalom, 1987, pp.373-75.

18. See Chapter 10.

19. In a collection of Ongpin's (1988) major speeches and interviews there is not a single reference to agrarian reform until late January 1987.

20. 'Remarks delivered to the Carnegie Endowment,' 7 April 1986 (Ongpin, 1988, p.81).

21. *Ibon Facts and Figures*, no. 193 (31 August 1986).

22. Dy, 1986.

23. US House of Representatives, 1986 (29 April), pp.26-27.

24. *Ibon Facts and Figures*, no. 193 (31 August 1986).

25. 'Aquino Interviewed on Commitment to Change,' *La Reppublica* (Rome), 11 March 1986. Reproduced in Foreign Broadcast and Information Service, Daily Report: Asia-Pacific, 13 March 1986; cited in Bello, 1987, p.85.

26. 'Address to the Board of Directors,' Asian Development Bank, 30 April 1986. Reprinted in US House of Representatives, 1986 (30 April), p.233.

27. *MB* (22 May 1986) cited in *Ibon Facts and Figures*, no.189 (30 June 1986), p.4.

28. *BD* (6 June 1986) cited in *Ibon Facts and Figures*, no.189 (30 June 1986), pp.4-5.

29. *BT* (5 March 1986).

30. MAF, 1986, pp.2-4. The plan also endorsed security of tenure on uplands and the return of tribal lands.

31. Interview (anonimity requested) 10 May 1991.

32. *Ibon Facts and Figures*, no. 193 (31 August 1986), p.1.

33. Kiunisala, 1987, pp.16-17.

34. Interview with Philip Juico, former Secretary of Agrarian Reform, Makati, 16 August 1989.

35. Interview with Ex-Mayor Inocencio Uy, Roxas, Isabela, 20 June 1989. See Chapter 10, section 10.2.2 for a discussion of Uy's voluntary offer to sell.

36. Monsod, 1986, pp.75-76.

37. Alburo et al, 1986 and NEDA, 1986a. For a discussion of both documents see *Ibon Facts and Figures*, no.191 (31 July 1986) and Nemenzo, 1988, pp.242-45.

38. Interview, Solita Monsod, 9 May 1991.
39. Interview, Solita Monsod, 9 May 1991.
40. NEDA, 1986a, p.17, emphasis is mine.
41. 'Development Policies and Business Opportunities,' 12th Business Conference at Philippine Plaza, 27 November 1986 (Ongpin, 1988, pp.91-93).
42. NEDA, 1986b, pp.95-101. The physical projections of the plan are discussed in more detail in the next chapter.
43. The most blatant of these was the statement that 'Under land surveys, a total area of 3,375,000 hectares is projected to be subdivided into farm and homelots during the Plan period'. Neda, 1986b, p.97. Closer examination of the plan's Table 3.5 revealed that the figure had to refer to the *number of lots*, or some other multiple of an estimated 375,500 hectares, to be covered by a 'land capability-suitability classification survey'.
44. NEDA, 1986b, pp.99-100.
45. NEDA, 1986b, Annexe 3.2.
46. *BD* (18 February 1987).
47. NEDA, 1986b, p.101.
48. *MC* (20 June 1986) cited in *Ibon Facts and Figures*, no.191 (31 July 1986), p.6.
49. Presidential [PCGR], 1986a and 1986b, pp.34-38.
50. Presidential [PCGR], 1986b, p.38.
51. Interview, Conrado Estrella, former Minister of Agrarian Reform, Makati, 26 February 1989.
52. Presidential [PCGR], 1986b, pp.38-56.
53. Interview, Gerardo Bulatao, Assistant Secretary, DAR, 21 November 1988.
54. FAO, 1987a.
55. Interview with Jaime Tadeo, 16 September 1987, Manila.
56. Initially a list of over 1,000 potential delegates was drawn up. Executive Secretary Joker Arroyo and Fulgencio Factoran apparently played a central role in the final selection, which accounts for the fact that many were lawyers close to Arroyo. The President and her advisers chose 44 delegates, reserving five places for Marcos' KBL and one place for the pro-Marcos Iglesia ni Kristo, but the latter declined the invitation and former Senator and KBL strong-man Alejandro Almendras withdrew in order to take part in coming elections. This left a total of 48.
57. Floor Leader Napoleon G. Rama was a close friend to Ninoy Aquino (Burton, 1989, p.56), as was ex-Senator Francisco A. Rodrigo. Bernas had become very close to the President, and Lorenzo M. Sumulong was her uncle.
58. Romero, who was said to be the foremost authority on women and legal rights (Aguilar, 1987, p.53) and had been a classmate of Arroyo, later became presidential counsel.
59. Ahmad Domocao Alonto, Aldofo S. Azcuña (later to become Presidential spokesman), José F.S. Bengzon Jr., José D. Calderon, Hilario G. Davide Jr., Alberto M.K. Jamir, José N. Nolledo, Napoleon G. Rama, Rustico F. de los Reyes Jr. and José E. Suarez.
60. Many politicians, notably Raul Manglapus, declined to participate since they would be barred from running for office for at least a year. *Former senators*: Ahmad Domocao Alonto, Ambrosio B. Padilla, Francisco A. Rodrigo (also close to the Church hierarchy), Decoroso R. Rosales, Lorenzo Sumulong; *former Congressmen*: Hilario G. Davide Jr., José B. Laurel Jr. (Salvador's elder brother and guardian of the clan), Regalado E. Maambong (KBL member), Blas F. Ople (KBL member); *former justices*: Cecilia Muñoz-Palma (also an MP after 1984), Roberto R. Concepcion; *conservative Catholic*: Manila prelate Monsignor Teodoro C. Bacani, Bernardo Villegas (both close to the business community), Teresa Nieva of NAMFREL; *business*: José F.S. Bengzon, Jr. (corporate lawyer and relative of the Health Minister), Ricardo Romulo and Christian S. Monsod.
61. Ancestor Sotero Laurel was at the Malolos Congress, which drafted the constitution of the short-lived Philippine Republic in 1898; José P. Laurel was a delegate at the 1934 Constitutional Convention; and Sotero H. Laurel was a delegate to the 1971 Convention. One

wonders if the appointment of Vicente B. Foz, a rather innocuous journalist of the *Manila Bulletin*, to the 1986 Commission was primarily inspired by the presence of Vicente Foz, elected from Ilocos Sur, at the Malolos Convention in 1898.

62. This discussion is based largely on two articles on the committee debates written by Francisco Lara (Lara 1986a and 1986b).

63. Aside from Tadeo (who voted against the Constitution), these appear to have been Ponciano L. Bennagen (nationalist and anthropologist), Lino Brocka (film maker who walked out in protest), Edmundo G. Garcia (social democrat and political scientist), José Luis Martin C. Gascon (social democratic UP student leader), Minda Luz M. Quesada (grass roots health worker), José E. Suarez (nationalist who voted against the Constitution), Rene V. Sarmiento (human rights lawyer) and Christine Tan (Catholic sister and urban poor organizer).

64. Interview, Jaime Tadeo, Muntinlupa Prison, 7 May 1991.

65. *The Constitution of the Republic of the Philippines*, hereafter referred to as the Constitution, adopted by the Constitutional Commission of 1986, Article 13, Section 4.

66. Lara, 1986a, p.18.

67. Lara, 1986a, pp.24–25.

68. Lara, 1986a, p.5.

69. Tolk, 1989, p.18 citing Bernas, 1988, Vol.II, p.479.

70. Tolk, 1989, p.19.

71. Lara, 1986a, pp.14–15, citing the Journal of the Constitutional Commission (hereafter JCC), 7 August 1986, p.13.

72. Constitution, Article 13, Section 6.

73. JCC, 7 August 1986, p.33 cited in Lara 1986a and 1986b.

74. On Rodrigo's background see Constantino, 1978, p.297. He was the commissioner referred to by Joker Arroyo as one of the US Embassy's 'people in the Con-Com', in the embarrassing taped telephone conversations between President Aquino, Locsin and Arroyo, released to the press by former Marcos supporter Homobono Adaza. See Jonathan Steele's report in the *Guardian* (26 January 1987) and Constantino, 1987, p.149.

75. Originally both commissioners along with Romulo, Padilla and de los Reyes wanted to leave even more leeway by stating 'priorities *and other conditions* to be determined by Congress'. Lara, 1986, p.11, citing the JCC p.33.

76. Lara, 1986b, pp.4–5.

77. Constitution, Section 4.

78. Lara, 1986b, p.5. PBSP was chaired by Andres Soriano III, chairman of the board of one of the Philippines' largest corporations, San Miguel. On Villegas, see Chapter 5, section 5.9.

79. Lara, 1986b, p.6.

80. Lara, 1986b, p.7.

81. See the 1935 Constitution, Article 13, section 4 and the 1973 Constitution, Article 14, section 13.

82. See Chapter 1.

83. Tolk, 1989, p.29. Constitution, Article III, Section 9.

84. Lara, 1986a, p.23.

85. Lara, 1986a, p.23.

86. Nationalist film-maker, Lino Brocka, who had supported Tadeo in the CSJ, resigned in protest from the Commission in September.

87. Abueva, José V. 'Yes to the 1986 Constitution: Perspectives on Self-Determination, Democratization, Nation-Building and Contributing to Peaceful Change in the World,' 14 January 1987. *PDI* 19 Jan 1987, p.7.

88. Abueva, 1986, p.3.

7

THE PEASANT MOVEMENT AND THE DEBATE OVER PRESIDENTIAL ACTION ON AGRARIAN REFORM

7.1 Introduction

While the Constitutional debate on agrarian reform set severe constraints on future presidential action, the most important debate occurred over the President's executive order, to be issued in July 1987. Although the Constitution gave Congress a final say over the shape of reform, the President had the power to initiate a programme, and her executive order would set the pace for future Congressional action. The debate over presidential action that took place during the first half of 1987 was precipitated by an extensive and successful peasant campaign to place reform on the national agenda. The establishment of the Congress for a People's Agrarian Reform (CPAR) represented an unprecedented level of unity within the peasant movement.

Advocates of the liberal approach to reform were able to gain a much more prominent position in the Executive during this period than they had throughout 1986. The course of the debate over the executive order brought into clear relief the nature of the Aquino administration and the responsibility of various members of Cabinet for the direction taken in agrarian reform policy. It also revealed characteristics of the Philippine state, as well as the major sources of societal support for the state, which help to explain the government's stance on agrarian reform.

7.2 Peasant movement demands redistributive reform

After the new government was established, peasant organizations wasted little time in pressing their demands for swift action on agrarian reform. Leaders from the conservative peasant organizations that had previously supported and worked within Marcos' limited programme met with journalists to explain their proposals for reform. These they had drawn up with the assistance of MAR officials.[1] Like officials in the government, their vision of reform remained entirely within the confines of Marcos era legislation. However, at the grass-roots a much more radical set of agrarian reform demands was articulated at conferences held all over the country during the first six months of the new government, involving tens of thousands of peasants and their supporters, as well as Church and non-governmental organizations (NGOs).[2]

Immediately after the fall of Marcos, NGOs linked to the social democratic NGO coalition, Philippine Partnership for the Development of Human Resources in Rural Areas (PHILDHRRA), participated in a series of local

217

meetings throughout the country, culminating in a national forum on 14 March. Following the meeting, PHILDHRRA launched a series of Consultations on Agrarian Reform and Rural Development (CARRD) from the village to the national level. These involved some 10,000 participants and culminated in a National Consultation on Agrarian Reform and Rural Development on 7-8 August.[3]

These efforts were actively endorsed by the FAO and the Asian NGO Coalition for Agrarian Reform and Rural Development (ANGOC) chaired by Dioscoro L. Umali, the long-time advocate of the liberal approach to reform who had hosted Ladejinsky during his visits to the Philippines in the Marcos years.[4] The meetings articulated demands that were forwarded to the PCGR Survey Team at the Ministry of Agrarian Reform, the CSJ, which was debating the Constitutional provisions on agrarian reform, and Minister Solita Monsod's NEDA, which was drafting the country's five-year economic plan.

The most articulate and forceful set of demands on agrarian reform to emerge from the grass-roots during this early period was presented by the militant peasant organization, the KMP. The KMP was formally organized in 1985 as an alliance of local peasant organizations that had adopted an unambiguous national democratic platform. While their claim to 750,000 members was no doubt exaggerated, they were clearly the largest organized bloc among the peasantry, since many of the more moderate groups often had only a 'paper membership'. Many veteran peasant leaders were active in the KMP.

On 18 March 1986, KMP leaders met with Agriculture Minister Ramon Mitra and presented a list of five demands: 'genuine land reform'; an end to 'foreign monopoly and control in agriculture'; reduced farm input prices and increased farm produce prices; support services for peasant farmers; and a guarantee of the 'democratic rights' of peasants to organize and participate in decision-making free from military repression.[5] On 6 June the KMP National Council approved a comprehensive and detailed *Program For Genuine Land Reform* that was submitted to the President three days later.[6] The plan called for free distribution of land to agricultural tenants, impoverished small farmers and farmworkers; priority to women for the use and ownership of land; protection of ancestral land rights of indigenous minorities; selective compensation to former owners; nationalization of lands controlled by foreign transnational corporations; introduction of cooperatives and support services to develop the productivity of agriculture; and complementary programmes of industrialization.

KMP leaders recognized that proposals such as 'free distribution' and 'selective compensation', which were essentially elements of a revolutionary approach, would not be adopted by the Aquino government. In March Tadeo said, 'it would seem too radical to speak right away of free distribution of land'.[7] The KMP was willing to go along with a liberal approach to reform, which was what Tadeo had advocated within the Constitutional Commission. With no action and no clear policy stand on agrarian reform on the part of the government, the KMP launched nationwide 'organized land occupations' on 26

September 1986.[8] Other peasant organizations also decided to occupy idle and abandoned lands in an attempt to force the government to make good its promises for reform.[9]

On 21 October, the anniversary of the Marcos land reform, the KMP organized a demonstration at Mendiola Bridge, which leads to Malacañang, the presidential palace. They demanded an audience with the President to discuss immediate action on agrarian reform. They were met with barricades and hundreds of riot police and military troops. According to DAR official Gerardo Bulatao, it was Executive Secretary Joker Arroyo who 'stopped the President from meeting with the KMP'. Bulatao said that several DAR officials had heard about the KMP rally, found out what their demands were, and prepared an answer for the President. Minister Alvarez went to the President with the proposal that she meet the KMP. Arroyo was there and dismissed the suggestion saying, 'Land Reform, *saka na iyan* ['it's not a priority']'.[10] This was not the first time that Arroyo had blocked Malacañang from acting on the issue. According to Bulatao, Arroyo 'sat on proposed legislation' in June 1986 and 'was idle again in August'.[11] Arroyo's opposition to swift action on redistributive reform coincided with the position of his rivals in Cabinet, as well as the views of the military.

7.3 The military and a shift to the right

During 1986, the AFP under General Fidel Ramos attempted to restore its tarnished image after its participation in almost fifteen years of dictatorial rule. Ramos spoke about the 'New Armed Forces of the Philippines' which was 'undertaking a program of moral reorientation of its officers and men'.[12] He pledged the loyalty of the New AFP to the civilian government and spoke of its determination to defeat the communist insurgency. He warned against entering peace talks with the NDF. Instead, he proposed a new strategic counterinsurgency plan labelled '*Mamamayan*' (People), which combined the goals of national reconciliation with security and development. In the old days, he said, development had given priority to the 'haves' and now it must give priority to the 'have nots', in the military as well as among the civilian population. Yet he did not outline any redistributive goals.

Despite objections from the military and the US, the government followed up the release of political prisoners in February and March 1986 with efforts to initiate talks with the NDF. The first open act of protest from AFP officers was launched by General José Zumel, a Marcos loyalist, and Arturo Tolentino, Marcos' vice-presidential candidate. The 'Manila Hotel' 'coup attempt' on 6 July was quickly put down by General Ramos. However, the start of formal talks between the government and the NDF on 5 August led to a more serious plot by RAM officers and Defence Minister Enrile.[13]

In November, in order to get the military's backing to head off the plot and remove Enrile, the President had to accede to military demands for the removal of several liberal democrats from the Cabinet. The President dismissed Local

Government Minister Aquilino Pimentel and Labour Minister Augusto Sanchez, the only two left-of-centre Cabinet ministers with powerful portfolios.[14] They had been opposed not only by the military, but also the domestic and foreign business community.[15] Jaime Ferrer, a veteran of the anti-Huk counterinsurgency war in the 1950s, replaced Pimentel in the Ministry of Local Government, and Franklin Drilon, who had been a Deputy Minister of Labour with a good relationship with the TNCs, replaced Sanchez. Another veteran of the 1950s and a critic of Marcos, General Rafael Ileto, was appointed Minister of Defense. These appointments increased the number of active supporters of the conservative approach to reform within the Cabinet.

On 27 November government and NDF representatives signed an agreement for a 60-day cease-fire and peace talks to begin on 8 December. The NDF put land reform at the top of its agenda for discussions. However, the Aquino government still gave no indication that it was prepared to make agrarian reform a priority in its own policy. The military was loath to endorse any programme which included government cooperation with the militant peasant movement. The military and US officials regarded the KMP as no more than a 'front' for the underground CPP.[16] Such a label is inappropriate, however, since the KMP was composed almost entirely of peasants whose local organizations throughout the archipelago were carrying out organizational work responsive to the everyday conditions of their members.[17] By categorizing militant peasant organizations as front groups, the military pre-empted those in MAR who argued that such groups should be involved in the implementation of agrarian reform.

The increasing role of the AFP in the Aquino government reinforced its bias against redistributive reform. When AFP officers endorsed economic reforms as part of the counterinsurgency effort, their policies resembled those of the business community and landowners. Brigadier General Luis A. Villa-Real, a veteran of the counterinsurgency war in the 1950s and head of the Philippine branch of the World Anti-Communist League, spoke only about the 'redistribution of economic benefits' not land or other assets.[18]

By the end of 1986, Minister Alvarez was still talking about agrarian reform in terms of a more thorough implementation of the Marcos programme, which would only 'eventually' be expanded to 'cover all arable public and private lands'.[19] On 14 December, President Aquino issued Memorandum No.56 asking Alvarez to head a task force to study the land-sharing programme put forward by acting Governor Daniel Lacson in Negros Occidental.[20] Also in December Monsod set up an Inter-Agency Task Force on Agrarian Reform (IATFAR), mainly concerned with calculating financial requirements for agrarian reform as it was formulated within the draft Constitution. However, these moves fell far short of peasant demands for early executive action to implement a comprehensive redistributive programme.

7.4 Mendiola massacre prompts government action

During the campaign leading up to the plebiscite on the Constitution on 2 February 1987, President Aquino engaged in classic patronage politics by using the occasion to distribute emancipation patents (EPs) to tenants on rice and corn lands covered by the Marcos programme.[21] According to one local DAR official, thousands of EPs ready for distribution in 1986 were held back to be re-issued under the signature of President Aquino:

> After Alvarez took over there was a verbal order from Manila. All EPs and Certificates of Agricultural Leasehold were to be held in abeyance and then were to be returned to the central office where they would be re-issued with the signature of President Aquino. They distributed these in their name, not in the name of Marcos.[22]

The KMP, still demanding an audience with the President to discuss its proposals for reform, set up a camp in front of the MAR buildings from 15 to 22 January. On 19 January, they held a congress in Quezon City and reported on the progress of their own land occupations. Tadeo met with Alvarez and the encounter ended in a shouting match.

On 22 January 1987, the KMP led a demonstration of 15,000 peasants to Malacañang and Jaime Tadeo vowed that they would be deterred no longer. Once again they were met at the Mendiola Bridge with barbed wire, police and a contingent of marines, but this time the troops opened fire. Nineteen peasants were killed in what became known as the 'Mendiola Bridge Massacre', as soldiers and plain-clothes gunmen hidden in the crowd of onlookers fired on the unarmed demonstrators.[23] Some government and US officials claimed that the left provoked the violence.[24] It is far more likely that the armed forces wanted to send a message to the militant peasant movement and their supporters and at the same time pre-empt any extension of the cease-fire with the NDF. Brigadier General Ramon E. Montaño, who was supposedly sanctioned for his part in the massacre and removed from the Philippine Constabulary Capitol Command, was later promoted to head the National Capitol Region Defense Command (NCRDC), set up as an anti-coup force to control all the armed forces in Metro Manila.[25]

The massacre was met with outrage by grass-roots organizations, many of whom had supported Aquino. The following day José Diokno and three other officials resigned from the Presidential Human Rights Commission and Maria Serena Diokno resigned as government peace negotiator. This backlash, together with the impending end of the cease-fire with the NDF, convinced the government that it had to act on the reform issue. Once again, it was peasant mobilization that propelled the government to take action.

7.4.1 The government's first draft programme

The day after Mendiola, the Inter-Agency Task Force on Agrarian Reform (IATFAR) recruited new members and quickly put together a proposal for an expanded reform programme.[26] Work on the January 23 document had clearly begun before the massacre, as part of an effort to raise foreign development assistance for the agrarian reform component of NEDA's *Medium Term Plan*. Its title, 'Accelerated Land Reform Project', indicated that it had been drafted as one project among many to be financed by foreign aid. However, it became the first of many draft versions of a proposed agrarian reform programme to be debated over the next seven months. After Mendiola, many in the Cabinet believed that it had become a political imperative for President Aquino to issue an executive order (EO) on agrarian reform before the May election and July convocation of a new Congress.[27]

The January 23 draft elaborated the main programme elements that would be debated in all subsequent drafts of a presidential executive order on agrarian reform. A four-phase programme was proposed, to be implemented in only five years and covering all private and public agricultural lands (see Table 7.1). 'Program A' involved the completion of the Marcos reform on about half a million hectares of tenanted rice and corn lands (over 7 hectares) and would be completed in the first two years. Also during the first two years, 'Program B' involved the redistribution of nearly a million hectares of other private lands that were idle or abandoned, foreclosed or forecloseable, sequestered by the government, or expropriated under the long-standing 'Landed Estates' programme. Programs A and B could be accomplished under existing legislation.

The January 'project' document stated that 'Program C', covering nearly four million hectares of privately owned lands, was not part of the project proposal, but rather to be implemented only after legislation would be passed by the new Congress.[28] 'Program D', covering public lands, was also not part of the proposal and was said to require further study. The January draft still remained within the confines of existing legislation and was silent on the controversial issue of retention limits and landowner compensation.[29] However, for the first time, it offered a clear and quantified projection for expanding the government programme to include *all private lands*, rather than following the general landowner proposition that public lands should be covered first. It also proposed a rapid implementation of reform within a six-year time frame. On the level of universality of coverage and timing it was not far from the liberal approach.

Cabinet members were sharply divided over the content of the programme and the proposed executive order. The advocates of the liberal approach in the lower echelons of government dusted off the proposals made in 1986 and lobbied for an executive order that would be a full-blown agrarian reform law, incorporating all four 'Programs' mentioned in the January draft, and enacted through the President's legislative powers. They knew that Congress could later amend such a law, but they felt that strong action by the President would make it more difficult for Congress to enact a watered-down programme. Cabinet member and NEDA Director Solita Monsod championed their cause.

The majority who backed a conservative approach were divided between those who believed that the President should limit her action to a Proclamation

Table 7.1: Accelerated Land Reform Project (23 January 1987)

Type of Land	Hectares	Time Frame	Legislation
Program A	**557,000**	**1987-1989**	Marcos PD 27
Rice & Corn Lands	557,000		(and RA 3844)
Program B	**939,000**	**1987-1989**	Existing
			legislation
Voluntary Offers	300,000		(RA 3844)
Idle & Abandoned	189,000		(LOI 227)
Expropriated[a]	100,000		(RA 3844)
Foreclosed(able)	300,000		
Sequestered	50,000		
Program C	**3,852,000**	**1989-1992**	New
- Haciendas under	2,333,000		legislation
labour administration			required.
- Other tenanted lands	957,000		(RA 1199)
- Tenanted rice & corn	562,000		
less than 7 hectares			
Programme D[b]			
(Still to be Defined)			CA 141
Public Lands			and new
			legislation
Total Programme Scope	**5,348,000**		

[a]Refers to Landed Estates over 24 hectares covered by the 1963 Code of Agrarian Reforms (as amended in 1971) RA 3844.
[b]In February DAR said 5,000,000 hectares of public alienable and disposable lands suitable for agriculture to be covered: 'logged-over areas', 'unnecessary military & civilian reservations' and 'areas of cancelled/expired' public land leases.
Source: 'Accelerated Land Reform Project', Integrated-Agency Task Force on Agrarian Reform (Manila: 23 January 1987) and 'The Aquino Government's Genuine & Comprehensive Agrarian Reform', Department of Agrarian Reform (February 1987).

announcing the main thrusts of a programme, which would be defined and passed into law later by Congress, and those who felt that she should pass legislation concerning only Programs A and B in the January draft - the acceleration of the implementation of existing agrarian reform laws.[30] The debate over the proposed executive order touched on all the main defining characteristics of agrarian reform, including: the scope and timing of the programme; retention limits; voluntary land transfer and corporate stock sharing; compensation to owners and payment by beneficiaries; programme finance; and beneficiary participation.

7.4.2 Cabinet Action Committee launches public debate

The Mendiola Massacre cast a dark shadow over the Aquino government and put into question its proclaimed intention to be a government based on 'people power'. On 26 January, some 30,000 people staged an 'indignation rally' and marched to the gates of Malacañang. The government wanted to repair the damage done to its credibility, and for the first time in history it allowed the demonstration to cross the Mendiola Bridge and proceed to within 20 yards of the presidential palace. Earlier, President Aquino had met with KMP leader Jaime Tadeo to make arrangements. Several government ministers and close advisers to the President went out and joined hands with the demonstrators in order to defuse the confrontational atmosphere of the rally.[31]

Two events allowed the government to avoid the Mendiola Massacre's potentially devastating impact on its credibility among the peasantry and the grass-roots movement. On 27 January, Marcos 'loyalist' troops under the leadership of intelligence officer Col. Oscar Canlas, staged a revolt attacking Villamor Air Base in Manila and occupying the Channel 7 television building. This allowed the government to reclaim the centrist ground in the face of challenges from the right and the left, leaving the impression that Mendiola was the responsibility of military rather than civilian leaders. On 2 February, Aquino received an overwhelming vote of confidence in the Constitutional plebiscite, which was passed with a resounding 75 per cent 'yes vote'.[32] Thus the government maintained its popular image.

On 27 January, Finance Minister Jaime Ongpin made his first major call for agrarian reform at a Paris meeting of the World Bank's Consultative Group on the Philippines. In his opening remarks he described the government's 'centre-piece' programme in very different terms than he had throughout 1986. He asked the aid donors to take special note of 'what promises to be the most important area of our economic recovery and one in which we have a unique opportunity to make a truly historic change, namely Land Reform'.[33] He told the donors that the government would need $500 million in assistance to launch the plan. At the meeting it was decided that a World Bank Mission should visit the country to advise on the design of an agrarian reform programme and that a mini-consultative conference of aid donors should be held in April in Japan to follow up on foreign assistance for reform.[34] Both Monsod and Bulatao believed that Ongpin used reform simply as one more means to raise the overall level of foreign aid funds flowing into the country.[35]

A further sign of the government's belief that urgent action on reform was now needed came on 28 January when President Aquino called for the establishment of a Cabinet Action Committee (CAC) on agrarian reform.[36] The CAC met on 4 February in what would be the first of many long sessions debating successive drafts of an executive order on agrarian reform.[37] Its members were primarily drawn from the NEDA, DAR, the DA and the Institute of Agrarian Studies of the University of the Philippines at Los Baños (see Table 7.2). They immediately made specific proposals concerning Programs A and B in the January draft. Their memorandum to the President was revealing in that it 'endorsed for presidential approval' two draft executive orders concerning the distribution of 'foreclosed properties' and 'idle and abandoned lands' that had been submitted to the Office of the President as early as 29 May and 22 August 1986. This provided yet more evidence that the President's staff, under Joker Arroyo, had been deliberately blocking all reform proposals.

Table 7.2: Personnel in the Cabinet Action Committee (CAC) and the Inter-Agency Task Force on Agrarian Reform (IATFR)

Name	Department	Position	Participation	
S.C. Monsod	NEDA	Director General	CAC	
W.G. Nuqui	NEDA	Assist. Director General	CAC	
M. Adriano	NEDA		CAC	IATFAR
J.C. Medina Jr.	DAR	Acting Secretary (OIC)	CAC	
S. Pejo	DAR	Acting Assist. Secretary	CAC	IATFAR
V.G. Bulatao	DAR	Chief Planning Services	CAC	IATFAR
L. Serrano[a]	DAR	Assist. Sec. Admin. Affairs	CAC	
C.G. Dominguez[b]	DENR DA	Secretary	CAC	
P.E. Juico[b]	DA DENR	Undersecretary	CAC	
B. Tolentino	DA	Agricultural Credit	CAC	
F.S. Factoran Jr	DENR	Secretary	CAC	
R.M. Umali	DENR	Nat. Res. Manag. Centre	CAC	
R.K. Katigbak	DF	Undersecretary	CAC	
S.H. Bello III	DJ	Undersecretary	CAC	
M.S. Sarmiento	OP	Assist. Ex.Sec. for Legis.	CAC	
Q.S. Doromal[c]	PCGG	Commissioner	CAC	
R.A. Diaz[d]	LBP	Vice-Pres. Agriculture	CAC	
L. Cornista	UPLB	Instit. of Agrarian Studies	CAC	
L. Pealba	UPLB			
V. Saguin	UPLB			
M. Mangahas	SWS	Economist		IATFAR
C. Sabio				IATFAR

[a]Hardly participated in meetings
[b]Dominguez served first as DENR Secretary and later as DA Secretary while Juico was initially representative for the DA and later for DENR.
[c]Not mentioned by Bulatao, but in Manila Chronicle (20 July 1987).
[d]Not mentioned by Bulatao, but in Business Day (21 May 1987)
Source: Interview, Gerardo Bulatao, Assistant Secretary, DAR, 24 November 1988.

Arroyo's lack of interest in pursuing agrarian reform was further reflected by the fact that his aide, Assistant Executive Secretary for Legal Affairs Mariano S. Sarmiento, attended only two of the many CAC meetings.[38]

Solita Monsod assumed the chair of the CAC after peasant leader Jaime Tadeo, in a meeting with the President after Mendiola, said that he could not work with Alvarez.[39] Dominguez replaced Mitra as Secretary at the DA when the latter resigned to run for Congress, and soon took on the Chairmanship of the CAC at Monsod's request. Fulgencio Factoran, who had been Arroyo's Assistant Executive Secretary, was appointed as Secretary at the DENR. Eventually the Land Bank and the Department of Finance had representatives on the CAC, but they also maintained their own line to the President. The IATFAR met together with the CAC and became its day-to-day working body.[40] The major Cabinet advocates of the conservative approach to reform, such as Ongpin and Arroyo, did not participate in the CAC, while several supporters of the liberal approach were extremely active in both the CAC and the IATFAR (see Table 7.2).[41]

The CAC, under Monsod's leadership, attempted to work quickly to demonstrate that the government was committed to introducing an expanded agrarian reform programme. They even initiated a series of meetings with the KMP, beginning on 16 February.[42] In a letter to the CAC, KMP Chairman Jaime Tadeo stated, 'We have the impression that the government is yet non-committal,' about Programs C and D of the plan. After making a number of specific proposals, he stressed the KMP position in favour of 'free land distribution'. On landowner compensation, he stated that 'only small landowners who did not acquire their lands through deceit, intimidation and fraud, and who put in their savings to buy their lands should be compensated for by the government'. He said that the KMP would 'agree to a compensation package equal to affordable cost, only if, affordable cost determination is the prerogative of the peasant'.[43] However, in an effort to make their proposals palatable to the Cabinet, the CAC repeatedly reduced the estimate of private lands to be covered in draft proposals prepared from January through to the end of April. After only two weeks, on 2 March the KMP withdrew from the dialogue, citing government rigidity especially on the issue of landowner compensation, and proclaimed that its land occupations would be intensified.[44]

In the wake of this protest, the CAC included coverage of private and public lands (Programs C and D) in their draft plans but emphasized that they would require Congressional approval. In a 27 April draft plan, the CAC returned to the controversial proposal, originally made by the PCGR Survey Team and MAR in 1986, that landowners be paid compensation based on land values declared in their most recent tax return.[45] The CAC also proposed a system of progressive land taxation to encourage large owners to submit to reform, a uniform retention limit of 7 hectares for all privately owned lands, and a rapid six-year programme implementation schedule. The IATFAR decided to conduct public hearings on the draft plan between 27 April and 1 May, despite protest by some DAR Regional Directors who argued that they should wait until after the 11 May Congressional elections.[46] The CAC followed up the hearings with at least five drafts of the executive order written during May 1987.[47]

During the entire period between February 1986 and the signing of the executive order on 22 July 1987, Aquino's Cabinet only discussed agrarian reform once. It proved to be an explosive session. On 4 May 1987, agrarian reform was placed on the Cabinet agenda and Secretary Dominguez presented the 27 April draft. When he finished his presentation he was immediately confronted by Joker Arroyo, who launched a long diatribe against agrarian reform. According to Monsod, Arroyo called it 'communist inspired' and went on to deliver a full-blown defence of the conservative approach.[48] Then Secretary of Defence Rafael Ileto took the floor and read out a Defence Department position paper against agrarian reform. The paper argued that redistributive reform would cause greater instability in the country.[49] Ileto went on to recount how his own family had lost considerable land to their tenants under past reform programmes, and that these people were no longer even farming the lands themselves.[50] Monsod was taken aback by the vehement opposition expressed toward the programme by the conservative majority in Cabinet.

On 4 May, presumably after the Cabinet meeting, Ongpin expressed his own views of the 27 April draft in a memo to the President.[51] He said that the wide scope of the programme was 'confusing the international community'. In effect, he was saying that reform plans were worrying foreign investors and especially transnational agribusiness firms. He suggested drastically cutting proposed spending on the programme and changing its name from the 'Accelerated Land Reform Program' to the 'Integrated Agrarian Reform Program'. This would take the focus off the redistributive aspect of the plan. He also warned against breaking up large estates.

The President had originally asked the CAC to finalize the draft executive order by the end of May, though many in the Cabinet wanted her to delay any action. As the end of May approached, Monsod and those most active in the CAC were determined to hold the President to her deadline. In the 22 May and 25 May drafts, the CAC outlined much more favourable terms for beneficiaries to acquire land.[52] The 25 May draft provided for a rapidly implemented redistributive programme corresponding in large measure to the position advanced by the advocates of the liberal approach in the lower echelons of government since early 1986.

Mahar Mangahas of the IATFAR conducted a concerted campaign to secure support for the liberal approach embodied in these early drafts. At the end of March, he succeeded in getting the Bishops Businessmen's Conference (BBC) to organize a workshop on agrarian reform at the Asian Institute of Management (AIM). On 5 May, BBC National co-chairmen Bishop Cirilo R. Almario and Christian Monsod called on the President to sign the executive order before Congress convened. They explicitly supported the seven hectare retention limit, the transfer of large estates to collective ownership by their workers, land valuation based on the owners' tax declarations, and popular participation in all stages of reform implementation. They argued that these findings were based on national consultations in 24 provinces.[53]

The World Bank Mission on agrarian reform, which had visited the country in March, submitted its final report on 16 May. It contained a criticism of an early draft executive order and recommended a much more radical programme of reform, thus bolstering the case of those in the CAC who were advocating the liberal approach. The Bank's report was deliberately leaked to the media.[54] Solita Monsod went to the press on 19 May telling journalists she 'would cry' if Cabinet decided to leave the job of legislating on agrarian reform to Congress. She commented on the CAC's proposal saying, 'I rate it very high on feasibility, marketability, fairness and comprehensiveness'.[55] Two days later, she made the President's May deadline known to the press, in what was clearly an attempt to force a presidential signature on the EO.[56]

7.4.3 Congress for a People's Agrarian Reform

The peasant movement also launched a major campaign to get the 25 May draft approved. At a three day conference from 29 to 31 May 1987, the Congress for a People's Agrarian Reform (CPAR) was established, marking an unprecedented degree of unity not only among peasant organizations but also urban-based non-governmental organizations (NGOs). With the foundation of CPAR, the smaller and larger peasant groups decided to join forces to put pressure on the government. It was a coalition of thirteen major peasant organizations from across the political spectrum (see Table 7.3).[57] The coalition grew out of the campaigning work undertaken by peasant organizations and NGOs throughout 1986 and the first half of 1987. Its founding conference was endorsed by the Catholic Bishops' Conference of the Philippines and the government's National Economic Development Authority. Initial funds to organize the conference had been provided under a technical cooperation grant from the United Nations Food and Agriculture Organization.[58]

Since CPAR sought to unite both the radical and more moderate organizations it laid out a broad programme. The CPAR plan incorporated all the major aspects of the 1986 KMP proposal except the provision for 'free' land distribution, saying simply that the conditions under which land would be distributed should not be burdensome for the new owners.[59] The CPAR plan was originally drafted by long-time advocate of the liberal approach, Professor Dioscoro L. Umali, who had been actively supporting unity efforts since early 1986.[60] CPAR's leaders included some of the most seasoned peasant organizers in the country. Some, like Francisco Baltazar of the AMA, were Huk veterans involved in peasant organizing since the early 1950s. Uniting such figures as Rafael Mariano of the militant KMP and leading social-democratic peasant organizers like Feliciano Matienzo of KASAMA and Oscar Castillo of PAKI-SAMA, the CPAR could legitimately claim to speak for a wide section of the peasant movement.

By the end of May 1987, an impressive alliance had formed behind the liberal approach to agrarian reform, embodied in the CAC's 25 May draft executive order. An important minority of officials within the DAR and NEDA supported the draft, along with such organizations as the BBC and a wide alliance of peasant groups and urban-based NGOs who formed CPAR. Yet this was not the only lobby at work during this period. Landowners and agribusiness interests launched their own campaign and found a great deal of sympathy within the conservative majority in the Cabinet.

7.5 Alliance around the conservative approach

During the campaign leading up to the Congressional elections on 11 May, opponents of redistributive reform were relatively silent about the government's draft agrarian reform proposals. Once the elections were over, an alliance against redistributive reform began to emerge among landowners, agribusiness management, financial institutions and traditional politicians. While these groups had

Table 7.3: Peasant Organizations in the Congress for a People's Agrarian Reform (CPAR)

		Description and Leaders
National Democratic Orientation:		
AMIHAN	Pambansang Pederasyon ng Kababaihan Magbubukid	– KMP linked peasant women. * Lourdes Calma
KMP	Kilusan ng Magbubukid ng Pilipinas	– A national federation of peasant organizations. * Rafael Mariano (Jaime Tadeo)
NFSW-FGT	National Federation of Sugar Workers-Federation of General Trades	– Trade union based in Negros Occidental. * Gerundio Dago-ob (Serge Cherniguin)
PAMALAKAYA	Pambansang Lakas ng Kilusang Mamamalakayang Pilipinas	– A national federation of "fisher-folk" organizations. * Rodolfo Sambajon
Aligned to the old PKP:		
AMA	Aniban ng Manggagawa sa Agrikultura	– Based in Central Luzon. Member of SANDUGUAN. * Francisco Baltazar (Nick Mangiduyos)
KABAPA	Katipunan ng Bagong Pilipina	– AMA peasant women's organization. * Trinidad Domingo (Aida Lava)
KAMMMPI	Kapatiran ng Malalayang Maliliit na Mangingisda ng Pilipinas	– Fishermen's group based in Southern and Central Luzon. * Arturo Olegario
Social-Democratic Orientation:		
BAHANGGUNIAN	Bahanggunian ng Maliliit na Mangingisda sa Lawa ng Laguna	– Fishermen's organization based at Laguna lake. * Sofronio Balagtas
LMP	Lakas ng Magsasakang Pilipino	– Member of BANDILLA. Based in Camarines Sur. * Gregorio Nazarrea (Jun Olitquit)
LMMMP	Lakas ng Magsaska, Manggagawa, Mangingisda ng Pilipinas	– Linked to BANDILLA. Based Negros, Bukidnon and Laguna. * Laurentino Bascug
KASAMA	Katipunan ng mga Samahan ng Mamamayan	– Breakaway from FFF. Close to KMP and PHILDHRRA. * Feliciano Matienzo
PAKISAMA	Pambansang Kilusan ng mga Samahang Magsasaka	– Linked to BISIG. Based in Laguna and Neuva Ecija. * Oscar Castillo
Member of government-supported alliance SANDUGUAN:		
FFF*	Federation of Free Farmers	– National federation of farmer organizations. * Ben Granada (Jeremias Montemayor)
UFFAP	United Farmers and Fishermen's Association of the Philippines	– Member of SANDUGUAN. * Rustico Tagarda

* FFF left the CPAR soon after it was formed.

different interests, they slowly converged around a common set of proposals about agrarian reform that embodied the conservative approach. They won sympathy in the Aquino Cabinet and would go on to influence Congressional deliberations about reform.

7.5.1 Landowners opposed to redistributive reform

During the week after the elections the Confederation of Sugar Producers (CSP) and the Philippine Sugar Association (PSA) sent a telegram to the President asking her to delay action on agrarian reform until the Congress convened.[61] The Jalasig Sugarcane Planters' Association, based on Panay Island, sent a long letter to the President with the same message.[62] Its chairman, Eduardo Hernandez, said the CAC proposal was 'a hastily assembled land reform package', which 'might open the door to injustices committed on landowners, certainly not in conformity with the social justice and democratic orientation of our present government'.[63]

Just after the 25 May draft came out two leaders of the sugar industry, newly elected Congresswoman Hortensia Starke and Fred Elizalde, presided over a meeting of representatives of large and small landowner groups from across the country. The convention, at Makati's Intercontinental Hotel, passed a resolution demanding again that the President take no action before the convocation of Congress. Agricultural Secretary Carlos Dominguez and NEDA head Solita Monsod came to present the 25 May CAC draft to the landowners. They were told that the audience was fully aware of the government's programme and did not want to listen to another presentation, but wished the CAC to listen to their objections.

The large landowners pitched their arguments against land redistribution as a defence of the interests of small owners. Several small landowners addressed the conference to speak about their 'hard-earned land'. Eduardo Hernandez underlined how offensive he found provisions in the draft order that would penalize landowners with imprisonment for violations of the reform law:

> All our lives, we have been holding on to these lands and we have already suffered a lot...We worked hard for it...Suddenly we will become criminals.[64]

Hernandez was one of the most articulate spokespeople for the landowner lobby, who later became chairman of the Council of Agricultural Producers of the Philippines (CAPP). While he and other big landowners spoke to the interests of the very small owners, their own reality was quite different.

Hernandez was a 'third-generation' lawyer and past president of the Philippine Bar Association, educated in the US and Britain, and author of at least two hefty legal volumes.[65] He was typical of the biggest landowners in the country. While he chaired the CAPP he was also Executive vice-president of Alcorn International, a US-owned TNC involved in oil exploration. In 1988, he ran the affairs of the CAPP out of the plush offices of Alcorn, which occupy the 19th floor of the

Solidbank Building in Makati. From there he spoke about his 460 hectare sugar plantation on the southern island of Panay in Iloilo.

Like many urban-based landowners, Hernandez visited his estate at the weekends. He was incensed by those in the CAC and the DAR who accused him and his colleagues of being 'feudalistic', saying that his was a modern mechanized farming operation. Of his 100 permanent workers he said, 'I could do without them. I could buy a harvester for only P60,000, but the workers don't want it'. While claiming that, 'This talk of feudalism is nonsense', he regarded himself as his workers' protector:

> ...If anyone applies for a loan from me...If their mother is sick. I can't deny it. If she died I would be a dead man. It is a paternalistic system. But it works both ways.

He explained why he was against redistributing land to the landless peasants:

> There are many nitwits because of malnutrition. This is the reality...I see my neighbours. They use such primitive methods...The poor illiterate farmer will build a house with hollow blocks and a tin roof...But every day he walks by the river with beautiful stones. But he doesn't know how to make a house of stone....I often wonder to myself, if I were born in their place would I be like them?...I wouldn't be as poor. I would see that flat stone on my way home. I would pick one up each day and would have 365 by the end of a year. I would see the clay.
>
> ...The river is 200 to 300 meters from his field. He doesn't know how to make a water wheel to bring the water to his farm. The skill of making a thatched roof is not known. There is no knowledge of how to build a stone wall or to use a pulley or a fulcrum. It's always force against force...The poor see television and hear the radio. They are bombarded with fertilizers and pesticides. The poor fellow is overwhelmed. These things are foisted on him by the smart cookies from the capital.

He said that landless workers see the plight of these small farmers and have no desire to acquire land. They will take the land from the government only to sell it later.

Hernandez argued that it was acceptable to divide up rice and corn lands, but that other lands should be exempted. If the government wanted to redistribute property, he said, they should 'pay me cash for my land.' Otherwise the programme would amount to communistic confiscation. At the May convention, when Solita Monsod said that the Congress could always amend an agrarian reform law introduced by President Aquino through an executive order, Hernandez agreed. However, he said, 'once a law is already passed, you have sort of pre-empted an action to legislate'.[66]

7.5.2 Conservative reformists in Cabinet join the chorus

After several postponements, a Cabinet meeting was finally scheduled for 27

May 1987, when the CAC members believed that the President would sign the executive order. However, at one o'clock in the morning, while the CAC was putting the final touches on the draft executive order, Solita Monsod received a telephone call from Presidential Counsel Teodoro Locsin. According to Monsod, 'He said, tomorrow's meeting there is going to be a draft. It is not your draft, don't say a word. That's the line.' After six months of intensive work in the CAC, Monsod could not believe what she was hearing. There was to be no discussion, and Monsod and at least one other Cabinet member were informed that they were to accept the alternative draft or resign.[67]

The landowners' outcry provided ammunition for the opponents of the liberal approach in the Cabinet. In a memo to the President dated 28 May, Executive Secretary Joker Arroyo summarized the views of newly elected members of the House of Representatives who were lobbying for a delay in the President's executive order. He said that government funds would be better spent by rechannelling them to the basic needs of the rural poor, like potable water. That day, Presidential spokesman Teodoro Benigno told the press that Arroyo, Locsin, DENR Secretary Fulgencio Factoran and presidential assistant Flerida Ruth Romero were closetted in a room still debating 'the spirit and intent of the law'.[68]

Arroyo reportedly argued that there was a 'constitutional obstacle' to the President enacting a full-blown agrarian reform law through an executive order. He was reported as saying that the government had been 'stampeded' into legislating agrarian reform by the massacre at Mendiola.[69] On the single issue of agrarian reform the Cabinet seemed to approach consensus. Even antagonists like Arroyo and Ongpin seemed to be in agreement in their rejection of the 25 May draft. Only the three Cabinet members participating in the CAC seemed to dissent, and of these Monsod was more outspoken then either Factoran or Carlos Dominguez.

In the first week of June a new draft executive order incorporated many of the demands of the advocates of the conservative approach. Most importantly, the programme would be spread over ten years rather than five, which meant that landowners could retain control over larger amounts of land for a longer period of time and that the coverage of the bulk of private lands (Program C), would be put off until after the presidential elections in 1992. In addition, the new draft would allow landowners' compensation to be based primarily on their own declaration of the land's market value rather than assessments in their latest tax return.[70] This 3 June draft represented a decisive shift away from the liberal approach to reform. In response to landowner criticisms that the CAC's public hearings had been overshadowed by the Congressional election campaign, the President also ordered a new round of hearings.[71]

These changes still did not satisfy the landowners or the advocates of the conservative approach in Cabinet. On 5 June, Ongpin and Deogracias Vistan, the former in his capacity as Chairman and the latter as President of the Land Bank of the Philippines, submitted a separate draft executive order to the President.[72]

Their alternative eliminated any mention of landowner retention limits, deferring the coverage of private lands to an undetermined future date. They argued that such a measure would guarantee the continued productivity of the agricultural sector and eliminate landowner resistance. They also proposed tighter requirements on beneficiary payments for land. A few days later Vistan explained their draft, saying that they were acting on the President's wishes, 'we took the cue [when] the President said she wanted a program that "will not rock the boat too much, that will not create a national crisis," that kind of thing'.[73] At about the same time, Joker Arroyo, Vice-President Laurel, Trade and Industry Secretary José Concepcion and officials of the Sugar Regulatory Administration all publicly expressed their opposition to the inclusion of private lands and the seven hectare retention limit in the executive order.[74]

A more extreme opposition emanated from the sugar planters of Negros. Emboldened by disintegrating support in the Cabinet, they responded to the 3 June draft executive order by launching the Movement for an Independent Negros (MIN). On 6 June 1987, 100 sugar planters wearing black ski-masks organized a demonstration in Bacolod where they announced their intention to take up arms to defend their lands. The MIN's armed wing was rumoured to be closely connected with the anti-communist vigilante group known as El Tigre.[75] By mid-June, landowners began using the newly elected Representatives to lobby against redistributive reform before Congress opened.[76]

Throughout this period peasant organizations continued to urge the President to take into consideration their proposals. On 11 June a delegation from the Congress for a People's Agrarian Reform met with President Aquino to present their declaration of principles. They subjected each subsequent draft executive order to public scrutiny and criticism. Member organizations continued to hold public rallies and pickets to express their opposition to the increasingly pro-landowner orientation in the drafts.[77] These demonstrations reinforced the urgency for presidential action on reform and bolstered the position of those in the Cabinet who felt that the President had to act before Congress convened at the end of July. However, they did little to influence the shape of the final executive order.

At the end of the month, Solita Monsod attempted to defend the seven hectare retention limit against criticisms articulated by Ongpin and Vistan, arguing that anything higher might lead to land reform in reverse, where landowners whose land was covered by the Marcos programme would ask for parts of their land to be returned to them. As she delivered this message, the Makati Business Club presented its own position paper to the President. In it they echoed the Vistan-Ongpin letter calling for a 'middle course of action', which would initially limit the programme to sequestered, foreclosed, idle, abandoned, expropriated and alienable lands of the public domain. They too called for slashing the costs of the programme, while leaving other aspects for Congressional legislation.[78]

On 28 June, in an attempt to further placate the landowners, the draft

J

executive order was revised again. For the first time it included a separate section on 'Assistance to Landowners'. Priorities were reformulated to correspond with those recommended by the business community. Landowners would 'have the option to choose a contiguous retention area', receive tax exemptions if they voluntarily offered to sell their lands, and their children would be accorded priority in land redistribution.[79] This draft also attempted to pacify the financial community by specifying that forecloseable lands slotted for redistribution included only those lands foreclosed 'by *government* financial institutions'. Banks would be allowed to hold mortgage rights and the titles to agricultural lands offered to them as collateral for up to five years.[80] However, neither the landowners nor the bankers were convinced. Wilfrido Tecson, president of the Consolidated Bank and Trust Company (Solidbank) and a member of the Bankers Association of the Philippines, said that, faced with a government requirement for banks to channel 25 per cent of their lending to agriculture or invest in government treasury notes, banks would choose the latter because of their fear of agrarian reform. Tiros Antiporda Jr., president of Pilipinas Bank, asked the government to 'play it cool in including sugar and coconut croplands as well as aquaculture areas because of their foreign exchange earnings potentials'.[81]

During July 1987 there was a final confrontation among Cabinet members over the executive order. On 6 July, Vistan and Ongpin sent another 'open letter' to the President protesting the maintenance of a uniform seven hectare retention limit in the draft.[82] They amended their own draft executive order to include a specific section allowing agribusiness corporations to avoid land distribution by instituting a stock-sharing programme.[83] They again urged the President not to move hastily by including private lands in her executive order. They were convinced that the President had to issue an executive order before Congress opened, but were determined that it should not include any statement on retention limits or compensation. It was this position that emerged as the dominant one in Cabinet and it soon received the endorsement of the Catholic hierarchy.

On 14 July, 87 bishops gathered in the Catholic Bishop's Conference where they approved a pastoral letter calling for 'as comprehensive a program of agrarian reform as possible'. Both the timing of the letter and the repeated mention of action in the form of an 'executive order' or by 'legislative fiat' demonstrated the Bishops' support for presidential action before Congress convened. On the other hand, the Bishops limited their description of reform to 'sharing', stressing that any programme had to be 'realistic', and stated that peasants, 'in the interest of law and order, should not unjustly and forcibly pre-empt claims to lands in question prior to approval of the agrarian reform act'.[84] The language of the letter was later reflected in the President's proclamation on agrarian reform.[85] Thus, the bishops put their official stamp of approval on the conservative approach to reform around which the majority in Cabinet had united.

Despite the bishops' endorsement of presidential action, congressmen-elect still argued that the President should not take any action on reform before the opening of Congress. On 17 July, newly elected congressmen gathered at the old Batasan building for a briefing on agrarian reform. Former Cabinet member and newly elected Representative Antonio Cuenco, from Cebu, reported that 40 Congressmen believed that the President should not take any action on reform. Many opposed the seven hectare retention limit and all wanted still more public hearings.[86]

The following day, Solita Monsod and the CAC submitted a position paper to the President and the media directly opposing the recommendations of Ongpin and Vistan. They made a last-ditch effort to maintain the seven hectare limit. While the CAC had already retreated on most components of the liberal approach, their paper was still framed in liberal arguments. They said that retention limits had to be based on people rather than crop or soil characteristics which are both susceptible to change. The CAC argued that a programme which 'emphasizes productivity will sacrifice equity,' but 'the equity-enhancing' programme 'will lead to greater productivity'.[87]

Despite all the concessions made by the CAC, the tacit alliance that had emerged between landowners, agribusiness interests, bankers and the politicians provided the President with the opportunity to issue an executive order leaving most of the details of a new reform programme to Congress. Indeed, this approach was favoured by a majority in the Cabinet, which united such fierce rivals as Finance Secretary Ongpin and Executive Secretary Arroyo, and was sanctioned by the Catholic bishops. The LBP's draft, prepared by Vistan and Ongpin, was more important in drafting the final executive order than all the drafts prepared over seven months by the CAC. The President's own cynicism regarding the seemingly new commitment to agrarian reform after the Mendiola Massacre in January was demonstrated by the fact that after Alvarez resigned in early March, no new Secretary of Agrarian Reform was appointed until the executive order was issued on 22 July 1987.

7.6 Executive order 229

The President finally outlined her stand on agrarian reform by issuing executive order 229 (EO229) and Proclamation 131, on 22 July 1987, five days before Congress opened.[88] In the end, EO229 was written by Arroyo, Locsin, Vistan, Factoran, Deputy Executive Secretary Catalino Macaraig Jr., Justice Secretary Sedfrey Ordoñez and Constitutional Commissioner Adolfo Azcuna. The most influential texts on which it was based were the Vistan-Ongpin draft and a paper written by Ordoñez outlining constitutional obstacles to agrarian reform.[89] The President's executive order included concessions on almost every objection raised by the opponents of redistributive reform, and left the central issues of defining retention limits and the timetable, or 'priorities', of reform entirely to Congress.

During the seven months of debate over the executive order there was an important change in the manner in which the objectives of agrarian reform were described. In the 23 January draft, the 'equity' objective of reform was placed before 'productivity'.[90] In the 25 May draft the language of the Constitution was introduced, which stressed equitable distribution of 'opportunities' and wealth.[91] This was an important change recalling the President's own campaign speeches in 1986. From the point of view of the conservative approach to reform, it is more important to ensure that farmers and farmworkers have the opportunity for gainful employment than control over land. The 28 June draft cited the Constitution, arguing that agrarian reform was part of the national goal of a more equitable distribution of 'opportunities, incomes and wealth' and also, for the first time, included a reference to the 'ecological, developmental or equity considerations' limiting the scope of reform.[92] The final definition of reform objectives in Proclamation 131 mentioned only *increased productivity and increased incomes*. Those sections of the Constitution mentioning equity were no longer cited and the only mention of equity was in the constitutional clause limiting the scope of reform.[93]

In almost every draft executive order there was some mention of the state's objective to eliminate poverty.[94] The 28 June draft dropped all references to this objective and the 22 July presidential statements followed suit.[95] On the other hand, Proclamation 131 introduced new reform objectives, not previously mentioned in any of the drafts. For the first time it stated that the reform should be 'flexible' and 'realistic' and carried out in a spirit of 'harmony' between landowners and beneficiaries.[96]

7.6.1 Scope, timing and retention limits

Proclamation 131 stated that the Comprehensive Agrarian Reform Program (CARP) would cover 'regardless of tenurial arrangement and commodity produced, all public and private agricultural lands as provided in the Constitution'.[97] However, since it left the definition of priorities and retention limits to Congress, the Proclamation and EO229 remained silent on how much land would actually come under the programme scope. Nevertheless, throughout the debate over the executive order, a number of physical projections about the scope of reform were made which served as the basis for DAR's own planning (Table 7.4).

The most striking feature of the evolution of programme scope during 1987 is that the amount of private lands considered for coverage dropped from 5.3 million hectares in January to 2.5 million hectares in September. While there appears to have been a slight reversal of the downward trend between April and September, this was due only to the inflation of the amount of land still to be covered under Marcos's PD27 (Program A).[98] Overall, there was a drastic reduction throughout the period in the coverage of land in 'landed estates' run with hired labour and in tenanted farms. The area of landed estates was reduced from 2.3 million to 1.5 million and finally to only 634,000 hectares, while tenanted farms were reduced from 957,000 to 622,000 and finally to only 81,000 hectares.

Table 7.4: CARP Scope: Draft Executive Orders 1987 (hectares)

	January 23	March 13	April 27	[a]September
Program A (PD 27)	557,000	557,000	557,000	727,800
Rice Irrigated				254,700
Non-Irrigated				254,700
Corn				218,400
Beneficiaries	*397,856*	*398,000*	*397,856*	*519,857*
Program B	939,000	939,000	600,000	510,000
Voluntary Offers	300,000	300,000	50,000	250,000
Idle & Abandoned	189,000	189,000	200,000	200,000
Expropriated	100,000	100,000	100,000	
Foreclosed(able)	300,000	300,000	200,000	
Sequestered	50,000	50,000	50,000	60,000
Beneficiaries	*672,144*	*670,700*	*425,000*	*364,285*
Program C	3,852,000	2,138,500	1,280,000	1,280,000
Landed Estates[b]	2,333,000	1,516,450	634,000	634,000
Other tenanted lands	957,000	622,050	81,000	81,000
Tenanted rice & corn <7 ha.s	562,000			
Other Non-Tenanted			565,000	565,000
Beneficiaries		*1,188,100*	*640,000*	*640,000*
Sub-Total Private	5,348,000	3,634,500	2,437,000	2,517,800
Program D[c]		1,350,000	1,350,000	1,866,920
Government Owned[d]				50,000
Resettlement				467,420
Public A & D		1,350,000	1,350,000	1,349,500
Beneficiaries		*675,000*	*675,000*	*1,100,464*
Total Hectares	5,348,000	4,984,500	3,787,000	4,384,720
Beneficiaries		*2,931,800*	*2,137,856*	*2,624,606*

[a]Institute of Agrarian Studies, Los Baños, 'Selected Statistics for the Comprehensive Agrarian Reform Program' September, 1987. Program A (DAR and LBP Records); Program B (Estimates of PCGG and DAR); Program C (NCSO 1980 Census); Program D (DENR)
[b]Labelled 'haciendas under labour administration' until 20 April draft. These are presumably non-tenanted farms over 50 hectares.
[c]In addition public lands covered by the Integrated Social Forestry Program where beneficiaries would receive a stewardship contract rather than ownership: March 13 draft: 2,470,000 ha.s to 494,000 beneficiaries which was reduced in the April through September drafts: 170,000 ha.s to 234,000 beneficiaries.
[d]This was listed as part of Program B but has been placed here to separate public from private lands.
Source: Cabinet Action Committee, Integrated-Agency Task Force on Agrarian Reform and Department of Agrarian Reform, 1987.

The coverage of private agricultural lands was perhaps the most crucial indicator of changing intentions about the scope of reform. An interesting insight into both the intentions of those drafting the proposals and the inaccuracy of government statistics on landownership and agrarian reform is provided when the estimated scope of land coverage is considered in light of proposed retention limits. The 13 March draft postulated a retention limit of 24.99 hectares for landowners, leaving a total of 2.1 million hectares of private lands to be covered.[99] When the 27 April draft lowered the retention limit to seven hectares one would have expected a significant increase in the programme scope. Instead, it was reduced to only 1.3 million hectares.[100]

Program B was also significantly reduced in scope from 939,000 hectares in January to 510,000 hectares in September. The first reduction was made in the 27 April draft when what appeared to be an unrealistic estimate for 'voluntarily offered' land was scaled down.[101] However, by September that item was again increased after the 'voluntary' component of reform was emphasized in EO229. By September, 'Expropriated' and 'Foreclosed' lands entirely disappeared as separate categories.[102] All the drafts between May and June stated that lands foreclosed or foreclosable by *both* government and private financial institutions would be redistributed. However, the 28 June draft made it clear that only those lands forecloseable by government financial institutions would be covered by reform.[103]

The scope of reform depends not only on retention limits but also programme timing. With the 3 June draft and the extension of the programme until 1997, the 24.99 hectare limit would be implemented only in 1992 and the seven hectare limit only five years later. Extending the programme over a ten year period would allow landowners much more time to disguise their ownership of the land in smaller holdings under titles of friends and relatives. The longer programme period also meant that lower retention limits would not even come into force before the election of a new administration, which meant there was no guarantee that they would ever be enforced. While the President remained silent in EO229 on the problem of timing and priorities, the debate over the executive order introduced the formula for a ten-year reform programme with phased retention limits that would later be adopted in the law.

7.6.2 Landowner compensation and registration

In EO229 the President responded to landowners' worries about compensation by ensuring that the amount paid for land would be based primarily on the owner's own 'declaration of current fair market value'.[104] When the CAC first began its work, it was much closer to the liberal approach in regard to landowner compensation. The memorandum from its first meeting stated that landowners were entitled to 'reasonable compensation', rather than the Constitutional Commission's interpretation of 'just compensation' as equivalent to the market value.[105] In its early draft programmes there was no clear formula for determining reasonable or just compensation.

However, in the 27 April draft, the CAC took a bold step along the lines of the liberal approach, arguing for a special executive order on compensation. This would provide compensation based on 'the market value of the land as *determined by government assessors per the landowner's tax declaration*'.[106] Such a formulation appeared to conform to the Constitutional requirement of 'just compensation' based on 'market value'. Since landowners had almost always undervalued their lands in tax declarations, the formula would allow a significant redistribution of wealth and would considerably lessen the cost of implementation. There was also a quality of 'fairness' in this proposal, since landowners had long avoided paying their share of taxes. It was preferred over compensation based on the productive value of the land, as in PD27, because of the great delays which that formula caused in reform implementation.[107]

There was considerable legal precedence for adopting such a formula, most notably Marcos' PD76 of 1972.[108] However, just two days after the draft was released, the Supreme Court issued a decision declaring PD76 and all laws based on it as unconstitutional because it took too much discretion away from the Courts.[109] Political scientist David Wurfel argued that because of this ruling the CAC reverted to a compensation formula based on the landowners' own declaration of market value.[110] In fact, the tax-based compensation formula was maintained in five subsequent drafts of the executive order.[111] Compensation based on tax valuations was not in itself deemed unconstitutional. The Court struck down PD76 only because it 'infringed upon the right, under due process, to have just compensation reviewed in court'. In fact, the Court acknowledged the constitutionality of determining compensation on the basis of landowners' declared value for taxation purposes if subjected to judicial review.[112]

It was only after the landowner challenge at the end of May that the CAC in its 3 June draft stated, 'The LBP shall compensate the landowner an amount to be established by the government, which shall be *based on the owner's declaration of current fair market value*'.[113] EO229 maintained this formulation and offered an even more attractive instrument to landowners in the form of LBP bonds 'bearing market rates of interest that are aligned with 91-day treasury bills rates'.[114] Thus, the CAC's acceptance of the landowners' own declaration of market value as the basis for compensation was not made primarily in deference to legal authority as Wurfel argued. It was rather a political decision to accommodate the conservative approach to reform advanced by landowners, agribusiness and financial institutions.

In order to benefit from this offer the executive order required landowners to register their lands within 180 days. Registration would require a sworn statement on the size of land holdings, income received from the land, the names of all tenants and regular farmworkers, the terms of mortgages and leases, and the latest declared value of the land by the City or Provincial Assessor, as well as the 'current fair market value, which the owner wishes to receive'.[115] The succession of draft orders required the Register of Deeds to clear any land registered with the DAR, but this was eliminated from EO229, thus eliminating a major mechanism for preventing landowner evasive practices.

However, landowners had always attempted to avoid revealing how many tenants or farmworkers lived on their lands, or the terms of their employment, since this information could be used to assist in redistributing their property. They had also resisted stating their actual income from the land or the latest assessed value since this could provide a case for lower compensation than their own declared 'fair market value'. Ideally, this information should be verified by the producers themselves, which is one of the reasons why redistributive reform requires the full participation of peasant organizations. The executive order called for no such participation. Nonetheless, although compelling owners to make such revelations was very much a second best, it was one of the few clauses in EO229 that went against the owners' wishes.

7.6.3 Voluntary schemes and corporate stock distribution

EO229 gave owners the right both to receive compensation directly from the beneficiary and 'to enter into a voluntary agreement for direct transfer of their lands' to the beneficiaries.[116] Right from the start of debates on the executive order, provisions for voluntary land transfer were included.[117] However, in the 25 May draft, around which the advocates of the liberal approach attempted to rally support, 'voluntary land transfer' schemes had to ensure that beneficiaries would have majority control within nine years and full ownership in not more than 17 years.[118] All of the drafts included provisions to encourage landowners to voluntarily offer their lands to the government for sale. A similar provision in the final law was to lead to major scandals involving DAR fraudulent land deals.[119] The 28 June draft added a new incentive, making such transactions 'exempt from the payment of taxes and fees', which was retained in EO229.[120]

These provisions ignored one of the central lessons of past reforms in the Philippines and other Asian countries, like India, Japan, Taiwan and South Korea. When 'voluntary' agreements are permitted, the way is open for landowners to coerce their tenants and farmworkers to arrive at an agreement favourable to the owners.[121] In fact, a basic characteristic of the conservative approach is to confine agrarian reform, as much as possible, to such voluntary schemes.

Perhaps the most controversial section of EO229 was its provision allowing corporate landowners to avoid land redistribution by selling shares of stock to their workers. Workers would be given the 'right to purchase such proportion of the capital stock of the corporation that the land assets bear in relation to the corporation's total assets', and they would be given 'additional compensation which may be used for that purpose'.[122] This provision drew sharp criticism from the advocates of redistributive reform.[123] Criticisms centred on the fact that if a corporation could prove that its land assets represented, for instance, only 5 per cent of total assets, then only 5 per cent of the corporation's shares would be offered for distribution among the entire work-force of the company.[124]

It was striking, however, that criticism of this scheme was muted until the issuance of EO229. The soon-to-be-named Agrarian Reform Secretary Philip Juico, who participated in all the CAC's deliberations, later claimed that the option was not discussed by the CAC and appeared for the first time in the final version of EO229:

It didn't come up during those discussions as far as I recall...There was an end run. Somebody made an end run to the President and Executive Secretary Arroyo to include that. I think it was Mr. Vistan of [the] Land Bank and the late Secretary Ongpin of Finance. They brought it up one fine morning. It suddenly came out in the final copy of the executive order...Joker Arroyo welcomed it, based on the explanation that if you start redistributing lands you will destroy Philippine agriculture.[125]

However, as has already become clear, the corporate stock-sharing proposal did not appear out of the blue in EO229. In an earlier version it was advanced by Secretary Ongpin as his flag-ship proposal for agriculture throughout 1986 and the President's family was considering such a programme even before the government came to power.[126]

The stock-distribution concept was introduced, albeit in a discreet manner and a somewhat different form, as early as the 22 May draft executive order. During this period it was included as part of the 'voluntary land transfer' option.[127] It was retained slightly modified in the 25 May draft around which the advocates of the liberal model rallied.[128] This early statement of the stock-distribution option was more ambiguous than EO229 with regard to the percentage of the existing corporation's stock, which would have to be distributed to workers in order for the corporation to be exempt from outright land redistribution. However, the thinking behind this clause was revealed as early as March 1987, when the World Bank Mission was given a 'verbal briefing' and a 'working paper' describing a possible stock-distribution plan. The Mission reported that it involved transferring 'the property of the hacienda...to a corporation, initially wholly owned and controlled by the present owners'. Even at this early date, there was already a proposal to allow corporations to transfer their agricultural land assets to spin-off entities whose shares would then be gradually transferred to employees.[129]

In addition to Secretary Ongpin and the President's family, other agribusiness firms were pushing for such a plan. José Ma. T. Zabaleta, vice-president of the 'agro-marine' corporation, Gamboa Hermanos, Incorporated, claimed at least partial parentage of the stock-distribution scheme:

In the heat of the Land Reform discussions, I talked to the President of the Philippines and eventually wrote her a proposal wherein the objectives of Land Reform could be achieved by way of a shared ownership of the factors of production.[130]

One member of the IATFAR support staff involved in drafting the executive order emphasized that 'the late Finance Secretary Jaime Ongpin *was only one of the prime advocates* of the stock sharing option':

The agribusiness sector, in general (i.e., pineapple, banana, coconut, etc.) had strong interest on [sic] this provision. But most quarters have intimated that the real force behind it was the President's brother, Peping Cojuangco...First, this [was] simply a way out for Hacienda Luisita...Secondly, this was a clear concession to the big planters...[whose] political support was vital to the present dispensation.[131]

In early June, Ongpin's Undersecretary and long-time friend, Ramon K. Katigbak, who was the Finance delegate to the CAC, told the President that there were big opportunities for private business in the agrarian reform programme. He explained that the programme would include the option of a 'corporate farm model' where farmworkers could own land value through shares of stock. He said that while such a model was already allowed in the draft executive order, there should be additional provisions to make it more explicit.[132]

The provision for corporate stock-distribution that finally appeared in EO229 reproduced the exact wording included in the LBP draft executive order sent to the President by Ongpin and Vistan on 6 July 1987.[133] In their covering letter they explained the origin of the plan, but did not refer to Gamboa Hermanos by name:

> It is taken from a model of a large, corporate landowner (700 hectares) that has actually submitted a proposal for Land bank [sic] to finance the transfer of ownership equivalent to 30 per cent of the company's capital stock to its workers (30 per cent represents the value of the land in relation to the value of that firm's total assets). Furthermore, this firm has committed to increase the wages of its workers to make the cost of acquiring the shares very affordable.[134]

They introduced an important change in the stock-distribution plan. As it had been explained to the World Bank Mission in March and in subsequent draft EOs, stock-distribution would eventually transfer a *majority* of shares to beneficiaries. The Ongpin-Vistan plan reversed this by requiring a corporation to distribute only that amount of stock equivalent to the proportion of its land assets to total assets. This meant that corporations could comply with agrarian reform without transferring majority ownership to the farmworkers.

Foreign agribusiness corporations were left relatively undisturbed by EO229. The stock-distribution plan did not affect them, since companies like Del Monte Philippines, Dole Philippines and Sime Darby leased most of their lands from the government or other landowners.[135] EO229 stated that all leases on land covered by the programme would be respected but would be subject to review after five years.[136] The only real effect on TNC operations was that they were likely to be leasing their lands from different owners, who might increase the incredibly low rental rates that they had previously enjoyed.[137]

To cushion the political impact of the favourable treatment extended to large foreign and domestic agribusiness corporations that leased the bulk of their land, EO229 included a requirement that they engage in 'production sharing'. Individuals or corporations that operated farms on leased lands whose gross sales were greater than P5 million per annum were required to turn over 2.5 per cent of gross sales 'from the production/cultivation of such lands...as compensation to the farmworkers'.[138]

The claim by Juico and others that the corporate stock-distribution plan did not appear until the final version of EO229 was drafted at Malacañang was thus only partially true. Secretary Ongpin and others had made no secret of the fact that they believed such an approach was the best way both to preserve what they saw as the efficiency of the agribusiness sector, and to respond to the wishes of 'farm leaders, landowners, bankers, businessmen and government officials'.[139] José Zabaleta of Gamboa Hermanos said of the plan, 'I thought at the time [it] was the best way to approach *part of the problem*, limited to large agricultural corporations which worked with a social conscience'.[140] The final version of EO229, while catering to the views of such business leaders, also took into account pressures from the military.

7.6.4 Confrontation with the peasant movement

The executive order 'permanently disqualified' from participation in the pro-gramme 'all persons, associations, or entities who prematurely enter the land to avail themselves of the rights and benefits' of the programme.[141] With this clause the government effectively rejected cooperation with the peasant move-ment to implement reform and opted instead for a policy of confrontation. The clause was clearly designed to win the support of landowners, the business community and the military alike. It was directed at both organized and spontaneous actions by peasants who had been occupying idle, abandoned, foreclosed and sequestered lands in the face of government inaction on reform.[142] In the months following the issuance of EO229, the military, security forces hired by companies managing foreclosed lands, and vigilante groups all stepped up attacks on peasants involved in land occupations.

The wording of this provision was vague enough to allow it to be used with discretion. It could be implemented both to punish those organizations that took a stand against the government or which the military labelled as front groups of the communist underground, and to reward those that were generally supportive of the government. This direct challenge to the peasant movement was not inserted in any of the draft orders until the 28 June draft. That draft contained two contradictory provisions regarding peasant land occupations. A special section on 'Disqualifications' stated that, 'Persons who illegally enter and occupy land covered by this Program after *January 1, 1986* shall be disqualified'.[143] However, it also deemed as a 'Prohibited Act', 'entry and occupation with the use of force, intimidation or threat or by taking advantage of the absence or tolerance of the landowner or rightful possessor of any land covered by the CARP *after effectivity of this Order.*'[144]

The 28 June draft was thus unclear as to whether punishment would be meted out on peasants who occupied land after the government came to power but before the executive order was passed. It left no doubt, however, that the

243

intention of government was to oppose any militant peasant action. In fact, the second clause seemed to provide the basis for absentee landowners to reclaim land that may have been long abandoned and even wilfully turned over to the peasants. Its authors may have been targetting particularly those lands occupied under the wing of the revolutionary movement and its own reform programme.

EO229 was less sweeping in its description of those who could be excluded in this way. However, because it made no mention of the dates beyond which land occupations would be deemed grounds for disqualification, it was even harsher than the earlier draft. Until 28 June, all the draft orders had outlined sanctions against landowners, the courts or the military if they took evasive action or ejected prospective beneficiaries from the land.[145] These were gradually whittled down and finally discarded by the time EO229 was issued.[146]

EO229 also moved away from any significant involvement of the beneficiaries in the design and implementation of agrarian reform. In outlining the composition of the national and local bodies which would implement the programme, EO229 laid the basis for peasant representatives to be outnumbered by those from government agencies and other sectors, including landowners.[147] The first May draft described a 'Barangay People's Council' to be set up in every village, that would be responsible for participating in and supporting the implementation of CARP, evaluating and monitoring its progress and arbitrating agrarian conflicts.[148] The 25 May draft renamed this structure the 'Barangay Agrarian Reform Council' (BARC). Interestingly, the 28 June draft, which was otherwise generally close to the final version, explicitly stated that the BARCs would 'participate in the identification of agrarian reform beneficiaries, lands and landowners'.[149] This had been a major demand of peasant organizations, who knew that only local villagers could tell who really controlled the land. EO229, however, eliminated this proviso. It called instead for the establishment of a Presidential Agrarian Reform Council (PARC), which would include fourteen Cabinet members, the head of the LBP and representatives from among beneficiaries and landowners to be appointed by the President.[150]

7.7 Agrarian reform and counterinsurgency

While these provisions were designed to accommodate the wishes of the landowners, they also reflected the military's opposition to government cooperation with the peasant movement. During the period after the Mendiola Massacre when the executive order was being debated, military pressure on the government was growing. In the week following the Mendiola Massacre and the 27 January rebellion by loyalist officers, the Lupao Massacre in Nueva Ecija shocked the nation. The military had arrived in the village in pursuit of an NPA unit and had gunned down 17 civilians, four of whom were under 13 years old and two of whom were in their eighties. The NPA unit had fled the village long before the 100-strong detachment had arrived.[151] Hopes of casting the AFP as the 'New' Armed Forces were completely dashed.

Both the AFP and the United States made it clear to the government that they wanted civilian authorities to make a stronger commitment to the counterinsurgency campaign.[152] During the first months of the debate over the executive order, the Cabinet's approach to counterinsurgency differed significantly from the strategy adopted by the military. Cabinet officials stressed the contribution that agrarian reform could make to the counterinsurgency effort. This emphasis was consistent with the liberal approach to reform and reflected the early efforts of the CAC to cast the government programme in such terms. The first draft programme on 23 January denounced the past 'abuse of state prerogatives to grant land to the powerful and hence socially undeserving few'. It argued that land reform had 'given the subversive movement its most alluring talking point to attract the landless poor' and that its implementation by the government was the key to 'peace and reconciliation'.[153] The DAR's elaboration of this draft called for the distribution of 'unnecessary military... reservations', a position that was unlikely to endear them to the AFP.[154]

Even advocates of the conservative approach within the Cabinet spoke about agrarian reform in these terms. In his first major speech endorsing agrarian reform, Finance Secretary Jaime Ongpin stressed the connection between reform and the 'insurgency':

> As the rural misery has deepened, it has driven increasing numbers to violent protest..The insurgents' confidence in the new government has now drawn them to the conference table; and the government is bound in honour and in simple humanity to redress their legitimate grievances...[B]y the insurgents' own admission there is one policy action which will satisfy them more than anything else, and which is also unanimously recognized as legitimate and long overdue. This is, very simply, real and effective Land Reform.[155]

In March, while the US was stepping up pressure for a comprehensive counterinsurgency strategy, President Aquino declared that agrarian reform was the anchor of her anti-insurgency programme.[156] Just a week later, Secretary Ongpin also cast the expanded agrarian reform programme in these terms:

> Because of its relation to political unrest, we have a special concern for the problem of rural poverty. We have supplemented the Philippine Development Plan with an expanded, revitalized and accelerated land reform program...[157]

By the end of March, however, top representatives of the government had ceased talking about agrarian reform in such terms. Only the CAC attempted to maintain this thrust in its draft executive orders.

While the 27 April draft dropped any mention of the abuse of state power in the past, it did affirm that, 'The immediate implementation of the ALRP is very crucial. Delaying its implementation is expected to *exacerbate political and social unrest* in the country'.[158] From 25 May through 28 June, the draft executive orders affirmed that agrarian problems were the source of instability and violence in the countryside, and presented agrarian reform as part of the solution.[159] Apparently, only a minority in the business community accepted this linkage.[160]

245

In their final attempt to inject a clearer commitment to redistribution in the President's executive order, the CAC's 7 July position paper called on the liberal argument about the relationship between agrarian reform and counterinsurgency. The paper underlined the need for a genuinely redistributive approach to respond to 'the insurgency steadily growing in our countryside'. It emphasized that, 'If the land is not willingly shared, it will inevitably be forcibly taken'.[161]

On 22 July, however, the President made no such assertion, instead making only a general statement:

> [I]n the last analysis, the times undeniably call for change, and the need to undertake the agrarian reform program can no longer wait...the forces of history and the Constitution, the pressing needs of the times, the capabilities of the present and the age-old aspirations of the Filipino people demand such an agrarian reform program.[162]

As early as 11 February 1987, after the collapse of peace talks with the NDF, the President gave in to military demands and announced a policy of 'Total War' against the revolutionary movement. The AFP revived the paramilitary groups and CHDF, which had been so active during the Marcos regime, as an important tool in its counterinsurgency strategy.

'Vigilante groups' were set up in many parts of the country, sometimes closely linked with local landowner interests, like El Tigre in Negros Occidental.[163] After public outrage over the proliferation of these groups, Aquino ordered their disbandment, only to reverse her position under military and US pressure and approve 'unarmed' vigilante groups on 4 April.[164] Local Government Secretary Jaime Ferrer, who had been appointed at the end of 1986 after the military forced the dismissal of Aquilino Pimentel, actively promoted the assimilation of vigilante groups into new 'anti-communist citizens' action committees'. Ferrer, who was later assassinated, was clearly attempting to apply the lessons of the Magsaysay anti-Huk campaign, where counterinsurgency warfare had convinced the elite that redistributive agrarian reform was unnecessary.[165]

Early on in the debate over the executive order there had been some attempt to win the military over to the programme on the grounds of self-interest. Shortly before his resignation to run for Senate, Secretary Heherson Alvarez reassured the military that landless soldiers in active service, as well as retirees and veterans, would benefit from any reform programme.[166] However, military strategy was in essence to break the militant peasant movement rather than lure it into support for the government through redistributive reform. By taking a hard line against peasant initiatives and land occupations, EO229 seemed to endorse such a strategy.

7.8 Conclusion

The debate over the executive order throughout the first half of 1987 was in essence a debate between the conservative and liberal approaches to agrarian reform, put on the agenda as the result of peasant mobilization. The evolution of the debate shed considerable light on the nature of the Aquino administration as well as the nature of the Philippine state itself and its relation to specific interests and groups in society.

Throughout its first year in office the Aquino government had shown little interest in redistributive reform. The conservative approach to reform was dominant in Cabinet and the Constitutional Commission and the government seemed to believe that agrarian reform was not an urgent issue. Most extraordinary, the Cabinet only had one thorough discussion on reform before the executive order was signed in July 1987. Pressure for action on reform originated in the peasant movement, and it was action by the peasants and their urban supporters that struck at the government's complacency, finally bringing agrarian reform to the top of the policy agenda after the Mendiola Massacre. In addition, most of the Cabinet realised that it had to take some form of action on reform, after the break-down of talks with the NDF, whose own agenda had given prominence to agrarian reform.

For the first time, advocates of the liberal approach to reform received a hearing at the highest levels of government. The early drafts of the presidential executive order included provisions for the speedy implementation of a programme that would redistribute a significant portion of cultivated lands to tenants and farmworkers at reasonable cost and with minimum compensation to landowners. During this period the government also spoke about agrarian reform as the anchor of its counterinsurgency strategy. NEDA Director Solita Monsod and, to a lesser extent, Agriculture Secretary Carlos Dominguez championed the liberal approach in Cabinet. The 25 May draft embodied many of the tenets of the liberal approach and received the endorsement of the peasant and grass-roots movements as well as influential organizations like the BBC. There was widespread public support for presidential action to implement such an approach before the Congress convened.

Landowners and the political clans who relied on their support were relatively quiet as the debate over an executive order began, because the campaign for Congressional elections was already under way. After the elections on 11 May, landowner and big business opposition grew exponentially. While some among these groups and even in the Cabinet preferred to see no action at all on agrarian reform, a tacit alliance formed around the conservative approach to reform. Their main objective was to delay the expansion of reform to private lands (Program C), to extend the period of the reform plan, to ensure market value compensation and to devise means for corporate estates to be exempt from redistribution.

The conservative majority in the Cabinet, so much in evidence during the government's first year in office, reasserted itself and emerged strengthened after more centrist and left-leaning members were purged as a result of military pressure, or resigned to run for office in the Senate. Even Executive Secretary Joker Arroyo and Finance Secretary Jaime Ongpin, who were at logger-heads on almost every other issue, found common ground on the issue of agrarian reform.

Of the two, Arroyo appeared the most determined to block forceful presidential action on reform. He emanated from a big landowning family in Bicol and was extremely close to landowner leader Eduardo Hernandez, who no doubt influenced his thinking on reform.[167] However, it would be too simplistic to interpret his position strictly in these terms. Of more importance was the fact that Arroyo perceived himself as the power-broker of the President. He apparently believed that strong action on reform would create too many enemies among the powerful in society. More than anyone else in Cabinet, Arroyo seemed to believe that Aquino could shift the political responsibility for reform onto Congress and emerge above the fray. Arroyo, who had been a prominent figure among the 'parliament of the streets' in the last days of Marcos, became the shrewdest of politicians.

Secretary Ongpin was cut from a very different cloth. Where Arroyo went along with the conservative approach as second-best to dropping the issue altogether, after the Mendiola Massacre Ongpin realised that the President had to sign an executive order, but wanted it to be one of his own design. He became one of the main architects of the conservative approach embodied in EO229. Not long after he was forced to resign from the Cabinet in exchange for Arroyo's own resignation, and shortly before his suicide, Ongpin told journalist Sandra Burton that if the President did not move ahead with land reform and a co-ordinated military and economic offensive against the 'rebels in the country-side', the military would fill the vacuum.[168] Mirabel Ongpin said that after her husband was sure that he could not continue for long in the government, he was 'determined that he would keep on until he raised the money for land reform'.[169] Ongpin's attachment to the business community and his firm belief in the leading role of export-oriented corporate agribusiness led him to be the foremost advocate of the conservative approach in Cabinet.

Landowners and the corporate sector alike found solace in his positions. Eduardo Hernandez typified the biggest landowners in the country. He was both a 'gentleman-farmer' with a paternalist approach to the peasantry, and an executive of a foreign TNC, who could feel at home in any Western board room or university. Cory Aquino's own family, headed by her eldest brother, the publicly shy patron of the clan and head of the family corporations, Pedro Cojuangco, and represented on the political front by another brother, Congress-man José Cojuangco, were very much like Hernandez. They formed a powerful clan in Tarlac at the pinnacle of a network of patronage ties, and felt at home both as lords of their sugar estate and as captains of Philippine business in the plush surroundings of Makati.

The Aquino government's deference to the views of landowners and agribusi-ness reflected not only the class identities of its members and supporters, but also the character of the Philippine state itself. Advocates of the liberal approach to reform worked to enshrine in the executive order 'quasi-judicial powers' for the DAR. This issue was first raised in the recommendations of the PCGR Survey Team and the MAR back in 1986. The first May draft spelled out in detail the powers of the DAR to acquire land, to determine the application of the right of retention by landowners and the 'compensability' of their claims, and to preside over virtually every aspect of reform. The DAR's decisions would be binding and the only appeal would be to the Office of the President.[170]

This idea was based on the principle that a DAR transformed and working with peasant organizations, NGOs and a strong network of 'Barangay People's Councils' would be free from interference by the political networks behind elected members of government and the courts, which were known to be dominated by powerful local interests. By the time EO229 was issued, the 'quasi-judicial powers' of the DAR were described in three short sentences. The DAR would share jurisdiction with the DA and DENR, with many of the powers previously assigned to it transferred to the Presidential Council on Agrarian Reform. EO229 followed the Ongpin-Vistan proposal, stating that landowners would have the right to appeal to Regional Trial Courts on decisions taken by the DAR.[171] The attempt to create a state institution empowered to implement a redistributive reform, beyond the jurisdiction of powerful vested interests, was soundly defeated.

As during the Marcos years, those who occupied powerful positions within the state did not challenge the dominant landed and corporate interests. The military, which emerged as a major actor within the state, was also opposed to any programme that would have incorporated the militant peasant movement into the process of implementation. There was virtually no tradition of state action independent of the powerful political clans in society upon which the Aquino government could draw. It is not surprising that it was Solita Monsod, one of the few genuine technocrats in the Cabinet with weak links with all of the major power centres in society, who went the furthest in promoting a liberal redistributive programme.[172]

During the first half of 1987, President Aquino still had law-making powers and theoretically could have issued an executive order launching a redistributive programme, at least along the lines of the 25 May draft. While the Constitution guaranteed that Congress would have the right to amend any law introduced by the President, a strong endorsement by the executive could have reinforced the position of those advocating the liberal approach in the new legislative chamber. At this time President Aquino still retained a wealth of popular support and an image transcending her ties to the political clans. This was reflected in a comment made by KMP leader Jaime Tadeo when he met the President after the Mendiola Massacre, 'We assure you, Mrs. President, that the peasants love you'.[173]

Claims that the Cabinet Action Committee endorsed market-value compensation to landowners as a result of a legal decision by the Supreme Court, or that the executive order failed to promote a low retention limit due to Constitutional limitations, are clearly inaccurate. Rather, these were political decisions taken in deference to the interests of landowners and the business community. Although peasant mobilization had put reform on the agenda, the debate over the executive order demonstrated that the commitment of the President and her closest advisers to the conservative approach to agrarian reform had not significantly changed after the Mendiola Massacre. The President's executive order set the tone for the next major debate over reform that would take place in the newly reconstituted Congress.

Notes

1. The organizations were the Agrarian Reform Beneficiaries Association (ARBA), the Federation of Land Reform Beneficiaries Associations (FLRBA) and the Federation of Agricultural and Industrial Toiling Hands (FAITH). They asked Aquino to move quickly on reform and expand the old programme to cover all foreclosed lands and lands that had been left idle since 1980. These lands, they said, should be taken over by the government 'for redistribution and resale at cost' to the landless. *Malaya* (9 March 1986).

2. One series of meetings, involved peasant leaders, Church activists and former political prisoners. Transcripts of speeches and discussion were published in Sandoval ed., 1986. Another series was organized by Frank Sionil José, writer and long-time advocate of the liberal approach to reform. Transcripts of discussions were published in José's journal, *Solidarity*, No.s 106 and 107 (1986). This was one of 11 seminars held between March 1986 and January 1987, capped by a major conference on 7-8 February 1987 (José, ed., 1987).

3. PHILDHRRA, 1987, p.5; Umali, 1990, p.11.

4. ANGOC was created in 1979 as a result of the FAO's World Conference on Agrarian Reform and Rural Development (WCARRD).

5. Tadeo, 1986, pp.17-20.

6. Kilusang [KMP], 1986.

7. Tadeo, 1986, p. 17.

8. By April 1987, they claimed that more than 50,500 hectares had been occupied with 20,000 hectares already under cultivation. *Peasant Update International* (Manila: KMP, April 1987),p.1.

9. By September 1987, the *Pambansang Kilusan ng mga Samahang Magsasaka* (PAKISAMA) was occupying some 2,000 hectares in Mindanao; *Aniban ng Manggagawa sa Agrikultura* (AMA) was occupying 3,000 hectares in Central Luzon; United Farmers and Fishermen's Association of the Philippines (UFFAP) occupied 30,000 hectares in the Basilan region; and the *Lakas ng Magsasaka Manggagawa at Mangingisda ng Pilpinas* (LMMMP) was also said to be involved with land occupations. Interview with Dina Abad and Dinki Soliman of the Congress for a People's Agrarian Reform, Manila, September 1987.

10. Interview with Gerardo Bulatao, Assistant Secretary, DAR, 24 November 1988.

11. Interview with Bulatao, 11 September 1987.

12. Ramos, 1986, p.108.

13. On 9 November Lt.Col. Victor Corpus, former PMA instructor who had defected to the NPA but rejoined the AFP after his release from prison in 1986, revealed that RAM was planning a coup code-named 'God Save the Queen', which would leave Aquino as a figurehead in a military-civilian junta. On 22 November troops from Enrile's province, Cagayan, moved toward the capital.

14. Nemenzo, 1988, pp.261-68.

15. Nemenzo, 1988, p.238-39.

16. Interview with Gerardo Bulatao, Assistant Secretary, DAR, 24 January 1989. This was the personal view of Jack André, Economic Officer on the Philippine Desk, State Department, (Interview 5 December 1989).

17. Based on first-hand observations and visits with local KMP chapters on Luzon, Mindoro and Mindanao between 1987 and 1989. The relationship between the legal and underground peasant organizations are discussed further in the Conclusion.

18. Villa-Real, 1987, p.258.

19. Heherson Alvarez, 'A Report to the President' 3 November 1986, excerpts reprinted in DeDios et al, 1988, pp.780-82. Citation from Alvarez, 'Ministry Order No. 210-86', Series 1986, Ministry of Agrarian Reform.

20. Included were Mitra, Monsod, Lacson, and representatives of the Presidential Management Staff, Negros Council Forum and the Philippine National Bank, to whom many of the sugar planters were in debt. *Malaya* (17 December 1986).

21. *Malaya* (6 March 2987).

22. Interview, DAR official in Region II who requested anonymity, 17 May 1989.

23. *Peacemaker*, Vol.17, no.1 (Manila: January-March, 1987).

24. The 'Report of the Citizens' Mendiola Commission, Office of the President' (27 February 1987, reprinted in DeDios et al, 1988, p. 789) stated that, 'security officers of the police and military commanders were in civilian attire', and there 'was unnecessary firing by the police and military' in violation of the law, but also claimed that there was 'gunfire from both sides'. Jack André (Interview, 5 December 1989), who was serving at the US Embassy said, 'I saw Jaime Tadeo on TV saying if they try to stop us from getting to Malacañang, there will be blood in the street...What happens, they march and some guys get shot, there is talk - I think credible talk - of provocateers [sic] among these farmers - most of whom were not farmers - anyway some people got killed, very unfortunately'.

25. *PDI* (22 September 1987).

26. Inter-Agency Task Force on Agrarian Reform (IATFAR), 'Accelerated Land Reform Project' 23 January 1987 (hereafter, '23 January Draft'). The document indicated an expansion of the IATFAR to include the Agrarian Reform Institute at UP Los Baños, LBP, MAF, MAR, MF, MNR, NEDA and Mahar Mangahas's Social Weather Stations, Inc.

27. There were supposedly 16 or 17 drafts of the Executive Order (Interview, DAR Secretary Philip Juico, 16 August 1989). This analysis is based on an examination of eleven of these (which will be referred to by their dates) prepared between 23 January and 28 June 1987 and the final Executive Order, No.229, issued on 22 July 1987. The drafts only assumed the form of draft executive orders in May.

28. 23 January Draft, p.18. While stating that new legislation was required for Program C, DAR's February schematic cited RA1199 (Agricultural Tenancy Act of 1954) as part of its legal justification. Because this law merely regulated rentals on tenanted farms, it seems that, just as in the *Medium Term Plan*, the expansion of reform to private lands was still perceived mainly as land tenure regulation and not redistribution.

29. The document did offer a critical evaluation of the compensation process of past programmes and, while endorsing 'just compensation', it argued that beneficiary payments must be affordable (e.g., equal to or less than previous rental payments) (23 January Draft, pp.13,16).

30. *BD* (4 June 1987).

31. Customs Commissioner Bobby Tañada, Presidential Counsel Rene Saguisag, Executive Secretary Joker Arroyo, Audit Chairman Teofisto Guingona and Appointments Secretary Ching Escaler were among those who joined the demonstration (*Peacemaker*, January-March 1987). Jonathan Steele observed the momentary closeness between the government and the popular movement, saying, 'it almost seemed as though the Government had become the opposition, and the enemy, as before, were the troops, driven back but waiting discreetly in the wings'. *The Guardian* (27 January 1987).

32. See James Clad's report, *FEER* (12 February 1987) and Chapter 6.

33. Ongpin, 1988, p.97. This is the first statement on agrarian reform in the collection of Ongpin's most important speeches.

34. William C. Thiesenhusen confirmed in a letter to the author (6 March 1991) that Ongpin 'had asked for the [World Bank] team's evaluation at the Paris Club meetings'. The controversial World Bank Mission is discussed in Chapter 9. See the discussion on foreign assistance in Chapter 10.

35. Interviews, Solita Monsod, 9 May 1991 and Gerardo Bulatao, 24 November 1988.

36. The CAC initially included the DAR, DA, DENR, PCGG and NEDA. With the approval of the new Constitution on 2 February 1987, all Ministries were once again called 'Departments', and Ministers, 'Secretaries'.

37. Present at the meeting were DAR Secretary Alvarez, DENR Secretary Dominguez, DA Secretary Mitra, NEDA head Solita Monsod and PCGG chairman Jovito Salonga. Cabinet [CAC], 4 February 1987.

38. Interview with IATFAR member Gerardo Bulatao, 24 November 1988.

39. Interview, Solita Monsod, 9 May 1991.

40. Interview with IATFAR member Gerardo Bulatao, 21 November 1988.

41. The advocates of the liberal approach included Bulatao and Mangahas, who won over CAC chairperson Solita Monsod and most of her NEDA staff.

42. Cabinet [CAC], 16 February 1987.

43. Letter from Jaime Tadeo, Chairman KMP to the Cabinet Action Committee (CAC, 16 February 1987).

44. *Midweek* (3 June 1987). The KMP's decision was no doubt precipitated by the government's decision on 27 February to charge Jaime Tadeo with sedition for his part in the events leading up to the Mendiola Massacre.

45. 'Accelerated Land Reform Program: Program Brief,' Inter-Agency Task Force on Agrarian Reform, 27 April 1987 (hereafter, 27 April Draft).

46. NEDA, 'Memorandum from the Director of the Agricultural Staff to the Director General', 20 April 1987. Regional Directors were all hold-overs from the Marcos administration. DAR, 'Public Hearings Reactions to the Proposed Executive Order on Comprehensive Agrarian Reform Program', First Round, n.d.

47. Two undated drafts were written in early May and will be referred to as the 'May A' and 'May B' drafts, while a third was dated 20 May, a forth dated 22 May and a fifth dated 25 May.

48. Interview, Solita Monsod, 9 May 1991. Another Cabinet member (Interview 9 May 1991) confirmed Arroyo's outburst, but thought he said 'leftist'.

49. Interview, Solita Monsod, 9 May 1991.

50. Interview, Cabinet Member, 9 May 1991.

51. Ongpin, Memo to the President, 4 May 1987.

52. It proposed that beneficiaries would pay 80 per cent of the purchase price of the land over a period of 20 years at a zero rate of interest. This was reduced to a 17 year period in the 25 , May Draft. 22 May Draft, Section 17 and 25 May Draft, Section 11.

53. *BD* (15 May 1987).

54. The Bank based its report on the 13 March Draft executive order. See Chapter 9 for a discussion of the World Bank report.

55. *BD* (20 May 1987).

56. *MC* (22 May 1987).

57. The FFF quickly withdrew from the coalition and the majority of the farmer organizations in SANDUGUAN, an alliance created to work with the government during the Marcos years, did not participate.

58. United Nations FAO, 1988.

59. 'The People's Declaration of Agrarian Reform', Congress for a People's Agrarian Reform, Quezon City, 31 May 1987. The eight-point document was later elaborated into a detailed programme of agrarian reform.

60. See section 7.2 above. Umali headed the Ramon Magsaysay Foundation which prepared 'A Proposal for the National Agrarian Reform Program', 9 June 1987.

61. The CSP grouped together 44 planters' organizations, while the PSA was made up of 17 sugar milling companies from Luzon and the Visayas. *BD* (19 May 1987).

62. *BD* (19 May 1987). This group claimed a membership of 3,500.

63. *BD* (19 May 1987).

64. *BD* (29 May 1987).

65. The following citations are from an interview with Hernandez in his Makati office, 2 December 1988.

66. *BD* (29 May 1987).
67. Interview Solita Monsod, 9 May 1991. While there is some question about the date of the meeting, one other Cabinet member independently confirmed Monsod's story, saying that he also received a telephone call at about the same time in the morning (Interview, 9 May 1991).
68. *MC* (29 May 1987). Romero, who was a member of the Constitutional Commission (see Chapter 6) was the main contact used by US liberal reform advocate Roy Prosterman to channel his views to the President's office (see Chapter 9).
69. Malou Mangahas based this report on conversations with three other Cabinet members. *MC* (7 June 1987).
70. June 3 Draft, Sections 4 and 17.
71. *MC* (7 June 1987). See the CAC's summation of these hearings, 'Matrix of Comments/ Suggestions During the Second Round of National and Regional Consultations on the Proposed Executive Order on the CARP', which reported basically the same arguments as the first hearings.
72. The letter was reproduced in Council [CAPP], 1987a, pp.67-72.
73. *PDI* (Manila: 9 June 1987), p.8.
74. *BT* (5 June 1987).
75. *FEER* (25 June 1989).
76. *PDI* (Manila: 19 June 1987).
77. PHILDHRRA, 1987, p.12.
78. *Business Times* (25 June 1987).
79. 28 June Draft, Sections 2, 7, 11 and 15.
80. 28 June Draft, Section 2.
81. *Business Times* (29 June 1987). ,
82. The letter was reproduced in CAPP, 1987a, pp.73-76.
83. Land Bank of Philippines Draft, Section 8.
84. Catholic Bishops' Conference, 1987. Fifteen Bishops had met about a month before in Cagayan d'Oro, where they warned that Congress would be likely to avoid forceful action on agrarian reform and urged the President to sign an executive order (*Asian Wall Street Journal* 1 July 1987; *BT* 24 June 1987).
85. Proclamation No.131, 'Instituting a Comprehensive Agrarian Reform Program', 22 July 1987.
86. *MC* (18 July 1987). On the sentiments of Congressional representatives see *PDI* (19 June 1987).
87. The paper, dated 17 July 1987, was reprinted in *MC* (21 July 1987).
88. Proclamation No. 131, 'Instituting a Comprehensive Agrarian Reform Program', and Executive Order No.229, 'Providing the Mechanisms for the implementation of the Comprehensive Agrarian Reform Program', 22 July 1987.
89. Amando Doronila, *MC* 23 (July 1987).
90. 23 January Draft, p.15 and May A Draft, 'Preamble'. This was maintained in subsequent drafts until the end of May.
91. May 25 Draft, 'Preamble'. *Constitution*, Article XII, Section 1, Paragraph 1.
92. June 28 Draft, 'Preamble'.
93. Proclamation 131, 'Preamble'.
94. January 23 Draft, p.15 and after that in the 'Preamble' of subsequent drafts.
95. While several articles of the Constitution were cited in Proclamation 131 to justify agrarian reform, it dropped the reference to Article XII, Section 1, Paragraph 1 pertaining to the elimination of poverty, which had been included in previous drafts.
96. Proclamation 131, 'Preamble'.
97. Proclamation 131, Section 1.
98. If one discounts the 170,800 hectares added on to Program A, the September sub-total of private lands to be covered would total 2,347,000 hectares, maintaining the downward trend. See Chapter 4 for estimates of the Marcos programme and Chapter 10 for subsequent manipulation of these figures.

99. 13 March Draft, p.46.
100. 27 April Draft, 'Transitory Measures'. The World Bank Mission (1987b, pp.15, 56) had argued that the retention limit in the March Draft was far too high and claimed that by lowering it to seven hectares an additional 1.2 million hectares of land could be included in Program C.
101. The World Bank Mission (1987b, p.16) had advised cutting Program B by 50 per cent, saying, 'it seems most unlikely that 300,000 hectares of good quality land will be "voluntarily offered" for land reform'.
102. Those lands formerly included as 'foreclosed' were apparently added to voluntary offers, and 'expropriated' lands were integrated with the figure for resettlement under public lands.
103. May B Draft, Section 8; 28 June Draft, Section 2.
104. EO229, Section 6.
105. Cabinet [CAC], Memo to the President, 4 February 1987, p.3.
106. 27 April Draft, p.15. The CAC was following the earlier proposals of the PCGR Survey Team (see Chapter 6, section 6.4) as well as the World Bank Mission (1987b, pp.40-42).
107. See Chapter 4.
108. Marcos's PD76 (6 December 1972) stated that, 'For purposes of just compensation in cases of private property acquired by the Government for public use, the basis shall be the current and fair market value declared by the owner or administrator, or such market value as determined by the assessor, whichever is lower'. This was reiterated in subsequent PDs and endorsed by the Supreme Court during the Marcos years (World Bank, 1987b, pp.40-42; Tolk, 1989, pp.28-36).
109. Export Processing Zone Authority vrs Ceferino E. Dulay, 149 Supreme Court, Rep. Ann. 305, G.R. no. 59603, April 29, 1987. Cited by Tolk, 1989, p.27 and Wurfel, 1988, p.321.
110. Wurfel, 1988, p.321.
111. May A Draft, Section 10; May B Draft, Section 10; 20 May Draft, Section 9; 22 May Draft, Section 8; and 25 May Draft, Section 7.
112. Tolk, 1989, p.51, note 151 citing the Supreme Court decision: 'the rule introduced in PD76...does not upset the established concepts of justice or the constitutional provision on just compensation'. Tolk (pp.39-40), however, disapproved of linking agrarian reform compensation to taxation and proposed an alternative formula based on a return to an assessment of the productive value of the land.
113. 3 June Draft, Section 17.
114. EO229, Section 6. Section 18 stipulated that the Presidential Agrarian Reform Council would adopt rules concerning 'control mechanisms for evaluating the owner's declaration of current fair market value...taking into account current land transactions in the locality, the landowner's annual income from his land, and other factors', but the landowner's declaration remained the starting point.
115. EO229, Section 4. The early drafts also required owners to include their land title numbers but this was dropped on 20 May.
116. EO229, Sections 6 and 8.
117. In the 13 March Draft, there were no restrictions on the terms for such agreements, but land in excess of the retention limit had to be transferred within five years. In the first May draft this was labelled 'Voluntary Land-Sharing', requiring complete divestment in 15 years (May A Draft, Section 17; 20 May Draft, Section 12). The 20 May Draft (Sections 12 and 18) curiously reduced the period of 'Voluntary Land-sharing' to ten years, but added a new section on 'Voluntary Land Transfer', which allowed a voluntary transfer agreement to be completed in 'a period not more than *eighty (80) years*'.
118. 22 May Draft, Section 18; 25 May Draft, Section 8. Ike Pahm (letter to the author 22 February 1991), who worked as part of the support staff of the IATFAR from the Institute of Agrarian Studies at the University of the Philippines at Los Baños, said that people at the IAS and at DAR 'were not particularly keen' on the concept of voluntary land transfer 'because of

its tremendous ambiguity'. He said that the IATFAR reached a consensus on the need 'to make the transfer as quick as possible'. He pointed out that 'this was not included in the final executive order at all'.

119. See Chapter 10.
120. 28 June Draft, Section 11; EO229, Section 9.
121. In South Korea, voluntary land transfers contributed positively to reform implementation (see Chapter 3), but this was because the landowners were already convinced that they would lose their lands and therefore sold-out to tenants at a price just slightly better than what the government was offering.
122. EO229, Section 10.
123. *BS* (Manila: 2 December, 1987).
124. What is more, workers would only be given '*the right* to purchase' shares and offered additional compensation which they 'may' use for the purchase. It was conceivable that farmworkers, whose income was rarely enough to feed their families, might use additional compensation for consumption rather than spend it on a tiny proportion of the company's stocks.
125. Interview with Philip Juico, former Secretary of Agrarian Reform, 16 August 1989, Makati.
126. See Chapters 5, section 5.9 and Chapter 6, section 6.3.
127. The 22 May Draft (Section 11) stated, 'In case the voluntary transfer agreement involves gradual transfer of the land or *gradual divestment of shares of stocks* and other like instruments of ownership over the land, the majority portion of the land or majority control over the instruments of ownership should be transferred within a period of not more than fifteen years, and 100 per cent of the land or 100 per cent of the instruments should be transferred within a period of not more than thirty years'.
128. The 25 May Draft (Section 8), however, reduced the period by which the workers were to enjoy full-ownership to 17 years.
129. World Bank, 1987b, p.28.
130. José Ma. T. Zabaleta, Senior vice-president - Planning, Gamboa Hermanos Incorporated, in a letter to the author, 13 March 1991. His role was also underlined by Juico (Interview 16 August 1989, Makati).
131. Ike Pahm, Institute of Agrarian Studies, UP Los Baños, letter to the author 22 February 1991.
132. *Business Times* (2 June 1987).
133. LBP Draft, Section 8.
134. Letter to the President from Jaime Ongpin and Deogracias Vistan, chairman and president of the LBP, 6 July 1987, reprinted in Council (CAPP), 1987, pp.73-76.
135. See Chapter 10.
136. EO229, Section 11.
137. See Chapter 10.
138. The first mention of production sharing was in relation to provisions on the modification of public land use in the 25 May Draft, section 14. See Chapter 10 on the implementation of this scheme.
139. Ongpin-Vistan letter to the President, 6 July 1987.
140. Letter to the author (emphasis in original), 31 March 1991.
141. EO229, Section 22.
142. *MC* (20 February 1987). See Putzel and Cunnington, 1989.
143. 28 June Draft, Section 8.
144. 28 June Draft, Section 26.
145. For instance the 20 May Draft (Section 40) stated that DAR must give its approval before any judge or court ordered a cultivator evicted, and prohibited 'any member of the Armed Forces' from executing an order of eviction knowing it to be false. These prohibitions were later dropped.

146. EO229, Section 23 stated only that, 'Persons, associations, or entities who wilfully prevent or obstruct the implementation of CARP shall be liable for contempt'.

147. EO229, Sections 18 and 19 on the PARC and the BARCs. The BARC would consist of representatives from (1) farmer and farmworker beneficiaries; (2) non-beneficiaries; (3) agricultural cooperatives; (4) other farmer organizations; (5) Barangay Council; (6) NGOs; (7) landowners; (8) DA; (9) DENR; (10) DAR Agrarian Reform Technologist; (11) LBP. Whether the producers would actually be out-numbered would depend on the political strength of peasant organizations in a village, particularly *vis a vis* categories (2) (4) (5) and (6).

148. May A Draft, Section 21.

149. 25 May Draft, Section 18; 28 June Draft, Section 22.

150. EO229, Section 18. To be included were the Secretaries of the DAR, DA, DENR, DBM, DF, DOLE, DLG, DPWH, DTC, NEDA and the PCGG. Interestingly, in the 28 June Draft, the Executive Secretary was also made a member of PARC, and in EO229 included in its Executive Committee.

151. James Fenton, *Independent* (16 and 18 February 1987) and *Guardian* 16 February 1987.

152. See Chapter 9.

153. 23 January Draft, p.9.

154. See Table 7.1 above.

155. 'Opening Statement at the Consultative Group Meeting,' Paris, 27-28 January, 1987 (Ongpin, 1988, p.99).

156. Statement to journalists on 3 March 1987, reported by Renato Constantino, *Malaya* (6 March 1987).

157. Address for Carnegie Endowment Face to Face Program, 10 March 1987 (Ongpin, 1988, p.111).

158. 27 April Draft, p.16.

159. 25 May, 3 June, 28 June drafts in 'Preamble'.

160. Arthur N. Aguilar, a member of the conservative business group Manindigan, was one among this minority. On 26 May he urged rapid action by the President, 'Since agrarian reform would not only be the centerpiece of government programs but also an integral part to [sic] resolve communist insurgency, time is of the essence'. *BD* (26 May 1987).

161. The paper, dated 17 July 1987, was reprinted in *MC* (21 July 1987).

162. Proclamation No. 131, 'Preamble'.

163. Putzel, 1988, pp.53-55. For a comprehensive discussion see Lawyers Committee for Human Rights, 1988.

164. *Guardian* (17 March and 10 April 1987). See Chapter 8.

165. *IHT* (11 February 1987). On the Magsaysay campaign, see Chapter 3. Ferrer was assassinated on 3 August 1987 (Davis, 1989, p.13). While some suspected the NPA (Kessler, 1989, p.77), those arrested for the murder were linked to a gun-for-hire network in the national penitentiary. José Obusa, a medium security inmate at Muntinlupa prison, who had been released on a false summons from a judge in Quezon province, was positively identified as Ferrer's killer (*PDI* 30 September 1987).

166. *MC* (Manila: 20 February 1987).

167. DAR Undersecretary Salvador Pejo, who had been Director of Region V covering Bicol, reportedly said that Arroyo's family no longer owns much land there. Interviews, Solita Monsod, 9 May 1991, and Eduardo Hernandez, 2 December 1988.

168. Burton, 1989, p.429. Ongpin took his own life on 7 December 1987.

169. Letter to the author from Maria Isabel Ongpin, 28 October 1990. Mrs. Ongpin's description of her husband's thoughts about land reform were a testament both to his sincerity in pushing for action on reform in 1987 and his commitment to the main tenets of the conservative approach.

170. May A Draft, Section 19.
171. EO229, Section 17; LBP Draft, Section 17.
172. Monsod's determination was no doubt buttressed by the fact that a win on the issue of agrarian reform would strengthen her hand against Jaime Ongpin on issues of foreign debt and public finance, on which they were in vehement disagreement.
173. Jonathan Steele, *Guardian* (27 January 1987).

8

CONGRESS AND THE PASSAGE OF THE COMPREHENSIVE AGRARIAN REFORM LAW

8.1 Introduction

With the passage of executive order 229, President Aquino succeeded in shifting the political responsibility for reform to the newly established Congress, which seems to have been the strategy of her closest advisers from the start.[1] The opening of Congress on 27 July 1987 and the subsequent provincial-municipal elections on 18 January 1988 virtually completed the 'restoration' begun in February 1986. The new legislature assembled in an atmosphere of growing instability and disillusionment with the Aquino government. Urban and rural 'cause-oriented' groups had wanted more forceful executive action on reform before the convocation of Congress.

The young colonels who had rallied around Juan Ponce Enrile felt excluded from power and saw the growing popular protest movement as a pretext for the military to assert its authority. Members of the House of Representatives were anxious to safeguard the revival of the legislative branch within the state and with it their own power to disperse favours and consolidate support in their constituencies, particularly in light of upcoming local elections. Many of those elected to the Senate had served in Aquino's first Cabinet and hoped to remake their chamber, which had not met for fifteen years, in the image of the pre-martial law Senate - a terrain for national debate and a stepping stone to higher political office.

After their defeat on the executive order, advocates of the liberal approach to agrarian reform turned their attention to Congress. At the same time, leaders of the peasant movement let it be known that they were prepared to pursue their call for a 'people's agrarian reform' both inside and outside of the legislative process. The great national debate on agrarian reform was not yet over.

8.2 Restoration of Congress in the shadow of the military

The influence of traditional landowning families was demonstrated in the national elections to the newly constituted House of Representatives and Senate on 11 May 1987. Despite the centrality of the agrarian reform issue, only the left-leaning Partido ng Bayan (People's Party) and Alliance for New Politics included agrarian reform as a central issue in the campaign. Candidates supported by the government coalition as well as those in the right-wing opposition avoided campaigning on the issue, both to win the support of traditional

259

politicians centred among the landowners in the provinces and to avoid drawing the ire of the organized peasant movement.

After the vote was taken it was clear that the traditional politicians, organized more on the basis of provincial clans than parties, dominated the new House of Representatives. Of the 200 members elected, 129 were members of traditional clans, while another 38 were related to them.[2] While clans that had been out of favour under Marcos did better than erstwhile Marcos supporters, many of the latter were nonetheless elected. Conrado Estrella's dynasty remained intact, with both a son and grandson of the ex-Agrarian Reform chief elected to the House. Maria Clara Lobregat, ex-chair of the COCOFED, beat the administration-backed candidate in Zamboanga City. Many clan candidates who had formerly supported Marcos switched their loyalties to the new government.

Many of the representatives were members of large landowning families. When the 204 representatives were required publicly to declare their assets, 141 registered ownership of agricultural and residential land valued at P293.7 million. Two relatives of the President were among the wealthiest, with the President's sister-in-law, Teresa Aquino-Oreta, declaring P17.2 million, and her brother, José Cojuangco Jr., declaring P6.4 million worth of real estate. Ramon Mitra Jr. declared landed property of P3 million. However, even these figures almost certainly underestimated holdings since they did not reflect the amount of land owned by corporations in which these families had a major stake.[3]

The President's brother, José Cojuangco Jr., emerged at the head of the ruling coalition's political machine and was elected as a representative from Tarlac. He had engineered the defection of many former supporters of Marcos and Salvador Laurel to the government coalition. In a manner reminiscent of Marcos' Cabinet members' entry to the Interim Batasang Pambansa in 1978, many of Aquino's first Cabinet members took their place in the ranks of the House and especially the Senate. Ramon Mitra was elected from Palawan and, with the blessing of José Cojuangco, became Speaker of the House.[4] Jovito Salonga became Senate President, and even Juan Ponce Enrile, who had become leader of the right-wing opposition, succeeded in getting a place in the chamber.

Continuing peasant mobilization and EO229's 90-day deadline for Congressional action on agrarian reform combined to put reform legislation at the top of the congressional agenda.[5] The Congress for a People's Agrarian Reform established a 'tent city' outside congressional buildings to ensure that the new representatives would not attempt to postpone discussion of reform legislation. CPAR also began drafting its own bill outlining an agrarian reform programme.

Speaker Ramon Mitra named Sorsogon representative Bonifacio Gillego as head of the House Committee on Agrarian Reform. Senate President Jovito Salonga put Aquino's first Agrarian Reform chief, Heherson Alvarez, in charge of the Senate's counterpart committee. Both were given mandates to come up with draft reform legislation as quickly as possible. The main issues at stake were those that had been extensively debated around the executive order but left unresolved: the definition of retention limits, landowner compensation and the timing, or priorities, of reform.

Hardly had the Congress opened its doors when there were renewed and serious rumblings from the military. After the earlier, almost theatrical, coup attempts, on 27 August 1987 Col. Gregorio Honasan shocked the country with the first serious attempt by a group within the armed forces to challenge the seat of power. Following this attempted coup, President Aquino's government made numerous concessions to the armed forces in an effort to head-off further rebellions. The President reshuffled her Cabinet again, this time dismissing her controversial Executive Secretary, Joker Arroyo, whose resignation had been demanded by dissidents within the armed forces. The simultaneous dismissal of the late Jaime Ongpin (which was widely perceived as precipitating his suicide in December), and his replacement as Finance Secretary by Vicente Jayme, had less impact on the Cabinet's policy orientation, since both men shared a common policy approach. The President asked Congress for an across-the-board salary increase for military personnel and gave the armed forces more freedom to conduct the war in the countryside on their own terms. She backed away from threats to prosecute soldiers for human rights violations and appointed a number of retired officers to top posts in the government.[6]

President Aquino restated her commitment to the AFP's 'total war' strategy. In October she travelled to Davao where she declared her support for the vigilante groups, telling an *Alsa Masa* rally of 4,000, 'You here have set the example'.[7] The military's influence in government was further expanded in January 1988 when General Fidel Ramos replaced Rafael Ileto as Secretary of Defence. The Secretary of Agrarian Reform, Philip Juico, attempted to reassure the military that the government's plans for agrarian reform would not undermine counterinsurgency efforts. He told 750 cadets at the Philippine Military Academy that no reform would be implemented in areas influenced by communist rebels until they were first secured by the military.[8] In February, one DAR official reportedly claimed that an agreement had been made 'in principle' with the Department of Defense to give 30,000 soldiers priority in the distribution of sequestered lands.[9]

The military showed itself more committed than ever to suppress peasant unrest through firepower rather than reform. AFP spokesman, General Honesto Isleta expressed the military's alternative when he said, 'We want something like the National [sic] Security Act...in Malaysia and Singapore.'[10] The AFP leadership cited the internal security measures of these countries, which include the death penalty and indefinite detention without trial, as models.[11] As Congress began its deliberations over agrarian reform, the military showed no sign of backing away from its counterinsurgency strategy, which gave no place to redistributive agrarian reform. In August 1987, Senate President Jovito Salonga told a foreign journalist, 'You cannot have meaningful land reform in an atmosphere of such instability'.[12]

8.3 The House of Representatives and the landowners

Representative Bonifacio Gillego surprised many by the uncompromising stand he took in defence of a liberal model of reform during the House debate. He was an ex-military intelligence man who had taken a stand against Marcos during the 1971 Constitutional Convention. He was forced into exile in the US after martial law was declared and participated in the anti-Marcos movement there, playing a role in exposing Marcos' human rights violations, the workings of his military machine and even the President's fraudulent World War II medals. Mitra had to reward him with a committee chairmanship. Gillego would have preferred to sit on the defense committee, but Mitra wanted to avoid antagonizing the AFP and delegated him to agrarian reform, where Gillego had no experience. After resisting the appointment out of a feeling of *delicadeza* towards the President, since he had heard she wanted her uncle, Congressman Herminio Aquino, to take the Committee, Gillego finally accepted upon Mitra's insistence.[13]

The congressman proved to be a fast learner and soon sought out the advice of peasant leaders. At the first meeting of his Committee on 30 July 1987, Gillego announced that he and Speaker Mitra had already set up a small group, or 'select committee', to produce a draft bill to submit to the Committee. The small group included Eligio Tavanlar, José Medina from the DAR and UP Professor Alex Fernandez - all involved in the reform efforts of Marcos and previous administrations. Gillego said that they consulted the key draft versions of the executive order, position papers from the peasant movement, documents from the landowners and Roy Prosterman's book.[14] Knowing the House and his Committee to be dominated by those opposed to redistributive reform, Gillego was determined to get a head-start over the opposition and to produce the first working draft of legislation.

Of the 31 members who signed up for the House Committee, 18 were members of traditional political clans, seven were relatives of those clans and only six were new and relatively unattached to the traditional clans.[15] Gillego said that of the 31 members, not more than ten supported his approach to reform.[16] José Cojuangco himself joined in the early meetings of the Committee, as did other representatives of the landowners, including sugar and rubber planter Hortensia Starke, from Negros Occidental, and sugar planter Romeo Guanzon, also from Negros. Even the two Estrellas came to sit on the committee. Starke was very suspicious of the 'select committee' preparing the draft, saying, 'I thought I would be involved in this thing'. She did not like DAR involvement,'They should be executing what we legislate'. As it turned out, her fears were unfounded.

Gillego had known Tavanlar from their days together in Laos assisting the US war effort. Because Tavanlar had participated in Magsaysay's NARRA, the Macapagal and the Marcos reforms, Gillego assumed that he would be pro-reform. He had little knowledge at the time of the divergent positions in the DAR and believed that Medina also would push for rapid reform. But Tavanlar turned out to be much more favourable to the landowner reticence to redistribute private lands and ended up defending a conservative approach. At the Committee's next hearing, Tavanlar told them, 'reconciliation of the interests of the land owner and the land tiller should be the first attempt we should make. Now, the consequence of that is peace in the countryside...It is not so important for a person at the low level to own land, if you can assure him an increasing level of livelihood...[W]e should try to maintain production in our country today and do everything to increase it'.[17]

The landowners apparently could not believe their ears, and Rep. Rodolfo Albano, an old Marcos stalwart from Isabela, was quick to praise Tavanlar and looked forward to his draft legislation.[18] Gillego said that when Tavanlar aligned himself with the landowners he ignored him. The landowners, Starke and Guanzon, then recruited the aging consultant to their team.[19] Later DAR Assistant Secretary Gerry Bulatao, who was quietly advising congressmen in favour of the liberal approach, questioned Tavanlar's integrity saying, 'He hires himself out as a consultant to anyone'.[20] The landowners also ensured that the Committee was flooded with presentations from landowner organizations around the country. One of the first to be heard in Committee was Leo Carparas of the organization COLOR, the Council of Landowners for Orderly Reform, who argued that taking property was outright injustice. He was followed by Arsenio Acuña of the National Federation of Sugar Planters and the CAPP.

Only one formal hearing of the Committee was held with peasant leaders. The seasoned veteran of many years of peasant organizing, Ka Memong Patayan, vice-president of the KMP, argued that if landowners were to be compensated at all, the government should provide the funds. He advocated free distribution of lands to peasant beneficiaries.[21] Gillego remained in touch with peasant leaders and worked closely with CPAR members throughout the House debates. The efforts of the landowners and the approach of Tavanlar's draft legislation spurred on Rep. Gregorio Andolana from Agusan del Norte, who along with Vicente Garduce was one of only two congressmen elected from the left-leaning Partido ng Bayan slate, to file his own bill shortly after the first Committee meeting. It embodied, almost to the letter, the programme drafted by the Congress for a People's Agrarian Reform (CPAR).[22] The bill called for a quick five year implementation, a retention limit of no more than two hectares of land already personally cultivated by the owner, and compensation linked to the value declared in past tax declarations, the owner's declaration of fair market value and an estimation of past rents and unpaid work performed by cultivators.

The landowners were taken by surprise and accelerated work on their own version of reform. They introduced a bill in the second week of August which called for a 20 hectare retention limit and the exemption of all major export crops including sugar, coconuts, pineapple and bananas. The landowner programme also proposed delaying coverage of private lands until all public lands were distributed. Landowners would receive cash payment at market value for their lands as long as the funds were invested in industry or commerce. The landowner bill also reiterated EO229's provisions on corporate stock-sharing, and called for a strict application of sanctions against peasants occupying agricultural lands.[23]

On 14 August, Rep. Florencio Abad from the Gillego group, moved a motion to give the Chairman blanket authority to consolidate all bills so far filed in the House. The result was House Bill 400, drafted by Gillego and the supporters of the liberal approach. It made two major modifications of the Andolana-CPAR proposal as concessions to the landowners. It allowed a retention limit of seven hectares and stipulated that landowners need not personally cultivate retained land. It also allowed a corporate stock-sharing programme and production and profit-sharing, but only 'pending final land transfer'. However it proposed a rapid five year implementation period, provided no exemptions or deferments, included a sliding scale of compensation based on the size and manner of acquisition of a landowner's holdings, and contained mechanisms for full peasant involvement in the implementation of reform.[24] Gillego's bill was only able to win the support of ten members of the Committee, but by presenting it in the form of a Committee Report to the House on 17 August 1987, when several landowner representatives were absent, Gillego was able to get the bill to the floor of the main chamber with the signatures of 22 members of the House.[25]

Procedurally out-manoeuvred, the landowners quickly drafted a rival bill, closely following their earlier draft. It was officially submitted by Rep. Romeo Guanzon - a congressman from Negros Occidental who was also a big landowner and President of the National Federation of Sugar Planters - and had the endorsement of no less than 116 House members.[26] On 15 September the Liberal Party held a caucus to discuss what position it should take in the House. Senators Saguisag, Salonga and Ziga were all present. Eleven of the 21 in attendance voted to support a call to re-commit the Gillego bill to committee. On 20 September a motion was presented on the floor of the House proposing that HB400 be returned to Committee in light of the way it had been passed and the arrival of a rival bill endorsed by more than half the House. However, given the widespread popular support for reform, Mitra wanted legislation quickly and encouraged launching debate immediately on HB400. The vote on 21 September favoured proceeding with discussion of the Gillego bill. Thus HB400, which was closer to the principles of the liberal approach, would serve as the basis for debate in the House, while the advocates of Guanzon's landowner bill decided to defend their interests by proposing amendments.

Over the following six months a process of amendments to HB400 was undertaken within the House. Many of the provisions in rival landowner bills were gradually incorporated, in much the same fashion as the executive order had been transformed. At the end of September, Gillego and his colleagues made one crucial concession to the landowners, agreeing to enlarge the retention limit to seven hectares plus seven hectares for one legitimate heir. Gillego later regretted this, as well as the earlier concession allowing landowners to retain lands that they did not personally cultivate.[27] José Cojuangco played a low-profile role throughout the process. He withdrew from the House Committee after the first few sessions and was not even a signatory to the landowner bills originally presented in Congress. However, Gillego testified that as the amendment process got under way he was invited on more than one occasion to the Speaker's office, and Cojuangco was always present in these 'persuasion sessions'. Gillego commented, 'From the very start the group of landowners in Congress looked up to Peping for guidance or leadership'.[28] Cojuangco seemed to leave the public debate to Representatives Guanzon and Starke.

The landowner representatives lined up one after another for the interpellation of the bill and then to speak against it. The debate on the floor of the House during this period saw a head-on confrontation between the liberal and conservative approaches to reform, encompassing diametrically opposed views on the definition of reform, the nature of property rights, the role of productivity improvement and assumptions about peasant unrest and rebellion. Congressman Gillego's sponsorship speech on 21 September 1987 was an eloquent defense of the liberal approach. Setting his defence of reform squarely in the liberal tradition, and underlining the fact that the need for reform had long been known to the country's leaders, he said that everyone from 'the American land reform adviser to the Philippines in 1951 [a veiled reference to Robert Hardie], to Marcos and President Aquino herself recognized reform as crucial to achieving peace and development'.

During the debate that followed, Rep. Hortensia Starke, who personally owned sugar and rubber plantations in Negros and Mindanao, challenged Gillego on his definition of 'comprehensive agrarian reform'.[29] She echoed past proponents of the conservative approach to reform, arguing that 'agrarian...refers to anything that has to do with agriculture, and as you know agriculture also refers not only to land, but also to the labor that works on the land and to the machinery...and to all the other inputs...that go into production...So it is not necessarily referring to privately owned lands'. As for 'reform', Starke went on, 'when it refers to the farmer, it means to improve his economic status', while 'comprehensive' refers not only or necessarily to all lands, but 'to all components: marketing, organization, infrastructure, irrigation, and credit facilities'.

Gillego rose to the challenge, 'if we use the term 'agrarian''...[we] refer to a relationship and that relationship is not between man and land...[If] I am tilling this land that I do not own, I relate myself in a real sense not to the land that I till, but to you, my landowner...[I]n our relationship there is [a] situation that is pregnant with opportunities for abuse and exploitation...[T]he state comes in and corrects this unjust relationship'. Gillego continued, 'you added an adjective like comprehensive...What has been the...nature of reforms in the past? Limited'. He went on to explain that in the context of the failed reforms of the past, 'comprehensive' meant both public and private lands, regardless of tenurial arrangement, 'beyond rice and corn and this is what hurts. It goes to sugar, it goes to coconut, it goes to cash crops and all permanent crops'. Finally, Gillego

265

returned to Starke's definition of 'reform'. 'As a social or political concept...[it] would include institutional reform. And the institution involved here is owner-ship of property, and in the ownership of property there can only be one relationship. If property is land, you either owned the land or I work on the land which you owned.'

In much the same terms as Ladejinsky and other proponents of the liberal approach had used before him, Gillego argued that 'ownership of property is ownership of status, privilege and power'. '[W]hen there is a crisis that has historical roots in land hunger and land injustice...even a democratic government wedded as it is to the concept of protecting life, liberty and property, begins to reappraise its position vis-a-vis the concept of property...[E]ven during our time in the Constitutional Convention we talked [of] property in terms not of absolute ownership but in terms of stewardship...The use of police power, the right of eminent domain, these are all used by way of State intervention for the general welfare and the general rule'.

But later, Rep. Pablo Garcia, countered with a conservative defence of private property. He attacked what he called 'worn out and discredited slogans spawned at some other times and places such as "land for the landless"...Is there freedom when you can be compelled against your will to part with land which you have earned out of your honest toil, tears, sweat and blood?' He protested that the Constitution guarantees to 'protect the liberty and property' of the rich and the poor alike. And he appealed to natural law, 'If your land...is a gift of God...then only God not Congress, can take it away from you against your will'.[30]

The two approaches also clashed over the proper understanding of the role of increased agricultural productivity. In his sponsorship speech, Gillego argued that agrarian reform was not only a requisite of social justice, but the only means to advance the nation economically. 'Poverty', he said, 'is primarily the result of the highly unequal distribution of ownership and control over land resources...[T]he transfer of control over all farm activities to the direct producer will release hitherto under-utilized...productive capacities'. As a result, higher incomes 'will in turn expand the domestic market' and 'manufacturing will be encouraged to broaden its domestic activities', resulting in a 'self-sufficient and self-generating national economy effectively controlled by Filipinos'.

His vision was not shared by the landowner representatives. Rep. José Carlos Lacson said that reform should not include productive private lands, but that both public lands and these should be distributed 'as done in the FELDA scheme in Malaysia, using the landless settlers in the development process to train them and strengthen their commitment to the land'. On private lands, 'the tenurial relationship between the owner and tillers should be improved' and the latter given a 'home lot'. There should be production sharing, and when land is redistributed it should only be after 'ten to 15 years...using as a vehicle of ownership a farm cooperative or a corporation'.[31]

Finally, the opposing camps presented obverse assessments of the challenge of the revolutionary movement in the countryside. Gillego warned that a failure to redistribute land would result in 'an escalation of the fires of revolt currently engulfing the countryside'. 'Where there is poverty and suffering, there is discontent. And where there is discontent, violence breeds and festers. Our history reveals that rural unrest and insurgencies are the instinctive and often spontaneous responses of the peasantry to the conditions of land dispossession and resulting penury...[T]he clamor for land grows stronger and the once melancholy refrain sung by the toiling masses is fast becoming an inflammatory anthem of rage and fury'. Most of the Congressmen did not concur with the idea that a comprehensive redistributive reform was necessary to put down the revolutionary movement.

In a position resembling that of the AFP itself, Rep. Thelma Zosa-Almario argued against those who 'would have us believe that HB400 is the solution to the communist insurgency problem...[T]he communists will seek to wrest power from our constitutional government whether agrarian reform is implemented or not'.[32] Rep. Simplicio Domingo Jr. apparently agreed with Gillego's definition of 'agrarian', but came to a different conclusion. 'Agrarian...refers...to a situation...where unrest mars or threatens the good relationship of a considerable number of landowners and tenants'. However, he insisted that he did 'not see any actual or even imminent agrarian unrest or trouble' that would justify widespread redistributive reform. Instead, he proposed concentrating land reform only 'in areas where there is actual agrarian trouble or unrest' and exempting from reform lands 'devoted to the big plantation[s] of coconut, sugar, banana and pineapple'.[33]

One of the most extraordinary speeches was made by Maria Clara Lobregat, representative from Zamboanga City and erstwhile partner to Eduardo Cojuangco Jr. and Juan Ponce Enrile in the coconut monopoly of the Marcos years. She ensured the House, 'I speak not as a landowner', and went on to put her case, 'each human being is born with different talents so that not every Filipino wants to be a farmer'. Not all who cultivate land can own it, she argued, just as, 'Not all housemaids own the homes they work in. Not all drivers own the cars they drive. Now that is how life is'. She concluded her speech by asking the House to 'stop and consider' that for the landowners the loss of their land is like the loss of a child, and warned that the landowner may well 'demand a confrontation with his Representative in Congress to explain why such a law has been passed'.[34]

In early February the landowners went on a public offensive. The Council of Agricultural Producers of the Philippines (CAPP) denounced efforts in the House as, 'a blatant attempt to railroad the passage of a controversial, confiscatory, land ineffective agrarian reform law down the throats of many Filipinos who would be unjustly deprived of their hard-earned property due to this measure'.[35] José Cojuangco produced his own version of HB400 with consolidated amendments, reflecting most of the conservative proposals from the original landowner bills.[36] He held a closed-door caucus the following week to line up support for the amendments.[37] Cojuangco spoke publicly after this meeting and announced that he felt retention limits should be determined by Provincial Agrarian Reform Councils.[38]

During the week of 23 March 1988, amendments were introduced one after the other, allowing compensation to be based on the landowners' declaration of market value, putting off the distribution of private lands, and finally allowing a retention limit of seven hectares for the owner plus three hectares for *each* legal heir.[39] This prompted 14 of the original 22 sponsors of HB400 to withdraw their support for the bill. Majority floor leader, landowner and presidential relative, Francisco S. Sumulong, took over sponsorship of the bill. Gillego justified his withdrawal by saying that Congress was sending 'a signal to the people...[This] only confirmed the worst fears of our people that we are the bastion of conservatism at a time when radical reforms are needed'. Andolana commented, 'This is land to the landed and not land to the landless tiller'.[40]

Congresswoman Lorna Verano Yap surprised her colleagues when she asked, 'Who are these children who will be made beneficiaries of these lands? Some of them are learning ballet, some are going to the best schools abroad and maybe driving their own cars while the farmers cannot even own the land that they till...I am sick in my heart'.[41] The final bill was passed on the 21 April 1988, with 112 votes in favour and 47 votes opposed, and was immediately condemned by peasant organizations around the country. Jeremias Montemayor called the Comprehensive Agrarian Reform measure passed by the House, 'a comprehensive and genuine disaster', saying that landowners covered by the Marcos reform would demand lands back for their heirs.[42]

8.4 The Senate debate on reform

Debate in the other chamber of Congress followed a different and much less antagonistic course. The Senators, who did not have to worry about the views of landowners in local constituencies, held a more even-keeled debate, but also one where the conservative and liberal positions confronted one another. Fifteen of the original 24 senators participated in the Senate Committee. Senator Alvarez, apparently having learned after his brief stint at DAR that caution was the better course of action for one with political aspirations, defended a thoroughly conservative approach. His bill mirrored EO229 and allowed variable land retention limits from seven to 15 hectares, exemptions for orchards, prawn and fish farms, and pineapple and banana plantations; a schedule of implementation leaving private farm lands the last to be covered; and market value compensation for owners. It also called for mandatory inter-cropping on coconut lands in order to make them more productive, a plan for profit-sharing on corporate lands exempted from coverage, and a provision on voluntary land transfer so vague that it could accommodate corporate stock-sharing or any other arrangement concluded between owner and beneficiary.[43] The Senate then began conducting hearings throughout the country.[44]

In October, Senator Butz Aquino introduced a rival bill embodying most of the principles of the liberal approach. Like Gillego, Aquino established close contact with the peasant lobby groups. In an explanatory note accompanying the bill, Aquino specifically argued, 'Agrarian reform is also the long-term solution to insurgency. As long as the rural population remains poor and desperate, armed struggle will always appear attractive and justifiable'. He called for a three hectare retention limit on all lands and the prohibition of absentee ownership of any kind, also compensation based on owners' tax declarations and cash incentives to owners who voluntarily participate as well as to small owners. Profit sharing arrangements pending final transfer of the land were dictated with higher requirements placed on foreign agribusiness than domestic, and strict penalties for landowner violations as well as support services for beneficiaries were spelled out.[45]

True to the conservative approach, Alvarez called the Aquino bill 'politically unworkable' because it could result in social discord in the countryside, apparently assuming that social discord was not already a problem in the rural areas.[46] Senator Paterno threw his weight behind the Alvarez bill and Herrera backed off from presenting yet another version. In early November Alvarez introduced a new bill claiming to have taken into account all alternatives, but the basic components of his original proposal remained.[47] Aquino refused to budge and the two bills were further debated in Committee. However, on 17 December 1987, under pressure for legislative action, Alvarez called for a vote on yet another version of his bill, which retained all his original proposals on retention limits and exemptions.[48] In an extremely revealing vote, 10 of the 13 senators who were then members of the Committee voted to report the bill to the Senate floor, with only Aquino and Maceda writing dissenting opinions and Enrile refusing to sign 'for lack of comprehensive study and time'.[49]

The debate continued in the new year, but by February the Senators' intentions were becoming clear. They told Alvarez that the Senate should come up with a low retention limit, since the House was prepared to pass a 24 hectare limit.[50] Even Aquino had originally justified his three hectare limit as a bargaining chip with the House.[51] Under severe pressure from Senate President Jovito Salonga, the Senators agreed to amend their bill to lower the retention limit to five hectares. On 28 April 1988, 18 senators, including Alvarez and Aquino, voted for the bill, while Senators Osmeña, Enrile and Paterno - all opponents of redistributive reform - abstained.[52] They then appointed their members to the Joint House-Senate Conference Committee, called to reconcile the two bills, which held its first meeting on 12 May 1988.

Throughout Congressional deliberations the landowners engaged in an escalating campaign against those advocating a liberal approach, actively lobbying both chambers and holding rallies around the country. The landowners argued that agrarian reform was discriminatory toward the owners of rural property and would spell the ruin of the agricultural sector. The landowners claimed that, with their access to capital and education, only they could provide the necessary technological improvements to advance agricultural production. While they acknowledged the need to curb the abusive practices of some landowners and to

269

improve farmworkers' wages, they called on the government to limit redistribution to publicly-owned lands.[53] The large landowners launched a concerted appeal to the much more numerous small owners, attempting to stir up opposition to reform and to convince them that their interests were identical. They depicted the plight of the employee who had bought a small farm with retirement pay, or the owner-cultivator family who, after years of work as tenants, had bought their own land.[54] The big owners omitted to mention that the original House Bill 400 included provisions that were in the interests of small owner-cultivators.

The landowner campaign was not limited to calm argumentation, rather it was designed to put pressure on the Congress. In March 1988, when the Council of Agricultural Producers of the Philippines (CAPP) held their annual convention, 1,000 landowners from all over the country denounced efforts to draft a redistributive reform, declaring that the program 'will reduce this country to a nation of peasants'.[55] Later in the month, President Aquino went to address a convention of the National Federation of Sugar Planters (NFSP). Lawyer and outspoken planter representative, Arsenio Al. Acuña, hurled abuse at her, saying, 'Land reform is the biggest menopausal blunder of this President'.[56] After the President addressed the hostile crowd, Joey de la Paz, chairman of the NFSP's 'agrarian reform committee' stood up and declared, 'We will fight land reform. They will get our lands over our dead bodies'.

In April, the NFSP sponsored a television programme where Rep. Hortensia Starke warned that the Senate bill would ruin the nation.[57] As the Joint House and Senate Committee began to negotiate the final shape of the law, the NFSP held a convention in Bacolod, the capital of the sugar province of Negros Occidental, where 800 planters attended. Senator Osmeña openly campaigned against the Senate bill, urging the landowners to oppose the CARP and prepare to use the 1992 elections to hit back at the Senators responsible. He told the crowd, 'No dictator in Manila should tell you how much to retain of your land'.[58]

Upon seeing the final shape of both the Senate and House versions of the programme, peasant leader Jaime Tadeo told a rally of 20,000 farmers that both were 'hacienda bills' that would not 'uproot the peasant from poverty'.[59] Just days before the final House vote, the Congress for a People's Agrarian Reform launched a march to Congress with caravans starting from Irosin, Sorsogon in Gillego's home province and the northern province of Isabela. Peasants also announced demonstrations in Cebu City, Bacolod, Cagayan de Oro, Davao and the province of Mindoro Occidental. Revealing its own sympathies on the agrarian reform legislation, the military set up blockades preventing hundreds from joining in the motorcade bound for Congress. Bishop Bacani announced the Church's support for the demonstrations and urged the peasants to keep up pressure on the Congress.[60]

During the first week of meetings, the Senators in the Conference Committee speedily agreed to include the House provision allowing three hectares for each heir, as long as they were over 15 years old. The House then agreed to a five hectare retention limit. The Committee became deadlocked over the issue of timing. The Senators at first asked for private lands to be covered in the second year of the programme, while the House wanted this delayed until at least the fourth year, or beyond the term of the government.[61] With Congress due to adjourn in four days, the Senators gave way on the phasing of reform and an agreement was reached finalizing the law.[62]

On 7 June 1988, 152 members of the House voted for the law and only 20 against it, with four abstentions.[63] With their eyes on their future political prospects, several of those who had withdrawn sponsorship from HB400 voted in favour of the law. Boni Gillego and Florencio Abad, however, stood their ground and voted 'no'. When questioned why she decided to vote in favour of the legislation, Rep. Hortensia Starke said, 'There were more good things than bad. After 1992 we can have some amendments'. For Starke, the ten-year framework within the law was crucial to her decision, since it would allow the introduction of important amendments after 1992, when she and others were certain that the political complexion of the executive and the Senate would be different.[64] Seventeen Senators approved the law, while Estrada, Shahani, Aquino and Enrile absented themselves from the vote, Paterno abstained and Osmeña proudly voted no.[65] Although representatives of the Church had urged peasants to keep up their mobilization for reform, when the law was passed Cardinal Sin announced that he was 'very happy' with the outcome.[66]

It has been suggested that the final law agreed on by the Joint Senate-House Conference Committee was a 'compromise'. Many legislators themselves painted the law as a 'tolerable compromise' between the interests of the landless, represented most closely in the Senate bill, and the interests of the landowners, which dominated the House version.[67] Others argued that the Senate represented a more urban and industrially based section of the ruling class, and was biased in favour of plantations operated by the TNCs and a new breed of corporate and commercial local farm-owners, while the House represented local plantation owners.[68]

While these explanations have some validity, the Senate was in fact less committed to redistributive reform than most observers have realized. Senators, who were elected by a national, rather than a constituency vote, had less direct demands on them from landowner networks than did members of the House and they could afford to be bolder in their rhetoric about reform. There were several indications that the Senators, many of whom had presidential aspirations, believed that they could be more radical in their reform proposals because at the end of the day final legislation would be drawn up in Conference Committee with the House and they could be sure of obtaining a more conservative legislation without incurring any blame from the supporters of reform. In assessing the legislative outcome, CPAR leader Corazon Juliano-Soliman supported such an analysis, saying that besides Alvarez and Aquino, Senators were non-committal about reform.[69] Ultimately the Senators demonstrated their lack

271

of conviction by their quick agreement with the House on the final shape of the law.

Soliman suggested that a major reason why Congress did not do more was because there were few determined advocates of agrarian reform in the cities. While the peasants mounted an impressive campaign, they did not succeed in organizing the kind of pressure of 1971, which forced legislative action on reform against the wishes of the President.[70] Former DAR Assistant Secretary Gerry Bulatao offered a similar assessment, 'Pressure groups were only minimally felt during the drafting of the agrarian reform programme. Had people been more on the ball - if they had been more prepared to fight for specific points, they could have had more impact on the final programme'.[71] However, such a portrait seems to harbour illusions about what could be gained from Congress in 1988. In fact, the peasant lobby succeeded in keeping reform on the Congressional agenda and in getting far more out of Congress than they had in 1971.

What was most striking about the Senate-House confrontation and the legislative process as a whole was the emergent alliance between both chambers around an essentially conservative approach to reform. Soliman, herself, provided support for such a verdict in commenting on the legislative outcome. Land is a political power base, she said, and its redistribution 'would spell the end of political dynasties'. She continued, 'landowners have easy access to Congress ...They also meet members of Congress at social functions such as parties and family reunions. They speak the same language, share similar tastes, and laugh at the same jokes. It is not at all easy for them to go beyond their world and into that of the many who toil in the sun'.

8.5 Anatomy of the agrarian reform law

On 10 June 1988, President Aquino's signature made the CARP, or Republic Act 6657, the country's basic law on agrarian reform.[72] In her speech on that occasion the President said that she hoped that the Act would 'end all the acrimony and misgivings of the contending parties to the program'. Her words struck a note of irony when she said, 'Let us see the program not as a taking of property from some and a giving of it to others', since many felt that the law would, in fact, redistribute very little property. The President was watchful, even then, that her words would not antagonise the landowners, saying, 'The stewardship of the land that the landlords *were said to have neglected* shall now pass...to the tillers'.[73]

The bias in favour of landowners and agribusiness that characterised EO229 was even more pronounced in the new agrarian reform law. Like the executive order, the law reproduced the Constitutional principles of reform, but it also significantly amended them. The definition of 'agrarian reform' offered in the law reduced the centrality of land redistribution, defining reform as *either* the 'redistribution of lands' or 'production or profit sharing, labor administration, and the distribution of stock'.[74] This appeared to contradict the Constitution and the law's own assertion that 'the agrarian reform program is founded on the right of farmers and regular farmworkers, who are landless to own...the lands they till', and was reminiscent of earlier efforts to water-down the content of reform.[75]

While it was not surprising that the law reaffirmed the landowners' right to 'just compensation' for their lands, it went even further than EO229 in guaranteeing owners the right to dictate and receive the 'fair market value' of their land. Although the law stated that compensation would be determined in part on the original purchase price of the land, owners were no longer required to submit that information when they registered their lands.[76] The original House Bill 400 stated that both tenants' and owners' information about the land would be considered in deciding compensation levels, and any conflicting information would be decided on by People's Agrarian Reform Councils (PARCONs), controlled by peasant and NGO representatives. But the law completely abandoned the principle of peasant and NGO control of the implementing committees. Landowners would be paid in a combination of cash and Land Bank Bonds with very generous terms on the use of the bonds.[77]

Rather than giving the Department of Agrarian Reform (DAR) the final say on the level of compensation, landowners were permitted to contest DAR decisions on this and all matters in the courts.[78] The Supreme Court was given power to designate one branch of existing Regional Trial Courts in each province to act as 'Special Agrarian Courts', in much the same way as they had done in the 1950s. Decisions of the DAR and the Special Agrarian Courts could be reviewed by the Court of Appeals and then the Supreme Court. The law stipulated that, while agrarian reform cases were to receive priority, their hearing could be extended beyond the ten years of the programme's life.[79] Limiting DAR's powers of judicial review guaranteed that CARP would be bogged down in the courts for years to come.

The retention limits of five hectares per landowner plus three hectares for each heir over fifteen years of age meant an effective retention limit of between 11 and 14 hectares.[80] This greatly reduced the scope of reform, given the ability of landowners to disguise the size of their holdings through transfer of titles to relatives and clients. It also ensured that the many lands owned by smaller absentee owners would be exempted from coverage and opened the doors for considerable legal challenges to implementation. Under the law, landowners could choose the best portions of land for their own and their children's retention. While the law stated that children had to be 15 years old to qualify, it did not stipulate any date by which they had to attain this age, thus leaving room for further court challenges. Children were supposed to cultivate or 'manage' the land that they received, but since management can be claimed from quite far afield, the basis was laid for the continuation of absentee ownership. Tenants on land retained by the owners and their children were given one year to declare whether they wished to remain as tenants or be assigned land elsewhere under the programme. Given the average owner's influence over their tenants and the average tenant family's understandable doubt about unseen land

Table 8.1 Timetable for the Implementation of CARP

Programme years		Lands Covered
Phase 1	Years 1 - 4	Rice and corn lands under P.D.27.
		Idle and abandoned lands.
		Lands foreclosed by government financial institutions.
		Lands acquired by the Presidential Commission on Good Government.
		Private lands voluntarily offered.
Phase 2	Years 1 - 4	Public agricultural lands.
		Private lands in holdings greater than 50 hectares.
Phase 3	Years 4 - 7	Private lands in holdings 24 - 50 hectares.
	Years 6 - 10	Private lands in holdings less than 24 hectares.

Source: The Comprehensive Agrarian Reform Law of 1988, or Republic Act (RA)6657, Section 7.

in a strange locality, most tenants were likely to hesitate before leaving their owners' land.

Following the last versions of the executive order, before it abandoned any mention of phasing, the law was designed to be implemented over a period of ten years rather than the five that both the Gillego and Aquino bills had originally suggested. As illustrated in Table 8.1, it would initially cover mainly public lands and large private holdings, leaving the majority of lands legally listed as smaller holdings until the end of the programme, after the tenure of the administration had expired. This was a measure of the utmost importance in winning House approval for the law.

As listed in Table 8.1, Phase 1 and 2 of the programme appear to bring a large proportion of land under immediate distribution. However, closer scrutiny proves just the opposite. While the law guaranteed that landowners who received seven hectares under the Marcos programme would be allowed to retain their land, it did not specify whether these owners would be able to claim additional land for their children. As Montemayor had been quick to realize after heirs were included in the House bill, given the relatively large amount of rice and corn lands that were still to be covered, not even the beneficiaries of Marcos' PD27 could be guaranteed that landowners would not claim some of the rice and corn lands for their children.

As in EO229, foreclosed lands under Phase 1 included only lands held by *government* financial institutions and not those held by private banks. While the law provided private landowners with an additional 5 per cent of their compensation in cash if they voluntarily offered their lands, loopholes that permitted them to retain land acted as a counter-incentive. Even the amount of 'idle or abandoned' land available for redistribution under Phase 1 was not likely to be large since, according to the law, land had to have been left idle for 'a period of three years *immediately prior* to receipt of notice of acquisition by the government'.[81] Landowners, even if their land had been idle for ten years, could evade redistribution by putting it to some immediate agricultural use, or by asserting that it was abandoned 'by reason of *force majeure*', claiming that the presence of militant peasant organisations or the NPA prevented cultivation.

The law also reaffirmed the corporate stock distribution option outlined in EO229 and included in the final House bill.[82] A ten year deferment was allowed to owners whose lands were devoted to 'commercial livestock, poultry and swine raising, and aquaculture including saltbeds, fishponds and prawn ponds, fruit farms, orchards, vegetable and cut-flower farms, and cacao, coffee and rubber plantations'.[83] This opened the door to landowners to shift cultivation to these commercial endeavours in order to avoid redistribution. DAR was given the power to determine when 'the purposes for which this deferment is granted no longer exist', however nowhere were the purposes explicitly stated in the law, thus ensuring that DAR would have difficulty in defending a decision to cancel this exemption when challenged to do so in court by the landowners.

Finally, all private lands leased to domestic or transnational agribusiness corporations were also made exempt from redistribution for *ten years*, or until their lease expired. Even when the lease expired, the law stated that if 'it is not economically feasible and sound to divide the land' for redistribution, it would be distributed to workers' cooperatives. Nowhere was there a statement defining who would decide the feasibility of redistribution. The law also stipulated that such workers must then come to an agreement over a new lease or the old one would remain in force. This would virtually compel workers' cooperatives to conclude agreements with domestic and foreign agribusiness.

The language and content of the law expressed an explicit bias in favour of landowners, agribusiness corporations and traditional politically powerful families. Tenants who remained on retained lands would be subject to leasehold arrangements with no further measures to ensure their security. As declared in EO229, landowners were permitted to engage in 'voluntary transfer' agreements with all the ensuing problems of coercion. While the terms of payment for those who would eventually receive land under the programme appeared to favour the beneficiary, they were actually not as lenient as they appeared.

Beneficiaries would have a 30-year repayment period, with annual amortisation payments not to exceed the value of 5 per cent of gross production during the first five years and 10 per cent after that time. However, this was *gross*, not *net* production, and thus applied to produce without taking into account the cost of production. Given the high cost of farming, beneficiaries could not be certain that they would be able to pay. The original proposals of Ongpin and Vistan during the debate over the executive order were included in the law, giving the Land Bank the authority to foreclose land automatically if three annual payments were not made.[84]

In Gillego's original House bill, there were provisions for establishing Peoples' Agrarian Reform Councils that would be a channel for popular participation and a means to counter-balance the political power of landed interests. The law replaced this notion with the establishment of Provincial Agrarian Reform Coordinating Committees (PARCCOM), a proposal originally suggested by the President's brother, José Cojuangco.[85] The PARCCOMs were empowered to regulate the implementation of reform and to ensure that the priorities would be strictly adhered to by DAR, even if this meant that the programme could not be implemented within the ten year deadline. Only these provincial bodies were given the power to speed up the process of reform. In reality the PARCCOMs opened a door for provincial politicians to short-circuit the reform process.[86]

8.6 The peasants' alternative to CARP

When the final law was signed by the President, the Congress for a People's Agrarian Reform rejected it as fundamentally opposed to the interests of the rural poor. On 26 June, CPAR sponsored a multi-sectoral conference bringing together 600 delegates from all over the country. They included representatives of peasant, worker, student and other sectoral organizations as well as many of the NGOs that had supported CPAR's work over the preceding year. The following day the conference adopted 'The People's Agrarian Reform Code' (PARCODE) as an alternative to the government's programme.

The PARCODE incorporated most of the provisions of earlier proposals made by the peasant movement. It set a maximum five hectare retention limit for landowners who cultivated their own land, but guaranteed that the tillers' right to own land would take precedence over the owners' right to land retention. Tenancy would be totally abolished. The programme called for 'selective and progressive' compensation based on the assessed value of the land in landowners' tax declarations. It would compensate small landowners at a higher rate than large owners. Beneficiaries would be ensured affordable amortization payments and would be provided with support services. CPAR's Code stipulated a short five year implementation period. It contained specific provisions for 'fisherfolk', women and indigenous peoples, and proposed establishing a structure of People's Agrarian Reform Councils (PARCONs) to ensure full peasant participation in reform implementation.[87]

PARCODE was still, in essence, a liberal reform. It recognized the right of landowners to compensation for their lands and the principle that beneficiaries should pay for the lands they received.[88] However, unlike the proposals traditionally advanced by advocates of the liberal approach, the Code called for peasant and other people's organizations to play a leading role in the implementation process. Like all liberal reforms, the outcome of an effort to implement a programme like PARCODE would depend on the strength of the people's organizations. This would determine whether such a programme resulted primarily in 'co-opting' or 'empowering' rural producers. Aside from the member organizations of CPAR, well-known figures put their signatures to CARP, including Rep. Bonifacio Gillego, social-democratic leader Noberto Gonzales, BAYAN leader Eta Rosales, BISIG representative Francisco Nemenzo,

BANDILA representative Chito Gascon, and the House representative for women, Teresita Deles. Signatories also included noted advocates of the liberal approach to reform, such as Mahar Mangahas and the Asian Institute of Management's Gaston Ortigas.[89]

The conference launched a campaign to collect 2.5 million signatures calling for a referendum that would reject the government's agrarian reform law and adopt the PARCODE in its place. CPAR based this campaign on a provision in the Constitution that allows for a referendum, 'whereby the people can directly propose and enact laws or approve or reject any act or law or part thereof passed by the Congress', after a petition is signed by 10 per cent of registered voters.[90] However, the PARCODE contained at least one crucial legal flaw in its final provision or 'effectivity clause'.[91] In reference to Article VI, Section 32 of the Constitution, PARCODE stated that a petition of ten per cent of the voters would be sufficient to repeal CARP and implement PARCODE. In fact, the Constitution states only that a referendum can be held '*after* the registration of a petition' signed by ten per cent of voters. What is more, the Constitution empowers Congress to determine the mechanism to hold such a referendum. In other words, even if successful, CPAR's signature campaign could do no more than provide the basis to hold a referendum and could not, in itself, cause the repeal of CARP.

Subsequently, the signature campaign proceeded in fits and starts and the major member organizations of CPAR never seemed to take it very seriously.[92] Even if they were to succeed in collecting the required number of signatures for a referendum in a legally acceptable form, it was unrealistic for the peasant groups to believe that they could win such a contest. The dominant position of political clans within the state was such that any contest through the ballot box would almost certainly turn out against the peasants' radical proposals. In the first place, the same Congress that passed CARP into law would have control over setting up the referendum. Since landowners would oppose provisions in the PARCODE (such as that stipulating selective compensation) as unconstitutional, Congress would be unlikely to include PARCODE as an option in the referendum. In fact, landowner representatives had already expressed their confidence that they would win a plebiscite on agrarian reform. Earlier in the year, when appearing on a television programme sponsored by the National Federation of Sugarcane Planters, Rep. Hortensia Starke had called for such a referendum.[93]

No doubt the main intent of the peasant movement in articulating PAR-CODE was to present an acceptable and 'theoretically attainable' alternative to CARP as the basis on which to mobilize both the peasantry and its supporters. In addition to launching this campaign on a national level, the peasant organizations continued their actions on the ground. KMP leader Jaime Tadeo said that starving farmers could not wait for the implementation of PARCODE, and called on peasants to continue land occupations, rent strikes and crop seizures.[94] Over the next year, many peasant groups launched their own local initiatives to demonstrate that measures called for in PARCODE could improve the livelihood of the landless rural poor. They also used PARCODE to explain the failings of the government's own programme.[95]

8.7 Conclusion

The debate over agrarian reform in Congress covered much the same ground as the earlier Cabinet confrontation between advocates of the liberal and conservative approaches. Many of the participants in drafting reform legislation were the same as those who had been involved with the early drafts of the executive order. DAR officials on both sides of the debate, as well as other experts and officials involved in drafting the reform legislation of previous governments, served as resource people to congressmen and senators. Peasant organizations, the Congress for a People's Agrarian Reform and non-governmental organizations played an active role in lobbying Congress to adopt a liberal model of reform. At the same time, landowners ensured that their organizations got a wide hearing in Congress and that politicians would have no doubt about the consequences of voting for something more than a conservative reform.

The advocates of the liberal approach attempted to revive proposals, presented early on in the debate over the President's executive order, for a rapidly implemented programme covering all agricultural lands that would bring about lasting change in the countryside. At the same time, most members of Congress were naturally inclined to the conservative approach and they drew on the proposals already elaborated and endorsed during the previous year by the President's closest advisers. Lacking strong presidential support, and with the military playing an increasingly powerful role within the state, those in Congress advocating a return to the liberal approach contained in the early draft executive orders were virtually ensured of defeat from the outset. Their continuing presence in the debate was largely due to the determined mobilization of the peasant movement and its supporters, which even Congress could not entirely ignore. However, escalating dissent within the armed forces during this period reinforced what appeared to be more of a consensus around the conservative approach than a compromise between pro-landowner and pro-peasant positions.

The inability of the legislative institutions of the state to establish authority over its military institutions and to transcend the interests of major power centres in society was strikingly illustrated during the course of the agrarian reform debate. The victory of advocates of the conservative approach in both the executive and legislature was determined primarily by the continued dominance of powerful Filipino interests opposed to redistributive reform. The outcome was, however, also influenced, as it had been in the past, by the action and inaction of the major foreign actor in the country, the United States.

Notes

1. The President said as much when she signed the final legislation, 'It was my intention from the start to assign the substantive portions of the program to those who would be most affected and therefore most informed about them, the people themselves through their elected representatives' (Aquino, 10 June 1988).

2. Institute [IPD], 1987.

3. Data was not available to distinguish agricultural from residential property. Only 40 claimed to be landless. Cristina Pastor, *MC* (10 April 1988).

4. Institute [IPD], 1987, part 2.

5. EO229, Section 18.

6. In March 1988 the President restated her intention to do away with the regional unified commands in order to give local commanders more authority (*Reuters* 22 March 1988). On human rights violations by the military and failure to prosecute see Amnesty International, 1988. On military personnel appointed to top government jobs see Shelia S. Coronel's discussion in the MC (20 September 1987).

7. *Reuters*, 23 October 1987.

8. *PDI* (28 February 1988).

9. *Malaya* (7 February 1988).

10. He was referring to the Internal Security Act.

11. *Reuters* (16 February 1988).

12. Burton, 1989, p.427.

13. Interview, Bonifacio Gillego, 26 August 1989. Gillego (1988) recounted other reasons for his hesitance, including his perception that it was a 'no-win' issue.

14. The small group had at their disposal the following documents: Draft Executive Orders dated 25 May, 3 June, 28 June, the draft prepared by the LBP as well as a 'June 11 Landowner draft'; the June report from the World Bank; papers from NGOs, KMP and PHILDHRRA; Prosterman and Riedinger (1987) and a land reform primer written by Mariano Tirol. House Committee on Agrarian Reform, Minutes, 30 July 1987.

15. House Committee, Minutes, 30 July and 4 August 1987; IPD, 1987.

16. Gillego, 1988a, p.3. Included in their number was the group that Gillego called the 'magnificent seven': Gregorio Andolana of Cotabato, Vicente Garduce of Samar, Oscar Rodriguez of Pampanga, Raul Roco of Camarines Sur, Edcel Lagman of Albay, Florencio Abad of Batanes, and Romeo Angeles, the peasant sectoral representative to Congress.

17. House Committee Minutes, 4 August 1987.

18. House Committee Minutes, 4 August 1987.

19. Gillego said Tavanlar had called him asking to participate (Interview, 26 August 1989) but Mendoza (1988, p.7) stated that Mitra had first met with Tavanlar.

20. Interview, Gerardo Bulatao, 24 November 1988.

21. *Trends Register* (15 August 1988), p.3.

22. House Bill (HB) 65, filed 27 July to 4 August.

23. House Bill 319, filed 10 to 14 August.

24. House Bill 400.

25. House Committee on Agrarian Reform, Committee Report No. 4, 17 August 1987.

26. House Bill 941. Guanzon declared P5 million in real estate holdings (note 3 above) and inherited leadership of the NFSP from his friend, Marcos ally and Negros 'warlord', the late Armando C. Gustilo (Interview Arsenio Acuña, 26 February 1989).

27. Interview, Gillego, 26 August 1989.

28. Interview, Gillego, 26 August 1989.

29. The debate that follows is from the Congressional Record, 19 November 1987, 5:40pm to 8:00pm.

30. *Torno en contra* Speech of Congressman Pablo Garcia, March 1988.

31. *Torno en contra* Speech of Congressman José Carlos Lacson, 8 March 1988.

32. *Turno en contra* Speech of Congresswoman Thelma Zosa-Almario 7 March 1988.

33. *Turno en contra* Speech of Congressman Simplicio Domingo Jr. 2 March 1988.

34. Privilege Speech of Rep. Maria Clara Lobregat, 15 March 1988.

35. *Malaya* 6 February 1988.

36. HB400, 8 February 1988, with hand-written note, 'Cojuangco Proposal'. HB319 seemed to be the model, as the text eliminated a schedule for implementation, returned to a 24 hectare retention limit, exempted orchards, aquaculture, poultry, pasture, livestock and agro-forestry, and stated that 'areas earmarked for urban expansion...shall not be physically redistributed'. It favoured fair market compensation and expansion of the Courts' role, thus limiting DAR's decisional powers, and of course inserted the corporate stock-sharing proposal.

37. *Malaya* (16 February 1988).

38. *MC* (26 February 1988).

39. The key amendment on retention limits introduced by Rep. Adelbert W. Antonino, from an old political clan in South Cotabato, was endorsed by 118 representatives against 49, illustrating the power of the landowner bloc.

40. *MC* (25 March 1988).

41. *Chronicle on Sunday* 27 March 1988.

42. *Malaya* (23 April 1988).

43. Senate Bill (SB) 16, introduced in early August 1987. It seems that Alvarez updated his original version of SB16 sometime in September to make it appear slightly less pro-landowner (SB16, second version). No Senate bill ever specifically spelled out the corporate stock-sharing option.

44. Between 11 August and 25 September 1987, hearings were held on coconut lands, sugar lands, aquaculture, financing and plantations. A special hearing was held in Bacolod Negros. A meeting was held with the Committee on Natural Resources, and a hearing was conducted to take into account the position of the Sanduguan coalition of peasant organizations. Notes from Alvarez Office, October 1987.

45. Senate Bill 123, 1 October 1987.

46. *BS* (14 October 1987).

47. Senate Bill 133, November 1987.

48. Senate Bill 249, 17 December 1987.

49. Senate Committee on Agrarian Reform, Report No. 103, 17 December 1987. Maceda's dissenting opinion demonstrated a surprising sophistication and knowledge about reform for one who was seldom involved either before or after in any advocacy around the issue.

50. *BS* (27 February 1988).

51. Aquino said, 'If the Senate comes up with a seven hectare retention limit from the start, the House would just come up with an even higher number'. *BW* (15 October 1987).

52. Senator Pimentel was absent.

53. This argument was best expressed by Delfin N. Mercader, vice-president of the United Cebu Landowners Association (UCLA), in an article in the *MB* (20-12-87), published in full in Council [CAPP], 1987.

54. Constantino, 1987.

55. *MC* (7 March 1988).

56. *MC* (27 March 1988) and interview, Arsenio Acuña, 26 February 1989.

57. *MC* (17 April 1988).

58. *MC, Malaya* (15 May 1988).

59. *Political Monitor* (16 May 1988).

60. *Malaya* (17-18 April 1988), *MC* (16 April 1988) *Philippine Human Rights Update*, No.8 (April 15 1988).

61. *MC* (20, 30, 31 May 1988).

62. *MC* (7 June 1988).

63. *FT* (9 June 1988), *MC* (29 June 1988).

64. Interview, Rep. Hortensia Starke, 6 December 1988.

65. *MC, Malaya* (8 June 1988)

66. *MC* (9 June 1988).

67. *MC* (9 June 1988).

68. Hayami et al, 1990, pp.75-76, 81-82.

69. Soliman, 1988.
70. Soliman, 1988.
71. Interview, Gerardo Bulatao, 23 November 1988.
72. The Comprehensive Agrarian Reform Law of 1988, or Republic Act 6657. Further references will refer to Sections of the law.
73. Aquino, 10 June 1988.
74. Section 3.
75. Section 2.
76. Sections 17 and 14.
77. Section 18. They would be paid between 25 per cent and 35 per cent in cash, depending on the size of their holdings and whether they offered their lands to the government voluntarily. They could opt to receive shares of stock in government controlled corporations, or tax credits or Land Bank bonds that would enjoy market interest rates aligned with 91-day treasury bills and be eminently negotiable.
78. Section 18.
79. Sections 54-62.
80. Section 6.
81. Section 3, emphasis added.
82. Section 31.
83. Section 11.
84. Section 26.
85. Section 44. *MC* (26 February 1988).
86. This clause recalls the power given to local governments to stall the implementation of Quezon and Magsaysay's programmes.
87. 'An Act Instituting a People's Agrarian Reform Program and Providing the Mechanisms for its Implementation', Manila: 26 June 1988.
88. In fact, whereas HB400 had called for no compensation for holdings above 50 hectares, PARCODE allowed 10 per cent of assessed market value.
89. *MC* (27 June 1988).
90. *Constitution*, Article 6, Section 32.
91. PARCODE, Section 22.
92. Nevertheless, the signature campaign continued as a major preoccupation of CPAR's work. See Congress [CPAR], 1990.
93. *MC* (17 April 1988).
94. *MC* (27 June 1988).
95. *Agrarian Reform Monitor*, vol.1, no.3 (1989), p.2.

THE US AND AGRARIAN REFORM DURING THE AQUINO YEARS

9.1 Introduction

The US played an important, if not always open, role in influencing the policy orientation of the new Aquino government. From the time Aquino took office until Congress passed the CARP in July 1988, US advocates of the liberal and conservative approaches to reform were active in the debate. Yet the interpretation of the US role during the Aquino years has been just as unclear as it was during the Marcos years. Benedict Anderson, in an otherwise insightful analysis of the new government, said that 'the World Bank, along with senior Japanese and American officials' were arguing 'in favour of a land-reform that hopefully would destroy the basis of NPA rural power'.[1] This gave the impression that the US was whole-heartedly behind the reform. Others, however, argued that US land law expert Roy Prosterman, who had returned to the Philippines, was not advocating 'genuine' agrarian reform. As in the earlier period, the confusion emanated from a failure to identify distinct and conflicting approaches to agrarian reform among US actors.

While in the earlier debates on reform during the 1950s, 1960s and 1970s, the Cold War was still being hotly contested, by the late 1980s it was running out of steam. Since US thinking on agrarian reform had been greatly influenced by its perception of international communism, one might have thought that animosity toward redistributive reform would have subsided in Washington. Certainly Roy Prosterman believed that he could make a strong case for redistributive reform as a major tool to bring about development and stability after the fall of the Marcos dictatorship. However, the US State and Defence Departments, the United States Agency for International Development (USAID) and the conservative right in the United States appeared to have a different assessment of what was needed.

9.2 The return of the liberal reformer Roy Prosterman

After an eleven year absence, Roy Prosterman and his assistant Jeff Riedinger, arrived in Manila in March 1986, just weeks after the Aquino government had come to power. Prosterman saw in the new government an opportunity to learn from the mistakes of the Marcos era and rapidly to implement a programme of agrarian reform that would undermine both the communist-led New People's Army and the radical peasant movement. Prosterman's goal - to use redistributive reform as a means to undermine revolutionary movements – had not changed by the late 1980s.[2]

For this reason he once again became a target of those campaigning against US intervention in the country. His critics correctly identified his motives, but two misconceptions continued to plague their analysis of his role. First, they assumed that because Prosterman was opposed to revolution, his proposals for agrarian reform were somehow not 'genuine'. Second, they assumed that Prosterman's proposals for implementing reform were endorsed by the US government as part of its counterinsurgency strategy in the country.[3] In fact, the policy proposals that he made during the Aquino debate over reform paralleled those made by Filipino advocates of the liberal approach, and if adopted they would have laid the basis for significant redistributive reform. However, his proposals were not endorsed by either the Philippine government or US policy-makers.

While it is unclear what attitude the US embassy took towards Prosterman's visits to the Philippines in 1986, it does appear that Prosterman arrived in Manila without an invitation from anyone in the Aquino government.[4] With no one yet named as Minister of Agrarian Reform, he managed to meet with then Minister of Agriculture Ramon Mitra, whose office had the most influence in shaping the government's early agricultural policy. He submitted his first report to Mitra on 31 March 1986.[5] Much of this report was devoted to calculations of the dimension of the problem (number of landless tenants and farmworkers, land available, etc.) and an inventory of what had and had not been accomplished by the Marcos reform.

However, Prosterman and Riedinger raised a number of crucial policy questions which they believed the government had to consider if it was really intent on implementing a redistributive programme. They singled out the necessity of establishing a constitutional framework conducive to reform. Anticipating the crucial role of the Constitutional Convention in laying the basis for reform, they stated, 'it is clear that policy decisions on some of the issues...could either be facilitated or made impossible, depending on choices made in constitutional drafting'. In this respect they underlined the importance of endowing farmworkers as well as tenants with the right to benefit from land redistribution.[6] They clearly recognized that any reform programme that did not benefit the expanding ranks of farmworkers would fail both in alleviating rural poverty and in securing political stability.

They also opposed the government's intention to delay the redistribution of commercial crop lands, arguing that all crop lands must be subject to redistribution. They emphasized the need to deal firmly with landowners, since it was the government's soft stand toward landlords that had brought the implementation of the Marcos programme to a virtual standstill. Landowners had blocked redistribution of their land by endless appeals in the courts. Prosterman and Riedinger stated that the government should, 'announce that landlords who continue to present objections found to be frivolous or dilatory would lose, say,

75 per cent of their compensation as a penalty (landlords would have 30 days to re-assess and withdraw existing protests or objections)'.[7] Their advice appeared to fall on deaf ears during this first trip (March–April 1986). No one had yet been appointed as Minister of Agrarian Reform and Mitra had decided against a call for a new programme.[8]

Later in the year Prosterman met the law professor Flerida Ruth Romero when she gave a talk at the University of Washington. As a member of the Constitutional Commission and later as Presidential Counsel, she proved to be an important contact who ensured that Prosterman's papers were well circulated in the commission and the government.[9] Prosterman and Riedinger returned to the country again in June and July 1986, when they travelled to Negros Occidental. There they met with Governor Daniel Lacson and leading sugar planters such as Romeo Guanzon, who would later play such an active role in opposing the proposals for liberal reform. They worked with the government-endorsed National Congress of Unions in the Sugar Industry of the Philippines (NACU-SIP). Evidently they had contact with Edgardo Estacio who had written many of the National Federation of Sugar Workers' (NFSW) position papers on agrarian reform, but later led a split in the union and local CPP branch.[10] In Manila, Romero facilitated discussion between Prosterman and Riedinger and members of the Constitutional Commission. On that trip they also saw Jeremias Montemayor and others in the Federation of Free Farmers whom Prosterman had known from the early 1970s. They had brief discussions with other peasant organizations and their supporters.[11] The new agrarian reform chief Heherson Alvarez saw them on that occasion, as did José Medina, whom Prosterman knew well from the Marcos years.

The most important visits of the two US liberal reform advocates were made in 1987, while debate over the executive order was on-going. They met with Solita Monsod when she was playing a leading role in the Cabinet Action Committee, and Prosterman later commented, 'Of all the people we met, she seemed by far the most genuinely supportive of land reform'.[12] Monsod also found Prosterman's proposals helpful at this juncture.[13] While the post of DAR secretary was again vacant during their visit, Prosterman and Riedinger had discussions with two of those being proposed for the position, Bernardo Villegas and Mahar Mangahas, whom Prosterman had met during the 1970s.[14] Prosterman also confronted the defenders of the conservative approach, finding Finance Undersecretary, Ramon Katigbak 'very hostile to land reform'. Later Prosterman commented, 'He favoured large plantation agriculture...[and] his family owns large lands'.[15]

Prosterman wrote a series of memos between March and May 1987, commenting on successive draft executive orders produced by the CAC. Most revealing were his comments on the 3 June draft of the executive order - one of the last drafts that had already removed most of the liberals' proposals.[16] His proposed revisions of the draft executive order fell into four broad categories: opposing concessions to the landowners, opposing concessions* to agribusiness, limiting the power of the courts to delay reform and granting farmworkers the right to benefit from land redistribution.

He opposed the graduated retention limits included in the early drafts of the executive order and argued for an immediately effective seven hectare limit on *all* privately owned lands.[17] He deleted the provision allowing compensation at the landowner's 'declaration of current fair market value', and proposed a return to compensation based on the value declared by owners in their tax declarations. Prosterman proposed a compromise for landowners whose undervaluation of the land in tax returns was extreme, suggesting that they could choose to have the land compensated at a rate of three and a third times the gross value of the harvest - a formula similar to that adopted in Japan and Taiwan.

The Prosterman amendments also called for landowners to include a separate statement with their land registration, detailing all lands disposed of or acquired after 31 December 1986 together with the names of those from whom they purchased the land or to whom they sold it. This was another attempt to fill a loophole in the executive order that would allow landowners to disguise their holdings by 'selling' them to family members and supporters. Recognizing the pitfalls of allowing voluntary agreements between landowners and potential beneficiaries, Prosterman deleted all references to this form of land transfer. He knew from past experiences that allowing 'voluntary' transfers would sanction the continuation of landowners' coercive powers over their tenants.

In the draft that Prosterman examined, the provision for corporate landowners had not yet explicitly been included.[18] But Prosterman did suggest that all lease, management, contract and mortgage agreements over private lands be immediately ended. Instead, those corporations or individuals (who were not eligible beneficiaries of reform) who held a contract or lease covering any portion of the land would be entitled to share in the landowners' compensation. This would release lands leased by agribusiness corporations for redistribution. Prosterman recognized the necessity of redistributing certain modern farms intact to farmworker cooperatives, rather than splitting them up into smallholdings. However, he stressed that cooperative redistribution would be a 'transitional' arrangement and any long-term cooperative ownership or management of the redistributed lands had to be sanctioned by the beneficiaries themselves.[19]

Prosterman also included amendments that would have greatly reduced the power of landowners to use the courts to delay the implementation of reform. While he maintained the owners' right to appeal actions taken by the Department of Agrarian Reform (DAR), his revisions would have ensured that the DAR could immediately implement its decisions and not be required to wait on the outcome of appeals. He also specified that, while the courts were empowered to review the level of compensation offered to the landowner, their decision on what would be 'just compensation' had to be based on the above mentioned criteria for compensation.

Finally Prosterman amended the definition of those who could benefit from reform and specifically included farmworkers and subtenants as reform beneficiaries. Prosterman emphasized that 'temporary or seasonal workers who regularly work during particular times or seasons on this property and reside in the vicinity' must be included as beneficiaries. He also required landowners to list the names of these temporary workers along with tenants and permanent workers when they registered their lands. The absence of this provision in all the government drafts and its final programme was one of the most important limitations in its whole approach to reform.

Prosterman's proposals demonstrated his commitment to promoting a thoroughly redistributive reform along the lines of the liberal approach. However, Monsod judged his efforts as a 'useless exercise' at that point in time.[20] Much of what he suggested had been included in earlier drafts of the executive order and was cut out after the 1 June 'putsch' by the advocates of the conservative approach. Monsod's judgement seems to have been accurate since none of his proposals were incorporated in the final executive order or subsequently in the law. Shortly after he submitted these proposals Prosterman fled the country, having been informed that landowners had delivered a 'death threat' against him.[21] While Prosterman's proposals for a liberal redistributive reform received short shrift from most of those in government, he was not the only foreigner urging the adoption of such a formula.

9.3 The World Bank and the liberal approach

In a surprising departure from its past indifference to redistributive reform, the World Bank submitted reports to the government in March and May 1987 that called for a radical redistributive reform along the lines of the liberal approach.[22] Traditionally, the Bank had a pessimistic and wary attitude toward reforms and during the 1970s they never fully endorsed the Marcos programme.[23] However, after Finance Secretary Jaime Ongpin placed agrarian reform at the centre of his appeals for foreign aid at the World Bank Consultative Group meeting in January 1987, the Bank decided to send a mission to the country in March to make recommendations on the government's reform plans.[24] What was most surprising was the inclusion in the Mission of some long-time advocates of liberal redistributive reform.[25]

The Bank mission was extremely critical of the government's draft reform plan and raised many of the same points as Prosterman.[26] They strongly opposed attempts to put off the distribution of private lands until the latter stages of the programme, saying that such a course of action would lead to failure. Landowners could be counted on to take evasive action, the report said, and it concluded that, 'the proposed sequencing virtually guarantees that when the time comes for beginning Program C [the distribution of private lands], the basis for it will have ceased to exist'. The mission emphasized that a successful programme had to be implemented swiftly. Like Prosterman and the Filipino liberal reformers, the report said that proposed efforts to phase in retention limits 'would encourage evasions' and recommended a single uniform retention limit of seven hectares.[27]

The report pointed out that the proposed programme's heavy reliance on landowners' 'voluntary' offers, as well as the distribution of 'idle and abandoned lands', was entirely unsound. The mission argued that, 'It is difficult to find reasons why landowners in large numbers should voluntarily offer their land...unless it were unproductive and with a market value less than the present value of the compensation package offered by Government', and added that most abandoned lands were 'unlikely to be fertile'.[28] The report also criticized the allowance of direct agreements between owners and beneficiaries, saying 'the legal nexus between landowner and beneficiary should be broken'.[29] Having been shown an early version of the corporate stock-sharing plan, the mission concluded that the plan would be 'financially attractive only to those landowners who believed that they had a good chance of avoiding the transfer element of the scheme over its 30-year life', and advised that such ideas be dropped.[30] Overall, the Bank found the government's estimate of public lands available for distribution to be very much exaggerated.

The Bank's mission also called attention to the problem of 'just compensation', arguing that successful agrarian reform programmes have always 'included a confiscatory element'. They endorsed proposals that compensation be based on the owners' declaration of value in past tax returns or the assessed value, 'whichever is lower'.[31] They called for softening the terms of repayment by beneficiaries, warning that as they stood, 'most of the beneficiaries will not receive any immediate increase in disposable income,' and might even be worse off. In fact, the Bank recommended a once only upfront payment from the beneficiary of P600 per hectare. While this was an incredibly small sum, the Bank calculated that the government could earn more this way than through a 30-year amortization period, with a low collection rate and a high cost of collecting small periodic payments. The Bank mission also argued that the programme must be based on peasant involvement, 'unless genuine local participation is built into the program, peasant beneficiaries are likely to regard the ALRP as just another unrealistic program emanating from Manila'.[32]

Like Prosterman, the Bank mission noted that an effective redistributive reform could help to undermine the revolutionary movement, 'to the extent that the land reform program succeeds in its stated objective of removing one of the main sources of instability in rural areas, it thereby removes the need for a possible substantial expansion of civil defense expenditures'. While the report argued that the Bank's own Articles of Association prevented it from financing compensation payments to landowners, 'to the extent that the government accords priority to the ALRP, there is no reason to believe that they [aid agencies] would not be ready and willing to allocate new aid to such a high priority program'.[33]

The mission's recommendations mirrored many that Prosterman had been making and were even more radical on the issue of compensation to landowners. Prosterman himself may have influenced the report.[34] The highly critical tone of the Bank's report as well as its radical recommendations quickly drew the fire of the conservatives.[35] Even Monsod found the report overly critical of the government's proposals, and when she heard its recommendation to distribute land almost for free, she apparently told them 'You are out of your minds'.[36] The initial response of some on the left was similar to their reaction to Prosterman. Nationalist author, Letizia Constantino, commented, 'the World Bank is not taking this position for altruistic reasons. It believes that a successful land reform program will fight insurgency and restore normalcy - two preconditions sought by foreign investors'.[37] It is true that the Bank is not known for its altruistic motives (though some of the participants in the mission may have possessed them), but if the government had adopted its recommendations the final programme could have been far more redistributive in character.

Given the Bank's past ambivalence and even antagonism toward redistributive reform, it is difficult to understand why it recommended the implementation of such a radical liberal approach. Even when Ladejinsky was working for the Bank, the institution had never endorsed such a recommendation to a developing country government. In 1986, after Marcos had fled the country, the World Bank had published an important three-volume study on the Philippines laying out a framework for economic recovery. Only one paragraph had mentioned land reform as a 'long-term issue that would need further study by the Government'.[38] One explanation for the mission's report might be that it was simply the conclusion of mission members and did not represent the views of the Bank. However, there are two problems with such a point of view. First, it is reasonable to assume that when the Bank in Washington appoints members to a mission it does so with an implicit understanding of the type of report that it wishes to see produced.[39] Secondly, three members of the mission were on the Bank's staff and the Bank officially endorsed the report to the Philippine government.[40]

A more cynical explanation might be that the Bank knew full well that the government was unlikely to allow an effective redistributive programme. Having been the target of much criticism within the Philippines for its past support to Marcos, the Bank therefore appointed the mission as an exercise in public relations. Lending credence to such an interpretation is the fact that the local mission of the Bank stationed in Manila felt that the mission's report was not realistic and did not take it very seriously.[41] However, even after CARP was passed into law, the Bank's Asia director continued to urge the government to find ways to speed up implementation and distribute more lands. He referred back to the mission report saying, 'While the "one-payment" proposal may have been unfeasible, we do feel that a much shorter payment period of three to five years, on an amount affordable to the farmer should be applied'.[42]

While the Bank was working in the framework of the government's essentially conservative programme, it would seem that the mission and its recommendations for a liberal reform had won genuine endorsement, at least among some in the Bank. However, the same could not be said for the US government, where, outside of the US House of Representatives, both the Bank mission's report and Prosterman's recommendations were ignored in favour of a traditional conservative approach.

9.4 The Reagan Administration and the conservative approach

After Reagan's White House finally decided to abandon Marcos, and Aquino established her government, there was considerable debate in Washington around the orientation of US assistance to the new government. Prosterman's proposals on agrarian reform enjoyed a degree of support in the US House of Representatives Committee on Foreign Affairs and among some influential members of the academic community. However, while the US executive branch was somewhat divided over its assessment of the new government and the best strategy for the US to pursue, there was nonetheless general consensus in the administration for a conservative approach to agrarian reform.

In early 1986, the US House of Representatives held it first major hearings on foreign assistance to the Philippines after the ascendancy of the Aquino administration. Congressman Stephan Solarz, as Chairman of the Foreign Affairs Subcommittee on Asia and the Pacific region, chaired the hearings. Solarz's staff knew Prosterman from his work on agrarian reform in El Salvador in the early 1980s. US involvement in the limited agrarian reform programme there had provoked an important debate in Congress, where Senator Jesse Helms had led a campaign opposing US funding for redistributive reform. On that occasion, Prosterman and his supporters were actually able to win US assistance to the programme as part of their efforts to put down the radical peasant movement. They had even forced an amendment to the US Foreign Assistance Act, which permitted US funding for compensation to landowners if the President deemed it in the US national interest.[43]

Solarz raised the issue of US funding for agrarian reform during the first hearing on the Philippines on 29 April 1986. At that hearing the most vocal witness in favour of funding reform was the political scientist Carl Landé, who professed knowledge of the views of both the US Embassy and the US military command in the Philippines. He suggested that funds be used to encourage the Aquino government to take action on reform, saying, 'land reform is one of the main cards in the deck of the Communist New People's Army...and to the degree that land reform is neglected, I think the radical opposition is going to be greatly strengthened'.[44] When Solarz suggested that perhaps it was not good to make aid conditional, Landé proposed that the best way to proceed would be to offer 'additional funds' for land reform. Gustav Ranis, who was less sanguine about reform, nonetheless said, 'it would be very nice...if [President Aquino]-...said as soon as possible "we would have a land reform in sugar, even if it affects our own estate"'.[45]

However, in the next hearing, while witnesses from the State Department, the US Agency for International Development (USAID) and the Department of Defence all spoke of needed reforms, not one of their prepared presentations mentioned a need for agrarian reform. Testimony from the State and Defence

Departments echoed long-standing differences over US strategy in the Philippines. Generally, the State Department saw the need to abandon Marcos earlier than did the Pentagon, the National Security Council and the White House, and it was more open to Aquino's policy of negotiation with the NPA.[46] However, by mid-1987 a consensus had developed between all departments in favour of an all-out counterinsurgency drive in which redistributive reform played no part.[47]

Richard Armitage, a former Ambassador to the Philippines who had assumed the post of Assistant Secretary of Defence for International Security Affairs, praised speedy reforms within the armed forces, emphasizing that they had been 'renamed the "New" Armed Forces of the Philippines'. He argued that the 'New' AFP had 'refurbished its image within the Philippines and certainly among its colleagues in the US Department of Defence'. Later in the year, after several coup attempts were uncovered within its ranks, not even the AFP command kept the label 'New'. Armitage was not so generous to the Aquino government, criticizing it for its failure to embrace 'the need for a total integrated counterinsurgency package'.[48] He was particularly critical of early moves by Aquino toward negotiations with the communist movement and attempts to check the authority of the Armed Forces.[49]

The statement of John Monjo, Deputy Assistant Secretary of State for East Asia and Pacific Affairs, was more conciliatory to the Aquino government. Monjo acknowledged the need for 'an amnesty component' in a 'comprehensive counter-insurgency strategy', but Armitage's prepared statement cast doubt on the effectiveness of such measures. Monjo focused more on the problems of poverty and 'military abuses' and underlined the need for 'military reforms aimed at restoring discipline and respect for human rights' as well as the need for 'reformist local governments'. Armitage emphasized that local governments had to work with the military and the Church to fight the insurgency. Differences between State and Defence concerned the appropriate mix of military, economic and political components to achieve success in counterinsurgency. However, neither saw redistributive reform as an essential part of solving problems of unrest and poverty.[50]

The Reagan administration's aid programme was described by Charles Greenleaf, Assistant Administrator in the Bureau for Asia and the Near East in the USAID. He said that the programme 'was developed following a trip to the Philippines in mid-March [1986] by a senior Administration team headed by A.I.D. Administrator M. Peter McPherson'.[51] Armitage stated that 'detailed consultations on military assistance...were an important part of the McPherson Mission'. He said that military aid was crucial and warned, 'Failure to provide this aid would be the greatest of tragedies if it resulted in a communist triumph'.

In addition to its concern for stepping up the counterinsurgency campaign and endorsing the lead role of the military in those efforts, the administration outlined the achievements made by the Aquino government in economic reform. Assistant Secretary Monjo praised the 'market-oriented economic team within the Aquino government', which he said, 'is already seeking to promote deregulation and liberalization of the economy.' He said that they had identified the key areas of economic reform: allowing the peso to respond to foreign exchange market forces; cancelling decrees setting up monopolies in such sectors as sugar, coconuts, chemicals, etc; dismantling public sector financial entities and privatizing numerous public corporations; liberalizing import restrictions, including removal of bureaucratic restraints on trade; eliminating price controls on certain agricultural products and establishing an efficient stabilization program for basic food commodities.[52] Not surprisingly, these reflected the general macro-economic reform package presented to the country by the IMF.[53]

Monjo's only other reference to the problems in the agricultural sector was a brief acknowledgement that, 'Traditional plantation agriculture is in trouble'. When Congressman Stephan Solarz questioned the witnesses about land reform, Greenleaf responded in a guarded fashion, 'Clearly land reform is one of the topics that the new government will consider', but he quickly added that it 'is extremely difficult to implement land reform programs'. He said that it was necessary to wait and see what the Aquino government wanted to do about agrarian reform. Echoing the early US reaction to reform after Marcos declared martial law, the USAID official added that, 'we're prepared, of course, to...look at what they have and to consider assistance in this area'.[54]

During Aquino's first year in office, the Reagan Administration's overall formula for addressing the problems of rural unrest and economic stagnation in the Philippines remained unchanged. It aimed to develop a counterinsurgency strategy combining the efficient use of military force and effective local government, and to institute economic reforms that would encourage foreign and domestic agribusiness to take the lead in rural development. The bias against redistributive agrarian reform was evident in assessments made by individual officials at the State Department, the Pentagon and USAID, which had direct responsibility for managing the Reagan administration's foreign assistance programme.

9.4.1 The State Department on the politics and economics of reform

One State Department official argued that while the Department recognized that 'CARP was a political imperative', it did not believe that agrarian reform would improve the economic prospects of either the Philippines or US corporations active there. In fact, he appeared to equate the economic prospects of the country with the prospects for US corporate investment. He commented, 'We applauded and encouraged agrarian reform efforts, but we looked for ways to preserve the profitability and economic viability of major American agribusiness multinational corporations'.[55] John H. Andre, Economic Officer at the State Department's Philippine Desk, who was on the Embassy staff during the first two years of the Aquino administration, was even more categorical than his colleague.[56] He said that in his personal opinion, 'while...it may be true, particularly tactically, that you can't solve the insurgency problem without some land reform, this is not the route to economic development in the Philippines'.

Given limited US funds for aid to the country, Andre said, 'I'd have to say that land reform would not, in my own view, rank very high'. He confirmed that no one at the Philippine desk had the particular responsibility of following developments around agrarian reform. In much the same way as Filipino landowners, Andre contrasted the issue of agrarian reform with that of job creation, saying, 'I view land reform as being maybe one element, but certainly a smaller one to the imperative of creating more jobs'. While differences existed between the State Department and the Pentagon, Andre argued, 'On land reform specifically, the issue doesn't come up to create inter-agency conflict. I don't think there is any difference between State and the DoD'.[57]

9.4.2 The Pentagon on reform and counterinsurgency

Officials at the Pentagon were also circumspect about the importance of agrarian reform in solving the problems of the Philippines. They addressed the agrarian reform issue only in 1987, after Aquino launched a public debate over the draft executive order. In testimony before the House in March 1987, Richard Armitage acknowledged that agrarian reform was an important component of the Communist Party's programme in the Philippines. He told the committee, 'as a general proposition with insurgencies and agrarian economies, land reform is a siren song to the have-nots. I would say there's no more effective method of propagandizing than for the NPA to call for land reform now that Marcos is gone'.[58]

Congressman Stephan Solarz then asked him if he believed that, 'a well thought out comprehensive agrarian reform program initiated by the government, could constitute an important and effective component of a counter-insurgency program?' He answered that it could, but with one qualification, 'It would be effective if combined - as I understand the Aquino government's intent - with a *non-confiscatory policy*, and one that is carefully explained to all the people'.[59] The bottom-line for US officials was that agrarian reform must involve market-value compensation to landowners, thus making programmes expensive and essentially non-redistributive.

One Pentagon official explained more clearly the attitude of the Defence Department toward agrarian reform in the Philippines:

Agrarian reform is not at the top of the list of solutions or causes of the insurgency. Every person in the Department of Defence (DOD) has their own perception of this...If I had to pick one solution above all the others I would put local government at the top of the list. The insurgents make gains largely by default. There is no presence of government...With or without land reform, if the local government core is not more responsive to local needs then there will be no solution to the insurgency.[60]

9.4.3 USAID and agrarian reform

In USAID, which has the responsibility for administering all US-funded development programmes in the Philippines, the bias against agrarian reform was clear cut. USAID was extremely reluctant to become involved in the Aquino government's programme. John Blackton, acting AID director in 1987, resisted pressure on the agency to support a programme of agrarian reform.[61] In March 1987, when Congressman Solarz was intensifying his campaign to secure US funding for reform, he invited USAID to Congress. He questioned James Norris, Deputy Assistant Administrator for Asia and the Near East, about the agency's attitude toward reform. Norris responded carefully:

> The Government of the Philippines has identified land reform as one of its top priorities, and is currently developing a detailed land reform program which is expected to be completed this spring. We recognize that this is an important issue in the Philippines, both economically and politically, and we plan to review carefully any proposal the government develops.
>
> We are, however, also very much aware that land reform is a sensitive subject which holds different meanings for each country and must be approached in the context of each country's own experiences and circumstances. Effective land reform programs have been exceedingly difficult to formulate and implement.[62]

Solarz pushed him, asking whether if inputs, credit and expertise were available 'such a program would be useful, not only in responding politically to the desire of the landless for land, but would also increase agricultural production...Do you agree with that, Mr. Norris?' Norris betrayed his scepticism answering, 'It's very difficult not to agree when the premise is that everything is done right. The difficulty with land reform is frequently everything isn't done right'.

When Solarz began closer questioning, Norris's ambivalence became even more clear. Solarz asked if he had any idea of how much unutilized arable land there was in the Philippines and Norris responded, 'We have no data on that'. When Solarz suggested that there were a million acres of abandoned land, Norris responded, 'We have no details'. Solarz asked if he knew how many landless labourers there were and Norris answered, 'No'. 'And do you know how many tenant farmers there are?' asked Solarz, to which Norris responded, 'I don't have that data either'. Solarz asked if he knew what tenants had to pay in land rent, 'No,' responded Norris. Solarz then nearly exploded, saying:

> ...it might be a good idea for you to begin to spend some time trying to learn a little bit more about this problem. Clearly if there is going to be some kind of agrarian reform, AID will be asked to play a part in it; and our capacity to play such a part will be enhanced if there was some awareness in AID of the dimensions of the problem, and the difficulties which obviously exist in dealing with it.[63]

At that point Gaston Sigur, Assistant Secretary of State for East Asia and Pacific

Affairs, told Solarz that while they appreciated the concern of Congress, they would rather wait before allocating funds to agrarian reform and in general they opposed any sort of earmarking.

9.4.4 The US Government and the CARP

After the attempted coup against President Aquino in August 1987, Solarz held another set of hearings to assess the situation in the country. In the December 1987 hearing, Solarz asked Assistant Secretary of State David Lambertson to present an assessment of the debate in the Philippine Congress over agrarian reform. Lambertson obscured the differences between the opposing bills being discussed, stating, 'All of them are genuine land reform bills'. He betrayed the State Department's own bias in relation to the debate when he said that the Philippine Congress was now having to confront 'some of the realities of the complexity of enacting land reform'. These included, 'variations in productivity of land around the Philippines...[and] variations, therefore, in the price that has to be paid... [and] the retention limits for different kinds of crops'.[64]

What Lambertson described as the 'realities' of reform were, in fact, the realities as perceived by the landowner block in the House of Representatives and Alvarez in the Senate. Solarz asked him whether it was true that the Philippine House was dominated by landlord interests. Lambertson responded that the fact that Congress was debating agrarian reform at all 'belies that notion, at least to some extent'. By minimizing the differences between the bills under discussion in the Philippines and simply stating that all would result in 'genuine land reform', Lambertson completely obfuscated the Congressional debate. By this time obfuscation seemed to envelop all the administration's actions in relation to agrarian reform in the Philippines.

USAID's reluctance to get involved with agrarian reform was so strong, according to NEDA Director Solita Monsod, that they actually misrepresented US Congressional opinion to the Philippine government. While Solarz had been leading a Congressional effort to get the Reagan administration to provide funding for agrarian reform, USAID-Manila had been telling Monsod that his agency could not do more on agrarian reform because Congress was unwilling. Monsod said she found out, by chance, that USAID had been called to Congress and grilled on its attitude toward reform, 'One of our NEDA staff was there at the time and went to Congress and was flabbergasted about what she heard'. Monsod called in Fred Sheck from the USAID office in Manila and confronted him, 'They were telling us one thing and telling Congress the other. He was rather shamefaced'.[65]

Much to the dismay of USAID, in December 1987 the House voted to earmark $100 million in additional US foreign assistance to be dispersed in two equal parts in 1988 and 1989 and to be spent exclusively on agrarian reform.[66] Solarz thus managed, against the protestations of the executive, to get a minimal amount of additional funding for agrarian reform as an incentive to the Philippine government to speed up deliberations, as Carl Landé had originally proposed. Solarz had echoed the words of Prosterman when he had introduced the legislation in the House:

> Recognizing the overriding importance of an agrarian reform program as an essential element of any effective counter-insurgency program, and based on the view that if the Philippines does not implement agrarian reform, there is likely to be an agrarian revolution, the Subcommittee report recommends an additional $50 million in fiscal year 1988 and another $50 million in fiscal year 1989 to help fund an agrarian reform program by the Philippines.[67]

Dispersal of the funds was made conditional on the Philippine Government coming up with an 'effective' programme and ensuring that a majority of funds would be secured from other sources. It was understood that no part of the money would be spent on compensating landowners.[68] In the end, because CARP was not passed into law in time for the 1988 allocation, the US 'Agrarian Reform Support Program' (ARSP) consisted of only $50 million for 1989. This represented only 0.8 per cent of the expected $6.5 billion dollars in foreign funding needed for the programme, and no more than 10.4 per cent of US foreign assistance to the country that year[69].

9.4.5 The liberal comeback and the conservative response

After RA6657 was passed by the Philippine Congress and the period of implementation began, Prosterman still felt it worth trying to encourage a more vigorous implementation of reform.[70] While he found the law 'very weak', he argued in a paper written ten days after the law was signed, that it was 'still potentially salvagable'. Just as landowners looked for loopholes to evade redistribution, Prosterman identified loopholes in the language of the law that could be exploited by a determined executive power. The two most important, he claimed, involved the Presidential Agrarian Reform Council's power to vary the retention limit allowed to owners in order to bring more land under the programme's coverage, and the administrative power of DAR to prevent huge compensation claims by landowners.

He also called for measures to prohibit tenant evictions, to speed up programme implementation rather than stretch it over the ten year period, to prohibit conversion to deferred crops, and to prevent landowner attempts to declare coconut lands as 'fruit farms' which would then fall under the ten-year deferment. He wanted penalties to be applied to landowners who violated these rules, and assurance that landowners could not gain control over provincial and *barangay* agrarian reform councils. Finally, he said that 'it is vitally important that administrators adopt' the modern methods of land titling based on aerial photo-maps and computerized processing, since traditional methods 'would overwhelm the administrative system and drastically slow down any reform'.

Near the end of 1988, Prosterman made one last appeal for concerted action by President Aquino to try to save the reform, saying that the very 'future of Philippine democracy' was at stake.[71] He echoed his calls of the mid-1970s saying, 'The results of failure will be continued low agricultural productivity, persistent rural poverty, and an NPA insurgency constantly invigorated by the support of an aggrieved and impoverished peasantry'. He marshalled considerable evidence, predicting a level of reform implementation under the law that would be even less than 'the wholly failed 1956-63 program under Ngo Dinh Diem in South Vietnam'. Only if 'Mrs. Aquino chooses to personally intervene' in the process of implementation could the reform be salvaged.

But by this time Prosterman was whistling in the wind. His verdict that the reform could still accomplish goals of raising productivity and achieving political stability was based on a total lack of appreciation for the character of the Philippine state and President Aquino's own government. While he said that PARC had the administrative power to hasten reform implementation, he ignored the law's provision that this could be done only upon 'recommendation by the Provincial Agrarian Reform Coordinating Committees'. These committees were already subject to influence from provincial political power networks. Because the President, and Congress after her, had already decided to give in to so many of the landowners' demands, the landowner lobby was strengthened. It therefore had enough basis in the Constitution and the law to prevent any subtle manipulation of the law's language to lower retention limits or reduce compensation levels to the landowners. Prosterman was appealing to the President to use executive power to save the law, when the character of the law had largely been shaped by the President's own family and her closest supporters.

Prosterman's protestations were also dismissed in Washington, much as they had been in the 1970s. One USAID official involved in the Philippine programme commented that 'only Prosterman, and a few other people' believed that agrarian reform could make a positive economic contribution in the country. He stated that, 'to the extent that agrarian reform meant redistribution of land - which from Prosterman's point of view is about all it means, or should mean if you're using the term properly - our analysis had suggested that redistribution of land was not the answer to poverty, inequity or stagnation in rural areas'. Prosterman had simply got it wrong. As for the World Bank mission and report, he believed that it 'was an example of what happens when you mistakenly try, as a foreign agency, to take the lead in pointing the way on a highly controversial issue...the World Bank...[was] absolutely blasted out of the water'.[72] Even a member of Solarz's staff felt that Prosterman was 'too involved to be of any relevance', and he added, 'He is a bit of a missionary on land reform'.[73] He suggested that perhaps Solarz also had placed too much importance on the issue, and felt that the congressional, provincial and local elections of 1987-1988 were a more important tool for establishing the Aquino government's legitimacy and weakening the insurgency.

Thus, while the United States had a small aid programme in support of CARP, no one in the US government was enthusiastic about the programme. The text of the US-funded Agrarian Reform Support Programme (ARSP) was in one sense an extraordinary document.[74] While the programme was ostensibly designed to assist CARP, the programme document elaborated all the reasons why agrarian reform would not do much good for the country. The text spelled out that the goal of the USAID Mission's strategy in the Philippines was, 'to work with the GOP and the Philippine private sector to improve living standards in the country's rural areas'. It then actually stated that, 'support to CARP will not necessarily directly improve agricultural productivity, generate greater employment or increase rural income levels'.

Within the text of the programme USAID also wanted to make sure that no precedent was set in terms of either long-term Agency support for agrarian reform in the Philippines or support for it in other countries. The document therefore reiterated Agency policy, which views 'land tenure and land reform as being marginal rather than fundamental in importance; that is, many other policies (e.g. farm-gate prices, credit, marketing mechanisms, etc.) are seen as being at least of equal importance with regard to achieving rural development'.[75] The text went on to say that 'a strong implication' of this policy was that 'the conditions under which A.I.D. would support redistributive land reform will arise very infrequently'.

As if the point had not been made clearly enough, the text noted that in discussions between the Agency and the Philippine government, 'in most situations, it will be more appropriate, politically and economically, to pursue types of policies besides land reform'. USAID even felt obliged to assert that, 'In fact, A.I.D. is carrying out an extensive and effective policy dialogue with the GOP on improving agricultural policies under other programs and projects'. This portion of the text ended with the curious statement that Agency policy provided no guidance 'for a politicized situation of land maldistribution which ARSP indirectly addresses'.[76] In June 1988, when negotiations over the programme began in earnest, a telegram from the State Department to Ambassador Nicholas Platt (1988-1991) in Manila instructed the USAID mission to negotiate the use of the $50 million for 'non-sensitive' components of the CARP, 'such as roads and credit,' and to ensure that 'the AID program will not reimburse land acquisition or other sensitive components'.[77]

In late 1989, after the implementation of the ARSP had already begun, Agency officials in Washington did not hide their reticence about the programme, saying, 'The agency doesn't see agrarian reform as one of the better solutions to solving problems in the "ag" sector, but see it as marginal'.[78] They went on to explain that in their view landholdings were generally not large in the Philippines. Secondly, population was growing so fast that only the development of off-farm employment opportunities could accommodate the increased work force. Finally, agriculture was characterized by a preponderance of low-value traditional crops like coconut, rice and corn, and productivity was low. None of those problems, they argued, could be solved by agrarian reform. They felt that the $50 million could have been better spent on other programmes. While the USAID mission never took a formal position during the agrarian reform debate, USAID officials said that in informal discussions they found that Philippine officials in the Philippine Council for Agricultural Resources, Research and Development (PCARRD) and the Department of Agriculture were very sympathetic with their views.

9.5 The US private sector, the conservative movement and counterinsurgency

While US government officials were reticent about agrarian reform, the private sector with interests in the Philippines was adamantly opposed to the measure. The Executive Vice-president of the American Chamber of Commerce in the Philippines (ACCP), J. Marsh Thomson, said that US investors were interested in agribusiness in the country, but that all the talk of agrarian reform was having a dampening effect on the flow of new investments. Rather than creating doubt with threats of land redistribution, he argued, the government ought to be promoting the military's counterinsurgency drive, which could only strengthen foreign investors' confidence.[79] The ACCP had a great deal of influence at the US Embassy. As Jack Andre at the State Department said, the Embassy has a 'constant exchange' of views with the Chamber.[80]

The US banking community had only one interest in mind from the moment Aquino took office. This was expressed in March 1986, in testimony before the US House by David Pflug of Manufacturers Hanover Trust, the bank at the head of the group of 480 banks with debt exposure in the country. His view was that the US Government should place only one condition on providing aid to the Aquino Administration:

I would simply say that I would recommend to the government that they make...the disbursement [of increased aid] contingent on achieving an agreed program with the World Bank and the IMF.[81]

For the most part, US corporations were careful not to speak openly about the CARP. It was clear, however, that large corporations like Dole and Del Monte were very concerned over the direction that agrarian reform would take.

When Congressman Gillego's House Committee was debating reform legislation, Dole Philippines, quietly but determinedly, attempted to influence their deliberations. Gillego was invited to meet with them at the Manila Hotel and later Congressmen Andolana and Garduce, also from the nationalist bloc, met the Dole management. Gillego decided to travel to Dole's plantation in South Cotabato to hold meetings with the workers. He thought that he would be sitting down with trade union leaders, but instead found a well-prepared mass meeting arranged by the management. Gillego commented that, 'The manner of questioning seems to have been orchestrated and directed to show they did not want reform in that place'.[82]

The conservative movement in the United States was also actively involved in lobbying the government on Philippine policy after Aquino came to power. This took on particular importance due to the trend that developed during the

Reagan years toward the 'privatisation' of covert action, which saw an increased involvement by individuals and organizations of the conservative movement in Central Intelligence Agency (CIA) operations abroad.[83] Just as the advocates of the liberal approach to reform, like Roy Prosterman, became involved in reform implementation or work on the ground with like-minded Filipinos, so the advocates of the conservative approach appear to have become actively involved in the implementation of their option.

On 12 January 1986, the National Defense Council Foundation (NDCF) became one of the first organizations in the US conservative movement to throw its weight behind Corazon Aquino's campaign for the Presidency. The NDCF, founded in 1978, described itself as 'a conservative anti-Communist Washington-area non-profit research and educational organization'.[84] Its Executive Director was retired Major Frederick Andrew Messing Jr., who had spent 21 years in the armed forces, most of them with Special Forces or Special Operations. The NDCF's own publicity described him as 'a recognized expert on Low Intensity Warfare'.[85] Messing, who won his spurs in Vietnam in the late 1960s, prided himself on having visited 21 zones of conflict throughout the third world, with 50 trips to El Salvador alone. When the NDCF declared its support for Aquino's challenge against Marcos, Messing told the press that he would travel to the Philippines to campaign for Aquino.[86]

His efforts were evidently greatly appreciated as demonstrated by a telegram he received from the President's brother-in-law, Butz Aquino, and Bobby Hernandez in March 1986, thanking him for 'invaluable assistance extended to our cause of freedom and democracy'. They told him that his 'Timing was almost perfect' and that they hoped to see him soon.[87] In his small office in Alexandria (Virginia), a photo of Messing and President Aquino was placed beside photos of him with Richard Nixon, Ronald Reagan and George Bush, as well as in the field with the Nicaraguan contras and a variety of other similar forces.[88] Messing was a self-styled 'protegé' of the legendary Edward Lansdale, having 'studied' with Lansdale during the last four years of his life, and his views toward agrarian reform and counterinsurgency paralleled those of his mentor.[89]

Like Lansdale, Messing felt that the US government tended to rely too heavily on purely military solutions to peasant protest movements. He echoed Lansdale, saying:

> When guerrillas decide that they are going to risk their lives, you don't take it lightly. There's social, political and economic injustices that have to be redressed. Guerrilla movements don't spring up for the hell of it. There gotta be a hard core group of really crabby people.

He criticized the US government for not developing a 'multi-dimensional approach' to counterinsurgency and incorporating social, political, macro and micro economic, and military security measures. He felt that the US government should back a programme that integrated rural development projects with political reforms and well-developed military special operations.

Messing felt that Prosterman did not understand that landowners should be allies in the process, saying, 'This guy Prosterman down there - the blood of El Salvador is on his hands, because the agrarian reform program in El Salvador became so divisive and so inequitable and so brutal, the way they implemented it'. On CARP he was critical toward the President for exempting her own family's *hacienda* from redistribution. At the same time, he said, 'it's got to be designed so the person having their land confiscated from them has got to be completely satisfied that they came out a winner'.

For Messing, agrarian reform without market value compensation was worse than no programme at all, 'all you are doing is promoting economic, political, social and military security turmoil'. The only way to win a war against a guerrilla movement, he said, 'is to co-opt them, make them part of the system'. Messing developed close contact with certain officers in the AFP from about 1985. He said, 'The smartest son-of-a-bitch in the Philippines is General Biazon, the head of the Marines in Metro Manila'. Referring to Biazon's counterinsurgency campaign, which involved infiltrating the communist movement and establishing civilian paramilitary groups in Mindanao, Messing commented, 'He did the most successful program in Davao'.

For Messing and others in his network, land distribution should be selectively applied in areas where peasant unrest was most acute. This was the view expressed by retired US Army General Richard G. Stilwell when he returned from a visit to the Philippines in 1987. Stilwell had once been commander of US troops in South Korea and was Deputy Undersecretary at Defence in the early Reagan years.[90] He reportedly travelled to Manila just before the coup attempt against the Aquino government in August 1987.[91] Stilwell argued that the Communist Party's strength was increasing due to the persistence of correctable but neglected problems of poverty, including 'an unsatisfied popular hunger for land'. Until these problems were addressed, he argued, the insurgency would continue to grow.[92] Yet, like Lansdale before them, Stilwell and Messing's proposals fell short of promoting redistributive reform.

Among the organizations of the conservative movement in the US, the Heritage Foundation, whose plush offices stand just opposite Capitol Hill, became particularly interested in the Philippines after 1986. Formed in 1974, with backing from prominent US conservatives like Joseph Coors, Paul Weylich and Richard Mellon Scaife, the Foundation was a leading 'new right' think-tank and important lobby group in Congress.[93] Richard Fisher, policy analyst at the Foundation's Centre for Asian Studies, had forceful ideas about agrarian reform.[94] Fisher said the Foundation didn't oppose agrarian reform per se, 'but if redistribution leads to the break down of rural society, like for example in Negros where it may very well do that, then it is something to be opposed. Certainly it should not be funded by American tax-payers'. He felt that redistribution could lead to the 'empowerment of the local Communist movements'.

The dynamic force for development in Negros Occidental, Fisher argued, was the 'rural middle class', whom he identified as 'the landowners or hacienda owners', those with 'talents and that commitment to the community'. He echoed the planters themselves, saying that he favoured, 'a limited land reform program that focused primarily on government lands'. However, 'Beyond that, to roll into Negros, chop up the haciendas or roll into Mindanao and then chop up the banana plantations. I think that if that happens, it would lead to economic and political disaster'. When asked who in the Philippines shared his views, he said he liked the 'ideas of Governor Lacson [Negros Occidental] in particular who advocates a minimum land reform program', and mentioned that banana grower Roberto Sebastian of Marsman Plantations in Mindanao was 'a very, very dear friend'.[95]

According to Fisher, the US Congress did not put more effort into opposing the approval of funds for agrarian reform for two reasons. First, it was clear that no US money would go into landowner compensation but would only be spent on infrastructure and support services, which did not contradict normal USAID practice. Secondly, it was only $50 million, a tiny portion of the programme's overall funding needs and a small percentage of the overall US aid programme. Fisher said, 'As long as we're not being asked to shoulder a major proportion of that program, then I don't think it will become a major issue'.

Fisher outlined the Foundation's proposals for a strategy in the Philippines, saying, 'The path to growth in the Philippines is not redistributing all this land, but decentralization, import-export liberalization...[and] pacification of the countryside'. By pacification, he said, he did not 'mean killing all the communists', but 'enabling local government to become a reality', providing livelihood projects, and building infrastructure. He said that he believed the AFP's strategy of deploying Special Operations Teams and Civilian Armed Forces Geographical Units (CAFGUs), better known as vigilantes, was 'eminently sensible'. The major problem was that 'the AFP doesn't even have enough guns, much less radios, much less medicines, trucks [and] jeeps'. Fisher was wholly supportive of the growing role of landowners in Negros in the funding of military operations, saying, 'sure they are funding the protection of their crops - they have no choice. The government doesn't have the wherewithal to defend these areas in Negros...I think it's healthy, because it demonstrates that these people care enough to defend what they have and it means they have that level of commitment to the community'.

Both the NDCF and the Heritage Foundation were part of a network of institutions deeply involved in US intervention in Central America. Messing and Stilwell were just two of a number of retired Special Forces and CIA operatives, including Major-General John K. Singlaub and Ray Cline, all connected with US covert operations against Nicaragua, who visited and wrote about the Philippines after 1986.[96] Their approach to counterinsurgency, while sometimes distinct from the official views of the Pentagon, provided support to those promoting a conservative approach to agrarian reform in the Philippines during the Aquino years.

9.6 Conclusion

United States involvement in the politics of the Philippines did not stop with their assistance in transporting Marcos out of the country in February 1986. The US government and private actors influenced the course of the debate over agrarian reform during the Aquino administration's first two years. US advocates of both the liberal and conservative approaches to reform maintained contact with like-minded Philippine officials and actively promoted their policy options. However, the advocates of the conservative approach appeared to be even more dominant than they had been during the early debate over reform in the Marcos martial law years.

Prosterman was back in the Philippines and succeeded in establishing contacts in the upper echelons of the Aquino government. Contrary to the views of some on the left, the policy option he outlined was clearly in favour of a genuinely redistributive reform. His liberal approach gained some headway as the US Congress actually debated assistance to agrarian reform. However, an aid package of only $50 million was approved for 1989. What is more, ARSP funding was opposed by the USAID which was responsible for implementing the aid programme.

The World Bank mission's recommendations on the agrarian reform programme were not taken seriously by either the Philippine or the US government. However, they did represent a shift in at least middle-ranking Bank officials' attitude toward the liberal approach to reform. While the overall lending programme of the Bank continued to support traditional prescriptions for structural adjustment, official endorsement of the mission's recommendations on reform indicated that there was perhaps a renewed interest in agrarian reform within the institution.[97] While the liberal approach to reform was clearly in a minority, it was still a live option with enthusiastic supporters.

At the same time, once again the weaknesses of the liberal approach were in evidence. Prosterman clearly underestimated the forces arrayed against reform in both Manila and in Washington. His own 'anti-communist' orientation led him to work mainly with government-supported peasant organizations like NACUSA in Negros and the FFF. He had little interest in the growing campaign of CPAR and their alternative 'People's Agrarian Reform'. Unlike some Filipino advocates of the liberal approach, such as Congressman Bonifacio Gillego, Prosterman showed little understanding that the grass-roots peasant movement was really the only force committed to redistributive reform. Prosterman's ultimate influence during the Aquino debate was far less pronounced than it had been during the early years of the Marcos reform.

While there were some differences between the policy of the US State and Defence Departments toward the Philippines in the early Aquino period, the animosity toward redistributive reform appeared to be shared by all the major agencies of the US government. Support for the conservative approach was expressed in both economic and political terms. The US attached considerable conditionality to its financial aid, but this focussed on liberalising trade, curbing

303

state subsidies and reforming the military, rather than on agrarian reform. US officials devoted most of their attention to pressuring the Aquino administration to work more closely with the military in the implementation of a co-ordinated programme of counterinsurgency. USAID's own opposition to redistributive reform was so pronounced that they actually distorted the views of the US Congress in their discussions with the Philippine government.

The conservative movement in the United States had clearly defined ideas about agrarian reform. They opposed the liberal approach on ideological grounds related to their notions of the sanctity of private property, as well as on political military-security grounds. The network of US conservative organizations so active in Central America turned up in the Philippines after February 1986. They sought to consolidate the new Aquino government in their own image. While both Messing and Prosterman were devoted to defeating communism, they had distinctly different strategic assessments of how that goal could be achieved. Their differences were strikingly parallel to those between Lansdale and the Ladejinsky-disciple Robert Hardie in the Philippines in the mid-1950s.

The United States probably had less potential to influence the outcome of the debate over agrarian reform during the Aquino period than they had after Marcos declared martial law. At the time US support had been crucial to Marcos, and US leverage was therefore probably greater. Still, in the months after Aquino came to power and had greatest scope for action, strong endorsement of redistributive reform by the US might have strengthened the position of the liberal reformers. The Aquino government was anxious at the time to win universal support in Washington. In this context, US animosity toward the liberal approach to reform helped to consolidate the position of the proponents of the conservative approach within the Aquino government.

The US government appeared to be confident that the renewed legitimacy of the Philippine government under Aquino, combined with the prominent place of the military in the state, would be sufficient to undermine the radical peasant movement and ensure a degree of stability in the country. They clearly felt that there was no need to upset the balance of forces in the Philippine government itself, which was weighted firmly in favour of landowners and agribusiness corporate interests. Even Congressman Solarz dropped the issue of agrarian reform after the passage of the small aid programme. Dominant US attitudes on reform strengthened the conservatives' hand, not only in the debate over reform policy, but also during the following years, as implementation of the much attenuated agrarian reform law was under way.

Notes

1. Anderson, 1988, p.27.
2. For a full statement of his strategy see Prosterman and Riedinger, 1987, chapter 1.
3. Robin Broad, John Cavanagh and Chip Fay, at a press conference in late 1986 said,

'Prosterman's efforts were not attempts at genuine land reform. Rather, his advice was explicitly designed to appease increasingly radicalized peasants and stem large-scale uprisings.' Cited by Lopez, 1986.

4. Prosterman certainly knew the US Ambassador Stephen Bosworth (1984–1988). While working on agrarian reform in El Salvador in the early 1980s, he evidently met Bosworth, who had been Deputy at the State Department's Latin America desk and then Chairman of the Secretary's Policy Planning Council.

5. Prosterman and Riedinger, 1986.

6. Prosterman and Riedinger, 1986.

7. Prosterman and Riedinger, 1986.

8. See Chapter 6, section 6.3.

9. Interview, Roy Prosterman, 30 November 1989. See Chapter 6, section 6.5.1 and Chapter 7, section 7.5.2.

10. Edgardo Estacio later served as a witness for the Bacolod police chief in charges levelled against 11 members of the NFSW (*The Visayan Daily Star*, 12 October 1988).

11. They met with those involved in CPAR including the KMP staff, Dinky Soliman and Felipe Romero of the non-governmental organization ACES, as well as Oscar Castillo of PAKI-SAMA. Conversation with Jeff Riedinger, 25 February 1989.

12. Interview Roy Prosterman, 30 November 1989.

13. Interview Solita Monsod, 9 May 1991.

14. Villegas and Mangahas were on opposing sides of the agrarian reform issue. See Chapters 5, 6 and 7.

15. Interview Roy Prosterman, 30 November 1989.

16. Prosterman presented to the government a revised version of the 1987 3 June Draft Executive Order. His revision was dated 26 June 1987. He clearly indicated all the deleted wording and all his revisions. Prosterman's name does not appear on the text, but his authorship was confirmed by an official of the Department of Agrarian Reform in September 1988.

17. He deleted the clause stipulating that landowners could retain up to 50 hectares until 1990, 24 hectares until 1992 and seven hectares in 1997.

18. See Chapter 7, section 7.6.3.

19. For his position on cooperatives see Prosterman and Riedinger, 1987, p.219 and passim.

20. Interview, Solita Monsod, 9 May 1991.

21. The rumour mills of Manila looked on his flight humorously, saying that the threat was not a serious one, but the assassination of one of Prosterman's co-workers in El Salvador in 1981 (Prosterman and Riedinger, 1987, p.158) probably explains why he took it to heart.

22. The first report was the 'World Bank Land Reform Mission: Preliminary Conclusions', marked 'Confidential' and dated 25 March, 1987 (World Bank, 1987). The second was a longer report, 'Agrarian Reform in the Philippines: An Assessment of the Proposal for an Accelerated Land Reform Program', 12 May 1987 (World Bank, 1987b).

23. See Chapter 4, especially section 4.4.2.

24. See Chapter 7, section 7.4.2. The mission included Martin Karcher, Senior Economist, Projects Department in the East Asia and Pacific Regional Office of the Bank, as mission leader; Mohan Gopal, Legal Counsel, and David Jarvis, Loan Officer in the Philippine Division, also Bank employees; John H. Duloy, an Australian consultant; Sein Lin, Director of the US Lincoln Institute of Land Policy; and William Thiesenhusen of the Land Tenure Center at the University of Wisconsin.

25. Both Thiesenhusen (1971, 1990) and Lin (1972) were academic specialists on reform who had a long history of involvement in promoting an essentially liberal approach.

26. The mission had seen a draft of the 'Proposal for an Accelerated Land Reform Program', prepared in early March 1987.

27. World Bank, 1987b, p.56.

28. World Bank, 1987b, p.16, 28.

29. World Bank, 1987b, pp.34-36.
30. World Bank, 1987b, p.30.
31. World Bank, 1987b, p.40.
32. World Bank, 1987b, p.53.
33. World Bank, 1987b, p.74.
34. Prosterman (Interview, 30 November 1989) met with the mission in Washington and said that he also had good meetings with the Philippine desk at the Bank.
35. *PDI* (19 June 1987).
36. Interview, Solita Monsod, 9 May 1991.
37. Constantino, 1987.
38. World Bank, 1986, vol.2, p.123.
39. This is not meant to suggest that Bank consultants lack integrity, but merely that the Bank generally knows where an academic or other consultant stands based on their past work and hires them accordingly.
40. If the mission report had been internal to the Bank alone, or if only their preliminary report had been presented to the government, the conclusion might have been different. However, the final report was forwarded to the government by Gautam S. Kaji, Director Country Department II Asia Region, at the Washington office.
41. Interview, Manuel Lim, World Bank office Manila, 25 September 1987.
42. Gautam S. Kaji, Director Country Dept.II Asia Reg., letter to DAR Secretary Philip Juico, 4 April 1989.
43. In 1962 the Foreign Assistance Act was amended to prevent US funding the compensation for expropriated property. It was amended in 1985 to allow such funding if the US President deemed it in the national interest (US Foreign Assistance Act of 1961 as amended, Section 620g, in US Congress 1989, p.200).
44. US House of Representatives, 1986 (April 29), p.21.
45. US House of Representatives, 1986 (April 29), p.30. This view was reiterated a year later by David Joel Steinberg, President of Long Island University, who said, 'There is a symbolic importance about what she does with her own lands or her family's lands which transcends immediate public relations'. Rudiger Dornbusch of MIT and John Thomas of Harvard also told the committee that reform was urgent, especially on Hacienda Luisita. US House of Representatives, 1987 (12 March).
46. See Chapter 5 on divisions in the US administration in the last days of Marcos. For the divergence of opinion during the early days of the Aquino administration, see *FEER* (9 April 1987).
47. See Sheila Coronel, *MC* (19 September 1987).
48. US House of Representatives, 1986 (15 May), pp.94-95.
49. US House of Representatives, 1986 (15 May) p.133.
50. In December 1987, after rumours that the US had provided covert support to military rebels who staged a coup in August 1987, Assistant Secretary of State Lambertson asserted that the State and Defence Departments were at one in both their analysis of the Philippines and their support for the Aquino Administration. US House of Representatives, 1987a.
51. US House of Representatives, 1986 (15 May), p.116.
52. US House of Representatives, 1986 (15 May), p.82.
53. Government of the Republic of the Philippines, 1987, 'Memorandum on Economic Policy', and National [NEPA], 1986.
54. US House of Representatives, 1986 (15 May), p.158.
55. Interview with a member of the Bureau of Intelligence and Research, Department of State, Washington, 6 December 1989.
56. Interview, John H. Andre II, Country Officer, Office of Philippine Affairs, Department of State, 5 December 1989.
57. Andre's view was not shared by a colleague in the Bureau of Intelligence and Research

(Interview, 6 December 1989), who argued that, 'The Department of Defence has been more negative toward the Comprehensive Agrarian Reform Programme, as they have been toward all the Aquino programmes, than has State'.

58. US House of Representatives, 1987 (17 March), p.912.
59. Emphasis added. US House of Representatives, 1987 (17 March), p.913.
60. Interview with a Pentagon official, Washington, 13 December 1989.
61. Interview with AID consultants who preferred to remain anonymous (Manila, September 1987).
62. US House of Representatives, 1987 (17 March), p.884.
63. US House of Representatives, 1987 (17 March), pp.914-915.
64. US House of Representatives, 1987a (2 December), p.43.
65. Interview, Solita Monsod, 9 May 1991.
66. *Congressional Record*, House (10 December 1987), pp.H1148-51, H1194-96,
67. US House of Representatives, 1987 (18 March), p.948.
68. This was to avoid a concerted opposition from Senator Jesse Helms and other opponents of agrarian reform.
69. On programme budget see Chapter 10. US foreign assistance in 1989 was estimated at $479 million, almost a quarter of which was in military aid (USAID, 1989b).
70. The following summarizes the main points in Prosterman and Hanstad, unpublished paper, 1988a. These papers were delivered to the government and widely circulated in Manila.
71. Prosterman and Hanstad, unpublished paper 1988b.
72. Interview, USAID officials, Washington D.C., November 1989.
73. Interview with Solarz aide, Washington D.C., December 1989.
74. USAID, 1989.
75. The ARSP (USAID, 1989, p.29) was referring to USAID Policy Determination (PD)-13 and Bureau for Program and Policy Coordination (PPC) guidance.
76. USAID, 1989, p.29.
77. State Department to Embassy, 28 June 1988, telegram.
78. Interview with USAID officials in Washington, 28 November 1989.
79. *BW* (Manila: 12 January 1988).
80. Interview, John H. Andre II, Country Officer, Office of Philippine Affairs, Department of State, 5 December 1989.
81. US House of Representatives, 1986 (29 April), p.21.
82. Interview, Bonifacio Gillego, 26 August 1989.
83. Johnson, 1989, p.19.
84. National [NDCF], 12 January 1986.
85. National [NDCF] publicity brochure, n.d.
86. *Boston Globe* (13 January 1986).
87. Butz Aquino and Bobby Hernandez telegram to Andy Messing Jr., 5 March 1986, NDCF files.
88. According to Messing (Interview, 6 December 1989), the photo with Aquino was taken in 1988. The following account is based on the author's interview with Messing.
89. Lansdale, who was on the board of the NDCF, died in 1988.
90. Bonner, 1988, p.337.
91. *PDI* (5 October 1987).
92. Stilwell, 1987.
93. *Foundation News* (March-April 1979) and Barry et al, 1986, pp.37-38.
94. Interview, Richard Fisher, 29 November 1989.
95. On Sebastian, see Chapter 10.

96. On Central America, see Barry et al, 1986 and the Christic Institute, 1988. For a description of Singlaub in the Philippines, see Putzel, 1988, pp.63-65; and on the overall activities of the US right in the Philippines, see Marti, 1987.
97. Further evidence of the interest came when the Bank commissioned Clive Bell (1989) to write a background paper on agrarian reform for the 1990 *World Development Report*.

IMPLEMENTING CARP: CONTENDING POSITIONS WITHIN THE STATE

10.1 Introduction

With the conservative approach to reform firmly enshrined in law and endorsed by the United States, the Aquino government set about implementing the new agrarian reform programme. A review of its implementation demonstrates how the Comprehensive Agrarian Reform Program (CARP) actually came to serve the interests of certain factions of the elite and sheds further light on the character of the Philippine state. Debates between the advocates of the liberal and conservative approaches within state institutions continued during the early stages of implementation. However, both the orientation of state officials and powerful vested interests in society would bring the debate to a decisive conclusion.

Throughout the remainder of Aquino's term in office, she continued to affirm that CARP was the 'centre-piece' of her government's economic and social programme. Landowners and domestic and foreign agribusiness interests adjusted to the conditions imposed by CARP and sought to turn the law to their own advantage. The President's family continued to play a leading role in these efforts by implementing CARP on their own estate. CARP required the immediate transfer of public lands leased by transnational corporations to their workers, a move that many in government hoped would reap an early political dividend and show the administration's commitment to the reform process. The government also sought to enlist an unprecedented amount of foreign aid for CARP implementation. By early 1991, just a year and a half before scheduled national elections, government representatives were claiming that 82 per cent of the programme's targets for the period had been met. However, the reality of CARP implementation gives rise to a very different assessment of its accomplishments.

10.2 Conservatives and liberals in the state

During the early years of reform implementation the state remained divided along a number of different fault lines. Major divisions developed within the Department of Agrarian Reform (DAR) and between it and other state institutions, including the military, the Department of Finance and the Land Bank. Advocates of the liberal approach felt that even within the context of a conservative reform law, significant advances could be made in land redistribution. CARP still made the headlines after the passage of the law, but the content of the headlines changed considerably. Landowners remained intent on ensuring that liberal reformers in government were not able to make significant headway in implementing land redistribution, and they sought common cause with others both inside and outside state institutions.

10.2.1 Contending positions in the DAR

After leaving the post of DAR Secretary vacant for nearly five months, President Aquino appointed Philip Juico on 23 July 1987, the day after she signed her executive order. Juico was recommended for the job by his boss, Agriculture Secretary Carlos Dominguez. Juico, who was a friend of the presidential family and the prime mover in Aquino's media bureau during her election campaign, came from an agribusiness background. He had worked both in the private sector and in government with the late Arturo Tanco, Marcos' Agriculture Secretary.[1] According to one Cabinet member, his major qualification was the fact that he would 'follow and not give...any lip' to the President, an important quality at that time given the Cabinet disputes between Ongpin, Arroyo and Monsod.[2]

Juico was a more active manager than his predecessor and brought several new people into the upper echelons of the Department, but most of the old bureaucracy remained in place. He was hesitant to introduce sweeping changes and believed that his role was to 'harmonize [the] competing interests' of landowners and the targeted reform beneficiaries.[3] While Juico had some familiarity with agrarian reform through his participation as Undersecretary in the Cabinet Action Committee drafting the executive order, he relied heavily on Undersecretary José Medina, long-time second-in-command at the Department, to provide the orientation for implementing first the executive order and then the new agrarian reform law.

Medina had worked within the context of conservative reform throughout the Marcos years, and he continued to defend the approach, and DAR's record, after the new administration assumed power. He had been in charge of DAR during the first three months of the Aquino administration and during the five months following Alvarez's resignation. For Medina, CARP was merely an evolutionary extension of Marcos' reform programme, the implementation of which remained essentially a 'documentation process' to be carried out by central state institutions. He repackaged the old formula for Juico as a 'new' DAR strategy, called the 'Systems Approach and Management By Results'. His strategy involved organizing DAR officials at the municipal and provincial levels into teams, each assigned to a different function. One would identify land to be covered, another would determine its productivity, another its value, another would organize the Barangay Agrarian Reform Committee (BARC) and so on.[4] Since Medina was in charge of Field Operations, he had control over 91 per cent of the DAR organization.[5]

Medina's strategy was challenged by advocates of the liberal approach, led by Assistant Secretary Gerardo Bulatao, who had entered the DAR during the early months of the Aquino administration and had lobbied in vain for earlier and more decisive legislation. Bulatao and his supporters first gained influence in DAR's Education Bureau and then in the Bureau responsible for support services to beneficiaries. Like past advocates of liberal reform, they believed that they could make gains even within the context of a flawed reform programme. Bulatao criticized Medina's strategy as bureaucratic and defended a 'Community Based Approach' to reform implementation, which focussed on work with peasant and non-governmental organizations (NGOs).

The liberal reformers argued that DAR should be organized on a geographical rather than a functional basis. Local teams would work with the beneficiaries to implement all aspects of the programme, from land identification, through valuation, title distribution and the provision of support services. This argument had first been advanced in 1986 by Bulatao and others sent into DAR by the Presidential Commission on Governmental Reorganization, when they described the role of local Agrarian Reform Teams.[6] While Bulatao acknowledged that it was necessary to have specialists at the provincial level, those in the field had to be 'generalists who are aware of each sub-programme'. This resembled the way that Land Commissions had operated in Japan, where the liberal approach had been successfully implemented.[7] For Bulatao, 'Unless the priority is put where farmers are organized none of this will work'.[8] Bulatao, like Bonifacio Gillego in the House, departed from the earlier position of the liberal reformers, especially Americans like Prosterman, in advocating a bottom-up approach centred on the peasants' own organizations.

In early 1989, Bulatao was already aware that he was being out-manoeuvred. He said, 'Our community-based strategy is technically being done in 60 provinces, but Medina sits on top. For him NGOs and people's organizations don't exist...The hard-sell of Medina is working, even with Juico. He will reverse the community-based approach'.[9] While Bulatao had some protection from Juico since they had attended La Salle high school together, Medina represented a dominant majority in the DAR bureaucracy. Even after he was forced to leave his post in 1989, his bureaucratic strategy retained its dominance.

The DAR was also involved in inter-agency competition within the state. The Department had long been viewed as one of the weakest government agencies. President Aquino contributed to this by leaving the post of Secretary vacant at the outset of her administration and again for the first half of 1987. After Juico was appointed to DAR, Land Bank president Diogracias Vistan continuously challenged his authority and DAR's responsibility in determining such matters as landowner compensation.[10] Juico was preoccupied with endearing himself to the President and displaying formal accomplishments by his department. Right from the start, Juico, like Estrella before him, was less concerned with reform content than with positive propaganda on CARP and the immediate political impact of DAR's activities on the networks that provided support for the Aquino administration. This is what made 'voluntary land transfers', allowed under the law, so attractive to the Secretary.

10.2.2 Voluntary Offers and the demise of Juico

Secretary Juico apparently believed that DAR could achieve the quickest results at the least political cost by focusing on the implementation of CARP provisions encouraging 'voluntary land transfer' and employing the law's allowance of generous compensation to landowners. After the passage of EO229 and throughout the first year of implementation of the agrarian reform law, DAR officials around the country concentrated on completing the Marcos programme and soliciting from landowners 'Voluntary Offers to Sell' (VOS) their land.[11] By September 1989, DAR Central Office reported that officials had succeeded in soliciting more than 126,000 hectares of voluntary offers from landowners (see Table 10.1).[12] Juico's decision to concentrate on VOS brought the basic weaknesses of CARP quickly to the fore and opened DAR to attack by other state agencies and landowners anxious to discredit the government's programme.

Under the compensation formula finally included in the law and the early guide-lines of DAR, landowners could secure even *more than market-value* compensation for their lands. DAR's working formula for determining market-value compensation under EO229 (22 July 1987 to 10 June 1988) was based on an assessment of the owner's declared market value, the owner's declaration of the net income of the land and DAR's calculation of value as determined by the sale of comparable lands. With the passage of RA6657 in June 1988, DAR decided that the value of land would be determined by averaging three estimates of market value: the 'assessed market value' (AMV) reported in a landowner's most recent tax declaration, the 'market value' (MV) as an average of three sales of comparable land in the vicinity of a landholding inflated by the consumer price index, and the owner's own 'declaration of fair market value' (DMV) made during the government's land registration programme, *Listasaka I and II*, between 1987 and 1988. While the compensation formula included a safeguard against extreme over-valuation in the owner's own declaration, it still permitted compensation at up to 33 per cent more than market value (see Figure 10.1).

Such a compensation formula might have guaranteed against excessive compensation, in terms of the market-value criteria enunciated in the law, if state institutions like DAR or the tax bureaux were immune to landowner influence. However, DAR officials were urged to demonstrate results by closing as many deals as possible with landowners. There were several ways in which the formula was abused. First, DAR officials often chose to establish market value (MV) as an average of three sales of highly-valued land, labelling the sales as 'comparable'. The arbitrary character of their choice along with the tendency for land speculation demonstrated the unsoundness of using 'comparable sales' as an element in the compensation formula. Secondly, landowners were able to pay just one tax instalment on the basis of an inflated land value and thus raise the level of 'assessed market value' (AMV). The nearer that assessed value was to the market value, the higher could be their own declared value and the resulting compensation. There was no obligation for landowners to pay unpaid tax arrears at the inflated level, but beneficiaries who received the land would be required

Table 10.1: Voluntary Offers to Sell Under the CARP (1987-1989)

Region	Area Offered (Ha.s)	Number of Offers	Number Offers >100 Ha.s	Number of Corporations	Number of Banks	Area Acquired (Ha.s)	Number Offers Acquired	Average Value/Ha. (Pesos)
1 Ilocos	747	31	2	2	1	7.9	1	7,789.32
2 Cagayan	1553	60	4	2	24	146.7	9	21,609.26
3 Central Luzon	22944	155	30	7	42	26.4	3	9,621.82
4 S. Tagalog	29131	126	42	19	5	350.0	9	14,810.35
5 Bicol	39290	173	27	12	0	838.3	32	20,951.01
6 W. Visayas	8934	56	12	4	1	519.9	7	18,999.54
7 C. Visayas	2384	12	5	2	0	0	0	0
8 E. Visayas	988	14	2	1	0	0	0	0
9 W. Mindanao	1501	27	3	2	0	0	0	0
10 N. Mindanao	5733	55	8	5	0	305.5	7	27,161.18
11 S. Mindanao	3687	55	9	7	2	125.8	8	23,306.01
12 C. Mindanao	7799	87	10	6	0	0	0	0
Cordillera A.R.	1500	2	2	1	0	0	0	0
Total*	**126191**	**853**	**156**	**70**	**75**	**2320.5**	**76**	

*These were only offers compiled by Central Office through September 1989. Of the offers not paid for, appearing for the first time in the September 1989 list, only those greater than 20 hectares are included here. All corporate offers are included but the numerous small offers from banking institutions in the September 1989 list are not included. Lists from provincial offices in Region 5, Region 6 and Region 2 reveal that far more had been offered by September 1989.

Source: DAR Central Office. Reports on Voluntary Offers to Sell: (1) September 28 - December 31 1987; (2) November 1988; (3) Weekly Reports: November 7-11, November 14-18 1988; (4) June 1989; (5) September 1989.

Figure 10.1: Landowner Compensation: The Formula for Land Valuation Under RA6657

Three estimates of Market Value:
1) AMV   Assessed Market Value: reported in owner's latest tax declaration.
2) MV   Market Value: average of 3 sales of comparable land.
3) DMV   Declared Market Value: owner's own declaration of market value.

The formula: $\dfrac{AMV + MV + DMV}{3} = V$ (Value to be paid as Compensation)

The safeguard: if DMV > (AMV + MV) then compensation would be based on: (AMV + MV)/2 or guaranteed to be less than or equal to Market Value.
The condition for greater than market-value compensation: As long as AMV is 51% or more of the MV and the DMV is less than AMV + MV, then the owner will receive more than market value compensation. If the AMV is equal to the MV then it is possible for the owner to get up to 33.3% more than the MV.

Take two extreme examples:

AMV = 15,001   (15,001● 30,000● 45,000)/3 = 30,000.33
MV = 30,000   AMV + MV + DMV /3 = V (compensation)
DMV = 45,000   .001% > MV

AMV = 30,000   (30,000 + 30,000 + 59,999)/3 = 39,999.67
MV = 30,000   AMV + MV + DMV /3 = V (compensation)
DMV = 59,999   33% > MV

Source: Based on DAR, 'Guidelines on Land Valuation and Just Compensation', Draft Administrative Order, Series 1988 and Interview, Gerardo Bulatao, 24 January 1989.

to pay taxes at this level. Thirdly, because DAR officials discussed with landowners the level of comparable sales being chosen, landowners could both influence that choice and plan the most advantageous level for their 'declared market value' (DMV). The formula was therefore extremely susceptible to abuse by the landowners and opened the door to corrupt practices by DAR officials.

All the weaknesses of DAR's approach and the compensation formula came to public notice when the Land Bank of the Philippines (LBP) exposed the over-valuation of the 1,888 hectare Garchitorena Estate in Camarines Sur. The estate was originally owned by the once powerful Hispanic Garchitorena family, whose wealth originated in the abaca trade, but much of it had long since been declared pasture land.[13] In 1974, the family sold it to José Alberto, who used the land as collateral for a P1 million loan from the United Coconut Planters Bank (UCPB). One DAR official claimed that during the Marcos years the estate was offered for sale to the government, but was refused because the price demanded was too high for what was virtually non-arable land.[14] In 1985, when Alberto could not meet his payments he sold the estate to the UCPB for P1.4 million.[15] In April 1988, the UCPB decided to sell the land to Sharp International Marketing Inc. for P3.8 million.[16]

In May 1988, Sharp submitted a voluntary offer to sell the estate to DAR for P56 million, at a profit of over P52 million.[17] After purchasing the land at a price of P1,596 per hectare, the company's management went to the provincial tax office and paid taxes on the land stating that its value was P33,226 per hectare. In November, DAR officials, working with Sharp, changed the initial offer to P65 million.[18] DAR's Bureau of Land Acquisition recommended that an even higher valuation of P35,344 per hectare, or P66.7 million in total, be paid for the land. At the first meeting of a newly created DAR-LBP Compensation Clearing Committee on 28 December 1989, presided over by DAR Undersecretary Salvador Pejo, the claim was approved.[19] Within days Juico signed a deed of sale authorizing the Land Bank to pay Sharp P33,226 per hectare, or a total of P62.7 million, even more than Sharp's original offer, for what was largely sloping pasture lands.[20]

LBP president, Diogracias Vistan, returned the order for payment to DAR, saying that the amount was excessive. The Bank's own assessment in October 1988 had set the price per hectare at only P15,000, or less than half the value agreed by DAR. The President was informed about the deal on 1 April 1989 by Fr. Joaquin Bernas, and she met with Vistan and Juico on 5 April. Sharp then had the audacity to petition the Supreme Court to order DAR to pay the P62.7 million for the land.[21] Subsequently, Secretary Juico stopped the payment order and began an investigation of the deal. However, Vistan revealed the overpricing agreement to Congress and on 13 May 1989, Rep. Edcel Lagman told a joint House-Senate Committee the details, unleashing a scandal that brought the DAR's work virtually to a halt.

The fraud was accomplished by Sharp's falsification of the net income from the land, its extremely inflated declaration of the land's market value and by DAR officials' complicity not only in accepting these inflated figures, but in inflating them still further and in choosing an extremely high value of comparable sales. However, even without direct fraud by DAR officials, the compensation formula adopted would have allowed an extremely inflated price.[22] After the episode was made public, no less than four government investigations ensued. It was revealed that Sharp had in fact not consummated the purchase of the lands from the UCPB until 5 December 1988, suggesting bank complicity in the fraud. The UCPB had additionally arranged to sell Sharp the 1,187 hectare Liboro Estate in Ragay, also in Camarines Sur.[23] The major financier behind both land deals was Romeo Santos, who had provided the funds for the land purchase to Sharp president Alex Lina. Santos had been selling land to DAR throughout the 1970s and 1980s.[24]

Romeo Santos was an associate of the President's brother, Congressman José Peping Cojuangco. He became close to the family when he organized the Laban in Bicol and played a pivotal role in President Aquino's campaign against Marcos in the region.[25] After Aquino came to office her brother had urged Santos' appointment as manager of the Manila International Airport. Santos also ran in the Congressional elections from Caloocan City, Metro Manila. The result of the election was contested and in late June 1989, the House Election Tribunal announced that it was about to proclaim Santos the winner.[26]

Santos had been selling lands in Camarines Sur to DAR at least since 1976-

77.[27] Like many landowners, Santos appeared to be heavily involved in land speculation. According to DAR records, he had obtained titles to most of the rice and corn lands that he sold to DAR under the Marcos reform programme only after the programme was launched in 1972. Most were acquired in the late 1970s and early 1980s, with one title obtained as late as 1988. The sale of lands covered by the Marcos programme could only be legally accomplished with the approval of DAR and the Registry of Deeds.

Santos was married to Maria Magdalena Garchitorena, whose family was the original owner of the Garchitorena estate and many other lands in Bicol. Andres Garchitorena headed the provincial Registry of Deeds during the 1970s and his signature appeared on many of the land titles obtained by Romeo Santos. As for DAR, Santos had met Salvador Pejo, who was Regional Director in Bicol, in 1975. Pejo said that DAR 'didn't mind if he got the title after 1972'.[28] Another indication of Santos' land speculation was the fact that several of the land titles in his files at DAR had huge mortgages attached to them, suggesting that he acquired the land to raise funds for other economic activities.

On 12 October 1987, Santos sent a letter to DAR offering to sell, under the VOS component of CARP in EO229, 1,145 hectares of land in Camarines Sur for P34.3 million, or P29,959 per hectare. Of this land, 975 hectares had already been covered by the Marcos PD27 programme. Much of the land was unirrigated corn land, but DAR had approved its value at a uniform P25,000 per hectare in 1985. Both the high value accorded to corn land and that fact that the land was uniformly valued seemed to contradict the requirement that land value be determined by the land's productivity. The Land Bank opposed the valuation, saying that Santos had over-reported the productivity of the land and that beneficiaries had been coerced to accept the value.[29] Pejo and at least one other DAR official subsequently involved in the Garchitorena land scam had endorsed the stated value of the land.[30] Over 345 hectares of the land originally covered by PD27 had already been foreclosed by the Philippine National Bank, but later Pejo asserted that Santos had redeemed the lands before submitting them under the VOS.[31]

On 27 August 1987, Pejo, who had already been appointed Assistant Secretary for Field Services in DAR central office, wrote a letter to the Land Bank stating that Santos had requested that his claim folders for lands covered by PD27 be withdrawn from the bank. On 29 September, Jesus Diaz, vice-president of the LBP, returned the folders to DAR and less than two weeks later Santos resubmitted these lands, along with others, to the DAR as a voluntary offer inflating their already controversially high value. As well as Pejo, at least one other DAR official later involved in the Garchitorena case endorsed his request.[32] By June 1989, Santos had received payment for 188 hectares of land under VOS, the majority of which was paid at P27,000 per hectare.[33]

Clearly, the worst abuses of the VOS programme were centred in Bicol (Region 5). Table 10.1 reveals that the region covered 31 per cent of all land offered and 36 per cent of all land acquired during the two-year drive to solicit voluntary offers. However, similar abuses occurred throughout the country. In Region 5 as well as in most other regions, the land offered under the VOS programme fell into one or more of the following categories: rice and corn land already covered by the Marcos programme, land of low productive value, land about to be foreclosed by the banks or whose title was unclear, and land in areas where the New People's Army was actively implementing its own 'Revolutionary Agrarian Reform Programme'.

While there were many cases of owners, like Romeo Santos, resubmitting as VOS lands covered but not yet paid for by Marcos' PD27, other voluntary offers consisted of rice and corn lands that had escaped DAR's attention. Inocencio Uy, ex-Mayor of Roxas, Isabela was typical of most large landowners. In 1989, besides running a big and profitable lumber business, he had at least 200 hectares of rice, corn and tobacco land in the towns of Burgos, Roxas, Quirino and Mallig. He had acquired most of the land in the 1950s and 1960s from indebted peasants or from the Development Bank of the Philippines, which had already foreclosed the lands of original peasant settlers. The rice lands were still under a 50-50 sharing arrangement, despite the fact that such lands should have been covered by PD27 and that such sharecropping was legally outlawed by Macapagal's 1963 Code of Agrarian Reform. Uy offered the lands to the government under VOS for P65,000 per hectare, but DAR endorsed them at P33,000 to P36,000 per hectare. He said, 'They told me you can make some bargains later on. It is up to me to negotiate'. On lands that should have been covered by the Marcos programme, he planned to make a lucrative sale to DAR and to retain at least 30 hectares for his six children.[34]

Most lands offered under VOS were of poor quality and many were in isolated areas where the NPA was active. The Garchitorena estate was mainly pasture land. There was another 200 hectare property in the same town of similar quality offered under VOS.[35] According to the NPA command operating in the region, by 1985 over 2,000 hectares had been foreclosed in the town and were being farmed by more than 200 peasants, who initially paid a share to the bank while the local bank manager turned over taxes to the NPA.[36] When the bank stopped collecting rents, the peasants paid taxes directly to the NPA. The underground movement was active in all the towns where Santos' land was located. Tigaon, where Santos held title to many lands, was the seat of the NPA's first Armed Propaganda Unit in the Bicol region.[37]

In Negros Occidental, one team visited 7,356 hectares of voluntarily offered lands. They reported that all were located no less than 20 kilometres from the highway, usually mountainous and had poor soil quality. They noted that these were contested lands with a strong presence of military and vigilante groups.[38] Negros had its own land-scam where DAR officials purchased the 374 hectare Villasor Estate for P7.7 million, or an average of P20,517 per hectare. This was mostly abandoned, upland property, which was originally offered by Guillermo Villasor and the Araneta family for P3 million. DAR officials had more than doubled the price.[39] At a DAR conference, officials said that they had valued that part of the estate devoted to sugar at P33,000 per hectare and coconut lands at P5,000 per hectare.[40] However, DAR records revealed that none of the land was planted to sugar.

As in Camarines Sur, many of the Negros lands had already been abandoned by owners and subjected to the NPA's own reform programme. Roy Aguilar offered 1,021 hectares of land in the town of Sagay. He originally owned only 80 hectares and expanded his holdings by ejecting settlers during the Marcos years, when the price of sugar was high.[41] According to the outspoken Bishop Antonio Fortich, Aguilar told the bishop that he had already 'distributed the land to the people' because of 'pressure from the people in the hills'. The bishop recounted that Aguilar, 'felt he was no longer safe there'.[42] The land was being farmed by peasants and Aguilar was simply trying to cash in on the VOS programme. Several other major properties offered in Negros were already being farmed either by sugar workers or other peasants in the upland areas.[43]

Throughout the country owners offered to sell to DAR lands for which they had no clear title. In Negros Occidental, Rosario L. Cooper submitted a VOS covering 2,092 hectares in Vallerhermosa, which was mainly pasture land. Sugar workers believed that the Coopers had only held it as a concession from the government.[44] Hermina Manipol offered to sell 7,000 hectares in Nueva Ecija to the DAR, reportedly for P60,000 per hectare, until it was discovered that the land was part of the AFP's Fort Magsaysay.[45] Another offer of over 1,000 hectares made by a Mr. Paterno in Camarines Sur was later discovered to be national park land.[46]

The controversy unleashed by investigations into the VOS programme forced Secretary Juico to resign. While there was no evidence of his direct involvement in the land-scam, he presided over its implementation.[47] The VOS experience demonstrated the degree to which state institutions like the DAR and the tax offices were penetrated and manipulated by landowning interests. It showed that many landowners held lands primarily for speculative purposes and as a source of mortgage capital, and that their dubious dealings with DAR had been going on for a long time. The Land Bank's role in exposing DAR corruption by no means meant that it was committed to land redistribution.

On the contrary, the Bank, as an instrument of the Department of Finance, had worked first to limit the redistributive content of the programme and then to slow down its implementation. Throughout 1988 and early 1989, LBP president, Diogracias Vistan, had been sparring with Juico over the orientation of CARP implementation and the division of power between the LBP and the DAR within the government. Vistan used the controversy to bring down the DAR Secretary and to secure LBP dominance over the land valuation procedure. Subsequently, the Bank was given full responsibility over land valuation, weakening DAR's position still further.[48]

While most public attention around the VOS controversy was focused on the action of corrupt officials, it was the conservative orientation of the law and of DAR itself that lay at the root of the crisis. The law's focus on providing market-value compensation and encouraging voluntary land transfer opened the doors to corruption. The law and DAR put no importance on involving peasant beneficiaries in the land valuation process. Undersecretary Medina's 'Systems Approach and Management By Results' incorporated a 'doctrine of completed staff work' that led Juico directly into the land-scam trap. It stated that a department head should receive work in a completed form and be required to do no more than affix his approval or disapproval, such that 'completed staff work results in a single document prepared for the signature of the chief without accompanying comment'.[49] Juico followed this method and lost his position.

Voluntary offers became the focus of government activity because the conservative approach adopted was based on placating the landowners. Secretary Juico said that he concentrated on voluntary offers, 'precisely because I didn't want to use the compulsory acquisition powers of government'. He went on to stress that, 'Agrarian reform is not the only thing that is happening to this country. I didn't want to add to the tense atmosphere'. Juico said that he restricted DAR work to VOS because, 'We were not too sure where the military stood in this whole thing'.[50] His successor illustrated that DAR sought to accommodate not only the landowners but also the military.

10.2.3 Santiago, the military and counterinsurgency

June 1989 saw the government preparing for a meeting of the World Bank Consultative Group in Tokyo in early July. The government had hoped to make funding for CARP central to its efforts to raise increased foreign aid, and the scandal around Garchitorena threatened to undermine that strategy. On 30 June 1989, in an effort to restore the credibility of the agrarian reform programme, the President appointed graft-busting Miriam Defensor Santiago as the new DAR Secretary. Santiago had earned her reputation as a crusader against corruption while heading the Commission on Immigration and Deportation (CID). A lawyer by profession, she had been the youngest woman ever appointed to the bench when, at the age of 37 in 1983, she was named a judge at the Quezon City Regional Trial Court.

Acting DAR Secretary Benjamin Leong welcomed her appointment, as did influential Congressional figures.[51] However, the liberal reformers inside DAR were much more circumspect. While Assistant Secretary Gerardo Bulatao believed that her appointment was a politically logical decision by the President, he cast doubt on her ability to move forward agrarian reform, saying that she was 'the third secretary we have had who knows nothing about agrarian reform':

> She is urban based, but what does she understand about rural development? She is a lawyer, but doesn't know agrarian law. She has a head on her shoulders, but does she have a heart for the poor?

Bulatao argued that the problem at DAR was not principally one of graft but of ineptitude. He said that there were major questions of orientation and organization that the new Secretary would have to confront. She would have to decide priorities for land redistribution, given the problems encountered in VOS. Of 11,000 Barangay Agrarian Reform Councils (BARCs), 10,000 were not yet active, and Bulatao felt that action to consolidate them would be central to reform implementation. He wondered whether Santiago would move to compulsory acquisition in areas where peasant organizations were strong, or concentrate on areas where the landowners were least resistant. Finally, because of her reputation for working closely with the military, Bulatao wondered, 'Will she militarize the DAR, linking it with the counterinsurgency program or not identify the program with the military, even if land reform may have a counterinsurgency effect?'[52]

Santiago was adept at working with the media and she quickly attempted to enhance her image among the peasant groups. Soon after her appointment she acknowledged the 'serious flaws in the law against which I am powerless'.[53] She said that she recognized the superiority of the People's Agrarian Reform Code (PARCODE) put forward by the Congress for a People's Agrarian Reform (CPAR), but argued that it would be inappropriate to ask the President to endorse such a programme since it would not 'survive legislative scrutiny' in Congress.[54] Santiago, who clearly had ambitions for higher political office, also wanted to endear herself to the landowners. She affirmed that while RA6657 stated that the highest consideration must be given to the welfare of landless farmers and farmworkers, the law seeks 'a balance between the interests of the land-owners and those of the farmers'.[55] Adopting the conservative framework of the law, which defined agrarian reform as essentially a government-sponsored market transaction in land, Santiago said that the major way of speeding up implementation was to pay off the owners promptly, 'If I show them the colour of the government's money, I'm sure things will be a lot faster'.[56]

For the liberal reformers in DAR, the way to speed up the implementation of CARP was to rely increasingly on the peasant organizations. Officials like Bulatao felt that they could still make headway with reform if the energies of NGOs and peasant groups could be tapped. While Bulatao recognized that DAR could not encourage peasants to occupy lands, he felt that the government should attempt to bring existing land occupations under the wing of the reform programme. Even the most radical peasant organizations had demonstrated a willingness to work with the DAR, but the greatest barrier to their involvement was the role of the military. This was apparent both in the military's counterinsurgency strategy as well as their collaboration with landowners and agribusiness corporations.

The dominant conservative approach to reform was complemented by the military's practice of harassing those peasant organizations that occupied land and petitioned the government for its transfer.[57] Shortly after Aquino came to power in 1986, a local chapter of the militant peasant organization, the KMP, had occupied and tilled land sequestered from a former Marcos crony in Mamplasan, Laguna.[58] After long and difficult negotiations, the DAR had succeeded in establishing a working relationship with the peasants in order to bring them into the government's programme. DAR began discussing the possibility of transferring land on a collective basis to farmer beneficiaries, not only in Mamplasan but also in other large estates run by agribusiness corporations. In Mamplasan the military reacted by stationing a detachment right in the *barrio*. According to Bulatao, they actively discouraged farmers from signing an agreement for collective ownership, saying 'there must be individual ownership. To have a collective is communist'.[59] Arguing that agrarian reform was a subversive activity, they began breaking into seminars that DAR had organized with the peasants.

In August 1989, Secretary Santiago appeared to be taking a stand against the dominant military thinking and looked poised to confront the Department of Defence head-on. She publicly criticized the activities of the military detachment in Mamplasan, saying 'This is political illiteracy of the highest sort and should be categorized as a capital offence'. When Santiago threatened to arrest the military offenders, Defence Secretary Fidel Ramos reproached her for violating Cabinet courtesy and reminded her of her dependence on the military. He said that Santiago should not get so 'excited' and asked, 'if she is going to order the arrest of a military man, who is going to do the arresting?'[60]

Just two months later, Santiago, again with her eye on her future political career, seemed to have come to an understanding with General Ramos. In October 1989, a Memorandum of Agreement was signed between the Departments of Agrarian Reform and National Defence. It stated that the Armed Forces of the Philippines (AFP) would assist DAR in reclaiming lands illegally occupied by peasants or distributed by the New People's Army under their 'Revolutionary Agrarian Reform Program'. It also stated that farmers, their organizations and other non-governmental organizations wishing to conduct meetings on agrarian reform had to seek the permission of local military commanders.[61] One of Santiago's last acts as DAR Secretary was to declare that the Department had been infiltrated at the highest levels by communists and to make known her intention to root them out with the help of military intelligence.[62]

The military's counterinsurgency strategy called for the forced evacuation of entire peasant communities under the pretext of isolating the New People's Army, as in its 'Operation Thunderbolt' in Negros Occidental. This reduced still further the prospects for land redistribution under the CARP. The evacuations disrupted agricultural production and undermined peasant communities' efforts to build up organizations capable of implementing agrarian reform. Even the more astute counterinsurgency theorists in the AFP, who opposed the policy of 'search and destroy', limited their vision of agrarian reform to the conservative approach.[63]

Aside from the strategy-determined hostility to all versions of agrarian reform, the AFP appeared to maintain the relationship of mutual support with landowners and agribusiness so evident during the Marcos years. In Negros, the *hacenderos* put up a 'Sugar Development Foundation' (SDF), through which each landowner contributed P5 per picul of sugar milled to support the Philippine Constabulary Forward Command, one of the wealthiest paramilitary organizations in the country. This was one of many new paramilitary organizations, labelled Civilian Armed Forces Geographical Units (CAFGU), set up as part of the counterinsurgency effort sanctioned by President Aquino. Despite the fact that such a fund put into question the civilian government's control over the military, Negros Governor Daniel Lacson referred to the SDF as an indication that, 'People here decided to stand up for their freedom'.[64]

Representative Hortensia Starke explicitly opposed the liberal argument that agrarian reform could play a role in bringing about political stability. In a 'primer' on the topic, she wrote that increasing agricultural productivity rather than reform was a cure for insurgency.[65] Starke did not hide her own cooperation with the military and recounted how she contacted Defence Secretary Ramos to help her set up a CAFGU on her rubber plantation in Mindanao. She also facilitated what she called 'god-father' arrangements between local officials and ex-members of the NPA in Negros Occidental. She explained that those quitting the NPA did not want to be seen contacting military authorities, so she would 'give a little money to them...and send them to the mayor or vice-mayor'.[66]

In Mindanao many big agribusiness corporations financed the establishment of CAFGUs on their plantations and provided regular finance to Army infantry battalions stationed close by. One local official in Sto Tomas, Davao, praised Marsman Estates Plantation Inc., one of Del Monte's biggest banana growers, for all the help that they had extended in setting up the CAFGU:

> The CAFGU was set up by Capt. Alberto. There is one company with 88 men, organized in platoons. Marsman provided financing. The company is contributing P5,000 to P7,000 per week for maintenance. Marsman helps the 641st Battalion of the AFP with food subsistence. If a vehicle breaks down the company repairs it. They hire the CAFGU as security guards on the plantation.[67]

According to some workers on the plantation, the company used the threat of violence to dictate the outcome of a trade union certification campaign. This saw the National Federation of Labour challenging the incumbent, which was perceived by many as a company union. The workers said, 'People supporting NFL during the campaign even received death threats'.[68] Marsman Plantations president, Roberto Sebastian, was chairman of the Philippine Banana Growers Association and a major figure in the lobby against redistributive reform throughout the debates in the executive and legislature. He felt that the country needed a strong political leader like Singapore's Lee Kuan-yew, who could lead the military in establishing peace and order and in creating a good climate for agribusiness investment.[69]

A similar strategy of cooperation developed between the management of the

NDC-Guthrie oil palm plantation in Agusan del Sur and the local military command. The corporation enjoyed a close relationship with the 8th Infantry Battalion headquartered in nearby Rosario. A company, consisting of about 60 soldiers, was stationed just outside the plantation gate. According to NGPI Deputy Manager, Cesar Alaban, the corporation used its security budget to provide living quarters and rice and repair the vehicles for the Army contingent. In addition to employing a security force of 45 men armed with M-16s, the company also financed the establishment of a 21-man 'special CAFGU', put up solely for the protection of the plantation.[70]

NDC-Guthrie General Manager John Lee said, 'As part of our contribution to the national effort of the Philippines, we are supporting the formation of a special CAFGU unit for the plantation which comes under the direct control of the military'. He explained that the CAFGU enhanced the size of the 8th Infantry Battalion and acted as a 'stay-behind force for the military' especially to protect the company's mill, which had come under attack from the NPA in the past. But Lee emphasized, 'We don't want to involve ourselves in the politics of the NPA...We are trying to ensure that the peace and order situation is peaceful on the plantation without any abuses whatsoever'.[71] Local Church activists in the surrounding towns, however, had a different attitude toward military-corporation cooperation. They feared that military operations which evacuated large numbers of peasants from the land would facilitate agribusiness use of the lands in a manner similar to the corporate expansion in Mindanao in the 1970s and early 1980s.[72]

The continuing relationships between landowners, private corporations and the military illustrated the fractured character of the Philippine state. The military remained a centre of power within the state rather than an institution subordinate to the President. The agreement struck between DAR and the DND during Santiago's tenure illustrated the military's authority within the state. At the same time, the military worked closely with particular private interests to the point where they received significant funding from landowners and agribusiness corporations. In both its strategic orientation and its institutional interests, the AFP as a whole remained locked in a conservative approach to reform.

10.2.4 Routing the liberal reformers and the arrest of Jaime Tadeo

Despite the subordination of the DAR within the state, landowners and their representatives in Congress remained intent on ensuring that the implementation of CARP would gain no momentum. In October 1989, as DAR recovered from the Garchitorena land-scam, the Congressional Commission on Appointments refused to confirm the appointment of Santiago as DAR Secretary. Senator John Osmeña, who had consistently opposed all versions of the agrarian reform law, led the Congressional assault on Santiago.[73] Opposition to Santiago represented both an attempt by Senators and Congressmen to keep a damper on DAR, and an effort to undermine Santiago's political ambitions. The controversy was eclipsed when the Aquino government was shaken by a major attempted *coup d'etat* led by Colonel Gregorio Honasan during the first week of December 1989.[74] The government attempted to return to its normal business as quickly as possible after the coup was put down and Congress scheduled another meeting of the Appointments Commission on 20 December 1989.

On 19 December, DAR organized a rally of 8,000 farmers and DAR workers at the Ultra Stadium in Manila, where Santiago attempted to fight back against her Congressional detractors and pressure them to confirm her position.[75] Instead, the Commission by-passed discussion of her case altogether, which meant that the President would have to resubmit her appointment to a new session of Congress in January.[76] On 30 December, President Aquino made a speech to the nation and the world in an effort to restore confidence in her government. Her speech, laying out the government's immediate recovery programme, was particularly addressed to foreign investors and the military and she made no mention of agrarian reform.[77]

Two episodes in the first half of 1990 illustrated the final triumph of the conservative approach within the institutions of the state. The first was the controversy over the appointment of Representative Florencio Abad as DAR Secretary. The second was the arrest and imprisonment of the nation's most well-known peasant leader, Jaime Tadeo. The two events taken together were a virtual declaration of war against the peasant movement.

As a result of the December coup attempt, which had demonstrated the vulnerability and growing unpopularity of Aquino's administration, the President launched yet another Cabinet shuffle in January 1990. The general complexion of the Cabinet remained the same, designed primarily to reassure the domestic and international business community.[78] However, in a surprise move, the President decided to avoid any further controversy over Santiago, and appointed long-time liberal reform advocate Congressman Florencio 'Butch' Abad as Secretary of Agrarian Reform. Abad came from a political family and was elected to Congress in 1987 on the Liberal Party ticket as the sole representative of the country's smallest province, Batanes, which occupies several desolate islands off the northern coast of Luzon.

Identifying with social-democracy, Abad had been involved with assisting moderate peasant organizations since his student days at Ateneo in the mid-1970s and had been imprisoned for a short period during martial law.[79] As adviser to Fr. Bernas on the Constitutional Commission, he contributed to the Jesuit superior's stance in support of liberal reform. Abad was Gillego's assistant chairman during the House debate on agrarian reform, where he campaigned for a zero land retention limit and voted against the final law because of its concessions to landowners.

At the same time as she appointed Abad, the President's office weakened the position of DAR within the Cabinet. Abad's appointment was paired with the nomination of Senen Bacani to the powerful post of Secretary of Agriculture. Bacani was Vice-president and General Manager of Dole Philippines from 1983 until the end of 1988, when he was appointed Vice-president for Operations of the newly established Dole Asia Inc. He could be expected to appease the agribusiness sector if it had any worries about Abad. Vicente Jayme was elevated to the newly created position of Presidential Executive Coordinator for Economic and Financial Affairs. This was in response to the business community's desire, expressed during a meeting with the President in mid-December 1989, to have one 'economic czar' in charge of policy.[80] Thus the position of DAR Secretary was made more marginal.

Nevertheless, the appointment of Abad was a departure from the past. It was clearly designed to win over the centre-left in the peasant movement, which had grown increasingly estranged from the government and was playing an instrumental role in the broad CPAR coalition. Abad's appointment could provide credibility to the government's programme and the DAR. However, the President's office knew that the DAR Secretary would have to work within the constraints imposed by the law and his Department's subordination to the more powerful economic departments, the Land Bank and the military. The liberal reformers in DAR, led by Gerry Bulatao, nonetheless believed that his appointment would enhance their position and provide a chance to make real gains in land redistribution.

Abad made it known that he would stretch the law as far as it would go in favour of the landless peasants. He worried the landowners at the start of his tenure by calling for a more speedy implementation of land transfer and cooperation with peasant organizations. He proposed forgiving past debts of agrarian reform beneficiaries and asked the Cabinet for more cooperation in implementing the programme. He drew the ire of the military when, in response to a demand from the militant KMP, he said that he would review the pact between DAR and the DND which allowed a military hand in CARP implementation. He also confronted military opposition to government sponsorship of collective ownership, saying that he would 'issue an administrative order granting mother titles to organized peasant groups and cooperatives to facilitate a quicker distribution of lands to beneficiaries'.[81]

Congress responded to the liberal reform advocates' renewed effort to breath some life into CARP by refusing to confirm Abad's appointment. At the same time, the conservative majority within the DAR itself began a rear-guard action to undermine the position of their new boss. The show-down between Abad and the landowner representatives in Congress occurred over the issue of landowner applications to convert agricultural lands to industrial use. At the centre of the controversy was the 230 hectare Langkaan Estate in Dasmariñas, Cavite, owned by the government's National Development Corporation (NDC). In 1989, DAR municipal officers decided to acquire the estate after receiving an application from those farming the land. NDC opposed the DAR decision, announcing that it was engaged in a joint venture with the Japanese Marubeni Corporation to develop an industrial estate on the land.[82]

The NDC argued that the land was already reclassified as industrial in the Cavite land-use plan approved in 1980. José Concepcion, who as Secretary of the

Department of Trade and Industry (DTI) also headed the NDC, took a clear stand against the DAR. Secretary Abad opposed the conversion, stating that these were prime agricultural lands and only DAR could approve their conversion. He and his supporters pointed out that huge land areas had been technically reclassified as industrial during the 1980s under the authority of Imelda Marcos' Ministry of Human Settlements. If these paper reclassifications were allowed to stand in law, they argued, then vast areas of the most fertile land in the country could be exempted from agrarian reform.[83] However, on 14 February 1990, Justice Secretary Franklin Drilon offered a legal opinion stating that DAR had no jurisdiction over reclassifications approved before the passage of CARP in June 1988. In an early referendum among farmers on the estate they voted against conversion. However, a second referendum was conducted which mobilized a greater number of participants. This time they were told by the NDC-Marubeni group that they would be offered P55,000 per hectare and they approved conversion in a vote of 94 to 28. Abad's supporters argued that farmers had been paid even before the vote.[84]

Abad stood his ground and received the unqualified support of the entire spectrum of farmers' organizations in the country.[85] However, the ruling LDP party in the House led a campaign to prevent Abad's appointment, accusing him of being too pro-farmer. They assumed the rhetoric of nationalism and charged that Abad was against industrialization.[86] The President decided to endorse the DTI position on the land conversion issue, saying only that the 28 farmers who were against it should be allowed to keep their farms. Abad said that he would abide by her decision and Aquino asked Congress to approve Abad's appointment.[87] However, Congress continued to defer their decision. José Cojuangco mobilized the ruling LDP party members in Congress, the League of Mayors and the League of Governors in opposition to Abad. Secretaries Bacani and Drilon also pronounced their disapproval of DAR's treatment of the land conversion issue.[88] House Speaker Ramon Mitra, in opposing Abad's appointment, referred to the advocates of the liberal approach in DAR as leftists and communists.[89]

On 1 April 1990, landowners organized in the Land Upmost Productivity Association, whose acronym LUPA means land, held their national convention. LUPA president, Horacio Marasigan, expressed the landowners' opposition to Abad, saying that they would rather tolerate the suspended Undersecretary Jun Medina as DAR chief.[90] Encouraged by the overall political climate, a group of DAR employees petitioned Congress to oppose Abad's appointment, on the grounds that he was reorganizing the DAR to 'build a team' of officials around his own approach to reform. The group pronounced its support for Undersecretary Benjamin T. Leong.[91]

After the Commission on Appointments deferred action on Abad's case for the seventh time, on 4 April 1990 the Secretary resigned. Leong was subsequently appointed by the President without opposition. Most of the advocates of the liberal approach to reform still working in DAR saw Abad's departure as the final straw. They organized a demonstration in front of DAR's central office holding up a mock coffin proclaiming the 'death of agrarian reform'.[92] Most of them resigned their posts during the following months. Peasant organizations allied in the CPAR condemned the government for forcing Abad's resignation.[93] This brought to an end the division within the executive institutions of the state between the advocates of the conservative and liberal approach. The triumph of the conservatives within the state was complete.

Just one month later, the government arrested peasant leader Jaime Tadeo, chairman of the KMP.[94] The government had clearly been looking for a way to silence Tadeo after his outspoken opposition to the Constitution in 1986 and his leadership of the peasant movement in opposing the government's stand on agrarian reform. He had been charged with sedition after the Mendiola Massacre in January 1987.[95] On 10 May 1990, officers of the National Bureau of Investigation gained entrance to the KMP offices by pretending to be DAR officials. Once inside, they announced their identity and told Tadeo that he was being 'invited' for questioning relating to a demonstration organized by the KMP at the DAR headquarters earlier that month. Tadeo was only arrested after he was in custody and the charge was sedition. Much to his lawyers' surprise, the government then announced that he was being held in connection with a conviction on the charge of misappropriation of funds (estafa) first levelled against him by the Marcos government in 1982.

Tadeo was originally charged with misappropriating funds of a cooperative under his management just days after he led an important demonstration against the Marcos government. According to Amnesty International, 'It was widely believed at the time that the charges were filed against Tadeo in order to silence his criticism and to weaken his organizational base'.[96] The government filed both a civil and a criminal case against Tadeo in early 1982. His case was taken up by noted human rights lawyers, including former Senator José Diokno. In 1985, the civil case was dismissed for lack of evidence.[97] Nevertheless, the government decided to pursue the criminal case, which supposedly required even more evidence for a conviction. After Tadeo was appointed to the Constitutional Commission, his lawyers believed that the old charges would be dropped.

However, on 4 May 1987, a lower court found Tadeo guilty.[98] The decision was taken while he was leading a campaign criticising the President's draft executive order on agrarian reform. The Court of Appeals upheld the decision in January 1989.[99] In January 1990 the 2nd Division of the Supreme Court refused to review the case and on 25 April 1990 refused a motion for reconsideration. Ironically, one of the judges who sat in judgement on Tadeo was Associate Justice Florenz D. Regalado, who had also participated in the Constitutional Commission. Regalado was one of the most outspoken advocates of landowners' rights on the Constitutional Commission and one of those most opposed to Tadeo's views on agrarian reform.[100]

After his arrest, Tadeo was taken to the maximum security National Penitentiary at Muntinlupa, just outside Manila. After his incarceration, the government dropped all charges related to his political activities. However, the peasant leader was condemned to serve a sentence of 4 to 18 years branded as a criminal. Clearly, the government was attempting to label Tadeo as a criminal in order to discredit him in the eyes of the peasants and the public at large. His imprisonment was denounced by the entire peasant movement, as well as human rights activists at home and abroad. Despite the fact that his only hope for release was a presidential pardon, a year after he was imprisoned Tadeo maintained his vigorous criticism of President Aquino, saying that she 'is running the country like her own *hacienda*'. He even managed to laugh at his jailer, saying, 'I asked Cory Aquino for land for the peasants and she gave me "Muntinlupa", which in Tagalog means the 'smallest piece of land'.

In the eyes of President Aquino, Tadeo should no doubt have shown gratitude for his appointment to the Constitutional Commission by toning down his criticisms of the government. Tadeo's victimisation seemed to be at least partly due to the vindictiveness of a President who could not adequately respond to his well argued demands for agrarian reform and instead allowed his imprisonment for a criminal charge brought almost a decade earlier by the Marcos government.

10.3 Landowners, domestic agribusiness and the transnationals

The alliance in the state around the conservative approach to reform was a reflection of the dominant position of landowning families and corporations in society. The concentration of control over agricultural land in the hands of a relatively small portion of the population was coupled with other important oligopolies in the rural economy. The unequal distribution of economic power was mirrored by the concentration of political power in the political clans that dominated Congress. As the landowners and agribusiness corporations sought to delay and slow down the implementation of CARP, they used its provisions on corporate stock-sharing, commercial crop exemptions and lease-back arrangements to their own advantage. While doing all that they could to weaken DAR in the short-term, they also began to lay out their own plans for the future.

10.3.1 Landowners, rural oligopolies and political clans

By the late 1980s, aside from the significant concentration of control over land, there were also important oligopolies at every level of production and trading in agriculture. This made agriculture profitable to a relatively small number of elite families, while the sector as a whole received low priority in terms of investment, credit and research and development. The largest landowners and agricultural corporations concentrated whatever resources they put into agriculture on the production, and especially trading, of export commodities, often in combination with transnational capital.[101] The investments of these families and companies in agriculture and agricultural trade was concentrated on those commodities that enjoyed high prices in the international market. Table 10.2 shows the relative growth of particular high value export products.

Table 10.2: Top 25 Agricultural Exports (1980-1986 By Growth Rate)*

| Commodity | (Value US$ '000) | | Growth Rate |
	1980	1986	(%)**
Shrimps and Prawns	20,681.49	130,828.09	30.85
Ramie - Raw/Semi-Processed	4,559.78	22,257.58	30.24
Coffee (Robusta)	-	104,722.58	-
Seaweeds - Dried	8,339.91	22,477.19	17.97
Pineapples - Fresh	10,131.91	20,613.62	12.57
Pineapple Concentrates	9,014.03	18,237.51	12.46
Banana Crackers & Chips	4,814.96	9,634.51	12.26
Tuna - processed	29,486.33	49,614.69	9.06
Natural Rubber	8,505.82	10,056.56	2.83
Bananas - Fresh	114,184.43	130,221.64	2.21
Mangoes - Fresh	6,482.61	6,956.36	1.18
Pineapples - in Syrup	82,098.05	83,517.00	0.29
Coconut Oil - Residue	81,390.54	74,757.22	-1.41
Tobacco - Unmanufactured	28,819.04	20,967.43	-5.16
Coconut Oil - Crude	536,834.82	326,298.25	-7.96
Cocoa	17,912.26	10,666.54	-8.28
Abaca - Hand-stripped	18,042.30	9,183.62	-10.64
Molasses - Indelible	32,868.18	16,384.44	-10.96
Cocoa Butter - Fat & Oil	16,575.86	7,243.57	-12.89
Desicated Coconut	115,991.23	44,269.47	-14.83
Copra (not flour/meals)	47,253.05	17,599.62	-15.18
Lauan - White (rough)	81,457.72	23,281.34	-18.84
Coffee (Ecelsa, Liberica)	43,795.79	12,345.17	-19.03
Tuna - Frozen	68,326.17	13,464.26	-23.72
Centrifugal Sugar	557,274.34	86,795.58	-26.65

*The choice of commodity is based on top 25 in 1986
**Compounded annual Growth Rates. Source: Agribusiness Fact Book 1986. Manila: Centre for Research and Communications, 1987, p. 191.

Oligopolistic power was not limited to national economic and political actors, but was also exercised on a smaller scale at the provincial, municipal and *barrio* levels. In the rice sector, the Philippine Peasant Institute (PPI) played a major role in exposing the existence of a cartel of seven rice trading firms, which it claimed was capable of fixing the price of rice as it controlled a network stretching out to the provinces.[102] Small farmers and tenants were at the mercy of local merchants, who often sold the inputs for farming, bought the produce after harvest and controlled the *barrio* folk through a web of unending debt in the process. Small farmers paid high prices for inputs and received low prices for their harvest.[103] The small amount of credit extended to the agricultural sector went mainly to large landowners. Peasants were forced to rely on informal lenders, be they merchants, moneylenders, big landowners or their more well-off small-owner neighbours.[104]

Typically elite families on the provincial level derived their wealth from landownership, export-oriented crop production, logging concessions, control over provincial transport (including bus-lines, port facilities and trucking), trade in agricultural inputs and produce, ownership of rice mills and granaries, ranching, construction and control over *huweteng* (gambling rackets). Elite clans powerful at the national level had branches into all of these provincial sources of wealth and were also involved in urban real estate, the wholesale/retail trade, shipping, agricultural and non-agricultural exports, protected manufacturing enterprises, mining concessions and joint ventures with foreign corporations in both production and commerce.

The 1989 profile of landowners with holdings of over 50 hectares in one town in Sorsogon demonstrates the extent to which those who monopolized control over land were uninvolved in agriculture and had access to other major sources of income (Table 10.3). There were likely to be more owners with large landholdings in the town who had either not registered with DAR, or who had divided titles among relatives and friends. Nevertheless, the peasants residing there felt that the sample was representative. Only Mateo appeared to be actively involved in managing his coconut plantation, and his family earned most of its income from the operation of a lucrative restaurant franchise with the principal bus company servicing the province. They also owned one of the province's most important holiday resorts.[105]

The commanding role played by landowners, big merchants and agribusiness corporations in the rural economy ensured their dominance within the political realm. Even the agribusiness corporations were keen to cultivate their relations with local political clans and to look after their position in local government. The head of NDC-Guthrie's Community Relations Department, José Bunilla, was elected vice-mayor in the municipality where the plantation was located. Some of its foremen sat on local *barangay* councils.[106]

The landowner lobby in Congress had decided to vote for the agrarian reform law because they believed that in its final version the law would scarcely be able to touch private agricultural estates before the end of the Aquino administration. While some landowners mounted an early challenge to the law in the Supreme Court, in 1989 Eduardo Hernandez, chairman of the Council of Agricultural Producers in the Philippines, argued that it was not time for a court challenge. He pointed out that the Court was highly susceptible to the dominant political climate. There would be time enough later to challenge the constitutionality of CARP with regard to the expropriation of private lands.[107]

However, as early as 1990 the Supreme Court began to issue rulings in favour of the landowners which were likely to delay CARP implementation still further. First, the Court ruled that lands could only be transferred from owners to the government upon payment of full compensation. Secondly, landowners covered by PD27 who were unable to exercise their right to retain lands would be granted retention rights under the new law. This gave reality to the early fears of FFF leader Jeremias Montemayor that the new law would allow landowners covered by the Marcos programme to reclaim lands transferred to beneficiaries. Finally, the Court granted an injunction to livestock, swine and poultry farmers against coverage of their land by CARP.[108]

It was less likely that any amendments to the law would be passed by

Table 10.3: Profile Owners: Landholdings Over 50 Hectares Irosin, Sorsogon (Registered with DAR 1989)

Name of Owner	Hectares	Profession	Manner Acquired	Crops & Residence
Astillero, Ireneo	214.2	Deceased		Tenanted coconut/abaca. Family stays in town & Manila.
Calinisan, Melanio	102.9	Contractor	Married into landed family.	Tenanted coconut/abaca/citrus and rice. Stays in town.
De Castro, Rosita	65.1	Town handicraft business.		Coconut land. Stays in town.
Dorotan, Vicente	64.0	Physician	Hacendero family.	Control of land divided among heirs.
Erquiaga Development Corporation	394.4		Santiago Erquiaga owned. His widow married Meyer.	Idle: 1 caretaker. Mostly upland. Under VOS, but challenged by Pilar landowner Mary Ann Reynoso.
Gabito, Jesus	60.8	Grocery/ Merchant.	Bought from Erquiaga.	Kalamansi.
Gacias, Gleceria G.	77.4	Professionals		1/3 rice; 2/3 coconut. Stays in town.
Gallanosa, Isidro	74.8	Deceased	Hacendero family.	Lost control of lands.
Gallanosa, Pedro	60.8		Son of Isidro.	Peasants say family only controls house lot now.
Gamis, Macario	50.1	Deceased.	Was one of biggest owners	Tenanted coconut and rice. Lived in Gabao as does widow.
Imperial, Gerardo	55.3	Bakery.		Stays in town. More land in Bulan.
Locsin, Mariano	106.1	Deceased	Land acquired in part through arienda system (lending to poor farmers).	Mainly coconut. Family always resided Legaspi City. Land under VOS.
Mateo, Suzette G.	239.7	Restaurant chain & holiday resort.	Father acquired land 1954-80. Sold 6 ha.s in Rizal to buy 500 here.Hot springs bought from Erquiaga.	Coconut w/coffee, banana. Brother manages farm.
Michelena, Narciso	91.0	Pharmacy/ Video	Coconut/abaca/small rice.	Stays in town. Brother is mayor.
Ortube Development Corporation	298.5	Political Family		Coconut/abaca
Planca & Sons	81.4			Owner lives in Gabao.
Total	**2036.5**	**(Approximately 16% of total farm area in Irosin)**		

Source: DAR, Provincial Office, Sorsogon. Interviews landowners and peasants in Irosin, March 1989.

Congress until after the 1992 elections. Representative Hortensia Starke said that rather than embarrass President Aquino, the landowners would simply work to delay the implementation of the law. Amendments could be made to it after the 1992 elections, when a new President and Senate would be more favourable to the process.[109] Representative José Cojuangco nevertheless introduced a number of amendments in the House which, although they were all delegated to the Agrarian Reform Committee for debate, demonstrated the direction in which the landowners hoped to modify the legislation.

Cojuangco's plans to amend the law focused principally on implementation being decentralised to provincial governments or Congressional districts.[110] He had worked for the insertion of the Provincial Agrarian Reform Councils in RA6657. They were the only body empowered with accelerating the implementation of CARP. They were also placed in charge of coordinating with the private sector and NGOs. The political implications were important since it would be these bodies that could undertake a process of selection of NGOs in the future. According to Gerry Bulatao, almost 85 per cent of the PARCONs were set up by mid-1989, but they remained largely inactive.[111] This was the thrust behind the proposals of Governor Lacson in Negros Occidental, the centre of sugar production in the country. In fact, in March 1989 he succeeded in winning DAR acquiescence to his '10 per cent Now!' programme, which would allow landowners to voluntarily offer 10 per cent of their land to CARP, thus avoiding coverage of the remainder of their lands until some future date.[112] However, the Governor said that he would support all efforts to amend CARP and allocate total control over the programme to provincial authorities.[113]

As early as April 1990, landowners invited eight presidential hopefuls to speak at one of their national conventions and vowed to support only those candidates in the 1992 elections who would be responsive to their demands around CARP. Only Vice-President Laurel and Senator Enrile attended, but other candidates were likely to take the landowners seriously as the elections approached.[114] The landowners remained an important lobby group and major actors within the provincial patronage networks at the heart of the electoral system. Since most large landowners were convinced that no amendments would be possible until after the 1992 elections, they concentrated on employing those provisions in the law that would safeguard their control over their lands in the meantime.

10.3.2 Corporate stock-sharing and Hacienda Luisita

After the passage of the agrarian reform law, the biggest landowners and agribusiness corporations turned their eyes to the President's family estate, Hacienda Luisita, and its proposal to comply with CARP through corporate stock-sharing. Throughout the debate over reform, the President's family along with other large landowning interests had worked hard to include this provision. According to Rolando Dy of the Center for Research and Communication, the plan was progressive in that it would force corporate farms to increase their capital investment in their farms or lose control of the enterprise to their workers.[115] However, a closer examination of the application of the plan to the country's most talked-about corporate farm, Hacienda Luisita, demonstrates the fallacy of Dy's argument. In fact, given accepted and legal corporate accounting practices, it was virtually impossible under the CARP for workers to gain a majority share in any agribusiness corporation.[116]

The law allowed an existing corporate farm to establish a 'spin-off' corporation for purposes of stock distribution. The Cojuangcos established Hacienda

Luisita Inc. (HLI) on 1 August 1988, just one month after CARP was passed. It was the newest of a string of Cojuangco companies set up to profit from the formerly Tabacalera-owned properties in Tarlac. These included: the Central Azucarera de Tarlac; Tarlac Distillery Corporation; Luisita Marketing; Central Azucarera de Tarlac Reality Corporation; Luisita Realty Corporation; Luisita Golf and Country Club; the Tarlac Development Corporation (TADECO), by which the Hacienda itself was formerly owned; and José Cojuangco & Sons, which sat atop all the others and had a management contract with each of the sister companies.[117] Thus HLI became but a small part of the empire originally built in Concepcion, Tarlac, by Tabacalera.

Only 4,914 hectares of the original 6,431 hectare property were transferred to HLI from TADECO at the time that the new corporation was established. This was allowed by the law, since only the 'lands actually devoted to agricultural activities' were covered by CARP. The Cojuangco family had already transferred some of the land to other uses. The agricultural land was valued at P40,000 per hectare or a total of P196,630,000. Since this represented one-third of the new corporation's total assets, the workers at Hacienda Luisita were entitled to one-third of the shares of stock of HLI, and the Cojuangco family was guaranteed control of the corporation (Table 10.4).

The most questionable aspect of the deal was the determination of HLI's non-land assets, which made up two-thirds of the company's total assets. By inflating the value of 'non-land assets', any agribusiness corporation could ensure that non-land assets would always total more than land assets. This was what allowed the owners of Hacienda Luisita to maintain full control over the estate under the CARP. What they did was 'legal' in that it followed accepted corporate accounting practices. However, an examination of those practices demonstrates why the corporate stock-sharing programme was incompatible with the objectives of redistributive agrarian reform.

Looking at HLI's statement of assets (Table 10.4) shows clearly why it was easy for any corporation to ensure that its non-land assets were greater than its land assets. First, 'the standing crop' was counted as a non-land asset. This is one of the biggest items in any corporate farm's balance sheet. For Hacienda Luisita, it totalled approximately P103 million, or about 18 per cent of the total assets of the company. If this item alone was counted as part of the value of the land, which the law arguably should have required, then the workers would have been able to gain majority control of the company. The value of the standing crop is an extremely variable factor depending on a company's production plans, the weather, market prospects and, in the case of HLI and most agribusiness plantations, fluctuating international prices. It therefore seems to be a highly questionable basis on which to determine the value of a corporation and the ratio of wealth and ownership that should be distributed to the farmworkers to achieve 'just distribution'.

Secondly, 'Accounts due from affiliates' and 'Long-term Notes Receivable' represented payments that HLI was to receive from other Cojuangco companies.

Table 10.4 Hacienda Luisita Inc. Balance Sheet (1988-1989)

ASSETS		% of Total Assets	Amount (Pesos)
1) Total Current Assets			162,638,993
of which:			
a) Standing Crop:	103,088,495	18%	
of which:			
Raw Sugar Inventory	17,307,070		
Profit on sale of sugar	17,781,425		
Other Costs of Growing Crops[a]	68,000,000		
b) Cash on hand/in banks[a]	6,000,000	1%	
c) Accts due from affiliates[a]	8,500,000	1%	
d) Other Current Assets	45,050,498	8%	
2) Long-term Notes Receivable		5%	28,063,417
3) Property & Equipment			
Agricultural Land[b]		33%	196,630,000
Building & Machinery		14%	84,624,810
4) Other Assets			
Residential Land[c]		10%	60,462,000
Land Improvements (roads, rail, etc)[d]		10%	58,135,000
TOTAL ASSETS			**590,554,220**
LIABILITIES			
Current Liabilities[e]			199,282,758
Long Term Debt			36,140,000
Capital Stock to be issued			355,131,462
TOTAL LIABILITY (Inc. Capital Stock)			**590,554,220**

[a]Approximate, based on an extrapolation from TADECO's Balance Sheet.
[b]169 parcels with an area of 4,915.7466 ha.s, valued at P40,000,000/ha.
[c]An appraisal on 14 February 1989 of 11 lots totalling 120.9234. These lands were valued at P500,002.48/ha.
[d]187 lots totalling 265.7495, or a value of P218,758.64/ha.
[e]Includes: Notes payable and Accounts payable, icluding: Current portion long-term debt due to affiliated companies.
Source: Securities and Exchange Commission, Manila, 1989.

It would have been easy for the incorporators of HLI to ascribe a high value to charges to sister companies in order to increase the value of non-land assets. What is more, the 'Long-term Notes Receivable', worth P28 million, represented the sale of part of the Hacienda's land to the Cojuangco's Central Azucarera de Tarlac. Finally, two items included under 'Other Assets' on the HLI balance sheet show how a company could manipulate accounting practices to raise the value of 'non-agricultural land assets'. The first was a tract of 120.9 hectares of 'residential land' valued at P60,462,000, or P500,000 per hectare. This item was listed as being worth only P55,040 in TADECO's balance sheet as late as 30 June 1988. The second was a tract of 265.7 hectares of 'land improvements', covering roads, railway tracks and the like, which was valued at P58,135,000, or P218,759 per hectare. In 1988, this item was valued by TADECO at only P5,619,753.

The CRC's argument on the 'progressive nature' of this option was flawed on two counts. Firstly, the stock-sharing provision would not force the owners of corporate farms to invest more in the land. They could maintain control simply by manipulating the accounts of the corporation and ensuring that non-land assets were valued higher than agricultural land. Secondly, it is not desirable that agricultural operations in a country like the Philippines should be highly capitalized. Agrarian reform can be used as a tool for development precisely because it can encourage more intensive use of the land and the full utilization of abundant labour while economizing on scarce capital resources. From this perspective the corporate stock-sharing plan provided a means to perpetuate a model of plantation farming inappropriate to development needs in the country.

An overwhelming majority of workers (90 per cent) voted in favour of the plan in a referendum in November 1989.[118] The outcome of the vote was entirely predictable. The balance of power in the country favoured families like the Cojuangcos. The problem was not really that the farmworkers on the *hacienda* were denied the freedom of expression or the right to choose, as one peasant organization charged.[119] It was rather that farmworkers, tenants and the landless rural poor continued to be denied an environment that would allow them to identify what their choices were.[120] On 11 May 1989, DAR, the Tarlac Development Corporation, the newly formed Hacienda Luisita Inc. and the farmworkers on the Hacienda signed a Memorandum of Agreement to institute the corporate stock sharing scheme. Secretary Juico praised the deal, saying that it would serve as a model for other large estates, and would 'finally lay to rest the CARP issue at Hacienda Luisita'.[121]

Atty. Arsenio Acuña, a leader of the National Federation of Sugar Planters, said that throughout the debate on agrarian reform he 'followed Peping Cojuangco and his activities'. Acuña was teaching law in Bacolod before martial law, where he met Armando Gustilo, who later became Marcos' trusted warlord in northern Negros. In 1972 Acuña joined the firm of Marcos crony Ricardo Silverio, Philippine Finance Sterling (Philfinancing), and was soon able to put up his own finance company. When the sugar industry went into recession, he bought seven *haciendas* totalling about 1,000 hectares.[122] He said that all were originally owned by his family holding company, the Maria Clara Land Development and Holdings Corporation.[123] However, before the law was passed he incorporated each one separately.[124] For instance, his 318 hectare Hacienda Palma in the south of Negros was transferred to another family corporation, the Palma Kabankalan Agricultural Corporation, registered on 15 February 1988.[125]

While remaining opposed to CARP, Acuña was not worried for his own estates since he felt that distributing paper stocks to the workers would not significantly lessen his profits. He said that he had 100 hectares that were appropriate for prawn farming, half of which were already developed. Only one of his *haciendas* was organized by the militant trade union, the NFSW, after an eight year certification struggle. They concluded a collective agreement in September 1988, when Acuña told them that they would receive a stock certificate and their local president could attend the meetings of the company's board.[126] However, farmworkers on the *hacienda* said that DAR never met with them, nor had there been a Barangay Agrarian Reform Council established, and they had not received any stock certificate or extra payment as a result of CARP.[127]

By September 1990, DAR had received applications for corporate stock-distribution from only 83 corporations. By early 1991, the Presidential Agrarian Reform Council was ready to approve just six of these.[128] The future of the scheme was put into question with the filing of a House bill proposing to amend CARP.[129] However, the bill was probably deposited in order to create a Congressional stalemate, so that other proposed amendments from José Cojuangco would not be entertained. While DAR had earlier set a deadline for applications to the stock-sharing programme, as mandated by law, all such deadlines appear to have been abandoned in practice. There were reports of a rapid increase in the number of agricultural corporations established after the passing of EO229, but their owners probably delayed filing applications with DAR in order to wait and see just how far the programme would be implemented.

Corporate landowners also sought to exempt their lands from CARP coverage by applying for a ten-year deferment granted to those producing high-value export crops. Landowners hoped that before this period expired, the law would be changed either to extend considerably the period of deferment, or to exempt the properties permanently.[130] These corporations, and others awaiting coverage under other aspects of the law, were required to engage in production and profit sharing with their workers if their annual sales exceeded P5 million per year. The law required that they pay their employees three per cent of gross sales and ten per cent of net profits after taxes if they realized a profit.[131]

While some big landowners and corporations were displeased with this clause, it seemed to be due to accounting difficulties rather than any significant redistribution of income. Farmworkers would enjoy only an extremely meagre increase in their income, as statistics from the first year and a half of the programme demonstrated (See Table 10.5). The average income increase for farmworkers covered during this period was P71.00 per month. The highest amount received was P133.00 at the Philippine Rubber Company Inc., while among the lowest was P37.00 at the Eurasia Match Inc., owned by right-wing opposition leader, Senator Juan Ponce Enrile. The most that a worker could receive at Hacienda Luisita before the adoption of the corporate stock-sharing programme was P73 per month.

Very few firms complied with this provision of CARP. While it was reported

Table 10.5: Production/Profit Sharing Compliance 15 March 1989

CORPORATION	CROP	AREA (Ha.)	PROVINCE	PRODUCTION SHARING EO229 (Pesos)	PRODUCTION SHARING RA6657EO+CARP* (Pesos)	PROFIT SHARING RA6657 (Pesos)	TOTAL (Pesos)	NUMBER Benef	AMOUNT Per/Ben (Pesos)	AMOUNT Per/Ben/Month (Pesos)
P.B. Dizon & Sons	Banana	-	Davao d.N	860972	0	0	860972	880	978	P 61
Phil. Rubber Proj. Co Inc	Rubber	-	Zamboanga S.	0	594144	124104	718248	337	2131	P 133
Mindanao Rubber Co. Inc	Rubber	-	Zamboanga S.	0	503724	47973	551697	273	2021	P 126
Zamboanga Rubber Co.	Rubber	-	Zamboanga S.	0	327933	0	327933	229	1432	P 89
Dole Phils	Pinneapple	-	S. Cotabato	4713325	2215670	769278	7297273	8000	912	P 57
King Plantation Co.	Copra/Rubber Charcoal/Cattle Piggery/Nuts	852	S. Cotabato	0	121135	0	121135	159	762	P 47
San Miguel Corp	Feed/Lives	252	S. Cotabato	0	3029900	0	3859200	463	769	P 48
San Miguel Corp	Hyb. Corn	194	S. Cotabato	84800	67200	0	152000	221	687	P 43
San Jose Sugar Dev. Corp	Sugar	-	Negros Occ.	423563	364268	0	787831	869	907	P 57
Gamboa Hermanos Inc.	Sugar	-	Negros Occ.	890789	1308375	0	2191164	1168	1883	P 117
C-J Yulo & Sons Inc	Sugar/Coconut Coffee	-	Laguna	0	0	299556	299556	429	698	P 44
Eurasia Match Inc (Enrile)	Copra/Cacao Rubber/Pepper	969	Basilan	300711	0	0	300711	500	601	P 37
Cocoland Development Corp	Coco/Cacao Coffee/Pepper	1690	Basilan	403568	0	0	403568	550	734	P 45
Tarlac Development Corp	Sugar	-	Tarlac	5489818	0	0	5489818	4683	1172	P 73
Golden Farms Inc	Banana	-	Davao	0	566204	0	566204	987	574	P 72†
Checkered Farms Inc.	Banana	-	Davao	544728	0	0	544728	1230	443	P 56†
Diamond Farms Inc.	Banana	-	Davao	456871	0	0	456871	1955	234	P 30†

* Aggregate Period is 29 August 1987 to 31 December 1988.

† The Amount paid per beneficiary per month is doubled since these companies only paid 50% of what was due to their workers.

Source: Department of Agrarian Reform. 15 March 1989.

that 64 firms had submitted documents to DAR by 15 March 1989, only 21 had made any payments to their workers, and 34 submitted no more than the name of their corporation.[132] By December 1990, 56 companies had reported compliance with the scheme. DAR said that these companies had distributed P99.71 million in profit shares to some 76,032 beneficiaries.[133] Considering that the programme covered 41 months in arrears, it meant that each beneficiary had received an average increase in their income of only P31.99 per month. Profit sharing could easily be avoided through accounting practices that reduced profits to a minimum. Given DAR's difficulties in accomplishing its targets, it seemed unlikely that serious progress would be made in monitoring this aspect of the programme.

10.3.3 Transnationals and the workers' cooperatives

Another means whereby corporations could comply with CARP was to redistribute ownership of the land they farmed to cooperatives formed by their employees. The cooperatives would then engage in a 'lease-back' arrangement whereby the employees themselves would earn the rental income from the land. This formula was encouraged on the government-owned lands leased by transnational corporations (TNCs), like Dole and Del Monte. The TNCs had long enjoyed a favoured status in Philippine agriculture and were able to lease lands from government at nominal rates. While CARP was designed to increase the rental fees paid by these corporations and redirect rental income to the corporate employees, it was also meant to reassure the companies that they had a future in the country. Under the new law, there was no limit to the amount of lands that a foreign or domestic agribusiness corporation could lease from Filipino landowners. The Department of Agrarian Reform established cooperatives among the employees of the TNCs as part of a general thrust in CARP implementation to revive and expand the moribund government-sponsored cooperative movement of the Marcos years.

The TNCs came into the public eye soon after the passage of CARP when farmers in Impasug-ong, Bukidnon, launched a campaign to 'Stop the Expansion and Exploitation by Del Monte' (SEED). The controversy reached the national newspapers just a month after CARP was signed, when farmers stood in front of Del Monte bulldozers that were attempting to plough 93 hectares of land as part of an expansion area for the corporation's giant pineapple operations in the province.[134] The Del Monte pineapple operation in the community totalled some 500 hectares of land first leased by the company from private owners in 1984. According to SEED organizers, protesters who met with the Del Monte officials in 1984 were told that the company would not expand beyond the 500 hectares.

Farmers charged that the new expansion drive had begun in 1987 as an attempt to circumvent agrarian reform. They said that the company was leasing land from absentee owners whose land was foreclosable by the banks. Tenants cultivating the land would be expelled in order to plant it to pineapples.

Thereafter, such land could be exempted from CARP coverage by the ten-year deferment for commercial crops. The SEED campaign organizers also claimed that the expansion of pineapple production would displace local food production, introduce chemicals harmful to surrounding farmers and disrupt the life of the Lumad, or indigenous peoples' communities, in the area. The company denied all the farmers' accusations and affirmed its rights to lease land from any willing private landowner. They asserted that a meeting of the tribal council in Impasug-ong in 1987 had welcomed the corporate expansion.

Campaign organizers succeeded in obtaining the support of local municipal councils, Church organizers and members of Congress, thus forcing the government to take action. In a meeting between the company, campaign organizers and DAR officials it was agreed that no further expansion would be carried out until DAR set guidelines governing the implementation of agrarian reform on lands leased by multinational corporations. However, the implementation of CARP on the lands farmed by the TNCs concentrated almost exclusively on the rights of the corporation and its workers, providing little solace to farmers worried about the future expansion of the plantations' operations.

Under CARP, the government was mandated to immediately distribute to workers' cooperatives government-owned land leased to multi-national corporations. An initial round of contacts with the management of Dole Philippines, Del Monte Philippines and the National Development Corporation-Guthrie Plantations, all located in Mindanao, was undertaken by DAR shortly after the law was passed. In September 1988, the National Development Corporation (NDC) came to an agreement with DAR to 'sell' a portion of the lands leased by the corporations to the government for redistribution under CARP.[135] In what appeared to be a move to gain early positive publicity for the CARP, DAR decided to effect a rapid transfer of the lands to worker cooperatives and to organize a Presidential visit to Mindanao to distribute the Certificate of Land Ownership Awards (CLOAs) at the earliest possible date.

Distributing collective titles to the land would guarantee that the TNC estates would not be broken up. However, the law mandated that workers should be able to choose whether to receive collective title to the land through cooperatives or to receive individual titles. DAR had to ensure at least formal compliance from the workers and the establishment of cooperatives on each of the plantations. The cooperatives set up by the DAR at Del Monte and NDC-Guthrie plantations in December 1988 were good examples of the character of the new cooperative movement that emerged through the CARP.

On 29 July 1988, shortly after the law was passed, Secretary Juico visited the 19,000 hectare Del Monte pineapple plantation in Bukidnon to announce that it would be one of the first areas to be covered by CARP. Meetings were subsequently held with management to obtain a list of the work-force and determine who would be qualified to receive land, and to begin discussing the company's future rental payments to the workers. According to the leader of the cooperative at Del Monte, the employees did not hear from DAR officials again until 30 November.[136] That day DAR provincial director, Mrs. Antonieta R. Borra, arrived at the plantation and notified management and the union that the President would be visiting Mindanao in three weeks to distribute land titles to the workers.[137] A cooperative therefore had to be established immediately and she made arrangements to return the following day to preside over its incorporation.

Despite the requirement that incorporators of a cooperative should be democratically elected by the workers, the board and presidents of the two unions on the plantation, the WATU and the ALU, quickly met and chose 50 delegates to act as 'incorporators'.[138] Thirty-two were selected from the plantation and 18 from the cannery. By-laws and articles of incorporation prepared beforehand by DAR lawyers were signed on 1 December 1988.[139] Mr. Reynor D. Casiño, who was chosen as the cooperative's president, worked in the management. He was directly subordinate to Adrian Pabayo, Industrial and Community Relations Manager, who was the major actor on the company's side in negotiating with the cooperative over the price that the company would pay to lease the land.

Not only was the cooperative set up overnight, it appeared to be under the direct influence, if not control, of the management. Even DAR Region X Director, Jun Limbo, said that the elections were characterised by 'automatic nominations'. He said that it was clear that the 'management dictates', but added that it was 'understandable that management will want to have their choice', since they had invested so much in the plantation.[140] Workers commented that they did not understand how the cooperative was established and were not consulted about its by-laws and policies.[141]

At the two 4,000 hectare NDC-Guthrie oil palm plantations in Agusan del Sur a similar situation developed.[142] There DAR's work to establish separate cooperatives on each of the plantations complemented corporate officials' efforts to ensure 'labour peace' and the subordination of labour organization to the management. On NDC-Guthrie Estates Inc. (NGEI), the militant Kilusang Mayo Uno (KMU) had succeeded in winning the union elections, while NDC-Guthrie Plantations Inc. (NGPI) was still unionized with the much more timid Federation for Free Workers (FFW). Cesar Alaban, Deputy Manager in charge of NGPI, said that having two unions caused certain complications and asserted the management's preference for the FFW. However, he added, 'But [it] works two ways. If you have two unions there will be division'.[143]

DAR began setting up the cooperatives in Agusan del Sur as early as September 1988. Together with the management, they organized a meeting of about 25 *kapataz* (foremen) and supervisors at NGPI to act as a core group for organizing the cooperative. DAR explained the advantages of receiving the lands under a collective title and leasing them back to the company rather than receiving individual titles. DAR presented the meeting with the draft articles of incorporation and, given the composition of those present, they decided to change the draft allowing management personnel as well as workers to be active members of the cooperative. While the incorporators did stipulate that managers with the power to hire and fire workers would be excluded, in practice this referred only to the then General Manager, John Lee, while all the rest of upper-level management was allowed to participate. This core group then called a meeting of workers for 1 December 1988.

The management and the core group mobilized about 400 workers to attend the meeting, or 52 per cent of the 769 employees who qualified for cooperative membership.[144] They elected nine members to the cooperative's board, ensuring that there were two representatives from each of the plantation's four 1,000 hectare divisions and one from the mill. The vote, made with raised hands rather than by secret ballot as DAR had suggested, elected to the board five supervisors, two *kapataz* and only two general workers.[145] Joel Benedicto, a Senior Field Supervisor, was elected president of the cooperative.[146] At the company's other plantation, NGEI, a similar cooperative was established which by-passed the militant trade union altogether.

While DAR prohibited union officials from being elected to leading positions within the new cooperatives, they sanctioned the election of management personnel. DAR Undersecretary Salvador Pejo, argued that union members had been excluded because, 'My real objective was completely free beneficiary organizations who could really decide for themselves'.[147] DAR's action might be interpreted as a means to by-pass the many 'yellow' unions found in the agribusiness sector, but their decision to allow management participation in the cooperatives belies such a conclusion. In fact DAR Region X Director, Jun Limbo, saw the cooperatives as a means to undermine radical trade-unionism, saying, 'We expect that the unions will disappear if the cooperatives are firmly established'.[148]

At first it appeared that DAR would establish the same kind of cooperative at the 12,000 hectare Dole pineapple plantation in South Cotabato, which was unionized by the militant National Federation of Labour, affiliated to the KMU.[149] In June 1988, Undersecretary Pejo and Assistant Secretary Tamparong contacted Bong Malonzo, national leader of the NFL, to form a task force on the implementation of CARP at Dole, chaired by NFL Deputy head Abrahim Dar. After a series of meetings, on 29 November 1988 about 30 employees gathered at the home of one of the management employees involved in the task force to form the cooperative. The personnel department of the company participated in inviting employees to attend. DAR informed the meeting of the ban on union officials being elected as officers of the cooperative. Mr. Dar was incensed and walked out of the meeting. The meeting elected four representatives of the cannery workers, two from the finance department, one from engineering, two from the operations unit, two industrial workers and only four agricultural workers.

The union threatened industrial action and protests if DAR recognized the cooperative. With the president due to visit in less than two weeks, South Cotabato Governor Ismael D. Sueno and DAR Region XI Director Delugdug intervened in the debate. On 3 December 1988, they held a meeting with union representatives and the original cooperative board, and it was agreed to hold another election where 11 of the 15 board members would come from among the hourly paid workers who made up 73 per cent of the work-force, three from the salaried employees and one from management.[150] NFL officials later boasted, 'The control of the DARBCI [Dole Agrarian Reform Beneficiaries Cooperative, Inc.] is under control of the union'.[151] While the cooperatives at Del Monte and NDC-Guthrie appeared to be creatures of the management, the cooperative at Dole was evidently an instrument of the union. Nowhere did the cooperatives appear to be autonomous organizations of farmworkers making informed decisions about the future of the lands over which they received titles.

On 12 December, President Aquino visited Butuan City in Agusan del Norte and South Cotabato to preside over the distribution of Certificate of Land Ownership Awards (CLOAs) covering 24,250 hectares to representatives of the cooperatives at Del Monte, the NDC-Guthrie plantations and Dole (Table 10.6). Although the CLOAs were meant to cover a majority of the lands leased by these companies from the NDC, the worker cooperatives did not immediately receive title to the entire amount. Firstly, CARP allowed each corporation to maintain their old lease on 1,000 hectares of the government land until 1992. Secondly, DAR had trouble arranging for legal titles over the portion of lands to be transferred.

The cooperative at Dole received the legal title to only 67 per cent of the land covered by the President's CLOA (Table 10.6).[152] Director Dalugdug explained that NDC had leased 530 lots to Dole and many of these were untitled. He said that NDC had never bothered to properly title these lots after they obtained them from original owners or settlers who had either sold them 'willingly or were coerced'. In fact, a group of about 100 former owners were protesting the distribution of these lands to the worker cooperative at Dole.[153] Given the history of land acquisition at the NDC-Guthrie estates, similar protests were lodged with DAR by owners who said that they were compelled to sell to the NDC when the plantation was established in the late 1970s.

Thirdly, under CARP, the TNCs were allowed to maintain existing leases with private owners until their lease expired, but not for more than ten years. However, the Provincial Agrarian Reform Officer in Bukidnon, Antonieta Borra, said that the law was contradictory, because private owners of land planted to pineapple were allowed to apply for commercial crop deferment for a minimum of ten years. She said that she told Del Monte management that they should advise the owners who were leasing land to them to apply for this deferment.[154] In Del Monte's case, the majority of its land was leased from private owners, while for Dole the figure was about 26 per cent (Table 10.6). According to members of the cooperative, much of this land was owned by company officials.[155] It seemed likely that the TNCs would not have to significantly readjust their relations with private landowners for at least ten years.

Table 10.6 Land Transfer, TNCs in Mindanao (1988)

	Dole	Del Monte	NDC-Guthrie NGPI	NGEI	Total
Privately Owned (Hectares)	3185	10465	0	0	13650
NDC Owned (Hectares)	9124	8700	4249	4081	26153
Total Area	**12309**	**19165**	**4249**	**4081**	**39804**
NDC Area Purchased	**8964**	**8020**	**3348**	**3918**	**24250**
Title Received[a]	5976				
Still to Receive	2988				
NDC Area Not Purchased[b]	**160**	**680**	**901**	**163**	**1904**
Total Employees	8831	10617	1003	852	21303
Beneficiaries of Transfer	7063	8955	706	662	17386
Lease Rate with NDC (per ha.)[c]	800	760	567		
Lease Rate private (per ha.)	1500	1500			
Price (per ha.) paid to NDC[d]	8000	8000	6000	6000	

[a]DARBCI members, Interview, 8 May 1989, reported area on land title.
[b]Del Monte management said they retained 1,000 hectares of NDC land in Camp Philips (Inteview, Adrian Pabayo, 24 May 1989).
[c]The rent paid by NDC-Guthrie was supplemented with 1.5% of sales (Interview NGPI Cooperative, 29 May 1989). DAR placed it at P1,000 per ha.
[d]Paid out of CARP budget to NDC.
Source: DAR, 'A Historic Visit to South Cotabato and Butuan City' 12 December 1988; price per hectares reported in *Philippine Daily Inquirer* (14 February 1989).

Negotiations with the companies over the 'lease-back' rental rate that they would have to pay for land covered by CARP began in mid–October 1989, even before the cooperatives were formed.[156] DAR began the negotiations by meeting with Del Monte and Dole together. Of course, the two TNCs put forward a unified position, arguing that they could not rent the lands for more than what they paid private landowners, which was P1,500 per hectare. By December, they raised this to P1,770 by adding a P200 production bonus and an offer to pay land tax, which could increase at seven per cent per annum, with a lease lasting 12 years.[157] DAR's initial position was for a rental rate of P4,500 per hectare, increasing in line with inflation and a lease lasting nine years. NDC-Guthrie was asking for a 25 year lease at P600 per hectare with a production bonus of between P300 and P1,200.[158]

Not surprisingly, on 21 February 1989 the Del Monte cooperative, which was headed by Rey Casiño, the direct subordinate of Adrian Pabayo who was part of the management's negotiating team, signed a 'growers' contract' conceding to all of the management's demands. They even increased the time period of the lease to 25 years.[159] The company was furious when Secretary Juico wrote to say that he was suspending action on the 'growers' contract' because the rental period was too long and the rental rate along with the annual increment were too small.[160] The company argued that both national and local DAR officials

343

had told them to proceed with negotiations with the cooperative, and that if freely entered into by both parties DAR would not interfere.[161] The local DAR provincial chief, Antonieta Borra, was very sympathetic with the company, which she said was being reasonable and providing many benefits to their workers. She advised the company to convince DAR Central Office by explaining the benefits that workers would receive.[162]

The cooperative at NGPI in Agusan del Sur was just as accommodating, saying simply that they would not even ask for negotiation over the lease-back price as long as the company proposed at least P1,000 per hectare.[163] Only the cooperative at Dole, which was independent of the management, decided to publicly confront the corporation and demand a P7,000 per hectare lease to last only three years, in order to keep their options open in terms of transforming the plantation to another form of production. In addition, they asked for 12 per cent of net profits, that 75 per cent of labour requirements be allocated to the cooperative, that they be given an exclusive contract for hauling fruits, and that a 300 hectare experimental farm be set aside for their use.[164] Dole Industrial Relations chief Mani Lopez laughed in response to this proposal, saying, 'No crop in the Philippines can give you a return big enough to allow such a rental fee...We couldn't think of such a rent unless they are silver-plated pineapples'. He said, 'CARP is a headache', but believed that in the end the employees would be reasonable, arguing that these demands were coming 'from the outside', and singling out NFL national leader Bong Malonzo.[165]

The Dole cooperative remained convinced that they could extract a far higher rental rate from the company than it was offering, and were certain that the company would not pick up and move production to Thailand or Kenya as it was threatening. However, their position was weakened by the existence of the management dominated cooperative at Del Monte. The controversy proved embarrassing for the central government, which had wanted to use the distribution of titles over land rented by TNCs as positive propaganda for the CARP. Secretary Juico and Undersecretary Pejo, who had both been involved with DAR's negotiations with the TNCs, believed that the companies were involved in promoting the media hysteria around the Garchitorena land scam leading to their ouster.[166] In August 1989, Secretary Santiago was more accommodating, saying, 'If the farmers find the terms of such an arrangement beneficial, there is no moral basis for the Government to intervene'.[167] During his short tenure at DAR, Abad was not outspoken on the continuing controversy over the lease-back negotiations. The liberal reformers recognized that workers on the plantations were already better paid than most surrounding workers and felt that the whole strategy of covering these estates first was wrong.[168]

By January 1990, Dole workers were so frustrated over the DAR's lack of support in their efforts to negotiate a land lease agreement with the company that they declared their intention to return to the government the land granted to them under CARP.[169] Such an action would have been extremely embarrassing to DAR and the government. In October 1990, DAR Secretary Benjamin Leong attempted to bring the matter to a conclusion, stating that the Department would mandate a contract for both corporations providing for a P3,000 per hectare rental rate to be increased at seven per cent per annum, with a special provision for 'extraordinary inflation' that would require a greater annual increment. In addition, there would be a P200 production bonus per hectare and the lease would last for ten years, with the companies paying property taxes.[170] However, Del Monte had already been paying its cooperative according to the 'grower contract' signed in 1989, and along with Dole, they were likely to challenge DAR's decision in the courts.

DAR had originally decided to concentrate on the government-owned TNC lands in order to achieve early positive publicity for the CARP. However, because their conservative framework placed so little importance on the position of beneficiaries, the hastily formed cooperatives were generally dominated by management. It was the outspoken and uncompromising position of the Dole workers' cooperative, only formed due to the strength of their militant union, which upset the plans for speedy implementation. The cooperatives formed at Del Monte and NDC-Guthrie were the norm under CARP and resembled the organization of workers at Hacienda Luisita. In fact, there appeared to be a concerted effort to promote such pliant cooperatives in other aspects of CARP implementation.

The government promoted with great fanfare the cooperative established in Tarlac by former NPA leader Burnabe Buscayno, known as Commander Dante, who had decided to support President Aquino upon his release from prison in 1986. The cooperative brought together 5,000 farmers tilling 10,000 hectares in the Tarlac Integrated People's Livelihood Program and Foundation established between August and October 1988. With generous loans from the Land Bank and provision of support services by government, farmers in Dante's cooperative were reported to have been able to triple their rice production.[171] Dante told one interviewer, 'We have eliminated four layers of profiteers between the farmers and the consumers'.[172] However, while the positive reports about the cooperative no doubt reflected a real success story, it was highly unlikely that such a model could be reproduced elsewhere.

First, as long-time NPA commander, Dante had a wide following in Tarlac built up through years of underground organizing. The favourable terrain for the establishment of his cooperative was therefore a direct result of the earlier revolutionary work. Second, establishing a cooperative of that size impinges on the interests of local money-lenders and merchants. Dante had the protection of the President and her family's political network in Tarlac which kept local oligopolists at a distance. Finally, he had the support of the military who were using him as an example of the 'rebel returned to the fold'. Throughout 1988 and 1989, Dante appeared on full-page advertisements in the Manila press promoting the Land Bank. Dante's cooperative was therefore unique.

During 1989, under the auspices of CARP, many of the shells of the moribund *Samahang Nayon* cooperatives established under Marcos were being revived or transformed into 'multi-purpose cooperatives' by DAR and Department of Agriculture officials (DA). Often the same leaders were appointed to head the new Barangay Agrarian Reform Councils (BARCs) called for under CARP. In Region 11 in Mindanao, the revival of these moribund cooperatives formed a major part of the Regional DAR Director's plans, as they did in Region 2 in the north.[173] Nothing in the CARP would prevent the reassertion of control over these organizations by the same corrupt political networks that controlled them during the Marcos years.

10.4 Financing CARP: foreign aid and the conservative approach to reform

The bias in favour of landowners and domestic agribusiness in both the design of CARP and the manner of its early implementation was also reflected in the budget of the programme. The agrarian reform plan as finally passed by Congress was an extravagantly expensive programme for a developing country facing declining terms of trade for its exports and a foreign debt of $28 billion. The only way that such a plan could be implemented was with massive aid from abroad. During the Aquino years, the United States had an influence over the orientation of all international aid to the country that far outstripped its own declining financial contribution. Its own bias in favour of a conservative approach to reform was able to influence the leanings of other foreign donors. Whatever the intention of donors, their aid to CARP-related programmes could only reinforce the conservative approach embodied in the law and the existing patterns of domination in the countryside.

10.4.1 The CARP budget and foreign aid

The ten-year budget for CARP called for a net cash requirement of P221.1 billion or $10.35 billion. Of this, P80.6 billion, or $3.77 billion, represented the net cost for land acquisition and distribution activities. Most of this sum would be paid out as compensation to landowners. The government was to spend P80.125 billion, or $3.751 billion, in compensation to landowners, of which P2.771 billion, or 3.5 per cent, would be covered by land amortization payments from beneficiaries through 1997, and the remaining 96.5 per cent by other sources. The government hoped to recover some of this expenditure from amortization payments over the 30 years after 1997. Manila sought to enlist foreign support for the programme by stressing that funds needed for landowner compensation would be raised only through internal sources.

As can be seen in Table 10.7, 63 per cent of the total CARP budget, or $6.53 billion, was to be spent on support services. The government expected to raise this entire amount from foreign grants and loans.[174] During the life of the Aquino administration, until 1992, the Government hoped to raise no less than $2.6 billion from Official Development Assistance (ODA), mainly in grants and soft loans, to support the CARP. Thus ODA, and possibly new foreign

Table 10.7: Comprehensive Agrarian Reform Program Cashflow by Activity, 1987-1997 (US$ Millions)

Activities	TOTAL (1987-97)	Actual 1987	1988-92	1993-97
OUTFLOWS				
Preliminary Activities	**43.1**	**1.97**	**35.77**	**5.34**
Land Acquisition and Distribution	**3,774.4**	**5.38**	**751.54**	**3,017.46**
Compensation[a]	3,621.4	3.89	699.06	2,918.50
Other Costs	153.0	1.49	52.48	98.96
Support Activities	**6,533.5**	**4.49**	**2,549.11**	**3,979.92**
Extension	706.4	-	239.70	466.72
Credit[b]	2,694.8	1.92	1,149.67	1,543.26
Infrastructure	1,217.2	-	449.48	767.65
Institutional Strengthening	1,827.9	2.57	630.34	1,194.94
Research & Development	19.1	-	11.80	7.35
Data Base	68.1	-	68.12	-
TOTAL OUTFLOWS	*10,351.0*	*11.84*	*3,336.42*	*7,002.72*
INFLOWS				
Sale of Assets	**2,345.5**	**98.31**	**1,779.03**	**468.16**
PCGG[c]	1,322.6	11.70	842.70	468.16
APT[d]	1,022.9	86.61	936.33	-
TOTAL INFLOWS	*2,345.5*	*98.31*	*1,779.03*	*468.16*
NET CASH FLOW	**(8,005.5)**	**86.47**	**(1,557.39)**	**(6,534.56)**
Funding Needs				
Domestic Funding	1,428.9			
Foreign Funding	6,576.6	6.49	2,584.88	3,985.26

The peso sums are converted at P21.36 to $1.00.
[a]Net of Collections from amortization payments by beneficiaries.
[b]Net of collections and income from loan repayments.
[c]Presidential Commission on Good Government - sequestered assets.
[d]Asset Privatisation Trust - sale of government assets.
Source: *The Comprehensive Agrarian Reform Program of the Philippines*, Vol.1, 'Implementing Program and Budget, 1988-1997', Manila: Presidential Agrarian Reform Council (March 1989).

borrowing, was considered as fundamental to the implementation of CARP.

What is more, the potential contribution of CARP ODA to poverty alleviation and sustainable rural development was necessarily limited by the content of the government's programme. Looking at the budget in Table 10.7, CARP called for a net expenditure on landowner compensation that was greater than the combined expenditure for credit and extension services to beneficiaries of the programme. The $1.2 billion budget for 'Infrastructure', representing almost 20 per cent of expected foreign donor contributions, would serve the interests of large landowners and agribusinesses at least as much as beneficiaries. In other words, regardless of donors' intentions, foreign assistance could only reinforce the biases in the CARP.

By the end of 1990, the government's own fund-raising for CARP had fallen far below expectations. The government planned to raise $444.76 million per year between 1988 and 1992 from the sale of assets (Table 10.7). However, from mid-1987 through to the end of 1990, the *total* sale of assets amounted to only $570 million.[175] Efforts to enlist foreign financing were even less successful. Between 1987 and 1990 the Government was able to attract foreign commitments of only $95.8 million to its agrarian reform programme (Table 10.8). Of this, 52 per cent came from the United States, while 33 per cent was advanced by the Netherlands.[176]

Only seven per cent of foreign assistance to CARP was provided by Japan. Despite the clearly positive impact of agrarian reform within Japan's own development experience, it expressed no particular support to those advocating redistributive reform in the Philippines. A further $59 million in CARP aid was under some form of negotiation as of July 1989. Initial reports on foreign aid committed to CARP had been considerably higher, but still nowhere near the amount projected in the budget.[177] Foreign assistance actually committed represented the ridiculously small amount of only 0.004 per cent of the $2.58 billion that government planners hoped to raise for CARP between 1988 and 1992 (Table 10.7).

The very concept of the CARP, based on high levels of compensation to landowners and a centralized top-down formula of programme implementation, made it dependent for success on securing new grants and loans from bilateral and multilateral donors. According to DAR officials, throughout 1988 and early 1989 most donors were delaying a promise of funds until the launching of the Multilateral Aid Initiative (MAI), which was scheduled to take place at a meeting of the World Bank Consultative Group in Tokyo in July 1989.

In the months leading up to the Consultative Group meeting in Tokyo that was to launch the MAI, DAR was racked by the Garchitorena scandal. One of the first CARP projects to have been planned under the Japanese Technical Cooperation Program was an Integrated Rural Land Consolidation Project, to be implemented on estates that the government had acquired through the 'voluntary offers to sell' scheme in CARP. Needless to say, a Japanese delegation in the country at the time of the scandal was not pleased to find that all the estates to be covered by their project were involved in the land scams. The Japanese decided to delay further assistance until the Tokyo meeting. The future of the programme therefore became hostage to the MAI, which in turn was shaped largely by its American initiators.

After the land scandals, the Aquino Government scrambled to put the Department of Agrarian Reform in order for the Tokyo meeting by appointing a new Secretary. Decisions on funding for CARP were nonetheless postponed by the Consultative Group until a future Mini-Consultative Group meeting. This was originally scheduled for January 1990 but had to be delayed after the attempted coup d'etat in December 1989. In the end, no special meeting was ever held with donors on the CARP. The US bias in favour of a conservative approach to agrarian reform certainly influenced deliberations over the nature of

Table 10.8: Foreign Assistance to CARP (1987-1990)

Donor	US $ Millions	Type	Description
United States	50.00	Grant	USAID Agrarian Reform Support Programme (Dollars for Budget support; pesos to support activities for Operation Land Transfer)
Netherlands	31.72	Commodity Grant	Dutch Rural Development Assistance Programme (including Dutch-Asean Fertilizer programme). (Sale of fertilizer - proceeds to CARP) (1988-1991)
Japan	6.77		JICA: of which:
	0.53	Commodity Grant	- Kennedy Round II Grant for construction DAR Database Building
	1.17	Grant	- Feasibility Study: Assistance for the Integrated Jala-Jala Rural Development Project. (US$ 27.8 million project) (1989-1990)
	5.07	Grant	- Master Plan Study for Integrated Central Luzon Rural Development Project
FAO-Italy	6.17	Grant	Technical Support to Agrarian Reform and Rural Development (1989-1991)
ADB-OECF	0.45	Loan	Reforestation Project in DAR Resettlement Areas
UNFPA	0.15	Grant	Integrating Population-Related Concern in Training and Extension System of DAR (Australia)
	0.12	Grant	AIDAB: Natural Resources Management and Development Project-Land Administration Component (1989-1991)
South Korea	0.42	Grant	Training Seminar on Korean Agrarian Reform Experience
TOTAL	**95.80**		
PIPELINE			
Japan	4.26	Grant	JICA: Integrated Database Support to DAR
Sweden	4.72	Grant	Swedsurvey Cadastral Support
Denmark	0.17	Grant	DANIDA: Feasibility Study Grant for CARP in Bukidnon
Italy	50.00	1989-91	Protocol I Redefined: Area integrated projects in Regions X and XII for CARP beneficiaries. (Under discussion for 2 years)
World Bank	0.22	Loan	WB Loan did feasibility: Nucleus Estate-Outgrowers Project in CARP areas. (US$ 80 million project)
TOTAL Pipeline 59.37			

Source: Department of Agrarian Reform, 'Official Development Assistance Program for the Comprehensive Agrarian Reform Program', February 1991.

aid included in the MAI by other bilateral donors. In the end, the MAI followed the general prescription for structural adjustment laid out by the IMF from the outset of the Aquino government. The one structural adjustment never mentioned in these programmes was redistributive agrarian reform.[178]

10.4.2 ODA and the status quo

The overall thrust of foreign aid during the Aquino years marginalized agrarian reform in favour of macro-economic structural adjustment programmes. Much of the aid donated to the Philippines was at least as important to the donors as it was to the recipient. The motivation behind the fertilizer commodity programme launched by Canada was clearly expressed by the Canadian International Development Agency (CIDA) in its 1988 Country Programme. One of the goals of CIDA's commodity assistance programme was 'to maintain continuity of the Canadian potash supply' to the Philippines.[179] Foreign assistance that was actually related to CARP went mainly to nucleus farming, institution building and livelihood projects that were likely to delay rather than hasten needed redistributive reforms.

A considerable portion of ODA funds were directed into 'livelihood projects' for farmworkers and rural communities. The Canadian $100 million ODA project between 1986 and 1989 was one example. Canada's early financing of the Negros Rural Development Fund (NRDF) was widely perceived by the NGO community as providing a respite for the sugar planters and diverting attention from the need for more fundamental reforms on the poverty stricken island.[180] While Canada initially acknowledged that mistakes had been made in the implementation of NRDF, by November 1989 officials in Ottawa spoke of the programme as an overwhelming success.[181] Later the Canadian International Development Agency (CIDA) funded a pilot project under Governor Lacson's Ten-Year Development Programme. The project, which was the brainchild of Sixto K. Roxas, involved setting up an Economic District Management System (EDMS) linking five municipalities in the province.

The EDMS concept was supposed to be based on a new approach to development that would group together municipalities based on a comprehensive analysis of their natural economic potential, rather than the arbitrary borders formed between them for political expediency. Communities would be organized from the bottom up to participate in forms of production (pig raising, horticulture, cattle rearing, etc.) on contract with corporations.[182] The concept envisaged the participation of rural families with access to tiny garden plots, whose household head was often employed as a farmworker, diversifying their economic activity in order to increase incomes.[183]

Such a programme would have a great potential within the context of redistributive reform. However, without such reform it seemed to be little more than a way to relieve the pressure on wages and to undercut demands among farmworkers for access to land. In fact, in Negros Occidental, where the Governor consistently opposed a comprehensive redistributive programme, that appeared to be the objective.[184] The map of the entire province was to be redrawn, dividing it into Economic Districts based on the sophisticated resource mapping outlined in the model. However, after the intervention of Congressmen and Mayors, the zones were realigned to correspond exactly with existing congressional districts.[185] The EDMS became just another label applied to the existing structure of social and economic power in the country, and a means of channelling foreign aid funds into the hands of existing municipal councils and the patronage networks associated with them.

Members of the Negros Council for People's Development also believed that EDMS complemented the military's counterinsurgency programme by undermining existing militant organizations.[186] Their fears seemed to be corroborated when the US consultant Earl Kulp, who clearly saw such development work as one component of counterinsurgency, was hired by the project and travelled to Negros in 1989.[187] However, there is no evidence to suggest that EDMS project organizers were themselves directly involved in any collaborative effort with the military or US counterinsurgency experts, as was borne out by the dismissal of Kulp after only a short stay in Negros. Rather, it would seem that the project design dovetailed with military objectives in the province, and for that reason received unsolicited support from counterinsurgency strategists.

Other 'income generating' livelihood projects, such as those piloted in Negros and elsewhere by organizations like USAID and the corporate financed NGO, Philippine Business for Social Progress, appeared to fulfil the same function as the EDMS.[188] By providing a small supplement to the subsistence of the landless and near-landless rural poor, they would maintain the essential structure of a production system based on cheap labour and oriented toward the world market. The 'Kalakalan 20' programme, introduced by Congressman Oscar Orbos in 1989, had a similar thrust. It provided incentives for establishing small rural manufacturing enterprises in the countryside, with labour paid below minimum wage and production oriented for export. All of these programmes could act as a positive counterpart to a liberal redistributive reform. However, in the absence of widespread land redistribution, they appeared simply to provide low-wage employment, so helping to maintain the basic subsistence level of rural families within an export-oriented economy that needs no major expansion of domestic demand.

Other livelihood schemes funded by ODA were more blatant in their political motives. In the communities surrounding Del Monte's pineapple plantation and one of its major banana contract grower's plantation, Marsman Estates Inc., USAID and the companies launched a series of highly publicized community development projects. The biggest landowners were themselves involved with promoting similar livelihood projects. In fact, landowners in Negros and elsewhere were establishing NGOs to gain access to aid money.[189] Hortensia Starke's Movement for Justice on Land Reform, which she confided was really a 'one woman show', was just such an endeavour. By the end of 1988 she had money coming in from the Universities of Louisiana and Hawaii.[190] While donors might have been well-intentioned in their efforts to relieve poverty through such projects, local politicians, landowners and corporations saw them as mechanisms to help safeguard the status quo in property ownership. They were also often used to undercut the community activities of less well-funded grass-roots organizations.

Another area through which the government attempted to attract foreign assistance to CARP was in the promotion of the nucleus farm model on large estates. In many parts of the third world during the late 1970s and throughout the 1980s, growing population pressure on the land has meant that the establishment of new large landholdings by agribusiness corporations has become politically sensitive. Domestic and foreign corporations responded creatively to this development, moving increasingly toward new forms of contract growing. The most important of these was the nucleus estate model. This was pioneered by the British Commonwealth Development Corporation in Kenya in the late 1940s.[191] It was developed as a government-directed resettlement programme on virgin lands by the Federal Land Development Authority (FELDA) in Malaysia from the 1960s to the present.[192]

Essentially, the nucleus estate model involves establishing a large estate and processing plant surrounded by small holders growing the plantation crop under direction from central management. Forms have varied, from a situation where a large nucleus estate finds its production only supplemented by the small contract farmers, to one where the nucleus consists of only a processing plant and all produce is grown by surrounding small farmers. From the conservative perspective, the model has been seen primarily as a means for existing large estates to expand their future production.

In late 1988, the Commonwealth Development Corporation, under an $80,000 contract with the UK Overseas Development Administration, presented a proposal to DAR and the Land Bank to set up a nucleus farming programme among reform beneficiaries.[193] The CDC proposal drew on the positive and negative lessons of a number of nucleus estate schemes in which the Corporation had experience, in order to present a framework most suitable to Philippine conditions. The specific model proposed would 'avoid the most capital-intensive production technologies', encourage 'diversified production systems' rather than mono-crop systems, and concentrate on establishing 'processing facilities' rather than nucleus estates. 'Where possible' producers would have an opportunity 'to purchase an ownership stake' in the facility. Attention would be accorded to 'equitable distribution of revenue' and project planning would 'be done with the farmers and not for them'.

Following up on the project proposal, a World Bank mission visited the Philippines in June 1989 to develop a project for a 'nucleus estate management system'. They visited agricultural estates in Mindanao and Negros to identify the potential for such a system.[194] Subsequently a proposal was accepted for a World Bank pilot nucleus farming project at Matling Development Corporation in Lanao del Sur.[195] As of February 1991, the nucleus estate plan was the only

Table 10.9: Nucleus Estate Projects 1991

Estate	Crop	Area Nucleus	Area Outgrowers	Description
Agusan Plantations Inc	oil palm	1427		Agusan del Sur The API was owned by Leonardo Ty and Malaysian group headed by Keck. Plan to establish oil mill, whereas currently all palm fruit milled at NDC-Guthrie. Outgrowers located in Bunawan and Trento.
Tagnanan Estate	coconut/ cacao	312	1005	Davao del Norte
ZREC College Rubber Estate	rubber	330	670	Zamboanga del Norte Nucleus set up within the 1,000 hectares leased by the Zamboanga National Agricultural College Rubber Estate Corp and outgrowers in 20 km radius.
Lacaron Estate	coconut/ cacao	694	2500	Davao del Sur Doromal family lease contract with Philippine Cocoa Estates Corp. (joint venture set up by Jaime Ongpin's Benguet Management Corp and Sime Darby just before the 1986 elections) which operates the nucleus, eventually to be taken over by workers.
UP-NDC Basilan Plantation Inc.	rubber	2292	400	Basilan
Gamboa Hermanos	black pepper	112		Negros Occidental
San Carlos Fruits Corp.	fruit trees			Pangasinan
JMC Farms Inc.	fruit trees	570	864	Oriental Mindoro Nucleus managed by Globan Fruits Development Corp, while CADECOR/Land Bank control the outgrowing area.

Others without feasibility studies:
Licaros Estate Rubber Plantation
Golden Country Farm Development Project

TOTAL		5737	5439	

Source: Department of Agrarian Reform, 'Official Development Assistance Program for the Comprehensive Agrarian Reform Program', February 1991.

CARP project in which the Bank was directly involved. By 1991, the government had finished feasibility studies for eight estates covering a total of about 11,000 hectares (Table 10.9).

The nucleus estates plan was listed as one of CARP's five major projects in its appeal for foreign funding in 1991. Clearly, in the context of a liberal redistributive agrarian reform programme, a proposal such as that presented by CDC would be a means to mobilize the agribusiness sector in support of a large and newly established body of farmer and cooperative beneficiaries. However, in

353

the context of the CARP, the pursuit of the nucleus farming scheme was more likely to be another means for further expansion of agribusiness control of land and people. Discussions with the management of NDC-Guthrie Plantations Inc. and Del Monte Philippines, revealed that both companies planned further expansion of their operations through some form of out-growing or contract growing among agrarian reform beneficiaries.

The management of NDC-Guthrie, in which CDC and the IFC had a major loan exposure, reviewed the CDC proposal. In fact, one NDC official suggested that the proposal was drawn up in close connection with CDC plans to purchase an equity stake in NGPI, and was meant in part to sell the idea of the equity purchase to the CDC board.[196] NDC-Guthrie General Manager, John Lee, said that 'the corporation supports the concept of nucleus farming' and that the NDC had been actively pursuing the idea with the government and the CDC. The management felt that such a project would benefit the local community and 'assist in improving the overall security situation in the area'. Lee said that there were 'on-going discussions with CDC on this and contacts have been made with local government officials to gain their support'.[197] A review of the lists of lands Voluntarily Offered for Sale in the towns of Rosario and San Francisco, adjacent to the NGPI-NGEI oil palm estates, revealed that hundreds of hectares would be purchased by the government for distribution under CARP.[198] It was not unlikely that DAR would introduce a contract growing arrangement between these beneficiaries and the oil palm estate.

The Del Monte management also expressed interest in expanding its 2,000 hectares planted to papaya through a similar outgrowers' scheme. In 1989, they were drawing up plans for the scheme with the Department of Agriculture and the Management Association Foundation of the Philippines.[199] Gamboa Hermanos Inc., which was influential in shaping the corporate stock-sharing programme under CARP, also proposed to set up a 112 hectare nucleus estate in San Carlos, Negros Occidental, devoted to the cultivation of black pepper (Table 10.9). The company owned over 1,200 hectares in the area, devoted mainly to sugar production and covered by CARP under the corporate stock-sharing programme.[200] The nucleus estate would apparently be set up on the 113 hectare farm of its subsidiary, Highgrains Farms, Inc., which was established under the Marcos corporate farm programme in 1974 to produce rice. The company began expanding to black pepper in the mid-1980s and the nucleus estate programme of government would allow a rapid development in that direction.

Another nucleus estate planned on the 1,427 hectare Agusan Plantations Inc. appeared to provide government support for what were long-term expansion plans by the investors. The estate was established in 1982 as a joint venture between the government's NDC, a group of Filipino investors led by Leonardo Ty and the Singaporean firm Keck Seng Plantations. In 1988, NDC reduced its stock in the corporation and the Ty group increased theirs in order to insure a majority Filipino ownership.[201] The corporation leased 2,200 hectares from the NDC and DAR planned to redistribute ownership to a cooperative of workers just as at the NDC-Guthrie estates. By gaining government support under the nucleus estates programme, the company could finally put up a long-planned palm oil mill.[202]

Almost $2 billion of the funds that the government hoped to raise from foreign donors for the CARP were to be directed toward 'institution building and strengthening' (Table 10.7). A great percentage of these funds was certain to go directly to financing central agencies of the Philippine government. Most of the rest would be directed toward enhancing the capacity of regional, provincial and municipal development councils and establishing cooperatives. One of USAID's biggest accounts in the country, amounting to over $200 million, was a long-standing project to finance Municipal and Regional Development Funds. However, such councils remained the domain of municipal and provincial political power networks and the funds directed to them were likely to be appropriated directly into the patronage system of the political clans.

Foreign donors were anxious to provide small amounts of such support to the worker cooperatives set up under CARP. Representatives from the EC, CIDA and the Italian Cooperative Association all visited the cooperatives set up on the TNC plantations. In fact, farmworkers at Dole Philippines were approached by ODA donors without even having sought their assistance.[203] For ODA donors, providing money for institution strengthening was premised on the assumption that a democratic government had been established in Manila which needed support to consolidate under threats from both the right and the left.[204] However, channelling funds into such institutional strengthening projects in the absence of a realignment of power relations in the agricultural sector would more likely reinforce a balance of power decidedly against the rural poor.

10.5 The evolving scope and accomplishments of CARP

By the end of 1990, only a year and a half before national elections in May 1992, the Aquino government had fallen far short of its own conservative targets for land redistribution. While the design of CARP made it an extremely expensive programme and the government's fund raising - both through the sale of assets and the solicitation of foreign aid - fell abysmally short of requirements, poor performance was not due to a lack of funds. In fact, by September 1990, there was a surplus of P8.011 billion, or $286 million, in the CARP fund which remained unspent. The causes of sluggish programme implementation lay elsewhere.

At first sight the scope of CARP coverage appeared impressive. As shown in Table 10.10, over ten years CARP would 'cover' 10.3 million hectares of land, more than the reported total farm area.[205] However, the first insight into the real scope of CARP lay in the identification of what was meant by 'coverage' under the programme. First, the figures in Table 10.10 include land slated for redistribution by all previous agrarian reform programmes but which had not been distributed by the time the Aquino government came to power. These included lands under Marcos' PD27 and earlier resettlement programmes which

Table 10.10: Comparative Projections of the Scope of CARP (1987-1997) Area (Hectares) Number of Beneficiaries*

	1987 Target Total	1988 Target Total	1990 Target Total	1990 Target 1987-92	1990 Target 1993-97
Private Lands					
Rice & Corn					
(Marcos Programme)	727800	727800	727800	727800	0
Beneficiaries	*519857*	*522675*	*522675*	*522675*	*0*
Idle and Abandoned	200000	250000	250000	125175	124825
Voluntary Offers**	250000	400000	0	0	0
PCGG Sequestered	60000	2500	2500	1415	1085
Beneficiaries	*364285*	*217500*	*84165*	*42198*	*41967*
Privately Held	1280000	1887300	2287300	586250	1701050
Holdings >50 ha.s	634000	534400	706303	195372	510931
Holdings 5.01-24.00 ha.s	646000***	1049800	1063581	221611	841970
Holdings 24.01-50.00 ha.s		303100	517416	169267	348149
Beneficiaries	*640000*	*629102*	*762430*	*195416*	*567014*
Sub-total Private	**2517800**	**3267600**	**3267600**	**1440640**	**1826960**
Beneficiaries	*1524142*	*1369277*	*1369270*	*760289*	*608981*
Public Lands					
Government-Owned	50000	74500	74500	37302	37198
Public A/D + Leased	1349500	4595000	4595000	2300000	2295000
Integrated Social Forestry	1170000	1880000	1880000	885000	995000
Resettlement	467420	478500	478500	338458	140042
Sub-total Public	**3036920**	**7028000**	**7028000**	**3560760**	**3467240**
Beneficiaries	*1256274*	*2532001*	*2532001*	*1281691*	*1250310*
TOTAL	**5554720**	**10295600**	**10295600**	**5001400**	**5294200**
Beneficiaries	*2780416*	*3901278*	*3901271*	*2041980*	*1859291*

*Beneficiaries include the landowners' heirs who will receive 3 hectares each. Estimates represent 'agency capability' rather than the phasing requirements of RA6657.
**From 1989 'Voluntarily Offered' land was included in private lands as follows: 171903 hectares with lands >50 ha.s, 13781 ha.s with 5.01-24.00, and 214316 ha.s with 24.01-50.00 ha.s.
***81000 hectares listed as tenanted lands and 565000 as non-tenanted. Sources: 1987: Institute of Agrarian Studies, 'Selected Statistics for the Comprehensive Agrarian Reform (September 1987)'. 1988: DAR, 'Annual Land Distribution Projections and Projection of Beneficiaries' 1988. 1990: DAR, 'The CARP of the Philippines: An Overview and Status of Implementation,' (February 1991).

came to 1.2 million hectares. Second, 63 per cent of the lands listed under CARP 'coverage' in the Table, or almost 6.5 million hectares, were logged over, pasture and forested public lands, most of which were not slated for redistribution at all but rather to be 'covered' by various forms of stewardship contracts.

Third, the private lands 'covered' by CARP listed in Table 10.10 included corporate lands that would either be subject only to corporate stock redistribution, such as the President's Hacienda Luisita, or exempted for ten years and 'covered' by CARP only through production and profit sharing, like Senator Enrile's 970 hectare Eurasia Match Inc. estate in Basilan. Fourth, the CARP programme scope was flawed by the double-counting of land, where lands listed under the Marcos programme, or as idle and abandoned areas, were also included under the category of 'privately held' lands, as the earlier discussion of the VOS programme illustrated. Finally, both the CARP 'coverage' of private lands in the Table and the number of targeted beneficiaries included all those lands that would be distributed to the *heirs of the landowners* themselves, under the law's provision that allowed each heir to retain three hectares. Thus the announced scope of CARP was very deceptive indeed.

The final official scope of CARP was fixed in 1988, after the adoption of the law. Table 10.10 illustrates some important changes which occurred in the planned scope between 1987 and 1988. The most important was the increase in the coverage of private lands from 2.51 million hectares to 3.26 million hectares. This was accomplished by almost doubling the amount of lands that the government felt would be voluntarily offered by landowners, by slightly increasing the estimated amount of idle and abandoned lands and by increasing the coverage of other privately held lands by 67 per cent. After the Garchitorena land scam, the category of 'voluntary offers' was eliminated and these lands were subsumed within the 'privately held' category. Apparently the reason for the 67 per cent increase in privately held lands was the inclusion of all those lands that would be retained by the landowners' heirs.

Interestingly, the scope of coverage of sequestered lands was reduced from 60,000 hectares to only 2,500 hectares. The sequestered lands of Danding Cojuangco totalled well over the 16,000 hectares that he had received in his 'land swap' during the Marcos years.[206] In Negros Occidental alone, the Presidential Commission on Good Government reportedly sequestered 9,538 hectares of land belonging to Cojuangco and to Marcos' 'sugar king' Roberto S. Benedicto.[207] The government never explained why the area of sequestered lands to be included in CARP was reduced so drastically. While peasant organizations occupied some of the sequestered lands, thus forcing the government to take them under consideration for CARP coverage, the peasant movement surprisingly put little emphasis on demanding a government accounting of these lands.[208] The most likely explanation was that former owners of the lands obtained by Marcos and associates were able to reassert their control over the lands through deals with the Aquino government.

Central to understanding the scope of the government's conservative agrarian reform programme is the identification of the amount of private lands to be covered during the life of the Aquino administration. Since the strategy of the landowners was to delay programme implementation until after the 1992 national elections, the significance of the programme would be determined mainly by what could be accomplished before the elections. Putting aside the rice and corn lands covered by the Marcos programme, CARP was to cover about 2.6 million hectares of private lands between 1987 and 1997. However, during the life of the administration (1987-1992), only 713,000 hectares, or 27 per cent, of these lands were slated for coverage under CARP. Next to the minimum of 1.8 million hectares of land in holdings over 100 hectares in size, the scope of coverage during the Aquino administration appeared to be insignificant.[209] Even the official scope of the programme put off the major portion of private land redistribution to an uncertain future under a new administration.

If the scope of the Aquino programme looked modest, accomplishments through 1990 were even more limited. Every year after CARP was passed, the serving DAR secretary announced that annual targets could not be met.[210] They never readjusted the final scope of the programme, but it became increasingly apparent that more and more land would be covered only under a new administration. This was reflected in DAR's accomplishment report in February 1991, reported in Table 10.11. In 1991, CARP's target covering the period of 1987-1990 was significantly reduced, but the overall scope of the programme was maintained.[211] At first sight, CARP accomplishment over the period as reported in Table 10.11 appears impressive in terms of its revised target, with 86 per cent of targeted area and 77 per cent of targeted beneficiaries covered. Even the coverage of aggregate private lands was reported at 55 per cent of targeted area and 63 per cent of beneficiaries.

However, appearances can be deceptive. The apparently positive overall performance was derived almost exclusively from the performance on public lands. These were covered by DAR's long-standing programmes to establish land settlements and distribute landed estates acquired over the previous 40 years, and on-going projects of the Department of Energy and Natural Resources to issue stewardship contracts and free patents on forested and other public lands. The positive performance on private lands was due almost entirely to the continued reporting of the Marcos programme under CARP, where documents covering 80 per cent of targeted rice and corn lands were distributed to beneficiaries.

Reported accomplishments on lands covered for the first time under CARP demonstrated the extent to which the Aquino government's conservative model of reform left private lands untouched. Table 10.11 shows that no idle or abandoned lands were distributed throughout the entire period, despite the fact that these were slated as a top priority under the programme. The most likely explanation was that landowners were successfully mounting court challenges over the ownership of most of these lands. Throughout 1987-1990, only 9,949 hectares of privately held lands, or 4.6 per cent of the revised target, were distributed. Hacienda Luisita alone, which was covered only by the stock-sharing programme, represented 4,914 hectares, or almost 50 per cent of the total. Voluntarily offered land acquired between 1987 and 1989, amounted to 2,320 hectares, or 23 per cent of private land accomplishments (Table 10.1). Outside of the lands covered by the Marcos programme, all private lands represented only 0.66 per cent of the total area covered during the period. Of the government-owned lands covered, more than 30 per cent represented the three NDC estates

Table 10.11: CARP Accomplishments 1987-1990 Area (Hectares) and Number of Beneficiaries

	1988 Target 1987-90	1991 Target 1987-90	Area/Benef Covered 1987-90	% of Total Covered 1987-90	% 1988 Target	% 1991 Target
Private Lands						
Rice & Corn						
(Marcos Programmme)	570143	511642	411453	26.3	72.2	80.4
Beneficiaries	*410063*	*373518*	*311267*	*42.8*	*75.9*	*83.3*
Idle and Abandoned	50515	38286	0	0	0.0	0.0
PCGG Sequestered	765	2050	878	0.06	114.8	42.8
Beneficiaries	*17094*	*57604*	*1292*	*0.18*	*7.6*	*2.2*
Private farms of which	**189824**	**216081**	**9949**	**0.6**	**5.2**	**4.6**
>50 ha.s	65601					
5.01-24.00 ha.s	63407					
24.01-50.00 ha.s	60816					
Beneficiaries	*63277*	*75741*	*5655*	*0.78*	*8.9*	*7.5*
Sub-total Private	**811247**	**768059**	**422280**	**26.9**	**52.1**	**55.0**
Beneficiaries	*490434*	*506863*	*318214*	*43.7*	*64.9*	*62.8*
Public Lands						
Government-Owned	15054	16751	82222	5.2	546.2	490.8
Public A/D + Leased	1050000	865669	484239	30.9	46.1	55.9
ISF*	519000	n.a.	378330	24.2	72.9	n.a.
Resettlement & Landed Estates**	188458	170479	198358	12.7	105.3	116.4
Sub-total Public	**1772512**	**1052899**	**1143149**	**73.0**	**64.5**	**108.6**
Beneficiaries	*634103*	*431050*	*408850*	*56.2*	*64.5*	*94.8*
TOTAL AREA (1987-1990)	**2583759**	**1820958**	**1565429**	**100.0**	**60.6**	**85.9**
Total Beneficiaries	*1124537*	*937913*	*727064*	*100.0*	*64.6*	*77.5*

*Integrated Social Forestry is carried out by the DENR and distributes 25-year Stewardship contracts not exceeding 7 hectares to beneficiaries.
**This includes land covered under the old Resettlement and Landed Estates Programmes, the latter which was not necessarily public land.
Source: DAR, 'CARP of the Philippines: An Overview and Status of Implementation', Table 3 and p.16. (February 1991).

leased to Dole, Del Monte and NDC-Guthrie and distributed to the workers' cooperatives for lease-back to the companies.

The slow pace of private land coverage under CARP was encouraged from the earliest stages of implementation by Secretary Juico's decision to concentrate exclusively on completing the distribution of rice and corn lands and soliciting voluntary offers to sell. On 3 August 1989, Secretary Santiago announced a striking departure from this policy, saying that she would immediately begin the compulsory acquisition of private lands over 50 hectares. The Secretary said that 81,241 hectares of land would be purchased under this programme by the end of 1989.[212] At the top of the list were to be 8,000 hectares of land owned by the President's family in Tarlac. Santiago's announcement appeared to reflect a more aggressive stand by government on the implementation of agrarian reform and a commitment to accelerate the process. However, once again the limitations of the law itself constrained any action that DAR may wish to have taken. The announcement that 8,000 hectares of the Cojuangco family lands were to be acquired appears to have been timed to cushion the imminent approval of the stock transfer programme at Hacienda Luisita, which would allow the family to maintain control over the estate.

In fact, closer scrutiny of the Cojuangco lands slated for compulsory acquisition revealed that only 1,844 hectares belonged to the José Cojuangco branch of the family, which owned Hacienda Luisita. What is more, the list did not include lands owned by the family's major corporations: Luisita Realty Corporation, Central Azucarera de Tarlac Realty Corporation and José Cojuangco Enterprises, which reportedly had large holdings throughout Central Luzon.[213] By November 1989, DAR announced that only 1,021 hectares would be acquired from the heirs of José Cojuangco II and this would be through the family's *voluntary offer to sell*, not compulsory acquisition.[214] While Santiago had said that the government would pay P18,586 per hectare for the land under compulsory acquisition, the family asked for P40,000 per hectare under its VOS. In fact, many of these lands had already been covered by Marcos' PD27.[215]

In February 1991, DAR Secretary Benjamin Leong reported that a further 100,650 hectares of lands foreclosed by government institutions had been turned over to the DAR. He said that 116,000 hectares of private lands voluntarily offered to the government were in various stages of acquisition, and Notices of Acquisition had been issued for 54,216 hectares of private lands to be covered by compulsory acquisition.[216] If the acquisition, processing and distribution of these lands could somehow be accomplished within two years, DAR would have reached 40 per cent of the target for private land redistribution (excluding lands covered by the Marcos programme) set for 1992, and 11 per cent of the target for the ten year period. However, it was unclear in Leong's report whether the foreclosed lands were actually distinct from the lands he mentioned as voluntarily offered. As early as 1987, DAR began including all foreclosed lands covered by CARP under the category of voluntary offers. What is more, while notices of acquisition may have been issued on the 54,000 hectares of private lands, these could still be contested within the courts. The actual potential for further distribution of privately owned lands outside of those covered by the Marcos programme was therefore extremely limited.

One of the stumbling blocks to faster implementation of even the conservative reform was the continuing inadequacy of land records and the lack of knowledge about who actually owned agricultural land. While data collected in the government's land registration programmes, *Listasaka I & II*, provided a better indication of the concentration of landholdings than did the 1980 Census data, it remained incomplete, since a great number of landowners either did not register or understated their holdings.[217] For instance, Mayor Oscar Escudero of Casiguran, Sorsogon, was not listed among those owners registered as holding more than 50 hectares, but he offered 154 hectares to the government under VOS.[218] Another glaring example emerged from an examination of the VOS statistics. In Region 3, the area of land in holdings above 100 hectares offered to the government under VOS amounted to 164 per cent of the total landholdings above 100 hectares registered in the *Listasaka* programme.[219]

Despite the fact that major agrarian reform legislation had been on the books for 30 years, successive governments never undertook the necessary measures to document private agricultural holdings. In January 1989, Assistant-Secretary Gerry Bulatao reported that although Secretary Juico and the Executive Committee of the Presidential Agrarian Reform Council had decided to undertake the documentation of landholdings, absolutely nothing had been done.[220] The study and documentation of landholdings in the country would be a mammoth undertaking, involving cross-checking *Listasaka* data with data in the provincial Registries of Deeds and the Tax Offices, and corroborating these with local residents. Project workers in the EDMS programme in Negros Occidental demonstrated that such a task was possible when they carried it out for the five municipalities contained within their pilot project.[221] However, it appeared to be decidedly against the government's conservative approach to devote the necessary time and resources to such an endeavour. On a national scale, such an undertaking could only be accomplished with the full participation and initiative of the grass-roots peasant organizations and NGOs, which was ruled out by those who defended the conservative approach.

10.6 Conclusion

The first three years of CARP implementation demonstrated both the extent to which the conservative approach to reform served the interests of landowners and agribusiness corporations, and the degree to which these groups had penetrated the fractured institutions of the Philippine state. While liberal reformers believed that they could still 'do good' by working within the government for the implementation of CARP, the alliance in the state around the conservative approach doomed their efforts from the start. Most of the DAR bureaucracy survived from the Marcos years, and it had little interest in the liberal minority's efforts to work with peasant organizations on reform implementation.

The majority in DAR and the other line agencies, like the Department of Finance and the Department of Trade and Industry, could not see reform as anything more than an incremental process of documentation of government-sponsored market transactions in land. While Secretary Juico showed the proper deference to agribusiness interests and limited his work in DAR to the confines of the conservative approach, he still came under attack by the Department of Finance, acting through the Land Bank, which wanted to ensure DAR's subordinate position within the government. The military opposed the liberal reformers' efforts as well, and their opposition was based both on their strategic conception of counterinsurgency and their practical links with landowners and agribusiness corporations. The AFP was able to ensure DAR's subordination to itself, just as the officers worked to assert the military's own preeminence within

N

the state more generally.

The advocates of the liberal approach to reform who worked within the government during the early Aquino years developed an orientation distinct from those in the past, who had appeared to be motivated more by their desire to undermine radical peasant organization than to redistribute lands to the landless. Nevertheless, the liberal reformers acted as 'good will ambassadors' among the peasants for a state that was committed to a conservative programme. If landowners and their representatives had been more astute, they would have seen that the limits of the law itself were enough to protect their interests, and that a Secretary like Florencio Abad, supported by a minority in DAR, would provide legitimacy to the government and sew disunity in the peasant movement. However, every gain made by the opponents of redistributive reform encouraged them to go still further in their efforts to ensure that CARP would not get off the ground.

CARP implementation revealed the extent to which the state was penetrated by both domestic and foreign private interests as well as the interests of foreign state actors. The influence of private interests within DAR itself was demonstrated not only through the corruption which exploded into public view through the Garchitorena land scam, but also in DAR officials' relationship with agribusiness corporations. Although Juico was forced to take a strong public stand against Del Monte, the provincial agrarian reform officer in Bukidnon was advising the corporation on the best means to maintain control over land leased from private owners. Landowners and corporations also penetrated other state institutions like the military. Thus, while the military had its own independent identity within the state, its battalions became dependent on funding from important private interests, as was seen in both Negros and Mindanao. The same private interests exercised influence at every level of national, provincial and local government. Even largely foreign linked corporations, like Marsman Estates and NDC-Guthrie, were able to influence local politics.

The extent of the state's reliance on bilateral and multilateral donors also made it extremely vulnerable to foreign interests. However, while the government bent over backwards to make the language of CARP amenable to foreign donors and to ensure them that the programme was not confiscatory, still little foreign aid was forthcoming. Through the Multilateral Aid Initiative the US was able to amplify its influence despite the dwindling amounts of aid it provided to the government. Japan, which had become the country's most important official lender, showed no more enthusiasm for redistributive reform than had the US, despite its own positive experience with the liberal model. If anything, Japan's aid programme was even more tied to the promotion of Japanese private interests than was the US programme.

During its first three years of implementation, CARP was barely able to touch privately owned lands. Most of the lands that did come under DAR's authority had been covered by previous reform legislation. The basic structures of property relations and agricultural production were not altered by CARP. While TNCs had to pay a slightly higher rent for the land that they used, they were also allowed unlimited expansion of lands under their control. The claim that provisions within CARP, like the corporate stock-sharing scheme, would act as an incentive to modernization was both ill-conceived and unfounded. The President's family was able to secure control over its own sugar estate, and it led the way for other big owners like Arsenio Acuña to legitimate the control of lands acquired during the Marcos years. The corporate stock-sharing programme illustrated how the country's corporation and property laws were fundamentally biased against the landless.

Within the CARP there emerged a new thrust to undermine independent peasant organizations and trade unions through the launching of management controlled cooperatives on the large plantations and the revival of moribund government sponsored cooperatives among the small farmers. While workers were given the formal right to choose whether to lease back lands granted to them by the government or to accept corporate stock-sharing programmes from estate owners, no environment was created in which they could come to know what their choices really were. Without a shift in the balance of forces in the rural economy, the plantation workers were no more likely to choose to confront the TNCs or powerful families than tenants were likely to confront the terms for voluntary reform offered by their landlords.

The various programmes promoted by foreign aid donors, like Roxas' Economic Districts, or the CDC's nucleus farming models, could play a positive role within the context of a redistributive reform that empowered the rural majority. However, introduced within the context of conservative reform, they tended to serve as vehicles for the consolidation of existing power relations in rural society. Landowners and the families controlling agribusiness corporations were able to achieve their objective of slowing down CARP implementation long enough to amend or discard the law under a new administration after the 1992 elections. Much as landowner spokesman Eduardo Hernandez had predicted, as the political climate shifted after the scandals which engulfed DAR, the Supreme Court began to issue rulings in favour of the landowners.

However, during the implementation of CARP it also became clear that progress in land redistribution could only be made where the independent organizations of the peasantry were strong. The VOS programme was riddled with graft and corruption and marginal lands were sold to DAR at high prices, but it also demonstrated that landowners were more than willing to part with lands where peasants were organized or where the underground NPA had begun to implement its own agrarian reform programme. There would have been no controversy over the lease-back conditions, which the management-dominated cooperatives set up by DAR were ready to engage in with the TNCs, if the Dole workers' trade union had not expressed its forceful public opposition to the contracts.

In the Philippines, where the state lacks cohesion and is penetrated by private and foreign interests, it would appear that the only way in which the liberal model of reform could be successfully implemented would be with the full involvement of the grass-roots peasant movement. Only then could the efforts of landowners to over-value their lands be checked or an accurate assessment of landownership be made. The liberal reform advocates who were forced out of government during the implementation of CARP saw that the way forward was in an alliance first with the grass-roots. It is perhaps there that hope lies for future efforts to implement agrarian reform.

Notes

1. Interview, Philip Juico, 16 August 1989.
2. The Cabinet member prefers anonymity, but this assessment was confirmed by Gerardo Bulatao (Interview, 11 September 1987), who believed that Juico was good for the job. On disputes see Chapter 7.
3. Nine of the 13 Regional DAR Directors and 80 per cent of Provincial Agrarian Reform Officers were carry-overs from the Marcos years (Interview, Philip Juico, 16 August 1989).
4. Interview, José Medina, 17 March 1989 and DAR, 1988a.
5. Interview, Gerardo Bulatao, 3 May 1989.
6. Presidential [PCGR], 1986, p.37.
7. See Chapter 3.
8. Interview, Gerardo Bulatao, 2 September 1989.
9. Interview, Gerardo Bulatao, 21 March 1989.
10. The struggle between Vistan and Juico was evident in the minutes of meetings of the Presidential Agrarian Reform Council (Presidential [PARC], 1988-1989).
11. Interviews with provincial and municipal DAR officials in 1989.
12. An examination of DAR regional statistics on voluntary offers (Regions 2, 5, 6, 10 and 11) revealed that the total of lands offered was far higher, but these were not yet included in Central Office reports.
13. Owen, 1984, p.111. Mariano Garchitorena declared it pasture land (MC 6 June 1989).
14. Jovelina L. Serdan, Chair, DAR Committee on LBP Acquired Estates (PDI 3 June 1989).
15. Juico reportedly confirmed this in testimony before the Feria Committee set up to investigate the Garchitorena case (Malaya 26 June 1989).
16. Malaya (26 June 1989). Sharp was reportedly a dormant company for 17 years. Its chief officer was Alex Lina. Also among incorporators were Dennis Oscolio, Arthur Alcasid, Hilario Lim and Nevin Oca. The company had a paid up capital of only P15,000 (PDI 18 May 1989).
17. Juico (9 June 1989) testified that Sharp originally offered to sell the land for P56 million and that DAR's Juvenal Raguini admitted to changing the amount to P65 million.
18. Juico, 9 June 1989.
19. Joint DAR-LBP Special Order 552 creating Compensation Clearing Committee (CCC), 27 December 1988 (PDI, 3 June 1989).
20. DAR Central Office, June 1989.
21. PDI (23 May 1989). On 29 May the Supreme Court referred the petition to the Court of Appeals (PDI 30 May 1989).
22. Juico testified that the problem arose because the land had been valued according to a formula mandated by EO229, since it had been offered before the passage of the law (PDI 25 May 1989). Under this formula the main components considered were: P34,431, Sharp's declared market value; P45,610, Sharp's declared net income per hectare; and P32,000, the value of comparable sales (Yambot, 1989; Juico, 9 June 1989). But even if the later compensation formula had been employed using Sharp's original offer [P33,226 (Sharp's tax declaration,

AMV) + P29,661 (Sharp's declared value, DMV) + P32,000 (comparable sales, MV) = 94,887/3 = P31,629 per ha., or a total of P59.7 million], the valuation would have been almost as high as what DAR offered to pay Sharp under the old formula after officials altered the figures.

23. Testimony of UCPB officials before the Feria Commission in June 1989 (*MC* 28 June 1989).
24. Feria Commission Report, cited in *MC* (1 July 1989).
25. Interview with V. Francisco Varua, Vice-president for Marketing, José Cojuangco & Sons, Inc. (Makati, 31 July 1989).
26. *MB* (26 June 1989). With the eruption of the land scandal the Tribunal evidently changed its mind.
27. The following account is based on a review of Romeo Santos' folders at the DAR Land Transfer Centre in June-July 1989.
28. Interview, Salvador Pejo, 29 August 1989.
29. Letter of Teofilo T. Santos of the LBP to José Medina, then Deputy Minister of Agrarian Reform (2 April 1986). The LBP official asked DAR to verify a LBP task force report that found that, 'Farmers who were placed in the area were "threatened" in meetings conducted by MAR that if they were not agreeable to the price of P25,000 per hectare they can be evicted and replaced with other farmers'.
30. On 30 September 1985, Vicente G. Azana, District Officer of DAR, approved the valuation and on 27 November 1985, Pejo sent 'Land Valuation of Romeo Santos Estate at Salvacion, Tigaon, C.S.' to Secretary Estrella, also endorsing the P25,000 per hectare. Pejo wrote again to Medina on 14 April 1986, reiterating his support for the Santos valuation and claiming the LBP had been inciting farmers to protest that the value was too high.
31. Memorandum by DAR's Demefrio M. Argosino Jr. (23 April 1986). Interview, Salvador Pejo, 29 August 1989.
32. Silvestre Gabot of DAR wrote to the Land Bank (20 October 1987) recommending that the Santos claim be paid under Administrative Order No. 2, 1987, regulating VOS. LBP Vice-president, Jesus F. Diaz, expressed reservations over such a course of action in a letter to Gabot dated 12 November 1987.
33. DAR Central Office, June 1989. Only 30 hectares were paid at the lower price of P25,000 per hectare. In addition, 15 hectares of land submitted by Santos relatives in the same towns were paid at P27,000 per hectare.
34. According to the law, the limit would have been 23 hectares (five for the owner and three for each child). Interview, Ex-Mayor Inocencio Uy, Roxas, Isabela, 20 June 1989.
35. DAR records show that Florencio Rosales offered 190 hectares in Garchitorena.
36. Interview Ka Loida, Camarines Sur, 11 September 1989. Journalists visiting the estate reported that farmers cultivating the land said that they favoured the CPP land reform, since they paid only 15 per cent of their produce in taxes (*PDI* 10 June 1989).
37. Interview, Ka Mer, regional NPA Commander, September 1989.
38. DAR and PBSP, 1989.
39. Interview with Bishop Antonio Fortich, 4 August 1989.
40. DAR Conference Bacolod, 4 June 1989.
41. Interview, NFSW officials, 2 August 1989. Interview with farmers occupying the land, 3 August 1989.
42. Interview, Bishop Fortich, 4 August 1989.
43. Pepita Agricultural Corporation, 188 hectares; Pahangco Marketing Inc., 565.7 hectares; Rolando Macasa, 60 hectares; José Abueg, 42.2 hectares; Hermanas Sumbingco, 133.3 hectares.
44. Interview, NFSW officials, 2 August 1989.
45. DAR Central Office, November 1988; *PDI*, 7 June 1989. Justice Secretary Sedfrey Ordonez ordered her prosecution (*MC* 6 July 1989).
46. Offers reported in DAR Central Office, November 1989 and details of DAR reaction by David Wurfel, in conversation with the author, 26 July 1989.
47. However, DAR records raise some questions about Secretary Juico's family involvement in VOS. In November 1988 there were two voluntary offers to sell a total of 107 hectares of

land planted to sugar registered by a 'Norma Juico'. One was in Secretary Juico's home town of Porac, Pampanga and the other in Tarlac. In the September 1989 report the name on both these offers was changed to 'Norma Hewitt'. While the 43-hectare Porac property was valued by DAR at P9,399.04 per hectare, the Tarlac property was valued at P31,423.67 per hectare.

48. Executive Order 405, June 1990, cited in DAR, 1991a, p.15.
49. DAR, 1988a.
50. Interview, Philip Juico, 16 August 1989.
51. MC (1 July 1989).
52. Interview, Gerardo Bulatao, 4 July 1989. He suggested that she was close to General Mison, but she was also known to look favourably on some of those involved with the military dissidents in RAM.
53. PDI (21 July 1989).
54. Santiago commented, 'It is an intimately, superior piece of legislation because it is not a result of a compromise...It is rational, highly logical and consistent' (PDI 5 August 1989).
55. PDI (1 July 1989).
56. PDI (21 July 1989).
57. Putzel, 1990b, p.9.
58. Putzel and Cunnington, 1989, pp.85-89.
59. Interview, Bulatao, 30 November 1988 and 24 January 1989.
60. PDI (24 August 1989).
61. PDI (16 January 1990).
62. PDI (19 December 1989).
63. Lieutenant Colonel Victor Corpus (1989, pp.109, 186-87) proclaimed the general need for land reform as part of the counterinsurgency effort, but affirmed, like his US counterparts, that such a reform programme could not consist primarily of land redistribution. Instead, he proposed his own version of a corporate stock distribution plan where large estates would be run by 'a professional management team...with farmers as stockholders'.
64. Interview, Governor Daniel Lacson, 4 August 1989.
65. Starke, 1988, pp.3-4.
66. Interview, Rep. Hortensia Starke, 6 December 1988.
67. Interview, Sto Tomas official, 10 May 1989.
68. Interview, Marsman workers, 10 May 1989.
69. Interview, Roberto Sebastian, 10 May 1989.
70. Interview, Cesar Alaban, NDC-Guthrie, 27 May 1989. On the history of the plantation see Chapter 4.
71. Interview, John Lee, NDC-Guthrie, 29 May 1989.
72. Interview, Parish workers in San Francisco, Agusan del Sur, 27 May 1989.
73. Senators Osmeña and Enrile employed a seldom used clause in the old Agrarian Reform Code (RA3844, Section 50; RA6389 Section 9), which stated that anyone appointed as DAR Secretary had to have five years experience in agrarian reform work (MC 11 October 1989; DG 8 October 1989).
74. For background and details on the coup, see Putzel, 1990a and Philippine [PCIJ], 1990.
75. MC (26 December 1989).
76. MC (21 December 1989).
77. Aquino, 30 December 1989.
78. Adriano, 1990.
79. Manlogon, 1990; MC (7, 9 January 1990).
80. Adriano, 1990.
81. PDI (12, 16 January 1990)
82. Philippine [PPI], 1991b, pp.21-22.
83. DAR, 1990a.
84. PDI (14 March 1990).

85. All of the organizations in CPAR and the conservative Sanduguan coalitions as well as the FFF published a joint 'Declaration of the Peasantry on the Land Conversion Issue' *PDI* (9 March 1990).
86. *DG* (29 March 1990).
87. *PDI* (14 March 1990).
88. *PDI* (2 April 1990).
89. *PDI* (18 March 1990).
90. *MC* (2 April 1990)
91. *DG* (27 March 1990).
92. *PDI* (7 April 1990).
93. CPAR, 1990a.
94. Amnesty International (1990) pointed out that the arrest itself was questionable since no warrant was issued. On the Tadeo case, see also International Commission of Jurists, 1991, pp.51-52; de Quiros, 1991, pp.58-65; *Peasant Update* (May 1990).
95. See Chapter 7, section 7.4.
96. Amnesty International, 1990, p.5.
97. Regional Trial Court of Quezon City, Branch 101, Civil Case No. Q-39179, 27 September 1985.
98. Regional trial Court of Malolos, Bulacan, Branch 9 in a decision rendered on 4 May 1987.
99. Republic of the Philippines, Court of Appeals, Manila. Decision in 'People of the Philippines versus Jaime Tadeo,' (CA-G.R. CR. No. 05345) 31 January 1989.
100. On Regalado's role in the Con-com, see Chapter 6, section 6.5. Interview, Jaime Tadeo, Muntinlupa Prison, 7 May 1991.
101. Alternative [AFRIM], 1990, pp.30, 91. See also discussion in Putzel, 1991. On the overall concentration of land see Chapter 1.
102. *DG* (10 January 1990). The Confederation of Filipino Rice and Corn Associations denied the existence of the cartel in a letter to the Senate Committee on Agriculture (8 May 1991).
103. Lactao, 1988, p.24.
104. Floro, 1987; Lim, 1987; World Bank, 1987a, Vol.2 Annex 7.
105. Interview, Jaime Mateo, 28 March 1989.
106. Interview, Cesar Alaban, NGPI, 27 May 1989.
107. Interview, Eduardo Hernandez, 2 December 1988.
108. DAR, 1991a, p.14. On Montemayor's prediction see, Chapter 8, section 8.3.
109. Interview, Hortensia Starke, 6 December 1989.
110. *MB* (4 April 1990).
111. Interview, Gerardo Bulatao, 2 September 1989.
112. Governor Lacson's programme, which called on sugar planters to turn over 10 per cent of their land to their farmworkers, had originally been proposed under the '60:30:10' plan (Negros Occidental, 1987).
113. Interview, Governor Daniel Lacson, 4 August 1989.
114. *PDI* (2 April 1990).
115. Interview with Rolando Dy, Center for Research and Communication, September 1987.
116. The following analysis is based on an examination of Hacienda Luisita Incorporated 'Statement of Assets and Liabilities', filed with the Securities and Exchange Commission in May 1989, and the Statement of Assets and Liabilities of the Tarlac Development Corporation, 30 June 1988.
117. In addition, the Cojuangco family owned José Cojuangco Enterprises, which was set up to purchase lands in other areas and to handle other family enterprises. They also had an important share of Sugrains Inc., which was established in 1975 to manage several corporate farms under Marcos' General Order 47 on corporate rice production.
118. *MC* (8 November 1989).
119. The charge was made by the Assembliya ng mga Manggagawang Bukid ng Hasyenda Lusita

(AMBALUS), a group of farmworkers dissatisfied with the Luisita trade-union (*MC* 3 October 1989).

120. See Goodno (1991, chapter 1) for a description of working conditions on Hacienda Luisita.

121. *PDI* (12 May 1988).

122. Hacienda Palma (Kabankalan), Maria Clara and Cabanbanan (Bago), Serabia (Enrique Magalona), Pagassa, Da-u and Elinita (Cagay). Interview Avsenio Acuña, 26 February 1989.

123. According to records at the Securities and Exchange Commission (SEC), the company was established in 1979 and all incorporators and officers were Acuñas except for Ester and Manuel Arnaldo. While two independent informants said that in 1981 Hacienda Palma had been acquired from the Hispanic Sierra family by a corporation headed by retired General Romeo Espino, Marcos' AFP chief in the late 1970s, his name appears nowhere in the documents.

124. Interview Arsenio Acuña, 26 February 1989.

125. According to SEC records, all officers were members of the family.

126. Interview, National Federation of Sugar Workers officials, 2 August 1989.

127. Interview, farmworkers on Hacienda Palma, 5 August 1989.

128. DAR, 1991a, p.17.

129. HB31557.

130. Interview, Hortensia Starke, 6 December 1988.

131. Section 32, RA6657.

132. Presidential [PARC], 20 March 1989.

133. DAR, 1991a.

134. Sources on the controversy include PAKISAMA, 1988; Del Monte, 1988; Interview, Bienvenido Narcisso Jr. and Paul Paraguya, KAANIB Association, Impasug-ong, 23 May 1989; and Interview, Adrian Pabayo, Industrial and Community Relations Manager for Del Monte Philippines, 24 May 1989.

135. Interview, DAR Assistant Secretary Briccio Tamparong Jr., 21 August 1989. The NDC was a government-owned corporation and the lands in question were originally transferred to the corporation from the public domain through executive orders. See Chapters 2 and 4 above.

136. Interview, Reynor D. Casiño, 24 May 1989.

137. Interview, Antonieta Borra, 23 May 1989.

138. Plantation workers were members of the Associated Labour Unions (ALU), and cannery workers members of the Workers' Alliance of Trade Unions (WATU), both affiliated to the Trade Union Congress of the Philippines (TUCP), set up with Marcos' blessings in the 1970s (Emmanuel DeDios, 1988, p.140).

139. Interview, Reynor D. Casiño, 24 May 1989.

140. Interview, Jun Limbo, 25 May 1989.

141. Interview, a group of Del Monte workers, 24 May 1989.

142. On the history of the two plantations see Chapter 4.

143. Interview, Cesar Alaban, Deputy Manager in charge of NGPI, 29 May 1989.

144. There were 860 agricultural workers, 43 management personnel and 70 mill employees then working at NGPI, or a total of 973 (Data provided by NGPI management). Presumably 204 were disqualified as already owning lands.

145. Thus of some 17 senior staff personnel, five were elected, while the 27 *kapataz* had two representatives and the 833 labourers, 447 of whom were general workers, had only two representatives.

146. Interview, Joel Benedicto, Senior Field Supervisor and President of the cooperative, 28 May 1989.

147. Interview, Salvador Pejo, 29 August 1989.

148. Interview, Jun Limbo, 25 May 1989.

149. The salaried employees were unionized with the ALU.

150. Interview, Cynthia Belarma, member of first and second board of Dole Agrarian Reform Beneficiaries Cooperative, 8 May 1989.

151. Interview, National Federation of Labour officials, 8 May 1989.
152. Information on the title received by the other cooperatives was not available.
153. Interview, Percival C. Dalugdug, 9 May 1989.
154. Interview, Antonieta Borra, 23 May 1989.
155. They claimed that part of the land was owned by company officials through the Sarangani Reality Corporation, but this could not be confirmed (Interview, DARBCI, 8 May 1989).
156. Interview, Briccio Tamparong Jr., 21 August 1989.
157. Interview, Adrian Pabayo, 24 May 1989. Dole's private lease was for only 12 years but they wanted a longer guarantee from the cooperative (Interview, Mani Lopez, Director, Industrial Relations for Dole, 8 May 1989).
158. DAR, 1988c.
159. Del Monte Philippines, 21 February 1989.
160. Juico, Letter to Juan Sierra, Del Monte Philippines, 6 March 1989.
161. Interview, Adrian Pabayo, 24 May 1989.
162. Interview, Antonieta Borra, 23 May 1989.
163. Interview, Joel Benedicto, 28 May 1989.
164. Interview, DARBCI, 8 May 1989.
165. Interview, Mani Lopez, 8 May 1989.
166. Interview, Juico, 16 August 1989 and Pejo, 29 August 1989. There was no corroborating evidence for this claim.
167. *MC* (10 August 1989).
168. Interview, Gerardo Bulatao, 7 December 1988 and 4 January 1989.
169. *MC* (17 January 1990).
170. *BW* (31 October 1990).
171. *PDI* (18 March 1990).
172. Doyo, 1989.
173. Interviews with Percival C. Dalugdug, DAR Director Region XI, Davao City (9 May 1989), and with Alfredo A. Alog, DAR Provincial Officer for Isabela (22 June 1989).
174. Presidential [PARC], March 1989, vol.1. Foreign aid was also requested for the $43 million (0.4 per cent of the budget) to be spent on preliminary activities.
175. DAR, 1991b.
176. On the US Agrarian Reform Support Programme, see Chapter 9, section 9.4.4.
177. For an early summary of reports on ODA to CARP see Putzel, 1990b.
178. See Putzel, 1990b, pp.23-25.
179. CIDA, 'CIDA in the Philippines, Operational Projects, 1988.'
180. The most complete study of CIDA projects in the Philippines has been carried out by the Council for Peoples' Development (1988).
181. Interview, André Vinette, Canadian International Development Agency, Ottawa, 17 November 1989.
182. The strategy is most fully explained in a book published by Roxas' consultancy firm (Foundation [FCOMT], 1984).
183. Interview, Sixto K. Roxas, 4 and 26 September 1989.
184. For a detailed criticism of the EDMS programme in Negros see Broad [BIND], 1990.
185. Interview, Governor Daniel Lacson, 4 August 1989.
186. Interview, NCPD members, 5 April 1989.
187. On Kulp's counterinsurgency views, see Chapter 1, section 1.8.4. Kulp had evidently offered his services to Horacio Morales of the Philippine Rural Reconstruction Movement, who sent him to Sixto K. Roxas (Morales, in conversation with the author 22 September 1989). Kulp arrived in the Philippines in 1986 and, according to records in the Securities and Exchange Commission, in March 1987 established Zytek Manufacturing Inc., a biotechnology firm in Manila. Previously Kulp worked with USAID in Cambodia (1962-63), Saigon and Washington (1964-65; 1968-69), Thailand (1965-67) and as a consultant in Uganda (1971-72),

Washington and Senegal (1973-76), Thailand (1976-79), Mali and Zaire (1981-82). Between 1983 and 1986 he worked with Hawaiian Agronomics International Inc., conducting joint venture studies on agribusiness projects in Thailand, Jamaica, Honduras and the Philippines.

188. *MC* (15 January 1990).

189. The municipal council in Bulan Sorsogon was busy working with local landowners to establish such aid, attracting NGOs in March 1989 (field visit).

190. Interview, Rep. Hortensia Starke, 6 December 1988.

191. Rendell, 1976; Morgan, 1980.

192. Sympathetic summaries of these experiences can be found in Graham and Floering (1984, Chapter 7) and Tiffin and Mortimore (1990).

193. Ellman and Greeley, 1989.

194. J.K. Templeton, World Bank, 1989.

195. Interview, Dorothy Tadeo, 11 August 1989.

196. Interview, R.A. Dazo, National Development Corporation, 19 May 1989.

197. Letter, John Lee to the author, 16 June 1989.

198. DAR, Region 10, Report on VOS, May 1989.

199. Interview, Adrian Pabayo, 24 May 1989.

200. Gamboa Hermanos, Inc., 1988, p.2.

201. Agusan Plantations Inc., General Information Sheet, at the Security and Exchange Commission, 1988.

202. Previously all its production was sold to NDC-Guthrie. Letter, John Lee to the author, 16 June 1989.

203. Interviews with farmworkers at Dole, May 1989.

204. Interview, N. MacDonald, CIDA Manila, 11 July 1988.

205. On total farm area see Chapter 1.

206. See Chapter 4.

207. *DG, MC* (28 January 1989).

208. At its second National Conference in 1987, the KMP called for an acceleration in the occupation of sequestered lands (*MC* 10 December 1987).

209. See Chapter 1, Table 1.9 for estimated landholdings.

210. For Santiago's announcement see *PDI* (30 August 1989); for Leong's announcements see *MC* (2 August 1991).

211. The reduction can be seen in Table 10.10. The report included a reiteration of the overall scope of the programme (DAR, 1991a).

212. The land was located in Santiago's five pilot provinces: Tarlac, Rizal, Nueva Ecija, Davao del Norte and Leyte provinces (*MC* 4 August 1989).

213. V. Francisco Varua, Vice-President of José Cojuangco & Sons, Inc. (Interview, 31 July 1989), said that JCE was the entity that had title to most of the lands outside of Hacienda Luisita, accumulated over the years by José Cojuangco II.

214. Leo Roque, DAR Land Acquisition Bureau (*MC* 24 January 1990).

215. Cojuangco records at DAR's Operation Land Transfer Center, 1989.

216. DAR, February, 1991a.

217. See Chapter 1 for a discussion of this data.

218. Provincial Agrarian Reform Office, Sorsogon, 1989. His VOS was listed among those submitted to DAR Central Office in November 1988 by the DAR Office in Region V.

219. This calculation is based on the latest tabulation of VOS in Region 3 in comparison with the aggregate Listasaka data.

220. Interview, Gerardo Bulatao, 24 January 1989.

221. Database for SALVAPUL BAMUR project, Negros Occidental, 1989. The author's research on landowners in Sorsogon province demonstrated that peasant communities have the most accurate knowledge of landownership.

11

CONCLUSION

ASSESSING THE CONSERVATIVE AND LIBERAL APPROACHES AND ALTERNATIVES FOR THE FUTURE

In recent years, it has become commonplace among those discussing development problems in the third world to dismiss redistributive agrarian reform as no longer relevant. They argue that conditions that prevailed in Japan, Taiwan and South Korea after World War II, where redistributive programmes played such an important role, no longer exist in the Philippines or other third world countries. It is argued that rapid population growth, the exhaustion of land frontiers and the growing numbers of landless labourers mean that programmes based on the redistribution of land to those who work on it can do little either to stem the growth of poverty, or to stimulate long-term economic development. The conservative argument has been put most forcefully by those who defend modern plantations and agricultural corporations as leaders in the future economic development of the third world within an increasingly international market place.

Contrary to such assertions, redistributive agrarian reform has remained relevant in the Philippines, despite changes in demographic and employment patterns and market conditions, for three inter-related reasons. First, a majority of the population continue to live in poverty-stricken rural areas, where they depend primarily on the agricultural sector for their living but enjoy no secure access to land. Second, inequality in ownership and control over land remains acute and is more extreme than most analysts have previously imagined. Third, and most important, agrarian reform remains relevant in the Philippines because both the legal peasant movement and the underground communist movement, built upon peasant support, have continued to organize and wage war around demands for land redistribution. They do so because skewed access to land is still an important source of not only economic deprivation, but also political domination. Agrarian reform has remained part of a wider struggle to empower the majority of people who are powerless in Philippine society.

Redistributive agrarian reform alone cannot solve the myriad of development problems in countries like the Philippines. In this respect, the conservatives' arguments about demographic change, the social and economic diversification of agricultural production, and changing world market conditions, drive home the fact that the world is a very different place to what it was in the 1940s and 1950s. Those in the Philippines and elsewhere who are demanding redistributive agrarian reforms now see the necessity for such reforms to be combined with programmes for the diversification of rural production. They now speak about agrarian reform as one component of a strategy for national development. There is an increasing awareness that such development must be based on environmental sustainability as well as justice. Redistributive agrarian reform cannot in itself ensure such a development path, but it appears to be a necessary condition for future progress in the Philippines.

Three sets of conclusions emerge out of this study of agrarian reform experience in the Philippines. They explain not only why so little land has been redistributed in the past, but also what prospects exist for future reforms in the archipelago and elsewhere in the third world. The first are empirical and analytical conclusions about the conservative and liberal approaches as they have been adopted by both Filipino and US actors. Second, are conclusions about the nature of state and society in the Philippines and the conditions under which the state might adopt liberal redistributive reform. Third, this study casts some light on prospects for the future, including whether the US is likely to change its attitude toward redistributive reforms or whether a military-led authoritarian regime or a revolutionary movement might be more likely agents for implementing such reforms.

11.1 The conservative and liberal approaches in retrospect

Ever since the Huk uprising in the 1950s, it has been the peasant movement, whether mobilized in legal peasant organizations or in the communist-led guerrilla army, which has kept agrarian reform on the state's policy agenda. Marcos pronounced his reform programme as the centre of his 'New Society' both to undermine the radical peasant movement and to win support for martial law among the more moderate organizations. The Aquino government did not move on agrarian reform until peasants put their lives on the line at Mendiola in January 1987, and it was their action that ensured that reform would be at the top of the Congressional agenda.

The clash between advocates of the conservative and liberal approaches to reform has characterised debates about reform among Philippine officials as well as US policy-makers since the 1950s. Advocates of the two positions were found in the committees that drafted reform legislation under Macapagal in 1963 and Marcos in 1972. The two positions were present in the coalition behind Aquino's presidential campaign and within state agencies under the new government. They clashed in debates in the Constitutional Commission, over the Executive Order, in Congress, and within DAR during the early stages of reform implementation. At each stage, US advocates of the liberal approach also challenged the conservative status quo. The fact that such a clash has recurred over time indicates that reform policy cannot be understood simply as determined by an existing 'mode of production', the class character of a regime, or the place a country holds in the 'world system'.

11.1.1 The conservatives

During the Marcos and Aquino years the conservative approach to reform has remained dominant in both state policy and the counsel given by US government officials. Under Marcos far more land was concentrated in the hands of large owners than was redistributed to tillers. The reform programme adopted by the Aquino government did not reflect a compromise between the interests and demands of landowners and the landless, but rather a *consensus* around the conservative approach. The exemptions and phasing of the CARP demonstrated its conservative character, and specific provisions on retention limits and corporate stock-sharing ensured the programme's limited scope. That consensus was reinforced by the dictates of the military, both as a result of the counterinsurgency strategy it adopted with US support and due to its own interests in consonance with those of other advocates of the conservative approach.

While advocates of the conservative approach achieved some success in putting down the revolutionary movement in the early 1950s and slowing the growth of the New People's Army in the immediate aftermath of the declaration of martial law, they were unable to offer any significant contribution to poverty alleviation, dynamic economic growth or long-term political stability. By the early 1990s, landlessness and inequality were more acute then ever and poverty still rampant. The accomplishments of resettlement programmes have been meagre and legislation instituting leasehold tenure has been impossible to enforce. Gains made through productivity enhancing programmes have neither fulfilled their potential nor proved to be sustainable over time.

The conservative approach facilitated the expansion of agribusiness. However, in the absence of redistributive reform this sector has not been able to fulfil its potential contribution to rural development. Counterinsurgency efforts based mainly on military action have helped to momentarily weaken revolutionary challenges to the state. However, each set-back suffered by peasant-based armed movements has led to a period of exponential growth of radical forces set on capturing state power.

11.1.2 The liberal approach

Experience in the Philippines also assists an evaluation of the weaknesses inherent in the liberal approach. While the liberals' formula of redistributive reform remains relevant to countries like the Philippines, its strategic vision is fundamentally flawed. Advocates of the liberal approach have consistently underestimated the influence of landowners over the state, both in their confidence in the ability of an authoritarian government to implement reform and in their belief that landowners could easily be won over to reform if the terms for compensation were attractive. They have also underestimated the bias against redistributive reform among US policy-makers. All evidence suggests that this same bias has been incorporated in the development models propagated by all the rich countries in their official development assistance to the third world.

The liberal reformers' anti-communist orientation led them to believe that peasant involvement could be achieved through the parentage of the state and by isolating and even destroying the radical peasant movement. The advocates of the liberal approach have been prone to compromise, believing they could still achieve their objectives in the context of conservative agrarian reform programmes. Thus they continued to work within the context of the Marcos programme long after it became clear that Marcos had little intention of redistributing lands. Similarly, during the Aquino years, advocates of liberal reform remained active in the DAR even when it became clear that CARP was essentially a conservative programme. In this respect they served as little more than good-will ambassadors for regimes whose overall reform programme included no significant land redistribution.

11.2 The state and society in the Philippines

Reform experience also casts light on the nature of the state and its relationship to society. Under Marcos, the state did not become autonomous from society, but was rather captured by a small faction of old and new oligarchs. Marcos relied on a network of patronage stretching from Manila to the *barrios* to enforce his authoritarian rule. The state bureaucracy remained captive to societal interests, as evidenced by DAR's activities during martial law and in the land-scams, and in the cooperation that DAR officials offered to agribusiness corporations during the implementation of the Aquino programme. The military's cooperation with landowners and agribusiness corporations during martial law continued in the post-Marcos period. It was virtually impossible to identify a dividing line, so often postulated in theory, between 'national' entrepreneurs, big landowners and foreign-linked business interests in relation to agrarian reform.

The failure to adopt and carry out a redistributive reform cannot be explained as simply a lack of 'state capacity'. The absence of a bureaucratic machinery capable of carrying out reform and the lack of adequate land records was the consequence of a particular balance of power: since the colonial period, landowning interests have shackled the bureaucracy and blocked every attempt at comprehensive land registration. However, the class character of the Philippine state is not a sufficient explanation for why redistributive reform was never adopted, particularly when considered in light of the South Korean experience.

The Marcos years proved that an authoritarian *form* of government has no special proclivity toward reform implementation. Neither is it meaningful to explain reform by the presence or absence of sufficient 'political will'. President Magsaysay was probably more committed to the goals of liberal reformers than was Syngman Rhee in South Korea. To say that a particular state failed to adopt a programme of agrarian reform because its leaders lacked 'political will', is, as Robert Chambers pointed out, 'a way of averting the eyes from ugly facts. It is a conveniently black box...[which] stops short of asking who gains and who loses what, when, where and how'.[1]

To explain the conditions under which politicians, state officials, or members of the state bureaucracy might adopt a liberal redistributive model of reform it is crucial to focus on their sources of support in society. In order to retain power, those people who govern must maintain their sources of support in both society and the institutions of the state itself. It is almost a tautology to point out that in most societies in need of agrarian reform, it is likely that landowners have considerable influence over the state.[2] People who hold commanding positions within the state are not likely to support redistributive reform policies, either individually or as part of a 'collectivity of state officials', except when such policies contribute to the maintenance of their position and power. In the case of societies in need of agrarian reform, such reforms are unlikely unless the very existence of the state is threatened, as it was in South Korea. It is for this reason that the degree of peasant mobilization, and the extent to which it presents a challenge to the very foundations of the state, would appear to be the crucial factor determining whether or not the state will adopt redistributive reform.

At most points in time in any society, individuals within state institutions, and the institutions themselves, must operate under severe constraints that limit and shape the content of the development strategies or reform policies that they can adopt.[3] But in the history of any society there are what can best be described as, 'historical moments of choice', short of revolution, when it is possible, inspired by development strategies or the dynamic role of individual leaders, to take political action that exceeds the bounds of normal constraints. This is likely only at times of crisis, when the normal consensus around which the powerful in society support the state is thrown into question. At such moments, political action can *potentially* shape the contours of the state and rearrange its pillars of support in society by significantly altering property rights and permitting such measures as the adoption of redistributive agrarian reform.

The declaration of martial law by Marcos in 1972 and Aquino's ascent to power in the 1986 'February Revolution' were such 'moments of historical choice', as was the Korean War. Both Marcos and Aquino commanded legislative powers and were in a position to re-shape the constitution. Marcos could potentially have brought his most important civilian backers behind a redistributive reform by guaranteeing them opportunities within non-agricultural sectors. What is more, Marcos was in a position to re-shape the military. However, he decided not to move in such a direction. During the first year of the Aquino government, her executive commanded overwhelming support from the population. The pressure points of the new regime remained unclear, leaving it relatively free to implement radical policies. By turning to the organized grass-roots movement, the government might have decided to adopt redistributive reform. This might have precipitated a split within the armed forces, but that occurred in any case. The contours of the split would have been different. However, President Aquino and her closest advisers did not make such a choice.

The threat posed by the radical peasant movement to the continued existence of the state was never strong enough to lead either Marcos or his US supporters to believe that redistributive reform was necessary. Under Aquino, the consensus around the conservative approach was reached essentially because those who occupied positions of authority within the state still believed that the large landowning families and foreign and domestic agribusiness corporations could take the lead in agricultural development, and that the peasant movement posed no serious threat to the state. The US government appeared to be confident that the renewed legitimacy of the Philippine government under Aquino, combined with the prominent place of the military in the state, would be sufficient to undermine the radical peasant movement and ensure a degree of stability in the country.

11.3 Prospects for agrarian reform

During the final years of the Aquino administration the world was engulfed in a process of rapid transformation. The decline and disappearance of the socialist systems throughout the Soviet bloc heralded a new era in international politics. These changes are bound to have an impact on the Philippines and on the role of the United States in the country. With the failure of the Aquino government to take up its unique opportunity to implement agrarian reform and its general failure to transcend the limits of traditional clan politics, both the military and the radical left offer alternative paths for the future. Amid these changes, landlessness and poverty continue to dominate the rural landscape in the Philippines, and calls for redistributive reform continue to be heard throughout the archipelago.

11.3.1 The end of the Cold War

With the end of the Cold War, it might be assumed that the United States would be more open to a change in attitude toward redistributive reform, or that other foreign powers may be more conducive to supporting such programmes. The attack on advocates of the liberal approach in the 1950s was largely based on the presumption that they were soft on communism and that reform itself would provide encouragement to the communists. This viewpoint has also been integral to dominant thinking on counterinsurgency. However, the US bias against redistributive reform runs deeper than its opposition to communism. One has only to look to the colonial experience in the Philippines that began before the Bolshevik Revolution. In fact, the US may prove firmer than ever in its opposition to redistributive reforms, since the only occasions on which it supported such programmes were when its perceived interests appeared to be challenged by communist-led revolutionary movements.

The US is no longer as dominant in the Philippines as it once was. Japan is quickly becoming the country's major foreign investor and is already its lead aid donor. However, the Japanese have shown no interest in agrarian reform despite their own experience with successful liberal reform after World War II. The US was able to influence the orientation of all the Western donors' aid programmes after 1986 through the Multilateral Aid Initiative. There is little sign that future initiatives for redistributive reform will receive significant encouragement from any foreign country. In many ways, the foreign aid programmes of the past have acted as an impediment to reform. In the absence of foreign aid, those who control the institutions of the state would have less room to avoid action on redistributive reforms demanded by the peasantry.

11.3.2 The armed forces and reform

After the nearly successful coup attempt against President Aquino's government in December 1989, for the first time military rebels launched their own call for agrarian reform. They criticized the Aquino government for its failure to implement meaningful agrarian reform and its maintenance of oligarchic rule. Since then members of the rebel Young Officers Union (YOU) and RAM have included agrarian reform along with nationalist opposition to the US in their own platform.[4] Some of the military rebels have even announced their intention to seek talks with the Communist Party around the possibility of establishing a united front.

While the rebel officers sought popular support by promising agrarian reform, their activities on other fronts demonstrated very different intentions. After the December 1989 coup attempt, initial statements by RAM went no further than proclaiming its commitment to 'promote the equitable distribution of the factors of production and the enjoyment of the fruits of development'.[5] This showed no more commitment to a policy of redistributive reform than the declarations made by the Aquino coalition back in 1985. Nevertheless, in April 1990, military rebel leader Col. Gregorio Honasan criticized the government for its failure to implement agrarian reform.[6]

However, Honasan's reform rhetoric was contradicted by RAM's actions. RAM Col. Alexandre Noble spoke of the alliance between his rebel forces and landowners opposed to agrarian reform organized in the Movement for a Federal Mindanao.[7] In fact, the 1989 coup attempt suggested that the military rebels would not hesitate to ally themselves with wealthy landowners to take power. It was widely believed that the return of Eduardo Cojuangco Jr. to the country just days before the coup reflected such an alliance. Cojuangco was able to build a network of patronage within the AFP during the 1970s and that network was believed to remain intact during the Aquino years.[8]

Members of the Young Officers' Union have been somewhat more consistent than RAM in calling for a reformist and nationalist agenda. From the days when RAM was plotting against the Marcos government, the military dissidents attempted to inject an ideological content into their movement by adopting the 'Filipino Ideology' expounded by Nilo Tayag. Tayag, a former Secretary General of the Communist Party who defected to Marcos, began giving lectures to the military in 1981. He argued that Communist ideology could only be defeated with a rival ideology, which he elaborated essentially in nationalist terms.[9] Tayag continued to organize the 'Democratic Front for Filipinism' and remained the leading ideologue for military dissidents in the YOU even after the failed coup attempts during the Aquino years.[10] The 'Filipino Ideology', however, makes no commitment to redistributive reform. It is more akin to the national industrialization strategy proposed by thinkers like Lichauco, which has proven hostile to agrarian reform.

Given the intimate links between many officers in the AFP and landowners and agribusiness corporations, factionalism within the military itself, and popular support for formal democratic institutions, it is highly unlikely that any military group could come to power without striking a substantive alliance with at least a section of the civilian elite. It is much more likely that any group installed in power through a military coup would confine its action on agrarian reform to the conservative approach.

11.3.3. Revolutionary agrarian reform

At the other end of the political spectrum, the communist movement has maintained a commitment to its own revolutionary redistributive agrarian programme.[11] Much of the Communist Party's support has been based on the fact that in regions where the communists are strong, they have drastically reduced the rents that tenants pay to landowners, curbed the exploitative practices of moneylenders and merchants and increased farmworkers' wages - the 'minimum goals' of the Party's land reform programme. In some areas they have redistributed idle and abandoned lands to the cultivators or encouraged owners to do so 'voluntarily' or through the government's agrarian reform programmes.[12]

The Party's 'maximum goal' is 'the free distribution of land to the tillers who have no land or who do not have enough land'. However, the Party was mindful of previous socialist experience and argued that the retention limit in a region should be determined by the amount of land owned by 'rich peasants'.[13] Since the early 1970s, when the Party suffered serious losses in the Bicol peninsula and other regions by trying to implement its maximum programme, it has usually limited its reform efforts to the minimum programme. During the early years of the Aquino administration the CPP did distribute land titles in some of the areas under its control. However, this was apparently undertaken only as a propaganda stunt and such areas were quickly singled out by the military as priority zones for attack. Party cadre have experimented with cooperative forms of production with varying degrees of success, and in recent years they claim to have made new efforts to develop more sophisticated socio-economic programmes.

Not only has the Communist Party's promotion of its agrarian programme kept agrarian reform on the national government's policy agenda, there is also some indication that the little land redistribution that occurred under the Marcos and Aquino programmes was implemented, at least in part, with CPP-NPA support. In December 1988, the underground PKM, or National Peasant Movement controlled by the Communist Party, issued a press release claiming responsibility for 80 per cent of the lands turned over to peasants in Central

Luzon under the Marcos programme.[14] Such a claim would appear spurious but for the fact that DAR officials throughout the country confirmed that they were often most successful in implementing the government's agrarian reform programmes in areas where the CPP-NPA were present.[15] The NPA has also effectively set up a protective umbrella for the development of legal peasant organizations. Without the presence of the NPA to counter the landowners' own private armies, such organizations would have had little chance to operate in many rural areas.

It is not hard to understand why the communist movement has survived in the Philippine countryside. In many areas, communist work has been based on meticulous and painstaking social investigation, involving not only the identification of social classes and their dynamics, but a careful examination of the history of the place, the everyday problems encountered (from the health of local residents to trouble with cattle rustlers) and the cultural and religious activities of the community. The communists have often provided the only form of local government and law enforcement. Many of their leading cadres at the local level came from relatively well-off families and have spent their entire adult lives living under strenuous conditions in the uplands. Peasant communities who have witnessed the work of these cadres over many years have developed a genuine respect for the movement. This has allowed the CPP to operate with impunity in many of the country's rural areas.

However, it is highly unlikely that the Communist Party would ever be able to seize and hold state power on its own, even if it does manage to survive the rapid decline of international socialism. What is more, there are serious shortcomings in its own vision of agrarian reform that cast doubt on both the feasibility and desirability of CPP leadership of the agrarian movement over the long-term. These shortcomings encompass the basic philosophical orientation of the communist movement as well as its particular vision of agrarian reform and its practice in the countryside.

Despite its long association with the peasantry, the communist movement has been unable to break from the classical Marxist creed that preaches the universal backwardness of peasants and their approach to production. This can been seen in the Party's basic writings, which incorporate the classic idealisation of 'proletarian' leadership and promote education of the peasantry in the proletarian world view. While the *Guide to Land Reform* stated that plots of land would be set aside for NPA units to farm, this seldom happened in CPP-controlled areas where peasant work was often frowned upon. One of the movement's leaders explained that when NPA cadres were found to have broken discipline, they were) *punished* by being forced to plant banana trees and engage in other peasant work.[16]

While the CPP's *Revolutionary Guide to Land Reform* stated that 'the people's democratic government shall issue new land titles' to the tillers, cadres in Bicol explained that they envisioned distributing only *ladyao*, or 'planting rights', to the peasants. In part this was because the war itself was still 'fluid' and the Party wanted to demonstrate that without state power it could not guarantee a redistribution. But they also wanted to impress upon the peasants that 'recipients must be amenable to a redistribution later'. Finally, the Party was still debating whether it should actually endow peasants with ownership-like rights over the land since this would mean a right to buy and sell land.

These are legitimate concerns. What is more worrying is what appears to be individual cadres' continuing uncritical faith in the superiority of collective farming, despite the experience of socialist countries. The National Democratic Front's draft programme in 1987-1988 mentioned only that a future government would 'encourage the formation of cooperatives in all areas of agricultural endeavours'. It said that beneficiaries would, 'in the main, determine among themselves whether they prefer to till lands individually or work them collectively' and that large plantations would be transformed into 'state farms which may be cooperatively managed by agricultural workers'. The language of the document indicated a continuing debate on the subject.[17] In areas under Party control there have been many positive experiences with cooperatives. It is often thought that the problems in establishing cooperatives under conditions of war (lack of funds, the constant threat of military encroachment) would be removed if the movement came to power. Few cadres consider that war-time conditions may, in fact, have made the peasants more open to cooperative endeavour because of external threats and that it would be difficult to maintain their enthusiasm under peaceful conditions.

More fundamentally problematic is the communist perspective on the relationship between state and civil society. Because the communists understand the state only as an instrument of class rule, they plan to replace the dominance of the 'bourgeoisie', landowners and 'foreign imperialists' with 'proletarian' dominance through a 'vanguard' party. Despite the advances made by Filipino communists in working with the peasantry, their understanding of classical theory has not been amended to include a different appreciation for the role that the peasant majority can play both in production and in governance. The Party's practice on the ground demonstrates that they continue to see peasant organizations in an instrumental fashion and as subordinate to the Party itself. All 'mass organizations' are still looked upon from the Leninist perspective, which dictates that they should become the mechanism for transmitting the Party's message to the people. There is no appreciation of the need to establish peasant organizations that are truly independent from the Party.

However, despite these basic problems, the Party continues to be the most important political force to promote the peasants' demand for land. In the absence of a strong peasant movement independent of the state and traditional political clans, the collapse of the CPP would mean a costly set-back for the peasant cause. While many find the violent route to social change advocated by the communist movement abhorrent, it must be remembered that traditional politics in the Philippines remain a source of daily violence, while the power of the AFP and paramilitary groups has long been directed against unorganised peasant communities.

11.3.4 Revolutionising the liberal approach

Redistributive agrarian reform could make a major contribution to future development and peace in the Philippines, primarily by strengthening the foundations of civil society. The liberal reformers always recognized this, but they cast it in terms of undermining communism rather than empowering people. While this study has underlined the continuities in agrarian reform debates during the post-war period, there has also been change. One of the positive repercussions of successive debates over state policy has been that the principles of redistributive reform have become increasingly accepted, and private property in land less and less sacrosanct.

Among the most significant developments during the Aquino years was the foundation and consolidation of the Congress for a People's Agrarian Reform (CPAR). This was important not only because it represented one of the only working coalitions among groups covering the centre-left political spectrum, but also because it became a platform for a new statement of an essentially liberal approach to agrarian reform. CPAR's agrarian reform programme differed from that of the traditional advocates of the liberal approach in that it prescribed a leading role for the peasant organizations independent of both the state and the dictates of any political party. Future support for such an option could conceivably come both from those reform-minded politicians, officials and activists disillusioned with the government's failure to seize a golden opportunity for agrarian reform, and radical activists disheartened by the failures of traditional communist movements.

While advocates of the liberal approach in the US seem as committed as ever to their traditional motivations, figures like Bonifacio Gillego, Gerry Bulatao and other Filipino advocates of the liberal approach during the Aquino years were - or became - aware of the need to turn to the grass-roots peasant movement to implement their option. Many activists in the Communist movement have also come to understand the value of establishing an independent peasant movement within a growing complex of independent cause-oriented and non-governmental organizations. Some of these are middle-class cadre who have left the movement, either as a result of disillusionment or sheer exhaustion, but remain committed to contributing to social change. Even more interesting are cadre who entered peasant organizations on assignment from the Party, but have come to the realisation while working in the sector that the organizations need to be allowed to develop their own independence.

The great danger in attempting to promote agrarian reform through independent peasant organizations remains one of cooptation by the state and the traditional political forces dominant within it. During the Aquino administration there was clearly an attempt by some state officials to create a classic 'third force' in an effort to weaken those demanding radical social reforms. This was seen in the use of Dante's cooperative in Tarlac by both the Land Bank and the military, in an effort to isolate the more radical peasant movement and gain legitimacy for the government's programmes. The same trend was evident in the new thrust toward NGOs initiated by international aid agencies during these years. The danger of cooptation was clearly illustrated during the period leading up to the 1992 national elections. Aside from Senator Salonga's campaign for the presidency, by early 1992 none of the major candidates dared to comment on agrarian reform, let alone include it in their electoral programmes.[18] Clearly, traditional electoral politics in the Philippines offered little hope as a vehicle for promoting redistributive agrarian reform.

The principal impediment to cooptation has remained the intransigence of both the traditional political clans and the military toward any concessions on agrarian reform. There was a possibility that the appointment of the liberal reformer Butch Abad as DAR Secretary in 1990 might have secured the liberals' participation in government and would have helped to legitimate the conservative approach embodied in the CARP. However, his appointment was blocked by landowners and the corporate sector. Ironically, their very intransigence may contribute to the emergence of a new movement for redistributive reform based within autonomous organizations of the peasantry.

The existence of the CPP has contributed to keeping the danger of cooptation at bay, since the Party continues to organize peasants around a radical redistributive programme. It has contributed to developing among peasants a sense of self-confidence and independence from traditional patrons, including both large and small landowners, upon whom peasant families have often had to rely for their very survival. Every independent initiative must measure up to the standard set by the underground movement if it has any hope of winning the confidence of the peasantry. Perhaps the greatest source of hope lies among the peasants themselves, since they have seen many false promises of reform. In the end, it will be the peasants who will keep redistributive agrarian reform on the agenda for as long as they continue to be confined to conditions of poverty and insecurity.

Notes

1. Chambers, 1983, p.161.
2. Herring (1983, p.218) made the point from a structuralist perspective, arguing that state autonomy with regard to land reform is limited because, 'Those who command the agricultural means of production control the surplus, and export earnings or import substitutes', which creates a 'structural dependence of regimes on landed classes'. See also Block (1977).
3. Thompson, 1965, p.279.
4. RAM, which led the revolt against Marcos and the serious coup attempts against the Aquino government, gave its acronym a new content when they changed their name to the Rebolusyunaryong Alyansang Makabayan (People's Revolutionary Alliance). On YOU's endorsement of agrarian reform see MC (16 May 1990 and 16 October 1991).
5. RAM-SFP, 1990, p.189.

6   Transcript of an interview with Col. Gregorio Honasan, 9 April 1990, furnished to the author.

7   *Independent* (20 January 1990).

8   Tiglao, 1990, pp.13,19-20.

9   Coronel, 1990, pp.54-56. Tayag's work was reflected in the book, *Filipino Ideology*, released under Marcos' name in 1983.

10   Gloria, 1990, pp.135-137.

11   CPP, 1972.

12   Discussions with CPP cadres in the Bicol region, 1989, and from the Cagayan Valley, 1989. See the accounts of: Goodno, 1991; Jones, 1989; Davis, 1989; Chapman, 1988; and Padilla 1988.

13   CPP, 1972, Chapters 2-5.

14   *PDI* (12 December 1988).

15   Interviews with regional, provincial and municipal DAR officials 1988 and 1989.

16   Interview, Ka Mer, Bicol region command, September 1989.

17   NDF, 1988, pp.13-26.

18   Salonga criticized the government's programme, saying 'the farmers will never get land' (*DG* 17 December 1991).

BIBLIOGRAPHY

1. Books, articles, conference papers

Abueva, José V. (1986) 'Images and Meanings of the February Revolution'. Paper presented at the Conference of Professors for Peace, Manila (August).

Abueva, José V. (1987) 'Yes to the 1986 Constitution: Perspectives on Self-Determination, Democratization, Nation-Building and Contributing to Peaceful Change in the World', 14 January. Reprinted, *Philippine Daily Inquirer* (19 January 1987, p.7).

Adriano, Fermin D. (1984) 'A Critique of the "Bureaucratic Authoritarian State" Thesis: The Case of the Philippines', *Journal of Contemporary Asia*, 14, no.4.

Adriano, Fermin (1990) 'The Power Game Behind the Cabinet Revamp', *Manila Chronicle* (7 January).

Agoncillo, Teodoro A. (1960) *Malolos: The Crisis of the Republic*. Quezon City: University of the Philippines.

Agoncillo, Teodoro A. (1974) *Filipino Nationalism, 1872-1970*. Quezon City: R.P. Garcia Publishing Co.

Aguilar, Delia D. (1987) 'The Social Construction of the Filipino Woman', *Diliman Review*, 35, no.7, pp.50-62.

Alburo, Florian A. *et al* (1986) *Economic Recovery and Long-Run Growth: Agenda for Reforms*. Quezon City: Philippine Institute for Development Studies.

Alternative Forum for Research in Mindanao (AFRIM) (1986) 'The NDC-Guthrie Plantations in the Philippines', *Mindanao Focus*, no.11 (September).

Alternative Forum for Research in Mindanao (AFRIM) (1990) *Mindanao Incorporated: A Primer and Directory of Major Corporations Operating in Mindanao*. Davao: AFRIM.

Amin, Samir (1981) *The Future of Maoism*. New York: Monthly Review Press.

Amnesty International (1981) *Report of an Amnesty International Mission to the Republic of the Philippines*. London: Amnesty International Publications (11-18 November).

Amnesty International (1988) *Philippines: Unlawful Killings by Military and Paramilitary Forces*. London: Amnesty International Publications (March).

Amnesty International (1990) *Philippines: Imprisonment of Peasant Leader - Jaime Tadeo*, summary, AI Index ASA 35/17/90. London: Amnesty International (June).

Amsden, Alice H. (1989) *Asia's Next Giant: South Korea and Late Industrialization*. Oxford: Oxford University Press.

Anderson, Benedict (1988) 'Cacique Democracy in the Philippines: Origins and Dreams', *New Left Review*, no.169 (May-June).

Aquino, Belinda A. (1987) *Politics of Plunder: The Philippines Under Marcos*. Quezon City: Great Books Trading and U.P. College of Public Administration.

Aquino, Benigno (1983) 'Statement to the US House of Representatives'. 'United States-Philippines Relations and the New Base and Aid Agreement', Hearing before the Committee on Foreign Affairs and its Subcommittee on Asian and Pacific Affairs. 98th Congress, First Session (24 June). Washington D.C.: US Government Printing Office, 1983, pp.74-89.

Aquino, Corazon C. (1986) 'Broken Promises in a Land of Promise', Speech Delivered at the Ateneo de Davao Gymnasium, Davao City, 16 January 1986 cited in *Malaya*, 17 February 1986.

Ban Sung Hwan *et al* (1980) *Rural Development*. Cambridge: Council on East Asian Studies, Harvard University.

Barraclough, Solon (1982) 'Seven Hypotheses Concerning Comparative Studies of Agrarian Reform', *Working Paper*. Geneva: United Nations Research Insitute for Social Development.

Barraclough, Solon, ed. (1973) *Agrarian Structure in Latin America: A Resume of the CIDA Land Tenure Studies of Argentina, Brazil, Chile, Colombia, Ecuador, Guatemala, Peru*. Lexington, MA: Lexington Books.

Barry, Tom, Deb Preusch and Beth Sims (1986) *The New Right Humanitarians*. Albuquerque, New Mexico: Inter-Hemispheric Education Resource Center.

Baskñas, Juanita P. and Rosa L. Niduaza, (1978) *Profile of Prospective Samahang Nayon Members in the Philippines*. Los Baños: IDRC and Agricultural Credit and Cooperative Institute, University of the Philippines (March).

Baytion, Ma. Corazon E., Enrico F. Esguerra and Alexander R. Magno (1989) 'Development Cooperation and the Aquino Administration', paper presented at the National Symposium on a Midterm Assessment of the Aquino Government, Asian Institute of Tourism (4 October).

Bell, Clive (1974) 'Ideology and Economic Interests in Indian Land Reform', in D. Lehmann, ed., *Agrarian Reform and Agrarian Reformism: Studies of Peru, Chile, China and India*. London: Faber and Faber.

Bello, Walden, David Kinley and Elaine Elinson (1982) *Development Debacle: The World Bank in the Philippines*. San Francisco: Institute for Food and Development Policy and the Philippine Solidarity Network.

Bello, Walden (1985) 'Edging Toward the Quagmire: The United States and the Philippine Crisis', *World Policy Journal* (1985-86), pp.29-58.

Bello, Walden (1987) *Creating the Third Force: U.S. Sponsored Low Intensity Conflict in the Philippines*. San Francisco: Institute for Food and Development Policy.

Bentham, Jeremy (1789) *An Introduction to the Principles of Morals and Legislation*. London: Athlone Press, 1970.

Bergamini, David (1972) *Japan's Imperial Conspiracy*. New York: Pocket Books.

Berry, A.R. and R.W. Cline (1979) *Agrarian Structure and Productivity in Developing Countries*. Baltimore: Johns Hopkins University Press.

Blair, Emma Helen and James Alexander Robertson, ed.s (1903-1919) *The Philippine Islands, 1493-1898*. Cleveland: Arthur H. Clark.

Block, Fred (1977) 'The Ruling Class Does Not Rule: Notes on the Marxist Theory of the State', *Socialist Revolution*, 33 (May-June), pp.6-28.

Bonner, Raymond (1988) *Waltzing With a Dictator: The Marcoses and the Making of American Policy*. First edition 1987. New York: Vintage Books.

Boyce, James (forthcoming) *The Philippines: The Political Economy of Growth and Impoverishment in the Marcos Era*. London: Macmillan.

Bredo, William (1970) 'Agrarian Reform in Vietnam: Vietcong and Government of Vietnam Strategies in Conflict', *Asian Survey*, 10, no.8 (August).

Broad, Robin (1988) *Unequal Alliance: The World Bank, the International Monetary Fund, and the Philippines*. Berkeley: University of California Press.

Brock, Peter (1988) 'Fundamentalist Expansion: An Historical Perspective', *WSCF Journal* (April).

Brockett, Charles D. (1988) *Land, Power and Poverty: Agrarian Transformation and Political Conflict in Central America*. London: Unwin Hyman.

Brown, Lester (1970) *Seeds of Change*. New York: Praeger.

Burbach, Roger and Patricia Flynn (1980) *Agribusiness in the Americas*. New York: Monthly Review Press.

Burton, Sandra (1989) *Impossible Dream: The Marcoses, The Aquinos, and the Unfinished Revolution*. New York: Warner Books.

Carr, Edward H. (1979) *The Russian Revolution from Lenin to Stalin*. London: Macmillan.

Castillo, Gelia T. (1975) *All in a Grain of Rice*. Laguna: Southeast Asian Regional Center for Graduate Study and Research in Agriculture.

Catholic Bishops' Conference of the Philippines (1987) 'Thirsting for Justice, A Pastoral Exhortation on Agrarian Reform', signed by Ricardo Cardinal Vidal, President, Tagaytay City (14 July).

Center for Research and Communications (CRC) (n.d.). Publicity brochure.

Center for Research and Communications (CRC) (1986) *Agribusiness Fact Book and Directory*. Manila: CRC.

Center for Research and Communications (CRC) (1990) *Agribusiness Fact Book and Directory*. Manila: CRC.

Chambers, Robert (1983) *Rural Development: Putting the Last First*. London and New York: Longman.

Chapman, William (1988) *Inside the Philippine Revolution*. London: I.B. Tauris & Co.

Chomsky, Noam and Edward S. Herman (1979) *After the Cataclysm: Postwar Indochina and the Reconstruction of Imperial Ideology*. Volume 2 of *The Political Economy of Human Rights*. Montreal: Black Rose Books.

Christic Institute (1988) *Inside the Shadow of Government*. Declaration of Plaintiffs' Counsel, US District Court, Miami Florida (31 March). Washington D.C.: Christic Institute.

Chutima, Gawin (1990) 'The Rise and Fall of the Communist Party of Thailand', *Occasional Paper No.12*. Canterbury: Centre of South-East Asian Studies, University of Kent.

Clad, James (1987) 'Soldiers of God', *Far Eastern Economic Review* (3 March).

Colayco, Maria Teresa (1987) *Crowning the Land: The History of Philippine Packing Corporation*. Makati: Philippine Packing Corporation.

Communist Party of the Philippines (1972) Executive Committee, 'Revolutionary Guide to Land Reform', published in 1972 along with 'Rules of the People's Revolutionary Government'.

Communist Party of the Philippines (1987) 'Statement of the Communist Party of the Philippines on the 18th Anniversary of the New People's Army', *Ang Bayan* (publication of the Central Committee), Special Issue (29 March).

Congress for a People's Agrarian Reform (CPAR) (1987) *People's Declaration of Agrarian Reform*, Quezon City, 31 May.

Congress for a People's Agrarian Reform (CPAR) (1990) in Grace P. Arcilla, ed., *Lupa at Buhay, Agrarian Reform in the Philippines*. Amsterdam: Philippine Development Forum, pp.59-64.

Congress for a People's Agrarian Reform (CPAR) (1990a) *Assessment of the Second Year of Republic Act 6657*. Quezon City: CPAR.

Constantino, Letizia (1987) 'Agrarian Reform', *Education Forum*, 7 (15-30 December).

Constantino, Renato (1969) *The Making of a Filipino*. Quezon City: Malaya Books.

Constantino, Renato (1970) *Dissent and Counter-Consciousness*. Quezon City.

Constantino, Renato (1975) *A History of the Philippines*. New York: Monthly Review Press.

Constantino, Renato and Letizia R. Constantino (1978) *The Philippines: The Continuing Past*. Quezon City: Foundation for Nationalist Studies.

Cordova, Violeta G. (1982) 'New Rice Technology and its Effect on Labour Use and Shares in Rice Production in Laguna, Philippines', in Geoffry B. Hainsworth, ed., *Village-Level Modernization in Southeast Asia*. Vancouver: University of British Columbia Press, pp.191-206.

Coronel, Sheila S. (1990) 'RAM: From reform to revolution', in *KUDETA: The Challenge to Philippine Democracy*. Manila: Philippine Center for Investigative Journalism, pp.51-86.

Corpus, Lt. Col. Victor (1989) *Silent War*. Quezon City: VNC Enterprises.

Council of Agricultural Producers of the Philippines (CAPP) (1987a) *Fact Sheet and Materials on the Comprehensive Agrarian Reform Program*. Manila: CAPP.

Council of Agricultural Producers of the Philippines (CAPP) (1987b) 'Position Paper on the Comprehensive Agrarian Reform Program', Manila: CAPP.

Council of Agricultural Producers of the Philippines (CAPP) (1988) 'Memorandum on Senate Bill 249', signed Eduardo F. Hernandez, Chairman (6 May). Manila: CAPP.

Council for People's Development (CPD) (1988) 'The Politics of Aid: The Case of Negros Rehabilitation and Development Fund', Quezon City.

Courtney, P.P. (1980) *Plantation Agriculture*. 2nd ed., London: Bell and Hymann.

Cummings, Bruce (1981) *The Origins of the Korean War, Liberation and the Emergence of Separate*

Regimes, vol.1. Princeton: Princeton University Press.

Davis, Leonard (1989) *Revolutionary Struggle in the Philippines*. London: Macmillan.

Davis, John H. and Ray A. Goldberg (1957) *A Concept of Agribusiness*. Boston: Harvard University, Graduate Scool of Business Administration.

De Dios, Aurora Javate-de, Petronilo Bn. Daroy and Lorna Kalaw-Tirol, ed.s (1988) *Dictatorship and Revolution: Roots of People's Power*. Manila: Conspectus.

de Dios, Emmanuel S. (1988) 'The Erosion of Dictatorship', in Aurora Javate-de Dios, Petronilo Bn. Daroy and Lorna Kalaw-Tirol, ed.s, *Dictatorship and Revolution: Roots of People's Power*. Manila: Conspectus, pp.70-131.

de Dios, Emmanuel S. and Carlos C. Bautista (1990) 'Of Cabbages and Kings: Analysing the Economy in the 1990s', University of the Philippines, School of Economics (14 February).

de Guzman, Raul P. and Mila A. Reforma (1988) *Government and Politics of the Philippines*. Singapore: Oxford University Press.

de Janvry, Alain (1981) *Agrarian Question and Reformism in Latin America*. Baltimore and London: Johns' Hopkins University Press.

de Jesus, Ed. C. (1980) *The Tobacco Monopoly in the Philippines*. Quezon City: Ateneo de Manila University Press.

de Jesus, Ed. C. (1982) 'Control and Compromise in the Cagayan Valley', in *Philippine Social History: Global Trade and Local Transformations*. Ed. Alfred W. McCoy and Ed. C. de Jesus. Quezon City: Ateneo de Manila University Press, pp. 21-37.

de la Torre, Edicio (1986) *Touching Ground, Taking Root: Theological and Political Reflections on the Philippine Struggle*. London: Catholic Institute for International Relations.

de los Reyes, Basilio N. (1972) 'Can Land Reform Succeed?' in Lynch, Frank, ed. *View from the Paddy: Empirical Studies of Philippine Rice Farming and Tenancy*. Philippine Sociological Review, 20, no.s 1 and 2 (January and April)

de Quiros, Conrado (1990) *Flowers from the Rubble*. Manila: Anvil Publishing.

Diokno, José (1987) *A Nation for Our Children: Human Rights, Nationalism, Sovereignty - The Selected Writings of José Diokno*. Quezon City: José W. Diokno Foundation and Claretian Publications.

Diokno, Ma. Serena I. (1988) 'Unity and Struggle', in Aurora Javate-de Dios, Petronilo Bn. Daroy and Lorna Kalaw-Tirol, ed.s, *Dictatorship and Revolution: Roots of People's Power*. Manila: Conspectus, pp.132-175.

Dore, Ronald P. (1959) *Land Reform in Japan*. London and New York: Oxford University Press.

Dorner, Peter (1972) *Land Reform and Economic Development*. Harmondsworth: Penguin Books, Ltd.

Doronila, Amando (1985) 'The Transformation of Patron-Client Relations and its Political Consequences in Postwar Philippines', *Journal of Southeast Asian Studies*, 16, no.1 (March), pp.99-116.

Douglas, Donald E. (1970) 'An Historical Survey of the Land Tenure Situation in the Philippines', *Solidarity*, 5 (July).

Doyo, Ma. Ceres P. (1989) 'Philippines: Bernabe 'Kumander Dante' Buscayno: From Arms to Farms', *Sunday Inquirer Magazine* (23 July).

Dy, Rolando (1986) 'Philippines: Some Approaches to Aid Utilization for Agricultural Development', Manila: Centre for Research and Communications.

Edgerton, Ronald K. (1984) 'Americans, Cowboys, and Cattlemen on the Mindanao Frontier,' in Peter Stanley, ed., *Reappraising an Empire: New Perspectives on Philippine-American History*. Cambridge, MA: Harvard Studies in American-East Asian Relations 10, pp.171-198.

El-Ghonemy, M. Riad (1990) *The Political Economy of Rural Poverty: The Case for Land Reform*. London: Routledge.

Estrella, Conrado (1969) *The Democratic Answer to the Philippine Agrarian Problem*. Manila: Solidaridad.

Estrella, Conrado (1971) 'New Guidelines for Land Reform', *Solidarity*, 6, no.7, pp.2-12.

Europa Publications (1987) *The Far East and Australasia*. London: Europa Publications.

Evans, Peter B. (1985) 'Transnational Linkages and the Economic Role of the State: An Analysis of Developing and Industrialized Nations in Post-World War II Period', in Peter B. Evans, Dietrich Rueschemeyer and Theda Skocpol, eds., *Bringing the State Back In*. Cambridge: Cambridge

University Press, pp.192-217.

Farmers' Assistance Board (FAB) (1978) *Green Revolution and Imperialism*. Quezon City: FAB.

Feder, Ernest (1971) *The Rape of the Peasantry: Latin America's Landholding System*. Garden City: Anchor Books.

Feder, Ernest (1983) *Perverse Development*. Quezon City: Nationalist Foundation.

Feder-Gershon, Tongroj Oncan, Yongyuth Chalamwong and Chira Hongladaron (1988). *Land Policies and Farm Productivity in Thailand*. Baltimore: Johns Hopkins University Press.

Fegan, Brian (1982) 'Land Reform and Technical Change in Central Luzon: Rice Industry Under Martial Law'. *Philippine Commodity Paper*, series no. 4 (September). Quezon City: Third World Studies Center, University of the Philippines.

Ferrer, Ricardo D. (1984) 'On the Mode of Production in the Philippines: Some Old-Fashion Questions on Marxism'. In *Marxism in the Philippines*. Ed. R.S. David. Quezon City: Third World Studies Center, University of the Philippines, pp.189-242.

Ferrer, Ricardo D. (1989) 'On the National Bourgeoisie in the Philippines: An Empirical Study', School of Economics, University of the Philippines.

Floro, Sagrario (1987) 'Technical Change, and the Structure of Informal Credit Market', paper at a conference, 'Differential Impact of Modern Rice Technology on Favorable and Unfavorable Production Environments', (23-25 March), International Rice Research Institute, Los Baños.

Forbes, W. Cameron (1928) *The Philippine Islands*. Boston and New York: Houghton Mifflin.

Foundation for Community Organization and Management Technology (1984) *Community-Based Organization and Management Technology*. Manila: FCOMT.

Francisco, Luzviminda (1973) 'The First Vietnam: The US-Philippine War of 1899', *Bulletin of Concerned Asian Scholars*, 5, no.4 (December) reprinted in Luzviminda Bartolome and Fast, 1985.

Francisco, Luzviminda B. and Jonathan S. Fast (1985) *Conspiracy for Empire: Big Business, Corruption and the Politics of Imperialism in America, 1876-1907*. Quezon City: Foundation for Nationalist Studies.

Franke, Richard and Barbara Chasin, (1990) 'Development Without Growth: The Kerala Experiment', *Technology Review* (April), pp.43-51.

Friend, Theodore (1965) *Between Two Empires: The Ordeal of the Philippines 1929-1946*. New Haven: Yale University Press.

Galbraith, J.K. (1951) 'Conditions for Economic Change in Under-Developed Countries', *Journal of Farm Economics*, 33, pp.689-696.

Galula, David (1964) *Counterinsurgency Warfare: Theory and Practice*. London and Dunmow: Pall Mall Press and Praeger.

George, Henry (1879) *Progress and Poverty: An Inquiry into the Cause of Industrial Depressions, and of Increase of Want with Increase of Wealth. - The Remedy*. London: Kegan Paul, Trench and Co., 1888.

George, Henry (1881) *The Irish Land Question*, published in 6th edition as *The Land Question*, London: W. Reeves, 1908.

Ghai, D., C. Kay and P. Peek (1988) *Labour and Development in Rural Cuba*. ILO Study. London: Macmillan.

Ghose, Ajit Kumar, ed. (1983) *Agrarian Reform in Contemporary Developing Countries*. London: Croom Helm.

Gillego, Bonifacio (1988) 'The Voice of 70% of the People', printed in two parts, *Manila Bulletin* (23, 28 February).

Gillego, Bonifacio (1988a) 'The Confessions of Bonifacio Gillego', *Alternative*, vol.2, no.s 2 and 3 (January-June), pp.3-6, 57.

Gittinger, J.P. (1961) 'United States Policy Toward Agrarian Reform in Underdeveloped Nations', *Land Economics*, 37, no.5 (December).

Gleeck, Lewis E. Jr. (1981) *Laguna in American Times: Coconuts and Revolucionarios*. Manila: Historical Conservation Society, XXXIV.

Gloria, Glenda (1990) 'YOU: The soldier as nationalist', in *KUDETA: The Challenge to Philippine Democracy*. Manila: Philippine Center for Investigative Journalism, pp.133-138.

Gonzaga, Violeta B. Lopez (1988) *The Resource Base for Agrarian Reform and Development in Negros*

Occidental. Bacolod: Lasalle Social Research Center.

Gonzaga, Violeta B. Lopez (1989) *The Socio-Politics of Sugar: Wealth, Power Formation and Change in Negros (1899-1985)*. Bacolod: University of St. La Salle.

Gonzales, Ana Miren and Mary Hollnsteiner (1976) *Filipino Women as Partners of Men in Progress and Development: A Survey of Empirical Data*, Quezon City: Institute of Philippine Culture.

Goodno, James B. (1991) *The Philippines: Land of Broken Promises*. London: Zed Books.

Gorz, André (1988) *Critique of Economic Reason*. Translated by Gillian Handyside and Chris Turner. London: Verso.

Graham, Edgar and Ingrid Floering (1984) *The Modern Plantation in the Third World*. London and Sidney: Croom Helm.

Griffin, Keith (1974, 1979) *The Political Economy of Agrarian Change: An Essay on the Green Revolution*. First and second editions. London: Macmillan.

Griffin, Keith (1976) *Land Concentration and Rural Poverty*. London: Macmillan Press.

Griffin, Keith (1989) *Alternative Strategies for Economic Development*. London: Macmillan.

Grindle, Merilee S. (1986) *State and Countryside: Development Policy and Agrarian Politics in Latin America*. Baltimore and London: Johns Hopkins University Press.

Guerrero, Amado (1970) *Philippine Society and Revolution*. 3rd. ed. Oakland, CA: International Association of Filipino Patriots, 1979.

Guthrie, G.M., ed. (1971) *The Psychology of Modernization in the Rural Philippines*. Institute of Philippine Culture (IPC) Papers, No.8. Quezon City: IPC, Ateneo de Manila University.

Gurr, Ted Robert (1970) *Why Men Rebel*. Princeton: Princeton University Press.

Halliday, Jon (1978) 'The Political Background', *Korea, North and South*. New York: Monthly Review Press.

Han Sungjoo (1974) *The Failure of Democracy in South Korea*. Berkeley: University of California Press.

Harkin, Duncan A. (1975) 'Strengths and Weaknesses of the Philippine Land Reform'. *SEADAG Papers on Problems of Development in Southeast Asia*. Rome: U.N. Food and Agriculture Organization.

Hawes, Gary (1987) *The Philippine State and the Marcos Regime: The Politics of Export*. Ithaca: Cornell University Press.

Hayami, Yujiro and Masao Kikuchi (1985) 'Directions of Agrarian Change: A View from Villages in the Philippines', in Mellor, J. and G. Desai, ed.s, *Agricultural Change and Rural Poverty*. Baltimore: Johns Hopkins University Press.

Hayami, Yujiro, Ma. Agnes R. Quisumbing and Lourdes S. Adriano (1990) *Toward an Alternative Land Reform Paradigm: A Philippine Perspective*. Manila: Ateneo de Manila University Press.

Heady, E.O. (1952) *Economics of Agricultural Production and Resource Use*. New York: Prentice-Hall.

Held, David (1989) *Political Theory and the Modern State: Essays on State, Power and Democracy*. Cambridge: Polity Press.

Henderson, Gregory (1968) *Korea, the Politics of the Vortex* Cambridge: Harvard University Press.

Herring, Ronald J. (1983) *Land to the Tiller: The Political Economy of Agrarian Reform in South Asia*. New Haven: Yale University Press.

Hewes, Lawrence I. (1955) *Japanese Land Reform Program*. Tokyo, 1950; rpt. Ames, Iowa: Iowa State College Press.

Hick, Steven (1987) *Land Our Life*. Quezon City: Claretian Publications.

Hickey, Gerald C. and John L. Wilkinson (1978) *Agrarian Reform in the Philippines*. Santa Monica: RAND Corporation.

Hinton, William (1966) *Fanshen: Documentary of Revolution in a Chinese Village*. New York: Random House, Vintage Books.

Hipolito, Raffy Rey (1989) 'Japanese Economic Power: Philippine Setting', *Diliman Review*, 37, no.2.

Hollnsteiner, Mary R. et al. (1978) 'Development from the Bottom Up, Mobilizing the Rural Poor for Self-Development', *Country Report on the Philippines*. Rome: U.N. Food and Agricultural Organization.

Huizer, Gerrit, (1972) 'Peasant Mobilization and Land Reform in Indonesia', The Hague: Institute of Social Studies, Occasional Paper (June).

Huntington, Samuel P. (1968) *Political Order in Changing Societies*. New Haven and London: Yale University Press.

Hutchcroft, Paul D. (1989) 'Subject of Neglect, Object of Plunder: The State in Philippine Political Economy'. Paper presented to the Third International Philippine Studies Conference, Quezon City, 13-17 July.

Hutchcroft, Paul D. (1990) 'A State Besieged: Historical Patterns of State-Elite Relations in the Philippines', *Issues and Letters*, 1, no.4.

IBON Databank (1988a) *Directory of TNCs in the Philippines*. Manila: IBON Databank Phils., Inc.

IBON Databank (1988b) *Land Reform in the Philippines*. Manila: IBON Databank Phils., Inc.

Ileto, Reynaldo C. (1979) *Pasyon and Revolution: Popular Movements in the Philippines, 1840-1910*. Quezon City: Ateneo de Manila University Press.

Inoferio, Jovito G. (1979) 'Impact of Public Agricultural Land Distribution on Farm Size Inequality in Palawan 1951-1955', *Discussion Paper* 7903. Quezon City: School of Economics, University of the Philippines.

Institute for Popular Democracy (IPD) (1990) Fact Sheet, 3 February.

International Commission of Jurists (1984) *The Philippines: Human Rights After Martial Law*. Geneva.

International Commission of Jurists (1991) *The Failed Promise: Human Rights in the Philippines Since the Revolution of 1986*. Geneva: International Commission of Jurists.

International Development and Research Centre (IDRC) (1978) *Profile of Prospective Samahang Nayon Members in the Philippines*. With the Department of Local Government and Community Development and the Agricultural Credit and Cooperative Institute. Laguna: University of the Philippines at Los Baños.

International Rice Research Institute (various years) *Annual Report*.

Ishikawa, Shigeru (1970) *Agricultural Development Strategies in Asia: Case Studies of the Philippines and Thailand*. Manila: Asian Development Bank.

Islam, R. (1983) 'Poverty, Income Distribution and Growth in Rural Thailand', in A.R. Khan and E. Lee, ed.s, *Poverty in Rural Asia*. Geneva: International Labour Organization.

Jackson, Karl (1986) 'Post-Colonial Rebellion and Counter-Insurgency in Southeast Asia', *Asian Survey* (pre-publication off-print provided by the author).

Jacobs, Norman (1985) *The Korean Road to Modernization and Development*. Chicago: University of Illinois Press.

Jacoby, Eric (1971) *Man and Land: the Essential Revolution*. New York: Alfred A. Knopf.

Jessop, Bob (1982) *The Capitalist State: Marxist Theories and Methods*. Oxford: Basil Blackwell.

Joaquin, Nick (1986) *The Aquinos of Tarlac: An Essay on History as Three Generations*. Third edition. Manila: Solar Publishing Corporation.

Joaquin, Nick (1990) *Jaime Ongpin: The Enigma, A Profile of the Filipino as Manager*. Makati: Jaime V. Ongpin Institute of Business and Government.

Johnson, Loch K. (1989) *America's Secret Power: The CIA in a Democratic Society*. Oxford: Oxford University Press.

Jones, Gregg, Jr. (1989) *Red Revolution: Inside the Philippine Guerrilla Movement*. London: Westview Press.

José, F. Sionel, ed. (1976) 'Agrarian Reform - How Far Have We Gone', *Solidarity*, 10, no.1 (January-February).

José, F. Sionel, ed. (1986) 'Agrarian Reform Now!' *Solidarity*, No.s 106-107.

José, F. Sionel, ed. (1987) *A Filipino Agenda for the 21st Century*. Solidarity Conference, 7-8 February, Manila. Manila: Solidaridad Publishing House.

José, Vivencio R., ed. (1982) *Mortgaging the Future: The World Bank and the IMF in the Philippines*. Quezon City: Foundation for Nationalist Studies.

Kerkvliet, Benedict, J. (1977) *The Huk Rebellion: A Study of Peasant Revolt in the Philippines*. Berkeley: University of California Press and Quezon City: New Day Publishers.

Kerkvliet, Benedict J. (1979) 'Land Reform: Emancipation or Counter-Insurgency', in D.A. Rosenberg, ed., *Marcos and Martial Law in the Philippines*. Ithaca and London: Cornell University

391

Press.

Kerkvliet, Benedict, J. (1990) *Everyday Politics in the Philippines: Class and Status in Relations in a Central Luzon Village*. Berkeley: University of California Press.

Kessler, Richard (1989) *Rebellion and Repression in the Philippines*. New Haven: Yale University Press.

Kikuchi, Masao, Luisa Maligalgig-Bambo and Yujiro Hayami (1977) *Evolution of the Land Tenure System in a Laguna Village*. Manila: Agricultural Economics Department of the International Rice Research Institute.

Kikuchi, Masao and Yujiro Hayami, (1982) 'Technological and Institutional Response and Income Shares Under Demographic Pressure: A Comparison of Indonesian and Philippine Villages', in Geoffry B. Hainsworth, ed., *Village-Level Modernization in Southeast Asia*. Vancouver: University of British Columbia Press, pp.173-190.

Kilusang Magbubukid ng Pilipinas (KMP - Philippine Peasant Movement) (1986) *Program for Genuine Land Reform*. Quezon City (June).

Kim Joungwon (1975) *Divided Korea: The Politics of Development 1945-1972*. Cambridge: Harvard University Press.

King, Russell (1977) *Land Reform: A World Survey*. London: G. Bell and Sons.

Kiunisala, Edward (1986) 'The Only Way to Progress and Peace', *Philippine Free Press* (14 June), reprinted in Orlino Sol. Palapac, ed., *Fresh Winds of Change in Agrarian Reform*. Quezon City: Public Information Division, Ministry of Agrarian Reform, pp.13-28.

Kohli, Atul (1987) *The State and Poverty in India: The Politics of Reform*. Cambridge: Cambridge University Press.

Kolko, Gabriel (1969) *Roots of America's Foreign Policy*. Boston: Beacon Press.

Kolko, Gabriel (1986) *Vietnam, Anatomy of a War, 1940-1975*. London: Allen and Unwin.

Koone, Harold D. and Lewis E. Gleeck (1970) *Land Reform in the Philippines*. Agency for International Development, Spring Review. Washington, D.C.: US Agency for International Development.

Kulp, Earl M. (1970) *Rural Development Planning: Systems Analysis and Working Method*. New York: Praeger Publishers.

Kulp, Earl M. (1977) *Designing and Managing Basic Agricultural Programs*. Indiana: International Development Institute, Indiana University.

Lactao, Ernesto (1988) 'The Marketing System in Cagayan Valley: Analysis in a Town on Monopoly and Cooperative', Food Watch Research Program. Quezon City: Philippine Peasant Institute (April).

Ladejinsky, Wolf (1934) 'The Collectivization of Agriculture in the Soviet Union', *Political Science Quarterly* (March, June), pp.1-43, 207-252.

Ladejinsky, Wolf (1938) 'Soviet State Farms', *Political Science Quarterly* (March, June), pp.60-82, 207-232.

Ladejinsky, Wolf (1970) 'Ironies of India's Green Revolution', *Foreign Affairs*, 48 (July).

Ladejinsky, Wolf I. (1977) *Agrarian Reform as Unfinished Business: The Selected Papers of Wolf Ladejinsky*. Ed. Louis J. Walinsky. Published for the International Bank for Reconstruction and Development/ The World Bank. New York and London: Oxford University Press.

- (1939) 'Japan's Agricultural Crisis', pp.39-48.
- (1939b) 'Agricultural Problems of India', pp.30-39.
- (1947) 'Farm Tenancy in Japan', pp.68-92.
- (1949) 'Land Commissions in Japan', pp.109-113.
- (1949a) 'Field Trip in Szechwan: Tenant Conditions and Rent Reduction Program', pp.113-129.
- (1950) 'Too Late to Save Asia,' pp.131-135.
- (1950a) 'Rural Reconstruction and the China Aid Act', pp.136-141.
- (1951) 'From a Landlord to a Land Reformer', pp.148-150.
- (1951a) 'Observations on Rural Conditions in Taiwan', pp.142-147.
- (1951b) 'The Plow Outbids the Sword in Asia', pp.151-154.
- (1952) 'Comments on Land Reform in India,' pp.189-197.
- (1953) 'Comment on the Report of the Ford Foundation Conference on Land Tenure', pp.198-201.

- (1954) 'Advancing Human Welfare', pp.204–214.
- (1955) 'Field Trip Observations in Central Vietnam, April 1955', pp.217–228.
- (1956) 'Toward a More Effective U.S. Aid Program in Vietnam', pp.275–278.
- (1957) 'Agrarian Revolution in Asia', pp.279–280.
- (1963) 'Visit to the Philippines', pp.325–331.
- (1964) 'Land Reform', pp.354–366.
- (1970) 'Comments on India', pp.474–475.
- (1974) 'Agrarian Reform in the Philippines', pp.550–557.

Ladejinsky, Wolf with Warren H. Leonard and Mark B. Williamson (1948) 'Prospects for Japanese Agriculture', *Foreign Agriculture* (November), pp.240–245.

Ladesma, José Ernesto (1989) 'A Beginner's Guide to Reading the LOI', *Diliman Review*, 37, no.2.

Lal, Deepak (1983) *The Poverty of Development Economics.* London: Institute of Economic Affairs, Hobart Paper No.16.

Land Tenure Center (1978) *Annual Report 1977-1978.* Madison, WI: University of Wisconsin.

Landé, Carl (1986) 'The Political Crisis', in John Bresnan, ed., *Crisis in the Philippines.* Princeton: Princeton University Press.

Landé, Carl (1964) *Leaders, Factions and Parties: The Structure of Philippine Politics.* Southeast Asian Studies Monograph Series, 6. New Haven: Yale University.

Lansdale, Major General Edward (1972) *In the Midst of War: An American's Mission to Southeast Asia.* New York: Harper and Row.

Lara, Francisco Jr. (1986a) 'Land Reform and the CON-COM: Landmarks and Loopholes', *Diliman Review*, 34, no.3.

Lara, Francisco Jr. (1986b) 'Land Reform in the Proposed Constitution: Landmarks and Loopholes', *Agricultural Policy Studies*, no.1. Quezon City: Philippine Peasant Institute.

Lawyers Committee for Human Rights (1988) *Vigilantes in the Philippines.* New York: Lawyers Committee for Human Rights.

Ledesma, Antonio J., S.J., Perla Q. Makil and Virginia A. Miralao, eds. (1983) *Second View from the Paddy.* Manila: Institute of Philippine Culture, Ateneo de Manila University.

Lee-Flores, Wilson (1987) 'The Ayalas: Business Conquistadors', *Manila Chronicle* (14 September), p.15.

Lee-Flores, Wilson (1988) 'Reflections on the Island's Miracles', *Solidarity*, no. 120 (October–December).

Lee Han-been (1968) *Korea: Time, Change and Administration.* Honolulu: East-West Press.

Lehmann, David, ed. (1974) *Agrarian Reform and Agrarian Reformism: Studies of Peru, Chile, China and India.* London: Faber and Faber.

Lehmann, David (1978) 'The Death of Land Reform: A Polemic', *World Development*, 6, no.3, pp.339–45.

Lewin, Moshe (1968) *Russian Peasants and Soviet Power.* Evanston: Northwestern University Press.

Lichauco, Alejandro A. (1982) 'The International Economic Order and the Philippine Experience', in Vivencio R., José, ed. *Mortgaging the Future: The World Bank and the IMF in the Philippines.* Quezon City: Foundation for Nationalist Studies, pp.12–48.

Lichauco, Alejandro A. (1988) *Nationalist Economics.* Quezon City: Institute for Rural Industrialization.

Lichbach, Mark Iriving (1989) 'An Evaluation of "Does Economic Inequality Breed Political Conflict?" Studies', *World Politics*.

Lim, Joseph (1987) 'Review of Literature on Rural Finance: A Sub-Reading', paper prepared for Presidential Committee on Rural Credit. Manila.

Lin, Sein, ed. (1972) *Readings in Land Reform.* Taipei: Good Friends Press.

Lindqvist, Sven (1979) *Land and Power in South America.* Harmondsworth: Penguin Books.

Lipton, Michael (1974) 'Towards a Theory of Land Reform', in David Lehman, ed., *Agrarian Reform and Agrarian Reformism.* London: Faber and Faber.

Lipton, Michael (1989) *New Seeds and Poor People.* London: Unwin Hyman.

P

Lloyd, Christopher (1986) *Explanation in Social History.* Oxford: Basil Blackwell.

Locke, John (1690) *Two Treatises of Government.* Edited by Peter Laslett. Cambridge: Cambridge University Press, 1988.

Long, E.J. (1952) 'Some theoretical Issues in Economic Development', *Journal of Farm Economics,* 34, pp.729-30.

Lopez, Jun (1986) 'Observers Say AFP to Focus on Negros', *Malaya.*

Luzon Secretariat of Social Action (LUSSA) (1983) *Countryside Report.* Manila: LUSSA.

Lynch, Frank (1968) 'Introduction' in Walden F. Bello and Maria Clara Roldan, ed.s, *Modernization: Its Impact in the Philippines.* Institute of Philippine Culture (IPC) Papers, No.4. Quezon City: IPC, Ateneo de Manila University.

Lynch, Frank, ed. (1972) *View from the Paddy: Empirical Studies of Philippine Rice Farming and Tenancy.* Philippine Sociological Review, 20, no.s 1 and 2 (January and April).

MacArthur, Douglas (1964) *Reminiscences.* New York: McGraw Hill Book Co.

MacKinnon, Catherine A. (1989) *Toward a Feminist Theory of the State.* Cambridge, MA: Harvard University Press.

Magallona, Merlin M. (1982) 'A Contribution to the Study of Feudalism and Capitalism in the Philippines'. In *Feudalism and Capitalism in the Philippines.* Quezon City: Foundation for Nationalist Studies, pp. 14-44.

Mahal Kong Pilipinas Foundation (1989) *Philippines Best 1000 Corporations.* Manila.

Mangahas, Mahar, Virgina A. Miralao and Romana P. de los Reyes, ed.s (1976) *Tenants, Lessees, Owners: Welfare Implications of Tenure Change.* Quezon City: IPC, Ateneo de Manila University.

Mangahas, Mahar (1987) 'Political Economy of Land Reform and Land Distribution in the Philippines', Center for Research and Communication, *Agrarian Reform: Experiences and Expectations.* Symposium Proceedings April-May 1987. Manila: Southeast Asian Science Foundation, pp.1-8.

Manglapus, Raul S. (1967) *Land of Bondage, Land of the Free: Social Revolution in the Philippines.* Manila: Solidaridad Publishing House.

Manlogon, Melanie (1990) 'A New Man for Agrarian Reform' *MIDWEEK* (24 January), pp.17-22.

Mao Tse-tung (1977) *A Critique of Soviet Economics.* New York: Monthly Review Press.

Marchetti, Victor and John D. Marks (1974) *The CIA and the Cult of Intelligence.* New York: Dell Publishing.

Marcos, Ferdinand (1980) *Third World Alternative,* Ministry of Public Information.

Marshall, Alfred (1890) *Principles of Economics.* London: Macmillan, 1952 edition.

Mason, Edward S. et al (1980) *The Economic and Social Modernization of the Republic of Korea.* Cambridge: Harvard University Press.

Mauri, Hector (1986) 'Land Reform: The Way to National Liberation: A Challenge and a Response', *Solidarity* No.s 106-07, pp.75-109.

Maxfield, Sylvia and James H. Nolt (1987) 'Protectionism and the Internationalization of Capital: US Sponsorship of Import Substitution Industrialization in the Philippines, Turkey and Argentina' mimeo (10 December).

May, Glenn A. (1980) *Social Engineering in the Philippines: The Aims, Execution, and Impact of American Colonial Policy, 1900-1913.* Westport and London: Greenwood Press.

May, Glenn A. (1987) *A Past Recovered.* Quezon City: New Day Publishers.

McCoy, Alfred W. (1971) 'Land Reform as Counter-Revolution: U.S. Foreign Policy and the Tenant'. *Bulletin of Concerned Asian Scholars,* 3, no.1, pp. 14-49.

McCoy, Alfred W. (1983) "In Extreme Unction': The Philippine Sugar Industry', in R.S. David, ed., *The Political Economy of Philippine Commodities.* Quezon City: Third World Studies Center, University of the Philippines, pp. 135-180.

McCoy, Alfred W. (1988) 'RAM Boys', published in three parts in *MIDWEEK* (21 September to 12 October).

McCoy, Alfred W. (1991) 'The Restoration of Planter Power in La Carlota City', in Benedict J. Kerkvliet and Resil B. Mojares, ed.s, *From Marcos to Aquino: Local Perspectives on Political Transition in the Philippines.* Manila: Ateneo de Manila University Press.

McLennan, Marshall S. (1982) 'Changing Human Ecology on the Central Luzon Plain: Nueva Ecija, 1705-1939', in Alfred W. McCoy and Ed. C. de Jesus, ed.s, *Philippine Social History: Global Trade and Local Transformations*. Quezon City: Ateneo de Manila University Press, pp. 57-90.

Medina, José C. Jr. (1975) 'The Philippines Experience with Land Reform Since 1972'. *SEADAG Papers*. Rome: U.N. Food and Agriculture Organization.

Mendoza, Edgar (1988) 'House Bill No. 400: A Chronology on its Rise and Fall', *Alternative*, 2, nos. 2 & 3 (January - June).

Mijares, Primitivo (1976) *The Conjugal Dictatorship of Ferdinand and Imelda Marcos I*. San Francisco: Union Square Publications, 1986.

Mill, J.S. (1848) *Principles of Political Economy with some of their applications to social philosophy*. Book II, New York: Reprints of Economic Classics, Augustus M. Kelly, Bookseller, 1965; Books IV and V, London: Penguin Books, 1970.

Miller, Stuart Chreighton (1984) 'The American Soldier and the Conquest of the Philippines', in Peter Stanley, ed., *Reappraising an Empire: New Perspectives on Philippine-American History*. Cambridge, MA: Harvard Studies in American-East Asian Relations 10, pp.13-34.

Miranda, Felipe B. and Ruben F. Ciron (1987) *Development and the Military in the Philippines*. Quezon City: Social Weather Stations, Inc.

Mitchell, C. Clyde (1949) 'Land Reform in South Korea' *Pacific Affairs*, 22, no.2, (June) reprinted in Sein Lin, ed., *Readings in Land Reform* (Taipei: Good Friends Press, 1972), p.345.

Mitchell, Edward J. (1967) 'Land Tenure and Rebellion: A Statistical Analysis of factors Affecting Government Control of South Vietnam', RAND Corporation memorandum 5181-ARPA. Santa Monica: RAND Corporation. Also published as, 'Inequity and Insurgency', *World Politics*, 20, no.3 (April 1968), pp.421-38.

Mitchell, Edward J. (1969) 'Some Econometrics of the Huk Rebellion', *American Political Science Review*, 63, pp.1159-71.

Monk, Paul (1990) *Truth and Power: Robert S. Hardie and Land Reform Debates in the Philippines, 1950-1987*. Clayton, Vic., Australia: Centre of Southeast Asian Studies, Monash Paper Number 20.

Monsod, Solita (1986) 'Rural Development Strategies Then and Now', in Romulo A. Sandoval, ed., *Prospects of Agrarian Reform Under the New Order*. Quezon City: Urban Rural Mission.

Montemayor, Jeremias (1986) 'Another Look at Agrarian Reform', *Solidarity*, No.s 106-07, pp.49-58.

Montgomery, John D. (1962) *The Politics of Foreign Aid*. New York: Frederick A. Praeger, Publisher.

Montgomery, John, ed. (1984) *International Dimensions of Land Reform*. Boulder: Westview Press.

Morgan, D.J. (1980) *The Official History of Colonial Development*. Vol.2, *Developing British Colonial Resources 1945-1951*. London: Macmillan.

Muijzenberg, Otto van den (1991) 'Tenant Emancipation, Diversification and Social Differentiation in Central Luzon', in Jan Breman and Sudipto Mundle, ed.s, *Rural Transformation in Asia*. Delhi: Oxford University Press, pp.313-337.

Murray, Francis J. Jr. (1972) 'Land Reform in the Philippines: An Overview', in Frank Lynch, ed., *View from the Paddy: Empirical Studies of Philippine Rice Farming and Tenancy*. Philippine Sociological Review, 20, no.s 1 and 2 (January and April).

Nagano, Yoshiko (1982) 'Formation of Sugarlandia in the Late 19th Century', *Philippines in the Third World, Papers*, no. 32. Quezon City: Third World Studies Center, University of the Philippines.

National Defense Council Foundation (NDCF) (n.d.) 'De Oppresso Libre' (Free the Oppressed), publicity brochure. Washington, D.C. and Arlington, VA.

National Democratic Front (NDF) (1988) *Land Reform in the Philippines: Aquino's Program and the NDF Alternative*. Selected articles from *Liberation*.

National Economic Protectionism Association (NEPA) (1986) 'The IMF Recovery Program', (September), reprinted in De Dios, Aurora Javate-de, Petronilo Bn. Daroy and Lorna Kalaw-Tirol, eds. *Dictatorship and Revolution: Roots of People's Power*. Manila: Conspectus, 1988, pp.805-809.

Naylor, Robin Thomas (1987) *Hot Money and the Politics of Debt*. New York: Linden Press/Simon and Schuster.

Nemenzo, Francisco (1984) 'Rectification Process in the Philippine Communist Movement', in Lim

Joo-Jock and Vani S. ed.s, *Armed Communist Movements in Southeast Asia*. Singapore: Institute of Southeast Asian Studies, University of Singapore.

Nemenzo, Francisco (1988) 'From Autocracy to Elite Democracy', in Aurora Javate-de Dios, Petronilo Bn. Daroy and Lorna Kalaw-Tirol, ed.s, *Dictatorship and Revolution: Roots of People's Power*. Manila: Conspectus, pp.221-268.

Noble, Lela Garner (1987) 'Muslim Grievances and the Muslim Rebellion', in Carl Landé, ed., *Rebuilding a Nation: Philippine Challenges and American Policy*. Washington, D.C.: Washington Institute Press, pp.417-434.

Nolledo, José N. (1990) *Principles of Agrarian Reforms, Cooperatives and Taxation*. Manila: National Book Store.

Nove, Alec (1983) *The Economics of Feasible Socialism*. London: George Allen and Unwin.

Nozick, Robert (1974) *Anarchy, State and Utopia*. Oxford: Blackwell.

O'Donnell, Guillermo (1978) 'State and Alliance in Argentina, 1956-76', *Journal of Development Studies*, 15 (October).

Ofreneo, Rene E. (1980) *Capitalism in Philippine Agriculture*. Quezon City: Foundation for Nationalist Studies.

Olson, Garry L. (1974) *U.S. Foreign Policy and the Third World Peasant: Land Reform in Asia and Latin America*. New York: Praeger Publishers.

Ongpin, Jaime (1988) *The Public Conscience of Jaime V. Ongpin*. A collection of his speeches. Manila: Jaime V. Ongpin Foundation.

Owen, Norman (1984) *Prosperity Without Progress: Manila Hemp and Material Life in the Colonial Philippines*. Manila: Ateneo de Manila University Press.

Overholt, William (1976) 'Land Reform in the Philippines'. *Asian Survey*, 16 (May), pp.443-44.

Packenham, Robert A. (1973) *Liberal America and the Third World*. Princeton, NJ: Princeton University Press.

Pagusara, Mariflor Parpan (1984) 'The Kalinga Ili: Cultural-Ecological Reflections on Indigenous Theoria and Praxis of Man-Nature Relationship', in *Papers and Proceedings of the 1st Cordillera Multi-Sectoral Land Congress, 11 to 14 March 1983*. Baguio City: Cordillera Consultative Committee.

PAKISAMA (1988) 'Stop the Expansion and Exploitation by Del Monte', pamphlet. Quezon City: Pambansang Kilusan ng mga Samahang Magsasaka.

Panganiban, Lilia C. (1971) *Land Reform Administrative Procedures in the Philippines*, prepared for USAID. Madison, WI: Land Tenure Center, University of Wisconsin, 1972.

Panse, V.G., ed. (1965) *Some Problems of Agricultural Census Taking with Special Reference to the Developing Countries*. Rome: UN FAO Statistics Division (February).

Parsons, Kenneth et al (1956) *Land Tenure*. Proclamation of the International Conference on Land Tenure and Related Problems in World Agriculture. Madison, WI: University of Wisconsin Press.

Parsons, Talcott (1946) 'Population and Social Structures', in Douglas Haring, ed., *Japan's Prospects*. Cambridge, MA: Harvard University Press.

Patnaik, Usha (1972) 'Economics of Farm Size and Farm Scale', *Economic and Political Weekly*, 7 (August), pp.31-33.

Pauker, Guy J. 'President Corazon Aquino: A Political and Personal Assessment', in Carl Landé, ed., *Rebuilding a Nation: Philippine Challenges and American Policy*. Washington, D.C.: Washington Institute Press, pp.291-312.

Payer, Cheryl (1982) *The World Bank: A Critical Analysis*. New York: Monthly Review Press.

Pentagon Papers (1971) as published by the *New York Times*. New York: Bantam Books.

Phelan, John Leddy (1959) *The Hispanization of the Philippines: Spanish Aims and Filipino Responses, 1565-1700*. Madison.

Philippine Center for Investigative Journalism (PCIJ) (1990) *KUDETA, The Challenge to Philippine Democracy*. Manila: PCIJ.

PHILDHRAA, 1987, *Agrarian Reform: Today's Imperative: A Special Supplement on the Congress for a People's Agrarian Reform*. Makati: Philippine Partnership for the Development of Human Resources in Rural Areas (Septemeber).

Philippine Peasant Institute (PPI) (1984) *The Green Revolution and Price Hikes*. Quezon City: PPI.

Philippine Peasant Instiute (PPI) (1991a) *The Regional Agricultural Situation* (April) Quezon City: PPI.

Philippine Peasant Institute (1991b) 'Land Conversions'. Quezon City: PPI.

Po, Blondie (1980) 'Rural Organizations and Rural Development: A Documentary Study', in Marie S. Fernandez, ed., *Rural Organizations in the Philippines*. Manila: Institute of Philippine Culture, Ateneo de Manila University.

Pomeroy, William (1974) *American Neocolonialism: Its Origins in the Philippines and Asia*. New York: International Publishers.

Prosterman, Roy L. (1966) 'Land Reform in Latin America: How to Have a Revolution Without a Revolution', *Washington Law Review*, 42, no.189.

Prosterman, Roy L. (1970) 'Land-to-the-Tiller in South Vietnam', *Asian Survey*, 10, no. 8 (August), pp.751-764.

Prosterman, Roy L. (1972) 'Land Reform as Foreign Aid', *Foreign Policy*, no.6 (Spring).

Prosterman, Roy L. (1976) 'Simplied Predictive Index of Rural Instability', *Comparative Politics*, 8 (April), pp. 339-352.

Prosterman, Roy L. and Jeffrey M. Riedinger (1987) *Land Reform and Democratic Development*. Baltimore and London: Johns Hopkins University Press.

Prouty, L. Fletcher (1973) *The Secret Team*. New Jersey: Prentice-Hall, Inc.

Putzel, James (1988) 'Prospects for Agrarian Reform Under the Aquino Government', in Mamerto Canlas, Mariano Miranda Jr. and James Putzel, *Land Poverty and Politics in the Philippines*. London: Catholic Institute for International Relations.

Putzel, James and John Cunnington (1989) *Gaining Ground: Agrarian Reform in the Philippines*. London: War on Want.

Putzel, James (1990a) 'Endgame in Manila', *The Tablet* (London), 6 January, pp.7-8.

Putzel, James (1990b) 'The Comprehensive Agrarian Reform Program: Why it Mattered Little Who Was in Charge', in Grace Arcilla, ed., *Lupa at Buhay: Agrarian Reform in the Philippines*. Amsterdam: Philippine Development Forum.

Putzel, James (1990c) 'The Politics of the Aquino Agrarian Reform Programme: Influence of Bilateral and Multilateral Donors', in J. Putzel, A. Quisumbing, F. Lara and W. Armstrong, *Agrarian Reform and Official Development Assistance in the Philippines*. Occasional Paper, no.13, Centre of South-East Asian Studies, Unversity of Kent.

Putzel, James (1991) 'Agrarian Reform and Agribusiness Under Aquino', Paper Prepared for the European Conference on Philippine Studies, 22-25 April 1991, Amsterdam.

Quirino, Carlos (1978) 'The Sugar Lands', *Filipino Heritage, The Making of a Nation*, 6, pp.1476-79.

Quisumbing, Agnes and Lourdes S. Adriano (1987) 'Tenurial Arrangements and Agricultural Heterogeneity: Implications for A.R.'. Seminar on Agricultural Policy Research, University of the Philippines at Los Baños Agricultural Policy Research Program, 25-26 September.

Race, Jeffrey (1972) *War Comes to Long An: Revolutionary Conflict in a Vietnamese Province*. Berkeley: University of California Press.

Rafael, Vicente L. (1988) *Contracting Colonialism*. Quezon City: Ateneo de Manila University Press.

RAM-SDP (1990) (Revolutionary Alliance for the Masses and Soldiers of the Filipino People 'Our Dreams Shall Never Die: Statement of National Aspirations', reprinted in, *KUDETA: The Challenge to Philippine Democracy*. Manila: Philippine Center for Investigative Journalism, pp.185-189.

Ramos, General Fidel V. (1986) 'Rebuilding Values: Foundation for Recovery', in Romulo A. Sandoval, ed., *Prospects of Agrarian Reform Under the New Order*. Quezon City: Urban Rural Mission.

Raper, Arthur (1951) 'Some Effects of Land Reform in Thirteen Japanese Villages', *Journal of Farm Economics*, 28, no.2, pp.177-182.

Ravanera, Roel R. (1990) 'Impact of an Agri-Based Transnational Enterprise on Peasants and Peasant Community: The Case of Del Monte in Bukidnon', *IAST Occasional Papers*, Series no.33. Institute of Agrarian Studies, College of Economics and Management. University of the Philippines at Los Baños.

Ravenholt, Albert (1981) 'Rural Mobilization for Modernization in South Korea', in Howard

Q

Handelman, ed., *The Politics of Agrarian Change in Asia and Latin America*. Bloomington: Indiana University Press.

Raventos, Emili Giralt (1981) *La Compañia General de Tabacos de Filipinas 1881-1991*. Barcelona: Compañia General de Tabacos de Filipinas.

Rendell, Sir Wiliam (1976) *The History of the Commonwealth Development Corporation 1948-1972*. London: Heinemann Educational Books.

Rhee Sang-Woo (1980) 'Land Reform in South Korea: A Macro-Level Policy Review', in Inayatullah, ed., *Land Reform: Some Asian Experiences*. Kaula Lumpur: Asian and Pacific Development Administration Centre, pp.319-350.

Richter, Linda K. (1982) *Land Reform and Tourism Development*. Cambridge, MA: Schenkman Publishing Co.

Riedinger, Jeffrey (1990) 'Philippine Land Reform in the 1980s', in Roy L. Prosterman, Mary N. Temple and Timothy Hanstad, ed.s, *Agrarian Reform and Grassroots Development*. Boulder and London: Lynne Rienner Publishers.

Rivera, Temario C. (1982) 'Rethinking the Philippine Social Formation', in *Feudalism and Capitalism in the Philippines*. Quezon City: Foundation for Nationalist Studies, pp. 1-13.

Rizal, José (1890) 'The Indolence of the Filipinos'. *Solidaridad*, (July-Sept); rpt. in G.F. Zaide, *José Rizal: Asia's First Apostle of Nationalism*. Manila: Red Star Book Store, 1970.

Rizal, José (1886) *Noli me Tangere*. Trans. León Ma. Guerrero. Hong Kong: Longman, 1961.

Rizal, José (1891) *El Filibusterismo*. Trans. León Ma. Guerrero. Hong Kong: Longman, 1965.

Rocamora, Joel and David O'Connor (1977) 'The U.S., Land Reform, and Rural Development in the Philippines', in Walden Bello and Severina Rivera, ed.s, *The Logistics of Repression*. Washington, D.C.: Friends of the Filipino People, pp. 63-92.

Rocamora, Joel (1990) 'Gigantic Hoax: The Philippine Aid Plan is Not What it Seems', *Solidaridad II*, no.3, 1989-1990 (Tokyo).

Rorty, James (1955) 'The Dossier of Wolf Ladejinsky: The Fair Rewards of Distinguished Civil Service'. *Commentary* (New York), 19 (April), pp. 326-334.

Rostow, Walter W. (1961) 'Guerrilla Warfare in the Underdeveloped Areas'. *Department of State Bulletin* (7 August).

Rostow, Walter W. (1966) *The Stages of Economic Growth: A Non-Communist Manifesto*. Cambridge: Cambridge University Press.

Roth, Dennis M. (1977) *The Friar Estates of the Philippines*. Albuquerque: University of New Mexico Press.

Roth, Dennis M. (1982) 'Church Lands in the Agrarian History of the Tagalog Region', in Alfred W. McCoy and C. de Jesus *Philippine Social History: Global Trade and Local Transformations*. Quezon City: Ateneo de Manila University Press, pp. 131-154.

Rueschemeyer, Dietrich and Peter B. Evans (1985) 'The State and Economic Transformation: Toward an Analysis of the Conditions Underlying Effective Intervention', in Peter B. Evans, Dietrich Rueschemeyer and Theda Skocpol, eds., *Bringing the State Back In*. Cambridge: Cambridge University Press, pp. 44-77.

Roxas, Sixto K. (1989) '37 Years of Rural Reconstruction in the Philippines', *Rural Reconstruction Forum*, 1, no.s 3-4.

Ruttan, Vernon W. (1966) 'Tenure and Productivity of Philippine Rice Producing Farms', *The Philippine Economic Journal*, 5, no.1.

Salamanca, Bonifacio S. (1984) *The Filipino Reaction to American Rule 1901-1913*. Quezon City: New Day.

Sandoval, Romulo A. ed. (1986) *Prospects of Agrarian Reform Under the New Order*. Quezon City: Urban Rural Mission.

Say, Michael G., ed. (1976) *VIP's of Philippine Business*. Manila: Mahal Kong Pilipinas Charitable Foundation Inc.

Schaller, Michael (1985) *The American Occupation of Japan: Origins of the Cold War in Asia*. Oxford: Oxford University Press.

Schalom, Stephen R. (1986) *The United States and the Philippines: A Study in Neocolonialism*. Manila: New Day (first published, Philadelphia: Institute for the Study of Human Issues, 1981).

Schirmer, Daniel B. (1972) *Republic or Empire: American Resistance to the Philippine War*. Cambridge, MA: Schenkman Publishing Company, Inc.

Schirmer, Daniel B. and Stephan R. Shalom (1987) *The Philippines Reader*. Quezon City: KEN, Inc.

Sen, Amartya (1981) *Poverty and Famines*. Oxford: Oxford University Press.

Shafer, D. Michael (1988) *Deadly Paradigms: The Failure of U.S. Counterinsurgency Policy*. Princeton: Princeton University Press.

Shillinglaw, Geoffrey (1974) 'Land Reform and Peasant Mobilization in Southern China, 1947-1950', in D. Lehmann, ed., *Agrarian Reform and Agrarian Reformism: Studies of Peru, Chile, China and India*. London: Faber and Faber.

Sihanouk, Prince Norodom (1974) *My War with the CIA: The Memoirs of Prince Norodom Sihanouk as related to Wilfred Burchett*. Harmondsworth: Penguin Books.

Simbulan, Roland G. (1983) *The Bases of Our Insecurity: A Study of the US Military Bases in the Philippines*. Manila: BALAI Fellowship Inc.

Sison, José Ma. (1965) *Struggle for National Democracy*. 2nd ed. Manila: Amado V. Hernandez Memorial Foundation, 1972.

Sison, José Ma. (1989) *The Philippine Revolution: The Leader's View*. New York: Crane Russak.

Skocpol, Theda (1979) *States and Social Revolutions*. Cambridge University Press.

Skocpol, Theda (1985) 'Bringing the State Back In: Strategies of Analysis in Current Research', in Peter B. Evans, Dietrich Rueschemeyer and Theda Skocpol, eds., *Bringing the State Back In*. Cambridge: Cambridge University Press.

Smith, Adam (1776) *The Wealth of Nations*. Harmondsworth: Penguin Books, 1970 edition.

Smith, Joseph B. (1976) *Portrait of a Cold Warrior*. New York: G.P. Putnam's Sons.

Social Weather Stations (1988) *October 1989 Survey Data on Ownership of Agricultural Land*. Quezon City: Social Weather Stations, Inc.

Soliman, Corazon Juliano (1988) 'A Promise Unfulfilled: Why Congress Has No Agrarian Reform', *Political Monitor*, 4, no.9.

Stanley, Peter W. (1974) *A Nation in the Making: The Philippines and the United States 1899-1921*. Cambridge, MA: Harvard University Press.

Stanley, Peter W., ed. (1984) *Reappraising an Empire: New Perspectives on Philippine-American History*. Cambridge, MA: Harvard Studies in American-East Asian Relations 10.

Starner, Frances Lucille (1961) *Magsaysay and the Philippine Peasantry*. Berkeley and Los Angeles: University of California Press.

Steinberg, David (1986) 'Tradition and Response', in John Bresnan, ed., *Crisis in the Philippines: The Marcos Era and Beyond*. Princeton: Princeton University Press.

Stepan, Alfred (1978) *The State and Society: Peru in Comparative Perspective*. Princeton: Princeton Univeristiy Press.

Stepan, Alfred (1985) 'State Power and the Strength of Civil Society in the Southern Cone of Latin America', in Peter B. Evans, Dietrich Rueschemeyer and Theda Skocpol, eds., *Bringing the State Back In*. Cambridge: Cambridge University Press.

Stilwell, Richard G. (1987) 'Communists Gain While Philippine Leaders Dawdle', *Policy Review* (Winter).

Sturtevant, David R. (1976) *Popular Uprisings in the Philippines, 1840-1940*. Ithaca and London: Cornell University Press.

Tadeo, Jaime (1986) 'Reflections on Genuine Land Reform', in Romulo A. Sandoval, ed., *Prospects of Agrarian Reform Under the New Order*. Quezon City: Rural Urban Missions.

Tadem, Eduardo C. (1986) 'The Coconut Industry in Mindanao', *Mindanao Focus*, no.12 (December), pp.4-58.

Tiglao, Rigoberto (1990) 'Rebellion from the barracks: The military as political force', in *KUDETA: The Challenge to Philippine Democracy*. Manila: Philippine Center for Investigative Journalism, pp.1-23.

Tai Hung-chao (1974) *Land Reform and Politics, A Comparative Analysis*. Berkeley: University of

California Press.

Takigawa, Tsutomu (1974) 'Notes on the Agrarian Reform in the Philippines Under the New Society'. *Discussion Paper*, no. 74-15. Quezon City: Institute of Economic Development and Research, School of Economics, University of the Philippines.

Taruc, Luis (1953) *Born of the People*. New York: International Publishers.

Taylor, George E. (1964) *The Philippines and the US: Problems of Partnership*. Published for the Council on Foreign Relations. New York: Praeger.

Technology and Livelihood Research Centre (1987) *Coconut*. Manila: National Bookstore.

Thiesenhusen, William C. (1971) 'Employment in Latin American Development', in Peter Dorner, ed., *Land Reform in Latin America: Issues and Cases*. Land Economics Monographs no.3. Madison: University of Wisconsin Press.

Thiesenhusen, William C. (1990) 'Recent Progress Toward Agrarian Reform in the Philippines', paper, Colloquim on Agrarian Reform, Sulu Hotel, Quezon City (26-30 March).

Thompson, E.P. (1965) 'The Peculiarities of the English', reprinted in his *Poverty of Theory and Other Essays*. New York: Monthly Review Press, 1978.

Thorpe, Andy (1990), 'Peasant Participation and Productivity: An Evaluation of Sandinista Agrarian Reform, 1979-1988', *Discussion Paper*, No.14. Portsmouth: Portsmouth Polytechnic, School of Economics.

Tiffen, Mary and Michael Mortimore (1990) *Theory and Practice in Plantation Agriculture: An Economic Review*, London: Overseas Development Institute.

Tiglao, Rigoberto (1981) *Looking Into Coconuts: The Philippine Coconut Industry*. Davao: Alternative Resource Centre.

Tjondronegoro, S.M.P. (1972) *Land Reform or Land Settlement: Shifts in Indonesia's Land Policy 1960-1970*. Madison: Land Tenure Center Paper 81.

Tolk, Jeffrey S. (1989) 'Retention Limits, Just Compensation, and Agrarian Reform Under the 1987 Philippine Constitution', Paper submitted to seminar, Pacific Community Legal Research, Harvard Law School (23 May).

Tuma, Elias H. (1966) *Twenty-Six Centuries of Agrarian Structure and Agrarian Reform*. Rome: U.N. Food and Agriculture Organization.

Twain, Mark (1972) *A Pen Warmed-Up in Hell: Mark Twain in Protest*, ed. by Frederick Anderson. New York: Harper and Row.

Umali, D.L. (1990) 'The Role of NGOs in the Philippine Agrarian Reform Program', paper, Colloquim on Agrarian Reform, Quezon City (26-30 March).

Valencia, Ernesto M. (1987) 'The Political Economy of Land Reform', in Manuel F. Montes and Lilia Quindoza Santiago, ed., *Where Has All the Power Gone? Synthesis*, no.2.

Van Naerssen, Tom (1991) 'The Squatter Movement and Access to Land in Metro Manila'. Paper presented to the European Conference of Philippine Studies, 22-25 April, Amsterdam.

Villa-Real, Luis A. (1987) 'Threats to National Security in the Year 2000', in F. Sionel José, ed., *A Filipino Agenda for the 21st Century*. Solidarity Conference, 7-8 February. Manila: Solidaridad Publishing House.

Villareal, Gabriel L. (1987) 'Two Coconut Levies - A Study in Contrasts', in 2 parts, *Manila Bulletin* (22-23 December).

Villegas, Bernardo M. (1985) 'Help Poor Filipinos Earn a Stake in the Future', *Wall Street Journal* (7 October), p.23.

Villegas, Bernardo M. (1987) 'Agrarian Reform and the 1987 Constitution', in Center for Research and Communication, *Agrarian Reform: Experiences and Expectations*. Symposium Proceedings April-May 1987. Manila: Southeast Asian Science Foundation.

Villegas, E.M. (1982) 'Debt Peonage and the New Society', in Vivencio R. José. ed., *Mortgaging the Future: The World Bank and the IMF in the Philippines*. Quezon City: Foundation for Nationalist Studies, pp.49-74.

Ward, Eric E. (1990) *Land Reform in Japan 1946-1950, the Allied Role*. Tokyo: Nobunkyo.

Warriner, Doreen (1948) *Land and Poverty in the Middle East*. London: Royal Institute of International

Affairs.

Warriner, Doreen (1969) *Land Reform in Principle and Practice*. Oxford: Clarendon Press.

Waswo, Anne (1988) 'The Transformation of Rural Society, 1900-1950', in *The Cambridge History of Japan*, volume 6, 'The Twentieth Century', Cambridge: Cambridge University Press, pp.541-605.

Weber, Max (1968) *Economy and Society*.

Whang In Joung (1982) 'Administration of Land Reform in Korea', *Working Paper*, no.8301. Seoul: Korea Development Institute.

Wheelock, Jaime (1991) 'Sandinista Agrarian Reform', paper presented to International Conference on Agrarian Reform, Manila (January).

Wickberg, Edgar (1965) *The Chinese in Philippine Life*. New Haven: Yale University Press.

Williamson, Mark B. (1951) 'Land Reform in Japan', *Journal of Farm Economics*, 28, no. 2 (May), pp. 169-182.

Wise, William M. (1987) 'The Philippine Military After Marcos', in Carl H. Landé, ed., *Rebuilding a Nation: Philippine Challenges and American Policy*. Washington, D.C.: Washington Institute Press, pp.435-448.

Worsely, Peter (1984) *The Three Worlds: Culture and World Development*. Chicago: University of Chicago Press.

Wurfel, David O. (1977) 'Philippine Agrarian Policy Today: Implementation and Political Impact'. *Occasional Paper*, no. 46. Singapore: Institute of Southeast Asian Studies, University of Singapore.

Wurfel, David O. (1983) 'The Development of Post-War Philippine Land Reform: Political and Sociological Explanations', in Antonio J. Ledesma, S.J., Perla Q. Makil and Virginia A. Miralao, eds., *Second View from the Paddy*. Manila: Institute of Philippine Culture, Ateneo de Manila University.

Wurfel, David O. (1988) *Filipino Politics: Development and Decay*. Ithaca: Cornell University Press.

Yambot, Mario M. (1989) 'How Much is Garchitorena Worth?' *Philippine Daily Inquirer* (27 May), p.5.

Yanaga, Chitoshi (1968) *Big Business in Japanese Politics*. New Haven: Yale University Press.

Yengoyan, Arcam A. and Perla Q. Makil, ed.s (1984) *Philippine Society and the Individual*. Michigan Papers on South and Southeast Asia, no.24. Ann Arbor: University of Michigan.

Yoshihara, Kunio (1988) *The Rise of Ersatz Capitalism in Southeast Asia*. Quezon City: Ateneo de Manila University Press.

Youngblood, Robert L. 'Church and State in the Philippines: Some Implications for United States Policy', in Carl H. Landé, ed., *Rebuilding a Nation: Philippine Challenges and American Policy*. Washington, D.C.: Wahsington Institute Press, pp.351-368.

Zinn, Howard (1980) *A People's History of the United States*. New York: Harper Colophon Books.

2. Philippine government documents

Most of the documents listed under the following six subsections are unpublished, except for legislative documents and presidential decrees which can be more easily located. In many cases, including 'draft executive orders' and DAR reports, these documents were furnished to the author by government officials and can rarely be found in any government archive.

2.1 Aquino - presidential issuances

Aquino, Corazon (10 June 1988) 'Speech During the Signing of the CARP Bill'.

Aquino, Corazon (30 December 1989), Speech on the state of the nation after the December coup attempt.

Executive Order No.229 (EO229), 'Providing the Mechanisms for the implementation of the Comprehensive Agrarian Reform Program', 22 July 1987.

Proclamation No. 131, 'Instituting a Comprehensive Agrarian Reform Program', 22 July 1987.

2.2 Draft executive orders on agrarian reform (January - July 1987)

Inter-Agency Task Force on Agrarian Reform (IATFAR), 'Accelerated Land Reform Project', 23

January 1987 (23 January Draft).

Inter-Agency Task Force on Agrarian Reform, 'Proposal for an Accelerated Land Reform Program', 13 March 1987 (13 March Draft).

Inter-Agency Task Force on Agrarian Reform, 'Accelerated Land Reform Program: Program Brief', 20 April 1987 (20 April Draft).

Inter-Agency Task Force on Agrarian Reform, 'Accelerated Land Reform Program: Program Brief', 27 April 1987 (27 April Draft).

Draft Executive Order, early May 1987 (May A Draft).

Draft Executive Order, early May 1987 (May B Draft).

Draft Executive Order, 20 May 1987.

Draft Executive Order, 22 May 1987.

Draft Executive Order, 25 May 1987.

Draft Executive Order, 3 June 1987.

Draft Executive Order, 28 June 1987.

Land Bank of Philippines Draft Executive Order, 6 July 1987 ('LBP Draft').

2.3 Department (Ministry) of Agrarian Reform

Agrarian Reform Coordinating Council (21 October 1972).

Alvarez, Heherson T. (1986) Ministry Memorandum Circular No.5, Series of 1986 'Authority to Issue/Distribute Emancipation Patents to Farmer-Beneficiaries Regardless of Amortization Payments' (7 May).

Alvarez, Heherson T. (1986a) 'Ministry Order No. 210-86', Series 1986.

DAR (1973) Memorandum to all Regional Directors on reports that landowners are ejecting tenants (9 January).

DAR (1973) Memorandum Circular No.31, 'Scheme for the Immediate Payment to Landowners' (26 December).

DAR (1987) 'The Aquino Government's Genuine and Comprehensive Agrarian Reform', xerox, February.

DAR (n.d. [1987]) 'Public Hearings Reactions to the Proposed Executive Order on Comprehensive Agrarian Reform Program', First Round.

DAR (1988) 'Guidelines on Land Valuation and Just Compensation', draft Administrative Order, Series 1988.

DAR (1988a) 'Instituting the Systems Approach and Management by Results for the Field Operations Group', draft Administrative Order.

DAR (1988b) Confidential 'Listasaka I: Final Report on Landholders Registration by Regions as of July 18 1988', mimeo.

DAR (2 December 1988c) 'Status Report DAR Activities on CARP Multinational Coverage as of 2 December 1988'.

DAR (1989) Regional Offices, Statistics on Voluntary Offers to Sell.

DAR (1 January 1989) Memorandum Agreement on the New Integrated Development Program for Nueva Ecija (IDP-NE), between DAR, National Agriculture and Fishery Council and Nueva Ecija Provincial Government.

DAR (15 March 1989) Production/Profit-Sharing Compliance.

DAR (20 March 1989) Memorandum for ExCom PARC from DAR Profit and Production Sharing Task Force. 'Status Report on Compliance with Production Sharing Under EO229 and Profit Sharing Under RA6657'.

DAR (1990a) 'Conversion of Agricultural Lands in Proposed Industrial Estates'; 'Implications on CARP Implementation of Proposed Special and Industrial Projects'; 'Summary of Approved Applications for Conversion of Agricultural Lands to Non-Agricultural Uses' (March).

DAR, (1991a) 'The Comprehensive Agrarian Reform Program of the Philippines: An Overview and Status of Implementation', xerox, DAR, (February).

DAR (1991b) 'Official Development Assistance Program for the Comprehensive Agrarian Reform

Program' (February).

DAR and PBSP (1989) 'Area Survey of the Voluntary Offer to Sell Properties' conducted December 1988 to January 1989, north and south of Negros Occidental.

DAR Central Office, Reports on Voluntary Offers to Sell:
  (1) September 28 - December 31 1987;
  (2) November 1988;
  (3) Weekly Reports: November 7-11, November 14-18, 1988;
  (4) June 1989;
  (5) September 1989.

DAR Land Transfer Centre, Records and Folders of Landowners.

DAR Provincial Agrarian Reform Office, Sorsogon (1989) 'Private Landholdings: Farmsize Category: 50 ha.s and above', Sorsogon City, Sorsogon (March).

DAR Region 10, Report on VOS, May 1989.

Estrella, Conrado (22 November 1972) Memorandum to the President, 'Final Draft of the Proposed Rules and Regulations to Implement Presidential Decree No.27'.

Estrella, Conrado (9 January 1973) 'Memorandum to all Regional Directors'.

Estrella, Conrado F. (1973) Department Memorandum No.15 (19 June).

Estrella, Conrado F. (1974), *The Meaning of Land Reform*. Quezon City: Ministry of Agrarian Reform.

Estrella, Conrado F. (1978) *Tenant Emancipation in the Philippines*. Quezon City: Ministry of Agrarian Reform.

Estrella, Conrado F. (1982) *Landmarks and Impact: Philippine Agrarian Reform*. Quezon City: Ministry of Agrarian Reform.

Juico, Philip (6 March 1989) Letter to Juan Sierra, Del Monte Philippines.

Juico, Philip (9 June 1989) Statement before the Senate-House Committee on Agrarian Reform, reprinted in *Midweek* (28 June 1989).

Juico, Philip (1989) *Transforming the Countryside*. Quezon City: Department of Agrarian Reform.

Labayen, Benjamin (11 March 1982) Minutes, Meeting of Advocate Group with Deputy Minister Benjamin Labayen, MAR.

Ministry of Agrarian Reform [circa 1980] *Primer on Agrarian Reform*.

MAR (1981) List of all claims approved by the Land Bank through 1981.

MAR (1983) The Operation Land Transfer Program of the Philippines: Process and Impact (Manila).

MAR (1985) *Land Reform Statistics*.

MAR (1986) *The Philippine Agrarian Reform Program: An Illustrated Guide*.

2.4 Marcos - presidential issuances

Proclamation No.1081 (21 September 1972) 'Proclamation on A State of Martial Law in the Philippines'.

Presidential Decree (PD) No.2 (26 September 1972) 'Proclaiming the Entire Country as a Land Reform Area'.

Presidential Decree (PD) No.27 (21 October 1972) 'Decreeing the Emancipation of Tenants from the Bondage of the Soil'.

Letter of Instruction (LOI) No.7 (November 1972) 'On Establishing a Bureau of Cooperatives'.

Memorandum, 123-72 (25 November 1972) to Conrado Estrella and Cesar Virata, Postponing 'Promulgation of the Rules and Regulations'.

Letter of Instruction (LOI) No.41 (27 November 1972) 'To the Secretary of National Defense'.

Presidential Decree (PD) No.76 (6 December 1972) 'Requiring...Sworn Statement on the True Value of...Property'.

Letter of Instruction (LOI) No.46 (7 December 1972) 'To Conrado Estrella'.

Presidential Decree (PD) No.85 (25 December) 'Creating the Agrarian Reform Support Fund'.

Letter of Instruction (LOI) No.52 (17 January 1973) 'To the Secretary of National Defense'.

Presidential Decree (PD) No.175 (11 April 1973) 'Strengthening the Cooperative Movement'.

General Order (GO) No.47 (27 May 1974) 'Requiring Domestic Corporations and Partnerships to Engage in Rice/Corn Production'.

Presidential Decree (PD) No.251 (21 July 1973) 'Amending Certain Provisions of RA3844'.

Presidential Decree (PD) No.582 (14 November 1974) 'To the Philippine Coconut Authority'.

Letter of Instruction (LOI) No.227 (16 November 1974) 'To the Secretary of Agrarian Reform'.

Letter of Instruction 1180-A (1981) (on Hda.s Santa Isabel and San Antonio)

Executive Order (EO) No.778

2.5 Legislative documents

Commonwealth Act (CA) No. 182, 1936, forming the National Development Corporation.

Commonwealth Act (CA) No. 141, 1936, public lands act (December).

Commonwealth Act (CA) No. 441, 1939, establishing National Land Settlement Administration (June).

Commonwealth Act (CA) No. 461, 1938, to expropriate private lands and establish the Rural Progress Administration.

Congressional Record.

House Bill (HB) 65, 1987, the 'CPAR bill' (July-August).

House Bill (HB) 319, 1987, the 'landowner bill' (August).

House Bill (HB) 400, 1987, basis for debate on a new law (August-September).

House Bill (HB) 400, 1988 with hand-written note, 'Cojuangco Proposal' ((8 February).

House Bill (HB) 941, 1987, the 'Guanzon bill'.

House Committee on Agrarian Reform, Committee Report No. 4 17 August 1987.

House Committee on Agrarian Reform, Minutes 1987-1988.

'Notes' from Senator Alvarez's Office, October 1987.

Philippine Organic Act, 1902, serving as the colony's 'constitution'.

Public Act No.2874, 1919, amending Philippine Organic Act.

Public Act (PA) No.4054, 1935, Rice Share Tenancy Act.

Public Act (PA) No.4133, 1933, Sugar Cane Tenancy Contract Act.

Republic Act (RA) No.926, 1953, Authorizing the President to convey lands and other property in payment of landed estates (20 June).

Republic Act (RA) No.3844, 1963, 'Agricultural Land Reform Code' (8 August).

Republic Act (RA) No.6389, 1971, Amending RA3844 and renaming the code, 'Code of Agrarian Reforms' (10 September).

Republic Act (RA) No.6657, 1988, 'The Comprehensive Agrarian Reform Law' (10 June).

Senate Bill (SB) No.16, 1987, the 'Alvarez bill' (August).

Senate Bill (SB) No.123, 1987, the 'Aquino bill' (1 October).

Senate Bill (SB) No.133, 1987, 1987, the 'Alvarez bill revised' (November).

Senate Bill (SB) No.249, 1987, the 'Amalgamated Senate bill' (December).

Senate Committee on Agrarian Reform, Report No. 103, 17 December 1987.

2.6 Other government documents

Cabinet Action Committee on Agrarian Reform (CAC) (4 February 1987) 'Memo to the President'.

Cabinet Action Committee on Agrarian Reform (CAC) (16 February 1987) 'CAC-KMP Dialogue: Tentative Agenda', Minister of Agrarian Reform Heherson Alvarez.

Cabinet Action Committee on Agrarian Reform (CAC) (n.d.) 'Matrix of Comments/Suggestions During the Second Round of National and Regional Consultations on the Proposed Executive Order on the CARP'.

Constitution of 1935.

Constitution of 1973.

Constitution of 1987.

Final Report of the Committee on the Assessment of the Agricultural Sector's Performance Under the Aquino Government (12 December 1989). University of the Philippines at Los Baños.

Government of the Republic of the Philippines (1987) 'Memorandum on Economic Policy', submitted to the International Monetary Fund (2 February).

Government of the Republic of the Philippines (January 1991) 'Progress Report on the Philippine Agenda for Sustained Growth and Development', Program for the Multilateral Aid Initiative.

Government Service Insurance System, Minutes of board of trustees, memoranda and resolutions 1957 and 1958.

Manila Regional Trial Court's 'Decision' Civil Case no. 131654.

Ministry of Agriculture and Food (MAF) (1986), *A Short Term Recovery Plan for the Rural Sector.* Quezon City: MAF (14 May).

National Census and Statistics Office (NCSO), various years.

National Census and Statistics Office (NCSO) (1988) Integrated Survey of Households (ISH).

National Economic Development Authority (NEDA) (1986a) 'Policy Agenda for People-Powered Development', *Philippine Development*, 13, no.4 (July-August).

National Economic and Development Authority (NEDA) (1986b), *Medium-Term Philippine Development Plan, 1987-1992* (Manila: NEDA, 1986),

National Economic and Development Authority (NEDA) (1986c), *Compendium of Philippine Social Statistics.*

National Economic and Development Authority (NEDA) (1987) 'Memorandum from the Director of the Agricultural Staff to the Director General' (20 April).

National Social Action Council (1986) *Briefing Manual.* Manila: NSAC.

Negros Occidental, Governor's Office (1987) 'The 60-30-10 Plan as a Land Reform Package for the Province of Negros Occidental'.

Ongpin, Jaime (4 May 1987) Memo to the President from Secretary of Finance Ongpin, 'Five Important Points about the Accelerated Land Reform Program'.

Presidential Agrarian Reform Council (PARC) (1988-1989). Minutes.

Presidential Agrarian Reform Council (PARC) (March 1989) *The Comprehensive Agrarian Reform Program of the Philippines*, Vol.1, 'Implementing Program and Budget, 1988-1997', Manila: Presidential Agrarian Reform Council.

Presidential Commission on Government Reorgranization (PCGR) (1986a) *Survey Team Report on the Ministry of Agrarian Reform.* Members: Victor Gerardo J. Bulatao, Ernesto M. Ordoñez, Eduardo C. Tadem (15 May).

Presidential Commission on Government Reorganization (1986b) Eduardo C. Tadem, *Handbook on the Reorganization Proposals of the Ministry of Agrarian Reform.* (December).

Securities and Exchange Commission, various corporate records.

US War Damage Commission (1949) Claim No. 1089800. Reference: Compania General de Tabacos de Filipinas. *Memorandum in Compliance with the Commission's Order Requiring Claimant to Show Proof of why it Should Not be Declared a Disqualified Claimant.* Prepared by Breed, Abbott and Morgan, New York, who were lawyers for the claimant. Manila [University of the Philippines Library, Diliman: Rare books].

3. Other unpublished documents

Alliance of Multi-Sectoral Organizations (1984) Joint Manifesto of Protest (27 July), pamphlet.

ANCA-Priests' Assembly Dialogue with Cojuangco, Carag, Diaz (15 December 1980) Transcription: archives of Bishop Purugganan, Diocese of Ilagan, Isabela.

ANCA Corporation, Articles of Incorporation, 1 April 1980.

Aquino, Butz and Bobby Hernandez telegram to Andy Messing Jr., 5 March 1986, NDCF files, Alexandria, VA.

Broad Initiatives for Negros Development (BIND) (1990) *Report on the Economic District Management System (EDMS): The Case of SAVAPUL BAMUR.* (February) Bacolod: BIND.

CIDA (Canadian International Development Agency) (1988) 'CIDA in the Philippines, Operational Projects, 1988'.

Confederation of Filipino Rice and Corn Associations (8 May 1991), a letter to the Senate

Committee on Agriculture.

Del Monte Philippines (21 July 1988) 'Notice to All Employees' from the Management, Del Monte Philippines, Inc.

Del Monte Philippines (21 February 1989) 'Grower Contract', signed with the Del Monte Agrarian Reform Beneficiaries Cooperative.

Diokno, José W., Senator (29 August 1980) Dialogue with the Hacienda San Antonio and Sta Isabel Farmers. Transcription: archives of Bishop Purugganan, Diocese of Ilagan, Isabela.

Ellman, Antony and Martin Greeley, 'Nucleus Estate Development in the Philippines: Report of a Consultancy Mission', Commonwealth Development Corporation under contract with the Overseas Development Administration (January 1989).

'Facts About the Anca Project', (13 December 1980), archives of Bishop Purugganan, Diocese of Ilagan, Isabela.

Gamboa Hermanos, Inc. (1987) 'A Proposal for Voluntary Land Reform Compliance'.

Gamboa Hermanos, Inc. (1988) 'Proposal for Compliance with the Comprehensive Agrarian Reform Law of 1988'.

Guerrero, Milagros (1977) 'Luzon at War: Contradictions in Philippine Society, 1898-1902', Ph.D. diss., University of Michigan.

Institute for Popular Democracy (IPD) (1987) Political Clans and Electoral Politics: A Preliminary Research. Quezon City.

Institute of Agrarian Studies (IAS) (1987) 'Selected Statistics for the Comprehensive Agrarian Reform Program', Los Baños: IAS, College of Economics and Management, University of the Philippines (September).

Marti, Rev. Thomas J., MM (1987) 'US Intervention in the Philippines: Threat and Challenge', article prepared for reflection of member congregations of the Association of Major Religious Superiors in the Philippines.

Padilla, Sabino G. Jr. (1988) 'Agrarian Revolution: Peasant Radicalization and Social Change in Bicol', Masters thesis, Department of Anthropology, University of the Philippines, Quezon City.

Partido Demokratiko-Soyalista ng Pilipinas (PDSP) (1987) 'Programme of Action' and 'Minimum Programme'. Documents from the National Congress of Reorganization, Quezon City, (10-13 December).

Prosterman, Roy L. and Charles Taylor (18 December 1972) 'Summary Briefing Memorandum on Estimated External Funding Needs for the Philippine Land Reform Program'.

Prosterman, Roy L. (29 April 1973) 'Revising the Approach to the 'Retention Limit'.

Prosterman, Roy L. and Charles Taylor (11 August 1974) 'Briefing Memorandum on the Current Status of Philippine Land Reform'.

Prosterman, Roy L. and Charles Taylor (12 March 1975) 'The Philippine Land Reform: What Needs to Be Done'.

Prosterman, Roy and Jeff Riedinger (1986) 'Preliminary Observations on Status and Needs for a Possible Philippine Land Reform', Memo to the Honorable Ramon Mitra, Minister of Agriculture (31 March).

Prosterman, Roy (1987) Revised version of 3 June Draft Executive Order on Agrarian Reform (26 June).

Prosterman, Roy and Timothy Hanstad (1988a) 'Analysis of Republic Act No.6657. The Philippine Land-Reform Law: Can an Effective Land Reform Result?' (20 June).

Prosterman, Roy and Timothy Hanstad (1988b) 'Whether Failure is Inevitable Under the New Philippine Land-Reform Law', Memo to file (3 November).

Putzel, James (1986) 'The Ladejinsky Model of Agrarian Reform' M.A. Thesis, Department of Political Science, McGill University, Montreal.

National Defence Council Foundation (NDCF) (1986) 'Defense Group Issues Statement on Elections in the Philippines', Press Release (12 January). NDCF Files, Alexandria, VA.

National Consultative Assembly of Peasant Organizations. 'The National Peasant Situation' and other documents. Sacred Heart Novitiate, Quezon City, August 7-12, 1984.

National Democratic Front, 'Program of the National Democratic Front', in circulation in 1987 and 1988.

Ramon Magsaysay Foundation, 'A Proposal for the National Agrarian Reform Program', 9 June 1987.

Sabug Jun (1989) 'The Religious Right: Sanctification of a Political Agenda', unpublished research paper at Department of Political Science, University of the Philippines.

Starke, Hortensia (1988) 'Primer on the Comprehensive Agrarian Reform', Part I and 'Continuation'.

Wurfel, David O. (1960) 'The Bell Report and After: A Study of the Political Problems of Social Reform Stimulated by Foreign Aid', Ph.D. thesis, Department of Political Science, Cornell University.

4. US government documents

Copies of much of the cable traffic cited below are deposited with the National Security Archive, Washington, D.C. Excerpts from some of them appear in The National Security Archive, The Making of U.S. Policy: The Philippines, The Marcos Years. Published on microfiche, 1990.

Bureau of Intelligence and Research at the State Department (15 January 1973), 'Intelligence Note'.

Byroade to State (24 October 1972). Embassy to State Department, signed Ambassador Henry Byroade (Ref 189396).

Byroade to State (27 September 1972). Embassy to State Department, signed Ambassador Henry Byroade (Manila 09178) 'Presidential Decree on Land Reform'.

Byroade to State (27 September 1972). Embassy to State Department, signed Ambassador Henry Byroade (Manila 09188) 'American Chamber Telegram to President Marcos'.

Byroade to State (24 October 1972). Embassy to State Department, signed Ambassador Henry Byroade (Ref 189396) 'Land Reform'.

Congressional Record, Library of Congress, Washington D.C.

Current Foreign Relations, No. 43 (25 October 1972).

Development Alternatives Inc. to State Department (1 December 1972). Donald R. Mickelwait Report: 'Philippine Insurgency and US Policy: American Interests and Options in the Philippines'. Only a limited part of this report was released. It was the version submitted to Jerome French (Office of Development Administration of Bureau for Technical Assistance of Agency for International Development) and attached French to Silverstone (Memo 29 March 1973).

Emerson, James P. (1956) *Land Reform Progress in the Philippines 1951-1955*. Manila: International Cooperation Administration.

Foreign Relations of the United States (1950), vol. 6 on East Asia and the Pacific. Washington D.C.: US Government Printing Office.

Hardie, Robert S. (1951) *Philippine Land Tenure Reform: Analysis and Recommendations*. Manila: United States of America, Special Technical and Economic Mission to the Philippines.

Henderson, H.E. (1959) 'U.S. Views on Agrarian Reform,' 9 November, 1959 in *United States State Department Bulletin* (December 14).

Murphy to State (30 January 1979). Embassy to State Department, signed Ambassador Richard W. Murphy (Manila 02199) 'An Assessment of Progress Toward the New Society'.

Murphy to John H. Sullivan (USAID Washington) (31 January 1980) [Appears to be mis-dated and should read 1981]. Letter to John H. Sullivan, Assistant Administrator Bureau for Asia, USAID, signed Ambassador Richard W. Murphy with enclosure, 'Country Development Strategy Statement, Financial Year 1982'.

'National Policy Paper on the Republic of the Philippines' (NPP) (1966). Submitted on 1 December 1965 and approved and signed by Secretary of State Dean Rusk on 3 March 1966.

Newsom to State (8 June 1977). Embassy to State Department, signed Ambassador David Newsom, 'Country Evaluation Plan: Economic Human Rights'.

State Department and USAID to Embassy (17 October 1972). EA/PHL: Sclowman, EA: A.W. Hummel Jr., EA/Phl: Reusher; EA: H.H.Barger, ASIA/KPA: C.Shook, 'Land Reform'.

State Department to Embassy (18 March 1975). Memo of Conversation: R.L. Prosterman, C.A. Taylor, Philip C. Habib (Assistant Secretary, Bureau of East Asian and Pacific Affairs), Benjamin A. Fleck (Director, Office of Philippine Affairs), 'Land Reform in the Philippines'.

State Department to Embassy (28 June 1988), telegram.

Sullivan to State (28 August 1974). Embassy to State Department, signed Ambassador William H. Sullivan (Ref Manila A-206), 'Land Reform'.

Sullivan to State (11 October 1974). Embassy to State Department, signed Ambassador William H. Sullivan (Manila 12243 111348Z), 'Wolf Ladejinsky's Visit'.

Sullivan to State (29 December 1975). Embassy to State Department, signed Ambassador William H. Sullivan (Manila A-345), 'Land for the Tiller? An Impression of Philippine Agrarian Policy'.

Tobias, Channing (1951) 'The Importance of Land Reform', US State Department Bulletin, 25 (October 22), pp.661-64.

US Embassy to State (29 January 1976). 'Third Year of Martial Law'.

Usher, Memorandum (13 April 1973). Memorandum of Conversation: Harry Goldberg, Department of International Affairs, AFL-CIO; Robert Senser EA/RA; Richard E. Usher, Director of Philippine Affairs at East Asia of State. 'Land Reform Program in the Philippines'.

USAID (1970) Spring Review on Land Reform. Washington, D.C.

USAID (4 February 1980) Shaver (USAID Washington) to Schwarzwalder (USAID-Manila). Memorandum from Fred Shaver (AID Washington) through Leon Vaughn to Anthony M. Schwarzwalder, Director AID-Philippines, 'Memorandum Survey Report No. 2-492-80-6, Agrarian Reform (Philippines), Project no. 492-0261'. Appendix, 'Effectiveness of Philippine Land Reform' 1979.

USAID (1989) 'Agrarian Reform Support Program (492-0431): Program Assistance Approval Document', USAID/Philippines (January).

USAID (1989b) Congressional Presentation Fiscal Year 1990, 2 volumes, USAID, Washington D.C. (10 January).

US Arms Control and Disarmament Agency (1982) World Military Expenditures and Arms Transfers, 1970-1979 (March).

US House of Representatives (1986) 'United States Policy Toward the Philippines and the Proposed Supplemental Aid Package', Hearings and Markup before the Committee on Foreign Affairs and its Subcommittee on Asian and Pacific Affairs. 99th Congress, Second Session on H.R.5081 (29 April, 15 May, 26 June and 23 July). Washington D.C.: US Government Printing Office.

US House of Representatives (1987) 'Foreign Assistance Legislation for Fiscal Years 1988-89 (Part 5)'. Hearings and Markup before the Committee on Foreign Affairs and its Subcommittee on Asian and Pacific Affairs. 100th Congress, First Session (25 February, 3,4,5,11,12,17,18 March). Washington D.C.: US Government Printing Office.

US House of Representatives (1987a) 'Current Situation in the Philippines'. Hearing before the Committee on Foreign Affairs and its Subcommittee on Asian and Pacific Affairs. 100th Congress, First Session (2 December). Washington D.C.: US Government Printing Office, 1988.

US Congress (1989) 'Legislation on Foreign Relations through 1988', Committee on Foreign Relations, US Senate and Committee on Foreign Affairs, US House of Representatives (February). Washington D.C.: US Government Printing Office.

US Senate (1984) 'The Situation in the Philippines', a Staff Report for the Committee on Foreign Relations. Washington, D.C.

Van Steenwyk, Mark A. (1975). A Study of Philippine Farmer Organizations (Manila: USAID, no. AID492-748) (February).

5. Multilateral agencies

Most of the World Bank documents cited below were obtained by the author from Philippine government officials.

Bell, Clive (1989) 'Land Reform, Tenancy, Productivity and Employment Aspects of Property

Rights in Land', World Bank Consultant, Background Paper for *World Development Report 1990*. Washington D.C.: World Bank.

International Labour Office (ILO) (1974) *Sharing In Development: A programme of employment, equity and growth for the Philippines*. Report of an inter-agency team financed by the United Nations Development programme and organised by the International Labour Office. Geneva: ILO.

Kaji, Gautam S., Director Country Dept.II Asia Region (4 April 1989). Letter to DAR Secretary Philip Juico.

Templeton, J.K. (26-30 June 1989) Aide-Memoire: 'Philippines Agrarian Reform Program, Observations on the Program and a Project Concept for World Bank Financing', World Bank, 28 June 1989. Series of Memoranda to the Assistant Secretary for Planning and Project Management, DAR, from the Project Management Service.

United Nations Food and Agricultural Organization (FAO) (1984) *FAO Production Yearbook 1983*. Rome: FAO.

United Nations Food and Agriculture Organization (FAO) (1987) *Report of the WCARRD Follow-up Inter-Agency Mission to the Philippines*, WCARRD Mission No.20 (March). Rome: FAO.

United Nations Food and Agriculture Organization (1988) 'Preparation of the Accelerated Land Reform Programme', Technical cooperation programme, terminal statement (ES:TCP/PHI/6760). Rome: FAO.

World Bank (1975) 'Land Reform', *Sector Policy Paper*. (Based on *Bank Policy on Land Reform*. Report No.440, 2 May 1974). Washington, D.C.

World Bank (1975a) *Appraisal of the Rural Development Project, Philippines*. Report No.633a-PH (14 March). Washington, D.C.

World Bank (1985) *World Development Report, 1985*. Oxford: Oxford University Press.

World Bank (1986) *The Philippines: A Framework for Economic Recovery* Report No. 6350-PH (5 November). Washington, D.C.

World Bank (1987) 'World Bank Land Reform Mission: Preliminary Conclusions', marked 'Confidential' (25 March).

World Bank (1987a) *Philippines Agricultural Strategy Review*. Report No. 6819-PH, vol.I and II (21 October). Washington D.C.

World Bank (1987b) *Agrarian Reform Issues in the Philippines: An Assessment of the Proposal for an Accelerated Land Reform*. Draft, Strictly Confidential. Report No.6776-PH (12 May). Projects Department: East Asia and Pacific Regional Office. Washington, D.C.

World Bank (1988a) *The Filipino Poor: What is to be Done?* Washington, D.C.

World Bank (1988b) *The Philippines The Challenge of Poverty*. Report No. 7144-PH (17 October). Country Department II Asia Region. Washington, D.C.

World Bank (1989a) *World Development Report*. Oxford: Oxford University Press.

World Bank (1989b) *Philippines Forestry, Fisheries, and Agricultural Resource Management Study (ffARM Study)*. Report No.7388-PH (17 January). Washington, D.C.

World Bank (1989c), *Philippines: Toward Sustaining Economic Recovery*. Report No.7438-PH (30 January). Washington, D.C.

6. Periodicals

Ang Bayan (Central Committee of the Communist Party of the Philippines)
Asian Wall Street Journal (AWSJ)
Boston Globe (BG)
Bulletin Today (BT)
Business Day (BD)
Business Star (BS)
Business Times
Business World (BW) (Manila)
Courrier
Daily Express (DE)

Daily Globe (DG)
Economist (London)
Far Eastern Economic Review (FEER)
Financial Times (London)
Guardian (London)
Ibon Facts and Figures
Independent (London)
International Herald Tribune (ITH)
Malaya
Manila Bulletin (MB)
Manila Chronicle (MC)
Manila Times (MT)
MIDWEEK
New York Times (NYT)
Peacemaker
Peasant Update International
Philippine Daily Inquirer (PDI)
Political Monitor
Veritas